Baseball GPA

Baseball GPA
A New Statistical Approach to Performance and Strategy

DAVID P. GERARD

McFarland & Company, Inc., Publishers
Jefferson, North Carolina, and London

The information used here was obtained free of charge from and is copyrighted by Retrosheet. Interested parties may contact Retrosheet at 20 Sunset R0ad, Newark DE 19711.

LIBRARY OF CONGRESS CATALOGUING-IN-PUBLICATION DATA

Gerard, David P., 1960–
Baseball GPA : a new statistical approach to performance and strategy / David P. Gerard.
    p.   cm.
Includes glossary and index.

ISBN 978-0-7864-7256-7

1. Baseball—Statistics. 2. Baseball—Records. I. Title.

GV877.G47 2013   796.357021—dc23   2013029110

BRITISH LIBRARY CATALOGUING DATA ARE AVAILABLE

© 2013 David P. Gerard. All rights reserved

No part of this book may be reproduced or transmitted in any form or by any means, electronic or mechanical, including photocopying or recording, or by any information storage and retrieval system, without permission in writing from the publisher.

On the cover: Circuit board image © 2013 Texture City

Manufactured in the United States of America

McFarland & Company, Inc., Publishers
Box 611, Jefferson, North Carolina 28640
www.mcfarlandpub.com

Table of Contents

Preface   1

Part I. GPA: The Basics

Statistics, Simple and Otherwise	5
Creating GPA	9
The 2010 through 2012 Seasons	23
Best Individual Seasons, 1952–2012	48
Ballpark Corrections	56
Baserunning Strategies	66
Applying Baserunning Corrections	73
Baserunning Corrections, 1952–2012	83

Part II. GPA and Baseball Eras

The Relationship Between GPA and Batting Average	93
Baseball Eras, 1952–2012	100
The Pitching Era, 1971–1984	105
The Steroid Era, 1994–2004	112

Part III. GPA, Game Strategy and the Baseball Game Simulator

The Baseball Game Simulator	117
Constructing the Best Lineup	121
Run Production	129
Winning Games	136
Chance in Baseball	144
Should They Have Walked Bonds?	149
The Sacrifice Bunt	164
Baserunning Revisited	174

Part IV. Using GPA

GPA and Wins Above Replacement	181
Who Should Have Won the Cy Young Award?	201
Who Should Have Won the MVP Award?	217
GPA and Free Agency	235
Jim Rice's 1984 Season	245
Conclusion	251
Glossary	255
Index	261

PREFACE

This book describes a new baseball statistic I call GPA, or Gross Productivity Average. The first third of the text describes how GPA was created; the rest of the book applies GPA to settle long-standing controversies in baseball. The information in this book will allow everyone from baseball professionals to average fans to better understand the game.

Growing up a Red Sox fan, I learned to live with memorable disappointments. The Red Sox lost Game 7 of the 1975 World Series to the Reds thanks to Joe Morgan's bloop single in the top of the ninth inning to score Ken Griffey with the go-ahead run. Bucky Dent's three-run home run over the Green Monster gave the Yankees the lead for good in the seventh inning of a one-game playoff at Fenway Park for the 1978 American League East title. The Red Sox were one out away from winning the 1986 World Series when the Mets staged a historic rally which culminated in Mookie Wilson hitting a slow ground ball under Red Sox first baseman Bill Buckner's glove to win Game 6. The Red Sox went on to lose the World Series two days later.

Those painful losses have stayed with me my whole life. I have continued to think and rethink about the poor strategic decisions I felt were made by Red Sox managers over the years. What was I seeing that they couldn't see? Could a statistic be invented that would enable teams to employ more effective strategies in key game situations and get better production out of their players?

Jim Rice was elected to the Hall of Fame in 2009 for a stellar career that lasted from 1974 to 1989 and included 382 home runs and a 0.298 batting average. During the 1984 season he had a 0.280 batting average with 122 RBI and 28 home runs. Ralph Houk, the Red Sox manager that year, clearly was happy with his production since he batted him third in the lineup for most of his 657 at-bats that year and rarely rested Rice. Even though the Red Sox led the league with a 0.283 team batting average, they finished in fourth place in the American League East.

What bothered me about Rice's 1984 season was that he grounded into a then-record 36 double plays and struck out 102 times while walking only 44 times. I found it hard to believe that the benefits of having him hit in the heart of a potent lineup were not outweighed by the rallies he killed and runners he left on base throughout the year. There were no statistics at the time that could definitively determine how much of a benefit Rice was to his team that year. I began to think about creating a baseball statistic that would more accurately reflect a player's productivity than the oft-cited, traditional statistics batting average, RBI, home runs and slugging average.

Bill James defined sabermetrics as "the search for objective knowledge about baseball." James pioneered the in-depth analysis of baseball statistics when he published his *Bill James Baseball Abstract* beginning in 1977. His first edition presented statistics compiled from box scores from the 1976 baseball season.

James was frustrated because it was difficult for him to obtain detailed play-by-play information from past baseball seasons. When he contacted the Elias Sports Bureau, the official American and National League statistician since the 1920s, James was denied the detailed play-by-play statistics he wanted for his *Baseball Abstract*. When I attempted to get detailed play-by-play data from Elias in the 1990s, I was likewise told it was unavailable to me.

James did not accept Elias's rejection. Instead, he started Project Scoresheet in the 1980s to gather and share detailed play-by-play data from scorecards created by fans at the ballpark and from fans watching the game on TV or listening on the radio. Project Scoresheet eventually folded, but Dave Smith, who had worked on Project Scoresheet during its final years, then formed Retrosheet (www.retrosheet.org), which today provides a free, comprehensive play-by-play database of almost all major league baseball games played from 1947 to the current season.

The GPA statistic was created from the play-by-play data of all games from 1997 to 2009. The data is adjusted so that average GPA is equal to the average batting average of all major league players from 2005 to 2008. It works out well that the average GPA and batting average of all major league players from 1952 to 2012 are virtually identical at 0.259. This sets a modern standard for major league players untainted by steroids. Reporting GPA on a scale similar to that used for batting average makes it easy for people to understand.

Baserunning can significantly affect a hitter's or pitcher's production for his team. How much did Rickey Henderson's record 130 stolen bases add to his productivity for the 1982 Athletics? Which players had the most and least productive single seasons on the base paths? How much production does a knuckleball pitcher lose from all the stolen bases he allows and wild pitches he throws? How has baserunning changed over the years? These questions can be answered using a baserunning correction that is applied to GPA.

The ballpark can have a dramatic effect on a hitter's or pitcher's production. How much did playing at Coors Field help the average hitter or hurt the average pitcher? This book describes a ballpark correction that allows a player's production as measured by GPA to be accurately adjusted for the mix of ballparks and the era in which he played. Corrections are provided for every major league ballpark used from 1952 to 2012.

Offensive production has varied greatly from era to era and to a lesser extent from season to season. Over the years rules changed, different stadiums came into use, baseballs were manufactured by different companies and to different specifications, managers employed new strategies and players grew bigger, stronger, and even more athletic. Because all these changes occurred over time, it is difficult to look at any one statistic from 1952 to 2012 and get a clear picture of the change in offensive production taking place.

How was offensive productivity affected during the pitching-dominated years from 1970 to 1984 and the Steroid Era (defined here as the 1994–2004 seasons)? During what year did steroid use most affect the game? How much of the increased offensive productivity seen from 1994 to 2004 was due to steroids? Gross Productivity Average can answer these questions using a technique to filter out the other changes occurring over time.

Some baseball strategies have been endlessly debated without any consensus reached as to how or when they should be applied — or whether they should be applied at all. Where should the best hitter bat in the lineup? When should a hitter be intentionally walked? When should a sacrifice bunt be attempted? How often does a runner need to be successful when advancing a base in order to justify the risk?

This book will describe a computerized game simulation, developed independently of GPA, that allows these questions to be answered and definitive guidelines created. As the simulation demonstrates, the number of runs a team scores and the number of games it wins are determined by the GPA of the players in the lineup. The simulator shows that every player with the same GPA is equally productive for the team no matter how many home runs or singles he hits, no matter how many times he strikes out or walks, no matter how many double plays he hits into.

With GPA, it is also possible to look back at every season from 1952 to 2012 and determine which player was the most deserving of the Cy Young and Most Valuable Player awards. How often was the judgment of the writers who voted for these awards correct? Has the writers' ability to choose the most deserving player improved over the years? What were the greatest injustices in the awards' histories?

The first draft of this book was written during the 2010 Major League Baseball (MLB) season. By the end of 2012, the Retrosheet database had been updated to include most of the games from the 1947 and 1951 seasons and all the games from the 2010 through 2012 seasons. Chapters have been updated to include the 2010 through 2012 data if its inclusion was helpful or significant.

My background is primarily in computer science, not statistics. It is not necessary to have a background in statistics to understand GPA or the information presented here. This book avoids complex statistical methods, relying instead on the computer to produce a comprehensive and easily understood evaluation of the play-by-play data in the Retrosheet database.

My hope is that both baseball professionals and the average fan will come to accept GPA as the new standard for evaluating a major league player's productivity.

Part I. GPA: The Basics

STATISTICS, SIMPLE AND OTHERWISE

Baseball statistics are the bricks and mortar of baseball dialogue and analysis. One reason baseball statistics are followed more closely than those of any other sport is that they allow us to compare players from different eras.

The practice of keeping records of player achievements was started in the 19th century by Henry Chadwick. Based on his experience with cricket, Chadwick devised the precursors to modern baseball statistics, including batting average, runs scored, and runs allowed (See Thorn and Palmer's *Hidden Game* of *Baseball* for a fuller discussion of Chadwick's early work.)

Throughout much of modern baseball, batters have been evaluated by several core statistics including batting average (BA), runs batted in (RBI), and home runs (HR). A player who leads the league in these three statistics is referred to as the "Triple Crown" winner. For pitchers, wins, earned run average (ERA) and strikeouts are the most commonly used statistics.

The core statistics were chosen because they are easy to calculate from data published in a box score. Hits, runs, at-bats and RBI totals are tabulated and simple arithmetic is used to calculate each statistic. This process was done by hand until 1969, when Macmillan printed its *Baseball Encyclopedia*, which used a computer to compile statistics for the first time.

The unfortunate truth for those who want to create an elegant, simple baseball statistic is that baseball is a complex game. A single statistic calculated from tallying a few events from a box score will not accurately reflect the game. Now that baseball statistics can be tabulated and calculated by computers, they no longer need to be simple calculations.

As I thought about the limitations of the current baseball statistics in widespread use, I came up with my list of requirements for the "perfect" baseball statistic. It should:

1. Reflect how each plate appearance contributes to a team's chance of scoring (and winning the game).
2. Adjust for the number of opportunities each player has (be an average).
3. Be easy for the casual baseball fan to understand.
4. Value extra base hits and RBI appropriately.
5. Reward reaching base by means other than a hit.
6. Reward moving runners over.

7. Penalize leaving runners on base and hitting into double plays.
8. Measure both pitchers' and batters' performances equally well.
9. Reward runners for stealing bases or advancing by other means.
10. Penalize a runner for being caught stealing or other mistakes.
11. Correct for the effect of playing in different ballparks.
12. Be easy to calculate.

Few baseball statistics today come close to meeting these goals. What follows is an overview of baseball statistics in common use today, along with their respective strengths and weaknesses, and one non-baseball measure that is more nearly analogous to Gross Productivity Average.

Batting Average (BA)
Hits/At-Bats

Batting average (BA) is the most widely used statistic to measure a batter's performance. BA is calculated by dividing the number of hits by the number of at-bats. The calculation for BA lumps each plate appearance (PA) into one of 3 outcomes: a hit, an out or a non-event. At-bats are calculated by adding the hits and outs and ignoring the non-events.

The value of a hit to the team's chance of winning the game can vary widely from a bases-empty single to a grand slam, yet they count equally in the BA statistic. Runs batted in and clutch hitting are not rewarded in the BA statistic. Outs can have vastly different impacts on a team's chance of winning the game. A triple play can take a team out of a potentially high-scoring inning, while a baserunner who reaches on an error (which counts as an out in the BA calculation) can start a scoring rally. Non-events (which are ignored in the BA calculation) such as walks or being hit by a pitch result in the same outcome as a single (runner on first base) yet are not rewarded in the BA statistic. The BA calculation counts a successful sacrifice bunt as a non-event, since a runner moves up but an out is recorded. A hitter making an out by hitting behind a runner and moving him over to second base counts as an out in the BA calculation, yet the result for the team is exactly the same as with the sacrifice bunt.

Runs Batted In (RBI)

A run batted in (RBI) is credited to the batter when a runner scores as a result of his PA. An RBI is not credited when the batter hits into a double play or when a fielding error allows the run to score.

The RBI statistic is not an average and reflects the number of opportunities that the batter had to drive in runs. A leadoff hitter will have significantly fewer opportunities to get a RBI than a hitter batting third. Runs that score on fielding errors count the same in the game score, yet are usually ignored in the RBI calculation. The RBI statistic does not reflect the missed opportunities the batter had to drive in runners. A player who played for two months and had 50 RBI had a very productive period, but another player with 50 RBI who batted third in the lineup all year was very unproductive.

Home Runs (HR)

A home run (HR) is credited to the batter when, as the result of his at-bat, he is able to touch all four bases without a fielding error being committed. In modern baseball, a HR is almost always achieved by hitting the ball (without touching the ground) over the outfield fence. Rarely, an inside-the-park HR can be achieved by touching all four bases while the ball remains in play on the field without a fielding error being committed.

The HR statistic reflects a player's power. It is not an average so a player with more PAs will have more chances to hit a HR. Players who hit HRs often strike out more and hit into more double plays, which may reduce the team's chances of winning games.

Earned Run Average (ERA)

Earned run average (ERA) is the most widely used statistic to measure a pitcher's performance. It is the average number of earned runs the pitcher allows for every nine innings he pitches (the length of most games). Some runs that score because of fielding errors are excluded from the ERA calculation.

Winning the game is the pitcher's primary goal, which he accomplishes largely by preventing runs from scoring. Earned run average meets many of the criteria we would expect in a useful baseball statistic. It has the advantage of being measured over many innings and reflects a pitcher's ability to prevent hitters from being productive, runners from advancing, and is easy for the casual fan to understand.

A major limitation of ERA is that runners left on base when a pitcher is removed from the game still count toward the removed pitcher's ERA if they subsequently score. A relief pitcher's strong performance can positively affect the ERA of the pitcher he replaces. A relief pitcher's own poor performance may not be reflected in his ERA when an inherited runner scores ending the game.

Slugging Average (SLG)
(Singles + Doubles × 2 + Triples × 3 + Homers × 4)/At-Bats

Slugging Average (SLG) is calculated by dividing total bases by at-bats. Singles count as one base, doubles count as two bases, triples as three bases and HRs as four bases. Walks are excluded from the SA calculation.

The statistic was created to reward hitters for extra-base hits, something it does fairly well. But a home run is generally not four times as valuable to the team as a single. Slugging average, then, over-corrects for a limitation of the batting average statistic while retaining all of its other problems.

On-base percentage (OBP)
(Hits + Bases-on-Balls + Hit-By-Pitch)/(At-Bats + BB + HBP + Sacrifice Flies)

On-base percentage (OBP) is a measure of how frequently a player safely reaches base. A walk and hit by pitch are counted the same as a hit in the OBP calculation, while sacrifice flies count the same as an out.

On-base percentage (OPB) was created to reward hitters for reaching base. Just like slugging average, OBP tries to correct for some of the limitations of the batting average statistic while retaining all of its other problems.

OPS = On-base percentage + Slugging Average

A relatively new baseball statistic is OPS, which adds a player's on-base percentage and slugging average.

Although this attempts to correct for two limitations of the batting average statistic, it introduces the limitations of the on-base percentage and slugging average statistics and retains many of the problems of the batting average statistic.

NFL Passer Rating
(Completion % + Yards/Attempt + TD % + Interception %) × 16.667

In 1971, the National Football League created the NFL Passer Rating to measure a quarterback's performance with a single statistic. A lot can be learned from examining their effort.

Each of the four categories is equally weighted and adjusted using a simple mathematical formula (www.profootballhof, passer rating, 3/2010) to a "score" from 0 to 2.375. A score of 0 indicates a poor performance, a score of 1 indicates an average performance, and a score of 2 indicates a superior performance. With a truly exceptional performance, it is possible to exceed a score of 2.00. An arbitrary maximum score of 2.375 was chosen. The four scores are added together and multiplied by 16.667, yielding an NFL Passer Rating that can range from 0 to 158.3 (2.375 × 4 × 16.667).

Category Scores	0	1	2.375
Completion Percentage	30%	50%	77.5%
Yards/Attempt	3	7	12.5
Touch Down Percentage	0%	5%	11.875%
Interception Percentage	9.5%	5.5%	0%

Table 1.1. NFL Passer Rating category scores.

The benchmarks for these statistics are based on historical averages, but they were combined in an arbitrary manner. There was no data to support counting each category equally toward the NFL Passer Rating. The arbitrary maximum scores penalize exceptionally good performances, while the arbitrary minimum scores reward exceptionally poor performances.

The NFL Passer Rating was scaled so an average score would be 66.7 (1 × 4 × 16.667), similar to a good completion percentage. It was felt that scores over 100 would be exceptionally rare. Over the years football evolved, and now the best quarterbacks over a season can achieve a passer rating over 100 and on occasion achieve a maximum passer rating of 158.3 for a single game.

Despite these limitations, the NFL Passer Rating was a pioneering effort in football statistics. Still, after almost 40 years in use, the NFL Passer Rating is a mystery to most NFL fans. Some have a vague understanding that a rating over 100 is very good, but few have a really good understanding of how it works.

Sabermetricians have come up with an alphabet soup of statistics to overcome the limitations of the traditional baseball statistics — BsR, eOBS, dERA, EqA, wOBA, DIPS, OBP, OPS, and WAR, among others. New problems have been introduced with each attempt, and none comes close to being the "perfect" baseball statistic.

Creating GPA

It is easy to win a baseball game—just score more runs than your opponent! Runs are the currency of baseball. A batter's offensive production should be measured by the number of runs he creates for his team. A pitcher's value should be measured by his ability to prevent opponents from scoring runs.

At its core, the GPA statistic measures the runs a batter produces for his team or runs a pitcher allows to score for the opposing team. To evaluate a plate appearance (PA), GPA compares the result of the PA to historical norms. The historical norm chosen is the average result from all major league players who faced a similar base-out state during the interleague era from 1997 to 2009. A base-out state refers to the number of outs that have been recorded and the bases that are occupied. There are seven ways the bases can be occupied: 1B, 2B, 3B, 1B + 2B, 1B + 3B, 2B + 3B and 1B + 2B + 3B. The bases can also be empty, of course, bringing the number of men-on-base scenarios to eight. In addition, there are three possibilities for the number of outs: none, one or two. There are a total of 24 base-out states (8 × 3). GPA is reported on a scale similar to that used for batting average to make it easier for people to understand.

The value of each PA to the team varies widely throughout the game. The base-out states where a player has the opportunity to impact a team's chances of winning the game the most or least are listed below. In each example, the average number of runs scored was based on over 8.5 million PAs from 1952 to 2009.

1. With bases loaded and no outs, teams score an average of 2.318 runs the rest of the inning. This average increases to 4.493 when the next batter hits a home run, but falls to 0 if the next batter hits into a triple play (the most impact).

2. With bases empty and 2 outs, teams score an average of 0.100 runs the rest of the inning. This average increases to 1.111 when the next batter hits a home run, but falls to 0 if he makes an out (the least impact).

To place a value on a player's PA it is necessary to understand how many runs historically have scored in that base-out state and how the result of the player's plate appearance increased or decreased the number of runs expected to score that inning.

Since 1952, baseball can be divided into three eras based on major rule or scheduling changes that were implemented as shown in Table 2.1.

In 1973 the designated hitter (DH) rule went into effect, permitting a team to designate another player to hit in place of the pitcher. The rationale for the DH rule was that, with a few exceptions, pitchers are usually weak hitters. Traditionally, a manager must decide when to let a pitcher bat and when to remove him, particularly later in the game when the team needs to score more runs. With the DH rule, pitchers tend to remain in the game longer and face a stronger lineup (Jeff Merron, ESPN.com, 3/2003).

	Pre-DH	*Early DH*	*Interleague*	*Total*
Began	1952	1973	1997	1952
Ended	1972	1996	2009	2009
Games	30,769	48,862	31,417	111,048
Games Missing	993	8	0	1001
Plate Appearances	2,342,513	3,740,975	2,431,049	8,514,537
Baserunning Events	67,785	151,773	79,221	298,779
Home Runs/PA	1.866	1.887	1.928	1.896

Table 2.1. Retrosheet data from 1952 to 2009 by eras.

The DH rule remains one of the most controversial topics in baseball, especially since it only applies to American League (AL) games and some interleague games. It also makes comparing statistics from one baseball era to another more difficult.

In 1997, a rule allowing interleague play during the regular season was implemented. Before the 1997 season, teams in the American League (AL) and National League (NL) did not meet during the regular season except for exhibition games that did not count in the official team standings or league records. From 1997 to 2012, there were 16 teams in the AL and 14 teams in the NL, an imbalance that resulted in each AL team playing 18 interleague games while each National League (NL) team played 12 to 18 most years. In 2013, the Houston Astros joined the American League, giving each league 15 teams with each team playing 20 interleague games.

GPA is based on the performance of all major league players during the interleague era from 1997 to 2009.

Baseball statistics have been more widely followed over the years than most sports because they allow one to compare a current player's achievements to players from past eras. Barry Bonds's 756th home run surpassing Hank Aaron's career record was viewed as a more monumental event than his subsequent home runs because of the historical achievement.

Gross Productivity Average can be used to look back on the past 61 years of baseball to provide some historical context. Still, the standard by which all current players are being judged is the one set by modern players from the interleague era.

To be effective, GPA needs to accurately reflect the value of each PA to the player's team. The most basic question is how much GPA should value a single, double, triple or home run.

	———*Run Expectancy by Era*———			
Event	*Pre-DH*	*Early DH*	*Interleague*	*Average*
Out	0.201	0.214	0.231	0.215
Single	0.916	0.945	1.001	0.952
Double	1.209	1.249	1.296	1.255
Triple	1.491	1.549	1.570	1.536
Home Run	1.866	1.887	1.928	1.896

Table 2.2. Runs expected after batting events, by era. Data from 1952 to 2009.

The average number of runs that are expected to score for the rest of the half-inning for that base-out state is called **run expectancy.** Run expectancy includes the runs that result from the PA and all subsequent runs that score during the half-inning. Gross Productivity Average is a measure of the change in run expectancy.

During the interleague era, teams scored 1.001 runs after a single 1.296 runs after a double, 1.570 runs after a triple and 1.928 runs after a home run. A double was worth 30 percent (1.296/1.001) more than a single, a triple 57 percent (1.570/1.001) more and a home run 93 percent (1.928/1.001) more.

The batting average statistic undervalues a home run by 99 percent (1.896 / 0.952 – 1.0) since it values a single and a home run equally. The slugging average statistic overvalues a home run by 101 percent (4 × 0.952 / 1.896 – 1.0) since it values a home run four times more than a single.

Table 2.2 does not include the five other ways besides a single that a batter can reach first base with the bases empty: a walk, an error, a passed ball or wild pitch after a strikeout, catcher's interference or hit by pitch. Are these events worth the same to the team as a single?

The six ways a runner can reach first base with no outs and the bases empty are shown in Table 2.3. Each event is shown along with the number of times that event occurred from 1952 to 2009 and the number of runs that scored the rest of that inning. The run expectancy is almost identical no matter how the batter reached first base. It does not matter to the team how a runner reaches base because the number of runs the team will score is almost identical.

Event	*Number*	*Runs Scored*	*Run Expectancy*
Single	333,595	287,919	0.863
Strike Out	1,706	1,465	0.859
Walk	155,063	135,014	0.871
Hit-by-Pitch	12,239	11,007	0.899
Catcher's Interference	160	127	0.794
Error	19,041	16,347	0.859

Table 2.3. Run expectancy by event. Events that allowed a runner to reach first base with bases empty and no outs. Data from 1952 to 2009.

The other 23 base-out states produce data similar to the bases-empty-and-no-outs base-out state that is shown in Table 2.3. The run expectancy does not change much no matter how a batter gets on base.

Gross Productivity Average counts all events that allow a runner to reach base equally. This rewards batters with skills not always recognized by current baseball statistics. Fielding errors are more likely to occur when a batter can run fast or hits ground balls (see Tom Ruane's article "Do Some Batters Reach on Errors More Than Others," Retrosheet.org, 7/4/2005) and is rewarded by GPA.

Consider the base-out state bases empty and no outs. There are five possible outcomes after a batter's plate appearance. He can make an out, be on one of three bases or score a run. This is called the *play result*. Each play result for the bases empty and no outs scenario is shown in the top portion of Table 2.4 along with the number of times it occurred and the run expectancy.

Before Runners			Before Outs	After Runners			After Outs	Runs	Number	Run Expectancy	Change in Run Expectancy
—	—	—	0	—	—	—	1	0	388,849	0.287	−0.249
—	—	—	0	1B	—	—	0	0	145,098	0.926	+0.390
—	—	—	0	—	2B	—	0	0	30,964	1.158	+0.622
—	—	—	0	—	—	3B	0	0	3,490	1.425	+0.889
—	—	—	0	—	—	—	0	1	17,975	1.546	+1.010
							Total/Average		586,376	0.536	0.000
—	—	—	1	—	—	—	2	0	279,352	0.110	−0.178
—	—	—	1	1B	—	—	1	0	102,724	0.562	+0.274
—	—	—	1	—	2B	—	1	0	20,556	0.699	+0.411
—	—	—	1	—	—	3B	1	0	2,312	0.951	+0.663
—	—	—	1	—	—	—	1	1	11,489	1.298	+1.010
							Total/Average		416,433	0.288	0.000
—	—	—	2	—	—	—	3	0	219,934	0.000	−0.111
—	—	—	2	1B	—	—	2	0	83,132	0.242	+0.131
—	—	—	2	—	2B	—	2	0	15,965	0.341	+0.230
—	—	—	2	—	—	3B	2	0	1,592	0.386	+0.275
—	—	—	2	—	—	—	2	1	9,349	1.120	+1.009
							Total/Average		329,972	0.111	0.000

Table 2.4. Run expectancy by play result with the bases empty. Change in run expectancy is calculated by taking the run expectancy for that play result and subtracting the average run expectancy for all play results for that base-out state. Data from 1997 to 2009.

At the start of an inning, a team's run expectancy is 0.536. If the first batter makes an out, the run expectancy falls to 0.287. That batter's out cost his team an average of 0.249 (0.536 − 0.287) runs. On the other hand, if the first batter hits a home run, the run expectancy rises to 1.546. That batter's home run increased his team's run production by an average of 1.010 (1.546 − 0.536) runs.

With the bases empty and two outs, a team's run expectancy is 0.111, far lower than with no outs. If the batter makes the third out, the inning is over and the run expectancy falls to 0. That batter cost his team an average of 0.111 (0.111 − 0.000) runs. On the other hand, a home run increases the team's run expectancy by 1.009 (1.120 − 0.111) runs, about the same as if he hit a home run with the bases empty and either no outs or one out.

The value of an event to the team depends on the base-out state. With the bases empty and no outs, hitting a home run is 2.59 (1.010 / 0.390) times as valuable as a single. With the bases empty and two outs, hitting a home run is 7.70 (1.009 / 0.131) times as valuable as a single.

Slugging average generally overvalues a home run, but with the bases empty and two outs it undervalues the home run relative to a single. None of the widely used baseball statistics reflect how the base-out state changes a batter's strategy at the plate. With bases empty and two outs, generally batters should try to hit a home run even if it increases their chance of making an out by up to 2.24 (0.249/0.111) times compared with the bases empty and no outs.

Change in run expectancy (ΔRE) would make an excellent statistic on its own and is closely related to GPA. It would overcome almost all of the limitations of traditional baseball statistics. The average major league player's ΔRE would be 0, and about half of the players would have a negative value. This would cause problems since negative numbers tend to confuse the average fan and ΔRE would require fans to learn a new scale for valuing performance (as with the NFL Passer Rating). If ΔRE were widely adopted and reported, it is likely that even after years of use the average fan would have only a vague understanding of the ΔRE scale.

The scale on which ΔRE is reported is arbitrary. In Table 2.5, the average ΔRE for each base-out state is adjusted to 0 so that play results from various base-out states can be compared. An adjustment is required so that all PAs and base-out states have the same average value. The range of values for ΔRE, both high and low, will vary greatly depending on the importance of the plate appearance. The bases-empty-and-two-outs scenario has a range of 1.120 runs while bases-loaded-and-no-outs has a range of 4.531 runs (see Table 2.10).

| ———Before——— | | ———After——— | | | | Run | Change in Run | |
Runners	Outs	Runners		Outs	Runs	Expectancy	Expectancy	GPA
— — —	0	— — —		1	0	0.287	−0.249	0.019
— — —	0	1B — —		0	0	0.926	+0.390	0.658
— — —	0	— 2B —		0	0	1.158	+0.622	0.890
— — —	0	— — 3B		0	0	1.425	+0.889	1.157
— — —	0	— — —		0	1	1.546	+1.010	1.279
			Average			0.536	0.000	0.268
— — —	1	— — —		2	0	0.110	−0.178	0.090
— — —	1	1B — —		1	0	0.562	+0.274	0.542
— — —	1	— 2B —		1	0	0.699	+0.411	0.680
— — —	1	— — 3B		1	0	0.951	+0.663	0.932
— — —	1	— — —		1	1	1.298	+1.010	1.279
			Average			0.288	0.000	0.268
— — —	2	— — —		3	0	0.000	−0.111	0.157
— — —	2	1B — —		2	0	0.242	+0.131	0.399
— — —	2	— 2B —		2	0	0.341	+0.230	0.499
— — —	2	— — 3B		2	0	0.386	+0.275	0.543
— — —	2	— — —		2	1	1.120	+1.009	1.278
			Average			0.111	0.000	0.268

Table 2.5. GPA by play result with the bases empty. Data from 1997 to 2009.

Gross productivity average overcomes the limitations of ΔRE by adjusting the values up by 0.26833, the correction factor required to make the batting average and GPA of all major league players from 2005 to 2008 nearly equal at 0.26642. There are a number of important reasons why the 2005–2008 seasons were chosen as the baseline era for GPA.

Anonymous steroid tests from the 2003 season showed positive results in between 5 and 7 percent of MLB players. During the 2004 season, a weak drug testing policy was implemented that could not catch MLB players who used steroids in the off-season or after their single random drug test during the season. It was not until the 2005 season that an effective steroid testing policy was implemented. It broadened the definition of banned substances, implemented multiple unannounced tests throughout the year, and suspended any player testing positive.

Adjusting the average GPA to equal the average batting average from 2005 to 2008 sets a modern standard untainted by steroids.

It works out well that the average GPA and batting average of all major league players from 1952 to 2012 are virtually identical at 0.259.

Before Runners	Outs	Play Results	Before Runners	Outs	Play Results	Before Runners	Outs	Play Results
— — —	0	5	— — —	1	5	— — —	2	5
1B — —	0	12	1B — —	1	12	1B — —	2	9
— 2B —	0	12	— 2B —	1	12	— 2B —	2	9
— — 3B	0	11	— — 3B	1	11	— — 3B	2	8
1B 2B —	0	20	1B 2B —	1	17	1B 2B —	2	11
1B — 3B	0	20	1B — 3B	1	17	1B — 3B	2	11
— 2B 3B	0	20	— 2B 3B	1	17	— 2B 3B	2	11
1B 2B 3B	0	25	1B 2B 3B	1	19	1B 2B 3B	2	12

Table 2.6. All 24 base-out states with the number of possible play results for each. There are a total of 311 base-out state and play-result combinations that can occur assuming runners only advance on the base paths.

The table at the end of this chapter provides the GPA values for all 311 base-out state and play-result combinations.

After each PA, both the batter and pitcher are assigned the same GPA value for the appropriate base-out state and play result. GPA is calculated for a batter by taking the total of all GPA values for all PAs as a batter and dividing by the number of PAs as a batter. Gross productivity average is calculated for a pitcher by taking the total GPA values for all batters faced (as a pitcher) and dividing by the number of batters faced (as a pitcher). Table 2.7 shows how GPA is calculated for three sample PAs.

PA Number	PA Result	Before Runners	Outs	After Runners	Outs	Runs	GPA Value
1	Walk	— — —	0	1B — —	0	0	0.653
2	Strikeout	1B — —	1	1B — —	2	0	−0.042
3	Ground Out	1B 2B —	0	— 2B 3B	1	0	0.174
						GPA	0.262

Table 2.7 Sample GPA calculation for three plate appearances. The GPA values come from the table at the end of this chapter.

Calculating GPA by hand would be time-consuming, but what baseball statistics are compiled by hand anymore? Using the computer, the calculation is easy.

So far, the data presented in this chapter is what was actually observed in major league baseball. This was done so the concept of GPA would be easier to understand.

By using the actually observed data, subtle information about base-out states may be preserved. With the bases empty, a home run results in an increase in observed run expectancy of about 1.010 runs no matter how many outs there were at the time. One might expect the run expectancy to have increased by 1.000 runs since only one run scored and the base-out state remained unchanged after the home run. Maybe a pitcher who gives up a home run is more likely to allow the next batter to score. Maybe this is just chance because not enough events exist to evaluate.

Table 2.8 shows the play results for the base-out state bases loaded and no outs. The play resulting in a runner on third base and three runs scoring has an observed run expectancy of 4.531, which is higher than the 4.491 run expectancy for a grand slam home run. The observed run expectancy after rare events may be inaccurate compared to more common events.

The accuracy of any estimate is directly related to the square root of the number of events sampled. Consider two events:

Creating GPA

1. With bases empty and no outs, the batter makes an out (occurred 388,849 times).
2. With bases loaded and no outs, the batter drives in 3 runs and one out is made (occurred 6 times).

The observed run expectancy of the first event is likely to be about 255 times more accurate than the second event. (The square root of (388,849/6) is about 255.)

— — Before — —				— — After — —						Run	Change in Run
Runners			Outs	Runners			Outs	Runs	Number	Expectancy	Expectancy
1B	2B	3B	0	1B	2B	3B	0	1	1,710	3.210	+1.191
1B	2B	3B	0	1B	2B	—	0	2	478	3.692	+1.673
1B	2B	3B	0	1B	—	3B	0	2	233	3.931	+1.912
1B	2B	3B	0	—	2B	3B	0	2	432	3.940	+1.921
1B	2B	3B	0	1B	—	—	0	3	0	x	x
1B	2B	3B	0	—	2B	—	0	3	141	4.121	+2.102
1B	2B	3B	0	—	—	3B	0	3	64	4.531	+2.512
1B	2B	3B	0	—	—	—	0	4	271	4.491	+2.472
1B	2B	3B	0	1B	2B	3B	1	0	3,072	1.580	−0.439
1B	2B	3B	0	1B	2B	—	1	1	720	1.946	−0.073
1B	2B	3B	0	1B	—	3B	1	1	1,012	2.194	+0.175
1B	2B	3B	0	—	2B	3B	1	1	421	2.470	+0.451
1B	2B	3B	0	1B	—	—	1	2	26	2.346	+0.327
1B	2B	3B	0	—	2B	—	1	2	33	2.727	+0.708
1B	2B	3B	0	—	—	3B	1	2	23	2.913	+0.894
1B	2B	3B	0	—	—	—	1	3	6	3.333	+1.314
1B	2B	3B	0	1B	2B	—	2	0	55	0.455	−1.564
1B	2B	3B	0	1B	—	3B	2	0	32	0.562	−1.457
1B	2B	3B	0	—	2B	3B	2	0	255	0.502	−1.517
1B	2B	3B	0	1B	—	—	2	1	14	1.571	−0.448
1B	2B	3B	0	—	2B	—	2	1	23	1.130	−0.889
1B	2B	3B	0	—	—	3B	2	1	748	1.320	−0.699
1B	2B	3B	0	—	—	—	2	2	3	2.000	−0.019
1B	2B	3B	0	x	x	x	3	0	2	0.000	−2.019
1B	2B	3B	0	x	x	x	3	1	1	1.000	−1.019
							Total/Average		9,775	2.345	0.000

Table 2.8. Run expectancy by play result with the bases loaded and no outs. Change in run expectancy is compared with the average run expectancy for that base-out state. Data from 1997 to 2009.

The observed run expectancy (RE) for each of the 24 base-out states is shown in Table 2.9. All the observed play results from that base-out state are combined to produce an average run expectancy (RE). Each base-out state occurred at least 6,817 times and most occurred tens or hundreds of thousands of times.

— — Before — —					— — Before — —					— — Before — —				
Runners			Outs	RE	Runners			Outs	RE	Runners			Outs	RE
—	—	—	0	0.536	—	—	—	1	0.288	—	—	—	2	0.111
1B	—	—	0	0.921	1B	—	—	1	0.553	1B	—	—	2	0.238
—	2B	—	0	1.166	—	2B	—	1	0.706	—	2B	—	2	0.340
—	—	3B	0	1.440	—	—	3B	1	0.981	—	—	3B	2	0.372
1B	2B	—	0	1.525	1B	2B	—	1	0.939	1B	2B	—	2	0.456
1B	—	3B	0	1.835	1B	—	3B	1	1.204	1B	—	3B	2	0.510
—	2B	3B	0	2.035	—	2B	3B	1	1.429	—	2B	3B	2	0.596
1B	2B	3B	0	2.345	1B	2B	3B	1	1.592	1B	2B	3B	2	0.783

Table 2.9. Run expectancy for each base-out state. Data from 1997 to 2009.

From the data in Table 2.9, the change in RE for any base-out state and play result can be calculated as follows:

1. Take the average RE of the base-out state after the play occurred.
2. Subtract the average RE of the base-out state before the play occurred.
3. Add the number of runs that scored.

A single with the bases empty and no outs results in an increase in RE from 0.536 to 0.921 or a change in RE of +0.385 (0.921 − 0.536 + 0). This is similar to the +0.390 actually observed. Both of these base-out states occurred hundreds of thousands of times and so the observed and calculated RE should be similar.

A triple with the bases loaded and no outs results in three runs and a decrease in RE from 2.345 to 1.440, or a change in RE of +2.095 (1.440 − 2.345 + 3). This is lower than the +2.512 RE actually observed. Since this base-out state occurred only 64 times it is not surprising that the observed RE is less accurate.

Table 2.10 shows the observed and calculated GPA for each play result for two base-out states. Does it matter which GPA we use?

The data presented in the next few chapters was tabulated using both observed and calculated GPA. With either method, most batters' GPA did not differ by more than 0.001 points and only rarely differed by up to 0.003 points. Calculated GPA, however, more accurately represents rare events than observed GPA.

— Before — Runners	Outs	*— — After — —* Runners			Outs	Runs	Number	*Observed* GPA	*Calculated* GPA
— — —	0	—	—	—	1	0	388,849	0.019	0.020
— — —	0	1B	—	—	0	0	145,098	0.658	0.653
— — —	0	—	2B	—	0	0	30,964	0.890	0.899
— — —	0	—	—	3B	0	0	3,490	1.157	1.172
— — —	0	—	—	—	0	1	17,975	1.279	1.269
					Total/Average		586,376	0.268	0.268
— — 3B	0	1B	—	3B	0	0	790	0.675	0.686
— — 3B	0	—	2B	3B	0	0	1	−0.172	0.887
— — 3B	0	1B	—	—	0	1	1,190	0.746	0.772
— — 3B	0	—	2B	—	0	1	360	1.145	1.018
— — 3B	0	—	—	3B	0	1	47	1.381	1.292
— — 3B	0	—	—	—	0	2	146	1.465	1.388
— — 3B	0	1B	—	—	1	0	39	−0.531	−0.595
— — 3B	0	—	2B	—	1	0	5	−0.572	−0.442
— — 3B	0	—	—	3B	1	0	2,593	−0.177	−0.167
— — 3B	0	—	—	—	1	1	1,618	0.141	0.139
— — 3B	0	—	—	—	2	0	28	−1.029	−1.038
					Total/Average		6,817	0.268	0.268

Table 2.10. Observed and calculated GPA from each play result from two base-out states. Data from 1997 to 2009.

One concern with using a calculated rather than an observed GPA is that subtle information in the data may be lost. Table 2.11. shows the 11 different base-out state and play result combinations that produced men on first and second (1B + 2B) with two outs. Does it matter what the base-out state was before the play occurred? Maybe pitchers who face bases-loaded scenarios with two outs and give up two runs are more likely to allow subsequent batters to drive in runs. Maybe pitchers who face a man on first (1B) with two outs and walk the next batter are less likely to allow subsequent batters to drive in runs. Both scenarios result in men on first and second with two outs.

All 311 base-out state and play results combinations were reviewed and it turns out that it was irrelevant how a base-out state arose. The more times an event occurred, the closer its observed RE was to the calculated RE.

—Before— Runners			Outs	—After— Runners			Outs	Runs	Number	Obs Run Expectancy	Calc Run Expectancy
1B	—	—	2	1B	2B	—	2	0	30,033	0.468	0.456
—	2B	—	2	1B	2B	—	2	0	17,009	0.454	0.456
1B	2B	—	2	1B	2B	—	2	1	4,153	1.444	1.456
1B	—	3B	2	1B	2B	—	2	1	3,987	1.461	1.456
—	2B	3B	2	1B	2B	—	2	1	15	1.333	1.456
1B	2B	3B	2	1B	2B	—	2	2	1,466	2.448	2.456
1B	2B	—	1	1B	2B	—	2	0	22,434	0.446	0.456
1B	—	3B	1	1B	2B	—	2	0	434	0.422	0.456
—	2B	3B	1	1B	2B	—	2	0	191	0.408	0.456
1B	2B	3B	1	1B	2B	—	2	1	1,967	1.462	1.456
1B	2B	3B	0	1B	2B	—	2	0	19	0.455	0.456
								Total	81,744		Runs 0.456

Table 2.11. Observed and calculated run expectancy for all base-out states and play result combinations resulting in runners on first and second base with two outs. Data from 1997 to 2009.

In summary, GPA is a measure of the change in run expectancy. Table 2.12 (which is really a set of tables) provides the GPA values for all 311 base-out state and play-result combinations. (Note that the values build in an assumption that the runners always advance.) The average GPA for all 24 base-out states is 0.268. The relative value of each plate appearance to the team is reflected in the range of GPA values for that base-out state.

1. Bases loaded and no outs can result in GPA values that range from −2.105 (triple play, no runs score) to 2.431 (grand slam home run)—a difference of 4.536.

2. Bases empty and two outs can result in GPA values that range from 0.159 (makes an out) to 1.269 (hits a home run)—a difference of 1.010.

Gross productivity average accounts for the fact that PAs that occur with bases loaded and no outs are about 4.5 times as important to the team as those that occur with bases empty and two outs.

With what has been discussed so far, GPA meets the first eight of the 12 criteria listed for the "perfect" baseball statistic (bold below). GPA is not easy to calculate, but that's why computers exist (strikeout below). The other three criteria will be discussed in the next few chapters.

1. Reflect how each plate appearance contributes to a team's chance of scoring (and winning the game).
2. Adjusts for the number of opportunities each player has (be an average).
3. Be easy for the casual baseball fan to understand.
4. Value extra base hits and RBI appropriately.
5. Reward reaching base by means other than a hit.
6. Reward moving runners over.
7. Penalize leaving runners on base and hitting into double plays.
8. Measure both pitchers' and batters' performances equally well.
9. Reward runners for stealing bases and or advancing by other means.

10. Penalize a runner for begin caught stealing or other mistakes.
11. Correct for the effect of playing in different ballparks.
12. ~~Be easy to calculate.~~

Table 2.12 RE and Calculated GPA for All 311 Base-Out State and Play Result Combinations

Runners	Outs	RE
— — —	0	0.536

After

Runners	Outs	Runs	GPA	RE
1B — —	0	0	0.653	0.921
— 2B —	0	0	0.899	1.166
— — 3B	0	0	1.172	1.440
— — —	0	1	1.269	1.536
— — —	1	0	0.020	0.288

Before

Runners	Outs	RE
— — —	1	0.288

After

Runners	Outs	Runs	GPA	RE
1B — —	1	0	0.535	0.553
— 2B —	1	0	0.688	0.706
— — 3B	1	0	0.963	0.981
— — —	1	1	1.269	1.288
— — —	2	0	0.093	0.111

Before

Runners	Outs	RE
— — —	2	0.111

After

Runners	Outs	Runs	GPA	RE
1B — —	2	0	0.397	0.238
— 2B —	2	0	0.499	0.340
— — 3B	2	0	0.531	0.372
— — —	2	1	1.269	1.111
— — —	3	0	0.159	0.000

Before

Runners	Outs	RE
1B — —	0	0.921

After

Runners	Outs	Runs	GPA	RE
1B 2B —	0	0	0.871	1.525
1B — 3B	0	0	1.181	1.835
— 2B 3B	0	0	1.382	2.035
1B — —	0	1	1.267	1.921
— 2B —	0	1	1.513	2.166
— — 3B	0	1	1.787	2.440
— — —	0	2	1.883	2.536
1B — —	1	0	-0.100	0.553
— 2B —	1	0	0.053	0.706
— — 3B	1	0	0.328	0.981
— — —	1	1	0.634	1.288
— — —	2	0	-0.542	0.111

Before

Runners	Outs	RE
1B — —	1	0.553

After

Runners	Outs	Runs	GPA	RE
1B 2B —	1	0	0.659	0.939
1B — 3B	1	0	0.924	1.204
— 2B 3B	1	0	1.148	1.429
1B — —	1	1	1.273	1.553
— 2B —	1	1	1.425	1.706
— — 3B	1	1	1.701	1.981
— — —	1	2	2.007	2.288
1B — —	2	0	-0.042	0.238
— 2B —	2	0	0.060	0.340
— — 3B	2	0	0.092	0.372
— — —	2	1	0.830	1.111
— — —	3	0	-0.281	0.000

Before

Runners	Outs	RE
1B — —	2	0.238

After

Runners	Outs	Runs	GPA	RE
1B 2B —	2	0	0.489	0.456
1B — 3B	2	0	0.543	0.510
— 2B 3B	2	0	0.630	0.596
1B — —	2	1	1.272	1.238
— 2B —	2	1	1.374	1.340
— — 3B	2	1	1.406	1.372
— — —	2	2	2.144	2.111
x x x	3	0	0.034	0.000
— — —	3	1	1.034	1.000

Before

Runners	Outs	RE
— 2B —	0	1.166

After

Runners	Outs	Runs	GPA	RE
1B 2B —	0	0	0.633	1.525
1B — 3B	0	0	0.943	1.835
— 2B 3B	0	0	1.143	2.035

Creating GPA

Runners	Outs	Runs	GPA	RE
1B — —	0	1	1.029	1.921
— 2B —	0	1	1.274	2.166
— — 3B	0	1	1.548	2.440
— — —	0	2	1.644	2.536
1B — —	1	0	−0.339	0.553
— 2B —	1	0	−0.186	0.706
— — 3B	1	0	0.089	0.981
— — —	1	1	0.396	1.288
— — —	2	0	−0.781	0.111

———— Before ————

Runners	Outs	RE
— 2B —	1	0.706

———— After ————

Runners	Outs	Runs	GPA	RE
1B 2B —	1	0	0.507	0.939
1B — 3B	1	0	0.772	1.204
— 2B 3B	1	0	0.996	1.429
1B — —	1	1	1.121	1.553
— 2B —	1	1	1.273	1.706
— — 3B	1	1	1.549	1.981
— — —	1	2	1.855	2.288
1B — —	2	0	−0.194	0.238
— 2B —	2	0	−0.092	0.340
— — 3B	2	0	−0.060	0.372
— — —	2	1	0.678	1.111
— — —	3	0	−0.433	0.000

———— Before ————

Runners	Outs	RE
— 2B —	2	0.340

———— After ————

Runners	Outs	Runs	GPA	RE
1B 2B —	2	0	0.386	0.456
1B — 3B	2	0	0.441	0.510
— 2B 3B	2	0	0.527	0.596
1B — —	2	1	1.169	1.238
— 2B —	2	1	1.271	1.340
— — 3B	2	1	1.303	1.372
— — —	2	2	2.042	2.111
x x x	3	0	−0.069	0.000
— — —	3	1	0.931	1.000

———— Before ————

Runners	Outs	RE
— — 3B	0	1.440

———— After ————

Runners	Outs	Runs	GPA	RE
1B — 3B	0	0	0.686	1.835
— 2B 3B	0	0	0.887	2.035
1B — —	0	1	0.772	1.921
— 2B —	0	1	1.018	2.166

Runners	Outs	Runs	GPA	RE
— — 3B	0	1	1.292	2.440
— — —	0	2	1.388	2.536
1B — —	1	0	−0.595	0.553
— 2B —	1	0	−0.442	0.706
— — 3B	1	0	−0.167	0.981
— — —	1	1	0.139	1.288
— — —	2	0	−1.037	0.111

———— Before ————

Runners	Outs	RE
— — 3B	1	0.981

———— After ————

Runners	Outs	Runs	GPA	RE
1B — 3B	1	0	0.494	1.204
— 2B 3B	1	0	0.719	1.429
1B — —	1	1	0.843	1.553
— 2B —	1	1	0.996	1.706
— — 3B	1	1	1.271	1.981
— — —	1	2	1.578	2.288
1B — —	2	0	−0.472	0.238
— 2B —	2	0	−0.369	0.340
— — 3B	2	0	−0.338	0.372
— — —	2	1	0.401	1.111
— — —	3	0	−0.710	0.000

———— Before ————

Runners	Outs	RE
— — 3B	2	0.372

———— After ————

Runners	Outs	Runs	GPA	RE
1B — 3B	2	0	0.411	0.510
1B — —	2	1	1.140	1.238
— 2B —	2	1	1.242	1.340
— — 3B	2	1	1.274	1.372
— — —	2	2	2.013	2.111
x x x	3	0	−0.098	0.000
— — —	3	1	0.902	1.000

———— Before ————

Runners	Outs	RE
1B 2B —	0	1.525

———— After ————

Runners	Outs	Runs	GPA	RE
1B 2B 3B	0	0	1.090	2.345
1B 2B —	0	1	1.270	2.525
1B — 3B	0	1	1.580	2.835
— 2B 3B	0	1	1.780	3.035
1B — —	0	2	1.666	2.921
— 2B —	0	2	1.911	3.166
— — 3B	0	2	2.185	3.440
— — —	0	3	2.281	3.536
1B 2B —	1	0	−0.316	0.939

Runners	Outs	Runs	GPA	RE
1B — 3B	1	0	−0.051	1.204
— 2B 3B	1	0	0.174	1.429
1B — —	1	1	0.298	1.553
— 2B —	1	1	0.451	1.706
— — 3B	1	1	0.726	1.981
— — —	1	2	1.033	2.288
1B — —	2	0	−1.017	0.238
— 2B —	2	0	−0.914	0.340
— — 3B	2	0	−0.883	0.372
— — —	2	1	−0.144	1.111
— — —	3	0	−1.255	0.000

––––Before––––

Runners	Outs	RE
1B 2B —	1	0.939

––––––After––––––

Runners	Outs	Runs	GPA	RE
1B 2B 3B	1	0	0.920	1.592
1B 2B —	1	1	1.267	1.939
1B — 3B	1	1	1.532	2.204
— 2B 3B	1	1	1.757	2.429
1B — —	1	2	1.881	2.553
— 2B —	1	2	2.034	2.706
— — 3B	1	2	2.309	2.981
— — —	1	3	2.615	3.288
1B 2B —	2	0	−0.217	0.456
1B — 3B	2	0	−0.163	0.510
— 2B 3B	2	0	−0.076	0.596
1B — —	2	1	0.566	1.238
— 2B —	2	1	0.668	1.340
— — 3B	2	1	0.700	1.372
— — —	2	2	1.439	2.111
x x x	3	0	−0.672	0.000
— — —	3	1	0.328	1.000

––––Before––––

Runners	Outs	RE
1B 2B —	2	0.456

––––––After––––––

Runners	Outs	Runs	GPA	RE
1B 2B 3B	2	0	0.598	0.783
1B 2B —	2	1	1.271	1.456
1B — 3B	2	1	1.325	1.510
— 2B 3B	2	1	1.412	1.596
1B — —	2	2	2.054	2.238
— 2B —	2	2	2.156	2.340
— — 3B	2	2	2.188	2.372
— — —	2	3	2.926	3.111
x x x	3	0	−0.185	0.000
x x x	3	1	0.815	1.000
— — —	3	2	1.815	2.000

––––Before––––

Runners	Outs	RE
1B — 3B	0	1.835

––––––After––––––

Runners	Outs	Runs	GPA	RE
1B 2B 3B	0	0	0.795	2.345
1B 2B —	0	1	0.974	2.525
1B — 3B	0	1	1.284	2.835
— 2B 3B	0	1	1.485	3.035
1B — —	0	2	1.370	2.921
— 2B —	0	2	1.616	3.166
— — 3B	0	2	1.890	3.440
— — —	0	3	1.986	3.536
1B 2B —	1	0	−0.611	0.939
1B — 3B	1	0	−0.346	1.204
— 2B 3B	1	0	−0.122	1.429
1B — —	1	1	0.003	1.553
— 2B —	1	1	0.156	1.706
— — 3B	1	1	0.431	1.981
— — —	1	2	0.737	2.288
1B — —	2	0	−1.312	0.238
— 2B —	2	0	−1.210	0.340
— — 3B	2	0	−1.178	0.372
— — —	2	1	−0.439	1.111
— — —	3	0	−1.550	0.000

––––Before––––

Runners	Outs	RE
1B — 3B	1	1.204

––––––After––––––

Runners	Outs	Runs	GPA	RE
1B 2B 3B	1	0	0.661	1.592
1B 2B —	1	1	1.008	1.939
1B — 3B	1	1	1.274	2.204
— 2B 3B	1	1	1.498	2.429
1B — —	1	2	1.623	2.553
— 2B —	1	2	1.775	2.706
— — 3B	1	2	2.050	2.981
— — —	1	3	2.357	3.288
1B 2B —	2	0	−0.475	0.456
1B — 3B	2	0	−0.421	0.510
— 2B 3B	2	0	−0.334	0.596
1B — —	2	1	0.308	1.238
— 2B —	2	1	0.410	1.340
— — 3B	2	1	0.442	1.372
— — —	2	2	1.180	2.111
x x x	3	0	−0.931	0.000
— — —	3	1	0.069	1.000

––––Before––––

Runners	Outs	RE
1B — 3B	2	0.510

Creating GPA

——————After——————

Runners			Outs	Runs	GPA	RE
1B	2B	3B	2	0	0.542	0.783
1B	2B	—	2	1	1.214	1.456
1B	—	3B	2	1	1.269	1.510
—	2B	3B	2	1	1.355	1.596
1B	—	—	2	2	1.997	2.238
—	2B	—	2	2	2.099	2.340
—	—	3B	2	2	2.131	2.372
—	—	—	2	3	2.870	3.111
x	x	x	3	0	−0.241	0.000
x	x	x	3	1	0.759	1.000
—	—	—	3	2	1.759	2.000

————Before————

Runners			Outs	RE
—	2B	3B	0	2.035

——————After——————

Runners			Outs	Runs	GPA	RE
1B	2B	3B	0	0	0.572	2.345
1B	2B	—	0	1	0.751	2.525
1B	—	3B	0	1	1.061	2.835
—	2B	3B	0	1	1.261	3.035
1B	—	—	0	2	1.147	2.921
—	2B	—	0	2	1.393	3.166
—	—	3B	0	2	1.666	3.440
—	—	—	0	3	1.762	3.536
1B	2B	—	1	0	−0.835	0.939
1B	—	3B	1	0	−0.569	1.204
—	2B	3B	1	0	−0.345	1.429
1B	—	—	1	1	−0.220	1.553
—	2B	—	1	1	−0.068	1.706
—	—	3B	1	1	0.207	1.981
—	—	—	1	2	0.514	2.288
—	2B	—	2	0	−1.433	0.340
—	—	3B	2	0	−1.401	0.372
—	—	—	2	1	−0.663	1.111

————Before————

Runners			Outs	RE
—	2B	3B	1	1.429

——————After——————

Runners			Outs	Runs	GPA	RE
1B	2B	3B	1	0	0.449	1.592
1B	2B	—	1	1	0.797	1.939
1B	—	3B	1	1	1.062	2.204
—	2B	3B	1	1	1.286	2.429
1B	—	—	1	2	1.411	2.553
—	2B	—	1	2	1.563	2.706
—	—	3B	1	2	1.839	2.981
—	—	—	1	3	2.145	3.288
1B	2B	—	2	0	−0.687	0.456
1B	—	3B	2	0	−0.633	0.510
—	2B	3B	2	0	−0.546	0.596

Runners			Outs	Runs	GPA	RE
1B	—	—	2	1	0.096	1.238
—	2B	—	2	1	0.198	1.340
—	—	3B	2	1	0.230	1.372
—	—	—	2	2	0.968	2.111
x	x	x	3	0	−1.143	0.000
—	—	—	3	1	−0.143	1.000

————Before————

Runners			Outs	RE
—	2B	3B	2	0.596

——————After——————

Runners			Outs	Runs	GPA	RE
1B	2B	3B	2	0	0.456	0.783
1B	2B	—	2	1	1.128	1.456
1B	—	3B	2	1	1.183	1.510
—	2B	3B	2	1	1.269	1.596
1B	—	—	2	2	1.911	2.238
—	2B	—	2	2	2.013	2.340
—	—	3B	2	2	2.045	2.372
—	—	—	2	3	2.784	3.111
x	x	x	3	0	−0.327	0.000
x	x	x	3	1	0.673	1.000
—	—	—	3	2	1.673	2.000

————Before————

Runners			Outs	RE
1B	2B	3B	0	2.345

——————After——————

Runners			Outs	Runs	GPA	RE
1B	2B	3B	0	1	1.240	3.345
1B	2B	—	0	2	1.419	3.525
1B	—	3B	0	2	1.730	3.835
—	2B	3B	0	2	1.930	4.035
—	2B	—	0	3	2.061	4.166
—	—	3B	0	3	2.335	4.440
—	—	—	0	4	2.431	4.536
1B	2B	3B	1	0	−0.513	1.592
1B	2B	—	1	1	−0.166	1.939
1B	—	3B	1	1	0.099	2.204
—	2B	3B	1	1	0.324	2.429
1B	—	—	1	2	0.448	2.553
—	2B	—	1	2	0.601	2.706
—	—	3B	1	2	0.876	2.981
—	—	—	1	3	1.182	3.288
1B	2B	—	2	0	−1.650	0.456
1B	—	3B	2	0	−1.595	0.510
—	2B	3B	2	0	−1.509	0.596
1B	—	—	2	1	−0.867	1.238
—	2B	—	2	1	−0.765	1.340
—	—	3B	2	1	−0.733	1.372
—	—	—	2	2	0.006	2.111
x	x	x	3	0	−2.105	0.000
—	—	—	3	1	−1.105	1.000

—————Before—————			
Runners	Outs		RE
1B 2B 3B	1		1.592

———————After———————				
Runners	Outs	Runs	GPA	RE
1B 2B 3B	1	1	1.250	2.592
1B 2B —	1	2	1.597	2.939
1B — 3B	1	2	1.862	3.204
— 2B 3B	1	2	2.087	3.429
1B — —	1	3	2.211	3.553
— 2B —	1	3	2.364	3.706
— — 3B	1	3	2.639	3.981
— — —	1	4	2.945	4.288
1B 2B 3B	2	0	−0.559	0.783
1B 2B —	2	1	0.113	1.456
1B — 3B	2	1	0.168	1.510
— 2B 3B	2	1	0.254	1.596
1B — —	2	2	0.896	2.238
— 2B —	2	2	0.998	2.340
— — 3B	2	2	1.030	2.372
— — —	2	3	1.769	3.111
x x x	3	0	−1.342	0.000
x x x	3	1	−0.342	1.000
— — —	3	2	0.658	2.000

—————Before—————			
Runners	Outs		RE
1B 2B 3B	2		0.783

———————After———————				
Runners	Outs	Runs	GPA	RE
1B 2B 3B	2	1	1.272	1.783
1B 2B —	2	2	1.945	2.456
1B — 3B	2	2	1.999	2.510
— 2B 3B	2	2	2.086	2.596
1B — —	2	3	2.728	3.238
— 2B —	2	3	2.830	3.340
— — 3B	2	3	2.862	3.372
— — —	2	4	3.600	4.111
x x x	3	0	−0.511	0.000
x x x	3	1	0.489	1.000
x x x	3	2	1.489	2.000
— — —	3	3	2.489	3.000

The 2010 through 2012 Seasons

The information in the first few chapters of this book lays the theoretical framework for GPA. This chapter presents actual data from the 2010, 2011 and 2012 seasons, and the next chapter uses GPA to identify the best seasons by individual batters and pitchers since 1952.

All batters with at least 500 plate appearances (PAs) in 2010, 2011 or 2012 are listed in tables 3.9-3.11, found toward the end of this chapter. Likewise pitchers with at least 500 batters faced are listed by season in tables 3.12–3.14, while selected relief pitchers with 200 or more batters faced are listed in tables 3.15–3.17.

The data in the tables just mentioned reveal how GPA measures productivity. Note the relationship between batting average (BA) and GPA. The average batter has about the same GPA as BA. Batters with a GPA greater than their BA are more productive than their BA would suggest. Players with a GPA lower than their BA are similarly less productive than the average player with that batting average.

A pitcher's GPA reflects his ability to prevent opposing batters from being productive. Pitchers with low GPAs are more productive for their teams while those with high GPAs are less productive. Tables 3.12–3.17 list ERA, which is the traditional measure of a pitcher's performance. Opponents' BA, on-base percentage (OBP) and slugging average (SLG) against these pitchers are also shown. Although these stats are not traditionally reported for pitchers, they can be useful measures of productivity.

How do we know that GPA is a useful baseball statistic? One that illuminates what is easily overlooked in on-field performance but doesn't fly in the face of all other indicators? The Most Valuable Player and Cy Young awards are a good place to start. Players with the best GPAs should also be among the leading candidates for the MVP and Cy Young awards.

The MVP Award is chosen by the Baseball Writers Association of America (BBWAA). In 1938, the BBWAA instituted the "ranked choice" method of voting for each league. Two baseball writers (three from 1928–1960) who cover each team vote. They rank the 10 most valuable players in their league from 1 to 10. The top-ranked player receives 14 points, the second-ranked player receives nine points, the third-ranked player receives eight points, and so on, with the 10th-ranked player receiving one point. The player in each league with the most points wins the MVP Award.

Buster Posey was tied for the highest GPA in the National League with Ryan Braun and Andrew McCutchen. Posey was voted MVP by the BBWAA for the 2012 season with 20 of 32 first place votes. Playing a demanding position such as catcher and the Giants' winning the division likely swayed the voters to choose Posey over Braun and McCutchen.

Player	Team	Year	GPA	BA	OBP	SLG	MVP Points	MVP Rank
Posey, Buster	SFG	2012	**0.333**	**0.336**	0.408	0.549	422	1
Braun, Ryan	MIL	2012	**0.333**	0.319	0.391	0.595	285	2
McCutchen, A.	PIT	2012	**0.333**	0.327	0.400	0.553	245	3
Stanton, Giancarlo	MIA	2012	0.329	0.290	0.361	**0.608**	7	24
Headley, Chase	SDP	2012	0.322	0.286	0.376	0.498	127	5
Craig, Allen	STL	2012	0.321	0.307	0.354	0.522	10	19
Cabrera, Melky	SFG	2012	0.320	0.346*	0.390	0.516		
Goldschmidt, Paul	ARI	2012	0.318	0.286	0.359	0.490		
Montero, Miguel	ARI	2012	0.317	0.286	0.391	0.438	1	32
Jones, Garrett	PIT	2012	0.316	0.274	0.317	0.516		
Ramirez, Aramis	MIL	2012	0.315	0.300	0.360	0.540	47	9
Molina, Yadier	STL	2012	0.314	0.315	0.373	0.501	241	4

Table 3.1. National League MVP voting from the 2012 season. (*Cabrera was not eligible for the batting title after testing positive for steroid use.)

The top three players ranked by GPA in 2012 were also the top three in the MVP voting. Giancarlo Stanton (formerly called Mike) was ranked fourth by GPA, but received few MVP votes, most likely because he had only 501 PAs and played for the last-place Marlins.

Miguel Cabrera won the AL MVP Award in 2012 despite having only the fifth-best GPA in the league. Cabrera had, however, become the first player since Carl Yastrzemski in 1967 to win the Triple Crown. Although Cabrera dominated the traditional statistics, there were many who felt Mike Trout was more deserving by virtue of his superior baserunning skills and fielding. If Trout's GPA is corrected by +0.015 for his baserunning contributions and Cabrera's is corrected by +0.002 for his baserunning contributions, a strong argument can be made that Trout should have been the AL MVP. Trout was widely viewed as a superior fielder to Cabrera, and played one of the most important defensive positions, but GPA does not directly measure each player's defensive contribution (see the "GPA and Wins Above Replacement" chapter).

Player	Team	Year	GPA	BA	OBP	SLG	MVP Points	MVP Rank
Encarnacion, E.	TOR	2012	**0.350**	0.280	0.384	0.557	33	11
Mauer, Joe	MIN	2012	0.334	0.319	**0.416**	0.446	6	19
Hamilton, Josh	TEX	2012	0.334	0.285	0.354	0.577	127	5
Fielder, Prince	DET	2012	0.333	0.313	0.412	0.528	56	9
Cabrera, Miguel	DET	2012	0.329	**0.330**	0.393	**0.606**	362	1
Trout, Mike	ANA	2012	0.328	0.326	0.399	0.564	281	2
Willingham, Josh	MIN	2012	0.323	0.260	0.366	0.524		
Murphy, David	TEX	2012	0.318	0.304	0.380	0.479		
Cespedes, Yoenis	OAK	2012	0.316	0.292	0.356	0.505	41	10
Cano, Robinson	NYY	2012	0.305	0.313	0.379	0.550	149	4
Beltre, Adrian	TEX	2012	0.305	0.321	0.359	0.561	210	3

Table 3.2. American League MVP voting from the 2012 season.

Edwin Encarnacion led the AL in GPA in 2012, but his low BA and the fact that he was primarily a designated hitter for the third-place Blue Jays likely led the writers to underappreciate his contributions. Trout's tGPA is 0.345 when corrected for his baserunning contributions and the ballparks in which he played; Encarnacion's score, by comparison, is unchanged at 0.350. Given his superior contributions in the field, it could be easily argued that Trout deserved the MVP over Encarnacion. Cabrera's tGPA of 0.331, it should be added, is well behind the corrected scores of both Trout and Encarnacion.

Ryan Braun had the highest GPA in the National League and was voted MVP by the BBWAA for the 2011 season, garnering 20 of 32 first-place votes.

Player	Team	Year	GPA	BA	OBP	SLG	MVP Points	MVP Rank
Braun, Ryan	MIL	2011	**0.351**	0.332	0.397	**0.597**	388	1
Berkman, Lance	STL	2011	0.348	0.301	0.412	0.547	118	7
Fielder, Prince	MIL	2011	0.345	0.299	0.415	0.566	229	3
Votto, Joey	CIN	2011	0.345	0.309	**0.416**	0.531	135	6
Kemp, Matt	LAD	2011	0.342	0.324	0.399	0.586	332	2
Gonzalez, Carlos	COL	2011	0.323	0.295	0.363	0.526		
Morse, Mike	WAS	2011	0.317	0.303	0.360	0.550	5	19
Beltran, Carlos	SFG	2011	0.314	0.300	0.385	0.525	3	20
Pence, Hunter	HOU	2011	0.310	0.314	0.370	0.502	10	16
Jones, Chipper	ATL	2011	0.309	0.275	0.344	0.470		
Upton, Justin	ARI	2011	0.307	0.289	0.369	0.529	214	4
Tulowitzki, Troy	COL	2011	0.306	0.302	0.372	0.544	69	8
Howard, Ryan	PHI	2011	0.305	0.253	0.346	0.488	39	10
:								
Pujols, Albert (17)	STL	2011	0.298	0.299	0.366	0.541	166	5

Table 3.3. National League MVP voting from the 2011 season.

Player	Team	Year	GPA	BA	OBP	SLG	MVP Points	MVP Rank
Verlander, Justin	DET	2011	0.208	Pitcher Won Award			280	1
Bautista, Jose	TOR	2011	**0.364**	0.302	0.447	**0.608**	231	3
Cabrera, Miguel	DET	2011	0.361	**0.344**	0.448	0.586	193	5
Ellsbury, Jacoby	BOS	2011	0.337	0.321	0.376	0.552	242	2
Martinez, Victor	DET	2011	0.336	0.330	0.380	0.470	7	16
Gonzalez, Adrian	BOS	2011	0.333	0.338	0.410	0.548	105	7
Cano, Robinson	NYY	2011	0.323	0.302	0.349	0.533	112	6
Hamilton, Josh	TEX	2011	0.318	0.298	0.346	0.536	1	22
Avila, Alex	DET	2011	0.316	0.295	0.389	0.506	13	12
Longoria, Evan	TBR	2011	0.316	0.244	0.355	0.495	27	10
Granderson, C.	NYY	2011	0.315	0.262	0.364	0.552	215	4
:								
Young, M. (15)	TEX	2011	0.311	0.338	0.380	0.474	96	8

Table 3.4. American League MVP voting from the 2011 season.

Justin Verlander won the AL MVP award in 2011 in a close vote over a number of position players. The choice of a position player or a pitcher for the MVP award is somewhat arbitrary. Pitchers have won 11 of 123 MVPs (8.9 percent) from 1952 to 2012. Every pitcher who won the award since 1956 also won the Cy Young. Each had a truly outstanding season as measured by GPA, except for Don Newcombe in 1956 (see the "Who Should Have Won the MVP?" chapter). Most pitchers won their MVP in years when no position players in their leagues had superior seasons.

Verlander led the majors in wins and strikeouts and the AL in ERA in 2011. Thirteen times since 1952 a pitcher has won this unofficial "triple crown" of pitching, but only once, when Sandy Koufax did it in 1963, did they also win the MVP Award. Jose Bautista and Miguel Cabrera each had superior 2011 seasons with GPAs similar to those of recent position players who won the MVP. Verlander's GPA of 0.208 was not even the best among AL starting pitchers, as Jered Weaver had a GPA of 0.206.

Jacoby Ellsbury ranked second in the MVP voting. His BA of 0.321 somewhat underrepresented his production, and he won a Gold Glove as the best-fielding AL center fielder in 2011; but even if Ellsbury's GPA is corrected by +0.006 points for his baserunning contributions, his GPA still falls far short of the league leaders.

Curtis Granderson ranked fourth in the MVP voting. He hit 41 home runs and had 119 RBIs for the AL East champion Yankees. Although his BA of 0.262 significantly underrepresented his production, his GPA of 0.315 was likewise still substantially below the league leaders.

The Cy Young Award (CYA) is an honor given to the best pitcher. From 1956 to 1966 only one pitcher in the major leagues was honored each season. Since 1967, one pitcher in each league has been honored. The award is chosen by the BBWAA, which selects two baseball writers who cover each team to vote. As of 2010, each writer ranks the five most outstanding pitchers in his league from one to five. The top-ranked player receives seven points, the second-ranked player receives four points, the third-ranked player receives three points, and so on, with the fifth-ranked player receiving one point. The pitcher in each league with the most points wins.

Player	Team	Year	W	SO	ERA	GPA	BA	OBP	— Cy Young — Points	Rank
Medlen, Kris	ATL	2012	10	120	**1.57**	**0.185**	0.208	0.243		
Kershaw, Clayton	LAD	2012	14	229	2.53	0.212	0.210	0.270	96	2
Dickey, R.A.	NYM	2012	20	**230**	2.73	0.218	0.226	0.278	209	1
Gonzalez, Gio	WAS	2012	**21**	207	2.89	0.219	**0.206**	0.283	93	3
Cain, Matt	SFG	2012	16	193	2.79	0.223	0.222	0.274	22	6
Zimmermann, J.	WAS	2012	12	153	2.94	0.224	0.251	0.297		
Cueto, Johnny	CIN	2012	19	170	2.78	0.225	0.252	0.302	75	4
Lohse, Kyle	STL	2012	16	143	2.86	0.225	0.239	0.274	6	7
Strasburg, S.	WAS	2012	15	197	3.16	0.230	0.230	0.291		
Lee, Cliff	PHI	2012	6	207	3.16	0.231	0.255	0.278		
Hamels, Cole	PHI	2012	17	216	3.05	0.231	0.237	0.285	1	8

Table 3.5. National League Cy Young voting from the 2012 season.

Kris Medlen had a GPA of 0.185 in 2012 which was by far the best among starting pitchers and one of the lowest ever by a starting pitcher. The Braves limited Medlen to 502 batters faced because of his 2010 reconstructive elbow surgery, and this took him out of contention for the CYA. The "GPA and Wins Above Replacement" chapter discusses how to value Medlen's production compared with starting pitchers with far more batters faced.

Clayton Kershaw, R.A. Dickey and Gio Gonzalez had the three lowest GPAs in 2012 among starters with at least 800 batters faced and finished in the top three in the NL voting. According to GPA, Kershaw deserved the hardware. Dickey had more wins, a traditional measure that still holds sway with writers, and pitched for the Mets, who play in the largest media market. No previous knuckleball pitcher had won the award, and Dickey's story of struggling to become an elite pitcher may have helped his Cy Young prospects.

Among starting pitchers, David Price led the AL in 2012 with a GPA of 0.211 and won the Cy Young. Justin Verlander was second in GPA and second in the voting.

Jered Weaver and Felix Hernandez finished fourth and fifth, respectively, in the GPA-based rankings of AL starting pitchers in 2012, and finished third and fourth in the Cy Young. The top five starting pitchers as ranked by GPA were among the top six in the voting. Fernando Rodney, a relief pitcher, finished fifth.

Player	Team	Year	W	SO	ERA	GPA	BA	OBP	Cy Young Points	Cy Young Rank
Price, David	TBR	2012	20	205	2.56	**0.211**	0.226	0.284	153	1
Verlander, Justin	DET	2012	17	*239*	2.64	0.218	0.217	0.270	149	2
Sale, Chris	CHW	2012	17	192	3.05	0.219	0.235	0.291	17	6
Weaver, Jered	ANA	2012	20	142	2.81	0.221	**0.214**	**0.265**	70	3
Hernandez, Felix	SEA	2012	13	223	3.06	0.223	0.241	0.296	41	4
Morrow, Brandon	TOR	2012	10	108	2.96	0.227	**0.214**	0.280		
Harrison, Matt	TEX	2012	18	133	3.29	0.232	0.258	0.309	2	8
Parker, Jarrod	OAK	2012	13	140	3.47	0.233	0.248	0.312		
Hellickson, J.	TBR	2012	10	124	3.10	0.234	0.244	0.307		
Peavy, Jake	CHW	2012	11	194	3.37	0.238	0.234	0.284		

Table 3.6. American League Cy Young voting from the 2012 season.

Among starting pitchers, Clayton Kershaw, Roy Halladay and Cliff Lee all had outstanding seasons, and similar GPAs, in 2011. Kershaw led the NL in wins, strikeouts and the majors in ERA, and also took home Cy Young. The top five starting pitchers ranked by GPA were also the top five in the Cy Young voting.

Player	Team	Year	W	SO	ERA	GPA	BA	OBP	Cy Young Points	Cy Young Rank
Halladay, Roy	PHI	2011	19	220	2.35	0.203	0.239	0.269	133	2
Kershaw, Clayton	LAD	2011	21	248	**2.28**	0.207	0.207	0.256	207	1
Lee, Cliff	PHI	2011	17	238	2.40	0.207	0.229	0.268	90	3
Hamels, Cole	PHI	2011	14	194	2.79	0.211	0.214	0.259	17	5
Kennedy, Ian	ARI	2011	21	198	2.88	0.214	0.227	0.281	76	4
Cueto, Johnny	CIN	2011	9	104	2.31	0.220	0.220	0.290		
Cain, Matt	SFG	2011	12	179	2.88	0.221	0.217	0.279	3	8
Luebke, Cory	SDP	2011	6	154	3.29	0.224	0.209	0.274		
Vogelsong, Ryan	SFG	2011	13	139	2.71	0.224	0.244	0.310		
Lincecum, Tim	SFG	2011	13	220	2.74	0.225	0.222	0.302	7	6
Worley, Vance	PHI	2011	11	119	3.01	0.225	0.237	0.303		
Jurrjens, Jair	ATL	2011	13	90	2.96	0.226	0.249	0.306		

Table 3.7. National League Cy Young voting from the 2011 season.

Player	Team	Year	W	SO	ERA	GPA	BA	OBP	Cy Young Points	Cy Young Rank
Weaver, Jered	ANA	2011	18	198	2.41	0.206	0.212	0.262	97	2
Verlander, Justin	DET	2011	**24**	**250**	2.40	0.208	0.192	0.242	196	1
Beckett, Josh	BOS	2011	13	175	2.89	0.212	0.211	0.273	3	9
Hellickson, Jerem	TBR	2011	13	117	2.95	0.220	0.210	0.287		
Shields, James	TBR	2011	16	225	2.82	0.221	0.217	0.273	66	3
Romero, Ricky	TOR	2011	15	178	2.92	0.223	0.216	0.296	2	10
Haren, Dan	ANA	2011	16	192	3.17	0.225	0.235	0.265	7	7
Sabathia, C.C. (10)	NYY	2011	19	230	3.00	0.230	0.255	0.305	63	4

Table 3.8. American League Cy Young voting from the 2011 season.

Jered Weaver and Justin Verlander led AL starting pitchers in GPA in 2011 and were also the top two in the CYA voting. Although Weaver had a slightly better GPA, Verlander led the majors in wins and strikeouts and led the AL in ERA. To no one's great surprise, he also won the AL Cy Young

League rankings based on GPA suggest that the writers did a good job selecting the MVP and Cy Young Award winners in 2011 and 2012. (The MVP and CYA winners from 1952 to 2012 are reviewed in the "Who Should Have Won The Cy Young Award?" and the "Who Should Have Won The MVP Award?" chapters.)

The average BA for the league in 2012 was 0.2545, while the average GPA was 0.2557—very similar. The average BA for the league in 2011 was 0.2551, while the average GPA was 0.2543 — again, very similar. What's more, the average BA for the league in 2010, 0.2574, was virtually identical to the league-average GPA, which was 0.2575. Compared with the baseline years of 2005 to 2008, the relationship between BA and GPA did not change from 2010 through 2012.

The following tables list the GPAs of: (1) all batters for the 2012, 2011 and 2010 seasons with at least 500 PAs; (2) all pitchers for the 2012, 2011 and 2010 seasons with at least 500 batters faced; and (3) select relief pitchers for the 2012, 2011 and 2010 seasons with at least 200 batters faced.

Table 3.9. Batters with 500+ Plate Appearances, 2012

Player	Team	Year	GPA	BA	OBP	SLG	PA	Hits	RBI	HR
Encarnacion, E.	TOR	2012	0.350	0.280	0.384	0.557	644	152	110	42
Mauer, Joe	MIN	2012	0.334	0.319	0.416	0.446	641	174	85	10
Hamilton, Josh	TEX	2012	0.334	0.285	0.354	0.577	636	160	128	43
Posey, Buster	SFG	2012	0.333	0.336	0.408	0.549	610	178	103	24
Fielder, Prince	DET	2012	0.333	0.313	0.412	0.528	690	182	108	30
McCutchen, A.	PIT	2012	0.333	0.327	0.400	0.553	673	194	96	31
Braun, Ryan	MIL	2012	0.333	0.319	0.391	0.595	677	191	112	41
Stanton, Giancarlo	MIA	2012	0.329	0.290	0.361	0.608	501	130	86	37
Cabrera, Miguel	DET	2012	0.329	0.330	0.393	0.606	697	205	139	44
Trout, Mike	ANA	2012	0.328	0.326	0.399	0.564	639	182	83	30
Willingham, Josh	MIN	2012	0.323	0.260	0.366	0.524	615	135	110	35
Headley, Chase	SDP	2012	0.322	0.286	0.376	0.498	699	173	115	31
Craig, Allen	STL	2012	0.321	0.307	0.354	0.522	514	144	92	22
Cabrera, Melky	SFG	2012	0.320	0.346	0.390	0.516	501	159	60	11
Goldschmidt, Paul	ARI	2012	0.318	0.286	0.359	0.490	587	147	82	20
Murphy, David	TEX	2012	0.318	0.304	0.380	0.479	521	139	61	15
Montero, Miguel	ARI	2012	0.317	0.286	0.391	0.438	573	139	88	15
Jones, Garrett	PIT	2012	0.316	0.274	0.317	0.516	515	130	86	27
Cespedes, Yoenis	OAK	2012	0.316	0.292	0.356	0.505	540	142	82	23
Ramirez, Aramis	MIL	2012	0.315	0.300	0.360	0.540	630	171	105	27
Molina, Yadier	STL	2012	0.314	0.315	0.373	0.501	563	159	76	22
Wright, David	NYM	2012	0.312	0.306	0.391	0.492	670	178	93	21
Holliday, Matt	STL	2012	0.310	0.295	0.379	0.497	688	177	102	27
Gonzalez, Adrian	LAD	2012	0.308	0.299	0.344	0.463	684	188	108	18
Cano, Robinson	NYY	2012	0.305	0.313	0.379	0.550	697	196	94	33
Beltre, Adrian	TEX	2012	0.305	0.321	0.359	0.561	654	194	102	36
Ethier, Andre	LAD	2012	0.304	0.284	0.351	0.460	618	158	89	20
Gonzalez, Carlos	COL	2012	0.304	0.303	0.371	0.510	579	157	85	22
Fowler, Dexter	COL	2012	0.303	0.300	0.389	0.474	530	136	53	13
Butler, Billy	KCR	2012	0.299	0.313	0.373	0.510	679	192	107	29

Player	Team	Year	GPA	BA	OBP	SLG	PA	Hits	RBI	HR
Zobrist, Ben	TBR	2012	0.297	0.270	0.377	0.471	668	151	74	20
Jackson, Austin	DET	2012	0.297	0.300	0.377	0.479	617	163	66	16
Ross, Cody	BOS	2012	0.296	0.267	0.326	0.481	528	127	81	22
Pujols, Albert	ANA	2012	0.295	0.285	0.343	0.516	670	173	105	30
Beltran, Carlos	STL	2012	0.295	0.269	0.346	0.495	619	147	97	32
LaRoche, Adam	WAS	2012	0.295	0.271	0.343	0.510	647	155	100	33
Zimmerman, Ryan	WAS	2012	0.294	0.282	0.346	0.478	641	163	95	25
Hunter, Torii	ANA	2012	0.294	0.313	0.365	0.451	584	167	92	16
Hill, Aaron	ARI	2012	0.294	0.302	0.360	0.522	668	184	85	26
Swisher, Nick	NYY	2012	0.294	0.272	0.364	0.473	624	146	93	24
Jay, Jon	STL	2012	0.293	0.305	0.373	0.400	502	135	40	4
Kubel, Jason	ARI	2012	0.292	0.253	0.327	0.506	571	128	90	30
Prado, Martin	ATL	2012	0.292	0.301	0.359	0.438	690	186	70	10
Heyward, Jason	ATL	2012	0.291	0.269	0.335	0.479	651	158	82	27
Granderson, C.	NYY	2012	0.290	0.232	0.319	0.492	684	138	106	43
Rios, Alex	CHW	2012	0.290	0.304	0.334	0.516	640	184	91	25
Desmond, Ian	WAS	2012	0.290	0.292	0.335	0.511	547	150	73	25
Dunn, Adam	CHW	2012	0.290	0.204	0.333	0.468	649	110	96	41
Hart, Corey	MIL	2012	0.289	0.270	0.334	0.507	622	152	83	30
Davis, Chris	BAL	2012	0.289	0.270	0.326	0.501	562	139	85	33
Soriano, Alfonso	CHC	2012	0.287	0.262	0.322	0.499	615	147	108	32
Choo, Shin-Soo	CLE	2012	0.286	0.283	0.373	0.441	686	169	67	16
Konerko, Paul	CHW	2012	0.285	0.298	0.371	0.486	598	159	75	26
Teixeira, Mark	NYY	2012	0.285	0.251	0.332	0.475	524	113	84	24
Walker, Neil	PIT	2012	0.285	0.280	0.342	0.426	530	132	69	14
Freeman, Freddie	ATL	2012	0.284	0.259	0.340	0.456	620	140	94	23
Morales, Kendry	ANA	2012	0.284	0.273	0.320	0.467	522	132	73	22
Jones, Adam	BAL	2012	0.283	0.287	0.334	0.505	697	186	82	32
Freese, David	STL	2012	0.283	0.293	0.372	0.467	567	147	79	20
Murphy, Dan	NYM	2012	0.282	0.291	0.332	0.403	612	166	65	6
Cruz, Nelson	TEX	2012	0.281	0.260	0.319	0.460	642	152	90	24
Uggla, Dan	ATL	2012	0.281	0.220	0.348	0.384	630	115	78	19
Pedroia, Dustin	BOS	2012	0.281	0.290	0.347	0.449	623	163	65	15
Trumbo, Mark	ANA	2012	0.280	0.268	0.317	0.491	586	146	95	32
Wieters, Matt	BAL	2012	0.280	0.249	0.329	0.435	593	131	83	23
Scutaro, Marco	COL	2012	0.279	0.306	0.348	0.405	683	190	74	7
Reyes, Jose	MIA	2012	0.279	0.287	0.347	0.433	716	184	57	11
Reynolds, Mark	BAL	2012	0.279	0.221	0.335	0.429	538	101	69	23
Brantley, Michael	CLE	2012	0.279	0.288	0.348	0.402	609	159	60	6
Gordon, Alex	KCR	2012	0.279	0.294	0.368	0.455	721	189	72	14
Lawrie, Brett	TOR	2012	0.278	0.273	0.324	0.405	536	135	48	11
Pierzynski, A.J.	CHW	2012	0.278	0.278	0.326	0.501	520	133	77	27
Jeter, Derek	NYY	2012	0.278	0.316	0.362	0.429	740	216	58	15
Castro, Starlin	CHC	2012	0.277	0.283	0.323	0.430	691	183	78	14
Alvarez, Pedro	PIT	2012	0.277	0.244	0.317	0.467	586	128	85	30
Callaspo, Alberto	ANA	2012	0.277	0.252	0.331	0.361	520	115	53	10
Seager, Kyle	SEA	2012	0.276	0.259	0.316	0.423	651	154	86	20
Kipnis, Jason	CLE	2012	0.276	0.257	0.335	0.379	672	152	76	14
DeJesus, David	CHC	2012	0.274	0.263	0.350	0.403	582	133	50	9
Upton, Justin	ARI	2012	0.274	0.280	0.355	0.430	628	155	67	17
Aoki, Norichika	MIL	2012	0.274	0.288	0.355	0.433	588	150	50	10
Pagan, Angel	SFG	2012	0.274	0.288	0.338	0.440	659	174	56	8
Rollins, Jimmy	PHI	2012	0.273	0.250	0.316	0.427	699	158	68	23
De Aza, Alejandro	CHW	2012	0.273	0.281	0.349	0.410	585	147	50	9

Player	Team	Year	GPA	BA	OBP	SLG	PA	Hits	RBI	HR
Bourn, Michael	ATL	2012	0.272	0.274	0.348	0.391	703	171	57	9
Harper, Bryce	WAS	2012	0.272	0.270	0.340	0.477	597	144	59	22
Bruce, Jay	CIN	2012	0.272	0.252	0.327	0.514	633	141	99	34
Andrus, Elvis	TEX	2012	0.271	0.286	0.349	0.378	711	180	62	3
Santana, Carlos	CLE	2012	0.271	0.252	0.365	0.420	609	128	76	18
Crisp, Coco	OAK	2012	0.271	0.259	0.325	0.418	508	118	46	11
Youkilis, Kevin	CHW	2012	0.270	0.235	0.336	0.409	509	103	60	19
Cabrera, Asdrubal	CLE	2012	0.269	0.270	0.338	0.423	616	150	68	16
Phillips, Brandon	CIN	2012	0.269	0.281	0.321	0.429	623	163	77	18
Johnson, Chris	HOU	2012	0.266	0.281	0.326	0.451	528	137	76	15
Pence, Hunter	PHI	2012	0.266	0.253	0.319	0.425	688	156	104	24
Span, Denard	MIN	2012	0.266	0.283	0.342	0.395	568	146	41	4
Alonso, Yonder	SDP	2012	0.266	0.273	0.348	0.393	619	150	62	9
Morneau, Justin	MIN	2012	0.264	0.267	0.333	0.440	570	135	77	19
Lee, Carlos	MIA	2012	0.263	0.264	0.332	0.365	615	145	77	9
Pena, Carlos	TBR	2012	0.263	0.197	0.330	0.354	600	98	61	19
Moustakas, Mike	KCR	2012	0.263	0.242	0.296	0.412	614	136	73	20
Kinsler, Ian	TEX	2012	0.263	0.256	0.326	0.423	731	168	72	19
Viciedo, Dayan	CHW	2012	0.262	0.255	0.300	0.444	543	129	78	25
Ramirez, Hanley	LAD	2012	0.260	0.257	0.322	0.437	667	155	92	24
Upton, B.J.	TBR	2012	0.260	0.246	0.298	0.454	633	141	78	28
Davis, Ike	NYM	2012	0.260	0.227	0.308	0.462	584	118	90	32
Rodriguez, Alex	NYY	2012	0.259	0.272	0.353	0.430	529	126	57	18
Ellis, A.J.	LAD	2012	0.258	0.270	0.373	0.414	505	114	52	13
Altuve, Jose	HOU	2012	0.257	0.290	0.340	0.399	630	167	37	7
Aybar, Erick	ANA	2012	0.256	0.290	0.324	0.416	554	150	45	8
Pacheco, Jordan	COL	2012	0.254	0.309	0.341	0.421	505	147	54	5
Saunders, Michael	SEA	2012	0.254	0.247	0.306	0.432	553	125	57	19
Doumit, Ryan	MIN	2012	0.254	0.275	0.320	0.461	528	133	75	18
Ramirez, Alexei	CHW	2012	0.253	0.265	0.287	0.364	621	157	73	9
Weeks, Rickie	MIL	2012	0.253	0.230	0.328	0.400	677	135	63	21
Kendrick, Howie	ANA	2012	0.253	0.287	0.325	0.400	594	158	67	8
Rasmus, Colby	TOR	2012	0.253	0.223	0.289	0.400	625	126	75	23
Barney, Darwin	CHC	2012	0.249	0.254	0.299	0.354	588	139	44	7
Aviles, Mike	BOS	2012	0.249	0.250	0.282	0.381	546	128	60	13
Johnson, Kelly	TOR	2012	0.247	0.225	0.313	0.365	581	114	55	16
Beckham, Gordon	CHW	2012	0.247	0.234	0.296	0.371	582	123	60	16
Espinosa, Danny	WAS	2012	0.247	0.247	0.315	0.402	658	147	56	17
Reddick, Josh	OAK	2012	0.246	0.242	0.305	0.463	673	148	85	32
Victorino, Shane	PHI	2012	0.246	0.255	0.321	0.383	666	152	55	11
Furcal, Rafael	STL	2012	0.246	0.264	0.325	0.346	531	126	49	5
Revere, Ben	MIN	2012	0.246	0.294	0.333	0.342	553	150	32	0
Hosmer, Eric	KCR	2012	0.246	0.232	0.304	0.359	598	124	60	14
Jennings, D.	TBR	2012	0.245	0.246	0.314	0.388	563	124	47	13
Escobar, Alcides	KCR	2012	0.245	0.293	0.331	0.390	648	177	52	5
Boesch, Brennan	DET	2012	0.245	0.240	0.286	0.372	503	113	54	12
Ackley, Dustin	SEA	2012	0.244	0.226	0.294	0.328	668	137	50	12
Young, Michael	TEX	2012	0.241	0.277	0.312	0.370	651	169	67	8
Tejada, Ruben	NYM	2012	0.239	0.289	0.333	0.351	501	134	25	1
Infante, Omar	DET	2012	0.239	0.274	0.300	0.419	588	152	53	12
Peralta, Jhonny	DET	2012	0.237	0.239	0.305	0.384	585	127	63	13
Carroll, Jamey	MIN	2012	0.237	0.268	0.343	0.317	537	126	40	1
Stubbs, Drew	CIN	2012	0.236	0.213	0.277	0.333	544	105	40	14
Maybin, Cameron	SDP	2012	0.236	0.243	0.306	0.349	561	123	45	8

Player	Team	Year	GPA	BA	OBP	SLG	PA	Hits	RBI	HR
Suzuki, Ichiro	SEA	2012	0.231	0.283	0.307	0.390	663	178	55	9
Montero, Jesus	SEA	2012	0.231	0.260	0.298	0.386	553	134	62	15
Hardy, J.J.	BAL	2012	0.228	0.238	0.282	0.389	713	158	68	22
Young, Delmon	DET	2012	0.222	0.267	0.296	0.411	608	153	74	18
Smoak, Justin	SEA	2012	0.222	0.217	0.290	0.364	535	105	51	19
Cozart, Zack	CIN	2012	0.221	0.246	0.288	0.399	600	138	35	15
Francoeur, Jeff	KCR	2012	0.221	0.235	0.287	0.378	603	132	49	16
Escobar, Yunel	TOR	2012	0.220	0.253	0.300	0.344	608	141	51	9
Kotchman, Casey	CLE	2012	0.210	0.229	0.280	0.333	500	106	55	12
Weeks, Jemile	OAK	2012	0.202	0.221	0.305	0.304	511	98	20	2
Average			0.2557	0.2545	0.3190	0.4053				

Table 3.10. Batters with 500+ Plate Appearances, 2011

Player	Team	Year	GPA	BA	OBP	SLG	PA	Hits	RBI	HR
Bautista, Jose	TOR	2011	0.364	0.302	0.447	0.608	655	155	103	43
Cabrera, Miguel	DET	2011	0.361	0.344	0.448	0.586	688	197	105	30
Braun, Ryan	MIL	2011	0.351	0.332	0.397	0.597	629	187	111	33
Berkman, Lance	STL	2011	0.348	0.301	0.412	0.547	587	147	94	31
Fielder, Prince	MIL	2011	0.345	0.299	0.415	0.566	692	170	120	38
Votto, Joey	CIN	2011	0.345	0.309	0.416	0.531	719	185	103	29
Kemp, Matt	LAD	2011	0.342	0.324	0.399	0.586	689	195	126	39
Ellsbury, Jacoby	BOS	2011	0.337	0.321	0.376	0.552	732	212	105	32
Martinez, Victor	DET	2011	0.336	0.330	0.380	0.470	595	178	103	12
Gonzalez, Adrian	BOS	2011	0.333	0.338	0.410	0.548	715	213	117	27
Cano, Robinson	NYY	2011	0.323	0.302	0.349	0.533	681	188	118	28
Gonzalez, Carlos	COL	2011	0.323	0.295	0.363	0.526	542	142	92	26
Hamilton, Josh	TEX	2011	0.318	0.298	0.346	0.536	538	145	94	25
Morse, Mike	WAS	2011	0.317	0.303	0.360	0.550	575	158	95	31
Avila, Alex	DET	2011	0.316	0.295	0.389	0.506	551	137	82	19
Longoria, Evan	TBR	2011	0.316	0.244	0.355	0.495	574	118	99	31
Granderson, C.	NYY	2011	0.315	0.262	0.364	0.552	691	153	119	41
Ortiz, David	BOS	2011	0.315	0.309	0.398	0.554	605	162	96	29
Beltran, Carlos	SFG	2011	0.314	0.300	0.385	0.525	598	156	84	22
Teixeira, Mark	NYY	2011	0.313	0.248	0.341	0.494	684	146	111	39
Gordon, Alex	KCR	2011	0.312	0.303	0.376	0.502	690	185	87	23
Young, Michael	TEX	2011	0.311	0.338	0.380	0.474	689	213	106	11
Pence, Hunter	HOU	2011	0.310	0.314	0.370	0.502	668	190	97	22
Jones, Chipper	ATL	2011	0.309	0.275	0.344	0.470	512	125	70	18
Beltre, Adrian	TEX	2011	0.308	0.296	0.331	0.561	525	144	105	32
Youkilis, Kevin	BOS	2011	0.307	0.258	0.373	0.459	517	111	80	17
Upton, Justin	ARI	2011	0.307	0.289	0.369	0.529	674	171	88	31
Konerko, Paul	CHW	2011	0.306	0.300	0.388	0.517	639	163	105	31
Tulowitzki, Troy	COL	2011	0.306	0.302	0.372	0.544	606	162	105	30
Howard, Ryan	PHI	2011	0.305	0.253	0.346	0.488	644	141	116	33
Holliday, Matt	STL	2011	0.305	0.296	0.388	0.525	516	132	75	22
Pedroia, Dustin	BOS	2011	0.304	0.307	0.387	0.474	731	195	91	21
McCutchen, A.	PIT	2011	0.301	0.259	0.364	0.456	678	148	89	23
Ramirez, Aramis	CHC	2011	0.300	0.306	0.361	0.510	626	173	93	26
Zobrist, Ben	TBR	2011	0.299	0.269	0.353	0.469	674	158	91	20
Pujols, Albert	STL	2011	0.298	0.299	0.366	0.541	651	173	99	37
Montero, Miguel	ARI	2011	0.298	0.282	0.351	0.469	553	139	86	18
Victorino, Shane	PHI	2011	0.297	0.279	0.355	0.491	586	145	61	17
Butler, Billy	KCR	2011	0.295	0.291	0.361	0.461	673	174	95	19

Player	Team	Year	GPA	BA	OBP	SLG	PA	Hits	RBI	HR
Willingham, Josh	OAK	2011	0.295	0.246	0.332	0.477	563	120	98	29
Fowler, Dexter	COL	2011	0.295	0.266	0.363	0.432	563	128	45	5
Cabrera, Asdrubal	CLE	2011	0.293	0.273	0.332	0.460	667	165	92	25
Pena, Carlos	CHC	2011	0.292	0.225	0.357	0.462	606	111	80	28
Stanton, Mike	FLA	2011	0.292	0.262	0.356	0.537	601	135	87	34
Cruz, Nelson	TEX	2011	0.291	0.263	0.312	0.509	513	125	87	29
Reyes, Jose	NYM	2011	0.291	0.337	0.384	0.493	586	181	44	7
Escobar, Yunel	TOR	2011	0.290	0.290	0.369	0.413	590	149	48	11
Hart, Corey	MIL	2011	0.288	0.285	0.356	0.510	551	140	63	26
Joyce, Matthew	TBR	2011	0.288	0.277	0.347	0.478	522	128	75	19
Phillips, Brandon	CIN	2011	0.287	0.300	0.353	0.457	675	183	82	18
Roberts, Ryan	ARI	2011	0.286	0.249	0.341	0.427	555	120	65	19
Lee, Carlos	HOU	2011	0.284	0.275	0.342	0.446	653	161	94	18
Swisher, Nick	NYY	2011	0.283	0.260	0.374	0.449	635	137	85	23
Molina, Yadier	STL	2011	0.283	0.305	0.349	0.465	518	145	65	14
Cabrera, Melky	KCR	2011	0.283	0.305	0.339	0.470	706	201	87	18
Kinsler, Ian	TEX	2011	0.282	0.255	0.355	0.477	723	158	77	32
Freeman, Freddie	ATL	2011	0.282	0.282	0.346	0.448	635	161	76	21
Rollins, Jimmy	PHI	2011	0.281	0.268	0.338	0.399	631	152	63	16
Reynolds, Mark	BAL	2011	0.280	0.221	0.323	0.483	620	118	86	37
Jeter, Derek	NYY	2011	0.280	0.297	0.355	0.388	607	162	61	6
Smith, Seth	COL	2011	0.279	0.284	0.347	0.483	533	135	59	15
Ethier, Andre	LAD	2011	0.278	0.292	0.368	0.421	551	142	62	11
Damon, Johnny	TBR	2011	0.278	0.261	0.326	0.418	647	152	73	16
Kotchman, Casey	TBR	2011	0.277	0.306	0.378	0.422	563	153	48	10
McCann, Brian	ATL	2011	0.277	0.270	0.351	0.466	527	126	71	24
Jones, Adam	BAL	2011	0.277	0.280	0.319	0.466	618	159	83	25
Morrison, Logan	FLA	2011	0.277	0.247	0.330	0.468	525	114	72	23
Abreu, Bobby	ANA	2011	0.274	0.253	0.353	0.365	585	127	60	8
Walker, Neil	PIT	2011	0.274	0.273	0.334	0.408	662	163	83	12
Peralta, Jhonny	DET	2011	0.274	0.299	0.345	0.478	576	157	86	21
Bruce, Jay	CIN	2011	0.273	0.256	0.341	0.474	664	150	97	32
Weeks, Rickie	MIL	2011	0.273	0.269	0.350	0.468	515	122	49	20
Young, Chris	ARI	2011	0.273	0.236	0.331	0.420	659	134	71	20
Wieters, Matt	BAL	2011	0.273	0.262	0.328	0.450	551	131	68	22
Cuddyer, Michael	MIN	2011	0.273	0.284	0.346	0.459	584	150	70	20
Kendrick, Howie	ANA	2011	0.273	0.285	0.338	0.464	583	153	63	18
Santana, Carlos	CLE	2011	0.272	0.239	0.351	0.457	658	132	79	27
Hosmer, Eric	KCR	2011	0.272	0.293	0.334	0.465	563	153	78	19
Espinosa, Danny	WAS	2011	0.271	0.236	0.323	0.414	658	135	66	21
Castro, Starlin	CHC	2011	0.270	0.307	0.341	0.432	715	207	66	10
Markakis, Nick	BAL	2011	0.267	0.284	0.351	0.406	716	182	73	15
Trumbo, Mark	ANA	2011	0.266	0.254	0.291	0.477	573	137	87	29
Matsui, Hideki	OAK	2011	0.266	0.251	0.321	0.375	585	130	72	12
Lind, Adam	TOR	2011	0.266	0.251	0.295	0.439	542	125	87	26
Pennington, Cliff	OAK	2011	0.266	0.264	0.319	0.369	570	136	58	8
Bourn, Michael	HOU	2011	0.266	0.294	0.349	0.386	722	193	50	2
Hardy, J.J.	BAL	2011	0.265	0.269	0.310	0.491	567	142	80	30
Soriano, Alfonso	CHC	2011	0.265	0.244	0.289	0.469	508	116	88	26
Andrus, Elvis	TEX	2011	0.263	0.279	0.347	0.361	665	164	60	5
Callaspo, Alberto	ANA	2011	0.263	0.288	0.366	0.375	536	137	46	6
Francoeur, Jeff	KCR	2011	0.262	0.285	0.329	0.476	656	171	87	20
Loney, James	LAD	2011	0.262	0.288	0.339	0.416	582	153	65	12
Bonifacio, Emilio	FLA	2011	0.261	0.296	0.360	0.393	641	167	36	5

Player	Team	Year	GPA	BA	OBP	SLG	PA	Hits	RBI	HR
Hunter, Torii	ANA	2011	0.261	0.262	0.336	0.429	649	152	82	23
Uggla, Dan	ATL	2011	0.261	0.233	0.311	0.453	672	140	82	36
Johnson, Kelly	ARI	2011	0.260	0.222	0.304	0.413	613	121	58	21
Sanchez, Gaby	FLA	2011	0.259	0.266	0.352	0.427	661	152	78	19
Upton, B.J.	TBR	2011	0.259	0.243	0.331	0.429	640	136	81	23
Moreland, Mitch	TEX	2011	0.258	0.259	0.320	0.414	512	120	51	16
Pagan, Angel	NYM	2011	0.258	0.262	0.322	0.372	532	125	56	7
Rivera, Juan	TOR	2011	0.257	0.258	0.319	0.382	521	120	74	11
Maybin, Cameron	SDP	2011	0.257	0.264	0.323	0.393	568	136	40	9
Aybar, Erick	ANA	2011	0.256	0.279	0.322	0.421	605	155	59	10
Bourjos, Peter	ANA	2011	0.255	0.271	0.327	0.438	552	136	43	12
Jay, Jon	STL	2011	0.254	0.297	0.344	0.424	503	135	37	10
Ibanez, Raul	PHI	2011	0.252	0.245	0.289	0.419	575	131	84	20
Encarnacion, E.	TOR	2011	0.252	0.272	0.334	0.453	530	131	55	17
Rasmus, Colby	STL	2011	0.251	0.225	0.298	0.391	526	106	53	14
Pierre, Juan	CHW	2011	0.251	0.279	0.329	0.327	711	178	50	2
Prado, Martin	ATL	2011	0.250	0.260	0.302	0.385	590	143	57	13
Valencia, Danny	MIN	2011	0.250	0.246	0.294	0.383	608	139	72	15
Fukudome, K.	CHC	2011	0.250	0.262	0.342	0.370	603	139	35	8
Stubbs, Drew	CIN	2011	0.246	0.243	0.321	0.364	681	147	44	15
Ramirez, Alexei	CHW	2011	0.246	0.269	0.328	0.399	684	165	70	15
Gardner, Brett	NYY	2011	0.245	0.259	0.345	0.369	588	132	36	7
Huff, Aubrey	SFG	2011	0.244	0.246	0.306	0.370	579	128	59	12
Carroll, Jamey	LAD	2011	0.244	0.290	0.359	0.347	510	131	17	0
Crisp, Coco	OAK	2011	0.243	0.264	0.314	0.379	583	140	54	8
Jackson, Austin	DET	2011	0.243	0.249	0.317	0.374	668	147	45	10
DeJesus, David	OAK	2011	0.242	0.240	0.323	0.376	506	106	46	10
Werth, Jayson	WAS	2011	0.242	0.232	0.330	0.389	649	130	58	20
Barney, Darwin	CHC	2011	0.241	0.276	0.313	0.353	571	146	43	2
Polanco, Placido	PHI	2011	0.241	0.277	0.335	0.339	523	130	50	5
Bay, Jason	NYM	2011	0.240	0.245	0.329	0.374	509	109	57	12
Infante, Omar	FLA	2011	0.239	0.276	0.315	0.382	640	160	49	7
Andino, Robert	BAL	2011	0.239	0.263	0.327	0.344	511	120	36	5
Young, Delmon	MIN	2011	0.239	0.268	0.302	0.393	503	127	64	12
Crawford, Carl	BOS	2011	0.239	0.255	0.289	0.405	539	129	56	11
Pierzynski, A.J.	CHW	2011	0.239	0.287	0.323	0.405	500	133	48	8
Ludwick, Ryan	SDP	2011	0.238	0.237	0.310	0.363	558	116	75	13
Guerrero, V.	BAL	2011	0.236	0.290	0.317	0.416	590	163	63	13
Buck, John	FLA	2011	0.236	0.227	0.316	0.367	530	106	57	16
Wells, Vernon	ANA	2011	0.234	0.218	0.248	0.412	529	110	66	25
Beckham, Gordon	CHW	2011	0.233	0.230	0.296	0.337	557	115	44	10
Suzuki, Ichiro	SEA	2011	0.232	0.272	0.310	0.335	721	184	47	5
Hill, Aaron	TOR	2011	0.231	0.246	0.299	0.356	571	128	61	8
Desmond, Ian	WAS	2011	0.230	0.253	0.298	0.358	639	148	49	8
Bartlett, Jason	SDP	2011	0.225	0.245	0.308	0.307	618	136	40	2
Suzuki, Kurt	OAK	2011	0.218	0.237	0.301	0.385	515	109	44	14
Olivo, Miguel	SEA	2011	0.217	0.224	0.253	0.388	507	107	62	19
Escobar, Alcides	KCR	2011	0.217	0.254	0.290	0.343	598	139	46	4
Ellis, Mark	OAK	2011	0.214	0.248	0.288	0.346	519	119	41	7
Betancourt, Y.	MIL	2011	0.211	0.252	0.271	0.381	584	140	68	13
McGehee, Casey	MIL	2011	0.210	0.223	0.280	0.346	600	122	67	13
Gonzalez, Alex	ATL	2011	0.204	0.241	0.270	0.372	593	136	56	15
Rios, Alex	CHW	2011	0.191	0.227	0.265	0.348	570	122	44	13
Average			**0.2543**	**0.2551**	**0.3206**	**0.3990**				

Table 3.11. Batters with 500+ Plate Appearances, 2010

Player	Team	Year	GPA	BA	OBP	SLG	PA	Hits	RBI	HR
Votto, Joey	CIN	2010	0.368	0.324	0.424	0.600	648	177	113	37
Hamilton, Josh	TEX	2010	0.362	0.359	0.411	0.633	571	186	100	32
Cabrera, Miguel	DET	2010	0.357	0.328	0.420	0.622	648	180	126	38
Bautista, Jose	TOR	2010	0.341	0.260	0.378	0.617	683	148	124	54
Konerko, Paul	CHW	2010	0.336	0.312	0.393	0.584	631	171	111	39
Gonzalez, Carlos	COL	2010	0.335	0.336	0.376	0.598	636	197	117	34
Pujols, Albert	STL	2010	0.332	0.312	0.414	0.596	700	183	118	42
Gonzalez, Adrian	SDP	2010	0.332	0.298	0.393	0.511	693	176	101	31
Heyward, Jason	ATL	2010	0.328	0.277	0.393	0.456	623	144	72	18
Utley, Chase	PHI	2010	0.324	0.275	0.387	0.445	511	117	65	16
Cano, Robinson	NYY	2010	0.323	0.319	0.381	0.534	696	200	109	29
Tulowitzki, Troy	COL	2010	0.322	0.315	0.381	0.568	529	148	95	27
Rodriguez, Alex	NYY	2010	0.321	0.270	0.341	0.506	595	141	125	30
Holliday, Matt	STL	2010	0.317	0.312	0.390	0.532	675	186	103	28
Crawford, Carl	TBR	2010	0.316	0.307	0.356	0.495	663	184	90	19
Zimmerman, Ryan	WAS	2010	0.316	0.307	0.388	0.510	603	161	85	25
Choo, Shin-Soo	CLE	2010	0.316	0.300	0.401	0.484	646	165	90	22
Huff, Aubrey	SFG	2010	0.312	0.290	0.385	0.506	668	165	86	26
Braun, Ryan	MIL	2010	0.311	0.304	0.365	0.501	685	188	103	25
Teixeira, Mark	NYY	2010	0.310	0.256	0.365	0.481	712	154	108	33
Werth, Jayson	PHI	2010	0.310	0.296	0.388	0.532	652	164	85	27
Hart, Corey	MIL	2010	0.309	0.283	0.340	0.525	614	158	102	31
Swisher, Nick	NYY	2010	0.306	0.288	0.359	0.511	635	163	89	29
Matsui, Hideki	ANA	2010	0.305	0.274	0.361	0.459	558	132	84	21
Fielder, Prince	MIL	2010	0.304	0.261	0.401	0.471	714	151	83	32
Dunn, Adam	WAS	2010	0.304	0.260	0.356	0.536	648	145	103	38
Longoria, Evan	TBR	2010	0.304	0.294	0.372	0.507	661	169	104	22
Ortiz, David	BOS	2010	0.303	0.270	0.370	0.529	606	140	102	32
Mauer, Joe	MIN	2010	0.303	0.327	0.402	0.469	584	167	75	9
Uggla, Dan	FLA	2010	0.303	0.287	0.369	0.508	674	169	105	33
Ramirez, Hanley	FLA	2010	0.303	0.300	0.378	0.475	619	163	76	21
Young, Delmon	MIN	2010	0.302	0.298	0.333	0.493	613	170	112	21
Quentin, Carlos	CHW	2010	0.301	0.243	0.342	0.479	527	110	87	26
Guerrero, V.	TEX	2010	0.299	0.300	0.345	0.496	643	178	115	29
Rasmus, Colby	STL	2010	0.299	0.276	0.361	0.498	534	128	66	23
Howard, Ryan	PHI	2010	0.299	0.276	0.353	0.505	620	152	108	31
Ethier, Andre	LAD	2010	0.298	0.292	0.364	0.493	585	151	82	23
Sanchez, Gaby	FLA	2010	0.297	0.273	0.341	0.448	643	156	85	19
McCann, Brian	ATL	2010	0.295	0.269	0.375	0.453	566	129	77	21
Abreu, Bobby	ANA	2010	0.293	0.255	0.352	0.435	667	146	78	20
Johnson, Kelly	ARI	2010	0.292	0.284	0.370	0.496	671	166	71	26
Weeks, Rickie	MIL	2010	0.292	0.269	0.366	0.464	754	175	83	29
Hunter, Torii	ANA	2010	0.291	0.281	0.354	0.464	646	161	90	23
Drew, Stephen	ARI	2010	0.291	0.278	0.352	0.458	633	157	61	15
LaRoche, Adam	ARI	2010	0.291	0.261	0.320	0.468	615	146	100	25
Wright, David	NYM	2010	0.290	0.283	0.354	0.503	670	166	103	29
Soriano, Alfonso	CHC	2010	0.290	0.258	0.322	0.496	548	128	79	24
McCutchen, A.	PIT	2010	0.289	0.286	0.365	0.449	653	163	56	16
Beltre, Adrian	BOS	2010	0.289	0.321	0.365	0.553	641	189	102	28
Scott, Luke	BAL	2010	0.288	0.284	0.368	0.535	517	127	72	27
Ibanez, Raul	PHI	2010	0.288	0.275	0.349	0.444	636	154	83	16
Rolen, Scott	CIN	2010	0.288	0.285	0.358	0.497	537	134	83	20

Player	Team	Year	GPA	BA	OBP	SLG	PA	Hits	RBI	HR
Byrd, Marlon	CHC	2010	0.288	0.293	0.346	0.429	630	170	66	12
McGehee, Casey	MIL	2010	0.287	0.285	0.337	0.464	670	174	104	23
Pagan, Angel	NYM	2010	0.287	0.290	0.340	0.425	633	168	69	11
Gardner, Brett	NYY	2010	0.284	0.277	0.383	0.379	569	132	47	5
Torres, Andres	SFG	2010	0.283	0.268	0.343	0.479	570	136	63	16
Prado, Martin	ATL	2010	0.283	0.307	0.350	0.459	651	184	66	15
Pence, Hunter	HOU	2010	0.283	0.282	0.325	0.461	658	173	91	25
Pena, Carlos	TBR	2010	0.282	0.196	0.325	0.407	582	95	84	28
Wells, Vernon	TOR	2010	0.282	0.273	0.331	0.515	646	161	88	31
Young, Chris	ARI	2010	0.282	0.257	0.341	0.452	664	150	91	27
Butler, Billy	KCR	2010	0.281	0.318	0.388	0.469	678	189	78	15
Markakis, Nick	BAL	2010	0.280	0.297	0.370	0.436	709	187	60	12
Fowler, Dexter	COL	2010	0.280	0.260	0.347	0.410	505	114	36	6
Ludwick, Ryan	STL	2010	0.279	0.251	0.325	0.418	553	123	69	17
Young, Michael	TEX	2010	0.278	0.284	0.330	0.444	718	186	91	21
Granderson, C.	NYY	2010	0.278	0.247	0.324	0.468	528	115	67	24
Barton, Daric	OAK	2010	0.278	0.273	0.393	0.405	686	152	57	10
Davis, Ike	NYM	2010	0.278	0.264	0.351	0.440	601	138	71	19
Martinez, Victor	BOS	2010	0.278	0.302	0.351	0.493	538	149	79	20
Drew, J.D.	BOS	2010	0.278	0.255	0.341	0.452	546	122	68	22
Keppinger, Jeff	HOU	2010	0.277	0.288	0.351	0.393	575	148	59	6
Bruce, Jay	CIN	2010	0.275	0.281	0.353	0.493	573	143	70	25
Victorino, Shane	PHI	2010	0.275	0.259	0.327	0.429	648	152	69	18
Gomes, Jonny	CIN	2010	0.275	0.266	0.327	0.431	571	136	86	18
Overbay, Lyle	TOR	2010	0.274	0.243	0.329	0.433	608	130	67	20
Boesch, Brennan	DET	2010	0.271	0.256	0.320	0.416	512	119	67	14
Stubbs, Drew	CIN	2010	0.270	0.255	0.329	0.444	583	131	77	22
Upton, Justin	ARI	2010	0.270	0.273	0.356	0.442	571	135	69	17
Rios, Alex	CHW	2010	0.269	0.284	0.334	0.457	617	161	88	21
Loney, James	LAD	2010	0.268	0.267	0.329	0.395	648	157	88	10
Damon, Johnny	DET	2010	0.267	0.271	0.355	0.401	613	146	51	8
Reynolds, Mark	ARI	2010	0.266	0.198	0.320	0.433	596	99	85	32
Polanco, Placido	PHI	2010	0.266	0.298	0.339	0.386	602	165	52	6
Lee, Derrek	CHC	2010	0.264	0.260	0.347	0.428	626	142	80	19
Infante, Omar	ATL	2010	0.264	0.321	0.359	0.416	506	151	47	8
Jackson, Austin	DET	2010	0.263	0.293	0.345	0.400	675	181	41	4
Suzuki, Ichiro	SEA	2010	0.263	0.315	0.359	0.394	732	214	43	6
Reyes, Jose	NYM	2010	0.263	0.282	0.321	0.428	603	159	54	11
Peralta, Jhonny	CLE	2010	0.263	0.249	0.311	0.392	615	137	81	15
Lind, Adam	TOR	2010	0.263	0.237	0.287	0.425	613	135	72	23
Span, Denard	MIN	2010	0.262	0.264	0.331	0.348	705	166	58	3
Ramirez, Alexei	CHW	2010	0.262	0.282	0.313	0.431	626	165	70	18
Upton, B.J.	TBR	2010	0.261	0.237	0.322	0.424	610	127	62	18
Zobrist, Ben	TBR	2010	0.261	0.238	0.346	0.353	655	129	75	10
Podsednik, Scott	KCR	2010	0.261	0.297	0.342	0.382	595	160	51	6
Bourn, Michael	HOU	2010	0.260	0.265	0.341	0.346	605	142	38	2
Ramirez, Aramis	CHC	2010	0.260	0.241	0.294	0.452	507	112	83	25
Cuddyer, Michael	MIN	2010	0.260	0.271	0.336	0.417	675	165	81	14
Phillips, Brandon	CIN	2010	0.259	0.275	0.332	0.430	687	172	59	18
Desmond, Ian	WAS	2010	0.259	0.269	0.308	0.392	574	141	65	10
Ross, Cody	FLA	2010	0.258	0.269	0.322	0.413	569	141	65	14
Blake, Casey	LAD	2010	0.258	0.248	0.320	0.407	571	126	64	17
Jones, Adam	BAL	2010	0.257	0.284	0.325	0.442	621	165	69	19
Kubel, Jason	MIN	2010	0.257	0.249	0.323	0.427	582	129	92	21

Player	Team	Year	GPA	BA	OBP	SLG	PA	Hits	RBI	HR
Kendrick, Howie	ANA	2010	0.257	0.279	0.313	0.407	658	172	75	10
Scutaro, Marco	BOS	2010	0.256	0.275	0.333	0.388	695	174	56	11
Kemp, Matt	LAD	2010	0.255	0.249	0.310	0.450	668	150	89	28
Bartlett, Jason	TBR	2010	0.255	0.254	0.324	0.350	532	119	47	4
Betancourt, Y.	KCR	2010	0.254	0.259	0.288	0.405	588	144	78	16
Napoli, Mike	ANA	2010	0.254	0.238	0.316	0.468	510	108	68	26
Guillen, Jose	KCR	2010	0.253	0.258	0.314	0.416	577	135	77	19
Uribe, Juan	SFG	2010	0.253	0.248	0.310	0.440	575	129	85	24
Gonzalez, Alex	TOR	2010	0.253	0.250	0.294	0.447	640	149	88	23
Castro, Starlin	CHC	2010	0.252	0.300	0.347	0.408	506	139	41	3
Schumaker, Skip	STL	2010	0.252	0.265	0.328	0.338	529	126	42	5
Sandoval, Pablo	SFG	2010	0.251	0.268	0.323	0.409	616	151	63	13
Headley, Chase	SDP	2010	0.250	0.264	0.327	0.375	674	161	58	11
Molina, Yadier	STL	2010	0.249	0.262	0.329	0.342	521	122	62	6
Andrus, Elvis	TEX	2010	0.248	0.265	0.342	0.301	674	156	35	0
Lee, Carlos	HOU	2010	0.248	0.246	0.291	0.417	649	149	89	24
Jones, Garrett	PIT	2010	0.247	0.247	0.306	0.414	654	146	86	21
Inge, Brandon	DET	2010	0.247	0.247	0.321	0.397	580	127	70	13
Jeter, Derek	NYY	2010	0.247	0.270	0.340	0.370	739	179	67	10
Pennington, Cliff	OAK	2010	0.246	0.250	0.319	0.368	576	127	46	6
Pierre, Juan	CHW	2010	0.246	0.275	0.341	0.316	734	179	47	1
Wigginton, Ty	BAL	2010	0.245	0.248	0.312	0.415	649	144	76	22
Tejada, Miguel	SDP	2010	0.244	0.269	0.312	0.381	681	171	71	15
Hudson, Orlando	MIN	2010	0.242	0.268	0.338	0.372	559	133	37	6
Wieters, Matt	BAL	2010	0.242	0.249	0.319	0.377	502	111	55	11
Pierzynski, A.J.	CHW	2010	0.238	0.270	0.300	0.388	503	128	56	9
Suzuki, Kurt	OAK	2010	0.237	0.242	0.303	0.366	544	120	71	13
Hill, Aaron	TOR	2010	0.237	0.205	0.271	0.394	580	108	68	26
Davis, Rajai	OAK	2010	0.236	0.284	0.320	0.377	561	149	52	5
Francoeur, Jeff	TEX	2010	0.235	0.249	0.300	0.383	503	113	65	13
Figgins, Chone	SEA	2010	0.235	0.259	0.340	0.306	702	156	35	1
Cabrera, Melky	ATL	2010	0.234	0.255	0.317	0.354	509	117	42	4
Gutierrez, F.	SEA	2010	0.232	0.245	0.303	0.363	629	139	64	12
Callaspo, Alberto	KCR	2010	0.231	0.265	0.302	0.374	601	149	56	10
Escobar, Yunel	TOR	2010	0.229	0.256	0.337	0.318	567	127	35	4
Kouzmanoff, K.	OAK	2010	0.228	0.247	0.283	0.396	586	136	71	16
Morgan, Nyjer	WAS	2010	0.228	0.253	0.319	0.314	577	129	24	0
Cabrera, Orlando	CIN	2010	0.227	0.263	0.303	0.354	537	130	42	4
Theriot, Ryan	CHC	2010	0.227	0.270	0.321	0.312	640	158	29	2
Cedeno, Ronny	PIT	2010	0.223	0.256	0.293	0.382	502	120	38	8
Aybar, Erick	ANA	2010	0.218	0.253	0.306	0.330	589	135	29	5
Cantu, Jorge	TEX	2010	0.213	0.256	0.304	0.392	515	121	56	11
Lopez, Jose	SEA	2010	0.206	0.239	0.270	0.339	622	142	58	10
Izturis, Cesar	BAL	2010	0.198	0.230	0.277	0.268	513	109	28	1
Escobar, Alcides	MIL	2010	0.196	0.235	0.288	0.326	552	119	41	4
Average			0.2575	0.2574	0.3325	0.4028				

Table 3.12. Pitchers with 500+ Batters Faced, 2012

Player	Team	Year	ERA	GPA	BA	OBP	SLG	PA	Hits	RBI	HR
Medlen, Kris	ATL	2012	1.57	0.185	0.208	0.243	0.286	520	103	30	6
Price, David	TBR	2012	2.56	0.211	0.226	0.284	0.318	836	173	57	16
Kershaw, Clayton	LAD	2012	2.53	0.212	0.210	0.270	0.323	901	170	60	16
Dickey, R.A.	NYM	2012	2.73	0.218	0.226	0.278	0.362	927	192	70	24

Player	Team	Year	ERA	GPA	BA	OBP	SLG	PA	Hits	RBI	HR
Verlander, Justin	DET	2012	2.64	0.218	0.217	0.270	0.331	956	192	71	19
Gonzalez, Gio	WAS	2012	2.89	0.219	0.206	0.283	0.299	822	149	61	9
Sale, Chris	CHW	2012	3.05	0.219	0.235	0.291	0.370	772	167	59	19
Weaver, Jered	ANA	2012	2.81	0.221	0.214	0.265	0.340	739	147	55	20
Hernandez, Felix	SEA	2012	3.06	0.223	0.241	0.296	0.333	939	209	74	14
Cain, Matt	SFG	2012	2.79	0.223	0.222	0.274	0.361	876	177	66	21
Zimmermann, J.	WAS	2012	2.94	0.224	0.251	0.297	0.388	805	186	62	18
Cueto, Johnny	CIN	2012	2.78	0.225	0.252	0.302	0.366	888	205	64	15
Lohse, Kyle	STL	2012	2.86	0.225	0.239	0.274	0.368	864	192	63	19
Morrow, Brandon	TOR	2012	2.96	0.227	0.214	0.280	0.354	504	98	43	12
Strasburg, S.	WAS	2012	3.16	0.230	0.230	0.291	0.359	653	136	59	15
Lee, Cliff	PHI	2012	3.16	0.231	0.255	0.278	0.411	847	207	74	26
Hamels, Cole	PHI	2012	3.05	0.231	0.237	0.285	0.377	867	190	75	24
Harrison, Matt	TEX	2012	3.29	0.232	0.258	0.309	0.406	876	210	72	22
Parker, Jarrod	OAK	2012	3.47	0.233	0.248	0.312	0.358	751	166	64	11
Dempster, Ryan	TEX	2012	3.38	0.233	0.237	0.294	0.384	717	155	64	19
Hellickson, J.	TBR	2012	3.10	0.234	0.244	0.307	0.402	741	163	60	25
Latos, Mat	CIN	2012	3.48	0.237	0.230	0.291	0.390	858	179	80	25
Peavy, Jake	CHW	2012	3.37	0.238	0.234	0.284	0.387	882	191	81	27
Niese, Jonathon	NYM	2012	3.40	0.238	0.241	0.291	0.372	788	174	71	22
Greinke, Zack	ANA	2012	3.48	0.238	0.249	0.297	0.366	868	200	78	18
Vogelsong, Ryan	SFG	2012	3.37	0.239	0.242	0.309	0.379	788	171	69	17
Colon, Bartolo	OAK	2012	3.43	0.239	0.266	0.292	0.400	636	161	57	17
Iwakuma, Hisashi	SEA	2012	3.16	0.239	0.248	0.315	0.403	519	117	46	17
Miley, Wade	ARI	2012	3.33	0.240	0.255	0.290	0.395	807	193	73	14
Bumgarner, M.	SFG	2012	3.37	0.240	0.234	0.284	0.386	849	183	79	23
Johnson, Josh	MIA	2012	3.81	0.241	0.252	0.315	0.363	798	180	76	14
Vargas, Jason	SEA	2012	3.85	0.241	0.245	0.293	0.421	887	201	86	35
Burnett, A.J.	PIT	2012	3.51	0.241	0.246	0.307	0.361	851	189	75	18
Kuroda, Hiroki	NYY	2012	3.32	0.241	0.249	0.299	0.406	891	205	82	25
Capuano, Chris	LAD	2012	3.72	0.243	0.254	0.305	0.410	817	188	71	25
Detwiler, Ross	WAS	2012	3.40	0.244	0.241	0.304	0.377	686	149	66	15
Sabathia, C.C.	NYY	2012	3.38	0.244	0.238	0.285	0.381	833	184	83	22
Diamond, Scott	MIN	2012	3.54	0.244	0.274	0.308	0.423	714	184	73	17
Arroyo, Bronson	CIN	2012	3.74	0.244	0.267	0.301	0.421	835	209	81	26
Buehrle, Mark	MIA	2012	3.74	0.245	0.258	0.296	0.414	828	197	85	26
Gallardo, Yovani	MIL	2012	3.66	0.245	0.243	0.313	0.392	860	185	79	26
Maholm, Paul	CHC	2012	3.67	0.245	0.250	0.311	0.404	786	178	72	20
Sanchez, Anibal	DET	2012	3.86	0.246	0.265	0.310	0.405	820	200	75	20
Shields, James	TBR	2012	3.52	0.246	0.239	0.295	0.383	944	208	89	25
Harrell, Lucas	HOU	2012	3.76	0.247	0.253	0.322	0.363	827	185	77	13
Minor, Mike	ATL	2012	4.12	0.247	0.232	0.294	0.407	728	151	73	26
Samardzija, Jeff	CHC	2012	3.81	0.248	0.240	0.302	0.396	723	157	74	20
Estrada, Marco	MIL	2012	3.64	0.248	0.247	0.285	0.419	562	129	60	18
Garcia, Jaime	STL	2012	3.92	0.248	0.289	0.327	0.402	515	136	51	7
Cobb, Alex	TBR	2012	4.03	0.249	0.254	0.316	0.374	569	130	58	11
Quintana, Jose	CHW	2012	3.76	0.249	0.275	0.332	0.422	568	142	59	14
Cahill, Trevor	ARI	2012	3.78	0.249	0.250	0.325	0.380	839	184	80	16
Bailey, Homer	CIN	2012	3.68	0.250	0.256	0.306	0.412	874	206	85	26
Marcum, Shaun	MIL	2012	3.70	0.250	0.245	0.309	0.411	527	116	54	16
Hudson, Tim	ATL	2012	3.62	0.250	0.248	0.304	0.361	749	168	73	12
Fiers, Michael	MIL	2012	3.74	0.251	0.254	0.305	0.389	539	125	53	12
Fister, Doug	DET	2012	3.45	0.251	0.249	0.299	0.385	673	156	62	15
Scherzer, Max	DET	2012	3.74	0.252	0.250	0.312	0.409	787	179	73	23

Player	Team	Year	ERA	GPA	BA	OBP	SLG	PA	Hits	RBI	HR
Kendrick, Kyle	PHI	2012	3.90	0.252	0.254	0.315	0.416	674	154	68	20
Billingsley, Chad	LAD	2012	3.55	0.252	0.257	0.315	0.410	634	148	62	11
Lynn, Lance	STL	2012	3.78	0.252	0.253	0.327	0.401	744	168	72	16
Rodriguez, Wandy	HOU	2012	3.76	0.253	0.255	0.304	0.391	875	205	93	21
Darvish, Yu	TEX	2012	3.90	0.253	0.220	0.313	0.346	816	156	81	14
Moore, Matt	TBR	2012	3.81	0.253	0.238	0.326	0.380	759	158	75	18
Villanueva, C.	TOR	2012	4.16	0.254	0.242	0.312	0.446	521	113	56	23
Jackson, Edwin	WAS	2012	4.03	0.254	0.243	0.298	0.421	790	173	86	23
Westbrook, Jake	STL	2012	3.97	0.256	0.282	0.338	0.391	751	191	70	12
Wainwright, Adam	STL	2012	3.94	0.256	0.259	0.309	0.392	831	196	83	15
Harang, Aaron	LAD	2012	3.61	0.257	0.246	0.329	0.382	786	167	72	14
Volquez, Edinson	SDP	2012	4.14	0.257	0.236	0.344	0.362	802	160	77	14
Milone, Tom	OAK	2012	3.74	0.258	0.278	0.313	0.424	791	207	83	24
Zito, Barry	SFG	2012	4.15	0.258	0.263	0.332	0.426	799	186	77	20
Halladay, Roy	PHI	2012	4.49	0.258	0.261	0.306	0.407	646	155	75	18
Wilson, C.J.	ANA	2012	3.83	0.258	0.239	0.323	0.361	865	181	86	19
McDonald, James	PIT	2012	4.21	0.259	0.233	0.311	0.404	713	147	77	21
Richard, Clayton	SDP	2012	3.99	0.260	0.267	0.304	0.435	910	228	99	31
Wood, Travis	CHC	2012	4.27	0.260	0.232	0.305	0.441	649	133	74	25
Floyd, Gavin	CHW	2012	4.29	0.260	0.259	0.337	0.418	724	166	74	22
Kennedy, Ian	ARI	2012	4.02	0.261	0.266	0.322	0.453	899	216	94	28
Beavan, Blake	SEA	2012	4.43	0.262	0.281	0.317	0.475	638	168	71	23
Nolasco, Ricky	MIA	2012	4.48	0.264	0.285	0.331	0.423	832	214	94	18
Norris, Bud	HOU	2012	4.65	0.265	0.254	0.329	0.423	733	165	79	23
Buchholz, Clay	BOS	2012	4.56	0.265	0.263	0.330	0.426	802	187	84	25
Millwood, Kevin	SEA	2012	4.25	0.266	0.271	0.332	0.397	689	168	85	13
Saunders, Joe	ARI	2012	4.07	0.266	0.281	0.320	0.435	745	195	78	21
Haren, Dan	ANA	2012	4.33	0.266	0.275	0.312	0.463	747	190	84	28
Beckett, Josh	BOS	2012	4.65	0.267	0.264	0.319	0.423	730	174	84	21
Hughes, Phil	NYY	2012	4.23	0.268	0.259	0.305	0.460	815	196	95	35
Eovaldi, Nathan	LAD	2012	4.30	0.268	0.284	0.349	0.422	526	133	56	10
Williams, Jerome	ANA	2012	4.58	0.269	0.263	0.313	0.430	572	139	72	17
Mendoza, Luis	KCR	2012	4.23	0.269	0.278	0.348	0.411	709	176	72	15
Blanton, Joe	PHI	2012	4.71	0.270	0.273	0.306	0.453	806	207	93	29
Happ, J.A.	TOR	2012	4.79	0.271	0.264	0.332	0.455	627	147	72	19
Hanson, Tommy	ATL	2012	4.48	0.271	0.271	0.344	0.464	761	183	83	27
Correia, Kevin	PIT	2012	4.21	0.271	0.267	0.315	0.418	728	176	84	20
Lester, Jon	BOS	2012	4.82	0.273	0.273	0.331	0.442	876	216	108	25
Worley, Vance	PHI	2012	4.20	0.273	0.296	0.359	0.447	590	154	63	12
Leake, Mike	CIN	2012	4.58	0.275	0.287	0.326	0.479	757	201	90	26
Lincecum, Tim	SFG	2012	5.18	0.275	0.257	0.341	0.426	825	183	95	23
Holland, Derek	TEX	2012	4.67	0.276	0.243	0.299	0.446	730	162	91	32
Alvarez, H.	TOR	2012	4.85	0.277	0.290	0.339	0.473	807	216	97	29
Masterson, Justin	CLE	2012	4.93	0.279	0.269	0.348	0.388	906	212	114	18
Zambrano, Carlos	MIA	2012	4.49	0.279	0.251	0.356	0.358	591	123	71	9
McAllister, Zach	CLE	2012	4.24	0.279	0.268	0.318	0.449	543	133	69	19
Chen, Bruce	KCR	2012	5.07	0.281	0.281	0.328	0.486	827	215	102	33
Liriano, F.	MIN	2012	5.34	0.281	0.244	0.344	0.397	693	143	83	19
Lowe, Derek	CLE	2012	5.11	0.282	0.311	0.367	0.429	640	180	79	10
Doubront, Felix	BOS	2012	4.86	0.282	0.259	0.337	0.438	709	162	88	24
Porcello, Rick	DET	2012	4.59	0.283	0.310	0.353	0.455	783	226	96	16
Bedard, Erik	PIT	2012	5.01	0.283	0.263	0.341	0.418	557	129	67	14
Guthrie, Jeremy	COL	2012	4.76	0.284	0.288	0.340	0.483	788	206	98	30
Nova, Ivan	NYY	2012	5.02	0.285	0.288	0.349	0.511	748	194	92	28

Player	Team	Year	ERA	GPA	BA	OBP	SLG	PA	Hits	RBI	HR
Francis, Jeff	COL	2012	5.58	0.286	0.316	0.356	0.490	502	145	64	15
Santana, Ervin	ANA	2012	5.16	0.286	0.239	0.308	0.465	764	165	101	39
Jimenez, Ubaldo	CLE	2012	5.40	0.286	0.273	0.365	0.452	805	190	103	25
Feldman, Scott	TEX	2012	5.09	0.289	0.279	0.321	0.424	536	139	74	14
Hunter, Tommy	BAL	2012	5.45	0.291	0.302	0.337	0.527	573	161	76	32
Hochevar, Luke	KCR	2012	5.73	0.295	0.281	0.347	0.471	800	202	106	27
Lyles, Jordan	HOU	2012	5.09	0.298	0.279	0.332	0.440	628	159	84	20
Marquis, Jason	SDP	2012	5.22	0.300	0.289	0.346	0.497	561	146	77	23
Romero, Ricky	TOR	2012	5.77	0.301	0.282	0.381	0.440	829	198	98	21
Volstad, Chris	CHC	2012	6.31	0.306	0.306	0.365	0.482	507	137	78	16
Average			4.01	0.2557	0.2545	0.3190	0.4053				

Table 3.13. Pitchers with 500+ Batters Faced, 2011

Player	Team	Year	ERA	GPA	BA	OBP	SLG	PA	Hits	RBI	HR
Halladay, Roy	PHI	2011	2.35	0.203	0.239	0.269	0.313	933	208	60	10
Weaver, Jered	ANA	2011	2.41	0.206	0.212	0.262	0.336	926	182	62	20
Kershaw, Clayton	LAD	2011	2.28	0.207	0.207	0.256	0.298	912	174	59	15
Lee, Cliff	PHI	2011	2.40	0.207	0.229	0.268	0.339	920	197	64	18
Verlander, Justin	DET	2011	2.40	0.208	0.192	0.242	0.313	969	174	68	24
Hamels, Cole	PHI	2011	2.79	0.211	0.214	0.259	0.337	850	169	65	19
Beckett, Josh	BOS	2011	2.89	0.212	0.211	0.273	0.335	767	146	61	21
Kennedy, Ian	ARI	2011	2.88	0.214	0.227	0.281	0.361	900	186	68	19
Hellickson, J.	TBR	2011	2.95	0.220	0.210	0.287	0.373	774	146	56	21
Cueto, Johnny	CIN	2011	2.31	0.220	0.220	0.290	0.304	631	123	47	8
Shields, James	TBR	2011	2.82	0.221	0.217	0.273	0.350	975	195	72	26
Cain, Matt	SFG	2011	2.88	0.221	0.217	0.279	0.319	907	177	70	9
Romero, Ricky	TOR	2011	2.92	0.223	0.216	0.296	0.365	917	176	71	26
Luebke, Cory	SDP	2011	3.29	0.224	0.209	0.274	0.335	555	105	49	12
Vogelsong, Ryan	SFG	2011	2.71	0.224	0.244	0.310	0.361	752	164	57	15
Haren, Dan	ANA	2011	3.17	0.225	0.235	0.265	0.365	953	211	78	20
Lincecum, Tim	SFG	2011	2.74	0.225	0.222	0.302	0.344	900	176	66	15
Worley, Vance	PHI	2011	3.01	0.225	0.237	0.303	0.369	553	116	45	10
Jurrjens, Jair	ATL	2011	2.96	0.226	0.249	0.306	0.384	627	142	46	14
Fister, Doug	SEA	2011	2.83	0.227	0.237	0.278	0.339	875	193	69	11
Baker, Scott	MIN	2011	3.14	0.229	0.248	0.296	0.391	548	126	43	15
Sabathia, C.C.	NYY	2011	3.00	0.230	0.255	0.305	0.361	985	230	81	17
Kuroda, Hiroki	LAD	2011	3.07	0.231	0.254	0.300	0.415	838	196	70	24
Gonzalez, Gio	OAK	2011	3.12	0.232	0.230	0.318	0.336	864	175	64	17
Wilson, C.J.	TEX	2011	2.94	0.232	0.232	0.302	0.350	915	191	74	16
Hudson, Tim	ATL	2011	3.22	0.233	0.236	0.296	0.331	884	189	78	14
Collmenter, Josh	ARI	2011	3.38	0.233	0.237	0.278	0.374	621	137	52	17
Hanson, Tommy	ATL	2011	3.60	0.234	0.219	0.289	0.390	540	106	53	17
Zimmermann, J.	WAS	2011	3.18	0.235	0.251	0.294	0.377	662	154	49	12
Masterson, Justin	CLE	2011	3.21	0.237	0.257	0.318	0.349	908	211	68	11
Beachy, Brandon	ATL	2011	3.68	0.237	0.236	0.301	0.378	591	125	54	16
Santana, Ervin	ANA	2011	3.38	0.237	0.241	0.304	0.389	949	207	90	26
Humber, Philip	CHW	2011	3.75	0.238	0.243	0.294	0.357	676	151	59	14
Hernandez, Felix	SEA	2011	3.47	0.238	0.248	0.304	0.356	964	218	91	19
Pineda, Michael	SEA	2011	3.74	0.238	0.211	0.279	0.342	696	133	64	18
Latos, Mat	SDP	2011	3.47	0.239	0.233	0.292	0.363	799	168	69	16
Rodriguez, Wandy	HOU	2011	3.49	0.239	0.251	0.320	0.420	808	182	77	25
Carpenter, Chris	STL	2011	3.45	0.240	0.264	0.309	0.360	996	243	88	16
Lilly, Ted	LAD	2011	3.97	0.240	0.238	0.294	0.414	800	172	79	28

Player	Team	Year	ERA	GPA	BA	OBP	SLG	PA	Hits	RBI	HR
Dickey, R.A.	NYM	2011	3.28	0.241	0.256	0.308	0.382	876	202	82	18
McCarthy, B.	OAK	2011	3.32	0.241	0.258	0.281	0.377	690	168	63	11
Price, David	TBR	2011	3.49	0.241	0.230	0.289	0.370	918	192	86	22
Oswalt, Roy	PHI	2011	3.69	0.241	0.280	0.325	0.410	594	153	56	10
Lohse, Kyle	STL	2011	3.39	0.242	0.249	0.291	0.390	775	178	74	16
Lester, Jon	BOS	2011	3.47	0.242	0.234	0.316	0.374	799	166	69	20
Marcum, Shaun	MIL	2011	3.54	0.242	0.232	0.284	0.372	823	175	79	22
Karstens, Jeff	PIT	2011	3.38	0.243	0.263	0.302	0.419	668	163	66	22
Harrison, Matt	TEX	2011	3.39	0.244	0.257	0.312	0.374	772	180	69	13
Harang, Aaron	SDP	2011	3.64	0.244	0.269	0.331	0.427	719	175	67	20
Sanchez, Anibal	FLA	2011	3.67	0.244	0.250	0.313	0.398	830	187	80	20
Bumgarner, M.	SFG	2011	3.21	0.244	0.260	0.304	0.366	844	202	77	12
Wolf, Randy	MIL	2011	3.69	0.245	0.266	0.329	0.415	903	214	85	23
Chacin, Jhoulys	COL	2011	3.62	0.245	0.231	0.315	0.392	827	168	69	20
Jackson, Edwin	CHW	2011	3.79	0.245	0.290	0.342	0.427	861	225	86	16
Maholm, Paul	PIT	2011	3.66	0.245	0.262	0.321	0.390	687	160	63	11
Hudson, Daniel	ARI	2011	3.49	0.246	0.255	0.301	0.394	921	217	87	17
Leake, Mike	CIN	2011	3.86	0.247	0.250	0.298	0.416	693	159	68	23
Gallardo, Yovani	MIL	2011	3.52	0.247	0.245	0.296	0.390	865	193	85	27
Saunders, Joe	ARI	2011	3.69	0.247	0.266	0.324	0.438	874	210	83	29
Ogando, Alexi	TEX	2011	3.51	0.248	0.234	0.288	0.361	693	149	68	16
Stauffer, Tim	SDP	2011	3.73	0.248	0.258	0.316	0.413	777	180	70	20
Garza, Matt	CHC	2011	3.32	0.249	0.245	0.304	0.350	839	186	77	14
Buehrle, Mark	CHW	2011	3.59	0.249	0.277	0.315	0.414	858	221	84	21
Moscoso, G.	OAK	2011	3.38	0.249	0.212	0.270	0.346	526	102	52	14
Garcia, Freddy	NYY	2011	3.62	0.251	0.268	0.322	0.429	626	152	59	16
Greinke, Zack	MIL	2011	3.83	0.251	0.245	0.297	0.412	715	161	68	19
Chen, Bruce	KCR	2011	3.77	0.252	0.258	0.321	0.406	654	152	65	18
Tomlin, Josh	CLE	2011	4.25	0.252	0.248	0.274	0.438	662	157	71	24
Vazquez, Javier	FLA	2011	3.69	0.253	0.243	0.291	0.398	798	178	82	21
Floyd, Gavin	CHW	2011	4.37	0.253	0.247	0.297	0.388	798	180	90	22
Nova, Ivan	NYY	2011	3.70	0.253	0.258	0.322	0.384	704	163	66	13
Niemann, Jeff	TBR	2011	4.06	0.254	0.250	0.304	0.426	572	131	59	18
Morton, Charlie	PIT	2011	3.83	0.254	0.281	0.365	0.372	769	186	69	6
Vargas, Jason	SEA	2011	4.25	0.257	0.260	0.314	0.398	857	205	94	22
Garcia, Jaime	STL	2011	3.56	0.258	0.273	0.317	0.394	826	207	89	15
Lannan, John	WAS	2011	3.70	0.258	0.272	0.347	0.389	808	194	71	15
Norris, Bud	HOU	2011	3.77	0.258	0.250	0.321	0.412	795	177	83	24
Moseley, Dustin	SDP	2011	3.30	0.259	0.255	0.311	0.397	504	117	49	10
Cahill, Trevor	OAK	2011	4.16	0.259	0.269	0.340	0.398	901	214	94	19
Bedard, Erik	BOS	2011	3.62	0.260	0.241	0.309	0.371	541	118	56	14
Narveson, Chris	MIL	2011	4.45	0.260	0.257	0.326	0.409	699	160	74	17
Holland, Derek	TEX	2011	3.95	0.260	0.262	0.325	0.398	843	201	88	22
Danks, John	CHW	2011	4.33	0.262	0.274	0.325	0.427	728	182	77	19
Bailey, Homer	CIN	2011	4.43	0.264	0.264	0.312	0.416	561	136	66	18
Lewis, Colby	TEX	2011	4.40	0.264	0.244	0.299	0.439	839	187	95	35
Porcello, Rick	DET	2011	4.75	0.264	0.292	0.339	0.435	784	210	89	18
Hochevar, Luke	KCR	2011	4.68	0.265	0.252	0.313	0.429	835	192	93	23
Billingsley, Chad	LAD	2011	4.21	0.265	0.264	0.343	0.386	829	189	88	14
Davis, Wade	TBR	2011	4.45	0.265	0.267	0.330	0.441	795	190	85	23
Colon, Bartolo	NYY	2011	4.00	0.265	0.267	0.311	0.440	694	172	77	21
Scherzer, Max	DET	2011	4.43	0.265	0.272	0.325	0.455	833	207	94	29
Gee, Dillon	NYM	2011	4.43	0.266	0.248	0.338	0.401	706	150	78	18
McClellan, Kyle	STL	2011	4.19	0.267	0.260	0.319	0.431	607	143	68	21

The 2010 through 2012 Seasons

Player	Team	Year	ERA	GPA	BA	OBP	SLG	PA	Hits	RBI	HR
McDonald, James	PIT	2011	4.21	0.267	0.268	0.349	0.431	754	176	79	24
Capuano, Chris	NYM	2011	4.55	0.267	0.270	0.323	0.458	802	198	88	27
Pavano, Carl	MIN	2011	4.30	0.269	0.294	0.327	0.447	955	262	110	23
Marquis, Jason	WAS	2011	4.43	0.269	0.294	0.350	0.429	587	154	63	11
Myers, Brett	HOU	2011	4.46	0.269	0.267	0.315	0.437	917	226	114	31
Paulino, Felipe	KCR	2011	4.46	0.270	0.279	0.352	0.408	599	146	68	13
Dempster, Ryan	CHC	2011	4.80	0.270	0.271	0.343	0.445	881	211	101	23
Guthrie, Jeremy	BAL	2011	4.33	0.271	0.267	0.326	0.444	889	213	105	26
Pelfrey, Mike	NYM	2011	4.74	0.271	0.286	0.344	0.434	860	220	96	21
Hernandez, Livan	WAS	2011	4.47	0.271	0.291	0.337	0.434	751	199	85	16
Nolasco, Ricky	FLA	2011	4.67	0.272	0.295	0.331	0.440	891	244	103	20
Niese, Jonathon	NYM	2011	4.40	0.272	0.284	0.335	0.419	694	178	75	14
Carrasco, Carlos	CLE	2011	4.62	0.272	0.270	0.326	0.427	536	130	63	15
Cecil, Brett	TOR	2011	4.73	0.272	0.256	0.321	0.458	532	122	64	22
Zambrano, Carlos	CHC	2011	4.82	0.275	0.277	0.346	0.441	634	154	76	19
Wells, Randy	CHC	2011	4.99	0.276	0.269	0.328	0.438	583	141	72	23
Francis, Jeff	KCR	2011	4.82	0.276	0.301	0.337	0.457	803	224	95	19
Hammel, Jason	COL	2011	4.76	0.277	0.270	0.342	0.435	739	175	88	21
Liriano, F.	MIN	2011	5.09	0.277	0.249	0.350	0.376	591	125	67	14
Britton, Zachary	BAL	2011	4.61	0.277	0.276	0.342	0.393	666	162	79	12
Morrow, Brandon	TOR	2011	4.72	0.278	0.237	0.314	0.391	777	162	92	21
Volstad, Chris	FLA	2011	4.89	0.278	0.289	0.335	0.464	719	187	88	23
Jimenez, Ubaldo	COL	2011	4.68	0.280	0.254	0.333	0.419	822	186	101	17
Westbrook, Jake	STL	2011	4.66	0.280	0.290	0.355	0.435	809	208	94	16
Arroyo, Bronson	CIN	2011	5.07	0.281	0.286	0.327	0.527	855	227	111	46
Lowe, Derek	ATL	2011	5.05	0.281	0.285	0.347	0.406	830	212	100	14
Correia, Kevin	PIT	2011	4.79	0.282	0.287	0.331	0.461	660	175	78	24
Arrieta, Jake	BAL	2011	5.05	0.282	0.253	0.342	0.448	523	115	67	21
Burnett, A.J.	NYY	2011	5.15	0.283	0.260	0.339	0.464	837	190	104	31
Pineiro, Joel	ANA	2011	5.13	0.283	0.311	0.352	0.462	631	182	74	16
Chatwood, Tyler	ANA	2011	4.75	0.285	0.303	0.388	0.442	633	166	78	14
Penny, Brad	DET	2011	5.30	0.289	0.306	0.361	0.483	803	222	106	24
Happ, J.A.	HOU	2011	5.35	0.292	0.265	0.353	0.453	698	157	93	21
Duensing, Brian	MIN	2011	5.23	0.292	0.299	0.349	0.484	711	193	93	21
Blackburn, Nick	MIN	2011	4.49	0.297	0.305	0.363	0.467	670	183	81	19
Carmona, Fausto	CLE	2011	5.25	0.297	0.276	0.339	0.437	833	205	111	22
Wakefield, Tim	BOS	2011	5.12	0.297	0.267	0.324	0.470	677	163	98	25
Reyes, Jo-Jo	TOR	2011	5.57	0.304	0.303	0.362	0.490	641	176	92	21
Lackey, John	BOS	2011	6.41	0.304	0.308	0.375	0.477	743	203	106	20
Average			3.94	0.2543	0.2551	0.3206	0.3990				

Table 3.14. Pitchers with 500+ Batters Faced, 2010

Player	Team	Year	ERA	GPA	BA	OBP	SLG	PA	Hits	RBI	HR
Johnson, Josh	FLA	2010	2.30	0.208	0.229	0.282	0.325	744	155	47	7
Halladay, Roy	PHI	2010	2.44	0.209	0.245	0.271	0.373	993	231	69	24
Wainwright, Adam	STL	2010	2.42	0.211	0.224	0.274	0.330	910	186	65	15
Hernandez, Felix	SEA	2010	2.27	0.213	0.212	0.273	0.312	1001	194	72	17
Duensing, Brian	MIN	2010	2.62	0.216	0.247	0.301	0.365	535	122	38	11
Buchholz, Clay	BOS	2010	2.33	0.216	0.226	0.303	0.312	711	142	43	9
Hudson, Tim	ATL	2010	2.83	0.217	0.229	0.299	0.343	920	189	65	20
Oswalt, Roy	PHI	2010	2.76	0.217	0.213	0.268	0.346	837	162	63	19
Jimenez, Ubaldo	COL	2010	2.88	0.219	0.209	0.299	0.311	894	164	65	10
Latos, Mat	SDP	2010	2.92	0.220	0.217	0.272	0.330	748	150	57	16

Player	Team	Year	ERA	GPA	BA	OBP	SLG	PA	Hits	RBI	HR
Dickey, R.A.	NYM	2010	2.84	0.221	0.251	0.299	0.361	713	165	56	13
Price, David	TBR	2010	2.72	0.221	0.221	0.296	0.340	861	170	64	15
Santana, Johan	NYM	2010	2.98	0.221	0.240	0.292	0.356	817	179	66	16
Weaver, Jered	ANA	2010	3.01	0.222	0.222	0.267	0.355	905	187	70	23
Cain, Matt	SFG	2010	3.14	0.227	0.221	0.276	0.369	896	181	77	22
Hamels, Cole	PHI	2010	3.06	0.227	0.237	0.299	0.394	856	185	72	26
Cahill, Trevor	OAK	2010	2.97	0.229	0.220	0.287	0.332	783	155	68	19
Kershaw, Clayton	LAD	2010	2.91	0.229	0.214	0.295	0.320	848	160	67	13
Gonzalez, Gio	OAK	2010	3.23	0.229	0.229	0.316	0.329	851	171	68	15
Sabathia, C.C.	NYY	2010	3.18	0.229	0.239	0.301	0.355	970	209	82	20
Lincecum, Tim	SFG	2010	3.43	0.230	0.242	0.310	0.364	897	194	80	18
Verlander, Justin	DET	2010	3.37	0.231	0.228	0.291	0.339	925	190	76	14
Sanchez, Jonathan	SFG	2010	3.07	0.231	0.204	0.307	0.343	812	142	62	21
Wilson, C.J.	TEX	2010	3.35	0.232	0.217	0.311	0.311	850	161	69	10
Lee, Cliff	SEA	2010	3.18	0.234	0.240	0.255	0.363	843	195	74	16
Lester, Jon	BOS	2010	3.25	0.235	0.220	0.303	0.325	861	167	75	14
Liriano, F.	MIN	2010	3.62	0.236	0.252	0.315	0.355	806	184	70	9
Garcia, Jaime	STL	2010	2.70	0.237	0.243	0.315	0.323	695	151	53	9
Kuroda, Hiroki	LAD	2010	3.39	0.238	0.243	0.291	0.351	810	180	76	15
Myers, Brett	HOU	2010	3.14	0.239	0.248	0.303	0.379	936	212	79	20
Billingsley, Chad	LAD	2010	3.57	0.239	0.244	0.315	0.353	817	176	69	8
Hanson, Tommy	ATL	2010	3.33	0.239	0.239	0.301	0.347	845	182	79	14
Pavano, Carl	MIN	2010	3.75	0.239	0.266	0.300	0.417	906	227	88	24
Lilly, Ted	LAD	2010	3.62	0.240	0.229	0.278	0.421	785	165	79	32
Kennedy, Ian	ARI	2010	3.80	0.240	0.228	0.304	0.392	810	163	77	26
Zambrano, Carlos	CHC	2010	3.19	0.240	0.246	0.345	0.333	571	119	52	7
Scherzer, Max	DET	2010	3.50	0.241	0.244	0.316	0.383	800	174	72	20
Pettitte, Andy	NYY	2010	3.28	0.241	0.256	0.316	0.385	536	123	48	13
Lewis, Colby	TEX	2010	3.72	0.242	0.227	0.292	0.369	844	174	75	21
Vargas, Jason	SEA	2010	3.78	0.242	0.251	0.300	0.399	811	187	71	18
Hunter, Tommy	TEX	2010	3.73	0.243	0.255	0.304	0.436	536	126	45	21
Braden, Dallas	OAK	2010	3.50	0.244	0.249	0.294	0.373	781	180	70	17
Danks, John	CHW	2010	3.72	0.244	0.237	0.301	0.355	878	189	84	18
Cueto, Johnny	CIN	2010	3.64	0.245	0.257	0.319	0.408	780	181	75	19
Pelfrey, Mike	NYM	2010	3.66	0.245	0.275	0.337	0.398	870	213	78	12
Arroyo, Bronson	CIN	2010	3.88	0.245	0.234	0.289	0.389	880	188	90	29
Takahashi, H.	NYM	2010	3.54	0.245	0.252	0.314	0.398	516	116	52	13
Carpenter, Chris	STL	2010	3.22	0.245	0.244	0.302	0.377	969	214	88	21
Marcum, Shaun	TOR	2010	3.64	0.246	0.242	0.288	0.403	800	181	78	24
Richard, Clayton	SDP	2010	3.75	0.246	0.267	0.337	0.381	861	206	78	16
Davis, Wade	TBR	2010	4.07	0.246	0.255	0.323	0.433	722	165	70	24
Pineiro, Joel	ANA	2010	3.84	0.247	0.261	0.301	0.416	634	155	66	15
Garza, Matt	TBR	2010	3.91	0.247	0.248	0.308	0.420	855	193	83	28
Garland, Jon	SDP	2010	3.46	0.247	0.240	0.323	0.371	837	176	82	20
Guthrie, Jeremy	BAL	2010	3.83	0.248	0.243	0.298	0.416	872	193	85	25
Romero, Ricky	TOR	2010	3.73	0.248	0.242	0.320	0.354	882	189	86	15
Santana, Ervin	ANA	2010	3.92	0.249	0.259	0.324	0.420	954	221	95	27
Carmona, Fausto	CLE	2010	3.77	0.250	0.258	0.323	0.380	880	203	87	17
DeLaRosa, Jorge	COL	2010	4.22	0.251	0.235	0.324	0.413	512	105	51	15
Hughes, Phil	NYY	2010	4.19	0.252	0.244	0.302	0.400	730	162	78	25
Haren, Dan	ANA	2010	3.91	0.252	0.267	0.308	0.429	994	245	103	31
Niemann, Jeff	TBR	2010	4.39	0.253	0.242	0.312	0.412	733	159	79	25
Hernandez, Livan	WAS	2010	3.66	0.254	0.270	0.323	0.393	896	216	82	16
Gallardo, Yovani	MIL	2010	3.84	0.254	0.251	0.324	0.370	803	178	76	12

Player	Team	Year	ERA	GPA	BA	OBP	SLG	PA	Hits	RBI	HR
Chacin, Jhoulys	COL	2010	3.28	0.254	0.227	0.319	0.331	583	114	59	10
Sanchez, Anibal	FLA	2010	3.55	0.254	0.257	0.325	0.356	841	192	78	10
Matusz, Brian	BAL	2010	4.30	0.255	0.255	0.322	0.395	760	173	75	19
Dempster, Ryan	CHC	2010	3.85	0.256	0.244	0.323	0.388	918	198	92	25
Fister, Doug	SEA	2010	4.11	0.256	0.277	0.313	0.385	720	187	75	13
Floyd, Gavin	CHW	2010	4.08	0.257	0.274	0.331	0.388	798	199	81	14
Rodriguez, Wandy	HOU	2010	3.60	0.258	0.250	0.319	0.381	822	183	87	16
Chen, Bruce	KCR	2010	4.17	0.258	0.254	0.326	0.409	608	136	60	17
Zito, Barry	SFG	2010	4.15	0.259	0.250	0.329	0.396	848	184	82	20
Lowe, Derek	ATL	2010	4.00	0.259	0.273	0.330	0.398	824	204	84	18
Wolf, Randy	MIL	2010	4.17	0.259	0.258	0.333	0.430	936	213	100	29
Cecil, Brett	TOR	2010	4.22	0.259	0.264	0.317	0.416	726	175	82	18
Westbrook, Jake	CLE	2010	4.22	0.260	0.262	0.326	0.401	860	203	93	20
Jackson, Edwin	ARI	2010	4.47	0.261	0.265	0.333	0.402	902	214	95	21
Slowey, Kevin	MIN	2010	4.45	0.262	0.280	0.311	0.459	662	172	72	21
Wells, Randy	CHC	2010	4.26	0.262	0.273	0.333	0.413	843	209	91	19
LeBlanc, Wade	SDP	2010	4.25	0.262	0.279	0.340	0.478	625	157	67	24
Gorzelanny, Tom	CHC	2010	4.09	0.263	0.260	0.343	0.399	604	136	61	11
Buehrle, Mark	CHW	2010	4.28	0.263	0.295	0.332	0.418	897	246	94	17
Lackey, John	BOS	2010	4.40	0.264	0.277	0.339	0.426	930	233	98	18
Galarraga, Ar.	DET	2010	4.49	0.265	0.258	0.321	0.444	617	143	67	21
Garcia, Freddy	CHW	2010	4.64	0.265	0.279	0.329	0.475	671	171	78	23
Volstad, Chris	FLA	2010	4.58	0.265	0.277	0.340	0.415	758	187	81	17
Baker, Scott	MIN	2010	4.49	0.266	0.277	0.325	0.468	725	186	82	23
Matsuzaka, D.	BOS	2010	4.69	0.266	0.240	0.331	0.375	664	137	75	13
Greinke, Zack	KCR	2010	4.17	0.266	0.260	0.308	0.388	919	219	105	18
Hammel, Jason	COL	2010	4.81	0.267	0.287	0.335	0.420	770	201	87	18
Nolasco, Ricky	FLA	2010	4.51	0.268	0.273	0.309	0.456	665	169	76	24
Jurrjens, Jair	ATL	2010	4.64	0.270	0.270	0.333	0.458	500	120	54	13
Lannan, John	WAS	2010	4.65	0.271	0.302	0.357	0.441	643	175	75	14
Morrow, Brandon	TOR	2010	4.49	0.273	0.248	0.337	0.389	629	136	69	11
Niese, Jonathon	NYM	2010	4.20	0.273	0.280	0.346	0.437	770	192	87	20
Narveson, Chris	MIL	2010	4.99	0.273	0.266	0.330	0.431	724	172	82	21
Leake, Mike	CIN	2010	4.23	0.274	0.292	0.352	0.452	604	158	68	19
Masterson, Justin	CLE	2010	4.70	0.275	0.278	0.353	0.385	802	197	91	14
Mazzaro, Vin	OAK	2010	4.27	0.276	0.267	0.340	0.425	537	127	65	19
Karstens, Jeff	PIT	2010	4.92	0.277	0.300	0.333	0.504	525	146	66	21
Kendrick, Kyle	PHI	2010	4.73	0.278	0.283	0.329	0.477	771	199	93	26
Talbot, Mitch	CLE	2010	4.41	0.279	0.276	0.354	0.407	696	169	75	13
Porcello, Rick	DET	2010	4.92	0.280	0.288	0.333	0.419	700	188	84	18
Burnett, A.J.	NYY	2010	5.26	0.280	0.285	0.366	0.457	829	204	103	25
Blanton, Joe	PHI	2010	4.82	0.280	0.291	0.332	0.464	765	206	97	27
Correia, Kevin	SDP	2010	5.40	0.281	0.271	0.348	0.435	641	152	75	20
Saunders, Joe	ANA	2010	4.47	0.282	0.291	0.344	0.457	880	232	104	25
Sheets, Ben	OAK	2010	4.53	0.282	0.267	0.327	0.486	511	123	65	18
Harang, Aaron	CIN	2010	5.32	0.283	0.305	0.362	0.479	504	139	61	16
Bush, Dave	MIL	2010	4.54	0.284	0.286	0.346	0.481	781	198	97	28
Vazquez, Javier	NYY	2010	5.32	0.284	0.257	0.333	0.485	683	155	91	32
Davies, Kyle	KCR	2010	5.34	0.285	0.283	0.354	0.439	817	206	102	20
Norris, Bud	HOU	2010	4.92	0.286	0.256	0.346	0.412	683	151	90	18
Bergesen, Brad	BAL	2010	4.98	0.286	0.285	0.339	0.490	746	193	94	26
Cook, Aaron	COL	2010	5.08	0.286	0.290	0.357	0.402	572	147	71	11
Shields, James	TBR	2010	5.18	0.287	0.294	0.338	0.490	899	246	109	34
Stammen, Craig	WAS	2010	5.13	0.288	0.297	0.346	0.468	562	151	75	13

Player	Team	Year	ERA	GPA	BA	OBP	SLG	PA	Hits	RBI	HR
Parra, Manny	MIL	2010	4.94	0.288	0.281	0.363	0.453	560	135	73	18
Wakefield, Tim	BOS	2010	5.34	0.288	0.272	0.320	0.454	610	153	80	19
Lopez, Rodrigo	ARI	2010	5.00	0.289	0.286	0.333	0.500	874	227	116	37
Millwood, Kevin	BAL	2010	5.10	0.290	0.292	0.352	0.461	842	223	109	30
Bonderman, J.	DET	2010	5.53	0.290	0.277	0.342	0.448	754	187	97	25
Blackburn, Nick	MIN	2010	5.42	0.290	0.302	0.345	0.495	692	194	92	25
Maholm, Paul	PIT	2010	5.10	0.292	0.303	0.360	0.452	840	228	107	15
Beckett, Josh	BOS	2010	5.78	0.295	0.292	0.356	0.492	577	151	75	20
Kazmir, Scott	ANA	2010	5.94	0.298	0.271	0.367	0.474	682	158	93	25
Feldman, Scott	TEX	2010	5.48	0.298	0.313	0.363	0.486	641	181	87	18
Bannister, Brian	KCR	2010	6.34	0.311	0.302	0.365	0.503	581	158	81	23
Duke, Zach	PIT	2010	5.72	0.314	0.321	0.370	0.511	730	212	107	25
Rowland-Smith, R.	SEA	2010	6.75	0.334	0.314	0.379	0.575	510	141	83	25
Average			4.07	0.2575	0.2574	0.3325	0.4028				

Table 3.15. Select Relief Pitchers with 200+ Batters Faced, 2012

Player	Team	Year	ERA	GPA	BA	OBP	SLG	PA	Hits	RBI	HR
Rodney, Fernando	TBR	2012	0.60	0.142	0.167	0.219	0.198	282	43	9	2
Kimbrel, Craig	ATL	2012	1.01	0.143	0.126	0.186	0.172	231	27	6	3
Chapman, Aroldis	CIN	2012	1.51	0.173	0.141	0.225	0.226	276	35	15	4
Romo, Sergio	SFG	2012	1.79	0.181	0.185	0.235	0.290	215	37	17	5
Ziegler, Brad	ARI	2012	2.49	0.184	0.228	0.291	0.287	263	54	25	2
O'Flaherty, Eric	ATL	2012	1.73	0.185	0.229	0.300	0.302	230	47	15	3
McGee, Jake	TBR	2012	1.95	0.185	0.168	0.213	0.239	212	33	22	3
Frieri, Ernesto	ANA	2012	2.32	0.192	0.152	0.269	0.287	269	35	17	9
Soriano, Rafael	NYY	2012	2.26	0.192	0.217	0.287	0.352	279	55	17	6
Atchison, Scott	BOS	2012	1.58	0.193	0.223	0.256	0.293	200	42	18	2
O'Day, Darren	BAL	2012	2.28	0.194	0.202	0.254	0.360	263	49	20	6
Cook, Ryan	OAK	2012	2.09	0.194	0.166	0.256	0.261	288	42	20	4
Janssen, Casey	TOR	2012	2.54	0.194	0.195	0.241	0.323	242	44	18	7
Gregerson, Luke	SDP	2012	2.39	0.195	0.215	0.280	0.332	294	57	16	7
Jansen, Kenley	LAD	2012	2.35	0.195	0.146	0.230	0.274	252	33	19	6
Watson, Tony	PIT	2012	3.21	0.195	0.198	0.286	0.337	215	37	25	5
Norberto, Jordan	OAK	2012	2.60	0.196	0.200	0.284	0.330	212	37	19	5
Oliver, Darren	TOR	2012	2.06	0.196	0.214	0.282	0.294	221	43	13	3
Hanrahan, Joel	PIT	2012	2.72	0.198	0.187	0.307	0.341	254	40	18	8
Pestano, Vinnie	CLE	2012	2.57	0.199	0.207	0.283	0.348	286	53	22	7
Patton, Troy	BAL	2012	2.43	0.199	0.215	0.263	0.335	224	45	18	5
Burton, Jared	MIN	2012	2.18	0.201	0.186	0.255	0.294	245	41	17	5
Motte, Jason	STL	2012	2.75	0.204	0.191	0.245	0.331	279	49	26	9
Villarreal, Brayan	DET	2012	2.63	0.205	0.201	0.299	0.296	226	38	19	3
Boggs, Mitchell	STL	2012	2.21	0.205	0.211	0.279	0.291	296	56	24	5
Blevins, Jerry	OAK	2012	2.48	0.206	0.201	0.293	0.344	261	45	24	7
Ross, Robbie	TEX	2012	2.22	0.208	0.232	0.303	0.321	265	55	23	3
Wilhelmsen, Tom	SEA	2012	2.50	0.208	0.202	0.277	0.301	326	59	29	5
Grilli, Jason	PIT	2012	2.91	0.209	0.207	0.285	0.350	244	45	17	7
Putz, J.J.	ARI	2012	2.82	0.209	0.223	0.269	0.332	218	45	16	4
Stammen, Craig	WAS	2012	2.34	0.211	0.215	0.296	0.340	370	70	27	7
Betancourt, R.	COL	2012	2.81	0.212	0.241	0.278	0.377	236	53	22	6
Hernandez, David	ARI	2012	2.50	0.213	0.190	0.263	0.282	278	48	19	4
Broxton, Jonathan	KCR	2012	2.48	0.213	0.260	0.322	0.353	238	56	17	2
Lopez, Wilton	HOU	2012	2.17	0.213	0.250	0.277	0.348	260	61	22	4
Lyon, Brandon	TOR	2012	3.10	0.213	0.240	0.307	0.352	258	56	23	5

Player	Team	Year	ERA	GPA	BA	OBP	SLG	PA	Hits	RBI	HR
Davis, Wade	TBR	2012	2.43	0.213	0.189	0.271	0.299	284	48	22	5
Mattheus, Ryan	WAS	2012	2.85	0.214	0.241	0.300	0.409	265	57	26	8
Johnson, Jim	BAL	2012	2.49	0.214	0.220	0.272	0.284	269	55	24	3
Mujica, Edward	MIA	2012	2.76	0.215	0.230	0.268	0.374	258	56	25	7
Dotel, Octavio	DET	2012	3.57	0.215	0.230	0.272	0.346	234	50	21	3
Balfour, Grant	OAK	2012	2.41	0.215	0.160	0.242	0.253	289	41	27	4
Belisario, Ronald	LAD	2012	2.54	0.218	0.187	0.281	0.278	286	47	29	3
League, Brandon	SEA	2012	3.13	0.218	0.246	0.332	0.295	301	65	22	1
Miller, Jim	OAK	2012	2.59	0.219	0.217	0.327	0.361	211	39	20	6
Brach, Brad	SDP	2012	3.78	0.220	0.207	0.305	0.369	280	50	32	11
Strop, Pedro	BAL	2012	2.44	0.220	0.217	0.330	0.283	283	52	24	2
Santiago, Hector	CHW	2012	3.33	0.220	0.211	0.332	0.348	306	54	21	10
Nathan, Joe	TEX	2012	2.80	0.220	0.231	0.273	0.357	257	55	21	7
Pettitte, Andy	NYY	2012	2.87	0.220	0.232	0.286	0.346	303	65	23	8
Marshall, Sean	CIN	2012	2.51	0.222	0.232	0.289	0.308	256	55	22	3
Ogando, Alexi	TEX	2012	3.27	0.222	0.203	0.259	0.357	263	49	31	9
Perkins, Glen	MIN	2012	2.56	0.224	0.222	0.273	0.358	281	57	23	8
Papelbon, J.	PHI	2012	2.44	0.224	0.216	0.278	0.344	284	56	24	8
:											
Parra, Manny	MIL	2012	5.06	0.294	0.265	0.366	0.372	273	62	37	3
Qualls, Chad	PHI	2012	5.33	0.295	0.297	0.338	0.472	231	63	34	7
Hernandez, Livan	ATL	2012	6.42	0.298	0.317	0.354	0.536	292	84	48	15
Moscoso, G.	COL	2012	6.12	0.300	0.321	0.378	0.502	231	67	34	8
Gregg, Kevin	BAL	2012	4.95	0.300	0.291	0.385	0.453	200	50	32	6
Batista, Miguel	NYM	2012	4.44	0.301	0.283	0.382	0.429	244	58	30	6
Takahashi, H.	ANA	2012	5.01	0.301	0.251	0.300	0.472	212	49	33	8
Dunn, Michael	MIA	2012	4.91	0.307	0.283	0.379	0.428	208	49	31	3
Average			**4.01**	0.2557	0.2545	0.3190	0.4053				

Table 3.16. Selected Relief Pitchers with 200+ Batters Faced, 2011

Player	Team	Year	ERA	GPA	BA	OBP	SLG	PA	Hits	RBI	HR
Robertson, David	NYY	2011	1.08	0.147	0.170	0.280	0.226	272	40	16	1
Holland, Greg	KCR	2011	1.80	0.164	0.175	0.246	0.275	233	37	14	3
Clippard, Tyler	WAS	2011	1.83	0.171	0.162	0.228	0.307	329	48	26	11
Adams, Mike	TEX	2011	1.34	0.177	0.169	0.211	0.285	277	44	16	5
O'Flaherty, Eric	ATL	2011	0.98	0.182	0.221	0.283	0.288	301	59	16	2
Bastardo, Antonio	PHI	2011	2.64	0.182	0.144	0.242	0.282	225	28	14	6
Venters, Jonny	ATL	2011	1.84	0.186	0.176	0.289	0.219	357	53	22	2
Hanrahan, Joel	PIT	2011	1.83	0.186	0.220	0.267	0.276	274	56	17	1
Jansen, Kenley	LAD	2011	2.85	0.188	0.159	0.266	0.228	218	30	16	3
Putz, J.J.	ARI	2011	2.17	0.188	0.195	0.242	0.324	229	41	15	4
Casilla, Santiago	SFG	2011	1.74	0.191	0.183	0.290	0.244	211	33	12	1
Uehara, Koji	TEX	2011	2.35	0.192	0.164	0.194	0.341	243	38	21	11
Rivera, Mariano	NYY	2011	1.91	0.193	0.215	0.247	0.288	233	47	18	3
Valverde, Jose	DET	2011	2.24	0.193	0.198	0.298	0.282	301	52	19	5
Downs, Scott	ANA	2011	1.34	0.195	0.199	0.254	0.286	218	39	18	3
Balfour, Grant	OAK	2011	2.47	0.197	0.199	0.266	0.339	242	44	16	8
Axford, John	MIL	2011	1.95	0.198	0.212	0.276	0.281	305	59	18	4
Pestano, Vinnie	CLE	2011	2.32	0.198	0.184	0.272	0.305	250	41	20	5
Salas, Fernando	STL	2011	2.16	0.199	0.186	0.250	0.316	295	50	27	7
Motte, Jason	STL	2011	2.25	0.200	0.202	0.262	0.296	268	49	31	2
Kimbrel, Craig	ATL	2011	2.10	0.200	0.178	0.266	0.233	306	48	19	3
Marshall, Sean	CHC	2011	2.26	0.201	0.234	0.282	0.284	307	66	23	1

Player	Team	Year	ERA	GPA	BA	OBP	SLG	PA	Hits	RBI	HR
Rodriguez, F.J.	MIL	2011	2.64	0.203	0.243	0.311	0.351	307	67	25	4
Bell, Heath	SDP	2011	2.44	0.204	0.223	0.287	0.301	256	51	18	4
Coleman, Louis	KCR	2011	2.87	0.204	0.207	0.300	0.385	244	44	22	9
Bard, Daniel	BOS	2011	3.33	0.205	0.179	0.254	0.292	288	46	27	5
Farnsworth, Kyle	TBR	2011	2.18	0.205	0.211	0.261	0.347	231	45	23	5
Madson, Ryan	PHI	2011	2.37	0.205	0.243	0.296	0.297	246	54	18	2
Perkins, Glen	MIN	2011	2.48	0.206	0.244	0.310	0.333	253	55	22	2
Cordero, F.	CIN	2011	2.45	0.209	0.198	0.271	0.320	274	49	22	6
Sale, Chris	CHW	2011	2.79	0.209	0.203	0.284	0.328	288	52	22	6
Betancourt, R.	COL	2011	2.89	0.211	0.203	0.228	0.330	237	46	22	7
Crow, Aaron	KCR	2011	2.76	0.211	0.237	0.327	0.384	266	55	23	8
Aceves, Alfredo	BOS	2011	2.61	0.211	0.204	0.299	0.321	474	84	37	8
Storen, Drew	WAS	2011	2.75	0.211	0.204	0.262	0.337	303	57	21	8
Lopez, Javier	SFG	2011	2.72	0.212	0.221	0.324	0.279	222	42	18	0
Smith, Joe	CLE	2011	2.01	0.212	0.217	0.283	0.258	267	52	25	1
Crain, Jesse	CHW	2011	2.62	0.213	0.215	0.303	0.352	268	50	29	7
Peralta, Joel	TBR	2011	2.93	0.213	0.188	0.244	0.342	256	44	26	7
Ramirez, Ramon	SFG	2011	2.62	0.214	0.216	0.296	0.300	282	54	29	3
Hawkins, LaTroy	MIL	2011	2.42	0.214	0.260	0.296	0.328	204	50	13	1
Mujica, Edward	FLA	2011	2.96	0.217	0.233	0.274	0.364	297	64	26	7
Johnson, Jim	BAL	2011	2.67	0.217	0.238	0.285	0.342	366	80	35	5
Papelbon, Jonatha	BOS	2011	2.94	0.218	0.207	0.247	0.299	255	50	24	3
Benoit, Joaquin	DET	2011	2.95	0.218	0.218	0.275	0.306	241	47	29	5
MacDougal, Mike	LAD	2011	2.05	0.218	0.257	0.352	0.338	247	54	28	3
:											
Carrasco, D.J.	NYM	2011	6.02	0.294	0.337	0.403	0.508	225	67	34	7
Mijares, Jose	MIN	2011	4.41	0.297	0.275	0.377	0.420	228	53	31	4
Durbin, Chad	CLE	2011	5.27	0.300	0.306	0.363	0.509	318	86	48	12
Bergesen, Brad	BAL	2011	5.70	0.321	0.288	0.341	0.504	451	119	75	16
Berken, Jason	BAL	2011	4.79	0.327	0.318	0.383	0.561	223	63	43	10
Proctor, Scott	ATL	2011	6.92	0.336	0.313	0.423	0.594	201	50	37	11
Average			**3.94**	**0.2543**	**0.2551**	**0.3206**	**0.3990**				

Table 3.17. Selected Relief Pitchers with 200+ Batters Faced, 2010

Player	Team	Year	ERA	GPA	BA	OBP	SLG	PA	Hits	RBI	HR
Kuo, Hung-Chih	LAD	2010	1.20	0.151	0.139	0.211	0.192	229	29	10	1
Benoit, Joaquin	TBR	2010	1.34	0.152	0.147	0.189	0.265	217	30	11	6
Wagner, Billy	ATL	2010	1.30	0.178	0.159	0.238	0.255	268	38	14	5
Rhodes, Arthur	CIN	2010	2.29	0.180	0.196	0.265	0.309	217	38	16	4
Soria, Joakim	KCR	2010	1.78	0.183	0.216	0.266	0.302	270	53	15	4
Hensley, Clay	FLA	2010	2.16	0.184	0.200	0.286	0.281	307	54	15	3
Motte, Jason	STL	2010	2.24	0.184	0.220	0.285	0.333	208	41	19	5
Soriano, Rafael	TBR	2010	1.73	0.185	0.163	0.215	0.294	237	36	20	4
Wilson, Brian	SFG	2010	1.81	0.188	0.220	0.288	0.309	311	62	19	3
Lopez, Javier	PIT	2010	2.34	0.190	0.238	0.308	0.329	235	50	17	2
Thornton, Matt	CHW	2010	2.67	0.191	0.191	0.264	0.284	239	41	18	3
Feliz, Neftali	TEX	2010	2.73	0.192	0.176	0.246	0.269	269	43	20	5
Perez, Chris	CLE	2010	1.71	0.192	0.182	0.287	0.295	260	40	19	4
Bell, Heath	SDP	2010	1.93	0.193	0.221	0.300	0.285	287	56	16	1
Rivera, Mariano	NYY	2010	1.80	0.195	0.183	0.239	0.254	230	39	17	2
Bard, Daniel	BOS	2010	1.93	0.195	0.176	0.263	0.277	295	45	30	6
Adams, Mike	SDP	2010	1.76	0.197	0.196	0.265	0.261	268	48	14	2
Marmol, Carlos	CHC	2010	2.55	0.198	0.147	0.301	0.199	332	40	30	1

The 2010 through 2012 Seasons

Player	Team	Year	ERA	GPA	BA	OBP	SLG	PA	Hits	RBI	HR
Rodriguez, F.J.	NYM	2010	2.20	0.199	0.213	0.289	0.308	236	45	20	3
Burnett, Sean	WAS	2010	2.00	0.200	0.220	0.284	0.297	261	52	18	3
Gregerson, Luke	SDP	2010	3.22	0.202	0.170	0.223	0.301	297	47	31	8
Madson, Ryan	PHI	2010	2.55	0.206	0.212	0.274	0.308	217	42	16	4
Axford, John	MIL	2010	2.48	0.207	0.204	0.297	0.291	238	42	17	1
Meek, Evan	PIT	2010	2.14	0.207	0.185	0.273	0.273	324	53	28	5
Lyon, Brandon	HOU	2010	3.12	0.211	0.231	0.310	0.312	333	68	20	2
Sanches, Brian	FLA	2010	2.26	0.211	0.194	0.281	0.329	254	43	25	7
Downs, Scott	TOR	2010	2.64	0.212	0.211	0.270	0.314	241	47	19	3
Ramirez, Ramon	BOS	2010	2.99	0.213	0.207	0.280	0.351	284	52	22	7
Veras, Jose	FLA	2010	3.75	0.214	0.188	0.310	0.312	201	32	15	5
Marshall, Sean	CHC	2010	2.53	0.217	0.210	0.279	0.290	307	58	24	3
Jepsen, Kevin	ANA	2010	3.97	0.218	0.250	0.341	0.324	253	54	31	2
Oliver, Darren	TEX	2010	2.48	0.221	0.242	0.293	0.361	244	53	25	4
Breslow, Craig	OAK	2010	3.01	0.222	0.194	0.272	0.348	304	53	28	9
Hughes, Dusty	KCR	2010	3.83	0.222	0.273	0.351	0.380	252	59	24	3
Valverde, Jose	DET	2010	3.00	0.223	0.184	0.293	0.291	259	41	25	5
Guerrier, Matt	MIN	2010	3.17	0.223	0.219	0.285	0.340	286	56	33	7
Belisle, Matt	COL	2010	2.93	0.224	0.246	0.283	0.364	365	84	35	7
Saito, Takashi	ATL	2010	2.83	0.224	0.203	0.265	0.312	221	41	17	4
Rauch, Jon	MIN	2010	3.12	0.226	0.268	0.311	0.360	245	61	21	3
Aardsma, David	SEA	2010	3.44	0.228	0.198	0.308	0.323	202	33	18	5
Franklin, Ryan	STL	2010	3.46	0.230	0.230	0.270	0.391	264	57	25	7
Wood, Kerry	NYY	2010	3.13	0.230	0.210	0.337	0.317	201	35	17	4
Bonine, Eddie	DET	2010	4.63	0.306	0.305	0.360	0.458	303	84	45	7
Gallagher, Sean	SDP	2010	5.62	0.310	0.277	0.396	0.433	273	62	42	7
Tallet, Brian	TOR	2010	6.28	0.311	0.273	0.355	0.526	356	84	60	20
Russell, James	CHC	2010	4.78	0.317	0.279	0.324	0.497	219	55	43	11
Snell, Ian	SEA	2010	6.41	0.319	0.308	0.384	0.564	227	60	34	10
Average			4.07	0.2575	0.2574	0.3325	0.4028				

BEST INDIVIDUAL SEASONS, 1952–2012

The best 111 seasons as measured by GPA for both individual batters and pitchers from 1952 to 2012 are presented in this chapter. There are a few games missing from the Retrosheet database from 1952 to 1973 and the statistics listed here may differ slightly from the official statistics for those years.

As measured by GPA, Barry Bonds's 2001, 2002 and 2004 seasons were by far the most productive for a batter (with at least 500 PAs) since 1952. In that time, there were 21 batters who finished the season with a GPA over 0.400, none above 0.427. Bonds, by contrast, produced averages of 0.444 (2001), 0.457 (2002), and 0.471 (2004). He also leads the way among players with multiple seasons over 0.400, with five. (Others include Mickey Mantle, with four, and Ted Williams, Manny Ramirez, and Mark McGwire, with two apiece.)

Players who have admitted to steroid use or tested positive for them account for nine of these 21 seasons (Bonds, Ramirez, Giambi and McGwire). An additional two seasons (Helton and Walker) were posted by Rockies players who played in Coors Field before a humidor was used to store baseballs. During the pre-humidor era, Coors Field increased a batter's GPA substantially (0.059 points).

Seasons	Batters Top 111 GPA	Pct. Batters Top 111 GPA	Expected Pct. Batters	Team Seasons
1952 to 1961	17	15.3%	10.8%	162
1962 to 1971	10	9.0%	14.1%	212
1972 to 1981	7	6.3%	16.7%	250
1982 to 1993	7	6.3%	20.9%	314
1994 to 2004	56	50.4%	21.5%	322
2005 to 2012	14	12.6%	16.0%	240

Table 4.1. The top 111 seasons as measured by GPA for batters.

The era from 1994 to 2004 accounts for 50.4 percent (56 of 111) of the top batter seasons as measured by GPA. This is far greater than the 21.5 percent that would have been expected by chance alone. The expected percentage is adjusted for the number of teams playing each year and the length of each era. The chapter on what might this book refers to as the Steroid Era of 1994 to 2004 discusses what could account for these findings.

The era from 1962 to 1993 accounts for 21.6 percent (24 of 111) of the top seasons as measured by GPA for batters — far less than the 51.7 percent that would have been expected by chance alone. The chapter on the pitching-dominant era of 1971 to 1984 discusses what could account for these findings.

Pitchers Seasons	Pitchers Top 111 GPA	Expected Top 111 GPA	Team Pct. Pitchers	Seasons
1952 to 1961	6	5.4%	10.8%	162
1962 to 1971	47	42.3%	14.1%	212
1972 to 1981	23	20.7%	16.7%	250
1982 to 1993	17	15.3%	20.9%	314
1994 to 2004	11	9.9%	21.5%	322
2005 to 2012	7	6.3%	16.0%	240

Table 4.2. The top 111 seasons as measured by GPA for pitchers.

The top 111 seasons as measured by GPA for pitchers with 500+ batters faced are distributed in a pattern opposite that of the top 111 hitters. The era from 1962 to 1981 accounts for 63.1 percent (70 of 111) of the top seasons as measured by GPA for pitchers, as opposed to the 31.4 percent that would have been expected by chance alone.

The top 111 seasons as measured by GPA for relief pitchers with 200+ PAs includes only one from 1952 to 1961, Terry Fox's 1961 season. Top relief pitchers from 1962 to 1981 routinely faced 450 to 600 PAs per season compared to only about 300 batters faced for top relievers since 2000. The role of the relief pitcher, obviously, has evolved significantly over the past 50 years.

The following tables list the GPAs of the top 111 seasons by batters from the 1952 to 2012 with at least 500 PAs (Table 4.3); by pitchers with at least 500 batters faced (Table 4.4); and by relief pitchers with at least 200 batters faced (Table 4.5).

Table 4.3. Batters with 500+ Plate Appearances

Player	Team	Year	GPA	BA	OBP	SLG	PA	Hits	RBI	HR
Bonds, Barry	SFG	2004	0.471	0.362	0.609	0.812	617	135	101	45
Bonds, Barry	SFG	2002	0.457	0.370	0.582	0.799	612	149	110	46
Bonds, Barry	SFG	2001	0.444	0.328	0.515	0.863	664	156	137	73
Williams, Ted	BOS	1957	0.427	0.389	0.526	0.735	513	154	83	36
Helton, Todd	COL	2000	0.418	0.372	0.463	0.698	697	216	147	42
Williams, Ted	BOS	1954	0.416	0.345	0.516	0.628	504	127	86	27
Giambi, Jason	OAK	2000	0.413	0.333	0.476	0.647	664	170	137	43
Bonds, Barry	SFG	2003	0.413	0.341	0.529	0.749	550	133	90	45
Mantle, Mickey	NYY	1962	0.413	0.321	0.486	0.605	502	121	89	30
Mantle, Mickey	NYY	1956	0.412	0.353	0.464	0.705	652	188	130	52
Brett, George	KCR	1980	0.408	0.390	0.454	0.664	515	175	118	24
Ramirez, Manny	CLE	2000	0.406	0.351	0.457	0.697	532	154	122	38
Mantle, Mickey	NYY	1961	0.406	0.317	0.448	0.687	646	163	128	54
Walker, Larry	COL	1999	0.405	0.379	0.458	0.710	513	166	115	37
Mantle, Mickey	NYY	1957	0.404	0.365	0.512	0.665	623	173	94	34
McGwire, Mark	STL	1998	0.404	0.299	0.470	0.752	681	152	147	70
Thomas, Frank	CHW	1994	0.402	0.353	0.487	0.729	517	141	101	38
Bonds, Barry	SFG	1996	0.401	0.308	0.461	0.615	675	159	129	42
Ramirez, Manny	CLE	1999	0.401	0.333	0.442	0.663	640	174	165	44
Delgado, Carlos	TOR	2000	0.400	0.344	0.470	0.664	711	196	137	41
Martinez, Edgar	SEA	1995	0.400	0.356	0.479	0.628	639	182	113	29
Giambi, Jason	OAK	2001	0.399	0.342	0.477	0.660	671	178	120	38
Cash, Norm	DET	1961	0.398	0.361	0.487	0.662	673	193	132	41

Player	Team	Year	GPA	BA	OBP	SLG	PA	Hits	RBI	HR
Walker, Larry	COL	1997	0.397	0.366	0.452	0.720	664	208	130	49
Ramirez, Manny	BOS	2002	0.395	0.349	0.450	0.647	518	152	107	33
Sosa, Sammy	CHC	2001	0.395	0.328	0.437	0.737	711	189	160	64
McGwire, Mark	OAK	1996	0.393	0.312	0.467	0.730	548	132	113	52
Gentile, Jim	BAL	1961	0.391	0.302	0.423	0.646	601	147	141	46
Morgan, Joe	CIN	1976	0.390	0.320	0.444	0.576	599	151	111	27
McCovey, Willie	SFG	1969	0.388	0.320	0.453	0.656	623	157	126	45
Rodriguez, Alex	NYY	2007	0.385	0.314	0.422	0.645	708	183	156	54
Thomas, Frank	CHW	1997	0.385	0.347	0.456	0.611	649	184	125	35
Bonds, Barry	SFG	1993	0.385	0.336	0.458	0.677	674	181	123	46
McGwire, Mark	STL	1999	0.383	0.278	0.424	0.697	661	145	147	65
Pujols, Albert	STL	2006	0.382	0.331	0.431	0.671	634	177	137	49
Walker, Larry	COL	2001	0.382	0.350	0.449	0.662	601	174	123	38
Thome, Jim	CLE	2002	0.382	0.304	0.445	0.677	613	146	118	52
Rosen, Al	CLE	1953	0.382	0.336	0.422	0.613	688	201	144	43
Helton, Todd	COL	2003	0.382	0.358	0.458	0.630	703	209	117	33
Palmeiro, Rafael	TEX	1999	0.382	0.324	0.420	0.630	674	183	148	47
Martinez, Edgar	SEA	1996	0.381	0.327	0.464	0.595	634	163	103	26
Snider, Duke	BRO	1955	0.381	0.309	0.418	0.628	653	166	136	42
Berkman, Lance	HOU	2001	0.381	0.331	0.430	0.620	688	191	126	34
Sheffield, Gary	FLA	1996	0.380	0.314	0.465	0.624	677	163	120	42
Bonds, Barry	SFG	2000	0.380	0.306	0.440	0.688	607	147	106	49
Berkman, Lance	HOU	2006	0.379	0.315	0.420	0.621	646	169	136	45
Thomas, Frank	CHW	2000	0.378	0.328	0.436	0.625	707	191	143	43
Helton, Todd	COL	2001	0.377	0.336	0.432	0.685	697	197	146	49
Salmon, Tim	CAL	1995	0.377	0.330	0.429	0.594	638	177	105	34
Howard, Ryan	PHI	2006	0.377	0.313	0.425	0.659	704	182	149	58
Hafner, Travis	CLE	2006	0.377	0.308	0.439	0.659	564	140	117	42
Campanella, Roy	BRO	1953	0.377	0.312	0.395	0.611	590	162	142	41
Yastrzemski, Carl	BOS	1967	0.376	0.326	0.418	0.622	680	189	121	44
Gwynn, Tony	SDP	1997	0.376	0.372	0.409	0.547	651	220	119	17
Rodriguez, Alex	SEA	1996	0.376	0.358	0.414	0.631	677	215	123	36
Walker, Larry	COL	2002	0.376	0.338	0.421	0.602	553	161	104	26
Clark, Jack	STL	1987	0.375	0.286	0.459	0.597	559	120	106	35
Pujols, Albert	STL	2008	0.375	0.357	0.462	0.653	641	187	116	37
Pujols, Albert	STL	2003	0.375	0.359	0.439	0.667	685	212	124	43
Thomas, Frank	CHW	1996	0.374	0.349	0.459	0.626	649	184	134	40
Snider, Duke	BRO	1953	0.374	0.336	0.419	0.627	680	198	126	42
Sheffield, Gary	ATL	2003	0.374	0.330	0.419	0.604	678	190	132	39
Carew, Rod	MIN	1977	0.374	0.388	0.449	0.570	694	239	100	14
Morgan, Joe	CIN	1975	0.373	0.327	0.466	0.508	639	163	94	17
Ordonez, Magglio	DET	2007	0.373	0.363	0.434	0.595	679	216	139	28
Williams, Ted	BOS	1958	0.373	0.320	0.452	0.573	504	128	80	25
Pujols, Albert	STL	2009	0.373	0.327	0.443	0.658	700	186	135	47
Mantle, Mickey	NYY	1964	0.373	0.303	0.423	0.591	567	141	111	35
Kluszewski, Ted	CIN	1954	0.372	0.326	0.406	0.642	658	187	141	49
Gonzalez, Luis	ARI	2001	0.372	0.325	0.429	0.688	728	198	142	57
Piazza, Mike	LAD	1997	0.372	0.362	0.431	0.638	633	201	124	40
Bagwell, Jeff	HOU	1999	0.372	0.304	0.454	0.591	729	171	126	42
Ortiz, David	BOS	2005	0.372	0.300	0.397	0.604	713	180	148	47
Musial, Stan	STL	1954	0.372	0.335	0.426	0.644	545	155	108	34
Martinez, Edgar	SEA	2000	0.371	0.324	0.423	0.579	665	180	145	37
Giles, Brian	PIT	1999	0.371	0.315	0.418	0.614	627	164	115	39
Killebrew, H.	MIN	1969	0.371	0.276	0.427	0.584	709	153	140	49

Player	Team	Year	GPA	BA	OBP	SLG	PA	Hits	RBI	HR
Berkman, Lance	HOU	2002	0.370	0.292	0.405	0.578	692	169	128	42
McCovey, Willie	SFG	1970	0.370	0.289	0.444	0.612	638	143	126	39
Olerud, John	TOR	1993	0.370	0.363	0.473	0.599	679	200	107	24
Rodriguez, Alex	SEA	2000	0.370	0.316	0.420	0.606	672	175	132	41
Sheffield, Gary	LAD	2000	0.370	0.325	0.438	0.643	612	163	109	43
Belle, Albert	CLE	1996	0.370	0.311	0.410	0.623	715	187	148	48
Giles, Brian	PIT	2002	0.369	0.298	0.450	0.622	644	148	103	38
Robinson, Frank	CIN	1962	0.369	0.342	0.421	0.624	701	208	136	39
Delgado, Carlos	TOR	2003	0.369	0.302	0.426	0.593	705	172	145	42
Aaron, Hank	ATL	1971	0.368	0.324	0.410	0.670	546	152	112	45
Thomas, Frank	CHW	1993	0.368	0.317	0.426	0.607	676	174	128	41
Votto, Joey	CIN	2010	0.368	0.324	0.424	0.600	648	177	113	37
Williams, Billy	CHC	1972	0.368	0.333	0.398	0.606	650	191	122	37
Kent, Jeff	SFG	2000	0.368	0.334	0.424	0.596	695	196	125	33
Helton, Todd	COL	2004	0.367	0.347	0.469	0.620	683	190	96	32
Mantle, Mickey	NYY	1955	0.367	0.306	0.431	0.611	638	158	99	37
Ortiz, David	BOS	2007	0.367	0.332	0.445	0.621	667	182	117	35
Lynn, Fred	BOS	1979	0.367	0.333	0.423	0.637	622	177	122	39
Stargell, Willie	PIT	1971	0.367	0.295	0.398	0.628	606	151	125	48
Giambi, Jason	NYY	2002	0.366	0.314	0.435	0.598	689	176	122	41
Strawberry, D.	NYM	1987	0.366	0.284	0.398	0.583	640	151	104	39
Beltran, Carlos	NYM	2006	0.366	0.275	0.388	0.594	617	140	116	41
Caminiti, Ken	SDP	1996	0.365	0.326	0.408	0.621	639	178	130	40
Bonds, Barry	PIT	1992	0.365	0.311	0.456	0.624	612	147	103	34
Bonds, Barry	SFG	1998	0.365	0.303	0.438	0.609	697	167	122	37
Snider, Duke	BRO	1954	0.365	0.341	0.423	0.647	679	199	130	40
Galarraga, Andres	COL	1993	0.364	0.370	0.403	0.602	506	174	98	22
Allen, Dick	CHW	1972	0.364	0.308	0.420	0.603	609	156	113	37
Cabrera, Miguel	FLA	2006	0.364	0.339	0.430	0.568	676	195	114	26
Thome, Jim	CLE	1996	0.364	0.311	0.450	0.612	636	157	116	38
Bautista, Jose	TOR	2011	0.364	0.302	0.447	0.608	655	155	103	43
Mathews, Eddie	MLB	1953	0.364	0.289	0.385	0.596	501	125	91	35
Edmonds, Jim	STL	2004	0.363	0.301	0.418	0.643	612	150	111	42
Aaron, Hank	MLB	1963	0.363	0.319	0.391	0.581	700	197	126	42

Table 4.4. Pitchers with 500+ Batters Faced

Player	Team	Year	ERA	GPA	BA	OBP	SLG	PA	Hits	RBI	HR
Gibson, Bob	STL	1968	1.12	0.172	0.184	0.233	0.236	1161	198	43	11
Maddux, Greg	ATL	1995	1.63	0.173	0.197	0.224	0.258	785	147	35	8
Wilhelm, Hoyt	CHW	1965	1.80	0.175	0.175	0.226	0.277	549	88	35	11
Grant, Jim	OAK	1970	1.86	0.175	0.230	0.282	0.317	529	112	41	10
Corbett, Doug	MIN	1980	1.98	0.177	0.213	0.277	0.296	531	102	46	7
Gossage, Rich	PIT	1977	1.62	0.177	0.170	0.250	0.253	523	78	42	9
Gooden, Dwight	NYM	1985	1.53	0.180	0.201	0.254	0.270	1065	198	46	13
Martinez, Pedro	BOS	2000	1.74	0.182	0.167	0.213	0.259	817	128	41	17
Wilhelm, Hoyt	CHW	1964	1.99	0.182	0.202	0.252	0.282	510	94	32	7
Chance, Dean	LAA	1964	1.65	0.182	0.195	0.260	0.244	1093	194	50	7
Eichhorn, Mark	TOR	1986	1.72	0.185	0.192	0.261	0.288	612	105	49	8
Medlen, Kris	ATL	2012	1.57	0.185	0.208	0.243	0.286	520	103	30	6
Ryan, Nolan	HOU	1981	1.69	0.185	0.188	0.280	0.216	605	99	29	2
Tiant, Luis	CLE	1968	1.60	0.186	0.168	0.233	0.262	987	152	48	16
Koufax, Sandy	LAD	1963	1.88	0.186	0.189	0.230	0.271	1210	214	62	18
Hernandez, Gu.	DET	1984	1.92	0.187	0.194	0.252	0.254	548	96	36	6

Player	Team	Year	ERA	GPA	BA	OBP	SLG	PA	Hits	RBI	HR
Maddux, Greg	ATL	1994	1.56	0.188	0.207	0.243	0.259	774	150	38	4
Wood, Wilbur	CHW	1968	1.87	0.189	0.222	0.266	0.305	626	127	48	8
Rogers, Steve	MON	1973	1.54	0.190	0.199	0.274	0.278	526	93	24	5
Seaver, Tom	NYM	1971	1.76	0.190	0.206	0.252	0.297	1103	210	61	18
Koufax, Sandy	LAD	1966	1.73	0.190	0.205	0.252	0.294	1274	241	65	19
Perry, Gaylord	CLE	1972	1.92	0.191	0.205	0.261	0.296	1345	253	69	17
Kern, Jim	TEX	1979	1.57	0.191	0.198	0.288	0.261	578	99	51	5
McNally, Dave	BAL	1968	1.95	0.191	0.182	0.232	0.302	1038	175	61	24
Koufax, Sandy	LAD	1964	1.74	0.191	0.191	0.240	0.275	870	154	47	13
Nelson, Roger	KCR	1972	2.08	0.191	0.196	0.234	0.312	652	120	38	13
Farr, Steve	KCR	1990	1.98	0.191	0.220	0.301	0.295	515	99	38	6
Blue, Vida	OAK	1971	1.82	0.192	0.189	0.251	0.272	1207	209	69	19
Lee, Bob	LAA	1964	1.51	0.193	0.182	0.270	0.242	547	87	44	6
Sanders, Ken	MIL	1971	1.91	0.193	0.227	0.282	0.325	538	111	42	9
Guidry, Ron	NYY	1978	1.74	0.194	0.193	0.249	0.279	1057	187	49	13
Maddux, Greg	ATL	1997	2.20	0.194	0.236	0.256	0.311	893	200	56	9
Gossage, Rich	NYY	1978	2.01	0.194	0.187	0.277	0.288	543	87	48	9
Gossage, Rich	CHW	1975	1.84	0.195	0.201	0.306	0.252	583	99	52	3
Carlton, Steve	PHI	1972	1.97	0.195	0.207	0.257	0.291	1351	257	78	17
McLain, Denny	DET	1968	1.96	0.195	0.200	0.243	0.317	1288	241	82	31
Tudor, John	STL	1985	1.93	0.196	0.209	0.249	0.285	1062	209	59	14
Hunter, Jim	OAK	1972	2.04	0.196	0.189	0.241	0.296	1149	200	65	21
Perranoski, Ron	LAD	1963	1.67	0.197	0.231	0.298	0.302	541	112	48	7
Seaver, Tom	NYM	1973	2.08	0.197	0.206	0.252	0.313	1147	219	70	23
Koufax, Sandy	LAD	1965	2.04	0.197	0.179	0.227	0.280	1297	216	80	26
Horlen, Joe	CHW	1967	2.06	0.197	0.203	0.253	0.290	996	188	54	13
Hiller, John	DET	1968	2.39	0.197	0.200	0.279	0.309	518	92	31	9
Bolin, Bobby	SFG	1968	1.99	0.197	0.200	0.258	0.286	696	128	43	9
Peters, Gary	CHW	1966	1.98	0.198	0.212	0.260	0.301	801	156	43	11
Koosman, Jerry	NYM	1969	2.28	0.198	0.216	0.275	0.308	957	187	56	14
Nash, Jim	KCA	1966	2.06	0.198	0.204	0.276	0.314	516	95	29	6
Clemens, Roger	HOU	2005	1.87	0.198	0.198	0.261	0.284	838	151	45	11
Palmer, Jim	BAL	1972	2.07	0.198	0.217	0.268	0.308	1094	219	65	21
Brown, Kevin	FLA	1996	1.89	0.198	0.220	0.262	0.289	906	187	50	8
Scott, Mike	HOU	1986	2.22	0.198	0.186	0.242	0.291	1065	182	65	17
Schmidt, Jason	SFG	2003	2.34	0.199	0.200	0.250	0.316	819	152	50	14
Radatz, Dick	BOS	1963	2.04	0.199	0.201	0.285	0.284	541	94	47	9
Halladay, Roy	TOR	2005	2.41	0.199	0.225	0.260	0.326	553	118	37	11
Ryan, Nolan	CAL	1972	2.28	0.199	0.171	0.291	0.246	1154	166	68	14
Hall, Tom	MIN	1970	2.55	0.199	0.173	0.262	0.285	619	94	38	11
Clemens, Roger	TOR	1997	2.05	0.200	0.213	0.273	0.290	1044	204	59	9
Niekro, Joe	HOU	1982	2.47	0.200	0.229	0.278	0.303	1067	224	62	12
Clemens, Roger	BOS	1990	1.93	0.200	0.228	0.278	0.306	920	193	46	7
Martinez, Pedro	BOS	1999	2.07	0.200	0.205	0.248	0.288	835	160	51	9
Niekro, Phil	ATL	1967	1.80	0.200	0.209	0.267	0.280	793	151	53	9
Swift, Bill	SFG	1992	2.08	0.200	0.239	0.292	0.314	655	144	40	6
Carpenter, Chris	STL	2009	2.24	0.200	0.226	0.272	0.310	750	156	48	7
Sutton, Don	LAD	1980	2.20	0.200	0.211	0.257	0.330	833	163	54	20
Quisenberry, Dan	KCR	1983	1.81	0.200	0.229	0.243	0.315	536	118	47	6
Wilhelm, Hoyt	BAL	1959	2.19	0.200	0.224	0.299	0.307	903	178	59	13
Marichal, Juan	SFG	1965	2.13	0.200	0.205	0.239	0.318	1153	224	76	27
Taylor, Ron	STL	1963	2.84	0.200	0.243	0.289	0.372	540	119	45	10
Darwin, Danny	HOU	1990	2.21	0.200	0.225	0.266	0.331	646	136	44	11
Marichal, Juan	SFG	1966	2.23	0.201	0.202	0.230	0.312	1180	228	77	32

Best Individual Seasons, 1952–2012

Player	Team	Year	ERA	GPA	BA	OBP	SLG	PA	Hits	RBI	HR
Radatz, Dick	BOS	1962	2.24	0.201	0.211	0.279	0.338	504	95	47	9
Maddux, Greg	CHC	1992	2.18	0.201	0.210	0.272	0.279	1061	201	64	7
Reynolds, Allie	NYY	1952	2.12	0.201	0.207	0.290	0.279	735	135	46	6
Henry, Bill	CHC	1959	2.67	0.202	0.225	0.261	0.388	512	108	55	19
Sutton, Don	LAD	1972	2.08	0.202	0.189	0.240	0.271	1061	186	70	13
Fisher, Eddie	CHW	1965	2.40	0.202	0.205	0.259	0.302	646	118	53	13
Ellsworth, Dick	CHC	1963	2.11	0.202	0.210	0.262	0.281	1160	223	64	14
Martinez, Pedro	MON	1997	1.90	0.202	0.184	0.250	0.277	947	158	62	16
Martinez, Pedro	BOS	2003	2.22	0.203	0.215	0.272	0.314	749	147	48	7
Valenzuela, F.	LAD	1981	2.48	0.203	0.205	0.270	0.279	758	140	45	11
Peters, Gary	CHW	1963	2.33	0.203	0.216	0.277	0.286	978	192	54	9
Palmer, Jim	BAL	1975	2.09	0.203	0.216	0.266	0.316	1268	253	82	20
Nash, Jim	OAK	1968	2.28	0.203	0.219	0.269	0.339	910	185	55	18
Nolan, Gary	CIN	1972	1.99	0.203	0.227	0.259	0.336	689	147	41	13
McDowell, Sam	CLE	1965	2.18	0.203	0.185	0.286	0.244	1116	178	62	9
Halladay, Roy	PHI	2011	2.35	0.203	0.239	0.269	0.313	933	208	60	10
Palmer, Jim	BAL	1969	2.34	0.203	0.200	0.272	0.303	723	131	45	11
John, Tommy	CHW	1968	1.98	0.203	0.212	0.280	0.288	705	135	38	10
Short, Chris	PHI	1964	2.20	0.203	0.218	0.267	0.313	867	174	56	10
Seaver, Tom	NYM	1969	2.21	0.203	0.207	0.272	0.331	1089	202	66	24
Gibson, Bob	STL	1969	2.18	0.204	0.219	0.283	0.288	1270	251	78	12
Horlen, Joe	CHW	1964	1.88	0.204	0.190	0.248	0.264	815	142	48	11
Harris, Greg W.	SDP	1989	2.60	0.204	0.215	0.291	0.298	554	106	36	8
Black, Joe	BRO	1952	2.15	0.204	0.201	0.262	0.292	560	102	47	9
Hough, Charlie	LAD	1976	2.21	0.204	0.200	0.314	0.284	600	102	45	6
Wilhelm, Hoyt	CLE	1958	2.34	0.204	0.204	0.276	0.282	526	95	38	6
Harden, Rich	OAK	2008	2.07	0.204	0.183	0.270	0.287	595	96	37	11
Pierce, Billy	CHW	1955	1.97	0.204	0.212	0.276	0.312	835	161	48	16
Drysdale, Don	LAD	1964	2.18	0.204	0.207	0.255	0.283	1264	242	75	15
Knepper, Bob	HOU	1981	2.18	0.204	0.226	0.278	0.292	617	128	38	5
McGaffigan, Andy	MON	1987	2.39	0.204	0.235	0.303	0.320	500	105	38	5
Drysdale, Don	LAD	1968	1.94	0.205	0.226	0.279	0.285	901	187	51	10
Wood, Wilbur	CHW	1971	1.91	0.205	0.222	0.263	0.306	1316	272	81	21
Cone, David	NYM	1988	2.22	0.205	0.213	0.283	0.293	936	178	61	10
Leiter, Al	NYM	1998	2.47	0.205	0.216	0.298	0.306	789	151	46	8
Koosman, Jerry	NYM	1968	2.08	0.205	0.228	0.283	0.327	1058	221	65	16
Gooden, Dwight	NYM	1984	2.60	0.205	0.202	0.269	0.275	879	161	62	7
Tewksbury, Bob	STL	1992	2.16	0.205	0.248	0.265	0.353	915	217	58	15
Lincecum, Tim	SFG	2008	2.62	0.205	0.221	0.297	0.316	928	182	58	11
Buzhardt, John	CHW	1963	2.42	0.205	0.216	0.272	0.322	503	100	31	8
Caudill, Bill	CHC	1980	2.19	0.205	0.223	0.309	0.359	528	100	47	10

Table 4.5. Relief Pitchers with 200+ Batters Faced

Player	Team	Year	ERA	GPA	BA	OBP	SLG	PA	Hits	RBI	HR
Ryan, B.J.	TOR	2006	1.37	0.141	0.169	0.230	0.214	270	42	11	3
Rodney, Fernando	TBR	2012	0.60	0.142	0.167	0.219	0.198	282	43	9	2
Kimbrel, Craig	ATL	2012	1.01	0.143	0.126	0.186	0.172	231	27	6	3
Putz, J.J.	SEA	2007	1.38	0.145	0.153	0.202	0.252	260	37	16	6
Eckersley, Dennis	OAK	1990	0.61	0.147	0.160	0.172	0.226	262	41	12	2
Robertson, David	NYY	2011	1.08	0.147	0.170	0.280	0.226	272	40	16	1
Tatum, Ken	CAL	1969	1.36	0.147	0.172	0.276	0.220	342	51	16	1
Papelbon, Jonatha	BOS	2006	0.92	0.150	0.167	0.211	0.254	257	40	11	3
Kuo, Hong-Chih	LAD	2010	1.20	0.151	0.139	0.211	0.192	229	29	10	1

Player	Team	Year	ERA	GPA	BA	OBP	SLG	PA	Hits	RBI	HR
Hiller, John	DET	1973	1.44	0.152	0.198	0.260	0.278	498	89	30	7
Benoit, Joaquin	TBR	2010	1.34	0.152	0.147	0.189	0.265	217	30	11	6
Gagne, Eric	LAD	2003	1.20	0.158	0.133	0.199	0.176	306	37	10	2
Hoffman, Trevor	SDP	1998	1.48	0.158	0.165	0.232	0.229	274	41	16	2
Rivera, Mariano	NYY	2008	1.40	0.160	0.165	0.190	0.233	259	41	14	4
Mesa, Jose	CLE	1995	1.13	0.162	0.216	0.268	0.273	250	49	12	3
Eckersley, Dennis	OAK	1992	1.91	0.162	0.211	0.242	0.306	309	62	18	5
Ziegler, Brad	OAK	2008	1.06	0.162	0.236	0.311	0.327	229	47	12	2
Jackson, Mike	CLE	1998	1.55	0.163	0.195	0.252	0.290	239	43	12	4
Betancourt, R.	CLE	2007	1.47	0.163	0.183	0.208	0.277	289	51	16	4
Holland, Greg	KCR	2011	1.80	0.164	0.175	0.246	0.275	233	37	14	3
Fingers, Rollie	MIL	1981	1.04	0.164	0.198	0.235	0.277	297	55	19	3
Saito, Takashi	LAD	2007	1.40	0.166	0.151	0.209	0.239	234	33	14	5
Dibble, Rob	CIN	1989	2.09	0.166	0.176	0.261	0.250	401	62	32	4
Wagner, Billy	HOU	1999	1.57	0.167	0.135	0.208	0.212	286	35	15	5
Urbina, Ugueth	MON	1998	1.30	0.167	0.157	0.259	0.229	272	37	12	2
McGraw, Tug	PHI	1980	1.46	0.168	0.194	0.250	0.276	355	62	22	3
McGraw, Tug	NYM	1971	1.70	0.168	0.189	0.271	0.266	441	73	18	4
Nathan, Joe	MIN	2006	1.58	0.169	0.158	0.212	0.242	262	38	13	3
Nathan, Joe	MIN	2009	2.10	0.170	0.171	0.244	0.305	271	42	14	7
Olson, Gregg	BAL	1989	1.69	0.171	0.188	0.295	0.247	356	57	19	1
Clippard, Tyler	WAS	2011	1.83	0.171	0.162	0.228	0.307	329	48	26	11
Politte, Cliff	CHW	2005	2.00	0.171	0.181	0.254	0.323	262	42	23	7
Eckersley, Dennis	OAK	1989	1.40	0.172	0.162	0.175	0.258	206	32	19	5
Beck, Rod	SFG	1992	1.76	0.172	0.190	0.228	0.257	352	62	25	4
Lancaster, Les	CHC	1989	1.36	0.172	0.226	0.264	0.287	288	60	21	2
Romo, Vicente	CLE	1968	1.60	0.172	0.155	0.241	0.261	326	44	22	5
Donnelly, Brendan	ANA	2003	1.58	0.173	0.200	0.273	0.287	307	55	16	2
Chapman, Aroldis	CIN	2012	1.51	0.173	0.141	0.225	0.226	276	35	15	4
Thigpen, Bobby	CHW	1990	1.83	0.173	0.195	0.271	0.283	347	60	25	5
Papelbon, J.	BOS	2007	1.85	0.173	0.146	0.219	0.244	224	30	17	5
Rhodes, Arthur	SEA	2001	1.72	0.173	0.189	0.230	0.279	258	46	22	5
Harvey, Bryan	FLA	1993	1.70	0.174	0.186	0.222	0.240	264	45	21	4
Benitez, Armando	FLA	2004	1.29	0.174	0.152	0.220	0.257	262	36	19	6
Nathan, Joe	MIN	2004	1.62	0.174	0.187	0.259	0.257	284	48	14	3
Smoltz, John	ATL	2003	1.12	0.174	0.204	0.230	0.281	244	48	16	2
Gagne, Eric	LAD	2002	1.97	0.175	0.189	0.235	0.302	314	55	19	6
Myers, Randy	NYM	1988	1.72	0.175	0.190	0.248	0.278	261	45	25	5
Wagner, Billy	HOU	2003	1.78	0.175	0.169	0.234	0.266	335	52	17	8
Nen, Robb	SFG	2000	1.50	0.175	0.162	0.230	0.241	256	37	16	4
Wilhelm, Hoyt	CHW	1965	1.80	0.175	0.175	0.226	0.277	549	88	35	11
Grant, Jim	OAK	1970	1.86	0.175	0.230	0.282	0.317	529	112	41	10
Putz, J.J.	SEA	2006	2.30	0.176	0.207	0.245	0.284	303	59	25	4
Percival, Troy	CAL	1995	1.95	0.176	0.147	0.229	0.246	284	37	21	6
Brewer, Jim	LAD	1972	1.26	0.177	0.157	0.233	0.257	303	41	28	6
Lidge, Brad	HOU	2004	1.90	0.177	0.174	0.254	0.290	369	57	23	8
Gossage, Rich	PIT	1977	1.62	0.177	0.170	0.250	0.253	523	78	42	9
Rivera, Mariano	NYY	1999	1.83	0.177	0.176	0.239	0.237	268	43	17	2
Benitez, Armando	NYM	1999	1.85	0.177	0.148	0.260	0.236	312	40	21	4
Corbett, Doug	MIN	1980	1.98	0.177	0.213	0.277	0.296	531	102	46	7
Hasegawa, S.	SEA	2003	1.48	0.177	0.235	0.284	0.337	283	62	16	5
Sosa, Elias	LAD	1977	1.98	0.177	0.189	0.233	0.329	239	42	21	7
Adams, Mike	TEX	2011	1.34	0.177	0.169	0.211	0.285	277	44	16	5
Wetteland, John	MON	1993	1.37	0.178	0.188	0.260	0.276	344	58	23	3

Best Individual Seasons, 1952–2012

Player	Team	Year	ERA	GPA	BA	OBP	SLG	PA	Hits	RBI	HR
Olson, Gregg	BAL	1992	2.05	0.178	0.211	0.287	0.280	244	46	17	3
Sutter, Bruce	CHC	1977	1.34	0.178	0.183	0.231	0.271	411	69	34	5
Wagner, Billy	ATL	2010	1.30	0.178	0.159	0.238	0.255	268	38	14	5
Percival, Troy	CAL	1996	2.31	0.179	0.149	0.246	0.263	291	38	24	8
Bell, Heath	SDP	2007	2.02	0.179	0.185	0.257	0.246	363	60	27	3
Sambito, Joe	HOU	1981	1.84	0.179	0.192	0.269	0.299	255	43	14	4
Henke, Tom	TOR	1990	2.17	0.179	0.213	0.266	0.342	297	58	24	8
Eyre, Scott	SFG	2005	2.63	0.179	0.200	0.286	0.288	277	48	21	3
Howell, Jay	LAD	1989	1.58	0.180	0.211	0.266	0.289	312	60	19	3
Hoffman, Trevor	MIL	2009	1.83	0.180	0.183	0.240	0.241	210	35	15	2
Sutter, Bruce	STL	1984	1.54	0.180	0.245	0.281	0.344	477	109	34	9
Davis, Mark	SDP	1989	1.85	0.180	0.200	0.270	0.294	370	66	34	6
Miller, Stu	BAL	1965	1.89	0.180	0.207	0.265	0.293	462	87	32	5
Worrell, Todd	STL	1992	2.11	0.180	0.198	0.281	0.282	256	45	12	4
Fox, Terry	DET	1961	1.41	0.180	0.200	0.265	0.310	231	42	15	6
Rhodes, Arthur	CIN	2010	2.29	0.180	0.196	0.265	0.309	217	38	16	4
Hoffman, Trevor	SDP	2004	2.30	0.181	0.211	0.242	0.367	209	42	14	5
Rivera, Mariano	NYY	2009	1.76	0.181	0.197	0.237	0.311	257	48	17	7
Romo, Sergio	SFG	2012	1.79	0.181	0.185	0.235	0.290	215	37	17	5
Lyle, Sparky	NYY	1972	1.92	0.181	0.216	0.268	0.284	427	84	36	3
Rivera, Mariano	NYY	1998	1.91	0.181	0.215	0.270	0.309	246	48	17	3
Vande Berg, Ed	SEA	1982	2.25	0.181	0.207	0.296	0.303	303	54	18	5
Bailey, Andrew	OAK	2009	1.73	0.181	0.167	0.228	0.248	323	49	24	5
Montgomery, Jeff	KCR	1989	1.37	0.181	0.198	0.257	0.251	363	66	24	3
Henke, Tom	STL	1995	1.82	0.182	0.209	0.274	0.274	221	42	14	2
McClure, Bob	CAL	1989	1.55	0.182	0.212	0.270	0.283	205	39	19	2
Wilhelm, Hoyt	CHW	1964	1.99	0.182	0.202	0.252	0.282	510	94	32	7
O'Flaherty, Eric	ATL	2011	0.98	0.182	0.221	0.283	0.288	301	59	16	2
Gordon, Tom	NYY	2004	2.21	0.182	0.180	0.237	0.286	342	56	23	5
Bastardo, Antonio	PHI	2011	2.64	0.182	0.144	0.242	0.282	225	28	14	6
Nathan, Joe	MIN	2007	1.88	0.182	0.209	0.264	0.310	282	54	18	4
Hammond, Chris	ATL	2002	0.95	0.182	0.195	0.278	0.261	311	53	19	1
Camp, Rick	ATL	1981	1.78	0.182	0.239	0.271	0.337	304	68	21	5
Soria, Joakim	KCR	2010	1.78	0.183	0.216	0.266	0.302	270	53	15	4
Papelbon, J.	BOS	2009	1.85	0.183	0.213	0.289	0.311	285	54	18	5
Wagner, Billy	PHI	2005	1.51	0.183	0.165	0.229	0.265	297	45	21	6
Lilliquist, Derek	CLE	1992	1.75	0.183	0.187	0.253	0.306	239	39	18	5
Berenguer, Juan	ATL	1991	2.24	0.183	0.189	0.261	0.303	255	43	16	5
Myers, Randy	BAL	1997	1.51	0.184	0.217	0.289	0.286	241	47	18	2
Franklin, Ryan	STL	2009	1.92	0.184	0.220	0.296	0.296	250	49	14	2
Harvey, Bryan	CAL	1991	1.60	0.184	0.178	0.225	0.266	309	51	25	6
McBean, Al	PIT	1964	1.91	0.184	0.236	0.281	0.311	352	76	25	4
Hensley, Clay	FLA	2010	2.16	0.184	0.200	0.286	0.281	307	54	15	3
Wuertz, Michael	OAK	2009	2.63	0.184	0.188	0.248	0.319	304	52	26	6
Ziegler, Brad	ARI	2012	2.49	0.184	0.228	0.291	0.287	263	54	25	2
Groom, Buddy	BAL	2002	1.60	0.185	0.196	0.243	0.281	239	44	20	4
Eichhorn, Mark	TOR	1986	1.72	0.185	0.192	0.261	0.288	612	105	49	8
O'Flaherty, Eric	ATL	2012	1.73	0.185	0.229	0.300	0.302	230	47	15	3

BALLPARK CORRECTIONS

The next chapters describe the ballpark and baserunning corrections that can be applied to GPA to better reflect a player's total production for his team.

The ballpark can have a dramatic effect on a hitter's or pitcher's production. The distance from home plate to the fences, the amount of foul territory, and the hitting background are just some of the factors that influence the way a park plays. The weather and environment can also dramatically influence hitters and pitchers. If the wind blows out at Wrigley Field there will be more home runs and offensive production; if it blows in, there could be many fly-ball outs and a low score. In Denver, the thin air and low humidity have combined to make Coors Field a hitter's paradise — albeit one slightly less welcoming since the introduction of the humidor in 2002 — despite its spacious dimensions

Most attempts to correct for the differences among ballparks use crude calculations and call these corrections "ballpark factors." The most common approach is to compare the number of runs scored at home to the number of runs scored on the road. A simple ratio is created and that ratio is used to correct other statistics.

The problems that arise from this approach are:

1. There is no basis to assume that multiplying other statistics by the "ballpark factor" will make an appropriate correction.
2. Teams generally perform better at home than on the road. This difference must be taken into account when making any corrections.
3. Teams play other teams an uneven number of times. The corrections are biased toward the parks that teams play in most often.
4. The corrections are difficult for the casual baseball fan to understand.
5. The corrections tend to be very small numbers. It takes many events, usually over many seasons, to accurately measure the corrections.
6. Pitchers' plate appearances (as batters) can strongly bias the data. During interleague games, the designated hitter rule is used in American League parks but not National League parks.

Two calculations can be made to estimate the ballpark correction (BPC) for each ballpark. Each team's home batting GPA can be compared with its road batting GPA, and each team's home pitching GPA can be compared with its road pitching GPA. In this book, the average of both of these calculations is used to improve the accuracy of the BPCs.

A number of biases must be removed if the correction is to be accurate.

Players consistently perform better at home than on the road. From 1952 to 2012 the average batter had a 0.0105 *higher* GPA at home compared to their GPA on the road or conversely the average pitcher had a 0.0105 *lower* GPA at home compared to their GPA on the road. This difference was constant across eras. In the seasons before the DH came into being (1952 to 1972), it was 0.0101; in the first two decades of the DH era (1973 to 1996), 0.0114; and since the advent of interleague play (1997–2012), 0.0109.

Each of the two calculations can be adjusted for the difference between an average player's home and road GPAs over the era it is calculated using the following formulas:

$$BPC1 = \text{Road Batting GPA} - \text{Home Batting GPA} + \text{HmRdDifferential}$$
$$BPC2 = \text{Road Pitching GPA} - \text{Home Pitching GPA} - \text{HmRdDifferential}$$
$$BPC = (BPC1 + BPC2) \times 0.5$$

The difference between an average player's home and road GPAs (HmRdDifferential) does not effect the final BPC calculation since the differential is cancelled out when BPC1 and BPC2 are averaged.

	— — Uncorrected GPA — —				— Corrected GPA (0.0109) —			
	Home Bat	Road Bat	Home Pitch	Road Pitch	Home Bat	Road Bat	Home Pitch	Road Pitch
Progressive Field	0.275	0.270	0.265	0.278	0.270	0.276	0.270	0.273
Kauffman Stadium	0.269	0.255	0.281	0.284	0.264	0.261	0.287	0.278
Wrigley Field	0.277	0.261	0.269	0.279	0.271	0.267	0.275	0.273

	BPC1	BPC2	BPC	BPC1	BPC2
Progressive Field	0.005	−0.013	**−0.004**	−0.006	−0.003
Kauffman Stadium	0.014	−0.003	**0.006**	0.003	0.008
Wrigley Field	0.016	−0.010	**0.003**	0.004	0.002

Table 5.1. Ballpark correction values for selected stadiums. The calculations are shown both with and without a correction for the difference between an average player's home and road GPAs, but the final ballpark correction calculated is the same. Data from 1997 to 2012.

The number of times teams play each other is quite uneven. Division opponents play each other the most. Non-division opponents from the same league play each other a moderate number of times. Interleague opponents may play each other a few games each season, but during many seasons do not play a single game.

Table 5.2 shows the number of plate appearances (PAs) by Boston Red Sox batters and number faced by Red Sox pitchers from 1997 to 2009. The data is broken down by team faced and whether the PAs were at home or on the road.

If each PA counted equally in calculating the correction for Fenway Park, it would he heavily biased toward AL East parks. If the other four parks in the AL East favored the hitters, then Fenway Park's correction value would be inappropriately high. If the other four parks favored the pitchers, Fenway's correction value would be inappropriately low.

For the Red Sox from 1997 to 2009, a GPA ballpark correction is calculated against each of the 13 other teams in the American League. These team BPCs are then weighted to create an unbiased average BPC for all AL games.

Before 1997, when interleague play began, the BPCs could only be calculated relative to other teams in the same league. Since 1997, it is possible to use the data from interleague play to calculate BPCs relative to all teams in both leagues.

	American League					National League			
	—Home—		—Road—			—Home—		—Road—	
	Bat	*Pitch*	*Bat*	*Pitch*		*Bat*	*Pitch*	*Bat*	*Pitch*
Baltimore	4175	4169	4411	3996	Atlanta	868	974	981	956
Boston	x	x	x	x	Florida	584	568	333	311
New York	4221	4425	4255	4065	New York	444	433	317	309
Tampa Bay	3936	3872	4215	3849	Philadelphia	680	684	818	784
Toronto	4057	4213	4340	4126	Washington	372	315	427	433
Chicago	1935	1918	2315	2172	Chicago	0	0	119	102
Cleveland	2272	2245	2174	2943	Cincinnati	119	100	111	101
Detroit	2318	2326	2338	2178	Houston	137	133	120	104
Kansas City	2006	2016	2018	1854	Milwaukee	299	307	338	334
Minnesota	1864	1861	1927	1838	Pittsburg	113	117	109	104
					St. Louis	284	278	98	101
Anaheim	2360	2406	2159	2123	Arizona	215	229	119	106
Oakland	2549	2550	2399	2299	Colorado	225	233	127	102
Seattle	2068	2053	2551	2430	Los Angeles	104	122	104	96
Texas	2350	2329	2471	2322	San Diego	111	114	205	196
					San Francisco	109	111	113	106

Table 5.2. Plate appearances made by Boston hitters and batters faced by Boston pitchers. Data shown by home and road games against each team from 1997 to 2009.

If interleague and intraleague opponents were weighted equally in the calculation, then the correction would be overweighted with less accurate numbers from the opposite league. On average, the number of PAs against interleague opponents is about 10 percent of the total against intraleague opponents. Therefore, the correction will weight each interleague opponent 10 percent as much as each intraleague opponent.

For the 1997–2009 Red Sox, a BPC is calculated to account for 15 teams in the NL (the Cubs are ignored since they did not play at Fenway Park from 1997 to 2009). These 15 NL team BPCs are each multiplied by 0.1 and added to the 13 AL differentials. This sum is then divided by 14.5 (15 × 0.1 + 13) to calculate the final BPC for the Red Sox for this era.

Pitchers' PAs (as batters) are ignored since they tend to bias the data and make comparison between AL and NL parks more difficult.

In this book, the BPC is called a GPA ballpark correction (GPAbpc) value and is calculated for each ballpark relative to other ballparks. The second half of this chapter dicusses GPA ballpark corrections for individual players that are an average of the GPA ballpark correction values from the mix of ballparks in which that player played.

The GPA ballpark corrections for modern stadiums are sorted from highest to lowest in Table 5.3. A more comprehensive list of BPCs from 1952 to 2012 is provided in the table at the end of this chapter.

The park most favorable to hitters was Colorado's Coors Field, which had a GPAbpc of −0.059 from 1995 to 2001. In 2002, a humidor to store baseballs was introduced and from 2002 to 2012 the correction fell to −0.034 for Coors Field. Although this is still by far the highest of any modern park, it is no longer dramatically outside historical norms.

The Angels' 1961 season at Los Angeles' Wrigley Field had a correction of −0.030. Fenway Park from 1952 to 1972 had a BPC of −0.020.

The least-friendly park for hitters is San Diego's PETCO Park with a BPC of +0.024. PETCO Park's bias for pitchers differs little from Coors Field's bias for hitters.

In 2009, the new Yankee Stadium quickly acquired a reputation as park friendly to hitters because of the number of home runs being hit to right field. Through its first 23 games, 87 home runs were hit at the park, easily beating Minute Maid Park's previous record set in 2000. Commentator Peter Gammons denounced the new park as "one of the biggest jokes in baseball," and ESPN colleague Buster Olney described the stadium as being "on steroids."

An independent study in June 2009 concluded that the shape and height of the right-field wall, rather than the wind, was responsible for the proliferation of home runs at the new stadium. The pace slowed significantly as the season progressed, but a new single-season record of 237 home runs hit at a Yankee ballpark was set ("Design Cause of Stadium Homers, " MLB.com, 6/2009). This was tied for the 18th most during one season at a big league ballpark, but it fell far short of the record 303 homers hit at Coors Field in 1999.

New Yankee Stadium's GPA_{bpc} for 2009 was +0.003, little different from old Yankee Stadium's 1997–2008 correction of +0.004. Despite the home runs, new Yankee Stadium was slightly more favorable than average to pitchers during the 2009 season. At the time, some sports commentators had a hard time seeing the whole picture because they were fixated on a single aspect of the new park.

New Yankee Stadium's correction from 2009 to 2012 was −0.012, substantially greater than old Yankee Stadium. It takes a number of years to accurately measure a GPA ballpark correction, but it appears that New Yankee Stadium will favor hitters.

How much difference does including pitchers' PAs (as batters) make? It turns out that none of the corrections change by more than 0.001 points.

How much difference does excluding interleague play make? Most corrections change by 0.001 or less, but a few change by up to 0.003 points.

How much difference does counting all PAs equally make? This had the biggest effect, but all the changes were still less than 0.003 points.

The GPA_{bpc} tends to be less accurate when calculated over shorter intervals. The corrections are relative to other parks during that era. The corrections will evolve slowly as subtle changes occur at parks over the years and as new parks are built.

When a GPA ballpark correction value is greater than zero, the park favors pitchers over hitters; when it's less than zero, the park favors hitters instead.

In implementing GPA ballpark corrections for individual players, each PA has a GPA correction value added based on the park and year he made that plate appearance. The total correction is divided by the number of PAs, giving a ballpark correction for each player in GPA points. The correction data comes from Table 5.3 and the table at the end of this chapter.

Larry Walker won the 1997 MVP while playing for the Colorado Rockies. How much of an advantage did playing at Coors Field give him over fellow candidates Mike Piazza and Tony Gwynn, who played in parks that were much less favorable to hitters?

During the 1997 season, Walker had the highest GPA in the NL by 0.021 points. Walker's GPA falls to 0.367, however, when it is corrected for the ballparks in which he played. Comparing corrected GPAs among the top three players in the NL, Gwynn leads Piazza by 0.009 points and Walker by 0.018 points.

Team Name	Stadium Name	Seasons First	Seasons Last	Correction 1997–2012
Colorado	Coors Field	1995	2001	−0.059
Colorado	Coors Field (Humidor for Ball)	2002		−0.034
Texas	Rangers Ballpark in Arlington	1994		−0.015
Arizona	Chase Field	1998		−0.013
Yankees	Yankee Stadium II	2009		−0.012
Boston	Fenway Park	1952		−0.009
White Sox	U.S. Cellular Field	1991		−0.007
Cincinnati	Great American Ball Park	2003		−0.007
Kansas City	Kauffman Stadium	1973		−0.006
Miami	Marlins Park	2012		−0.005
Houston	Minute Maid Park	2000		−0.004
Cubs	Wrigley Field	1952		−0.003
Toronto	Rogers Centre	1990		−0.003
Philadelphia	Citizens Bank Park	2004		−0.003
Minnesota	Metrodome	1982	2009	−0.001
Milwaukee	Miller Park	2001		−0.001
Atlanta	Turner Field	1997		0.001
Washington	Nationals Park	2008		0.001
Pittsburgh	PNC Park	2001		0.002
Minnesota	Target Field	2010		0.002
Detroit	Comerica Park	2000		0.003
Yankees	Yankee Stadium I (Post-Renov)	1976	2008	0.004
Cleveland	Progressive Field	1994		0.004
Baltimore	Oriole Park at Camden Yards	1992		0.005
San Francisco	AT&T Park	2000		0.005
St. Louis	Busch Stadium III	2006		0.005
LA Angels	Angel Stadium of Anaheim	1966		0.006
Mets	Shea Stadium	1964	2008	0.007
Oakland	O.co Coliseum	1997		0.007
Mets	Citi Field	2009		0.007
Tampa Bay	Tropicana Field	1998		0.008
Florida	Sun Life Stadium	1993	2011	0.010
Dodgers	Dodger Stadium	1962		0.011
Seattle	Safeco Field	2000		0.015
Washington	RFK Stadium	2005	2007	0.018
San Diego	PETCO Park	2004		0.024

Table 5.3. GPA corrections calculated for ballparks in recent use. Corrections for parks not open from 1997 to 2012 are calculated for the era in which they were open.

Player	Team	Year	GPA	GPAbpc	cGPA	BA	MVP Points	MVP Rank
Walker, Larry	COL	1997	0.397	−0.030	0.367	0.366	359	1
Gwynn, Tony	SDP	1997	0.376	0.009	0.385	0.372	113	6
Piazza, Mike	LAD	1997	0.372	0.004	0.376	0.362	263	2
Bagwell, Jeff	HOU	1997	0.356	0.004	0.359	0.286	233	3
Bonds, Barry	SFG	1997	0.355	0.006	0.361	0.291	123	5
Lankford, Ray	STL	1997	0.349	−0.001	0.348	0.295		
Galarraga, Andres	COL	1997	0.343	−0.028	0.315	0.318	85	7
Olerud, John	NYM	1997	0.340	0.003	0.343	0.294		
Biggio, Craig	HOU	1997	0.336	0.004	0.339	0.309	157	4
Alou, Moises	FLA	1997	0.333	−0.002	0.331	0.292	60	10

Player	Team	Year	GPA	GPAbpc	cGPA	BA	MVP Points	MVP Rank
Jones, Chipper	ATL	1997	0.320	0.000	0.320	0.295	70	9
Kent, Jeff	SFG	1997	0.265	0.006	0.271	0.250	80	8

Table 5.4. National League MVP voting from the 1997 season. (The cGPA is the corrected GPA calculated by adding GPAbpc to GPA.)

At the time, the results of the voting for the 1997 NL MVP were controversial, with a number of writers feeling Piazza deserved the award. Gwynn actually had the best season as measured by GPA. Piazza may have been more deserving of the MVP Award because he was a catcher — a difficult defensive position to play.

Notice that the GPA ballpark correction for Walker is far lower than the −0.059 points for Coors Field at the time. He made about half his PAs on the road, which offset some of the advantage of playing at Coors Field. Andres Galarraga, who also played for the Rockies, had a lower BPC than Walker's because Galarraga's mix of PAs was 0.002 points less favorable than Walker's.

Player	Team	Year	GPA	GPAbpc	cGPA	BA	OBP	SLG	PA
Williams, Ted	BOS	1957	0.427	−0.009	0.417	0.389	0.526	0.735	513
Helton, Todd	COL	2000	0.418	−0.030	0.388	0.372	0.463	0.698	697
Williams, Ted	BOS	1954	0.416	−0.010	0.406	0.345	0.516	0.628	504
Williams, Ted	BOS	1999	0.405	−0.030	0.374	0.379	0.458	0.710	513
Walker, Larry	COL	1999	0.398	−0.006	0.393	0.361	0.487	0.662	673
Cash, Norm	DET	1961	0.398	−0.030	0.367	0.366	0.452	0.720	664
Walker, Larry	COL	1997	0.397	−0.029	0.353	0.350	0.449	0.662	601
Walker, Larry	COL	2001	0.382	−0.015	0.366	0.358	0.458	0.630	703
Helton, Todd	COL	2003	0.382	−0.007	0.375	0.324	0.420	0.630	674
Palmeiro, Rafael	TEX	1999	0.382	−0.007	0.375	0.324	0.420	0.630	674
Snider, Duke	BRO	1955	0.381	−0.008	0.373	0.309	0.418	0.628	653
Helton, Todd	COL	2001	0.377	−0.029	0.348	0.336	0.432	0.685	697
Campanella, Roy	BRO	1953	0.377	−0.008	0.369	0.312	0.395	0.611	590
Yastrzemski, Carl	BOS	1967	0.376	−0.009	0.367	0.326	0.418	0.622	680
Gwynn, Tony	SDP	1997	0.376	0.008	0.385	0.372	0.409	0.547	651
Walker, Larry	COL	2002	0.376	−0.016	0.361	0.338	0.421	0.602	553
Clark, Jack	STL	1987	0.375	0.006	0.381	0.286	0.459	0.597	559
Snider, Duke	BRO	1953	0.374	−0.008	0.367	0.336	0.419	0.627	680
Williams, Ted	BOS	1958	0.373	−0.011	0.362	0.320	0.452	0.573	504
Kluszewski, Ted	CIN	1954	0.372	−0.007	0.366	0.326	0.406	0.642	658
Gonzalez, Luis	ARI	2001	0.372	−0.008	0.364	0.325	0.429	0.688	728
Musial, Stan	STL	1954	0.372	−0.009	0.362	0.335	0.426	0.644	545
Martinez, Edgar	SEA	2000	0.371	0.007	0.378	0.324	0.423	0.579	665
Rodriguez, Alex	SEA	2000	0.370	0.007	0.377	0.316	0.420	0.606	672
Williams, Billy	CHC	1972	0.368	−0.006	0.362	0.333	0.398	0.606	650
Helton, Todd	COL	2004	0.367	−0.016	0.352	0.347	0.469	0.620	683
Lynn, Fred	BOS	1979	0.367	−0.008	0.359	0.333	0.423	0.637	622
Strawberry, D,	NYM	1987	0.366	0.008	0.374	0.284	0.398	0.583	640
Bonds, Barry	SFG	1998	0.365	0.006	0.371	0.303	0.438	0.609	697
Snider, Duke	BRO	1954	0.365	−0.008	0.357	0.341	0.423	0.647	679
Galarraga, Andres	COL	1993	0.364	−0.027	0.337	0.370	0.403	0.602	506
Cabrera, Miguel	FLA	2006	0.364	0.006	0.370	0.339	0.430	0.568	676

Table 5.5. The top 111 seasons by hitters with at least 500 plate appearances. Data from 1952 to 2012.

A reexamination of the top 111 seasons by GPA for hitters shows 31 had GPA ballpark corrections of ±0.006 or greater. For 24 of these 31 seasons, the GPAbpc was negative, indicating that the batters were substantially aided by the parks in which they played. Only two of the top 40 seasons as measured by GPA, Jack Clark's 1987 season and Gywnn's 1997 season, had positive ballpark corrections.

Player	Team	Year	ERA	GPA	GPAbpc	cGPA	BA	OBP	SLG
Gooden, Dwight	NYM	1985	1.53	0.180	0.008	0.188	0.201	0.254	0.270
Chance, Dean	LAA	1964	1.65	0.182	0.008	0.190	0.195	0.260	0.244
Ryan, Nolan	HOU	1981	1.69	0.185	0.010	0.196	0.188	0.280	0.216
Koufax, Sandy	LAD	1963	1.88	0.186	0.007	0.193	0.189	0.230	0.271
Koufax, Sandy	LAD	1966	1.73	0.190	0.009	0.200	0.205	0.252	0.294
Koufax, Sandy	LAD	1964	1.74	0.191	0.010	0.201	0.191	0.240	0.275
Blue, Vida	OAK	1971	1.82	0.192	0.006	0.197	0.189	0.251	0.272
Lee, Bob	LAA	1964	1.51	0.193	0.006	0.199	0.182	0.270	0.242
Tudor, John	STL	1985	1.93	0.196	0.007	0.203	0.209	0.249	0.285
Hunter, Jim	OAK	1972	2.04	0.196	0.007	0.203	0.189	0.241	0.296
Perranoski, Ron	LAD	1963	1.67	0.197	0.007	0.204	0.231	0.298	0.302
Seaver, Tom	NYM	1973	2.08	0.197	0.006	0.203	0.206	0.252	0.313
Koufax, Sandy	LAD	1965	2.04	0.197	0.009	0.206	0.179	0.227	0.280
Nash, Jim	KCA	1966	2.06	0.198	–0.006	0.192	0.204	0.276	0.314
Scott, Mike	HOU	1986	2.22	0.198	0.012	0.211	0.186	0.242	0.291
Radatz, Dick	BOS	1963	2.04	0.199	–0.010	0.189	0.201	0.285	0.284
Ryan, Nolan	CAL	1972	2.28	0.199	0.008	0.207	0.171	0.291	0.246
Niekro, Joe	HOU	1982	2.47	0.200	0.012	0.211	0.229	0.278	0.303
Clemens, Roger	BOS	1990	1.93	0.200	–0.007	0.193	0.228	0.278	0.306
Swift, Bill	SFG	1992	2.08	0.200	0.009	0.209	0.239	0.292	0.314
Sutton, Don	LAD	1980	2.20	0.200	0.011	0.211	0.211	0.257	0.330
Taylor, Ron	STL	1963	2.84	0.200	–0.008	0.193	0.243	0.289	0.372
Darwin, Danny	HOU	1990	2.21	0.200	0.012	0.212	0.225	0.266	0.331
Radatz, Dick	BOS	1962	2.24	0.201	–0.009	0.192	0.211	0.279	0.338
Henry, Bill	CHC	1959	2.67	0.202	–0.011	0.191	0.225	0.261	0.388
Sutton, Don	LAD	1972	2.08	0.202	0.011	0.213	0.189	0.240	0.271
Ellsworth, Dick	CHC	1963	2.11	0.202	–0.009	0.193	0.210	0.262	0.281
Valenzuela, F.	LAD	1981	2.48	0.203	0.013	0.215	0.205	0.270	0.279
Nolan, Gary	CIN	1972	1.99	0.203	0.009	0.212	0.227	0.259	0.336
Harris, Greg W.	SDP	1989	2.60	0.204	0.011	0.215	0.215	0.291	0.298
Hough, Charlie	LAD	1976	2.21	0.204	0.011	0.214	0.200	0.314	0.284
Drysdale, Don	LAD	1964	2.18	0.204	0.009	0.213	0.207	0.255	0.283
Knepper, Bob	HOU	1981	2.18	0.204	0.015	0.219	0.226	0.278	0.292
Drysdale, Don	LAD	1968	1.94	0.205	0.011	0.215	0.226	0.279	0.285
Cone, David	NYM	1988	2.22	0.205	0.008	0.213	0.213	0.283	0.293
Leiter, Al	NYM	1998	2.47	0.205	0.006	0.211	0.216	0.298	0.306
Gooden, Dwight	NYM	1984	2.60	0.205	0.008	0.213	0.202	0.269	0.275

Table 5.6. The top 111 seasons by pitchers with at least 500 batters faced. Data from 1952 to 2012.

Of the top 111 seasons by GPA for pitchers, 37 had ballpark corrections of ±0.006 or greater. For 30 of these 37 seasons, the GPAbpc was positive, indicating that the pitchers were substantially aided by the parks in which they played. Only two of the top 52 seasons, Jim Nash's 1966 season and Dick Radatz's 1963 season, had negative GPA ballpark corrections.

It is not surprising that many of the greatest seasons by hitters were aided by playing in ballparks favorable to hitters. Conversely, many of the greatest seasons by pitchers were aided by playing in ballparks that favored pitchers.

Since interleague play began in 1997, it is possible to compare the two leagues to see which is stronger. The AL has a 0.0070-point advantage (0.2698 – 0.2628) when all PAs, including those by pitchers, are accounted for. This difference is biased in favor of the AL by the DH rule. When PAs by pitchers (as batters) are excluded, the NL has a small advantage of 0.0023 (0.2721 – 0.2698) points. A small difference between the leagues is hard to interpret since so few of the games are between interleague opponents.

	GPA All Games		GPA Interleague Games	
	AL	NL	AL	NL
Including Pitchers	0.2698	0.2628	0.2688	0.2594
Excluding Pitchers	0.2698	0.2721	0.2744	0.2636

Table 5.7. Comparison of GPA for all games and for interleague games only. Data displayed by league from 1997 to 2012.

The best way to judge which league has been superior during the interleague era is by looking only at interleague games. Whether pitchers are included or excluded does not change the conclusion. The AL has been 0.0094 to 0.0108 GPA points superior to the NL. The AL's 2,081–1,883 record against the NL during this period is a more obvious indicator of the AL's superiority.

The following table shows GPAbpc by park and era. For each ballpark, a correction is calculated only for the years it was used during the pre–DH (1952–1972), early DH (1973–1996) and interleague eras (1997–2012). In the instances that a park was shared, a correction is shown for each team that played in that park (examples: Yankees in Shea Stadium from 1975–1976, Angels in Dodger Stadium from 1962–1965).

*Note — The White Sox played a few games in Milwaukee during 1968 and 1969. Oakland moved the plate 30 feet closer to the stands in 1969 and performed a series of major renovations from 1995 to 1996. Cincinnati in 1970, Pittsburgh in 1970, Toronto in 1989, and Seattle in 1999 split their seasons between two parks. Washington was an expansion team in 1961.

Table 5.8. Ballpark Corrections, 1952 to 2012

Team Name	Stadium Name	Seasons First	Seasons Last	GPA Corrections 1952-72	GPA Corrections 1973-96	GPA Corrections 1997-12
Arizona	Chase Field	1998				–0.013
Atlanta	Turner Field	1997				0.001
Atlanta	Atlanta-Fulton County	1966	1996	–0.006	–0.010	
Baltimore	Oriole Park at Camden Y	1992			–0.002	0.005
Baltimore	Memorial Stadium	1952	1991	0.005	0.008	
Bos. Braves	Braves Field	1952	1952	0.021		
Bos. Red Sox	Fenway Park	1952		–0.020	–0.015	–0.009
Brooklyn	Ebbets Field	1952	1957	–0.013		
Chi. Cubs	Wrigley Field	1952		–0.015	–0.009	–0.003
Chi. White Sox	U.S. Cellular Field	1991			0.009*	–0.007
Chi. White Sox	Comiskey Park	1952	1990	0.000	–0.002	
Cincinnati	Great American Ball Park	2003				–0.007

Team Name	Stadium Name	Seasons First	Seasons Last	GPA Corrections 1952–72	GPA Corrections 1973–96	GPA Corrections 1997–12
Cincinnati	Riverfront Stadium	1971	2002	0.015	0.001	–0.005
Cincinnati	Crosley Field	1952	1969	–0.010		
Cleveland	Progressive Field	1994			–0.000	0.004
Cleveland	Cleveland Stadium	1952	1993	–0.002	–0.001	
Colorado	Coors Field (Humidor)	2002				–0.034
Colorado	Coors Field	1995	2001		–0.074	–0.059
Colorado	Mile High Stadium	1993	1994		–0.049	
Detroit	Comerica Park	2000				0.003
Detroit	Tiger Stadium	1952	1999	–0.008	–0.002	–0.001
Florida	Sun Life Stadium	1993	2011		–0.004	0.010
Houston	Minute Maid Park	2000				–0.004
Houston	Houston Astrodome	1965	1999	0.010	0.020	0.009
Houston	Colt Stadium	1962	1964	0.015		
K.C. Athletics	Municipal Stadium	1955	1967	–0.007		
K.C. Royals	Kauffman Stadium	1973			–0.002	–0.006
K.C. Royals	Municipal Stadium	1969	1972	0.002		
L.A. Angels	Angel Stadium of Anaheim	1966		0.013	0.005	0.006
L.A. Angels	Dodger Stadium	1962	1965	0.017		
L.A. Angels	Wrigley Field	1961	1961	–0.029		
L.A. Dodgers	Dodger Stadium	1962		0.019	0.018	0.011
L.A. Dodgers	Los Angeles Memorial Co	1958	1961	–0.013		
Miami	Marlins Park	2012				–0.005
Mil. Braves	Milwaukee County Stadium	1953	1965	0.018		
Mil. Brewers	Miller Park	2001				–0.001
Mil. Brewers	Milwaukee County Stadium	1970	2000	0.002	0.002	–0.002
Minnesota	Target Field	2010				0.002
Minnesota	Metrodome	1982	2009		–0.009	–0.001
Minnesota	Metropolitan Stadium	1961	1981	–0.008	–0.008	
Montreal	Olympic Stadium	1977	2004		0.006	–0.003
Montreal	Jarry Park	1969	1976	–0.001	–0.013	
N.Y. Giants	Polo Grounds	1952	1957	–0.001		
N.Y. Mets	Citi Field	2009				0.007
N.Y. Mets	Shea Stadium	1964	2008	0.000	0.011	0.007
N.Y. Mets	Polo Grounds	1962	1963	–0.008		
N.Y. Yankees	Yankee Stadium II	2009				–0.012
N.Y. Yankees	Yankee Stadium I (Post R)	1976	2008		0.005	0.004
N.Y. Yankees	Shea Stadium	1974	1975		0.003	
N.Y. Yankees	Yankee Stadium I	1952	1973	0.011	0.000	
Oakland	O.co Coliseum	1997				0.007
Oakland	Oakland–Alameda County	1995	1996		0.010*	
Oakland	Oakland–Alameda County	1969	1994	0.011	0.016*	
Oakland	Oakland–Alameda County	1968	1968	0.006*		
Phil. Athletics	Connie Mack Stadium	1952	1954	–0.013		
Phil. Phillies	Citizens Bank Park	2004				–0.003
Phil. Phillies	Veterans Stadium	1971	2003	–0.001	0.000	0.004
Phil. Phillies	Connie Mack Stadium	1952	1970	–0.002		
Pittsburgh	PNC Park	2001				0.002
Pittsburgh	Three Rivers Stadium	1971	2000	–0.002*	–0.001	–0.001
Pittsburgh	Forbes Field	1952	1969	0.006*		
St. Louis	Busch Stadium III	2006				0.005
St. Louis	Busch Stadium II	1966	2005	–0.003	0.006	0.000
St. Louis	Busch Stadium I	1952	1965	–0.017		
San Diego	PETCO Park	2004				0.024

Team Name	Stadium Name	Seasons First	Seasons Last	GPA Corrections 1952–72	GPA Corrections 1973–96	GPA Corrections 1997–12
San Diego	Qualcomm Stadium	1969	2003	0.014	0.016	0.022
San Francisco	AT&T Park	2000				0.005
San Francisco	Candlestick Park	1960	1999	0.002	0.010	0.015
San Francisco	Seals Stadium	1958	1959	0.009		
Seattle Mariners	Safeco Field	2000				0.015*
Seattle Mariners	The Kingdome	1977	1998		−0.003	0.005*
Seattle Pilots	Sick's Stadium	1969	1969	−0.006		
Tampa Bay	Tropicana Field	1998				0.008
Texas	Rangers Ballpark in Arling	1994			−0.008	−0.015
Texas	Arlington Stadium	1972	1993	0.006	0.002	
Toronto	Rogers Centre	1990			−0.004*	−0.003
Toronto	Exhibition Stadium	1977	1988		−0.007*	
Wash. Nationals	Nationals Park	2008				0.001
Wash. Nationals	RFK Stadium	2005	2007			0.018
Wash. Senators	DC Stadium	1962	1971	0.007		
Wash. Senators	Griffith Stadium	1961	1961	0.018*		
Wash. Senators	Griffith Stadium	1952	1960	0.004		

BASERUNNING STRATEGIES

Before baserunning corrections are described, it is helpful to examine baserunning strategies.

How many times have you heard a broadcaster say that runners should never make the first or third out of an inning going to third base? Does this cardinal rule embody good baseball strategy?

When a runner is on base, he has to decide if advancing a base on a steal, passed ball, error, or wild pitch is worth the risk. This is a complex decision for the runner and has to be made in a split second.

A runner considering advancing a base needs to take into account the distance the ball gets away from the fielder, how fast he runs, the length of the fielder's throw, the strength of the fielder's arm, and most importantly the score and inning of the game.

A runner considering stealing a base needs to take into account his lead, the time it takes the pitcher to deliver the ball to the plate, the strength of the catcher's arm, and, again, the score and inning of the game.

| ——Before—— | | | | ——Before—— | | | | ——Before—— | | | |
Runners			Outs	RE	Runners			Outs	RE	Runners			Outs	RE
—	—	—	0	0.536	—	—	—	1	0.288	—	—	—	2	0.111
1B	—	—	0	0.921	1B	—	—	1	0.553	1B	—	—	2	0.238
—	2B	—	0	1.166	—	2B	—	1	0.706	—	2B	—	2	0.340
—	—	3B	0	1.440	—	—	3B	1	0.981	—	—	3B	2	0.372
1B	2B	—	0	1.525	1B	2B	—	1	0.939	1B	2B	—	2	0.456
1B	—	3B	0	1.835	1B	—	3B	1	1.204	1B	—	3B	2	0.510
—	2B	3B	0	2.035	—	2B	3B	1	1.429	—	2B	3B	2	0.596
1B	2B	3B	0	2.345	1B	2B	3B	1	1.592	1B	2B	3B	2	0.783

Table 6.1. Run expectancy for each base-out state. Data from 1997 to 2009.

At the end of close games, broadcasters are quick to blame runners for getting thrown out trying to steal third base or stretch a single into a double. They fail to realize that there is a risk-benefit ratio for any baserunning decision. What matters is knowing when the benefit justifies the risk.

With a man on first and no outs, the run expectancy (RE) is 0.921. If the runner advances to second base, the value increases to 1.166. If he is thrown out, it falls to 0.288, the run expectancy when the bases are empty with one out.

How often does the baserunner have to be successful to justify the risk?

$$\text{Success Rate} \times (1.166 - 0.921) = (1.0 - \text{Success Rate}) \times (0.921 - 0.288)$$
$$\text{Success Rate} = (0.921 - 0.288) / (1.166 - 0.288) = 0.721 = 72.1\%$$

In general with a man on first and no one out, a runner needs to be successful reaching second base at least 72.1 percent of the time to justify the risk. Toward the end of the game, the percentages will change depending on the score and the number of innings remaining.

| ——Before—— | | Percent | ——Before—— | | Percent | ——Before—— | | Percent |
Runners	Outs	Success	Runners	Outs	Success	Runners	Outs	Success
1B — —	0	72.1%	1B — —	1	74.3%	1B — —	2	70.0%
— 2B —	0	76.2%	— 2B —	1	68.4%	— 2B —	2	91.4%
— — 3B	0	92.3%	— — 3B	1	73.9%	— — 3B	2	33.5%

Table 6.2. The success rate required to attempt an advance with one runner on base. Data from 1997 to 2009.

Table 6.2 shows the nine base-out states with one runner on base. In six of nine of these base-out states, the runner needs to be successful 68–76 percent of the time to justify the risk.

With a man on third and no one out, the run expectancy is 1.440 and there is an 84.8 percent chance that one or more runs will score. Scoring increases the RE to 1.536 (1 run scored + 0.536 RE for a bases-empty, no-outs state), while getting thrown out reduces the RE to 0.288. The benefit of advancing from third base to score is modest (+0.096 runs); to justify the risk, the runner needs to be successful 92.3 percent of the time.

With a man on second and two outs, the run expectancy is 0.340 and there is a 22.5 percent chance that one or more runs will score. Advancing to third base increases the RE to 0.372, while getting thrown out reduces the RE to 0. To justify the risk for so small a benefit (+0.032 runs), the runner needs to be successful 91.4 percent of the time.

With a man on third and two outs, the RE is 0.372 and the likelihood that a run will score is 25.5 percent. Scoring increases the RE to 1.111 (one run scored + 0.111 RE with the bases empty and two outs); getting thrown out reduces the RE to 0. The benefit of scoring from third in this scenario is significant (+0.739 runs), and the runner needs to be successful only 33.5 percent of the time to justify the risk.

It turns out, then, that the rule against making the first or third out at third base makes sense roughly half of the time. Advancing from second to third base with no outs is justified if the runner is successful at least 76.2 percent of the time. Advancing from second to third base with two outs is justified only if the runner is successful at least 91.4 percent of the time. The rule is therefore good game strategy with two outs but bad strategy with no outs.

| ——Before—— | | Calc % | Stolen Bases | | Other Advances | | ——Total—— | |
Runners	Outs	Success	#	% Success	#	% Success	#	% Success
1B — —	0	72.1%	8,984	72.6%	4,291	75.5%	13,275	73.5%
— 2B —	0	76.2%	348	80.7%	918	89.0%	1,302	87.1%
— — 3B	0	92.3%	1	0.0%	67	91.0%	68	91.2%
1B — —	1	74.3%	11,659	72.2%	5,373	74.7%	17,032	73.0%
— 2B —	1	68.4%	1,697	75.0%	2,100	88.6%	3,797	82.5%
— — 3B	1	73.9%	100	11.0%	368	91.3%	468	74.1%
1B — —	2	70.0%	14,333	75.9%	6,920	77.9%	21,253	76.5%
— 2B —	2	91.4%	934	89.2%	2,359	93.9%	3,293	92.5%
— — 3B	2	33.5%	20	60.0%	572	92.3%	592	91.6%
	Total/Average		38,112	74.1%	22,968	80.4%	61,080	76.5%

Table 6.3. Calculated success rates required to attempt an advance with one runner on base and the actual rates for stealing a base and for advancing in other ways, excluding balks. Data from 1997 to 2009.

Table 6.3 shows the nine base-out states with one runner on base along with the calculated success rate needed to justify the risk of advancing a base. The actual success major league players had stealing bases or advancing a base in other ways is also shown for each of those nine base-out states. Balks are excluded since there is no risk of making an out after a balk is called.

Events classified in the Retrosheet database as "stolen base" or "caught stealing" are shown in the "Stolen Bases" column in Table 6.3. Note that when a failed hit-and-run play results in a runner being thrown out, the event is recorded by the scorer as "caught stealing." Other baserunning events such as pickoffs are not easy to classify and are included in the "Other Advances" column in Table 6.3. But a runner may be picked off while taking a large lead in anticipation of a stolen-base attempt; in that scenario, the event might be classified as a "pickoff" in the Retrosheet database, but an argument can be made that it should be considered a "caught stealing."

Major league players successfully advance on the base paths at about the rate required to justify the risk based on the base-out state. The only exception is scoring from third base with two outs, a scenario in which runners were successful 91.6 percent of the time, far greater than the rate of 33.5 percent required to justify the risk. Runners need to be much more aggressive in this base-out state.

With a man on third and one out, stealing home was successful only 11.0 percent of the time when a success rate of 73.9 percent is required to justify the risk. Presumably, most of these outs were the result of failed hit-and-run plays or failed squeeze bunts.

Other benefits of stealing include disrupting the pitcher's routine and advancing an extra base on a throwing error. About 5 percent of the time a throwing error allowed the runner to advance an extra base and 0.1 percent of the time to score from first base.

How often do multiple runners need to be successful trying to advance to justify the risk? The calculations are performed in the same manner as the base-out states with one runner on base. The data in Table 6.4 assumes that all the runners on base attempt to advance and the lead runner is thrown out if unsuccessful. The data in Table 6.5 assumes that only the lead runner attempts to advance and he is thrown out if unsuccessful.

——Before——			Outs	Percent Success	——Before——			Outs	Percent Success	——Before——			Outs	Percent Success
1B	2B	—	0	61.6%	1B	2B	—	1	55.0%	1B	2B	—	2	76.5%
1B	—	3B	0	77.3%	1B	—	3B	1	63.2%	1B	—	3B	2	38.1%
—	2B	3B	0	72.2%	—	2B	3B	1	65.7%	—	2B	3B	2	43.4%
1B	2B	3B	0	57.0%	1B	2B	3B	1	54.3%	1B	2B	3B	2	49.1%

Table 6.4. Success rates justifying an advance attempt with multiple runners on base. Assumes all runners advance and the lead runner is thrown out if unsuccessful. Data from 1997 to 2009.

——Before——			Outs	Percent Success	——Before——			Outs	Percent Success	——Before——			Outs	Percent Success
1B	2B	—	0	75.8%	1B	2B	—	1	72.6%	1B	2B	—	2	89.4%
1B	—	3B	0	93.7%	1B	—	3B	1	73.5%	1B	—	3B	2	41.2%
—	2B	3B	0	91.0%	—	2B	3B	1	79.7%	—	2B	3B	2	44.5%
1B	2B	3B	0	88.6%	1B	2B	3B	1	76.6%	1B	2B	3B	2	53.8%

Table 6.5. Success rates justifying an advance attempt with multiple runners on base. Assumes only the lead runner advances or is thrown out if unsuccessful. Data from 1997 to 2009.

With multiple runners on base the outcomes are more complex. Over 90 percent of the time, all the runners advance when the advance is successful. Only the lead runner advancing is the next-most-common successful outcome. About half the time the other runners are able to advance when an out is recorded on an attempt to advance a base.

Although not all encompassing, the range of success shown in Table 6.4 and Table 6.5 covers most of the situations that actually occur in major league games.

With multiple runners on base, major leaguers successfully advance on the base paths at about the rate required to justify the risk based on the base-out state. Again the only exception is scoring from third base with two outs, a base-out state in which runners were successful 87.9 to 91.4 percent of the time, far greater than the rate of 38.1 to 53.8 percent required to justify the risk. Runners need to be more aggressive in these base-out states.

| — — Before — — | | | Calc % | Stolen Bases | | Other Advances | | — — Total — — | |
Runners		Outs	Success	#	% Success	#	% Success	#	% Success
1B	2B	—	0	61.6%—75.8%	420	66.0%	974	83.5%	1,394	78.2%
1B	—	3B	0	77.3%—93.7%	464	88.2%	344	84.0%	808	86.4%
—	2B	3B	0	72.2%—91.0%	0	0.0%	103	91.3%	103	91.3%
1B	2B	3B	0	57.0%—86.6%	2	0.0%	135	92.6%	137	91.2%
1B	2B	—	1	55.0%—72.6%	1,210	71.2%	1,730	87.2%	2,940	80.6%
1B	—	3B	1	63.2%—73.5%	1,166	78.3%	829	76.8%	1,995	77.7%
—	2B	3B	1	65.7%—79.7%	25	0.0%	303	90.1%	328	83.2%
1B	2B	3B	1	54.3%—76.6%	12	0.0%	329	92.4%	341	89.1%
1B	2B	—	2	76.5%—89.4%	859	85.9%	2,100	90.3%	2,959	87.1%
1B	—	3B	2	38.1%—41.2%	2,096	87.3%	1,482	88.7%	3,578	87.9%
—	2B	3B	2	43.4%—44.5%	5	40.0%	322	92.2%	327	91.4%
1B	2B	3B	2	49.1%—53.8%	9	66.7%	439	90.7%	448	90.2%
			Total/Average	38,112	74.1%	22,968	80.4%	61,080	76.5%

Table 6.6. Calculated success rates justifying an advance attempt with multiple runners on base. Actual success rate stealing bases and advancing in other ways, excluding balks. Data from 1997 to 2009.

The first half of this chapter provides general guidance for baserunning strategies independent of the game score and number of innings remaining. The percentages are based on run expectancy, which balances the chance of scoring one run with the chance of having a big inning. For most games in the early and middle innings these percentages will apply.

At the end of a close game with the team trailing, the percentages will change because only one or two runs are needed. It is no longer necessary to consider the run expectancy because a big inning is not needed. Rather, the chance of scoring a small number of runs is more important.

In games when a team is far behind, the percentages change because multiple runs are needed to have a chance of winning the game. It is no longer necessary to consider run expectancy because an inning when only one run scores is not very helpful. Rather, the chance of scoring a large number of runs is more important. Runners will need to be more conservative on the base paths in these situations.

Table 6.7 shows the frequency of runs scored by base-out state. With a man on first and no one out, the run expectancy is 0.921. This figure is the average of the 57.24 percent of the time that no runs scored, the 16.98 percent that one run scored, the 13.03 percent that two runs scored, and so on up to the maximum number of runs scored in that base-out state.

--Before--			Run						
Runners		Outs	Expectancy	0	1	2	3	4	5+
—	—	—	0	0.536	0.7098	0.1555	0.0724	0.0343	0.0159	0.0122
1B	—	—	0	0.921	0.5724	0.1698	0.1303	0.0671	0.0334	0.0269
—	2B	—	0	1.166	0.3709	0.3476	0.1411	0.0756	0.0360	0.0288
—	—	3B	0	1.440	0.1517	0.5432	0.1508	0.0835	0.0374	0.0334
1B	2B	—	0	1.525	0.3671	0.2235	0.1578	0.1248	0.0687	0.0582
1B	—	3B	0	1.835	0.1363	0.4266	0.1631	0.1359	0.0725	0.0656
—	2B	3B	0	2.035	0.1369	0.2628	0.3040	0.1482	0.0778	0.0702
1B	2B	3B	0	2.345	0.1271	0.2759	0.2075	0.1375	0.1272	0.1249
—	—	—	1	0.288	0.8289	0.1010	0.0416	0.0170	0.0070	0.0044
1B	—	—	1	0.553	0.7241	0.1152	0.0915	0.0403	0.0173	0.0115
—	2B	—	1	0.706	0.5932	0.2334	0.0978	0.0447	0.0186	0.0123
—	—	3B	1	0.981	0.3386	0.4780	0.1012	0.0499	0.0189	0.0134
1B	2B	—	1	0.939	0.5804	0.1606	0.1063	0.0886	0.0377	0.0265
1B	—	3B	1	1.204	0.3511	0.3727	0.1156	0.0907	0.0407	0.0292
—	2B	3B	1	1.429	0.3109	0.2819	0.2212	0.0981	0.0528	0.0352
1B	2B	3B	1	1.592	0.3276	0.2618	0.1565	0.1025	0.0886	0.0630
—	—	—	2	0.111	0.9254	0.0500	0.0167	0.0052	0.0018	0.0009
1B	—	—	2	0.238	0.8710	0.0556	0.0496	0.0155	0.0055	0.0027
—	2B	—	2	0.340	0.7751	0.1501	0.0476	0.0176	0.0065	0.0030
—	—	3B	2	0.372	0.7451	0.1792	0.0484	0.0175	0.0065	0.0032
1B	2B	—	2	0.456	0.7669	0.1107	0.0555	0.0447	0.0149	0.0073
1B	—	3B	2	0.510	0.7252	0.1466	0.0561	0.0479	0.0169	0.0073
—	2B	3B	2	0.596	0.7370	0.0484	0.1369	0.0491	0.0196	0.0090
1B	2B	3B	2	0.783	0.6784	0.0886	0.1074	0.0560	0.0480	0.0217

Table 6.7. Run expectancy by base-out state and the frequency with which zero to five or more runs scored in each of those states. Data from 1997 to 2009.

--Before--			Run						
Runners		Outs	Expectancy	0	1	2	3	4	5+
—	—	—	0	0.536	0.7098	0.2902	0.1348	0.0624	0.0280	0.0122
1B	—	—	0	0.921	0.5724	0.4276	0.2578	0.1274	0.0603	0.0269
—	2B	—	0	1.166	0.3709	0.6291	0.2815	0.1404	0.0648	0.0288
—	—	3B	0	1.440	0.1517	0.8483	0.3051	0.1543	0.0709	0.0334
1B	2B	—	0	1.525	0.3671	0.6329	0.4094	0.2516	0.1269	0.0582
1B	—	3B	0	1.835	0.1363	0.8637	0.4371	0.2741	0.1381	0.0656
—	2B	3B	0	2.035	0.1369	0.8631	0.6003	0.2962	0.1480	0.0702
1B	2B	3B	0	2.345	0.1271	0.8729	0.5970	0.3896	0.2521	0.1249
—	—	—	1	0.288	0.8289	0.1711	0.0701	0.0284	0.0114	0.0044
1B	—	—	1	0.553	0.7241	0.2759	0.1607	0.0692	0.0289	0.0115
—	2B	—	1	0.706	0.5932	0.4068	0.1734	0.0756	0.0309	0.0123
—	—	3B	1	0.981	0.3386	0.6614	0.1834	0.0822	0.0323	0.0134
1B	2B	—	1	0.939	0.5804	0.4196	0.2591	0.1528	0.0642	0.0265
1B	—	3B	1	1.204	0.3511	0.6489	0.2763	0.1607	0.0700	0.0292
—	2B	3B	1	1.429	0.3109	0.6891	0.4072	0.1861	0.0880	0.0352
1B	2B	3B	1	1.592	0.3276	0.6724	0.4106	0.2541	0.1516	0.0630
—	—	—	2	0.111	0.9254	0.0746	0.0246	0.0079	0.0027	0.0009
1B	—	—	2	0.238	0.8710	0.1290	0.0734	0.0238	0.0082	0.0027
—	2B	—	2	0.340	0.7751	0.2249	0.0747	0.0271	0.0095	0.0030
—	—	3B	2	0.372	0.7451	0.2549	0.0757	0.0273	0.0097	0.0032
1B	2B	—	2	0.456	0.7669	0.2331	0.1224	0.0669	0.0222	0.0073
1B	—	3B	2	0.510	0.7252	0.2748	0.1282	0.0721	0.0242	0.0073
—	2B	3B	2	0.596	0.7370	0.2630	0.2146	0.0777	0.0286	0.0090
1B	2B	3B	2	0.783	0.6784	0.3216	0.2330	0.1257	0.0696	0.0217

Table 6.8. Run expectancy by base-out state and the frequency with which at least one to at least five runs scored in each. Data from 1997 to 2009.

Baserunning Strategies

Table 6.8 shows the frequencies of scoring at least one to at least five runs by base-out state. These numbers, useful for calculating the success rate required to attempt to advance a base late in a game, are used for the calculations below.

We can revisit the base-out state man-on-second, no-one out at the end of a close game. How often does the baserunner have to be successful advancing a base to justify the risk?

Success Rate = (Freq-Current − Freq-Failed) / (Freq-Success − Freq-Failed)
Success Rate = (0.6291 − 0.1711) / (0.8483 − 0.1711) = 0.676 = 67.6%

The above calculation is for the end a close game when one run is needed. With a man on second and no one out, the frequency at which one or more runs are scored is 0.6291 (Freq-Current). If the runner advances to third base, the frequency increases to 0.8482 (Freq-Success). If, however, he is thrown out, it falls to 0.1711 (Freq-Failed), the frequency for the bases-empty, one-out state.

| -- Before -- | | | Run | | | | | |
Runners			Outs	Expectancy	1+	2+	3+	4+	5+
1B	—	—	0	0.921	56.0%	88.8%	90.2%	91.6%	92.2%
—	2B	—	0	1.166	67.6%	96.0%	99.0%	100.0%	100.0%
—	—	3B	0	1.440	81.7%	100.0%	100.0%	100.0%	100.0%
1B	—	—	1	0.553	60.6%	91.5%	92.2%	92.9%	93.0%
—	2B	—	1	0.706	56.6%	93.7%	99.0%	100.0%	100.0%
—	—	3B	1	0.981	63.4%	100.0%	100.0%	100.0%	100.0%
1B	—	—	2	0.238	57.4%	98.3%	99.0%	100.0%	100.0%
—	2B	—	2	0.340	88.2%	98.7%	99.3%	100.0%	100.0%
—	—	3B	2	0.372	25.5%	100.0%	100.0%	100.0%	100.0%

Table 6.9. Success rates justifying an advance attempt at the end of a game, with one runner on base and one to five runs needed. The success rate is smoothed to provide consistent data. Data from 1997 to 2009.

| -- Before -- | | | Run | | | | | |
Runners			Outs	Expectancy	1+	2+	3+	4+	5+
1B	2B	—	0	1.525	49.6%	55.3%	79.8%	82.0%	84.0%
1B	—	3B	0	1.835	77.0%	57.9%	96.4%	97.9%	100.0%
—	2B	3B	0	2.035	59.6%	62.7%	96.0%	97.4%	98.8%
1B	2B	3B	0	2.345	59.1%	41.6%	48.6%	78.8%	79.5%
1B	2B	—	1	0.939	41.9%	55.5%	79.1%	81.6%	84.2%
1B	—	3B	1	1.204	54.7%	60.7%	91.3%	91.5%	93.9%
—	2B	3B	1	1.429	58.3%	56.6%	100.0%	100.0%	100.0%
1B	2B	3B	1	1.592	55.6%	41.3%	53.5%	78.1%	79.0%
1B	2B	—	2	0.456	88.6%	57.4%	86.1%	77.6%	81.1%
1B	—	3B	2	0.510	27.5%	57.0%	96.5%	98.0%	100.0%
—	2B	3B	2	0.596	26.3%	84.2%	100.0%	100.0%	100.0%
1B	2B	3B	2	0.783	32.2%	88.6%	58.6%	89.6%	91.0%

Table 6.10. Success rates justifying an advance attempt at the end of a game, with multiple runners on base and one to five runs needed. Assumes all runners advance and the lead runner is thrown out if unsuccessful. Success rate smoothed to provide consistent data. Data from 1997 to 2009.

If the team needs only one run, the player needs to advance from second to third successfully 67.6 percent of the time to justify the risk. This is less than the 76.2 percent calculated earlier in this chapter for the same base-out state when a specific number of runs is not needed. The 8.8 percent difference emerges because run expectancy factors in the chance of a big inning while the frequency of scoring one or more runs ignores it. Early in the game, having a big inning is important while late in the game scoring one run may be adequate.

At the end of a close game, the admonition against making the first or third out at third base holds when the team needs two or more runs. In that scenario the runner must be successful nearly 100 percent of the time. If, however, the team needs only one run and there are no outs, the runner might sometimes be better advised to make the attempt to advance to third.

With multiple runners on base, the outcomes are more complex at the end of games. The data in Table 6.10 assumes all the runners advance while the data in Table 6.11 assumes only the lead runner advances. Both tables assume the lead runner is thrown out if the advance is unsuccessful. Although not all encompassing, the range of success shown in both tables covers most of the situations that actually occur in major league games.

— — Before — — Runners	Outs	Run Expectancy	1+	2+	3+	4+	5+
1B 2B —	0	1.525	60.7%	90.0%	91.0%	92.0%	93.0%
1B — 3B	0	1.835	81.2%	100.0%	100.0%	100.0%	100.0%
— 2B 3B	0	2.035	76.9%	93.7%	100.0%	100.0%	100.0%
1B 2B 3B	0	2.345	78.1%	90.4%	92.3%	100.0%	100.0%
1B 2B —	1	0.939	55.9%	91.7%	94.2%	95.0%	95.5%
1B — 3B	1	1.204	59.7%	100.0%	100.0%	100.0%	100.0%
— 2B 3B	1	1.429	59.9%	100.0%	100.0%	100.0%	100.0%
1B 2B 3B	1	1.592	57.3%	97.0%	97.4%	99.1%	100.0%
1B 2B —	2	0.456	84.8%	95.5%	96.0%	97.0%	100.0%
1B — 3B	2	0.510	27.5%	99.4%	99.6%	100.0%	100.0%
— 2B 3B	2	0.596	26.3%	95.4%	100.0%	100.0%	100.0%
1B 2B 3B	2	0.783	32.2%	100.0%	100.0%	100.0%	100.0%

Table 6.11. Success rate justifying an advance attempt at the end of a game, with multiple runners on base and one to five runs needed. Assumes only the lead runner advances or is thrown out if unsuccessful. Success rate smoothed to provide consistent data. Data from 1997 to 2009.

This data is ideal for use in the bottom of the ninth inning when the home team knows exactly how many runs they need. What about the top of the ninth or earlier innings when trailing by multiple runs?

It is possible to calculate similar data for each half inning, but the number of data points gets so small that calculations become unreliable. Another approach is to calculate the chance of winning the game both if the runner successfully advances and if the runner is thrown out. This approach is used with simulated data in the "Baserunning Revisited" chapter in Part III.

Applying Baserunning Corrections

The benefit or harm to the team from baserunning events can vary widely. The Retrosheet database contains 298,779 baserunning events from 1952 to 2009. Although there were 28 times as many plate appearances (8,514,537) during that same period, the effect of those baserunning events on the team can be significant.

The goal of this chapter is to describe the baserunning corrections that can be applied to GPA to better reflect a player's total production for his team.

| — — Before — — | | | — — — After — — — | | | | | | Run | Change in Run |
Runners		Outs	Runners			Outs	Runs	Number	Expectancy	Expectancy
1B	—	0	—	—	—	1	0	3,513	0.288	−0.633
1B	—	0	1B	—	—	0	0	x	0.921	x
1B	—	0	—	2B	—	0	0	9,532	1.166	+0.245
1B	—	0	—	—	3B	0	0	624	1.440	+0.519
1B	—	0	—	—	—	0	1	10	1.536	+0.615
					Total/Average			13,679	0.953	+0.032
—	2B	0	—	—	—	1	0	168	0.288	−0.878
—	2B	0	—	2B	—	0	0	x	1.166	x
—	2B	0	—	—	3B	0	0	1,162	1.440	+0.274
—	2B	0	—	—	—	0	1	24	1.536	+0.370
					Total/Average			1,354	1.299	+0.133
—	—	3B	0	—	—	1	0	6	0.288	−1.152
—	—	3B	0	—	—	3B	0	0	x	1.440	x
—	—	3B	0	—	—	—	0	1	65	1.536	+0.096
					Total/Average			71	1.431	−0.010

Table 7.1. Attempts to advance with one runner on base and no outs. Data from 1997 to 2009 and includes balks.

With a man on first and no one out, the run expectancy (RE) is 0.921. If the runner successfully advances to second base, the RE increases by 0.245 runs to 1.166. Occasionally, the runner will make it to third base or score. If the runner is thrown out, the RE decreases by 0.633 runs to 0.288. The average change in RE for all attempts to advance a base with a man on first and no one out is +0.032 runs.

With a man on third and no one out, the run expectancy is 1.440 runs. If the runner scores, the RE increases by 0.096 runs to 1.536; if he is thrown out, the RE decreases by 1.152 runs to 0.288. The average change in RE with each attempt to advance a base was −0.010 runs.

The same analysis can be applied to the other 20 base-out states with runners on base. The average change in RE for the 78,531 events where runners attempted to advance a base during the interleague era from 1997 to 2009 was +0.071 runs.

There were 2,431,049 plate appearances (PAs) during the interleague era from 1997 to 2009. The average GPA for these PAs would change by +0.002 runs (78,531 / 2,431,049 × 0.071) if baserunning events were included. Although this is a very small number, certain players had much larger contributions from their baserunning events.

To create a baserunning correction, it is necessary to assign the change in RE from each baserunning event to each runner. With one baserunner the task is easy: any change in RE that occurs from a baserunning event is assigned to that runner. With multiple runners on base, the change in RE must be divided among the runners on base and the task is a bit more complex.

The following rules are used to divide the change in RE among the runners on base:

1. Any runners that advance are credited for the increase in RE created by their advancement.

2. Any runners that are thrown out are charged with the decrease in RE caused by being thrown out.

3. If the lead runner advances and other runners are thrown out, the lead runner's increase in RE will be reduced by the RE lost by the runners thrown out (but not be less than 0).

4. If the lead runner is thrown out and other runners advance, the lead runner's decrease in RE will be partially offset by the RE gained by the runners who advanced (but not be greater than 0).

5. If the batter strikes out or walks, the batter is credited only with the results of his PA. Any runner who attempts to advance after a strikeout or attempts to advance beyond the base he is entitled to reach after a walk is credited with the increase or decrease in RE created by his attempted advancement.

— — Before — —		— — — After — — —					Run	Change in Run
Runners	Outs	Runners			Outs	Runs	Number	Expectancy	Expectancy
1B — 3B	1	x x x			3	0	8	0.000	−1.204
1B — 3B	1	1B — —			2	0	41	0.238	−0.966
1B — 3B	1	— 2B —			2	0	99	0.340	−0.864
1B — 3B	1	— — 3B			2	0	280	0.372	−0.832
1B — 3B	1	— — —			2	1	17	1.111	−0.093
1B — 3B	1	1B — 3B			1	0	x	1.204	x
1B — 3B	1	— 2B 3B			1	0	1,093	1.429	+0.225
1B — 3B	1	1B — —			1	1	14	1.553	+0.349
1B — 3B	1	— 2B —			1	1	432	1.706	+0.502
1B — 3B	1	— — 3B			1	1	67	1.981	+0.777
1B — 3B	1	— — —			1	2	1	2.288	+1.084
					Total/Average		2,052	1.278	+0.074

Table 7.2. Attempts to advance a base with men on first and third and one out. Data from 1997 to 2009 and includes balks.

With men on first and third and one out, if both runners advance, the run expectancy increases from 1.204 to 1.706. The +0.502 increase in RE is divided between the runners as follows: The runner on third is credited with +0.341, or the difference in RE (1.553 −

1.204) had he alone advanced; and the runner on first is credited with the balance, or +0.147 (1.706 – 1.553).

If in the same base-out state only the runner on first base advances, the run expectancy increases from 1.204 to 1.429, and the +0.225 increase is credited to him alone.

If the runner on third scores but the runner on first is thrown out, the RE decreases from 1.204 to 1.111. The runner who was on third base gets no credit for advancing home and the runner who was put out is charged with the –0.093 decrease in run expectancy.

| — — Before — — | | — — — After — — — | | | | Change in Run | — Runner On — | |
Runners	Outs	Runners			Outs	Runs	Expectancy	First	Third
1B — 3B	1	x x x			3	0	–1.204	–0.238	–0.966
1B — 3B	1	1B — —			2	0	–0.966	0.000	–0.966
1B — 3B	1	— 2B —			2	0	–0.864	0.000	–0.864
1B — 3B	1	— — 3B			2	0	–0.832	0.000	–0.832
1B — 3B	1	— — —			2	1	–0.093	–0.093	0.000
1B — 3B	1	1B — 3B			1	0	x	x	x
1B — 3B	1	— 2B 3B			1	0	+0.225	+0.225	0.000
1B — 3B	1	1B — —			1	1	+0.349	0.000	+0.349
1B — 3B	1	— 2B —			1	1	+0.502	+0.153	+0.349
1B — 3B	1	— — 3B			1	1	+0.777	+0.428	+0.349
1B — 3B	1	— — —			1	2	+1.084	+0.735	+0.349

Table 7.3. The change in run expectancy assigned to each runner attempting to advance with men on first and third and no one out. Data from 1997 to 2009 and includes balks.

The change in run expectancy assigned to each runner attempting to advance with men on first and third and no one out is shown in Table 7.3. A similar calculation is made for the other 13 base-out states with multiple runners on base.

The baserunning correction for each batter is the total of all the changes in RE from baserunning events charged to him divided by the number of PAs. The baserunning correction for each pitcher is the total of all the changes in RE from baserunning events that occurred while he was pitching divided by the number of PAs he faced.

During the 2009 season there were 22 batters with baserunning corrections of at least +0.006. Most of these batters were speedy runners with many stolen bases. Jacoby Ellsbury led the majors with 70 stolen bases and had the highest baserunning correction (+0.013). Michael Bourn with 61 stolen bases and Carl Crawford with 60 stolen bases had the second- and third-highest number of stolen bases in the majors and the second- and third-highest baserunning corrections.

Ellsbury's baserunning events from 2009 are summarized in Table 7.5. He created more than nine runs for his team on the base paths. His stolen bases created more than 14 runs but were offset by the 6 runs the team lost when he was caught stealing. His advances on the base paths in other ways (e.g., wild pitches, balks) created more than 3 runs but were partially offset by the runs lost from the three times he was thrown out while not attempting a stolen base. On average, the GPA from his 693 PAs should be corrected by +0.013 (+9.234 / 693) to reflect his baserunning contributions.

How did Dan Uggla, who stole only two bases, have one of the highest baserunning corrections in the majors?

Table 7.6 shows that while the benefits of Uggla's two steals were offset by the one time he was caught stealing, he successfully advanced on the base paths in other ways 12 times without being thrown out. On average, the GPA from his 668 PAs should be corrected by +0.006 (+4.083 / 668) to reflect his baserunning contributions.

Player	Team	Year	GPA	GPAbrc	cGPA	BA	SB	CS	PA
Ellsbury, Jacoby	BOS	2009	0.270	0.013	0.283	0.301	70	12	693
Bourn, Michael	HOU	2009	0.266	0.012	0.278	0.285	61	12	678
Crawford, Carl	TBR	2009	0.286	0.011	0.296	0.305	60	16	672
Fowler, Dexter	COL	2009	0.267	0.010	0.277	0.266	27	10	518
Utley, Chase	PHI	2009	0.325	0.010	0.335	0.282	23	0	687
Winn, Randy	SFG	2009	0.257	0.009	0.266	0.262	16	2	597
Andrus, Elvis	TEX	2009	0.255	0.008	0.263	0.267	33	6	541
Choo, Shin-Soo	CLE	2009	0.306	0.007	0.313	0.300	21	2	685
Cruz, Nelson	TEX	2009	0.290	0.007	0.297	0.260	20	4	515
Kinsler, Ian	TEX	2009	0.304	0.007	0.311	0.253	31	5	640
Bay, Jason	BOS	2009	0.341	0.006	0.347	0.267	13	3	638
Wright, David	NYM	2009	0.307	0.006	0.314	0.307	27	9	618
Damon, Johnny	NYY	2009	0.307	0.006	0.313	0.282	12	0	626
Werth, Jayson	PHI	2009	0.301	0.006	0.307	0.268	20	3	676
Roberts, Brian	BAL	2009	0.290	0.006	0.296	0.283	30	7	717
Bartlett, Jason	TBR	2009	0.317	0.006	0.324	0.320	30	7	567
Rodriguez, Alex	NYY	2009	0.313	0.006	0.318	0.286	14	2	535
Upton, B.J.	TBR	2009	0.255	0.006	0.261	0.241	42	14	626
Rios, Alex	TOR	2009	0.237	0.006	0.242	0.247	24	5	633
Uggla, Dan	FLA	2009	0.273	0.006	0.279	0.243	2	1	668
Phillips, Brandon	CIN	2009	0.277	0.006	0.283	0.276	25	9	644
Matsui, Kazuo	HOU	2009	0.236	0.006	0.241	0.250	19	3	533
:									
Huff, Aubrey	BAL	2009	0.267	−0.003	0.265	0.241	0	6	597
Pence, Hunter	HOU	2009	0.258	−0.003	0.256	0.282	14	11	647
Barmes, Clint	COL	2009	0.249	−0.003	0.246	0.245	12	10	604
Escobar, Yunel	ATL	2009	0.297	−0.003	0.294	0.299	5	4	604
DeJesus, David	KCR	2009	0.287	−0.006	0.282	0.281	4	9	627
		Average	0.2637	0.0024	0.2661	0.2624			

Table 7.4. Batters with at least 500 plate appearances and baserunner corrections above +0.005 or below −0.002. Data from 2009.

Player	Event Type	Number	Total Δ RE	Average Δ RE	GPA Correction
Ellsbury, Jacoby	Stolen Base	70	+14.243	+0.203	0.0206
	Caught Stealing	12	−6.304	−0.525	−0.0091
	Other Advance	13	+3.045	+0.234	0.0044
	Other Out	3	−1.660	−0.553	−0.0024
	Total	98	+9.234	+0.095	0.0135

Table 7.5. Summary of Jacoby Ellsbury's baserunning events from 2009.

Player	Event Type	Number	Total Δ RE	Average Δ RE	GPA Correction
Uggla, Dan	Stolen Base	2	+0.255	+0.128	0.0004
	Caught Stealing	1	−0.238	−0.238	−0.0004
	Other Advance	12	+4.066	+0.339	0.0061
	Other Out	0	0.000	0.000	0.0000
	Total	15	+4.083	+0.272	0.0061

Table 7.6. Summary of Dan Uggla's baserunning events from 2009.

Player	Team	Year	GPA	GPAbrc	tGPA	BA	SB	CS	PA
Figgins, Chone	ANA	2009	0.297	0.001	0.298	0.298	42	17	729
Morgan, Nyjer	PIT	2009	0.258	0.002	0.260	0.307	42	7	533
Kemp, Matt	LAD	2009	0.306	0.003	0.308	0.297	34	8	667
Rollins, Jimmy	PHI	2009	0.248	0.004	0.252	0.250	31	8	725

Table 7.7. Players finishing in the top 10 in stolen bases but with baserunning corrections of less than +0.006. Data from 2009.

Four of the top 10 players in stolen bases during the 2009 season had baserunning corrections (GPAbrc) of less than +0.006.

Player	Event Type	Number	Total Δ RE	Average Δ RE	GPA Correction
Figgins, Chone	Stolen Base	42	+7.163	+0.171	0.0098
	Caught Stealing	17	−8.702	−0.512	−0.0119
	Other Advance	18	+4.844	+0.269	0.0066
	Other Out	5	−2.484	−0.497	−0.0034
	Total	82	+0.821	+0.010	0.0011

Table 7.8. Summary of Chone Figgins's baserunning events from 2009.

Chone Figgins was tied for the fourth in stolen bases in the majors in 2009, yet his baserunning correction of +0.0011 was below the MLB average of +0.0024. Table 7.8 shows that his 42 stolen bases created more than 7 runs but were more than offset by the 8.7 runs his team lost when he was caught stealing 17 times. By advancing in other ways on the base paths, he created enough runs to prevent his baserunning correction from being less than zero.

Nyjer Morgan was also tied for the fourth-highest number of stolen bases in the majors in 2009, and his baserunning correction of +0.0020 was, like Figgins's, slightly below the league average of +0.0024. Table 7.9 shows that his 42 stolen bases created almost 9 runs but were largely offset by the 8.4 runs the team lost when he was caught stealing 17 times.

Player	Event Type	Number	Total Δ RE	Average Δ RE	GPA Correction
Morgan, Nyjer	Stolen Base	42	+8.845	+0.211	0.0166
	Caught Stealing	17	−8.412	−0.495	−0.0158
	Other Advance	9	+2.351	+0.261	0.0044
	Other Out	5	−1.714	−0.343	−0.0032
	Total	73	+1.070	+0.015	0.0020

Table 7.9. Summary of Nyjer Morgan's baserunning events from 2009.

The worst baserunning correction from the 2009 season belonged to David DeJesus, whose baserunning events are shown in Table 7.10. He was caught stealing nine times, potentially costing his team more than 4 runs. On average, the GPA from his 627 PAs should be corrected by −0.006 (−3.538 / 627) to reflect the loss of run production from his baserunning.

Player	Event Type	Number	Total Δ RE	Average Δ RE	GPA Correction
DeJesus, David	Stolen Base	4	+0.561	+0.140	0.0009
	Caught Stealing	9	−4.143	−0.460	−0.0066
	Other Advance	6	+0.915	+0.153	0.0015
	Other Out	2	−0.871	−0.436	−0.0014
	Total	21	−3.538	−0.168	−0.0056

Table 7.10. Summary of David DeJesus's baserunning events from 2009.

Baserunning events that occur while a given pitcher is on the mound are rarely published. Even the number of stolen bases pitchers gave up during the season is seldom reported. Retrosheet.org, MLB.com, and most other baseball websites fail to provide it. Nevertheless, baserunning events can significantly affect the production a pitcher, just as they can a batter.

Player	Team	Year	ERA	GPA	GPAbrc	cGPA	SB	CS	BF
Contreras, Jose	CHW	2009	4.92	0.277	0.014	0.292	23	3	589
Wakefield, Tim	BOS	2009	4.58	0.254	0.010	0.264	22	3	572
Bannister, Brian	KCR	2009	4.73	0.273	0.009	0.282	14	1	668
Penny, Brad	BOS	2009	4.88	0.274	0.008	0.282	28	3	751
Hochevar, Luke	KCR	2009	6.55	0.313	0.007	0.319	18	4	631
Meche, Gil	KCR	2009	5.09	0.281	0.007	0.289	14	1	581
Davies, Kyle	KCR	2009	5.27	0.274	0.006	0.280	16	4	538
Chamberlain, Joba	NYY	2009	4.75	0.282	0.006	0.288	26	8	709
:									
Greinke, Zack	KCR	2009	2.16	0.207	−0.003	0.204	5	9	915
Carpenter, Chris	STL	2009	2.25	0.200	−0.003	0.197	2	4	750
Ohlendorf, Ross	PIT	2009	3.92	0.253	−0.003	0.250	11	8	725
Galarraga, Ar.	DET	2009	5.64	0.299	−0.003	0.296	3	5	642
Romero, Ricky	TOR	2009	4.30	0.264	−0.004	0.260	9	7	771
Cook, Aaron	COL	2009	4.16	0.262	−0.004	0.258	4	4	675
Verlander, Justin	DET	2009	3.45	0.242	−0.004	0.237	9	16	982
Average			4.31	0.2637	0.0024	0.2661			

Table 7.11. Pitchers with at least 500 batters faced and baserunner corrections above +0.005 or below −0.002. Data from 2009.

A few pitchers have baserunning corrections below zero, substantially better than the average baserunning correction of 0.002. These pitchers are so good at keeping runners from advancing that the runners that do attempt to advance on average harm their team's chance of scoring runs.

Pitchers with high baserunner corrections, on the other hand, are less productive for their teams because they allow runners to more easily advance on the base paths. Jose Contreras had the worst baserunning correction for any pitcher with at least 500 batters faced during the 2009 season. The baserunning events that occurred while he was pitching are shown in Table 7.12. Contreras is slow to deliver the baseball to the plate, which helped 23 runners to steal a base while only three runners were caught stealing. In addition, he had eight wild pitches and a passed ball. His baserunning correction of 0.014 is higher than Jacoby Ellsbury's baserunning correction of 0.013. When Contreras pitches, an average baserunner "improves" to the point that he is better than the league leader in stolen bases.

Player	Event Type	Number	Total Δ RE	Average Δ RE	GPA Correction
Contreras, Jose	Stolen Base	23	+4.219	+0.183	0.0072
	Caught Stealing	3	−0.585	−0.195	−0.0010
	Other Advance	9	+4.709	+0.523	0.0080
	Other Out	0	0.000	0.000	0.0000
	Total	35	+8.343	+0.238	0.0142

Table 7.12. Summary of the baserunning events that occurred while Jose Contreras was pitching. Data from 2009.

Tim Wakefield's primary pitch was a knuckleball, which is slow to reach the catcher. During the 2009 season he allowed 23 of 26 runners to steal a base, threw four wild pitches and had seven passed balls. Nearly six runs resulted from runners advancing against the pitcher, an average of 0.28 extra runs for each of the 21 games he started.

Player	Event Type	Number	Total Δ RE	Average Δ RE	GPA Correction
Wakefield, Tim	Stolen Base	22	+4.289	+0.195	0.0075
	Caught Stealing	3	−1.313	−0.438	−0.0023
	Other Advance	11	+2.856	+0.260	0.0050
	Other Out	0	0.000	0.000	0.0000
	Total	36	+5.832	+0.162	0.0102

Table 7.13. Summary of the baserunning events that occurred while Tim Wakefield was pitching. Data from 2009.

The best baserunning correction among pitchers with more than 500 batters faced belonged to Justin Verlander. During the 2009 sason, only nine of 25 runners successfully stole a base while he was pitching. (Four balks and eight wild pitches did offset some of the benefit from his ability to prevent runners from stealing bases.) While Verlander was pitching, runners trying to advance cost their team more than four runs, for an average of 0.12 runs for each of the 35 games he started.

Player	Event Type	Number	Total Δ RE	Average Δ RE	GPA Correction
Verlander, Justin	Stolen Base	9	+1.239	+0.138	0.0013
	Caught Stealing	16	−6.952	−0.435	−0.0071
	Other Advance	13	+3.055	+0.235	0.0031
	Other Out	3	−1.674	−0.558	−0.0017
	Total	36	−4.332	−0.106	−0.0044

Table 7.14. Summary of the baserunning events that occurred while Justin Verlander was pitching. Data from 2009.

Are baserunning corrections reproducible from year to year? For pitchers, the catcher they throw to is often the same throughout the season, and a catcher with a strong arm can influence a pitcher's baserunning correction significantly. For runners, events such as wild pitches or passed balls tend to be random events that do not occur often during the season. The runner's ability to advance when the opportunity presents itself is reflected in the baserunning correction.

Jacoby Ellsbury had the best baserunning correction (+0.013) of any runner during the 2009 season. It was the same as his 2008 correction, which had been good for fourth that season. In 2011, his baserunning correction of +0.006 was 20th best.

David DeJesus had the worst baserunning correction (−0.006) of any runner during the 2009 season. During the 2008 season he successfully stole 11 of 19 bases, which was far better than his 4 of 13 performance the following year but still resulted in a total change in run expectancy of −0.1 runs. DeJesus did advance on 14 wild pitches (a high number), and overall his 2008 season had a baserunning correction of +0.006 which was above average.

Justin Verlander had the best baserunning correction (−0.004) among pitchers with 500 or more batters faced in 2009. His baserunning corrections were 0.000 during the 2008 season, +0.001 during the 2010 season and +0.005 during the 2011 season.

Jose Contreras had the worst baserunning correction among pitchers in both 2008 (+0.010) and 2009 (+0.014).

What do these numbers show? Although a player's skills can change and there is some random variation, baserunning corrections tend to be reproducible from year to year.

Pitchers with 200 to 499 batters faced tend to be relievers, who often have runners on base when they come into the game. Since they face fewer batters, they will have fewer baserunning events and their baserunning corrections will tend to be a bit more random.

Player	Team	Year	ERA	GPA	GPAbpc	cGPA	SB	CS	BF
Jepsen, Kevin	ANA	2009	4.94	0.247	0.017	0.263	3	0	237
Wood, Kerry	CLE	2009	4.25	0.244	0.014	0.258	10	0	241
MacDougal, Mike	WAS	2009	4.31	0.273	0.014	0.287	5	1	246
Chavez, Jesse	PIT	2009	4.01	0.264	0.013	0.277	3	0	286
Stammen, Craig	WAS	2009	5.11	0.277	0.013	0.289	16	2	448
Purcey, David	TOR	2009	6.19	0.300	0.013	0.313	6	2	223
Bulger, Jason	ANA	2009	3.56	0.211	0.012	0.223	3	0	262
Meredith, Cla	SDP	2009	3.99	0.248	0.012	0.260	10	1	283
Perez, Chris	CLE	2009	4.26	0.259	0.012	0.271	7	4	239
Cabrera, Daniel	ARI	2009	6.00	0.329	0.012	0.341	3	1	258
Papelbon, J.	BOS	2009	1.85	0.183	0.011	0.194	9	1	285
Arias, Alberto	HOU	2009	3.35	0.227	0.011	0.237	3	0	209
League, Brandon	TOR	2009	4.58	0.258	0.011	0.269	9	1	313
Young, Chris	SDP	2009	5.21	0.277	0.011	0.288	19	0	336
Matsuzaka, D.	BOS	2009	5.76	0.283	0.011	0.294	7	0	283
Boyer, Blaine	ARI	2009	4.12	0.288	0.011	0.299	5	1	241
Lidge, Brad	PHI	2009	7.21	0.342	0.011	0.352	11	1	283
Average			4.32	0.2637	0.0024	0.2661			

Table 7.15. Pitchers with 200 to 499 batters faced and baserunner corrections of at least +0.011. Data from 2009.

During the 2009 season, Kevin Jepsen appeared in 54 games with 237 batters faced, all as a relief pitcher. He gave up three stolen bases but had six wild pitches and a passed ball. Jepsen's league-worst baserunning correction of +0.017 was largely attributed to his poor control. Almost four runs resulted from runners advancing, an average of 0.66 extra runs for each nine innings he pitched.

Player	Event Type	Number	Total Δ RE	Average Δ RE	GPA Correction
Jepsen, Kevin	Stolen Base	3	+0.888	+0.296	0.0037
	Caught Stealing	0	0.000	0.000	0.0000
	Other Advance	11	+3.451	+0.314	0.0146
	Other Out	1	−0.372	−0.372	−0.0016
	Total	15	+3.967	+0.264	0.0167

Table 7.16. Summary of the baserunning events that occurred while Kevin Jepsen was pitching. Data from 2009.

The best and worst baserunning corrections for batters and pitchers from the 2012 season are shown in the following tables.

Player	Team	Year	ERA	GPA	GPAbrc	cGPA	SB	CS	PA
McAllister, Zach	CLE	2012	4.24	0.279	0.010	0.289	15	1	543
Lincecum, Tim	SFG	2012	5.18	0.275	0.009	0.284	25	2	825
Cobb, Alex	TBR	2012	4.03	0.249	0.008	0.257	19	2	569
Jimenez, Ubaldo	CLE	2012	5.40	0.286	0.007	0.294	32	5	805

Applying Baserunning Corrections

Player	Team	Year	ERA	GPA	GPAbrc	cGPA	SB	CS	PA
Garcia, Jaime	STL	2012	3.92	0.248	0.007	0.255	4	5	515
Lowe, Derek	CLE	2012	5.11	0.282	0.007	0.289	7	2	640
Burnett, A.J.	PIT	2012	3.51	0.241	0.007	0.248	38	2	851
Feldman, Scott	TEX	2012	5.09	0.289	0.007	0.296	18	3	536
Liriano, F.	MIN	2012	5.34	0.281	0.006	0.287	15	2	693
Sanchez, Anibal	DET	2012	3.86	0.246	0.006	0.251	23	4	820
:									
Kershaw, Clayton	LAD	2012	2.53	0.212	−0.004	0.208	8	12	901
Cueto, Johnny	CIN	2012	2.78	0.225	−0.004	0.221	1	9	888
Mendoza, Luis	KCR	2012	4.23	0.269	−0.004	0.265	7	7	709
Lynn, Lance	STL	2012	3.78	0.252	−0.004	0.248	9	9	744
		Average	3.94	0.2543	0.0024	0.2568			

Table 7.17. Pitchers with at least 500 batters faced and baserunner corrections above +0.005 or below −0.003. Data from 2012.

Player	Team	Year	GPA	GPAbrc	cGPA	BA	SB	CS	PA
Crisp, Coco	OAK	2012	0.271	0.016	0.287	0.259	39	4	508
Trout, Mike	ANA	2012	0.328	0.015	0.342	0.326	*49*	5	639
Jennings, De.	TBR	2012	0.245	0.012	0.257	0.246	31	2	563
Zimmerman, Ryan	WAS	2012	0.294	0.010	0.304	0.282	5	2	641
Victorino, Shane	PHI	2012	0.246	0.009	0.255	0.255	39	6	666
Revere, Ben	MIN	2012	0.246	0.009	0.255	0.294	40	9	553
Kipnis, Jason	CLE	2012	0.276	0.008	0.284	0.257	31	7	672
Rollins, Jimmy	PHI	2012	0.273	0.008	0.280	0.250	30	5	699
Prado, Martin	ATL	2012	0.292	0.007	0.299	0.301	17	4	690
Upton, B.J.	TBR	2012	0.260	0.007	0.267	0.246	31	6	633
Stubbs, Drew	CIN	2012	0.236	0.007	0.244	0.213	30	7	544
Rodriguez, Alex	NYY	2012	0.259	0.007	0.266	0.272	13	1	529
Hunter, Torii	ANA	2012	0.294	0.007	0.301	0.313	9	1	584
Pagan, Angel	SFG	2012	0.274	0.007	0.280	0.288	29	7	659
Bourn, Michael	ATL	2012	0.272	0.006	0.279	0.274	42	*13*	703
Ramirez, Aramis	MIL	2012	0.315	0.006	0.321	0.300	9	2	630
Goldschmidt, Paul	ARI	2012	0.318	0.006	0.325	0.286	18	3	587
Altuve, Jose	HOU	2012	0.257	0.006	0.263	0.290	33	11	630
Saunders, Michael	SEA	2012	0.254	0.006	0.260	0.247	21	4	553
Escobar, Alcides	KCR	2012	0.245	0.006	0.251	0.293	35	5	648
Harper, Bryce	WAS	2012	0.272	0.006	0.278	0.270	18	6	597
Suzuki, Ichiro	SEA	2012	0.231	0.006	0.237	0.283	29	7	663
Gonzalez, Carlos	COL	2012	0.304	0.006	0.310	0.303	20	5	579
Headley, Chase	SDP	2012	0.322	0.006	0.327	0.286	17	6	699
Ackley, Dustin	SEA	2012	0.244	0.006	0.250	0.226	13	3	668
Reddick, Josh	OAK	2012	0.246	0.006	0.252	0.242	11	1	673
Johnson, Kelly	TOR	2012	0.247	0.006	0.253	0.225	14	2	581
:									
Reynolds, Mark	BAL	2012	0.279	−0.002	0.277	0.221	1	3	538
Trumbo, Mark	ANA	2012	0.280	−0.002	0.278	0.268	4	5	586
Cruz, Nelson	TEX	2012	0.281	−0.002	0.279	0.260	8	4	642
DeJesus, David	CHC	2012	0.274	−0.002	0.272	0.263	7	8	582
Davis, Ike	NYM	2012	0.260	−0.004	0.256	0.227	0	2	584
McCutchen, A.	PIT	2012	0.333	−0.004	0.329	0.327	20	12	673
		Average	0.2557	0.0026	0.2583	0.2545			

Table 7.18. Batters with at least 500 plate appearances and baserunner corrections above +0.005 or below −0.001. Data from 2012.

Player	Event Type	Number	Total Δ RE	Average Δ RE	GPA Correction
Trout, Mike	Stolen Base	49	+9.322	+0.190	0.0146
	Caught Stealing	5	−2.541	−0.508	−0.0040
	Other Advance	14	+4.391	+0.314	0.0069
	Other Out	3	−1.899	−0.633	−0.0030
	Total	71	+9.273	+0.131	0.0145

Table 7.19. Summary of Mike Trout's baserunning events from 2012.

Mike Trout lead the majors in stolen bases in 2012. His baserunning skills were one of the main arguments for selecting him over Miguel Cabrera for AL Most Valuable Player. Table 7.19 shows that his 49 stolen bases created 9.3 runs but were partially offset by the 2.5 runs his team lost when he was caught stealing five times. On average, the GPA from his 639 PAs should be corrected by +0.015 (+9.273 / 639) to reflect his baserunning contributions.

Baserunning Corrections, 1952–2012

The best and worst seasons as measured by baserunning corrections for both batters and pitchers from 1952 to 2012 are presented in this chapter. It should be noted that a few games are missing from the Retrosheet database from 1952 to 1973 and the statistics listed here may differ slightly from the official statistics for those years.

Player	Team	Year	GPA	GPAbrc	cGPA	BA	SB	CS	PA
Henderson, Rickey	OAK	1982	0.303	0.007	0.310	0.267	130	42	656
Brock, Lou	STL	1974	0.279	0.013	0.292	0.306	118	33	702
Coleman, Vince	STL	1985	0.247	0.016	0.263	0.267	110	25	692
Coleman, Vince	STL	1987	0.272	0.019	0.291	0.289	109	22	702
Henderson, Rickey	OAK	1983	0.296	0.021	0.317	0.292	108	19	622
Coleman, Vince	STL	1986	0.215	0.023	0.237	0.232	107	14	670
Wills, Maury	LAD	1962	0.266	0.025	0.291	0.299	104	13	759
Henderson, Rickey	OAK	1980	0.311	0.006	0.317	0.303	100	26	722
LeFlore, Ron	MON	1980	0.266	0.027	0.293	0.257	97	19	587
Ty Cobb	DET	1915				0.369	96	38	700
Moreno, Omar	PIT	1980	0.217	0.004	0.221	0.249	96	33	745
Wills, Maury	LAD	1965	0.245	0.003	0.248	0.286	94	31	711
Henderson, Rickey	NYY	1988	0.305	0.031	0.335	0.305	93	13	647
Raines, Tim	MON	1983	0.309	0.019	0.328	0.298	90	14	720

Table 8.1. Players with 90 or more stolen bases in a season since 1900.

Rickey Henderson set a modern record with 130 stolen bases in 1982. (Hugh Nicol still holds the all-time mark, 138, which he established in 1887.) The players with the greatest number of stolen bases in a season since 1900 are shown in Table 8.1. The table at the end of this chapter lists the best baserunning corrections for a season from 1952 to 2012. Interestingly, only five of the ten seasons found there are for players who stole more than 90 bases. Henderson's record-setting 1982 season, his 1980 season, Omar Moreno's 1980 season, and Maury Wills's 1965 season have baserunning corrections of +0.007 or less — not high enough to crack the top 8 from the 2012 season!

Player	Event Type	Number	Total Δ RE	Average Δ RE	GPA Correction
Henderson, Rickey	Stolen Base	93	+19.357	+0.208	0.0299
	Caught Stealing	13	−6.170	−0.475	−0.0095
	Other Advance	34	+8.610	+0.253	0.0133
	Other Out	5	−1.946	−0.389	−0.0030
	Total	15	+19.851	+0.137	0.0307

Table 8.2. Summary of Rickey Henderson's baserunning events from 1988.

Henderson's 1988 season merits a baserunning correction of +0.031, the highest by far since 1952. He created almost 20 runs for his team with his baserunning skills, or 0.14 runs for each of the 140 games in which he appeared.

Player	Event Type	Number	Total Δ RE	Average Δ RE	GPA Correction
Henderson, Rickey	Stolen Base	130	+25.552	+0.197	0.0390
	Caught Stealing	42	−22.987	−0.547	−0.0350
	Other Advance	16	+4.045	+0.253	0.0062
	Other Out	4	−2.137	−0.534	−0.0033
	Total	15	+4.473	+0.137	0.0068

Table 8.3. Summary of Rickey Henderson's baserunning events from 1982.

Despite having 37 more stolen bases in 1982, Henderson created 15.5 fewer runs with his baserunning skills than in 1988. His desire to set a major league record may have encouraged him to steal when the opportunities were not as good. Tim Raines led the league in 1982 with a baserunning correction of +0.014, while Henderson's +0.007 baserunning correction was only the 14th highest.

There were five players with 79 or more stolen bases during the 1980 season, far more than any other season in the modern era. The productivity from the baserunning skills of those players varied greatly.

Player	Event Type	Number	Total Δ RE	Average Δ RE	GPA Correction
Henderson, Rickey	Stolen Base	100	+20.160	+0.202	0.0279
	Caught Stealing	26	−14.236	−0.548	−0.0197
	Other Advance	13	+2.620	+0.202	0.0036
	Other Out	10	−4.552	−0.455	−0.0063
	Total	149	+3.992	+0.027	0.0055
LeFlore, Ron	Stolen Base	97	+22.606	+0.233	0.0385
	Caught Stealing	19	−9.110	−0.479	−0.0155
	Other Advance	20	+5.228	+0.261	0.0089
	Other Out	5	−2.772	−0.554	−0.0047
	Total	141	+15.952	+0.113	0.0272
Moreno, Omar	Stolen Base	96	+19.132	+0.199	0.0257
	Caught Stealing	33	−15.027	−0.455	−0.0202
	Other Advance	15	+3.152	+0.210	0.0042
	Other Out	6	−4.097	−0.683	−0.0055
	Total	150	+3.160	+0.021	0.0042
Wilson, Willie	Stolen Base	79	+15.427	+0.195	0.0207
	Caught Stealing	10	−4.572	−0.457	−0.0061
	Other Advance	16	+3.637	+0.227	0.0049
	Other Out	1	−0.442	−0.442	−0.0006
	Total	106	+14.050	+0.137	0.0189
Collins, Dave	Stolen Base	79	+17.966	+0.227	0.0293
	Caught Stealing	21	−11.740	−0.559	−0.0192
	Other Advance	15	+3.723	+0.248	0.0061
	Other Out	6	−3.610	−0.602	−0.0059
	Total	121	+6.339	+0.052	0.0103

Table 8.4. Players with 79 or more stolen bases during the 1980 season.

During the 1980 season, Ron LeFlore's 97 stolen bases were three behind major league leader Henderson. LeFlore's baserunning correction of +0.027, however, was the second-highest recorded from 1952 to 2012 and far exceeded Henderson's +0.006. LeFlore produced almost 16 runs for his team with his baserunning skills, or 0.11 for each of the 139 games in which he appeared. Henderson only produced four runs or 0.03 for each of the 158 games in which he appeared.

Player	Team	Year	GPA	GPAbrc	cGPA	BA	SB	CS	PA
Henderson, Rickey	OAK	1980	0.311	0.006	0.317	0.303	100	26	722
LeFlore, Ron	MON	1980	0.266	0.027	0.293	0.257	97	19	587
Moreno, Omar	PIT	1980	0.217	0.004	0.221	0.249	96	33	745
Wilson, Willie	KCR	1980	0.276	0.019	0.294	0.326	79	10	745
Collins, Dave	CIN	1980	0.258	0.010	0.268	0.303	79	21	613

Table 8.5. League leaders in stolen bases from the 1980 season.

Willie Wilson's 1980 baserunning correction of +0.019 was the 17th-highest recorded from 1952 to 2012 and trailed only LeFlore's baserunning correction for the same season. Wilson produced 14 runs for his team on the base paths or 0.09 for each of the 161 games in which he appeared.

Of the 127 players with at least 500 PAs during the 1980 season, Dave Collins's baserunning correction of +0.010 was 10th highest, Henderson's +0.006 was 17th highest, and Omar Moreno's +0.004 was 36th highest. Moreno's production on the base paths was quite unimpressive for someone who stole 96 bases. The average baserunning correction for the season was +0.001.

Ken Henderson's 1971 season seems out of place in the list of top baserunning corrections. He stole only 18 bases while being caught three times. He successfully advanced on the bases 19 times without being thrown out, including 13 wild pitches, two passed balls and two balks. These other advances resulted in almost six runs and explains why his 1971 season had such a high baserunning correction.

Player	Event Type	Number	Total Δ RE	Average Δ RE	GPA Correction
Henderson, Ken	Stolen Base	18	+3.158	+0.175	0.0053
	Caught Stealing	3	−0.830	−0.277	−0.0014
	Other Advance	19	+5.953	+0.313	0.0100
	Other Out	0	0.000	0.000	0.0000
	Total	40	+4.473	+0.137	0.0138

Table 8.6. Summary of Ken Henderson's baserunning events from 1971.

The benefit a team derives from a player's baserunning skills has more to do with the quality than the number of his stolen bases attempts. The 100 batters with baserunning corrections of +0.012 or higher are listed in the table at the end of this chapter. Everyone who made the list was successful stealing bases at least 76 percent of the time.

The top 100 seasons as measured by baserunning correction for runners with 500+ plate appearances are over-represented in the era from 1972 to 1993. This era accounts for 63 of 100 (63.0 percent) of the top seasons for runners, far more than the 37.6 percent of the top 100 seasons that would have been expected by chance alone. The seasons as measured by baserunning correction are distributed in a pattern different from that of the top seasons for hitters and pitchers as measured by GPA. Pitching dominated from 1962 to 1971, baserunning from 1972 to 1992, and hitting from 1994 to 2004.

Seasons	Runners Top 100 BRCs	Runners Top 100 BRCs	Expected Pct. Runners	Team Seasons
1952 to 1961	1	1.0%	10.8%	162
1962 to 1971	5	5.0%	14.1%	212
1972 to 1981	24	24.0%	16.7%	250
1982 to 1993	40	40.0%	20.9%	314
1994 to 2004	16	16.0%	21.5%	322
2005 to 2012	14	14.0%	16.0%	240

Table 8.7. Distribution of the top 100 seasons as measured by baserunning correction for batters.

The 51 best seasons as measured by baserunning correction for pitchers who faced 500 or more PAs are also shown in the table at the end of this chapter. Almost all of the pitchers named there allowed less than 50 percent of stolen base attempts to be successful.

Player	Event Type	Number	Total ΔRE	Average ΔRE	GPA Correction
Scott, Mike	Stolen Base	9	+0.698	+0.078	0.0013
	Caught Stealing	8	−3.578	−0.447	−0.0065
	Other Advance	5	+0.542	+0.108	0.0010
	Other Out	7	−3.463	−0.495	−0.0063
	Total	29	−5.801	−0.200	−0.0105

Table 8.8. Summary of the baserunning events that occurred while Mike Scott was pitching. Data from 1981.

Mike Scott's 1981 season, with a baserunning correction of −0.011, was the best of any pitcher who faced 500 or more PAs from 1952 to 2012. He picked off nine runners, and one runner who stole a base was thrown out as he tried to advance further. While Scott was pitching, runners trying to advance cost their teams almost six runs, or an average of 0.25 runs for each of the 23 games he started.

Player	Event Type	Number	Total ΔRE	Average ΔRE	GPA Correction
Garvin, Jerry	Stolen Base	9	+1.892	+0.210	0.0018
	Caught Stealing	19	−8.421	−0.443	−0.0081
	Other Advance	8	+2.879	+0.360	0.0028
	Other Out	12	−6.591	−0.549	−0.0063
	Total	48	−10.241	−0.213	−0.0098

Table 8.9. Summary of the baserunning events that occurred while Jerry Garvin was pitching. Data from 1977.

Jerry Garvin's 1977 season was perhaps even more impressive than Scott's 1981 performance, as Garvin faced 1,046 PAs, almost twice as many as Scott. Only nine of 28 runners stole bases while Garvin was pitching, resulting in a potential loss of 6.5 runs from their attempts. Only eight of 20 runners advanced in other ways, resulting in a potential loss of an additional 3.7 runs. Overall, more than 10 runs were potentially lost by opponents on the base paths, or 0.23 runs for each of his 44 starts.

How was Garvin so successful at preventing runners from advancing? His 1977 season was less successful when measured by a GPA of 0.273, an ERA of 4.20 and a 10-win, 18-loss record. Garvin's poor pitching allowed many batters to reach base. He set a single-season major league record by picking off 23 runners (many of which count as caught stealing) while four additional runners were thrown out trying to steal. He committed only two balks, threw two wild pitches, and had one passed ball.

Garvin's career, which lasted from 1977 to 1982, was otherwise undistinguished. He was primarily a relief pitcher from 1979 onward. In 1978, the only other season he faced more than 500 PAs, his baserunning correction of −0.004 was 10th best in baseball.

Six of the 10 worst seasons as measured by baserunning correction were posted by knuckleball pitchers. Joe Niekro had four of these seasons, and Hoyt Wilhelm and Tim Wakefield one each. Despite the production he allowed on the base paths, Niekro's 221 career wins make him one of the most successful knuckleball pitchers of all time.

Player	Event Type	Number	Total Δ RE	Average Δ RE	GPA Correction
Niekro, Joe	Stolen Base	19	+4.407	+0.232	0.0085
	Caught Stealing	2	−0.680	−0.340	−0.0013
	Other Advance	19	+5.807	+0.306	0.0113
	Other Out	1	−0.238	−0.238	−0.0005
	Total	41	+9.296	+0.227	0.0180

Table 8.10. Summary of the baserunning events that occurred while Joe Niekro was pitching. Data from 1976.

Niekro's 1977 baserunning correction of +0.018 was the worst of any pitcher who faced 500 or more PAs from 1952 to 2012. Nineteen of 21 runners stole bases while he was pitching, resulting in a potential gain of nearly four runs from their attempts. Nineteen of 20 runners advanced in other ways, potentially resulting in an additional 5.5 runs. Overall, more than nine potential runs were gained by opponents on the base paths, or 0.46 runs for every nine innings pitched.

Player	Event Type	Number	Total Δ RE	Average Δ RE	GPA Correction
Niekro, Joe	Stolen Base	31	+6.641	+0.214	0.0101
	Caught Stealing	6	−3.051	−0.509	−0.0047
	Other Advance	23	+8.442	+0.367	0.0129
	Other Out	1	−0.442	−0.442	−0.0007
	Total	61	+11.590	+0.190	0.0177

Table 8.11. Summary of the baserunning events that occurred while Joe Niekro was pitching. Data from 1987.

Niekro's 1987 season has a baserunning correction fractionally better than the one from 1976, but because he faced 139 more PAs in 1987, more potential runs were lost on the base paths that year. In 1987, he potentially lost 3.6 runs because of stolen bases, a total similar to 1976. Other advances from 1987 included 13 wild pitches and 10 passed balls, which potentially cost his team eight more runs. Overall, almost 12 runs were potentially gained by opponents on the base paths, or 0.43 runs for every one of his 27 appearances.

Knuckleball pitchers are not the only ones with poor baserunning corrections. Bobby Witt was known as a hard-throwing right-hander with control problems throughout his career. Many in Arlington, in fact, called him "Witt 'n Wild" as a play on the water park Wet 'n Wild, which was located next to Arlington Stadium. He led the league in walks three times and wild pitches twice.

Player	Event Type	Number	Total Δ RE	Average Δ RE	GPA Correction
Witt, Bobby	Stolen Base	44	+6.789	+0.154	0.0092
	Caught Stealing	4	−1.755	−0.439	−0.0024
	Other Advance	26	+7.566	+0.291	0.0102
	Other Out	0	0.000	0.000	0.0000
	Total	74	+12.600	+0.170	0.0170

Table 8.12. Summary of the baserunning events that occurred while Bobby Witt was pitching. Data from 1987.

Witt's 1987 season was, by baserunning correction, the third worst of any pitcher who faced 500 or more PAs from 1952 to 2012. He allowed 70 of 74 runners to advance during the season. Nearly 13 runs were potentially gained by opponents on the base paths, or 0.41 runs for every one of his 31 starts.

Witt's 1988 to 1991 seasons all had baserunning corrections between +0.010 and +0.013, each year ranking from worst to forth worst in the majors. Witt's walks and wild pitches dramatically declined after 1991. He also became better at stopping runners from stealing bases, allowing an average of 15 of 24 runners to steal a base from 1992 to 1999. He had fewer wild pitches and passed balls, but still an average of 10 of 11 runners advanced by means other than a stolen base during those years. From 1992 to 1999 his baserunning correction ranged from −0.001 to +0.004, which was similar to the league average of +0.002 during those years.

How many wins or losses are accounted for by the best or worst baserunning corrections? This topic is explored in greater depth in later chapters.

The following tables list the highest and lowest single-season GPA baserunning corrections from 1952 to 2012 for batters with at least 500 PAs and pitchers with at least 500 batters faced. GPAbrc is the GPA baserunning correction, while cGPA is the corrected GPA, calculated by adding GPAbrc to GPA.

Table 8.13. Batters with 500+ Plate Appearances

Player	Team	Year	GPA	GPAbrc	cGPA	BA	SB	CS	PA
Henderson, Rickey	NYY	1988	0.305	0.031	0.335	0.305	93	13	647
LeFlore, Ron	MON	1980	0.266	0.027	0.293	0.257	97	19	587
Law, Rudy	CHW	1983	0.271	0.026	0.297	0.283	77	12	551
Wills, Maury	LAD	1962	0.266	0.025	0.291	0.299	104	13	759
Lopes, Davey	LAD	1975	0.264	0.024	0.288	0.262	77	12	726
Wiggins, Al	SDP	1983	0.250	0.023	0.273	0.276	66	13	585
Coleman, Vince	STL	1986	0.215	0.023	0.237	0.232	107	14	670
Taveras, Willy	COL	2008	0.220	0.023	0.242	0.251	68	7	538
Henderson, Rickey	OAK	1983	0.296	0.021	0.317	0.292	108	19	622
Pettis, Gary	CAL	1985	0.257	0.021	0.278	0.257	56	9	516
Wilson, Willie	KCR	1979	0.262	0.021	0.282	0.315	83	12	640
Henderson, Rickey	NYY	1985	0.327	0.021	0.347	0.314	80	10	654
Wilson, Willie	KCR	1983	0.243	0.020	0.263	0.276	59	8	611
Womack, Tony	ARI	1999	0.255	0.020	0.275	0.277	72	13	684
Raines, Tim	MON	1983	0.309	0.019	0.328	0.298	90	14	720
Larkin, Barry	CIN	1995	0.326	0.019	0.344	0.319	51	5	567
Coleman, Vince	STL	1987	0.272	0.019	0.291	0.289	109	22	702
Wilson, Willie	KCR	1980	0.276	0.019	0.294	0.326	79	10	745
Lofton, Kenny	CLE	1994	0.324	0.019	0.343	0.349	60	12	523

Player	Team	Year	GPA	GPAbrc	cGPA	BA	SB	CS	PA
Grissom, Marquis	MON	1991	0.249	0.018	0.268	0.267	76	17	597
Campaneris, Bert	KCA	1966	0.251	0.018	0.269	0.267	52	10	606
Raines, Tim	MON	1986	0.307	0.018	0.325	0.334	70	9	664
Lopes, Davey	LAD	1978	0.267	0.018	0.284	0.278	45	4	665
Richards, Gene	SDP	1977	0.262	0.017	0.279	0.290	56	12	591
Wilson, Willie	KCR	1987	0.242	0.017	0.259	0.279	59	11	653
Duncan, Mariano	LAD	1985	0.217	0.017	0.234	0.244	38	8	620
Morgan, Joe	CIN	1975	0.373	0.017	0.390	0.327	67	10	639
Raines, Tim	MON	1987	0.332	0.017	0.349	0.330	50	5	627
Raines, Tim	MON	1985	0.286	0.017	0.302	0.320	70	9	665
Campaneris, Bert	OAK	1969	0.226	0.017	0.242	0.260	62	8	592
Cruz, Julio	SEA	1978	0.221	0.016	0.237	0.235	59	10	634
Pettis, Gary	DET	1988	0.223	0.016	0.239	0.2100	44	10	512
LeFlore, Ron	DET	1979	0.268	0.016	0.284	0.300	78	14	654
Morgan, Joe	CIN	1976	0.390	0.016	0.406	0.320	60	9	599
Brock, Lou	STL	1973	0.284	0.016	0.300	0.297	70	20	727
Coleman, Vince	STL	1985	0.247	0.016	0.263	0.267	110	25	692
Bourn, Michael	HOU	2010	0.260	0.016	0.276	0.265	52	11	605
Crisp, Coco	OAK	2012	0.271	0.016	0.287	0.259	39	4	508
Raines, Tim	MON	1984	0.291	0.015	0.306	0.309	75	10	718
Grissom, Marquis	MON	1992	0.258	0.015	0.274	0.276	78	13	707
Henderson, Rickey	OAK	1993	0.320	0.015	0.335	0.289	53	8	610
Hunter, Brian	SEA	1999	0.220	0.015	0.235	0.232	44	5	589
Bonds, Bobby	SFG	1972	0.269	0.015	0.284	0.259	44	6	697
Lofton, Kenny	CLE	1993	0.290	0.015	0.305	0.325	70	14	657
Crawford, Carl	TBR	2004	0.277	0.015	0.292	0.296	59	15	672
Cedeno, Cesar	HOU	1976	0.284	0.015	0.299	0.297	58	15	635
Suzuki, Ichiro	SEA	2006	0.279	0.015	0.294	0.322	45	2	752
Cedeno, Cesar	HOU	1977	0.264	0.015	0.279	0.279	61	14	598
Trout, Mike	ANA	2012	0.328	0.015	0.342	0.326	*49*	5	639
Wilson, Willie	KCR	1984	0.263	0.014	0.277	0.301	47	5	588
Davis, Eric	CIN	1988	0.313	0.014	0.328	0.273	35	3	543
Bradley, Phil	SEA	1987	0.273	0.014	0.288	0.297	40	10	702
Sanders, Deion	CIN	1997	0.232	0.014	0.246	0.273	56	13	509
Bowa, Larry	PHI	1977	0.214	0.014	0.229	0.280	32	3	675
Davis, Rajai	OAK	2010	0.236	0.014	0.250	0.284	50	11	561
Raines, Tim	MON	1982	0.264	0.014	0.278	0.277	78	16	731
Biggio, Craig	HOU	1994	0.327	0.014	0.341	0.318	39	4	511
Rollins, Jimmy	PHI	2008	0.273	0.014	0.287	0.277	47	3	625
Cuyler, Milt	DET	1991	0.236	0.014	0.250	0.257	41	10	546
LeFlore, Ron	DET	1978	0.267	0.014	0.281	0.297	68	16	741
Mays, Willie	SFG	1958	0.357	0.014	0.371	0.345	31	6	680
Davis, Eric	CIN	1987	0.352	0.014	0.366	0.293	50	6	562
Goodwin, Tom	COL	2000	0.270	0.014	0.284	0.263	55	10	606
Henderson, Ken	SFG	1971	0.274	0.014	0.288	0.264	18	3	598
Javier, Stan	OAK	1995	0.278	0.014	0.292	0.278	36	5	504
Henderson, Rickey	NYY	1989	0.315	0.014	0.329	0.274	77	14	674
Brock, Lou	STL	1971	0.287	0.014	0.301	0.313	64	19	721
Johnson, Lance	CHW	1995	0.276	0.014	0.290	0.306	40	6	645
Suzuki, Ichiro	SEA	2008	0.269	0.014	0.282	0.310	43	4	749
Ellsbury, Jacoby	BOS	2009	0.269	0.013	0.283	0.301	70	12	693
Taveras, Frank	PIT	1977	0.207	0.013	0.221	0.252	70	18	600
Raines, Tim	CHW	1992	0.302	0.013	0.316	0.294	45	6	644
Young, Eric	CHC	2000	0.261	0.013	0.274	0.297	54	7	690

Player	Team	Year	GPA	GPAbrc	cGPA	BA	SB	CS	PA
Alomar, Roberto	CLE	2000	0.284	0.013	0.298	0.310	39	4	697
Brock, Lou	STL	1974	0.279	0.013	0.292	0.306	118	33	702
Reyes, Jose	NYM	2011	0.291	0.013	0.304	0.337	39	7	586
Samuel, Juan	PHI	1984	0.250	0.013	0.264	0.272	72	15	737
Crawford, Carl	TBR	2006	0.301	0.013	0.314	0.305	58	9	653
Smith, Ozzie	STL	1988	0.263	0.013	0.276	0.270	57	9	669
Grissom, Marquis	MON	1994	0.265	0.013	0.278	0.288	36	6	521
Ellsbury, Jacoby	BOS	2008	0.245	0.013	0.258	0.280	50	11	609
Sandberg, Ryne	CHC	1985	0.297	0.013	0.310	0.305	54	11	673
Glanville, Doug	PHI	1999	0.293	0.013	0.306	0.325	34	2	692
Morgan, Joe	CIN	1977	0.326	0.013	0.339	0.288	49	10	645
Morgan, Joe	CIN	1973	0.327	0.013	0.340	0.290	67	15	693
Taveras, Frank	PIT	1976	0.224	0.013	0.237	0.258	58	11	573
Beltran, Carlos	KCR	2003	0.326	0.013	0.338	0.307	41	4	602
Jennings, De.	TBR	2012	0.245	0.012	0.257	0.246	31	2	563
Page, Mitchell	OAK	1977	0.313	0.012	0.326	0.307	42	5	592
Mumphrey, Jerry	SDP	1980	0.244	0.012	0.256	0.298	52	5	622
Coleman, Vince	STL	1990	0.243	0.012	0.256	0.292	77	17	539
Lofton, Kenny	CLE	1998	0.291	0.012	0.303	0.282	54	10	698
Rivers, Mickey	CAL	1975	0.273	0.012	0.286	0.284	70	14	672
Henderson, Rickey	OAK	1990	0.333	0.012	0.346	0.325	65	10	594
Daniels, Kal	CIN	1988	0.315	0.012	0.328	0.291	27	6	589
McGee, Willie	STL	1984	0.248	0.012	0.260	0.291	43	10	604
Gardner, Brett	NYY	2010	0.284	0.012	0.297	0.277	47	9	569
DeShields, Delino	MON	1993	0.273	0.012	0.285	0.295	43	10	562
Pettis, Gary	CAL	1986	0.268	0.012	0.280	0.258	50	13	628
Molitor, Paul	MIL	1988	0.305	0.012	0.317	0.312	41	10	691
:									
Lofton, Kenny	ATL	1997	0.303	−0.009	0.295	0.333	27	20	564
Helms, Tommy	CIN	1967	0.222	−0.009	0.213	0.274	5	11	530
Thomas, Derrell	SFG	1977	0.250	−0.009	0.241	0.267	15	13	568
McGee, Willie	STL	1986	0.255	−0.009	0.246	0.256	19	16	539
McCarver, Tim	STL	1969	0.258	−0.010	0.249	0.260	4	9	576
Cruz, Jose	HOU	1977	0.300	−0.010	0.291	0.299	44	23	661
Oliver, Al	PIT	1977	0.294	−0.010	0.284	0.308	13	16	622
Garcia, Damaso	TOR	1980	0.223	−0.010	0.213	0.278	13	13	565
Kuiper, Duane	CLE	1976	0.225	−0.011	0.214	0.263	10	17	555
Vaughn, Greg	MIL	1992	0.263	−0.012	0.251	0.228	15	15	573

Table 8.14. Pitchers with 500+ Batters Faced

Player	Team	Year	ERA	GPA	GPAbrc	cGPA	BA	SBa	CSa	PA
Scott, Mike	NYM	1981	3.91	0.261	−0.011	0.251	0.261	9	8	551
Garvin, Jerry	TOR	1977	4.20	0.273	−0.010	0.263	0.264	9	19	1046
Perry, Jim	CLE	1959	2.66	0.227	−0.009	0.218	0.223	2	10	620
Sain, Johnny	NYY	1952	3.44	0.260	−0.009	0.251	0.259	2	4	545
Marrero, Connie	WAS	1952	2.88	0.233	−0.009	0.224	0.249	5	7	770
Coleman, Joe	BAL	1954	3.63	0.264	−0.009	0.255	0.233	8	14	884
Ojeda, Bob	BOS	1984	4.01	0.261	−0.008	0.252	0.259	13	19	928
Welsh, Chris	SDP	1981	3.80	0.254	−0.008	0.246	0.264	10	10	512
Daal, Omar	ARI	1998	2.88	0.236	−0.008	0.228	0.245	2	12	664
Trout, Steve	CHC	1985	3.39	0.250	−0.008	0.242	0.270	7	13	601
Parque, Jim	CHW	1998	5.11	0.303	−0.008	0.295	0.299	6	9	507
Podres, Johnny	BRO	1953	4.23	0.286	−0.008	0.278	0.282	1	3	518

Player	Team	Year	ERA	GPA	GPAbrc	cGPA	BA	SBa	CSa	PA
Barr, Jim	SFG	1977	4.77	0.282	−0.008	0.274	0.306	17	14	1011
Tudor, John	STL	1986	2.93	0.237	−0.008	0.229	0.244	7	14	879
Hunter, Jim	OAK	1973	3.34	0.246	−0.008	0.238	0.232	4	18	1040
Leonhard, Dave	BAL	1968	3.14	0.231	−0.008	0.223	0.216	3	13	507
Michalak, Chris	TOR	2001	4.41	0.289	−0.008	0.281	0.293	5	5	610
Armstrong, Jack	CIN	1991	5.48	0.304	−0.008	0.296	0.293	11	8	611
Ojeda, Bob	NYM	1990	3.66	0.257	−0.008	0.249	0.272	14	11	500
Aase, Don	CAL	1978	4.05	0.257	−0.008	0.250	0.270	10	20	773
Pattin, Marty	MIL	1971	3.14	0.236	−0.008	0.229	0.234	12	23	1059
Redfern, Pete	MIN	1981	4.08	0.266	−0.007	0.259	0.261	3	12	601
Cuellar, Mike	BAL	1975	3.66	0.252	−0.007	0.244	0.249	6	20	1034
McNally, Dave	BAL	1972	2.95	0.231	−0.007	0.223	0.247	7	14	979
Smith, Bryn	MON	1983	2.50	0.226	−0.007	0.219	0.248	2	11	636
Langford, Rick	OAK	1978	3.44	0.254	−0.007	0.247	0.253	8	13	741
Talbot, Mitch	CLE	2010	4.41	0.279	−0.007	0.272	0.276	4	11	696
Vuckovich, Pete	MIL	1981	3.55	0.245	−0.007	0.237	0.249	10	14	620
McCaskill, Kirk	CAL	1990	3.25	0.254	−0.007	0.247	0.244	6	10	738
Gardner, Mark	MON	1991	3.86	0.261	−0.007	0.254	0.230	13	17	692
Burnside, Pete	DET	1960	4.29	0.264	−0.007	0.257	0.276	1	6	507
Shirley, Bob	SDP	1979	3.39	0.253	−0.007	0.246	0.257	8	20	843
Ferrarese, Don	PHI	1961	3.79	0.261	−0.007	0.254	0.234	3	9	587
Davis, Doug	TEX	2001	4.45	0.282	−0.007	0.275	0.295	6	11	828
Lolich, Mickey	DET	1974	4.16	0.266	−0.007	0.259	0.268	16	32	1263
Ellis, Dock	TEX	1978	4.20	0.279	−0.007	0.272	0.245	8	10	592
Honeycutt, Rick	TEX	1983	3.04	0.238	−0.007	0.231	0.269	9	16	865
Palmer, Jim	BAL	1977	2.92	0.225	−0.007	0.218	0.229	15	30	1269
Browning, Tom	CIN	1993	4.74	0.278	−0.007	0.271	0.333	4	7	505
Petry, Dan	DET	1984	3.25	0.246	−0.007	0.239	0.259	8	14	968
Collum, Jackie	CIN	1955	3.63	0.252	−0.007	0.245	0.254	0	2	546
Deshaies, Jim	MIN	1993	4.39	0.266	−0.007	0.260	0.264	7	18	770
Burris, Ray	CHC	1977	4.75	0.285	−0.007	0.278	0.305	12	17	970
Martinez, Pedro	MON	1995	3.53	0.245	−0.007	0.239	0.227	9	13	784
Blue, Vida	SFG	1986	3.27	0.248	−0.007	0.241	0.239	10	14	663
Bosman, Dick	TEX	1972	3.64	0.267	−0.007	0.260	0.273	4	12	738
Helling, Rick	TEX	1997	4.48	0.263	−0.007	0.256	0.233	7	13	550
Tudor, John	STL	1988	2.32	0.220	−0.007	0.213	0.257	9	10	794
Brett, Ken	CHW	1976	3.28	0.244	−0.006	0.238	0.233	11	15	835
Trout, Steve	CHC	1986	4.75	0.276	−0.006	0.269	0.298	20	16	711
McGregor, Scott	BAL	1984	3.94	0.261	−0.006	0.255	0.280	8	11	840
Witt, Bobby	TEX	1987	4.91	0.264	0.013	0.276	0.219	44	2	673
Wilhelm, Hoyt	BAL	1960	3.31	0.233	0.013	0.246	0.226	18	3	601
Hough, Charlie	TEX	1987	3.79	0.256	0.013	0.269	0.223	35	13	1231
Juden, Jeff	CLE	1997	4.46	0.262	0.013	0.275	0.257	49	6	706
Robertson, Rich	SFG	1970	4.85	0.271	0.013	0.284	0.277	19	2	830
Niekro, Joe	HOU	1983	3.48	0.232	0.013	0.245	0.241	45	9	1113
Juden, Jeff	ANA	1998	5.80	0.289	0.014	0.303	0.264	45	6	801
Candiotti, Tom	CLE	1987	4.78	0.276	0.014	0.290	0.250	25	5	888
Suppan, Jeff	BOS	1997	5.69	0.284	0.014	0.298	0.305	24	3	503
Bell, Rob	CIN	2000	5.00	0.273	0.014	0.287	0.243	18	1	618
Contreras, Jose	CHW	2009	4.92	0.277	0.014	0.291	0.272	23	3	589
Niekro, Joe	HOU	1985	3.83	0.242	0.014	0.256	0.249	47	7	983
Wakefield, Tim	BOS	2006	4.64	0.262	0.014	0.276	0.248	22	4	610
Dopson, John	BOS	1989	3.99	0.250	0.015	0.264	0.257	27	5	727

Player	Team	Year	ERA	GPA	GPAbrc	cGPA	BA	SBa	CSa	PA
Wilhelm, Hoyt	CHW	1964	1.99	0.182	0.015	0.196	0.202	7	1	510
Niekro, Joe	NYY	1986	4.87	0.285	0.015	0.300	0.275	23	1	571
Young, Chris	SDP	2007	3.12	0.219	0.015	0.234	0.192	43	0	705
McGowan, Dustin	TOR	2007	4.09	0.240	0.016	0.256	0.230	28	1	705
Witt, Bobby	TEX	1986	5.48	0.279	0.017	0.296	0.223	44	4	741
Niekro, Joe	MIN	1987	5.27	0.283	0.018	0.300	0.270	31	6	655
Niekro, Joe	HOU	1976	3.36	0.240	0.018	0.258	0.238	19	2	516

Part II. GPA and Baseball Eras

The Relationship Between GPA and Batting Average

The relationship between GPA and batting average (BA) is fixed so that the average GPA and BA from the 2005 to 2008 seasons are both 0.266. It sets a modern standard untainted by steroids and it works out well that the average GPA and BA of all major league players from 1952 to 2012 are virtually identical at 0.259.

Player	Team	Year	GPA	BA	GPA-BA	OPS	PA	RBI	HR
Bonds, Barry*	SFG	2001	0.443	0.328	0.115	0.515	664	137	73
Bonds, Barry*	SFG	2004	0.471	0.362	0.109	0.609	617	101	45
McGwire, Mark	STL	1998	0.404	0.299	0.105	0.470	681	147	70
McGwire, Mark	STL	1999	0.383	0.278	0.105	0.424	661	147	65
Giambi, Jason	NYY	2006	0.352	0.253	0.099	0.413	579	113	37
Bonds, Barry	SFG	1996	0.402	0.308	0.094	0.461	675	129	42
Killebrew, H.*	MIN	1969	0.370	0.276	0.094	0.427	709	140	49
Maris, Roger*	NYY	1961	0.362	0.269	0.093	0.372	698	141	61
Tettleton, Mickey	DET	1993	0.337	0.245	0.092	0.372	637	110	32
Killebrew, H.	MIN	1962	0.335	0.243	0.092	0.366	666	126	48
Mantle, Mickey*	NYY	1962	0.413	0.321	0.092	0.486	502	89	30
Beltran, Carlos	NYM	2006	0.366	0.275	0.091	0.388	617	116	41
Tenace, Gene	SDP	1978	0.315	0.224	0.091	0.392	515	61	16

Table 9.1. Batters with the greatest positive difference between GPA and BA for a season with at least 500 plate appearances. Data from 1952 to 2012 (*denotes MVP season).

An individual player's GPA and BA can vary greatly. Sluggers such as Barry Bonds can have a much higher GPA than BA since the production from their extra base hits are not reflected in the BA. Batters whose seasons had the greatest positive difference between GPA and BA are shown in Table 9.1. These include five seasons in which the batter won the MVP for his league and a solid but unspectacular 1978 season by Gene Tenace.

	ERA	GPA	BA	OBP	SLG	PA	Hits	RBI	HR
0 Outs	3.06	0.266	0.273	0.331	0.436	1,032K	252K	80.4K	29.8K
1 Out	5.01	0.266	0.268	0.334	0.422	992K	235K	136.1K	26.4K
2 Outs	5.10	0.266	0.250	0.334	0.400	962K	214K	129.8K	25.3K
Bases Empty	1.14	0.267	0.259	0.322	0.416	1,644K	389K	46.9K	46.9K
1st Only	2.89	0.266	0.278	0.336	0.438	539K	134K	43.7K	15.5K
2nd or 3rd	11.93	0.265	0.265	0.352	0.417	803K	177K	255.7K	19.2K
3rd, <2 Outs	22.60	0.264	0.329	0.368	0.505	167K	41K	102.9K	4.0K
Total	4.36	0.266	0.264	0.333	0.420	2,986K	701K	346.3K	81.5K

Table 9.2. Statistics by base-out state for all players from 1997 to 2012.

How the average player performed in each of the base-out states during the interleague era (1997–2012) is shown in Table 9.2. The GPA is about 0.266 no matter the base-out state, but BA varies significantly. With a runner on third base and less than two outs, batters hit 0.329, dramatically higher than the 0.259 they hit with the bases empty. On-base percentage (OBP) varies somewhat less and slugging average (SLG) somewhat more than batting average. When evaluating a player's performance, only GPA provides a measure unbiased by the base-out state.

	GPA	BA	OBP	SLG	PA	Hits	RBI	HR
0 Outs	0.414	0.338	0.456	0.851	182	50	35	21
1 Out	0.524	0.356	0.529	0.960	240	62	69	29
2 Outs	0.388	0.286	0.545	0.766	242	44	33	23
Bases Empty	0.390	0.295	0.454	0.849	359	82	46	46
1st Only	0.477	0.367	0.514	0.835	142	40	32	14
2nd or 3rd	0.535	0.382	0.650	0.944	163	34	59	13
3rd, <2 Outs	0.665	0.476	0.606	1.333	33	10	25	5
Total	0.444	0.328	0.515	0.863	664	156	137	73

Table 9.3. Statistics by base-out state for Barry Bonds's 2001 season.

Barry Bonds's 2001 season had the greatest difference between GPA and BA of any from 1952 to 2012. In all base-out states shown in Table 9.3, Bonds's production measured by GPA was greater than his batting average. His production was extraordinary with men on base, including a GPA of 0.665 with runners on third base and less than two outs.

	— Barry Bonds 2001—			— MLB Average 2001—		
	aGPA × FracPA	= GPA		aGPA × FracPA	= GPA	
Any Out	0.018	0.4834	0.009	−0.014	0.6603	−0.009
Strike Out	0.002	0.1370	0.000	−0.016	0.1722	−0.003
Double/Tr Play	−0.326	0.0120	−0.004	−0.555	0.0238	−0.013
Walk	0.538	0.2666	0.144	0.566	0.0845	0.048
HBP/Interference	0.547	0.0136	0.007	0.607	0.0102	0.006
Error	0.397	0.0015	0.001	0.780	0.0103	0.008
Any Hit	1.209	0.2349	0.284	0.920	0.2347	0.216
Single	0.714	0.0738	0.053	0.729	0.1534	0.112
Double	1.143	0.0482	0.055	1.045	0.0471	0.049
Triple	1.068	0.0030	0.003	1.323	0.0050	0.007
Home Run	1.574	0.1099	0.173	1.650	0.0292	0.048
Extra Base Hit	1.436	0.1611	0.231	1.279	0.0813	0.104
Total	0.444	1.0000	0.444	0.268	1.0000	0.268

Table 9.4. Barry Bonds's production by event compared with the major league average for 2001.

The events that resulted from plate appearances (PAs) for Bonds during the 2001 season are summarized in Table 9.4 alongside those of the average player that season, whose GPA was 0.176 (0.444 − 0.268) points lower. How did Bonds generate the second-highest GPA recorded for a season from 1952 to 2012? He hit a home run in 10.99 percent of his PAs, compared with 2.92 percent for the average player. That means that his record-setting 73 home runs contributed 0.173 points to his GPA, 0.125 (0.173 − 0.048) more than the home runs hit by an average player. Bonds walked 26.66 percent of his PAs compared with 8.45 percent for the average player. His then-single-season record of 177 walks (now third highest behind his own 2004 and 2002 seasons) contributed 0.144 points to his GPA, 0.96 (0.144 − 0.048) points higher than those of an average player.

Combine Bonds's production from his home runs and walks with his 3.52 percent (13.70 − 17.22) fewer strikeouts and 1.88 percent (1.20 − 2.38) fewer double and triple plays than the average player, and you get the second-highest single-season GPA of the past 60 years. The 0.116-point difference between his GPA of 0.444 and his BA of 0.328 represents the added production not reflected by the BA.

	GPA	BA	OBP	SLG	PA	Hits	RBI	HR
0 Outs	0.469	0.319	0.508	0.773	197	45	26	17
1 Out	0.539	0.435	0.665	0.991	188	47	45	17
2 Outs	0.417	0.347	0.651	0.702	232	43	30	11
Bases Empty	0.395	0.349	0.530	0.780	302	76	25	25
1st Only	0.552	0.369	0.586	0.786	128	31	21	9
2nd or 3rd	0.537	0.394	0.754	0.944	187	28	55	11
3rd, <2 Outs	0.688	0.500	0.778	1.500	36	5	19	3
Total	0.471	0.362	0.609	0.812	617	135	101	45

Table 9.5. Statistics by base-out state from Barry Bonds's 2004 season.

In 2004, Bonds had the second-greatest differential between GPA and BA of any player from 1952 to 2012. His production was again extraordinary with men on base, and it included a GPA of 0.688 with runners on third base and less than two outs.

The events that resulted in PAs for Bonds during the 2004 season are summarized in Table 9.6, along with those of the average major leaguer for that year. Bonds's GPA was 0.202 (0.471 − 0.269) points higher, as he hit a home run in 7.29 percent of his PAs compared with 2.89 percent for the average player. His 45 home runs contributed 0.121 points to his GPA, 0.073 (0.121 − 0.048) points higher than the home runs of an average player. He also walked in 37.60 percent of his PAs compared with 8.60 percent for the average player, as his single-season record of 232 bases on balls contributed 0.206 points to his GPA, 0.157 (0.206 − 0.049) points higher than the walks of an average player.

Combine Bonds's production from his home runs and walks with his 10.30 percent (6.48 − 16.78) fewer strikeouts and 1.88 percent (1.13 − 2.40) fewer double and triple plays than the average player and you get the highest single-season GPA from 1952 to 2012.

	— Barry Bonds 2004 —			— MLB Average 2004 —		
	aGPA	× FracPA	= GPA	aGPA	× FracPA	= GPA
Any Out	0.017	0.3809	0.006	−0.017	0.6584	−0.011
Strike Out	0.022	0.0648	0.001	−0.018	0.1678	−0.003
Double/Tr Play	−0.586	0.0113	−0.007	−0.565	0.0240	−0.014
Walks	0.549	0.3760	0.206	0.571	0.0860	0.049
HBP/Interference	0.648	0.0146	0.009	0.609	0.0099	0.006
Error	0.851	0.0097	0.008	0.790	0.0095	0.008
Any Hit	1.098	0.2188	0.240	0.919	0.2361	0.217
Single	0.711	0.0972	0.069	0.729	0.1552	0.113
Double	1.041	0.0438	0.046	1.046	0.0473	0.049
Triple	1.002	0.0049	0.005	1.314	0.0048	0.006
Home Run	1.656	0.0729	0.121	1.668	0.0289	0.048
Extra Base Hit	1.409	0.1216	0.171	1.284	0.0810	0.104
Total	0.471	1.0000	0.471	0.269	1.0000	0.269

Table 9.6. Barry Bonds's production by event compared with the major league average for 2004.

Bonds hit 0.362 en route to his second National League batting title, slugged 0.812 (fourth all time), and broke his on-base percentage record with a 0.609 average. Bonds won his fourth-consecutive MVP Award and his seventh overall. His offensive production in 2004 was by far the greatest in the history of baseball. His GPA was 0.014 points higher than his 2002 season (0.457) and 0.028 points higher than his 2001 season (0.443). It was also 0.044 points better than Ted Williams's 1957 season (0.427). (Williams was the only player besides Bonds in the top four seasons as measured by GPA from 1952 to 2012.)

Batters who have a lower GPA than BA tend to be those who drive in few runs or get few extra-base hits, strike out a lot, and hit into many double plays. Their lack of production is not reflected in their batting average. Batters with the greatest negative difference between GPA and BA are shown in Table 9.7. With the exception of Hal Lanier, most of these players had a good average; all, however, were otherwise weak hitters.

Player	Team	Year	GPA	BA	GPA-BA	OBP	PA	RBI	HR
Beckert, Glenn	CHC	1971	0.265	0.342	−0.077	0.367	570	42	2
Alou, Matty	NYY	1973	0.218	0.295	−0.077	0.338	550	29	2
Russell, Bill	LAD	1978	0.209	0.286	−0.077	0.320	672	46	3
Alou, Matty	PIT	1966	0.253	0.327	−0.074	0.355	531	25	2
Millan, Felix	ATL	1968	0.210	0.284	−0.074	0.311	540	29	1
Kaline, Al	DET	1954	0.204	0.276	−0.072	0.305	535	43	4
Lanier, Hal	SFG	1968	0.135	0.206	−0.071	0.222	518	27	0
Puckett, Kirby	MIN	1984	0.226	0.296	−0.070	0.320	583	31	0
Mueller, Don	NYG	1954	0.280	0.347	−0.067	0.367	609	67	4
Castillo, Luis	FLA	2000	0.268	0.334	−0.066	0.418	626	17	2
Sanguillen, Manny	PIT	1970	0.259	0.325	−0.066	0.344	510	61	7
Sanchez, Rey	KCR	2001	0.216	0.281	−0.065	0.300	579	37	0
Bowa, Larry	PHI	1977	0.215	0.280	−0.065	0.313	675	41	4

Table 9.7. Batters with the greatest negative difference between GPA and BA for a season with at least 500 PAs. Data from 1952 to 2012.

Glenn Beckert's 1971 season had the greatest negative difference between GPA and BA of any from 1952 to 2012. In all base-out states shown in Table 9.8, Beckert's production measured by GPA was less than his BA. His production was quite poor with runners on third base and less than two outs.

The events that resulted in PAs for Beckert during the 1971 season are summarized in Table 9.9, along with the average player's performance from 1971. Beckert did not strike out or walk much compared to the average player. Most of his hits were singles and that, combined with his lack of clutch hitting, resulted in a GPA 0.077 (0.265 − 0.342) points lower than his batting average.

	GPA	BA	OBP	SLG	PA	Hits	RBI	HR
0 Outs	0.290	0.367	0.384	0.444	202	66	13	2
1 Out	0.216	0.286	0.326	0.319	224	60	8	0
2 Outs	0.306	0.393	0.410	0.486	144	55	21	0
Bases Empty	0.268	0.330	0.369	0.401	344	107	1	1
1st Only	0.270	0.380	0.396	0.426	114	41	3	1
2nd or 3rd	0.251	0.337	0.330	0.398	112	33	38	0
3rd, <2 Outs	0.132	0.308	0.235	0.462	17	4	12	0
Total	0.265	0.342	0.367	0.406	570	181	42	2

Table 9.8. Statistics by base-out state from Glenn Beckert's 1971 season.

Beckert was an All-Star from 1969 to 1972 and was selected by the fans as a starter for the National League in the 1971 game. Voters may have allowed his high BA to blind them to his other statistics, which were less impressive.

	— Glenn Beckert 1971—			— MLB Average 1971—		
	aGPA	× FracPA	= GPA	aGPA	× FracPA	= GPA
Any Out	−0.006	0.6298	−0.004	−0.014	0.6748	−0.009
Strike Out	−0.042	0.0421	−0.002	−0.015	0.1420	−0.002
Double/Tr Play	−0.516	0.0298	−0.015	−0.547	0.0256	−0.014
Walks	0.582	0.0421	0.025	0.566	0.0856	0.048
HBP/Interference	0.000	0.0000	0.000	0.617	0.0057	0.004
Error	0.564	0.0105	0.006	0.757	0.0119	0.009
Any Hit	0.750	0.3175	0.238	0.871	0.2219	0.193
Single	0.710	0.2737	0.194	0.729	0.1632	0.119
Double	1.003	0.0316	0.032	1.028	0.0336	0.035
Triple	0.766	0.0088	0.007	1.298	0.0055	0.007
Home Run	1.576	0.0035	0.006	1.668	0.0196	0.033
Extra Base Hit	1.002	0.0439	0.044	1.267	0.0587	0.074
Total	**0.265**	**1.0000**	**0.265**	**0.245**	**1.0000**	**0.245**

Table 9.9. Glenn Beckert's production by event compared with the MLB average for 1971.

Player	Team	Year	GPA	BA	OPS	SLG	PA	RBI	HR
Beckert, Glenn	CHC	1970	0.230	0.288	0.323	0.349	632	36	3
Beckert, Glenn	CHC	1971	0.265	0.342	0.367	0.406	570	42	2
Morgan, Joe	HOU	1970	0.291	0.268	0.383	0.396	658	52	8
Morgan, Joe	HOU	1971	0.283	0.262	0.355	0.408	653	52	11
Hunt, Ron	SFG	1970	0.297	0.281	0.394	0.381	442	41	6
Hunt, Ron	MON	1971	0.294	0.280	0.401	0.357	631	38	5
Cash, Dave	PIT	1970	0.291	0.314	0.365	0.419	230	28	1
Cash, Dave	PIT	1971	0.264	0.289	0.349	0.354	532	34	2

Table 9.10. Statistics from select NL second basemen during the 1970 and 1971 seasons.

Although fans are not noted for their discrimination in choosing players for the All-Star game, Joe Morgan, Ron Hunt, and Dave Cash were other National League second basemen who had substantially more productive 1970 and 1971 seasons than Beckert.

	GPA	BA	OBP	SLG	PA	Hits	RBI	HR
0 Outs	0.125	0.174	0.209	0.194	177	27	7	0
1 Out	0.122	0.223	0.221	0.255	190	41	11	0
2 Outs	0.163	0.218	0.238	0.265	151	32	9	0
Bases Empty	0.196	0.219	0.241	0.258	291	62	0	0
1st Only	0.093	0.206	0.221	0.235	114	21	0	0
2nd or 3rd	0.018	0.168	0.174	0.188	113	17	27	0
3rd, <2 Outs	0.028	0.280	0.250	0.280	32	7	15	0
Total	0.135	0.206	0.222	0.239	518	100	27	0

Table 9.11. Statistics by base-out state from Hal Lanier's 1968 season.

As measured by GPA-BA differential, Hal Lanier's 1968 season was the seventh worst of the past 60 years. In all base-out states shown in Table 9.11, Lanier's production measured by GPA was less than his batting average. His production was bad with a runner on first and extremely poor with runners on second or third.

Lanier's plate appearances for 1968 season are broken down in Table 9.12, alongside those of the average player from 1968. Lanier, whose GPA was 0.071 (0.135 − 0.206) points lower than his BA, hit into 1.33 percent (3.67 − 2.34) more double plays than the average player, had 5.27 percent (2.32 – 7.59) fewer walks, and had fewer home runs, doubles, and triples. Even though Lanier had 4.78 percent (11.00 – 15.78) fewer strikeouts and an average number of singles, his GPA was only 0.135.

	— Hal Lanier 1968 —			— MLB Average 1968 —		
	aGPA	× FracPA	= GPA	aGPA	× FracPA	= GPA
Any Out	−0.022	0.7741	−0.017	−0.008	0.6918	−0.006
Strike Out	0.002	0.1100	0.000	−0.008	0.1578	−0.001
Double/Tr Play	−0.432	0.0367	−0.016	−0.560	0.0234	−0.013
Walks	0.593	0.0232	0.014	0.560	0.0759	0.042
HBP/Interference	0.000	0.0000	0.000	0.585	0.0065	0.004
Error	0.562	0.0097	0.005	0.753	0.0134	0.010
Any Hit	0.685	0.1931	0.132	0.849	0.2124	0.180
Single	0.654	0.1641	0.107	0.723	0.1582	0.114
Double	0.844	0.0270	0.023	0.993	0.0319	0.032
Triple	1.172	0.0019	0.002	1.231	0.0057	0.007
Home Run	0.000	0.0000	0.000	1.637	0.0167	0.027
Extra Base Hit	0.866	0.0290	0.025	1.216	0.0543	0.066
Total	**0.135**	**1.0000**	**0.135**	**0.231**	**1.0000**	**0.231**

Table 9.12. Hal Lanier's production by event compared to the major league average for 1968.

Lanier's GPA was 0.096 points lower than the average player's during the 1968 season, and his poor production contributed to the Giants' finishing nine games behind the Cardinals for the National League pennant.

Lanier's 0.135 GPA was by far the lowest for any batter with 500 or more PAs in a season from 1952 to 2012. (The next-lowest GPA was Mark Belanger's 0.164, also in in 1968.) Lanier's 1967 and 1969 seasons were also among the worst seasons measured by GPA from 1952 to 2012.

Player	Team	Year	GPA	BA	OPS	SLG	PA	RBI	HR
Lanier, Hal	SFG	1967	0.186	0.213	0.239	0.255	557	42	0
Wert, Don	DET	1968	0.186	0.200	0.258	0.299	589	37	12
Perez, Neifi	KCR	2002	0.184	0.236	0.260	0.303	585	37	3
Ramirez, Rafael	ATL	1986	0.183	0.240	0.273	0.335	530	33	8
Michael, Gene	NYY	1971	0.182	0.224	0.298	0.276	513	35	3
Foli, Tim	MON	1973	0.181	0.240	0.284	0.277	500	36	2
Tyson, Mike	STL	1973	0.181	0.243	0.279	0.299	506	33	1
Lanier, Hal	SFG	1969	0.176	0.228	0.263	0.251	537	35	0
Brosius, Scott	OAK	1997	0.176	0.203	0.259	0.317	526	41	11
Belanger, Mark	BAL	1968	0.164	0.208	0.271	0.248	530	21	2
Lanier, Hal	SFG	1968	0.135	0.206	0.222	0.239	518	27	0

Table 9.13. Batters with the lowest GPAs for a season with at least 500 PAs. Data from 1952 to 2012.

From 1952 to 2009 there were 6,701 batters with 500 or more PAs in a season. Those with the largest differences between GPA and BA for a single season were described earlier in this chapter and represent the 0.2 and 99.8 percentiles. Most batters have a much smaller difference between GPA and batting average.

Percentile	1st	10th	25th	50th	75th	90th	99th
GPA − BA	−0.053	−0.032	−0.017	+0.001	+0.019	+0.038	+0.070

Table 9.14. Percentiles for the difference between GPA and BA. Data from 1952 to 2009.

The difference between GPA and BA for 56 percent of batters is between −0.020 and +0.020 points (21st to 77th percentiles). For these batters, BA accurately reflects their offensive production. For the other 44 percent of batters, BA less accurately reflects their offensive production. For 1.7 percent of batters (0 to 1.7th percentile) BA over-represents their offensive production by at least 0.050 GPA points; for 5.0 percent (95.0th to 100th percentiles), BA under-represents it by at least 0.050 GPA points. The correlation coefficient between GPA and BA is +0.671, or a moderate positive association.

Baseball Eras, 1952 to 2012

Offensive production has varied greatly from era to era and to a lesser extent from season to season within an era. From 1952 to 2012 the league-wide batting average (BA) has varied from 0.236 to 0.271, the GPA from 0.231 to 0.278, and the home runs per plate appearance (HR/PA) from 0.0151 to 0.0299.

The table at the end of this chapter lists the major league averages by season for a number of statistical categories, including BA, GPA and HR/PA. Here, again, it's worth mentioning that a few games are missing from the Retrosheet database from 1952 to 1973, and the statistics listed here may differ slightly from the official statistics for those years.

Offensive production represents a balance between pitching and hitting. Many factors influence offensive production and could have contributed to the wide variation seen among seasons from 1952 to 2012.

Major League Baseball, for instance, has changed its rules over the decades, often with the apparent objective of increasing the number of runs scored. In addition, from 1960 to 1998, expansion increased the number of teams from 16 to 30. The mix of stadiums changed, as well, both as a result of expansion and as established teams replaced older stadiums with new ones. Artificial surfaces were introduced and more recently fell out of favor. Baseballs were manufactured in different ways. New strategies were employed including the introduction of new pitches and relief specialists. The biggest change may have been in the players themselves, as training methods and year-round dedication to staying in shape produced better athletes.

Because all these changes were occurring over time, it is difficult to look at any one statistic from 1952 to 2012 and get a clear picture of the change in offensive production taking place.

The clearest trend has been the improvement in baserunning. The average baserunning corrections were close to 0.0000 for most seasons in the early 1950s. In 1952 and 1954 the baserunning corrections were negative, meaning the average runner reduced the number of runs his team scored by attempting to steal a base or advance in other ways.

The number of stolen base attempts increased from 1,202 in 1952 (1.02 per game) to 3,537 in 1984 (1.68 per game) to a peak of 5,109 in 1987 (2.43 per game) to 4,365 in 2012 (1.80 per game). The net production from attempting to steal bases remained virtually unchanged from 1952 to 1984 with an average GPA baserunning correction from stolen base attempts of −0.0094 points. Potentially, about 133 runs were lost from runners attempting to steal a base in 1984, or an average of 0.06 runs per game.

Player	Event Type	Number	Total Δ RE	Average Δ RE	GPA Correction
1952 Season	Stolen Base	662	+120.168	+0.182	0.0015
	Caught Stealing	540	−233.062	−0.432	−0.0029
	Other Advance	799	+184.534	+0.231	0.0023
	Other Out	250	−135.575	−0.542	−0.0017
	Total	2,251	−63.935	−0.028	−0.0008
1988 Season	Stolen Base	3,301	+571.548	+0.173	0.0036
	Caught Stealing	1,414	−630.654	−0.446	−0.0040
	Other Advance	3,270	+679.055	+0.208	0.0043
	Other Out	323	−141.232	−0.437	−0.0009
	Total	8,308	+478.717	+0.058	0.0030
2008 Season	Stolen Base	2,798	+481.454	+0.172	0.0026
	Caught Stealing	1,033	−454.268	−0.440	−0.0024
	Other Advance	2,860	+573.945	+0.201	0.0031
	Other Out	270	−110.631	−0.410	−0.0006
	Total	2,251	+490.500	+0.070	0.0026

Table 10.1. Summary of baserunning events from the 1952, 1988, and 2008 seasons.

From 1985 to 2002 the net production from attempting to steal bases improved with an average GPA baserunning correction from stolen base attempts of −0.0061 points. From 2003 to 2012 the net production from attempting to steal bases averaged 0.0000 points. This improvement was attributable to more success stealing bases with the number of stolen base attempts remaining well below the peak levels of the late 1980s.

The improvement in baserunning over the years can be credited to improved production from, in roughly equal parts, stealing bases (less lost production) and advancing a base in other ways. The cause for this improvement is less clear. It is doubtful that runners are faster now than they were in the 1980s, when most of the single-season stolen base records were established. More likely an increased reliance on power hitting led to a more judicious use of the stolen base.

Power hitting as defined by HR/PA averaged 0.0229 from 1953 to 1966 with little variation. In 1967 and 1968 offensive production fell dramatically. By 1968, the HR/PA was 0.0167, BA was 0.236 and ERA was 2.98 — all period-low levels for 1952–2012.

There was a short-lived increase in HR/PA in 1969 and 1970, after the mound was lowered and the strike zone reduced; but from 1971 to 1984 there was again a drought in HR/PA, with an average of 0.0200 during those years.

Batting average improved from 1969 to 1972 to an average of 0.250, but it was not until the DH was introduced in 1973 that BA return to the levels seen during the 1950s. From 1973 to 1992 the average BA was 0.259. Earned run average followed a similar pattern, with an average ERA of 3.81 from 1973 to 1992, similar to that seen during the 1950s.

Before 1994, the highest HR/PA were 0.0249, during the 1961 season, and 0.0275, during the 1987 season. An unprecedented increase in HR/PA began in 1994, however, and every season after that saw the rate of HR/PA surpass 0.0260. The HR/PA from the 1996, 1999 to 2001, and 2004 seasons were 0.0280 to 0.0299, higher than had ever been seen before.

From 1994 to 2009 the ERA for each season has been 4.32 to 4.77, greater than any season from 1952 and 1993.

The BAs for the 1994 to 2000 seasons were 0.266 to 0.277, greater than any season since 1952. The BAs for the 2001 to 2011 seasons, on the other hand, were 0.255 to 0.269, higher than in most years but not dramatically higher than scattered seasons such as 1953 or 1979. Gross Productivity Average follows a pattern similar to BA during these years.

From individual statistics from each season since 1952 it is possible to say that from about 1967 to 1984 the balance favored pitchers over hitters and that since 1994 the balance has favored hitters over pitchers. The exact years these eras began and the magnitude of their effect are harder to precisely nail down.

In the previous chapter, the variation between GPA and BA for individual players was found to have ranged from −0.077 to +0.115 points. The higher the GPA relative to the BA, the more power and production a batter produces compared with an average player with that BA. The relationship between GPA and BA tends to remain constant from season to season, with only a small variation over time. From 1952 to 2012 the difference between GPA and BA for a whole season ranged from −0.0092 to +0.0073 points.

The advantage of looking at the difference between GPA and BA is that it removes most of the "noise" that makes other statistics hard to interpret from season to season. The mix of ballparks, changes in game strategy, and changes in rules tend to cancel out, allowing the long-term trends to emerge.

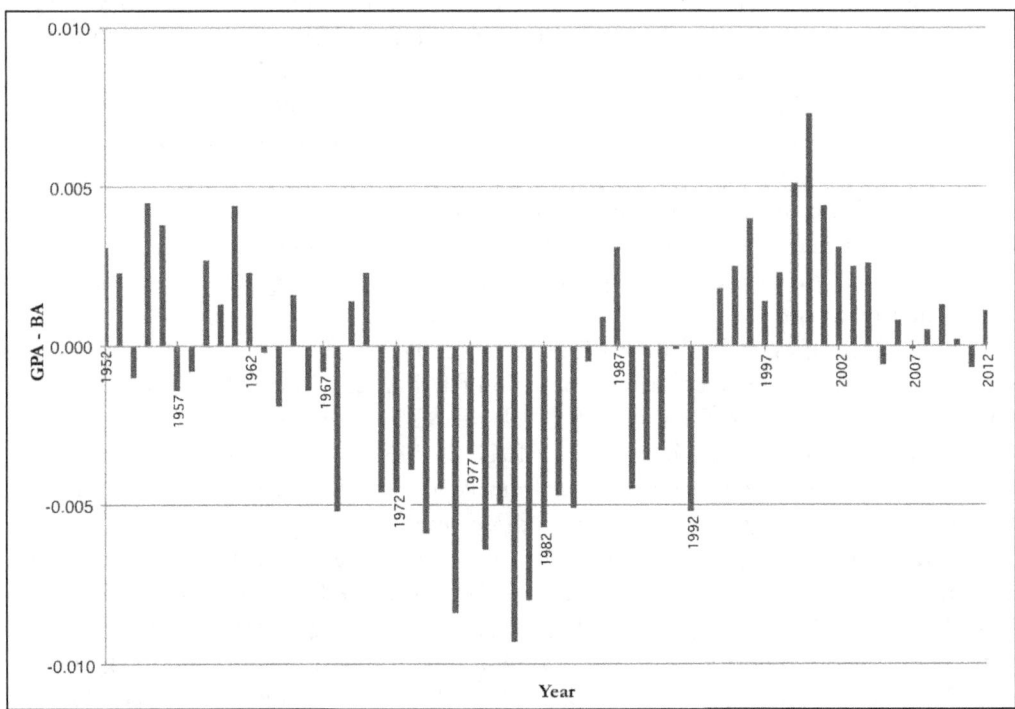

Figure 1. The difference between Gross Productivity Average and batting average for individual seasons from 1952 to 2012.

The average difference between GPA and BA was −0.0006 points from 1952 to 2012. From 1971 to 1984 there was an unprecedented string of 14 years in which the difference between GPA and BA was negative (average −0.0057 points). This book will refer to these years as the Pitching Era. From 1994 to 2004 there was an unprecedented string of 11 years in which the difference between GPA and BA was positive (average +0.0034 points), and this book will refer to those years as the Steroid Era.

Outside of the Pitching and Steroid eras, the average difference between GPA and BA was close to 0. From 1952 to 1970 the average difference between GPA and BA was +0.0008 points, from 1985 to 1993 it was −0.0016 points, and from 2005 to 2012 it was +0.0003 points.

What accounts for the significant change in offensive production over the past 60 years? The Pitching and Steroid eras will each be examined in the next two chapters.

In the table below, GPAbrc is the average GPA baserunning correction; cGPA is corrected GPA, or the sum of GPA + GPAbrc; and HR/PA is the fraction of PAs in which a home run was hit.

Table 10.2. Season Averages from 1952 to 2012

Year	ERA	GPA-BA	BA	GPA	GPAbrc	cGPA	OBP	SLG	HR/PA
1952	3.68	0.0031	0.2513	0.2544	−0.0008	0.2536	0.3264	0.3678	0.0179
1953	4.18	0.0023	0.2643	0.2666	0.0001	0.2667	0.3362	0.3978	0.0221
1954	3.91	−0.0010	0.2610	0.2600	−0.0003	0.2597	0.3329	0.3907	0.0207
1955	4.02	0.0045	0.2582	0.2627	0.0003	0.2630	0.3328	0.3934	0.0233
1956	3.99	0.0038	0.2581	0.2619	0.0004	0.2623	0.3319	0.3972	0.0240
1957	3.83	−0.0014	0.2573	0.2560	0.0003	0.2563	0.3241	0.3900	0.0229
1958	3.87	−0.0008	0.2578	0.2570	0.0004	0.2574	0.3249	0.3939	0.0238
1959	3.92	0.0027	0.2568	0.2595	0.0008	0.2603	0.3241	0.3923	0.0238
1960	3.82	0.0013	0.2550	0.2563	0.0009	0.2573	0.3238	0.3875	0.0224
1961	4.03	0.0044	0.2583	0.2627	0.0014	0.2641	0.3282	0.3992	0.0249
1962	3.97	0.0023	0.2578	0.2601	0.0017	0.2618	0.3261	0.3932	0.0240
1963	3.46	−0.0002	0.2461	0.2459	0.0015	0.2474	0.3088	0.3716	0.0221
1964	3.58	−0.0019	0.2505	0.2486	0.0016	0.2501	0.3126	0.3779	0.0225
1965	3.50	0.0016	0.2453	0.2469	0.0015	0.2484	0.3108	0.3715	0.0219
1966	3.52	−0.0014	0.2485	0.2471	0.0014	0.2485	0.3095	0.3760	0.0225
1967	3.31	−0.0008	0.2422	0.2414	0.0010	0.2424	0.3063	0.3572	0.0189
1968	2.98	−0.0052	0.2363	0.2311	0.0014	0.2325	0.2985	0.3400	0.0167
1969	3.61	0.0014	0.2482	0.2495	0.0018	0.2513	0.3201	0.3692	0.0210
1970	3.89	0.0023	0.2539	0.2562	0.0022	0.2584	0.3257	0.3854	0.0230
1971	3.47	−0.0046	0.2494	0.2448	0.0016	0.2464	0.3171	0.3656	0.0196
1972	3.26	−0.0046	0.2438	0.2392	0.0011	0.2403	0.3105	0.3539	0.0181
1973	3.74	−0.0039	0.2569	0.2531	0.0017	0.2548	0.3251	0.3785	0.0208
1974	3.62	−0.0059	0.2568	0.2509	0.0015	0.2524	0.3243	0.3691	0.0178
1975	3.70	−0.0045	0.2576	0.2531	0.0019	0.2550	0.3273	0.3740	0.0182
1976	3.51	−0.0084	0.2554	0.2471	0.0015	0.2486	0.3201	0.3610	0.0151
1977	3.99	−0.0034	0.2642	0.2608	0.0010	0.2617	0.3292	0.4011	0.0226
1978	3.68	−0.0064	0.2579	0.2515	0.0012	0.2526	0.3235	0.3786	0.0186
1979	4.00	−0.0050	0.2655	0.2605	0.0015	0.2620	0.3298	0.3975	0.0214
1980	3.84	−0.0093	0.2646	0.2553	0.0013	0.2566	0.3264	0.3878	0.0191
1981	3.58	−0.0080	0.2557	0.2477	0.0011	0.2488	0.3201	0.3686	0.0168
1982	3.86	−0.0057	0.2612	0.2555	0.0013	0.2568	0.3240	0.3887	0.0210
1983	3.86	−0.0047	0.2609	0.2561	0.0015	0.2576	0.3250	0.3893	0.0206
1984	3.81	−0.0051	0.2599	0.2548	0.0015	0.2563	0.3229	0.3847	0.0203
1985	3.89	−0.0005	0.2571	0.2565	0.0017	0.2582	0.3232	0.3910	0.0225
1986	3.97	0.0009	0.2577	0.2586	0.0017	0.2603	0.3259	0.3951	0.0237
1987	4.29	0.0031	0.2630	0.2661	0.0028	0.2689	0.3311	0.4154	0.0275
1988	3.73	−0.0045	0.2542	0.2498	0.0030	0.2528	0.3179	0.3777	0.0200

Year	ERA	GPA-BA	BA	GPA	GPAbrc	cGPA	OBP	SLG	HR/PA
1989	3.71	−0.0036	0.2541	0.2506	0.0023	0.2529	0.3196	0.3752	0.0193
1990	3.86	−0.0033	0.2579	0.2546	0.0021	0.2567	0.3246	0.3854	0.0207
1991	3.91	−0.0001	0.2557	0.2556	0.0017	0.2573	0.3234	0.3847	0.0210
1992	3.74	−0.0052	0.2557	0.2506	0.0016	0.2522	0.3224	0.3773	0.0189
1993	4.19	−0.0012	0.2651	0.2639	0.0017	0.2656	0.3323	0.4033	0.0231
1994	4.51	0.0018	0.2697	0.2715	0.0024	0.2739	0.3387	0.4243	0.0266
1995	4.45	0.0025	0.2668	0.2693	0.0026	0.2719	0.3378	0.4173	0.0260
1996	4.61	0.0040	0.2699	0.2739	0.0026	0.2765	0.3405	0.4267	0.0280
1997	4.39	0.0014	0.2668	0.2682	0.0018	0.2700	0.3368	0.4192	0.0264
1998	4.43	0.0023	0.2662	0.2685	0.0019	0.2705	0.3352	0.4202	0.0269
1999	4.71	0.0051	0.2712	0.2763	0.0022	0.2785	0.3445	0.4339	0.0291
2000	4.77	0.0073	0.2705	0.2777	0.0020	0.2798	0.3449	0.4371	0.0299
2001	4.42	0.0044	0.2640	0.2684	0.0019	0.2703	0.3322	0.4266	0.0292
2002	4.28	0.0031	0.2613	0.2645	0.0017	0.2661	0.3312	0.4167	0.0271
2003	4.40	0.0025	0.2642	0.2668	0.0022	0.2690	0.3326	0.4221	0.0278
2004	4.46	0.0026	0.2660	0.2687	0.0022	0.2709	0.3351	0.4278	0.0289
2005	4.29	−0.0006	0.2645	0.2639	0.0019	0.2658	0.3303	0.4189	0.0269
2006	4.52	0.0008	0.2693	0.2701	0.0023	0.2725	0.3366	0.4319	0.0286
2007	4.47	−0.0001	0.2681	0.2679	0.0027	0.2706	0.3358	0.4227	0.0263
2008	4.32	0.0005	0.2638	0.2643	0.0026	0.2669	0.3331	0.4162	0.0260
2009	4.32	0.0013	0.2624	0.2638	0.0024	0.2662	0.3329	0.4178	0.0270
2010	4.08	0.0002	0.2574	0.2575	0.0025	0.2601	0.3255	0.4028	0.0249
2011	3.94	−0.0007	0.2551	0.2543	0.0024	0.2568	0.3206	0.3990	0.0246
2012	4.01	0.0011	0.2545	0.2557	0.0026	0.2583	0.3190	0.4053	0.0268

THE PITCHING ERA, 1971 TO 1984

This book defines the Pitching Era as the unprecedented string of 14 years, from 1971 to 1984, in which the difference between GPA and BA for a whole season was negative (average −0.0057 points). During these years pitching was dominant over hitting. It can be argued that the Pitching Era began a few years earlier or ended a few years later. The 1968, 1988 to 1990 and 1992 seasons, for instance, all had GPA — BA differences of −0.0033 to −0.0057, significantly lower than any non–Pitching Era year from 1952 to 2012. The intervening years with GPA — BA differences close to 0 or positive, however, make it less certain these years should be included in the Pitching Era.

	ERA	*GPA*	*BA*	*OBP*	*SLG*	*PA*	*Hits*	*RBI*	*HR*
0 Outs	2.56	0.253	0.270	0.322	0.396	55,444	13,366	3,656	1,080
1 Out	4.54	0.256	0.269	0.327	0.393	53,715	12,882	6,889	1,028
2 Outs	4.49	0.258	0.254	0.329	0.374	52,051	11,896	6,383	979
Bases Empty	0.78	0.258	0.258	0.317	0.380	89,233	21,206	1,744	1,744
1st Only	2.39	0.256	0.288	0.333	0.418	28,285	7,284	1,891	610
2nd or 3rd	10.96	0.250	0.263	0.342	0.384	43,692	9,654	3,293	733
3rd, <2 Outs	21.23	0.250	0.331	0.359	0.478	9,120	2,225	5,503	161
Total	3.84	0.255	0.265	0.326	0.388	161,210	38,144	16,928	3,087

Table 11.1. Statistics by base-out state for the 1980 season.

The 1980 season was in the middle of the Pitching Era and saw a difference of −0.0093 points between GPA and BA, the most of any season from 1952 to 2012. The BA that year was 0.265, but the GPA was significantly lower for all base-out states, as shown in Table 11.1. Batters were particularly unproductive with men on second or third base, putting up a GPA of only 0.250, or 0.015 points lower than the BA for that year. Why was the GPA so much lower than the BA in 1980?

Table 11.2 summarizes the batting events for 1980 alongside the MLB average from 1952 to 2012, and it reveals that the GPA from the 1980 season was 0.004 points lower than the average for the 60-year period.

During the 1980 season, batters struck out 2.62 percent less frequently than in the average season, but they also walked less frequently by 0.44 percent. Batters had 1.07 percent more singles and 0.47 percent fewer extra-base hits than the average season.

Combine the lack of clutch hitting with fewer walks and fewer extra base hits and the 1980 season saw a −0.0093 difference between GPA and BA, the highest single-season difference from 1952 to 2012. That difference represents lost production that is not reflected in the batting average.

	— MLB Average 1980 —			— MLB Ave. 1952 to 2012 —		
	aGPA	× FracPA	= GPA	aGPA	× FracPA	= GPA
Any Out	−0.014	0.6650	−0.009	−0.015	0.6650	−0.010
Strike Out	−0.017	0.1246	−0.002	−0.017	0.1508	−0.003
Double/Tr Play	−0.558	0.0255	−0.014	−0.553	0.0246	−0.014
Walk	0.561	0.0818	0.046	0.569	0.0862	0.049
HBP/Interference	0.602	0.0042	0.003	0.605	0.0067	0.004
Error	0.767	0.0124	0.010	0.766	0.0115	0.009
Any Hit	0.873	0.2366	0.206	0.896	0.2306	0.207
Single	0.733	0.1714	0.126	0.733	0.1607	0.118
Double	1.020	0.0394	0.040	1.032	0.0408	0.042
Triple	1.315	0.0067	0.009	1.323	0.0057	0.008
Home Run	1.671	0.0191	0.032	1.670	0.0234	0.039
Extra Base Hit	1.241	0.0652	0.081	1.269	0.0699	0.088
Total	0.255	1.0000	0.255	0.259	1.0000	0.259

Table 11.2. Production by event from the 1980 season compared with the major league average from 1952 to 2012.

Over the years a number of factors have been identified to explain the apparent strength of pitching in the seventies and early eighties. Let's consider them one by one.

Ballparks

One theory explains the dominance of pitchers during this era by pointing to the mix of ballparks that came into use. Select data from the ballpark corrections chapter are shown in Table 11.3 for ballparks that opened between 1965 and 1977. The six expansion teams that began play in new parks averaged a ballpark correction of −0.001. Eight teams moved from old stadiums with average ballpark corrections of −0.001 into new stadiums with average ballpark corrections of −0.006.

Team	*Year*	*Old Park*	*GPAbpc*	*Year*	*New Park*	*GPAbpc*
Atlanta				1966	Atl.-Fulton County	0.010
Cincinnati	1970	Crosley Field	0.010	1971	Riverfront Stadium	−0.001
Houston	1964	Colt Stadium	−0.015	1965	Hou. Astrodome	−0.020
KC/Oak.	1967	Municipal Stadium	0.007	1969	Oak-Alameda Cnty	−0.016
LA Angels	1965	Dodger Stadium	−0.017	1966	Angel Stadium	−0.005
Mil Brewers				1970	Mil County Stad.	−0.002
Montreal				1977	Olympic Stadium	−0.006
Phil Phillies	1970	Connie Mack Stad.	0.002	1971	Veterans Stadium	0.001
Pittsburgh	1969	Forbes Field	−0.006	1971	Three Rivers Stad.	0.001
St. Louis	1965	Busch Stadium I	0.017	1966	Busch Stadium II	−0.006
San Diego				1969	Qualcomm Stad.	−0.016
Sea. Mariners				1977	The Kingdome	0.003
Toronto				1977	Exhibition Stad.	0.007
Wash./Texas	1971	DC Stadium	−0.007	1972	Arlington Stadium	−0.002

Table 11.3. Teams with new stadiums from 1965 to 1977. The second, third, and fourth columns show the old park name, last year in use, and GPA ballpark correction. The final three columns show the new park name, year it opened, and GPA ballpark correction from 1973 to 1992.

There were 22 major league teams by the 1977 season. Taken together, the 14 new stadiums from 1965 to 1977 account for a change in GPA of −0.002 points ((−0.001 × 6 +

(−0.006 − 0.001) × 8) / 22). The average GPA from 1952 to 1962 was 0.260 and fell to 0.254 from 1973 to 1992. The new stadiums probably accounted for about a third (−0.002 / −0.006) of the drop seen in GPA over this era.

Expansion

Major League Baseball gradually expanded from 16 teams in 1960 to 30 teams in 1998. One theory to account for the dominance of pitching during the era from 1971 to 1984 is that expansion diluted big league talent.

The expansion from 1961 to 1969 increased the number of teams from 16 to 24 and was followed by a period in which pitchers had a relative advantage over hitters; however, the expansion from 1977 to 1998 increased the number of teams from 24 to 30 and was followed by a period in which hitters had a relative advantage over pitchers. If the theory that major league talent was diluted by expansion were true, the change in the relative strengths of offense and defense would presumably be consistent.

Years	Teams	Expansion Teams
1952–1960	16	
1961	18	Los Angeles Angels, Washington Senators (Twins)
1962–1968	20	Houston Colts (Astros), New York Mets
1969–1976	24	KC Athletics, Wash. Nationals, SD Padres, Mil. Brewers
1977–1992	26	Toronto Blue Jays, Seattle Mariners
1993–1997	28	Florida Marlins, Colorado Rockies
1998–2013	30	Tampa Bay Rays, Arizona Diamondbacks

Table 11.4. Major league expansion teams from 1952 through to the present.

There are a number of other reasons that the "dilution of MLB talent" theory does not explain the dominance of pitching in the expansion years:

1. Pitching and hitting talent should both be diluted by expansion. Unless one benefits more than the other, no change in relative balance should be expected.

2. The pool from which MLB selects players has greatly expanded to include African Americans in the 1950s, Hispanic players from the 1960s to the 1990s, and most recently players from Korea and Japan.

3. The population of the United States has increased from 180 million in 1960 to 315 million today, about the same percentage increase as the number of teams in the majors.

4. Major League Baseball provides a much better wage now than in the 1950s for those who make it to the majors, and large signing bonuses are paid to promising young talent.

The arguments for the "dilution of MLB talent" theory include:

1. Baseball has more competition for the best athletes from football, basketball, and track and field, which attract many top athletes with a more glamorous image and good pay.

2. The number of African Americans in MLB fell from 17 percent in 1997 to 8 percent in 2007, less than the 12.3 percent of blacks in the general population of the U.S in 2007 (Lapchick et al., *The 2008 Racial and Gender Report Card: Major League Baseball*).

It is hard to see how MLB expansion could explain the changes in offensive production seen from era to era since 1952.

Improved Athletic Performance

Athletic performance has improved gradually over the last 60 years in virtually every sport in which an individual athletic accomplishment can be measured or timed. This is true even in sports such as baseball that are not very dependent on improved equipment to boost performance.

From the mid–1960s to the mid–1980s the baseball athlete almost certainly improved as well. During this time the balance between the pitcher and hitter went from being relatively even, to favoring pitchers, then back to being relatively even.

If improved athletic performance is to account for the dominance of pitchers during the era from 1971 to 1984, a number of contradictions have to be explained:

1. The improved athletic performance primarily benefited pitchers during the Pitching Era more than hitters, yet pitchers and hitters trained in the same facilities with the same training personnel.

2. The athletic performance of hitters caught up with pitchers by the late 1980s despite both pitchers and hitters trained in the same facilities with the same training personnel.

3. The dominance of pitching came on rather suddenly in the late 1960s. Improved athletic performance should cause a more gradual change in balance between pitchers and hitters.

It is hard to see how improved athletic performance of pitchers could explain the decreased offensive production seen during the Pitching Era.

Relief Pitching

Baseball game strategies have evolved over the years. One of the biggest changes has been the way pitchers are used in the game. The number of innings pitched by the league leader has gradually fallen from an average of 401 innings during the decade from 1910 to 1919 to 258 innings today. Over that same time the percentage of complete games fell from 79.0 percent to 4.4 percent (Rany Jazayerli, baseballprospectus.com, 3/2/2004).

For many years there were no pitching rotations and relievers. In 1876, George Bradley started all 64 games for the St. Louis Brown Stockings, completing 63 of them; his teammates threw four innings all year. Former starters like Firpo Marberry of the Washington Senators in the 1920s and Johnny Murphy of the New York Yankees in the 1930s did achieve distinction as relievers, but they were the exceptions.

Joe Page, a Yankee relief pitcher of the late 1940s, had two brilliant seasons as the Yankees won the World Series in 1947 and 1949 and stimulated interest in picking players who specialized in relief pitching.

In 1960, *The Sporting News* established its Fireman of the Year Award, to be given to the top relief pitcher in each league. The growing importance of relief pitchers was finally recognized by baseball in 1969 when the save became an official statistic for a relief pitcher who successfully held on to the lead (with certain stipulations).

The emergence of full-time relief pitchers gave teams the luxury of using their starting pitchers without having to worry about an emergency relief outing. Teams were able to plan what games their starting pitchers played days and weeks in advance and the pitching rotation was born.

In the 1950s, Casey Stengel routinely saved his best pitcher, Whitey Ford, to pitch against the best teams in the American League. Ford never started more than 33 games per year under Stengel. When Ralph Houk took over as manager in 1961, the Yankees went to a fixed rotation. In 1961, Ford started 39 games, threw 283 innings, and won 25 games — all career highs.

The emergence of relief pitchers potentially allowed a more skilled pitcher (or at least one with the platoon advantage) to face an opposing batter in late-game situations that were critical to the game's outcome. Starting pitchers evolved into players who pitched in a more regular rotation and for fewer innings. The combination of these factors could explain some of the dominance of pitchers from 1971 to 1984.

The Strike Zone

The definition of the strike zone has changed over the years. In 1963, it was defined as the space over home plate that is between the top of the batter's shoulders and his knees when he assumes his natural stance. In 1969, the strike zone was reduced vertically to the space between the batter's armpits and the top of his knees. In 1988, the strike zone shrank further, its upper limit defined by a horizontal line at the midpoint between the top of the shoulders and the top of the uniform pants. The lower level remained a line at the top of the knees until 1996, when it was lowered slightly from the top to the bottom of the knees.

While baseball rules provide a precise definition for the strike zone, in practice it is up to the umpire to judge whether a pitch passes through the zone. Historically, umpires have often called pitches according to a contemporary understanding of the strike zone rather than the official rulebook definition.

Many factors have contributed to the divergence of the official and conventional strike zones. In one example from the 1970s, umpires started wearing more compact chest protection, which allowed them to crouch lower and more easily call a low strike.

In 2001, MLB directed its umpires to call pitches according to the official definition rather than the conventional one. The umpires demonstrated limited compliance for a time. In 2002, QuesTec's Umpire Information System was implemented in a number of parks. It consists of four cameras placed around a ballpark that track the trajectory of each pitch. The data allows MLB executives to grade umpires on accuracy and help umpires learn the official strike zone. A new system called Zone Evaluation was implemented in all 30 MLB parks in 2009. It appears that the electronic systems are accomplishing their basic goals of returning the strike zone to its rule book definition ("Ball-Strike Monitor May Reopen Wounds," NYTimes.com, 3/31/2009).

Baseballs

Baseball is not a sport very dependent on the evolution of equipment. The basic bat and glove have changed little since the 1960s. Shoes and uniforms may have evolved, but they probably made only a minor contribution to the change in offensive production from era to era since 1952. One thing that has changed over the years is the baseball itself.

The cork-center baseball became the major league standard in 1911 and has been used since. This resulted in an explosion of offense. Following World War I, Babe Ruth emerged as the pre-eminent slugger of the new Live Ball Era.

In 1931, pitchers were given some recourse against the livelier ball when the ball changed again. A thin layer of rubber wrapped the cork center, slightly deadening the ball. The seams of the ball were raised as well to enable the pitcher to get a better grip on the ball for more rotation on breaking pitches.

Rawlings Sporting Goods started manufacturing baseballs in 1955 when it was bought out by Spalding. Both the American and National League balls were made by the same company, although they were stamped with the different names. Spalding was forced to sell Rawlings after an anti-trust investigation in 1968. Spalding continued to contract with Rawlings to manufacture baseballs until 1973, when they started to make the balls themselves.

For economic reasons, cowhide replaced horsehide as the baseball cover in 1974. Rawlings took back all manufacturing in 1976 and produced their baseballs in Taiwan and Haiti. Since 1990, Rawlings baseballs have been stitched in Costa Rica.

Major League Baseball has insisted that over the last 50 years the ball has not changed significantly. Whenever there has been a surge in offensive production, MLB consistently denies that a new livelier ball is responsible. Given all the changes that have occurred in the manufacturing of baseballs since 1955, can MLB be believed?

Researchers from the University of Rhode Island's Forensic Science Partnership examined baseballs used during the 1963, 1970, 1989, 1995, and 2000 seasons. Bounce tests on the balls revealed that the balls from 1995 and 2000 jumped significantly higher than their counterparts from 1963, 1970 and 1989.

The balls were then dissected. Compression tests on the pills (rubber/cork cores) showed the 1995 and 2000 balls were dramatically less stiff and more resilient. Bounce tests on the pills found that the average height of the bounces from the 1995 and 2000 pills was 83 and 82 inches, respectively; the pills from 1963, 1970, and 1989 balls bounced an average of 62 inches. The cork area of the pills appeared darker in balls from 1989, 1995, and 2000 than those from 1963 and 1970.

Fiber experts examined the woolen windings from the balls. According to MLB and Rawlings specifications, all three layers of windings should be made of wool. A large amount of synthetic fiber (probably polyester) was found in the balls from 1989, 1995, and 2000. The 1963 and 1970 balls fit the specifications better than the newer balls (Dennis Hilliard, uri.edu, 7/2001).

David Zavagno, president of Universal Medical Systems, Inc., claims to have used industrial X-ray and CT scanners to examine baseballs actually used in games from 1917 to 2007. His studies show a significant difference in composition of the balls over the years. Matthew N. Skoufalos (*Image*, 3/19/2007) discusses Zavagno's claims and raises doubts as to whether he actually performed the scans of the baseballs. There was no published data from Zavagno to support his claims.

A major limitation in these studies is that balls of different ages are being tested. It is unclear how much of the difference is attributable to changes in ball manufacturing techniques and how much to the effects of aging.

Only a limited number of balls were examined. More reliable studies would have examined a ball used in every season since the 1950s to see how suddenly the changes occurred. If the changes in the properties of the balls occurred suddenly, that would support the "manufacturing technique" theory. That theory would be further supported if the year the sudden changes occurred corresponded with (1) a known change in ball manufacture technique or manufacturing site or (2) a year when the observed difference between GPA and BA changed suddenly. If the changes in the performance of the balls occurred gradually over many years, it would suggest the observed changes came from aging of the balls.

Multiple factors probably came together to create the Pitching Era. Despite three major rule changes from 1969 to 1973 to boost offensive production, the difference between GPA and BA continued to be negative throughout the 14-year period.

New ballparks probably accounted for about a third of the falloff in offensive production. The emergence of relief pitchers and the pitching rotation likely also contributed to the dominance of pitching. And there is fair evidence that the baseball was less lively and that its composition changed with the end of the era.

Why the Pitching Era ended is less clear. One interpretation of the data is that the period that immediately followed, 1985 to 1993, which saw an average GPA of −0.0016 points, restored the balance between hitting and pitching to the levels seen in the 1950s and since 2005.

Another interpretation is that the Pitching Era faded and what has been referred to as the Steroid Era, which favored hitting, slowly took over. Other than a couple of aberrant seasons from 1985 to 1987, there is an almost linear increase in the difference between GPA and BA from 1980 (the peak of the Pitching Era) to 2000 (the peak of the Steroid Era).

The potential causes for increased offensive production during the Steroid Era are discussed in the next chapter.

The Steroid Era, 1994–2004

This book defines the Steroid Era as the unprecedented string of 11 years, from 1994 to 2004, in which the difference between GPA and BA for a whole season was positive (average +0.0034 points). The 1999 and 2000 seasons in the heart of the era had GPA − BA differences of +0.0051 and +0.0073, which were higher than any other seasons between 1952 and 2012. The 2001 season had a GPA − BA difference of +0.0044, which (other than 1999 and 2000) had only been matched by the 1955 season.

	ERA	GPA	BA	OBP	SLG	PA	Hits	RBI	HR
0 Outs	3.40	0.277	0.278	0.341	0.454	65,717	16,222	5,604	2,121
1 Out	5.47	0.279	0.274	0.346	0.436	63,117	15,092	9,316	1,776
2 Outs	5.53	0.277	0.258	0.347	0.421	61,427	13,932	8,815	1,796
Bases Empty	1.28	0.275	0.266	0.335	0.433	102,854	24,775	3,221	3,221
1st Only	3.18	0.281	0.286	0.350	0.457	34,991	8,846	3,050	1,098
2nd or 3rd	12.62	0.281	0.269	0.360	0.431	52,416	11,625	17,464	1,374
3rd, <2 Outs	24.20	0.293	0.337	0.373	0.532	10,982	2,708	7,124	314
Total	4.77	0.278	0.270	0.345	0.437	190,261	45,246	23,735	5,693

Table 12.1. Statistics by base-out state for the 2000 season.

The 2000 season was in the middle of the Steroid Era and had a difference of +0.0073 points between GPA and BA. The BA for the 2000 season was 0.270, but the GPA was significantly higher for all base-out states shown in Table 12.1. Batters were particularly productive in base-out states with a runner on third base and less than two outs, their GPA (0.293) climbing 0.023 points higher than the BA for that year. Why was the GPA so much higher than the BA in 2000?

The events that resulted from plate appearances (PAs) in the 2000 season are summarized in Table 12.2, along with the MLB average from 1952 to 2012. The GPA from the 2000 season was 0.019 points higher than the average GPA (aGPA) from 1952 to 2012.

During the 2000 season, batters struck out 1.30 percent more frequently but also walked 0.97 percent more often than the MLB average from 1952 to 2012. Batters likewise had 0.46 percent fewer singles but 0.60 percent more doubles and 0.65 percent more home runs than the MLB average.

Combine clutch hitting with more walks, doubles, and home runs and the 2000 season had the highest single-season difference between GPA and BA of any season from 1952 to 2012. The +0.0073-point difference between GPA and BA represents additional production not reflected in the batting average.

The Steroid Era, 1994 to 2004

	— MLB Average 2000 —			— MLB Avg. 1952 to 2012 —		
	aGPA	× FracPA	= GPA	aGPA	× FracPA	= GPA
Any Out	−0.020	0.6472	−0.013	−0.015	0.6650	−0.010
Strike Out	−0.022	0.1638	−0.004	−0.017	0.1508	−0.003
Double/Tr Play	−0.561	0.0248	−0.014	−0.553	0.0246	−0.014
Walk	0.577	0.0959	0.055	0.569	0.0862	0.049
HBP/Interference	0.612	0.0084	0.005	0.605	0.0067	0.004
Error	0.782	0.0108	0.008	0.766	0.0115	0.009
Any Hit	0.932	0.2378	0.222	0.896	0.2306	0.207
Single	0.739	0.1561	0.115	0.733	0.1607	0.118
Double	1.053	0.0468	0.049	1.032	0.0408	0.042
Triple	1.346	0.0050	0.007	1.323	0.0057	0.008
Home Run	1.683	0.0299	0.050	1.670	0.0234	0.039
Extra Base Hit	1.302	0.0817	0.106	1.269	0.0699	0.088
Total	0.278	1.0000	0.278	0.259	1.0000	0.259

Table 12.2. Production by event from the 2000 season compared with the major league average from 1952 to 2012.

So is the dominance of hitters in this era explained, at least in part, by the mix of baseball parks coming into use changed the game? Select data from the chapter on ballpark corrections are shown in Table 12.3 for ballparks that opened between 1991 and 2004. The four expansion teams that began play in new parks averaged a ballpark correction of 0.006. Fourteen teams moved from old stadiums with average ballpark corrections of −0.003 into new stadiums with average ballpark corrections of −0.003.

Team	Year	Old Park	GPAbpc	Year	New Park	GPAbpc
Arizona				1998	Chase Field	−0.001
Atlanta	1996	Atl.-Fulton County	0.010	1997	Turner Field	−0.001
Baltimore	1991	Memorial Stadium	−0.008	1992	Camden Yards	−0.006
Chicago (AL)	1990	Comiskey Park	0.002	1991	U.S. Cellular Field	0.005
Cincinnati	2002	Riverfront Stadium	−0.001	2003	Great Am. Ball Pk.	0.006
Cleveland	1993	Cleveland Stadium	0.001	1994	Progressive Field	−0.003
Colorado				1995	Coors Field	0.040
Detroit	1999	Tiger Stadium	0.002	2000	Comerica Park	−0.004
Florida				1993	Sun Life Stadium	−0.011
Houston	1999	Hou. Astrodome	−0.020	2000	Minute Maid Park	0.005
Milwaukee	2000	Mil. County Stad.	−0.002	2001	Miller Park	0.000
Oakland	1994	OAC (pre-renov)	−0.016	1997	OAC (post-renov)	−0.006
Philadelphia	2003	Veterans Stadium	0.000	2004	Citizens Bank Park	0.005
Pittsburgh	2000	Three Rivers Stad.	0.001	2001	PNC Park	0.000
San Diego	2003	Qualcomm Stad.	−0.016	2004	PETCO Park	−0.025
San Francisco	1999	Candlestick Park	−0.010	2000	AT&T Park	−0.001
Sea. Mariners	1998	The Kingdome	0.003	1999	Safeco Field	−0.013
Tampa Bay				1998	Tropicana Field	−0.005

Table 12.3. Teams with new stadiums from 1991 to 2004. The second, third, and fourth columns show the old park name, last year in use, and GPA ballpark correction for 1973 to 1996. The final three columns on the right show the new park name, the year it opened, and GPA ballpark correction from 1997 to 2009.

There were 30 MLB teams by the 1998 season. Taken together the 18 new stadiums from 1991 to 2004 account for a change in GPA of 0.000 points ((0.0058 × 4 + (−0.0026 − 0.0031) × 14) / 30). The average GPA from 1973 to 1992 was 0.254 and rose to 0.270

from 1993 to 2004. Therefore, the new parks do not account for any significant portion of the rise seen in GPA over this era.

The evidence that the ball may be livelier during the Steroid Era is discussed in the previous chapter. The "dilution of MLB talent" theory, which doesn't have the weight of evidence behind it, is discussed there as well.

The average baserunning correction during the Pitching Era was 0.0014 and improved to 0.0021 during the Steroid Era. Improved baserunning, which largely consisted of more success stealing bases, accounts for a 0.0007-point improvement in GPA during the 11-year period.

Anabolic steroids may improve a player's performance by helping to build muscle directly through a number of metabolic pathways and indirectly by promoting more aggressive behavior, including stimulating a player to practice more and with less fatigue for longer periods.

Anonymous steroid tests from the 2003 season showed that between 5 and 7 percent of the players were positive. Under the collective bargaining agreement that took effect on Sept. 30, 2002, random steroid testing was implemented for the 2004 season.

During the 2004 season, each player was tested only once a year and only during the season. A first positive steroid test resulted in treatment alone with no suspension, while a second positive brought a 15-day suspension. No players were suspended for steroid use during the 2004 season. It was still possible for players to use steroids in the off-season and after their random test during the season without any fear of being caught.

Largely because of the public and congressional outcry about their policy, Major League Basebabll and the players agreed to a new and tougher steroid-testing policy for the 2005 season. Banned substances now included steroids, steroid precursors, designer steroids, masking agents and diuretics. There would be unannounced mandatory tests of each player during the season. In addition, randomly selected players would be tested throughout the year, with no maximum number of tests per player. Any positive test would result in a suspension without pay.

We know that steroids were a widespread problem in baseball for a number of years until effective steroid testing was implemented for the 2005 season. That was also the season that the string of 11 years with a positive difference between GPA and BA was broken. From 2005 to 2012, the average GPA — BA difference has been close to 0, as it was during the mid–1980s and from 1952 to 1971.

As discussed in the previous chapter, athletic performance has improved gradually over the last 60 years in virtually every sport, including baseball, in which an individual athletic accomplishment can be measured or timed.

If improved athletic performance accounts for the transition from the Pitching Era to Steroid Era, the improvement should be gradual and spread over many years. From 1980 to 2000 (solid line in Figure 2) there was almost a linear increase in the GPA — BA differential. Some of this improvement is presumably from steroids and some from improved athletic performance unrelated to them.

From April 2005 to November 2012, there were 38 positive tests for steroids or other performance-enhancing drugs in major league players (www.baseball-almanac.com, accessed November 2012). Nine suspensions have come since April 2008, including two by Manny Ramirez. Because of the improved testing for performance-enhancing drugs, steroids were

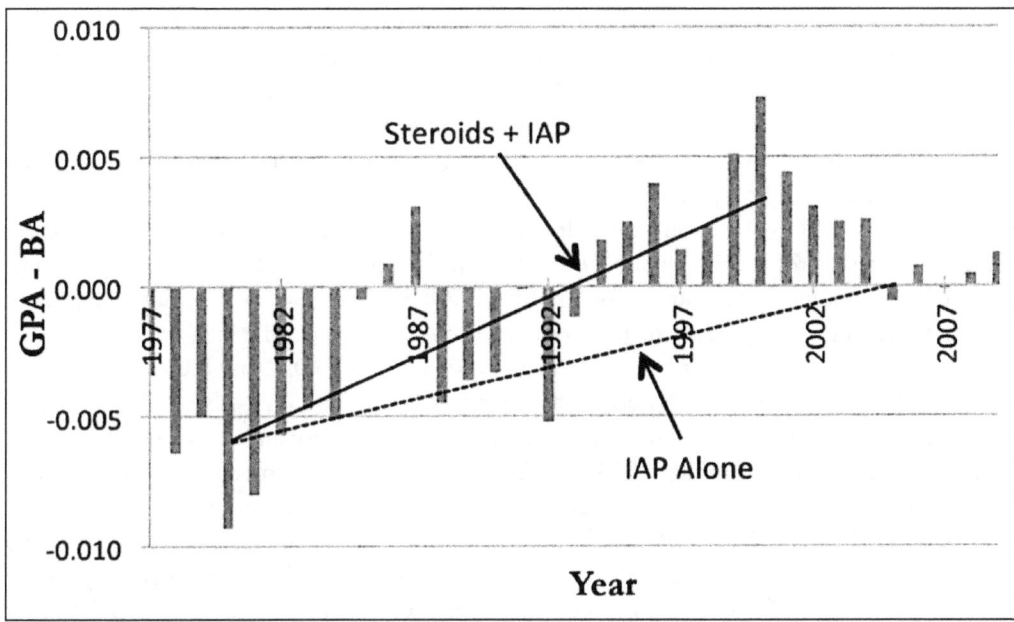

Figure 2. GPA — BA from individual seasons from 1977 to 2009. (The initialism "IAP" stands for improved athletic performance.)

almost certainly not a significant contributor to the athletic performance of the MLB player from 2005 to 2012. A few performance-enhancing drugs such as human growth hormone (HGH) still go undetected with the current MLB drug testing program, but it is not clear that HGH significantly boosts athletic performance as steroids do.

The improved performance of major league hitters from 1980 to 2005 (dash line in Figure 2) is likely attributable to improved athletic performance unrelated to steroids. The improved performance from 1980 to 2000 includes both the net effects of steroids and improved training methods. The difference between these lines is likely the net effect of steroids on the game of baseball during this era.

The GPA — BA differential increased 0.091 GPA points from the Pitching Era (average −0.0057 from 1971 to 1984) to the Steroid Era (average +0.0034 from 1994 to 2004). The average GPA — BA difference increased 0.0057 points from the Pitching Era to 2005 (−0.0057 to 0.0000).

It is assumed that improved athletic performance (including better baserunning) accounts for the slow and gradual improvement seen in GPA — BA from the Pitching Era to today. Of the increase in GPA — BA seen in the heart of the Steroid Era in 2000, 0.0046 GPA points (20 / 25 × 0.0057) was attributable to improved athletic performance and 0.0045 due to steroids (0.0091 − 0.0046). Of the 0.0046 points from improved athletic performance, 0.0007 is attributable improved baserunning and 0.0038 points to other benefits of improved training techniques.

A good estimate is that 7 percent of players were using steroids during this era (the high end of the range disclosed based on 2003 testing). Working from that estimate, the average steroid user would have seen a net increase in performance of 0.064 GPA points (0.0045/0.07).

There is some uncertainty in these estimates. The 0.0045-point improvement in GPA that is attributable to steroids is a net effect. The benefit hitters gained from using steroids may have been partially offset by the advantage some pitchers gained by using steroids. Individual hitters may have benefited from steroids more (if the 7 percent estimate is high) or less (if the 7 percent estimate is low), depending on the actual number of steroid users.

The percentage of players who used steroids and how long they used them during this era will never be known for certain. A low estimate of 5 percent can be chosen based on direct test results from 2003. A high estimate will be an informed guess, but 14 percent (double the high end of the range disclosed from 2003 testing) seems a reasonable guess.

If 5 percent to 14 percent of players were using steroids during this era, the average user would have seen a net increase in performance of between 0.032 and 0.090 GPA points.

The chapter "Chance in Baseball" demonstrates that the GPA—BA difference for a whole season can vary by ±0.0018 from its true value (in 90 percent of seasons) because of chance alone. The average GPA—BA difference during the pitching and steroids eras was used to provide a best estimate of the effects of those eras on production by hitters.

It is possible the GPA—BA difference of −0.0093 in 1980 was not attributable to chance alone but represented an actual trough of the Pitching Era. It is likewise possible that the differential of +0.0073 in 2000 represented an actual peak of the Steroid Era. If this were true, the GPA—BA difference would have increased 0.0163 GPA points from 1980 to 2000. Of that total, 0.0074 GPA points (20 / 25 × 0.0093) would be attributable to improved athletic performance and 0.0097 to steroids (0.0163 − 0.0074).

In summary, the difference between GPA and BA provides a unique measure of added production generated by extra base hits, clutch hitting and walks. Changes in the rules, equipment and mix of stadiums in use over time will tend to be filtered out by this statistic.

The increased muscle mass and power attributed to steroid use should increase production in a way accurately measured by the GPA—BA difference.

The 0.0091 points in added production seen from the Pitching Era to the Steroid Era (1980 to 2000) can be explained by three things: (1) improved athletic performance resulting from better training techniques (excluding baserunning), which probably accounted for 41.8 percent of the increase (0.0038 points); (2) improved baserunning, which accounted for 7.7 percent (0.0007 points); and (3) steroid use, which might have accounted for the other 38.5 percent (0.0035 points).

The GPA—BA difference suggests that steroid use might have peaked during the 2000 season, but it is possible that 0.0073-point increase is the result of chance alone.

Part III. GPA, Game Strategy and the Baseball Game Simulator

The Baseball Game Simulator

How many additional runs does a star such as Albert Pujols add to a team's production? In what position in the lineup should Pujols bat to generate the most runs for the team? If two hitters have the same GPA, one slugs a lot of home runs and the other is largely a singles hitter, do they each produce the same number of runs for the team?

These are complex questions that are not easily answered from information within the Retrosheet database. One can compare how many RBI the third and fourth positions in the lineup produce, but there are so many variables that change from game to game and from team to team that it is difficult to draw any valid conclusion from the data.

A game simulator has been created to address these and other complex questions. Unlike most other attempts to simulate baseball games, these simulators use the base-out state and play results to accurately reproduce the production of a lineup or simulate a game.

— — Before — —			Play	— — Before — —			Play	— — Before — —			Play
Runners		Outs	Results	Runners		Outs	Results	Runners		Outs	Results
— — —		0	5	— — —		1	5	— — —		2	5
1B — —		0	12	1B — —		1	12	1B — —		2	9
— 2B —		0	12	— 2B —		1	12	— 2B —		2	9
— — 3B		0	11	— — 3B		1	11	— — 3B		2	8
1B 2B —		0	20	1B 2B —		1	17	1B 2B —		2	11
1B — 3B		0	20	1B — 3B		1	17	1B — 3B		2	11
— 2B 3B		0	20	— 2B 3B		1	17	— 2B 3B		2	11
1B 2B 3B		0	25	1B 2B 3B		1	19	1B 2B 3B		2	12

Table 13.1. All 24 base-out states with the number of possible play results for each. There are a total of 311 base-out-state and play-result combinations that can occur assuming runners only advance on the base paths.

The game simulator described in this chapter uses a single lineup of nine batters. In a subsequent chapter, a second simulator is described that uses two different lineups of nine batters each to simulate a game. Each batter in the simulated lineup has his production simulated based on actual plate appearances (PAs). Those PAs can come from either an individual player or from many players whose PAs are combined. The PAs for each batter can come from a single season or a range of seasons. Games are nine innings, three outs per inning, and batters one to nine take their turns at-bat with the next player due up after the third out is made leading off the next inning.

| — — Before — — | | — — After — — | | | | Run | |
Runners	Outs	Runners	Outs	Runs	Number	Expectancy	FracPA
— — —	0	— — —	1	0	388,849	0.287	0.6631
— — —	0	1B — —	0	0	145,098	0.926	0.2474
— — —	0	— 2B —	0	0	30,964	1.158	0.0528
— — —	0	— — 3B	0	0	3,490	1.425	0.0060
— — —	0	— — —	0	1	17,975	1.546	0.0307
				Total/Average	586,376	0.536	1.0000

Table 13.2. Play results with the bases empty and no outs from 1997 to 2009.

For the first example, the batter's production will be simulated based on all PAs from all players from 1997 to 2009. The batter will be an average of all major league players from 1997 to 2009.

The historical play results with the bases empty and no outs, a base-out state that occurred 586,376 times from 1997 to 2009, are shown in Table 13.2. Batters had a 66.31 percent chance of making an out, a 24.74 percent chance of reaching first base, a 5.28 percent chance of reaching second base, a 0.60 percent chance of the reaching third base, and a 3.07 percent chance of scoring a run. A similar database of play results is created for each of the other 23 base-out states for the batter.

A second database of results is created for baserunning events for the batter when he is the lead runner.

From 1997 to 2009 there were 147,244 runners who had the opportunity to advance from first with no one out (see Table 13.3). Runners had a 2.39 percent chance of making an out, a 90.71 percent chance of remaining on first base, a 6.47 percent chance of advancing to second base, a 0.42 chance of advancing to third base, and a 0.01 chance of scoring a run before the next PA was complete. A similar database of play results is created for each of the other 20 base-out states when this player is the lead runner (no running events can occur if the bases are empty with 0, 1 or 2 outs).

| — — Before — — | | — — After — — | | | | Run | |
Runners	Outs	Runners	Outs	Runs	Number	Expectancy	FracPA
1B — —	0	— — —	1	0	3,513	0.288	0.0239
1B — —	0	1B — —	0	0	133,565	0.921	0.9071
1B — —	0	— 2B —	0	0	9,532	1.166	0.0647
1B — —	0	— — 3B	0	0	624	1.440	0.0042
1B — —	0	— — —	0	1	10	1.536	0.0001
				Total/Average	147,244	0.953	1.0000

Table 13.3. Baserunning events with a man on first and no one out from 1997 to 2009 (including balks).

The single-lineup game simulator runs as follows:

1. If runners are on-base, a running event (or no attempt to advance) is randomly selected from the lead runner's database of running events.

2. Step 1 is repeated until no attempt is made to advance by any runner or the bases are empty.

3. A randomly selected play result from that batter's database of play results for the current simulated base-out state is chosen.

	— Observed 1997 to 2009 —				— Simulated 1997 to 2009 —			
Lineup	PA	PA/Game	GPA	RBI+	PA	PA/Game	GPA	RBI+
Batter 1	766	4.73	0.267	67	768	4.74	0.268	82
Batter 2	749	4.62	0.271	78	749	4.62	0.268	83
Batter 3	731	4.51	0.306	109	731	4.51	0.268	89
Batter 4	714	4.41	0.303	116	713	4.40	0.268	93
Batter 5	698	4.31	0.283	101	696	4.30	0.268	89
Batter 6	680	4.20	0.270	88	679	4.19	0.268	85
Batter 7	662	4.09	0.256	80	662	4.09	0.268	83
Batter 8	643	3.97	0.246	71	644	3.98	0.269	82
Batter 9	624	3.85	0.201	54	626	3.86	0.268	79
Total/Average	696	4.30	0.2683	84.8	696	4.30	0.2684	85.1

Table 13.4. Observed data compared to simulated data by batter position in the lineup. Simulated lineup consists of nine batters, each an average of all players from 1997 to 2009. Data from 1997 to 2009.

The first simulated lineup will consist of nine identical batters, each of whose production will be simulated based on all PAs from all players from 1997 to 2009. The average production by lineup position for all 30 MLB teams from 1997 to 2009 is shown in the left half of Table 14.5, while the simulated production is shown in the right half.

The average number of outs per MLB game from 1997 to 2009 was 53.49, slightly lower than the 54 (9 × 2 × 3) expected in a nine-inning game. Games shortened by rain and the home team (when ahead) not batting in the bottom of the ninth inning were partially offset by extra inning games.

After the game simulator's data is adjusted for average game length of 53.49 outs, the simulated data is remarkably similar to that actually observed from 1997 to 2009. The number of PAs for each lineup position in the simulated lineup is virtually identical to the data actually observed.

Run production by each batter in the simulated lineup is measured by RBI+, which is the number of RBI plus any runs that score from a PA that are usually not counted in the RBI total. These include runs that score after an error and when a batter hits into a double play.

Managers tend to place their best hitters in the third and fourth positions in the lineup and their worst hitters at the bottom of the lineup. The simulated lineup had 9 batters of equal ability. For this reason, the distribution of RBI+ that is actually observed is more weighted toward the third to fifth batting slots than in the simulated lineup. Despite this difference, the average number of RBI+ for all nine batters in the simulated lineup is virtually identical (0.3 runs per season more for each batter) to the RBI+ actually observed.

	— — — — — — Fraction Run Distribution in an Inning — — — — — —								
Lineup	0	1	2	3	4	5	6	7	8
Observed	0.7101	0.1554	0.0723	0.0343	0.0159	0.0071	0.0030	0.0011	0.0005
Simulated	0.7085	0.1555	0.0734	0.0346	0.0159	0.0070	0.0030	0.0013	0.0005

Table 13.5. Observed data compared with simulated data by run distribution in an inning. The simulated lineup consists of nine batters, each an average of all players from 1997 to 2009.

Another way to compare actual and simulated games is to look at the distribution of runs scored in an inning. Simulated games are 0.16 percent less likely to have innings where no runs score, and that largely accounts for the 0.3 extra RBI+ per season for each batter in the simulated lineup.

A player can bat anywhere from first to ninth in a simulated lineup. That player's performance in the simulation will be based on the play results for each base-out state that arose from his simulated lineup position. If the mix of base-out states in the simulation differs from what he actually faced in games, his GPA in the simulation may vary slightly from his observed GPA in actual games.

As the number of games simulated increases, the data produced by the game simulator becomes more stable (that is, it does not change as the number of games simulated increases). Each example in this book was created by simulating 10,000,000 games, which produces data that is accurate to 0.01 percent.

Based on PAs, RBI+, and run distribution in an inning, the single-lineup baseball game simulator very accurately reflects baseball data that was actually observed from 1997 to 2009.

Constructing the Best Lineup

This chapter takes up another perennially asked question: In what position in the lineup should the best hitter bat to generate the most runs? Is it third or fourth, as the received wisdom suggests? Or have managers gotten it wrong all these years?

Lineup	*Observed 1997 to 2009*				*Simulated 1997 to 2009*			
	PA	GPA	GPAbrc	RBI+	PA	GPA	GPAbrc	RBI+
Batter 1	766	0.267	0.004	67	767	0.268	0.002	82
Batter 2	749	0.271	0.003	78	749	0.268	0.002	83
Batter 3	731	0.306	0.003	109	731	0.268	0.002	89
Batter 4	714	0.303	0.002	116	713	0.268	0.002	93
Batter 5	698	0.283	0.002	101	696	0.268	0.002	89
Batter 6	680	0.270	0.001	88	679	0.268	0.002	85
Batter 7	662	0.256	0.001	80	662	0.268	0.002	83
Batter 8	643	0.246	0.001	71	644	0.269	0.002	82
Batter 9	624	0.201	0.002	54	625	0.268	0.002	79
Total/Average	696	0.2683	0.0021	84.8	696	0.2684	0.0022	85.1

Table 14.1. Observed data compared with simulated data by batter position in the lineup. (Same data as in Table 13.5.)

Table 15.1 compares observed data from 1997 to 2009 with simulated data by batter position in the lineup. The simulated lineup consists of nine batters, each an average of all players from 1997 to 2009.

This simulation shows the fourth position in the lineup generates the most RBI+ per season. The third and fifth positions in the lineup each generate four fewer RBI+ per season than the fourth position. The third position in the lineup gets an average of 18 more PAs per season than the fourth position, but this increased opportunity is offset by fewer baserunners to drive in. The fifth position in the lineup sees an average of 17 fewer PAs than the fourth position, and this decreased opportunity is not offset by more baserunners to drive in.

Based on this simulation, the best hitter should bat fourth and the next two best hitters should bat third and fifth in no particular order. The fourth-best hitter should bat sixth. The fifth- and sixth-best hitters should bat second and seventh, in no particular order. The seventh- and eighth-best hitters should bat first and eighth in no particular order. The worst hitter should bat ninth.

Lineup	——————— Best to Worst Hitters in a Lineup ———————								
	1	2	3	4	5	6	7	8	9
Observed	6th	4th	1st	2nd	3rd	5th	7th	8th	9th
Simulated	7th/8th	5th/6th	2nd/3rd	1st	2nd/3rd	4th	5th/6th	7th/8th	9th

Table 14.2. Observed order managers bat their best to worst hitters compared with the order suggested by simulation. The simulated lineup consists of nine batters, each an average of all players from 1997 to 2009.

The actual order that managers bat their best to worst hitters (by GPA) differs from that suggested by the simulation. Managers tend to stack the top half of the lineup with their best hitters when this first simulation suggests that having them in the middle of the lineup might be more productive.

Player	Years	GPA	GPAbrc	cGPA	BA	OBP	Ave. Salary
Hernandez, R.	2001–2009	0.269	0.001	0.271	0.264	0.327	$4.285
Dellucci, David	2001–2009	0.269	0.002	0.271	0.249	0.336	$1.783
Johnson, Reed	2003–2009	0.269	0.003	0.272	0.282	0.344	$1.380
Upton, B.J.	2004–2009	0.269	0.005	0.274	0.266	0.352	$0.396
Baldelli, Rocco	2003–2009	0.269	0.005	0.274	0.279	0.324	$0.927
Weeks, Rickie	2003–2009	0.268	0.005	0.273	0.247	0.351	$1.453
Belliard, Ronnie	2001–2009	0.267	0.001	0.269	0.274	0.332	$1.587
Wigginton, Ty	2002–2009	0.267	0.001	0.268	0.271	0.328	$1.598
Biggio, Craig	2001–2007	0.267	0.005	0.272	0.265	0.333	$5.914

Table 14.3. Batters with average GPAs near 0.2684 from 2001 to 2009. Salaries in millions.

The approximate cost to field a lineup of average hitters based on a sample of hitters with GPAs near 0.2684 would be $2.147 million per player or $19.323 million for a lineup of nine players.

Player	Years	GPA	GPAbrc	cGPA	BA	OBP	Ave. Salary
Pujols, Albert	2001–2009	0.360	0.003	0.362	0.334	0.427	$8.326

Table 14.4. Albert Pujols's 2001 to 2009 season averages. Salaries in millions.

Another way to view the problem is to consider how much help adding Albert Pujols to various positions in the lineup would provide to a team of average hitters. For this set of simulations, Pujols's 6,082 PAs from the 2001 to 2009 seasons are pooled. The other eight batters are each an average of all players from 1997 to 2009. Pujols hit in the middle of a lineup of Cardinals players of varying abilities. The simulation places Pujols in base-out states in which his production was slightly higher than his actual GPA of 0.360.

The results of simulating games with lineups of eight average batters and Pujols are shown in Table 14.5. Pujols's production is shown on the left. The team's average production per player (including Pujols) is shown on the right.

The average number of PAs per season decreases as Pujols bats lower in the lineup. His production as measured by RBI+ (adjusting for the small differences in GPA) is greatest when he bats in the fourth position, next greatest in the third or fifth positions, next in the second or sixth positions, and so on. This is the same pattern seen in a lineup of nine average hitters. For Pujols, batting in the middle of the lineup maximizes his production.

Lineup	— — Simulated for Pujols — —				— — Simulated For Team — —			
	PA	GPA	GPAbrc	RBI+	PA	GPA	GPAbrc	RBI+
No Pujols					696	0.2684	0.0022	85.1
Pujols 1st	777	0.363	0.003	129	707	0.2796	0.0023	93.0
Pujols 2nd	759	0.364	0.003	131	707	0.2795	0.0023	93.0
Pujols 3rd	740	0.362	0.002	135	706	0.2790	0.0023	92.6
Pujols 4th	723	0.366	0.003	137	707	0.2793	0.0023	92.7
Pujols 5th	705	0.368	0.003	137	706	0.2795	0.0023	92.9
Pujols 6th	687	0.365	0.003	130	706	0.2788	0.0023	92.4
Pujols 7th	670	0.363	0.003	126	706	0.2784	0.0023	92.1
Pujols 8th	652	0.365	0.003	124	705	0.2783	0.0023	92.1
Pujols 9th	633	0.365	0.003	121	705	0.2781	0.0023	91.9

Table 14.5. Ten different simulated lineups. One is a simulation consisting of nine average players. Nine are simulations consisting of Albert Pujols batting in one of the nine positions in the lineup with the other eight positions filled with average players.

By adding Pujols to the lineup, the average RBI+ for the team increases from 85.1 to between 91.9 and 93.0. Pujols's presence makes a huge difference to team production, but where he actually bats has a smaller impact.

If Pujols bats first in the lineup, he produces 43.9 (129 − 85.1) more RBI+ than the average player he replaces, and his presence in the lineup creates opportunities for the other batters, who produce 27.2 (93.0 × 9 − 129 − 85.1 × 8) more RBI+ for the team. Team production increases by 62 percent because of Pujols's added production and 38 percent because of opportunities he creates for others with his presence in the lineup.

If Pujols bats fourth in the lineup, he produces 51.9 (137 − 85.1) more RBI+ than the average player, while his presence in the lineup creates opportunities for the other batters that produce 16.5 (92.7 × 9 − 137 − 85.1 × 8) more RBI+ for the team. Team production improves by 76 percent because of Pujols's added production and 24 percent because of opportunities he creates for others with his presence in the lineup.

As Pujols drops from first to fourth in the lineup, his production increases but overall team production falls when adjusted for Pujols's GPA. Team production falls in a linear manner as he is dropped from first to ninth in the lineup. Batting Pujols in the first or second positions in the lineup maximizes production for the whole team. The difference in production is quite small, however, with only 0.9 additional runs per season produced for the team by batting Pujols second versus fifth in the lineup ((93 − 92.9) × 9).

Pujols was a free agent after the 2011 season and signed a back-loaded contract for about $264 million dollars over 10 years. Pujols may be an unaffordable luxury for a team that consists of average players.

The team of average players has its overall GPA increase from 0.2684 to 0.2795 by placing Pujols fifth in the lineup. This is similar to the 0.2786 that would be expected by using the average GPA of Pujols and the eight average players ((0.360 + 0.2684 × 8) / 9).

Pujols's GPA of 0.360 is 0.092 points higher than the 0.268 GPA of the average player he replaces in the lineup. What about adding two players with GPAs of 0.314 (0.268 + 0.092 / 2) to the simulated lineup? The average GPA from the players in this new lineup is 0.2785 ((0.314 × 2 + 0.2684 × 7) / 9), similar to the lineup with Pujols. The two players with GPAs of 0.314 might be much more affordable for the team.

Player	Years	GPA	GPAbrc	tGPA	BA	OBP	Ave. Salary
Thomas, Frank	2001–2008	0.314	0.002	0.316	0.262	0.376	$7.184
Bay, Jason	2003–2009	0.314	0.004	0.319	0.280	0.376	$2.744

Table 14.6. Season averages for Frank Thomas from 2001 to 2009 and Jason Bay from 2003 to 2009.

Jason Bay and Frank Thomas had GPAs of 0.314 for the period from 2001 to 2009. Bay signed a four-year free-agent contract with the Mets for the 2010 to 2013 seasons for $8.625 million per season. Two players of this caliber might be obtained for half the price of signing Pujols.

	Simulated for Thomas+Bay				— — Simulated for Team — —			
Lineup	PA	GPA	GPAbrc	RBI+	PA	GPA	GPAbrc	RBI+
No T+B					696	0.2684	0.0022	85.1
T+B 1st and 2nd	770	0.314	0.003	107	708	0.2792	0.0025	93.1
T+B 2nd and 3rd	750	0.313	0.003	112	707	0.2789	0.0025	92.9
T+B 3rd and 4th	733	0.314	0.002	116	707	0.2789	0.0024	92.8
T+B 4th and 5th	715	0.315	0.003	116	707	0.2793	0.0023	92.8
T+B 5th and 6th	697	0.315	0.003	112	707	0.2787	0.0024	92.7
T+B 6th and 7th	680	0.315	0.003	108	706	0.2784	0.0024	92.4
T+B 7th and 8th	662	0.314	0.003	106	706	0.2781	0.0024	92.2
T+B 8th and 9th	644	0.315	0.003	104	706	0.2778	0.0024	92.0
T+B 1st and 5th	742	0.313	0.002	110	707	0.2787	0.0024	92.7

Table 14.7. Ten different simulated lineups. One is a lineup consisting of nine average players. Nine are simulations with Frank Thomas and Jason Bay in the lineup and the other seven positions filled with average players.

The results of simulating games with lineups of seven average batters and Thomas and Bay are shown in Table 14.7. Thomas and Bay's production is shown on the left (as the average of both players); the team's average production per player (including Thomas and Bay) is shown on the right.

The average number of PAs by Thomas and Bay decrease as they bat lower in the lineup. Their production, as measured by RBI+, follows the same pattern seen in a lineup of nine average hitters or eight average batters and Pujols.

Thomas and Bay increase the average RBI+ for the team from 85.1 to between 92.0 and 93.1, producing almost exactly the same effect as Pujols on a lineup of eight average batters.

If Thomas and Bay bat second and third in the lineup, they produce 53.8 ((112 − 85.1) × 2) more RBI+ than the average players they replace, while their presence in the lineup creates opportunities for the other batters that produce 16.4 (92.9 × 9 − 112 × 2 − 85.1 × 7) more RBI+ for the team. Team production increases 77 percent because of Thomas and Bay's added production and 23 percent because of opportunities they create for others with their presence in the lineup.

As Thomas and Bay drop from first and second to fourth and fifth in the lineup, their production increases, but overall team production falls. Team production falls in a linear manner, in fact, as they drop from the top to the bottom of the lineup. For Thomas and Bay, as for Pujols, batting in the middle of the lineup maximizes their production. Batting them in the first and second positions in the lineup maximizes production for the whole team.

Player	Years	GPA	GPAbrc	cGPA	BA	OBP	Ave. Salary
Pena, Carlos	2001–2009	0.300	0.002	0.302	0.247	0.355	$3.171
Sexson, Richie	2001–2008	0.299	0.001	0.300	0.258	0.348	$8.512
Lee, Carlos	2001–2009	0.297	0.002	0.299	0.290	0.346	$8.144

Table 14.8. Season averages for Carlos Pena and Carlos Lee from 2001 to 2009 and Richie Sexton from 2001 to 2008. Salaries in millions.

Carlos Pena, Richie Sexson and Carlos Lee are the three players who have GPAs closest to 0.299 for the period from 2001 to 2009. Pena signed a three-year contract with the Rays for the 2008 to 2010 seasons for $8.042 million per season; Sexton signed a four-year contract with the Mariners for the 2005 to 2008 seasons for $12.5 million per season but was released in 2008; and Lee signed a six-year free-agent contract with the Astros for the 2007 to 2012 seasons for $16.667 million per season.

One might think three players with GPAs of 0.299 would be more affordable than two players with GPAs of 0.314. It turns out that Pena, Sexson and Lee were paid more ($37.2 million/year) than Thomas and Bay ($15.8 million/year) and more than Pujols received as a free agent.

The results of simulating games with lineups of six average batters and Pena, Sexson and Lee are shown in Table 14.9. Pena, Sexson and Lee's production is shown on the left (as the average of all three players). The team's average production per player (including Pena, Sexson and Lee) is shown on the right.

	Simulated Pena, Sexson, Lee				— — *Simulated for Team* — —			
Lineup	PA	GPA	GPAbrc	RBI+	PA	GPA	GPAbrc	RBI+
No P+S+L					696	0.2684	0.0022	85.1
1st, 2nd and 3rd	755	0.302	0.002	107	702	0.2806	0.0019	93.7
2nd, 3rd and 4th	736	0.299	0.002	114	701	0.2792	0.0019	92.7
3rd, 4th and 5th	719	0.301	0.002	117	702	0.2795	0.0019	92.9
4th, 5th and 6th	702	0.303	0.002	116	702	0.2799	0.0019	93.3
5th, 6th and 7th	684	0.302	0.002	112	701	0.2792	0.0019	92.7
6th, 7th and 8th	666	0.302	0.002	109	701	0.2790	0.0019	92.6
7th, 8th and 9th	649	0.302	0.002	106	701	0.2788	0.0019	92.5
1st, 4th and 7th	719	0.300	0.002	113	701	0.2793	0.0019	92.8

Table 14.9. Nine different simulated lineups. One is a lineup consisting of nine average players. Nine are simulations with Carlos Pena, Carlos Lee and Richie Sexson in the lineup and the other six positions filled with average players.

The average number of PAs by Pena, Sexson and Lee decreases as they bat lower in the lineup. Their production, as measured by RBI+, follows the same pattern seen in a lineup of nine average hitters, eight average batters and Pujols, and seven average batters and Thomas and Bay.

Pena, Sexson and Lee increase the average RBI+ for the team from 85.1 to between 92.5 and 93.7, almost exactly the same amount by which Pujols improves a lineup of eight average batters.

If Pena, Lee and Sexson bat second, third and fourth in the lineup, they produce 65.7 ((107 − 85.1) × 2) more RBI+ than the average players they replace, while their presence in the lineup creates opportunities for the other batters that produces 11.7 (93.7 × 9 − 107 × 3 − 85.1 × 6) more RBI+ for the team. Team production is improved 85 percent by Pena,

Sexson and Lee's added production and 15 percent by opportunities they create for others with their presence in the lineup.

As Pena, Sexson and Lee drop from the top to the middle of the lineup, their production increases but overall team production falls when adjusted for their GPAs. Team production falls in a linear manner as they drop from the top to the bottom of the lineup. Here as in the scenarios with Pujols and with Bay and Thomas, batting these above-average hitters in the middle of the lineup maximizes their production. Batting them in the first, second and third positions in the lineup maximizes production for the whole team.

A similar simulation can be run with lineups of four players with GPAs of 0.291 (and 5 average players), five players with GPAs of 0.287, six players with GPAs of 0.284, seven players with GPAs of 0.281, or eight players with GPAs of 0.280, and in each instance the simulation will yield the same results. In all these cases, the average GPA of players in the lineup is 0.279. How about simulating a lineup of nine players with GPAs of 0.279?

Player	Years	GPA	GPAbrc	cGPA	BA	OBP	Ave. Salary
Lawton, Matt	2001–2006	0.280	0.002	0.282	0.261	0.359	$1.659
Clark, Tony	2001–2009	0.280	0.002	0.282	0.248	0.326	$7.848
Dye, Jermaine	2001–2009	0.280	0.002	0.281	0.269	0.337	$5.630
Cameron, Mike	2001–2009	0.279	0.003	0.282	0.251	0.340	$1.720
DeRosa, Mark	2001–2009	0.279	0.002	0.281	0.275	0.344	$9.600
Jones, Andruw	2001–2009	0.279	0.002	0.280	0.250	0.335	$2.281
Kearns, Austin	2001–2009	0.279	0.001	0.280	0.256	0.353	$4.473
Winn, Randy	2001–2009	0.279	0.003	0.282	0.289	0.346	$8.792
Hunter, Torii	2001–2009	0.278	0.004	0.282	0.275	0.332	$5.217

Table 14.10. Batters with average GPAs near 0.279 from 2001 to 2009. Salaries in millions.

The nine players who have GPAs closest to 0.279 for the period from 2001 to 2009 are listed in Table 14.10. During those years, each player had an average salary of $5.247 million per year, for a lineup totaling $47.2 million. These players are at various points in their careers during this period, and it isn't clear that a player with a GPA of 0.279 would cost $5.247 million on the free agent market.

The lineup of 0.279 GPA batters increases the average RBI+ total from 85.1 to 92.6, a 7.5-run improvement over a lineup of average batters (GPA 0.2684). It is similar in effect to adding Pujols to a lineup of eight average batters.

Even though all the batters have GPAs of about 0.279, the number of RBI+ varies from 81 to 107 in a pattern that differs from the other simulations in this chapter. The fourth batter in the lineup has the most RBI+ in the previous simulations, but Mark DeRosa has only 88 RBI+ in the simulated lineup of 0.279 GPA hitters. The eighth batter in the lineup has one of the lowest RBI+ totals in the previous simulations, but Torii Hunter has 107 RBI+ in the simulated lineup of 0.279 GPA hitters — more than anyone else.

It may seem that when constructing a lineup, hitters with the same GPA may not be interchangeable within the lineup. This issue was explored by creating lineups with the same hitter (with a GPA of about 0.279) in all nine lineup positions. With these lineups, production as measured by RBI+ is almost identical for each player when adjusted for the small differences seen in simulated GPA.

Constructing the Best Lineup

	Simulated 0.279 GPA Lineup				— — Simulated For Team — —			
Lineup	PA	GPA	GPAbrc	RBI+	PA	GPA	GPAbrc	RBI+
1st — Clark, Tony	771	0.278	0.002	100	700	0.2788	0.0023	92.6
2nd — Dye, Jermaine	753	0.282	0.003	101				
3rd — Cameron, Mike	734	0.278	0.001	90				
4th — DeRosa, Mark	717	0.277	0.002	88				
5th — Jones, Andruw	699	0.277	0.003	102				
6th — Kearns, Austin	682	0.277	0.003	83				
7th — Winn, Randy	665	0.278	0.002	81				
8th — Hunter, Torii	648	0.280	0.001	107				
9th — Lawton, Matt	629	0.282	0.002	92				

Table 14.11. Simulated lineup consisting of nine batters, each with a GPA of about 0.279 from 2001 to 2009.

The lineup with nine different hitters with GPAs of about 0.279 has an unexpected RBI+ pattern because some players contribute to their teams' production by getting on base and moving other runners over to create opportunities for others, while some contribute with extra base hits and home runs. Neither type of player, after taking into account his GPA, is more valuable to the team's overall production.

		— — Simulated for Team — —			
Player	Simulated Lineup	PA	GPA	GPAbrc	RBI+
Clark, Tony	All Lineup Positions 1st to 9th	684	0.2784	0.0017	92.0
Dye, Jermaine	All Lineup Positions 1st to 9th	701	0.2808	0.0018	94.1
Cameron, Mike	All Lineup Positions 1st to 9th	704	0.2777	0.0027	92.1
DeRosa, Mark	All Lineup Positions 1st to 9th	707	0.2809	0.0027	94.6
Jones, Andruw	All Lineup Positions 1st to 9th	698	0.2810	0.0016	93.6
Kearns, Austin	All Lineup Positions 1st to 9th	713	0.2781	0.0018	92.1
Winn, Randy	All Lineup Positions 1st to 9th	709	0.2820	0.0027	95.0
Hunter, Torii	All Lineup Positions 1st to 9th	687	0.2785	0.0034	92.2
Lawton, Matt	All Lineup Positions 1st to 9th	708	0.2868	0.0014	97.6

Table 14.12. Nine simulated lineups each consisting of one player in all nine lineup positions with a GPA of about 0.279.

In the first part of this chapter it was shown that placing the best player at the beginning of the lineup results in more total production for the team, while placing him in the middle of the lineup increases his RBI+ total but harms the team's overall productivity. With a mixed lineup of 0.279 GPA hitters, the number of RBI+ (or HR or BA) does not accurately reflect that player's contribution to total team productivity. Only GPA does.

Player	Years	GPA	GPAbrc	cGPA	BA	OBP	Ave. Salary
Utley, Chase	2003–2009	0.319	0.005	0.324	0.295	0.379	$4.167
Gonzalez, Luis	2001–2008	0.309	0.002	0.311	0.285	0.381	$7.333
Pena, Carlos	2001–2009	0.301	0.002	0.302	0.247	0.355	$3.171
Vidro, Jose	2001–2008	0.289	0.002	0.291	0.299	0.363	$6.125
Cameron, Mike	2001–2009	0.279	0.003	0.282	0.251	0.340	$1.720
Dellucci, David	2001–2009	0.269	0.002	0.271	0.249	0.336	$1.783
Helms, Wes	2001–2009	0.259	0.001	0.259	0.263	0.322	$1.659
Feliz, Pedro	2001–2009	0.249	0.001	0.250	0.254	0.293	$2.336
Barajas, Rod	2001–2009	0.240	0.002	0.242	0.238	0.284	$1.333

Table 14.13. Batters with GPAs from 0.240 to 0.318 from 2001 to 2009. Salaries in millions.

Nine players with GPAs of 0.240 to 0.319 for the period from 2001 to 2009 are listed in Table 14.13. Their average GPA is 0.279, as in the previous examples in this chapter. Their production varies widely from below average to well above average and may more closely resemble a real lineup of players. From 2001 to 2009, each player had an average salary of $3.292 million per year, for toal of $29.6 million for the lineup.

LineUp	*Simulated 0.240–0.319 Lineup*				*— — Simulated for Team — —*			
	PA	GPA	GPAbrc	RBI+	PA	GPA	GPAbrc	RBI+
1st — Utley, Chase	774	0.311	0.003	93	705	0.2795	0.0020	93.0
2nd — Gonzalez, Luis	757	0.311	0.003	95				
3rd — Pena, Carlos	739	0.299	0.002	111				
4th — Vidro, Jose	721	0.290	0.002	104				
5th — Cameron, Mike	704	0.277	0.001	101				
6th — Dellucci, David	688	0.267	0.001	95				
7th — Helms, Wes	671	0.258	0.001	77				
8th — Feliz, Pedro	652	0.250	0.002	87				
9th — Barajas, Rod	632	0.240	0.002	73				

Table 14.14. A simulated lineup consisting of nine batters with GPAs of 0.240 to 0.318 from 2001 to 2009. The best hitters are placed at the top of the lineup.

The lineup of 0.240 to 0.319 batters is simulated in two ways: (1) with the best hitters at the top of the lineup and (2) in the order favored by managers. The results are almost identical when corrected for the small difference in GPA each lineup produces in the simulation. Both lineups increase the average RBI+ for the team from 85.1 to 93.0 or 93.5 compared with a lineup of average (0.2684) batters. This increase is similar to the one observed by adding Pujols to a lineup of eight average batters.

LineUp	*Simulated 0.240–0.318 Lineup*				*— — Simulated For Team — —*			
	PA	GPA	GPAbrc	RBI+	PA	GPA	GPAbrc	RBI+
1st — Dellucci, David	775	0.266	0.003	76	705	0.2800	0.0020	93.5
2nd — Vidro, Jose	758	0.290	0.004	77				
3rd — Utley, Chase	739	0.318	0.002	110				
4th — Gonzalez, Luis	722	0.311	0.002	111				
5th — Pena, Carlos	706	0.301	0.002	120				
6th — Cameron, Mike	689	0.278	0.001	99				
7th — Helms, Wes	672	0.257	0.001	82				
8th — Feliz, Pedro	654	0.245	0.001	90				
9th — Barajas, Rod	634	0.241	0.002	73				

Table 14.15. A simulated lineup consisting of nine batters with GPAs of 0.240 to 0.318 from 2001 to 2009. The best hitters are in the middle of the lineup, in the order favored by managers.

From these simulated lineups it appears the best lineup is constructed by placing the best hitters at the top of the lineup, although the advantage over the traditional batting order, with the best hitters in the middle, is small. Over the course of a season, a lineup with the best hitters at the top of the lineup can score as many as three more runs per season or up to 0.002 more runs per game.

The upshot? The average GPA of the lineup is much more important than the order in which the individual players bat.

Players can contribute to their team's production by creating opportunities for others or driving in runs. Neither type of player, after taking into account his GPA, is more valuable to the team's overall production.

Run Production

What is the relationship between the average GPA of the whole lineup and the runs that lineup produces? This question will be answered in two ways: (1) by simulating lineups with batters all having the same GPA and (2) by examining historical team data for a season.

The GPA for a team has ranged from 0.231 to 0.280 for a whole season. Individual players can be used in simulated lineups with average GPAs above and below the range observed for teams for whole seasons.

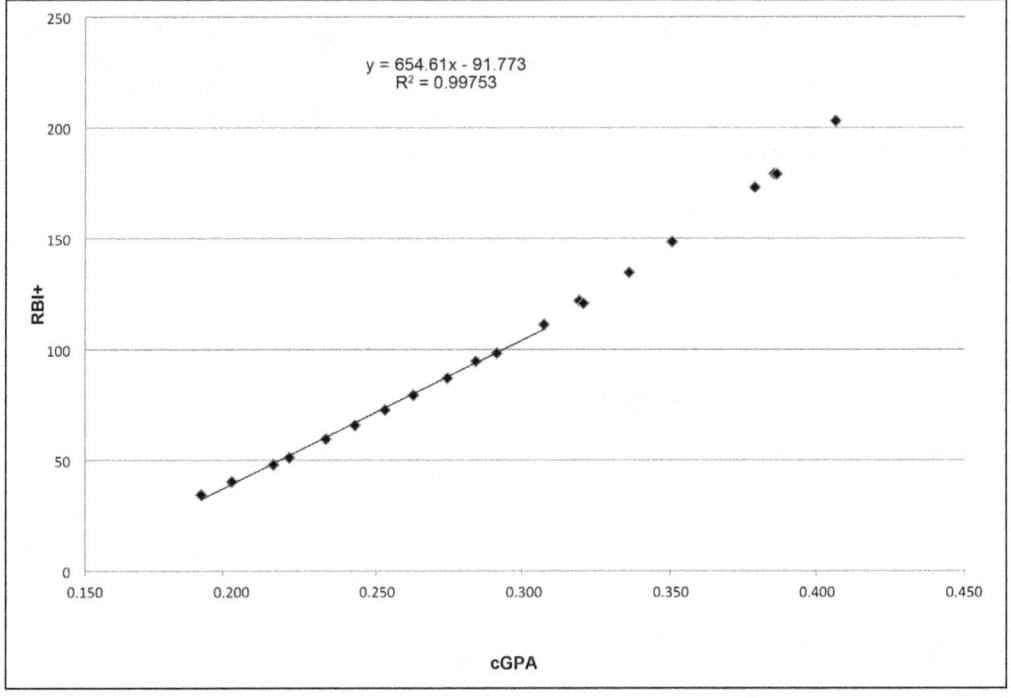

Figure 3. Corrected GPA (cGPA) vs RBI+ for simulated players or seasons in Table 16.1.

Simulating lineups of batters all with the same GPA confirms that there is an almost linear relationship between the lineup's average corrected GPA (cGPA), which is the sum of GPA and GPAbrc, and production as measured by RBI+ when the corrected GPA is less than 0.300. An R^2 of 0.9975 indicates that the regression line almost perfectly fits the data. (An R^2 is a statistical measure of how well the regression line approximates the real data points, with 0.0 denoting that it does not explain any variation and 1.0 denoting that it perfectly explains the observed variation.)

LineUp	Years	Observed Data			Simulated Data			
		GPA	GPAbrc	RBI+	PA	GPA	GPAbrc	RBI+
Lanier, Hal	1964–1973	0.1817	0.002	29	622	0.1873	0.0024	34.5
Flynn, Doug	1975–1985	0.1941	0.001	28	635	0.1999	0.0002	40.4
Ordonez, Rey	1996–2004	0.2108	0.001	34	651	0.2136	0.0008	48.0
Griffin, A.	1976–1993	0.2208	−0.001	32	644	0.2205	−0.0006	51.2
1968 Season		0.2311	0.0014	62	663	0.2310	0.0014	59.5
1967 Season		0.2414	0.0010	67	670	0.2414	0.0010	65.7
1978 Season		0.2515	0.0012	73	681	0.2515	0.0012	72.6
1956 Season		0.2619	0.0004	79	692	0.2619	0.0004	79.3
1994 Season		0.2715	0.0024	86	698	0.2715	0.0024	86.9
Dye, Jermaine	1996–2009	0.2809	0.002	78	702	0.2818	0.0018	94.6
Torre, Joe	1960–1977	0.2915	0.002	67	712	0.2882	0.0025	98.3
Puckett, Kirby	1984–1995	0.3012	0.002	94	721	0.3050	0.0018	111.2
Dunn, Adam	2001–2009	0.3115	0.002	88	756	0.3161	0.0026	121.9
Belle, Albert	1989–2000	0.3212	0.002	106	722	0.3182	0.0019	120.7
Musial, Stan	1952–1963	0.3311	0.001	77	761	0.3352	0.0004	134.6
Thomas, F.	1990–2008	0.3437	0.002	92	786	0.3481	0.0022	148.5
Mantle, M.	1952–1968	0.3559	0.003	94	834	0.3801	0.0050	179.2
Bonds, Barry	1986–2007	0.3645	0.005	93	822	0.3734	0.0052	173.1
McGwire, M.	1995–2001	0.3766	0.005	110	800	0.3845	0.0015	179.1
Williams, Ted	1952–1960	0.3930	0.002	64	871	0.4026	0.0036	203.0

Table 15.1. Gross Productivity Average vs. RBI+ for players or seasons shown in Figure 3.

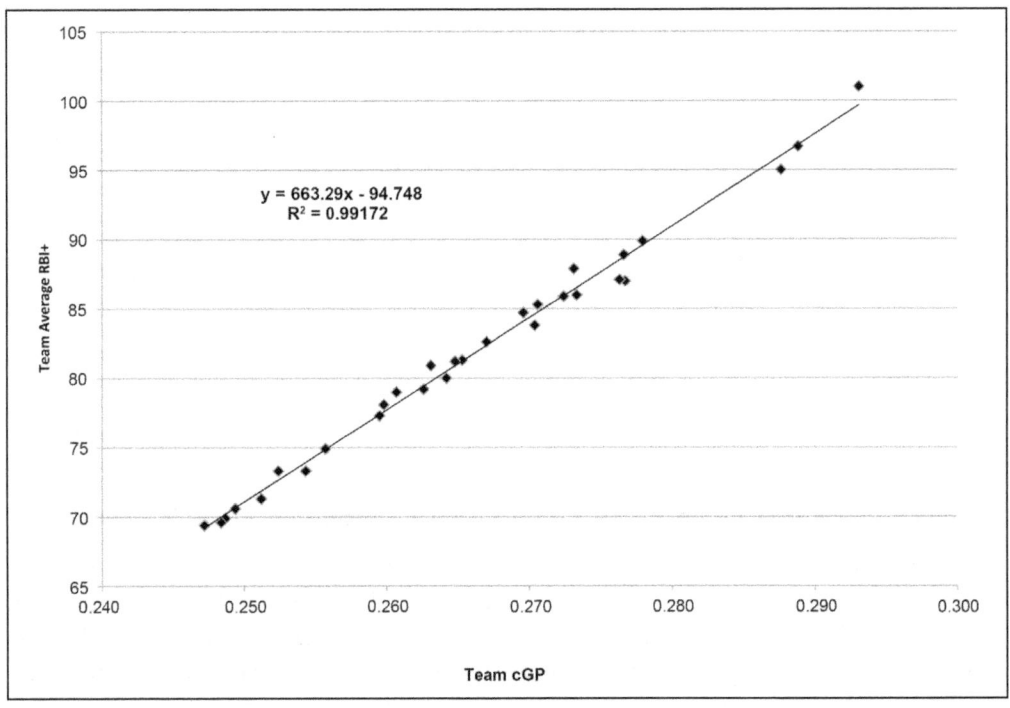

Figure 4. Corrected GPa (cGPA) vs. average RBI+ for teams from the 2009 season. (Data from Table 15.2).

Once the average cGPA of the lineup rises above 0.300, the relationship between cGPA and RBI+ is no longer linear. If you could fill a lineup with players like Albert Pujols, Ted Williams and Barry Bonds, that lineup would produce a few more runs than would be expected by just looking at the average corrected GPA of the whole lineup. How do actual team GPAs correlate with the number of RBI+ they produce during a season?

The actually observed team corrected GPA and RBI+ were very tightly correlated. An R^2 of 0.9917 indicates that the regression line almost perfectly fits the data. Although the simulated data had a slightly higher R^2 of 0.9975, this was the result of 10,000,000 simulated games while an actual season is only 162 games. A larger number of games would be expected to produce data that more accurately reflected a team's skill level.

Table 15.2 shows each team's corrected GPA and RBI+ from the 2009 season. The predicted RBI+ for each team is calculated based on the formula in Figure 3, which is derived from the simulated data. For most teams, RBI+ production is predicted almost exactly based on the whole team's corrected GPA. Tampa Bay had the largest deviation from the number of RBI+ expected of 2.4 runs per player or 21.6 runs per season (0.13 runs per game).

Team name	Year	Actual GPA	Actual GPAbrc	Actual tGPA	Actual RBI+	Predicted RBI+
NY Yankees	2009	0.2901	0.0030	0.2931	101.1	100.1
LA Angels	2009	0.2863	0.0024	0.2888	96.7	97.3
Boston	2009	0.2842	0.0034	0.2876	95.0	96.5
Philadelphia	2009	0.2748	0.0032	0.2779	89.9	90.1
Tampa Bay	2009	0.2727	0.0040	0.2767	87.0	89.4
Minnesota	2009	0.2738	0.0029	0.2766	88.9	89.3
Colorado	2009	0.2742	0.0021	0.2763	87.1	89.1
Texas	2009	0.2696	0.0037	0.2733	86.0	87.1
Toronto	2009	0.2698	0.0033	0.2731	87.9	87.0
Milwaukee	2009	0.2701	0.0022	0.2724	85.9	86.5
LA Dodgers	2009	0.2693	0.0013	0.2706	85.3	85.4
Florida	2009	0.2678	0.0027	0.2704	83.8	85.2
Cleveland	2009	0.2667	0.0029	0.2696	84.7	84.7
Oakland	2009	0.2631	0.0039	0.2670	82.6	83.0
Detroit	2009	0.2636	0.0018	0.2653	81.3	81.9
Baltimore	2009	0.2638	0.0010	0.2648	81.2	81.6
St. Louis	2009	0.2624	0.0018	0.2642	80.0	81.2
Atlanta	2009	0.2623	0.0009	0.2631	80.9	80.5
Chi. White Sox	2009	0.2604	0.0022	0.2626	79.2	80.1
Arizona	2009	0.2590	0.0018	0.2607	79.0	78.9
Washington	2009	0.2587	0.0010	0.2598	78.1	78.3
Chi. Cubs	2009	0.2586	0.0009	0.2595	77.3	78.1
Kansas City	2009	0.2535	0.0022	0.2557	74.9	75.6
NY Mets	2009	0.2509	0.0034	0.2543	73.3	74.7
Cincinnati	2009	0.2503	0.0022	0.2524	73.3	73.5
San Francisco	2009	0.2478	0.0035	0.2512	71.3	72.7
Houston	2009	0.2473	0.0022	0.2494	70.6	71.5
Seattle	2009	0.2464	0.0023	0.2487	69.9	71.0
Pittsburgh	2009	0.2460	0.0023	0.2484	69.6	70.8
San Diego	2009	0.2450	0.0023	0.2472	69.4	70.0
Average		0.2638	0.0024	0.2662	81.7	82.5

Table 15.2. Actual team GPA and RBI+ data from the 2009 season.

How well do BA, OBP and SLG correlate with offensive production as measured by RBI+?

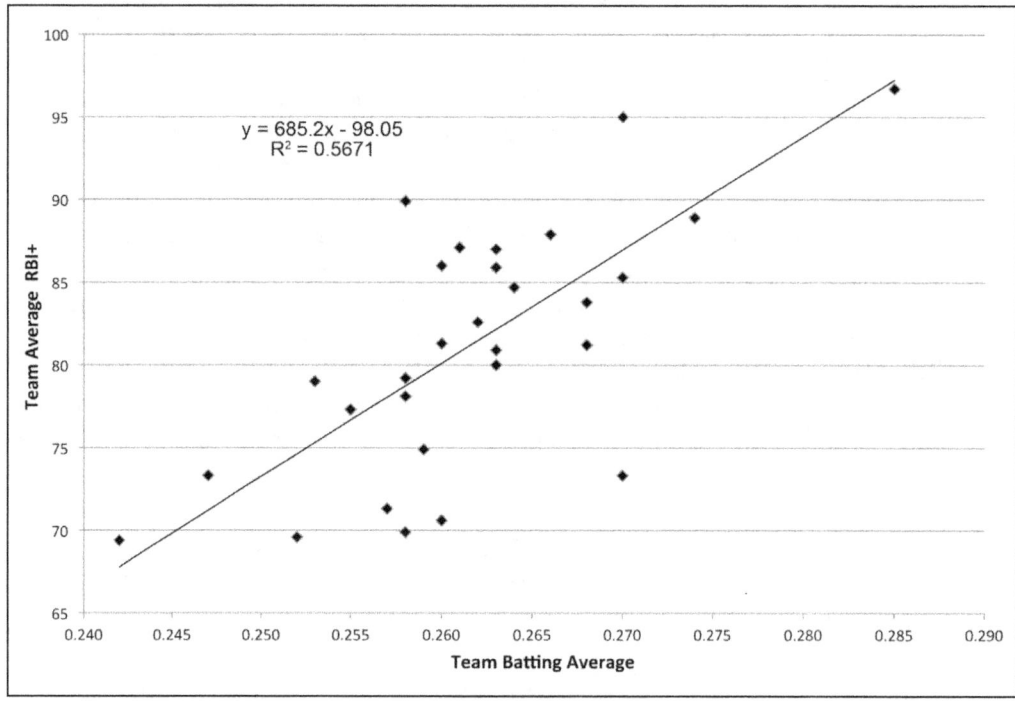

Figure 5. Batting average vs. average RBI+ for teams from the 2009 season.

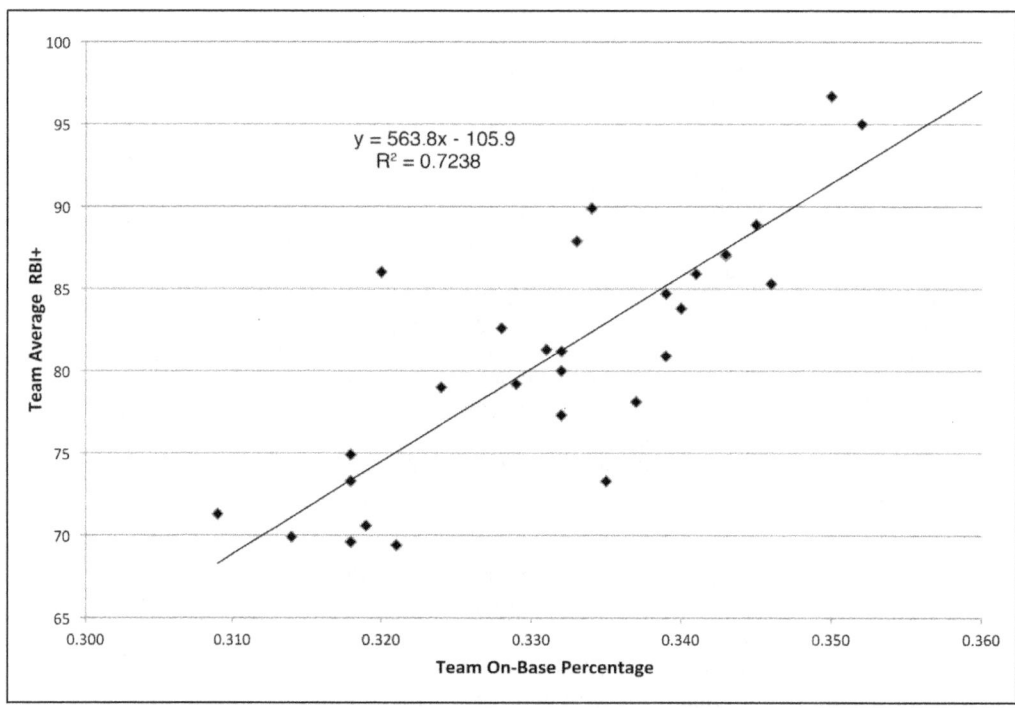

Figure 6. On-base percentage vs. average RBI+ for teams from the 2009 season.

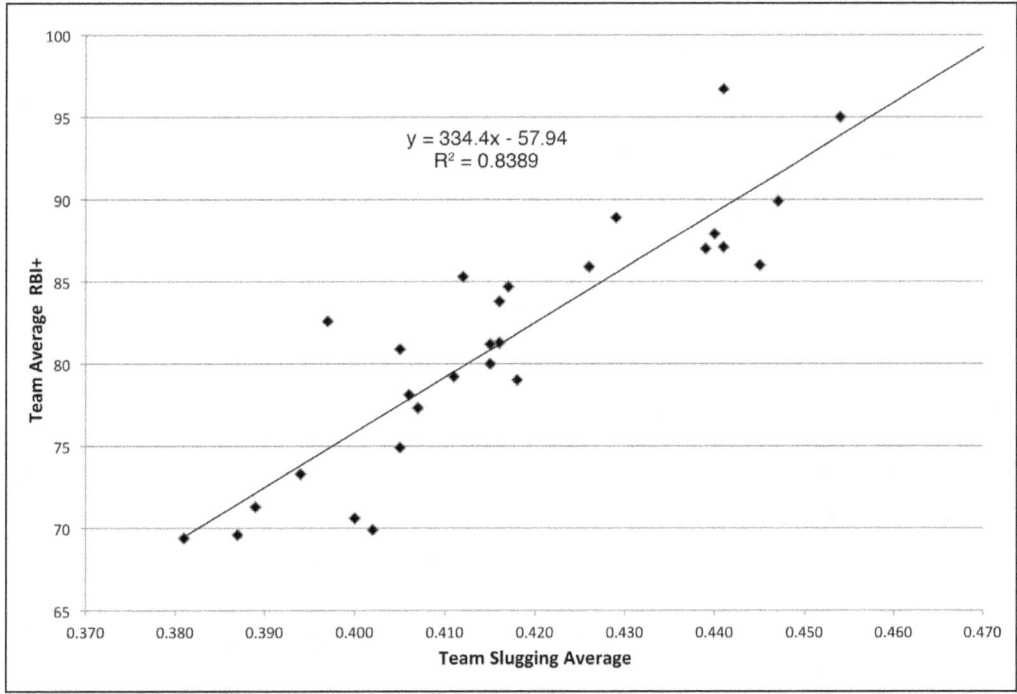

Figure 7. Slugging average vs. average RBI+ for teams from the 2009 season.

Team slugging average (SLG) had a moderate correlation ($R^2 = 0.8389$) with offensive production as measured by RBI+, followed by on-base percentage (OBP) ($R^2 = 0.7238$) and batting average ($R^2 = 0.5671$). None comes close to the very tight correlation seen with GPA ($R^2 = 0.9913$).

The last few chapters have focused on offensive production without considering the GPA of the pitchers.

How does the production of a pitching staff correlate with the team pitching GPA? Unlike batters, who are more productive when they have a high GPA, pitchers are more productive when they have a low GPA.

The actually observed team pitching corrected GPA and RBI+ allowed were very tightly correlated. An R^2 of 0.9909 indicates that the regression line fits the data almost perfectly. The total RBI+ allowed by each team for the season is divided by nine so that it is on the same scale as batters' RBI+.

Table 15.3 shows the total pitching GPA and RBI+ allowed for each team from the 2009 season. The predicted RBI+ allowed for each team is calculated based on the formula in Figure 3, derived from the simulated data. For most teams, RBI+ allowed is predicted almost exactly based on the total GPA of the team's pitchers. Pittsburgh had the largest deviation (2.1 RBI+) between predicted and actual RBI+ of any team, corresponding to 18.9 runs per season (0.12 runs per game).

The observed team ERA and RBI+ allowed were tightly correlated. An R^2 of 0.966 indicates that the regression line nicely fits the data, but the fit is not nearly as good as with team pitching GPA. This shows that although ERA is a good measure of pitching productivity, GPA measures pitching productivity much more accurately.

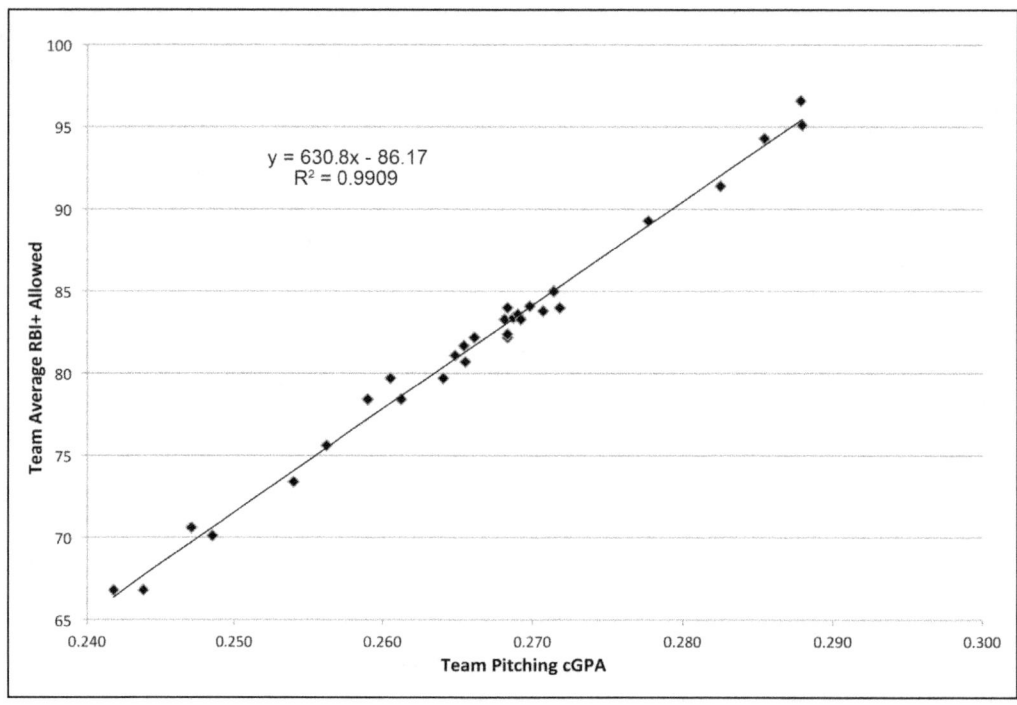

Figure 8. Team pitching cGPA vs. RBI+ allowed for the 2009 season. (Data from Table 15.3.)

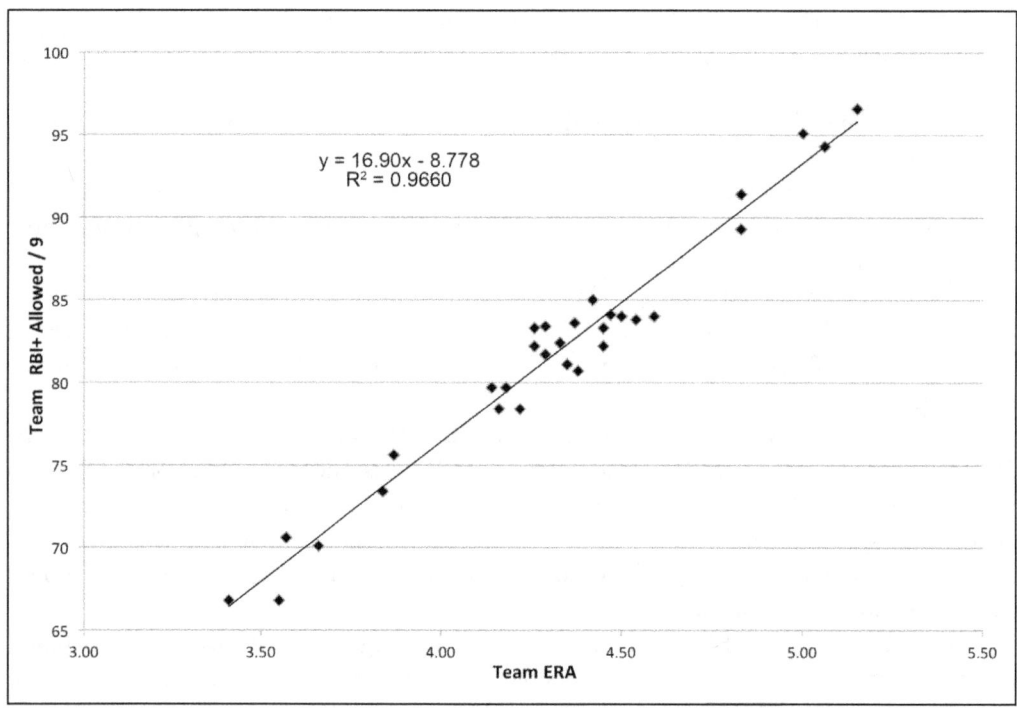

Figure 9. Team ERA vs. RBI+ allowed from the 2009 season.

| | | | ──────── Actual ──────── | | | | Predicted |
Team name	Year	ERA	GPA	GPAbrc	cGPA	RBI+	RBI+
Dodgers	2009	3.41	0.2395	0.0023	0.2418	66.8	66.5
San Francisco	2009	3.55	0.2416	0.0023	0.2439	66.8	67.9
Atlanta	2009	3.57	0.2460	0.0011	0.2471	70.6	70.0
St. Louis	2009	3.66	0.2475	0.0010	0.2485	70.1	70.9
Chic Cubs	2009	3.84	0.2518	0.0022	0.2540	73.4	74.5
Seattle	2009	3.87	0.2556	0.0006	0.2562	75.6	75.9
Philadelphia	2009	4.16	0.2581	0.0010	0.2590	78.4	77.8
Cincinnati	2009	4.18	0.2609	−0.0004	0.2605	79.7	78.8
Colorado	2009	4.22	0.2588	0.0023	0.2612	78.4	79.2
Chic White Sox	2009	4.14	0.2607	0.0033	0.2640	79.7	81.0
Boston	2009	4.35	0.2601	0.0046	0.2648	81.1	81.6
Detroit	2009	4.29	0.2642	0.0012	0.2654	81.7	82.0
Texas	2009	4.38	0.2624	0.0031	0.2655	80.7	82.0
NY Yankees	2009	4.26	0.2631	0.0030	0.2661	82.2	82.4
Oakland	2009	4.26	0.2659	0.0022	0.2681	83.3	83.7
Minnesota	2009	4.50	0.2660	0.0023	0.2683	84.0	83.9
LA Angels	2009	4.45	0.2636	0.0047	0.2683	82.2	83.9
Tampa Bay	2009	4.33	0.2660	0.0023	0.2683	82.4	83.9
Florida	2009	4.29	0.2659	0.0028	0.2687	83.4	84.1
San Diego	2009	4.37	0.2661	0.0029	0.2690	83.6	84.3
NY Mets	2009	4.45	0.2675	0.0017	0.2692	83.3	84.4
Toronto	2009	4.47	0.2683	0.0015	0.2698	84.1	84.8
Houston	2009	4.54	0.2687	0.0020	0.2707	83.8	85.4
Arizona	2009	4.42	0.2675	0.0039	0.2714	85.0	85.9
Pittsburgh	2009	4.59	0.2694	0.0024	0.2718	84.0	86.1
Milwaukee	2009	4.83	0.2751	0.0026	0.2777	89.3	90.0
Kansas City	2009	4.83	0.2785	0.0040	0.2825	91.4	93.2
Cleveland	2009	5.06	0.2813	0.0041	0.2854	94.3	95.1
Baltimore	2009	5.15	0.2855	0.0023	0.2878	96.6	96.6
Washington	2009	5.00	0.2843	0.0036	0.2879	95.1	96.7
Average		**4.31**	**0.2638**	**0.0024**	**0.2662**	**81.7**	**82.5**

Table 15.3. Observed team pitching GPA and RBI+ allowed from the 2009 season.

In summary, the GPA of the lineup accurately predicts offensive productivity as measured by RBI+. Team SLG correlates moderately well with offensive production as measured by RBI+, but OBP and BA correlate less well. None of the traditional statistics used in baseball comes close to the very tight correlation seen with GPA.

The GPA of the team's pitching staff accurately predicts the opponent's offensive productivity as measured by RBI+ allowed. Team ERA, on the other hand, is a good measure of the opponent's productivity but is not as tightly correlated.

WINNING GAMES

What is the relationship between the cumulative GPA of the lineup and winning games?

This question can be answered by simulating a game with two lineups, a visiting team and a home team. The GPA of the batters on each team can be adjusted to see how it affects the number of games each team wins. Whole MLB seasons have had GPAs ranging from 0.231 to 0.280. Individual players can be used in simulated lineups with average GPAs above and below the range observed for whole MLB seasons.

The two-lineup game simulator is similar to the one-lineup simulator used in the previous chapters but, in addition to simulating two lineups instead of one, it allows for extra innings. If a game is tied after nine innings, the simulated game continues until one team wins.

Rain-shortened games are simulated by randomly selecting games to call early after the top of the fifth inning is complete (subject to certain stipulations). The chance a game will be shortened is based on the number of games called early from 1997 to 2009, the date range supplying the data in tables 17.1–17.5. The number of innings and outs played before the game is called is likewise based on the length of shortened games from 1997 to 2009. During that era, 92 of 31,417 games (0.29 percent) were called before the top of the ninth inning was complete.

Lineup	*Fraction Inning Distribution in a Game*							
	4.5–6	*6–8 2/6*	*8.5–9*	*9.5–11*	*11.5–13*	*13.5–16*	*16.5–19*	*19.5+*
Observed	0.0005	0.0025	0.9144	0.0591	0.0173	0.0054	0.0008	0.0001
Simulated	0.0005	0.0025	0.9016	0.0683	0.0195	0.0065	0.0010	0.0002

Table 16.1. Observed innings in actual games compared to data from the two-lineup game simulator.

Lineup	*Outs Per Game*	*Runs Per Game*	*Pct. Home Wins*	*Visitor GPA*	*Home GPA*
Observed	53.49	9.57	53.98	0.2630	0.2738
Simulated	53.80	9.57	50.01	0.2684	0.2684

Table 16.2. Observed data compared with data from a two-lineup game simulator.

For the first example, the visitor and home lineups consist of nine batters, each an average of all players from 1997 to 2009. The average simulated game with these lineups includes 53.80 outs, slightly longer than the 53.49 outs observed in actual games. The home team wins 50.01 percent of the simulated games but 53.98 percent of actual games. The home-field advantage that real teams have contributes to shorter games, as the home team does not have to bat in the bottom of the ninth inning when ahead.

Fraction Run Distribution by Inning

Lineup	0	1	2	3	4	5	6	7	8
Observed	0.7101	0.1554	0.0723	0.0343	0.0159	0.0071	0.0030	0.0011	0.0005
Simulated	0.7085	0.1568	0.0731	0.0342	0.0156	0.0068	0.0029	0.0012	0.0005

Table 16.3. Observed runs by inning compared with data from a two-lineup game simulator.

There are other subtle differences between the two-lineup game simulator and actual game results. Actual games have slightly higher winning margins and are less likely to go into extra innings than the simulated games. The distribution of runs scored in an inning, however, is almost identical.

The GPAs for the simulated visitor and home lineups are the same at 0.2684, while actual visiting teams have a GPA of 0.2630 and actual home teams have a GPA of 0.2738. The difference in GPA between visiting and home teams corresponds to the home-field advantage seen in actual games and accounts for most of the differences seen between actual and simulated games.

Fraction Winning Margin Distribution

Lineup	1	2	3	4	5	6	7	8–12	13+
Observed	0.2773	0.1791	0.1464	0.1130	0.0839	0.0617	0.0459	0.0837	0.0090
Simulated	0.2925	0.1833	0.1441	0.1105	0.0827	0.0601	0.0426	0.0745	0.0097

Table 16.4. Observed winning margins in a game compared with data from a two-lineup game simulator.

So far the simulators have looked mostly at the GPA of the batters, ignoring the GPA of pitchers. They assume the GPA of batters does not change from inning to inning and game to game. In actual games, it is possible that the chance a batter will be successful may vary between plate appearances, depending on the pitcher faced. This variation may have contributed to the simulated games being slightly more competitive than actually observed games.

The results for the one- and two-lineup simulators are so close to the actually observed data that adding more complexity seems unjustified. The simulators can help us understand how to construct a lineup to score the most runs and ultimately win the most games. They can also be used to better understand ideal baseball strategies.

With the one-lineup simulator, the relationship between team GPA and run scoring was explored in the previous chapters. The two-lineup simulator can use the same approach to examine the relationship between team GPA and winning games. One lineup will consist of nine identical batters, each an individual player or a player representing the MLB average from a specific season. A second lineup will consist of nine batters, each an average of all players from 1997 to 2009.

There is an almost linear relationship between linuep cGPA (GPA + GPA baserunning correction) and the fraction of games won when the team cGPA is between 0.220 and 0.293. An R^2 of 0.9997 indicates that the regression line almost perfectly fits the data.

As the cGPA of the lineup rises above 0.300, the fraction of games won rises at a slower rate; as it falls below 0.220, the fraction of games won falls at a slower rate. The S-shaped curve formed is also called a sigmoid curve or logistic curve, and here it points to the fact that a team can win (or lose) only 162 games in a season, no matter how good (or bad).

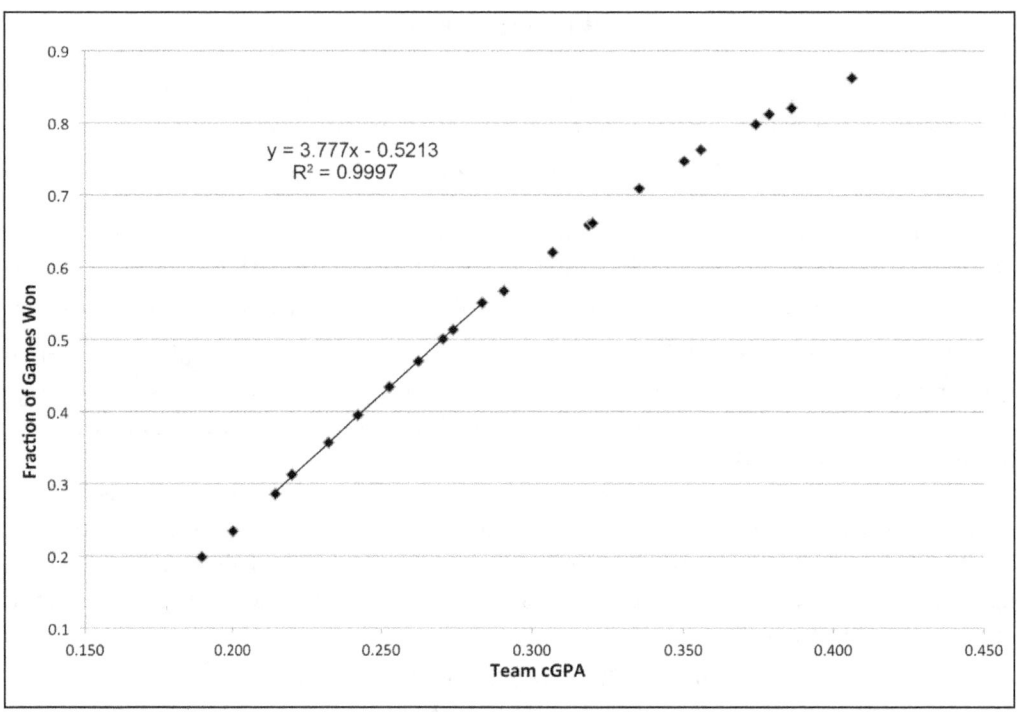

Figure 10. Team cGPA vs fraction of games won for simulated players or selected season averages (see data in Table 16.5). Lineups with these players or seasons are simulated against a second lineup consisting of nine batters, each an average of all players from 1997 to 2009.

LineUp	Years	Observed Data		Simulated Data				
		GPA	GPAbrc	GPA	GPAbrc	RBI+	WinFr	Wins
Lanier, Hal	1964–1973	0.1817	0.002	0.1873	0.0023	35.0	0.1989	32
Flynn, Doug	1975–1985	0.1941	0.001	0.1999	0.0002	40.8	0.2343	38
Ordonez, Rey	1996–2004	0.2108	0.001	0.2136	0.0008	48.5	0.2857	46
Griffin, A.	1976–1993	0.2208	−0.001	0.2206	−0.0006	51.6	0.3124	51
1968 Season		0.2311	0.0014	0.2310	0.0014	59.8	0.3572	58
1967 Season		0.2414	0.0010	0.2414	0.0010	65.8	0.3950	64
1978 Season		0.2515	0.0012	0.2515	0.0012	72.5	0.4340	70
1956 Season		0.2619	0.0004	0.2619	0.0004	79.1	0.4694	76
1997–2009 Seasons		0.2684	0.0021	0.2684	0.0022	84.6	0.5001	81
1994 Season		0.2715	0.0024	0.2716	0.0024	86.3	0.5129	83
Dye, Jermaine	1996–2009	0.2809	0.002	0.2818	0.0018	93.7	0.5509	89
Torre, Joe	1960–1977	0.2915	0.002	0.2882	0.0025	97.1	0.5671	92
Puckett, Kirby	1984–1995	0.3012	0.002	0.3050	0.0018	109.4	0.6205	101
Dunn, Adam	2001–2009	0.3115	0.002	0.3161	0.0026	119.5	0.6582	107
Belle, Albert	1989–2000	0.3212	0.002	0.3181	0.0019	118.4	0.6609	107
Musial, Stan	1952–1963	0.3311	0.001	0.3351	0.0004	131.3	0.7088	115
Thomas, F.	1990–2008	0.3437	0.002	0.3480	0.0022	144.2	0.7468	121
Berkman, L.	1997–2009	0.3466	0.002	0.3538	0.0019	147.6	0.7626	124
Pujols, Albert	2001–2009	0.3600	0.003	0.3711	0.0030	161.4	0.7979	129
Bonds, Barry	1986–2007	0.3645	0.005	0.3733	0.0052	167.1	0.8119	132
McGwire, M.	1995–2001	0.3766	0.005	0.3845	0.0015	172.8	0.8201	133
Williams, Ted	1952–1960	0.3930	0.002	0.4025	0.0036	194.8	0.8619	140

Table 16.5. Players and seasons used to fill all nine positions in simulated lineups. Simulated games were played against a lineup of average players. (Wins is the projected number of games won over a 162-game season.)

From 1952 to 2012, teams' cGPAs for a season have varied from a high of 0.308 for the 1953 Brooklyn Dodgers to a low of 0.217 for the 1963 Houston Astros. Virtually all teams since 1952 would fall in the linear portion of the curve in Figure 10, and the number of games a team wins could be predicted based on their team cGPA.

Table 16.6 shows the best and worst batting cGPAs (that is, not counting pitching cGPA) for teams between 1952 to 2012. Although there is a moderate correlation between the cGPAs and wins ($R^2 = 0.692$), team cGPA alone does not accurately predict wins. This is not surprising since team pitching was ignored in these calculations.

Player	Team	Year	GPA	GPAbrc	cGPA	BA	OBP	WinFr	Wins
Brooklyn Dodgers	BRO	1953	0.306	0.002	0.308	0.285	0.366	0.682	110
Cleveland Indians	CLE	1999	0.304	0.003	0.307	0.289	0.373	0.599	97
Seattle Mariners	SEA	1996	0.302	0.004	0.305	0.287	0.366	0.528	86
Chicago White Sox	CHW	2000	0.300	0.003	0.303	0.286	0.356	0.586	95
New York Yankees	NYY	1998	0.299	0.003	0.302	0.288	0.364	0.704	114
Colorado Rockies	COL	2000	0.299	0.003	0.302	0.294	0.362	0.506	82
Colorado Rockies	COL	1996	0.297	0.005	0.302	0.287	0.355	0.512	83
New York Yankees	NYY	2007	0.298	0.003	0.301	0.290	0.366	0.580	94
Cleveland Indians	CLE	1994*	0.297	0.003	0.300	0.290	0.351	0.593	96
New York Yankees	NYY	1994*	0.297	0.002	0.299	0.290	0.374	0.619	100
Oakland Athletics	OAK	2000	0.297	0.002	0.299	0.270	0.360	0.565	92
Boston Red Sox	BOS	2003	0.296	0.002	0.299	0.289	0.360	0.586	95
Texas Rangers	TEX	1999	0.295	0.004	0.299	0.293	0.361	0.586	95
Texas Rangers	TEX	1998	0.296	0.002	0.298	0.289	0.357	0.543	88
Cleveland Indians	CLE	1995*	0.295	0.003	0.298	0.291	0.361	0.694	112
Boston Red Sox	BOS	2004	0.295	0.003	0.298	0.282	0.360	0.605	98
:									
Houston Astros	HOU	1964	0.222	0.001	0.223	0.229	0.285	0.407	66
California Angels	CAL	1971	0.221	0.002	0.223	0.231	0.290	0.469	76
Cleveland Indians	CLE	1972	0.223	−0.002	0.222	0.234	0.293	0.462	72
Atlanta Braves	ATL	1968	0.221	0.001	0.222	0.248	0.303	0.500	81
Toronto Blue Jays	TOR	1981*	0.222	−0.001	0.221	0.226	0.286	0.349	57
New York Mets	NYM	1965	0.220	0.000	0.220	0.221	0.277	0.309	50
California Angels	CAL	1972	0.220	0.000	0.220	0.242	0.293	0.484	75
Texas Rangers	TEX	1972	0.220	0.000	0.220	0.217	0.290	0.351	54
San Diego Padres	SDP	1969	0.218	0.000	0.218	0.225	0.285	0.321	52
Los Angeles Dodgers	LAD	1968	0.217	0.000	0.217	0.230	0.288	0.469	76
Houston Astros	HOU	1963	0.214	0.003	0.217	0.220	0.283	0.407	66
New York Mets	NYM	1968	0.216	0.000	0.216	0.228	0.281	0.451	73
Chicago White Sox	CHW	1968	0.215	0.000	0.215	0.228	0.284	0.404	67
	Average		0.2587	0.0018	0.2604	0.2593	0.3268	0.500	81

Table 16.6. Best and worst batting cGPAs for teams between 1952 to 2012. (The asterisk [*] indicates a strike-shortened year.)

The same data presented in Figure 10 is displayed in Figure 11 as lineup net cGPA, which is the difference in cGPA between the simulated lineups. The regression line has been extended to include data from −0.050 to +0.050 net cGPA points and the correlation remains strong ($R^2 = 0.9979$).

Team net cGPA is defined as the difference between the cGPA of the batters and the cGPA of pitchers on that team. Historical teams will be examined to see how well their team net cGPA corresponded to games won. Table 16.7 shows the best and worst net cGPAs for teams between 1952 to 2012. There is a strong correlation between team net cGPAs and wins ($R^2 = 0.967$) for all teams over this sixty-year period.

Table 16.8 lists the teams from 1952 to 2012 with 103 or more wins (projected over a 162-game season) that did not make the list in Table 16.7. All have net cGPAs falling somewhere between +0.027 and +0.037 and came quite close to making the list.

Team	Year	— Batters — GPA	GPAbrc	— Pitchers — GPA	GPAbrc	Net cGPA	WinFr	Wins
New York Yankees	1998	0.299	0.003	0.248	0.001	0.052	0.704	114
Seattle Mariners	2001	0.292	0.003	0.243	0.001	0.051	0.716	116
Baltimore Orioles	1969	0.268	0.003	0.226	−0.001	0.046	0.673	109
Brooklyn Dodgers	1953	0.306	0.002	0.263	−0.001	0.046	0.682	110
New York Yankees	1953	0.285	−0.002	0.240	−0.002	0.045	0.656	106
Cleveland Indians	1954	0.272	−0.001	0.228	−0.001	0.044	0.721	117
Cleveland Indians	1995*	0.295	0.003	0.251	0.002	0.044	0.694	112
Atlanta Braves	1998	0.281	0.001	0.238	0.000	0.043	0.654	106
Houston Astros	1998	0.283	0.003	0.241	0.002	0.043	0.630	102
Cincinnati Reds	1975	0.276	0.005	0.236	0.003	0.042	0.667	108
Los Angeles Dodgers	1974	0.272	0.002	0.232	0.001	0.041	0.630	102
Oakland Athletics	2001	0.285	0.003	0.246	0.002	0.041	0.630	102
New York Yankees	1954	0.284	−0.001	0.241	−0.000	0.041	0.669	108
Baltimore Orioles	1970	0.271	0.002	0.234	0.001	0.039	0.667	108
New York Yankees	1961	0.279	0.002	0.241	0.001	0.039	0.673	109
New York Yankees	1956	0.291	0.000	0.253	−0.001	0.039	0.630	102
:								
New York Mets	1963	0.223	0.000	0.269	0.002	−0.049	0.315	51
Detroit Tigers	1996	0.268	0.002	0.318	0.002	−0.049	0.327	53
Oakland Athletics	1979	0.236	0.000	0.284	0.001	−0.050	0.333	54
San Diego Padres	1969	0.218	−0.000	0.265	0.002	−0.050	0.321	52
Detroit Tigers	2002	0.237	0.000	0.285	0.002	−0.051	0.342	55
Pittsburgh Pirates	1952	0.230	−0.003	0.281	−0.001	−0.054	0.325	53
Pittsburgh Pirates	1953	0.248	−0.001	0.300	0.003	−0.056	0.325	53
New York Mets	1962	0.243	0.000	0.296	0.003	−0.056	0.250	40
Philadelphia Athletics	1954	0.235	−0.001	0.291	0.000	−0.058	0.331	54
Pittsburgh Pirates	1954	0.243	−0.000	0.300	0.001	−0.058	0.344	56
Detroit Tigers	2003	0.236	0.001	0.293	0.002	−0.058	0.265	43
Pittsburgh Pirates	1955	0.226	−0.001	0.288	0.001	−0.064	0.390	63
Average		0.2587	0.0018	0.2587	0.0018	0.000	0.500	81

Table 16.7. Best and worst team net cGPAs from 1952 to 2012. (The asterisk [*] indicates a strike-shortened year.)

Team	Year	— Batters — GPA	GPAbrc	— Pitchers — GPA	GPAbrc	Tm Net cGPA	WinFr	Wins
New York Mets	1986	0.268	0.003	0.233	0.002	0.036	0.667	108
St. Louis Cardinals	2004	0.283	0.002	0.250	0.001	0.034	0.648	105
New York Yankees	1963	0.260	0.002	0.231	0.000	0.031	0.646	105
Detroit Tigers	1984	0.279	0.000	0.246	0.001	0.032	0.642	104
Oakland Athletics	1988	0.269	0.004	0.237	0.004	0.032	0.642	104
Atlanta Braves	1993	0.267	0.003	0.233	0.001	0.036	0.642	104
Detroit Tigers	1968	0.250	0.002	0.218	0.002	0.032	0.636	103
New York Yankees	1980	0.275	0.002	0.251	−0.001	0.037	0.636	103
Oakland Athletics	1990	0.262	0.002	0.234	0.002	0.028	0.636	103
New York Yankees	2009	0.290	0.003	0.263	0.003	0.027	0.636	103

Table 16.8. Teams with the most wins not listed in Table 17.11.

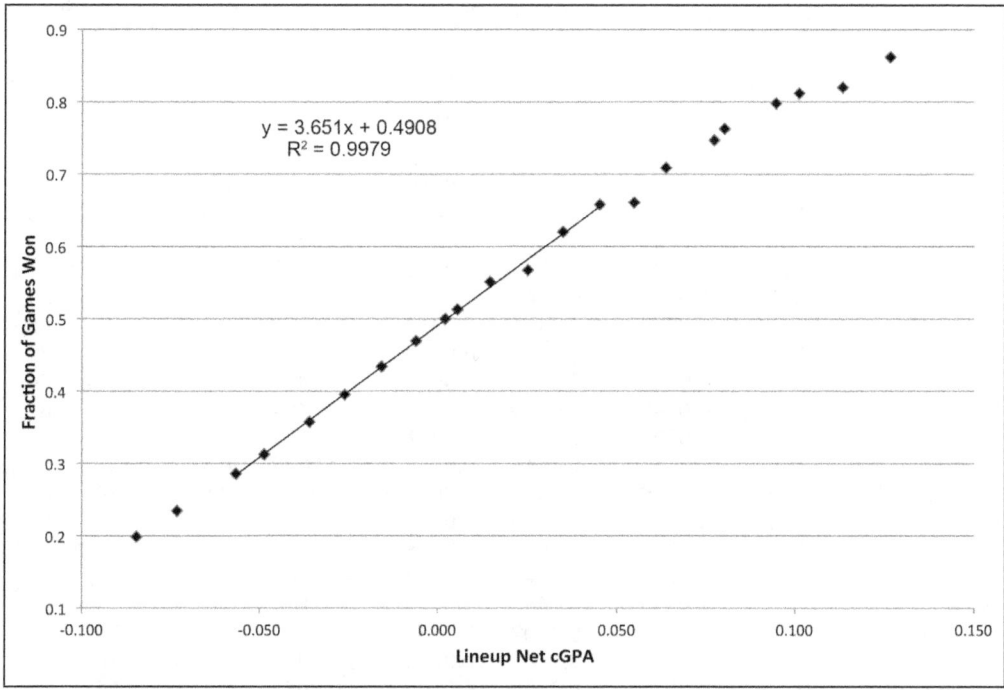

Figure 11. Lineup net cGPA vs fraction of games won for simulated players or seasons. Lineups with these players or seasons are simulated against a second lineup consisting of nine batters, each an average of all players from 1997 to 2009.

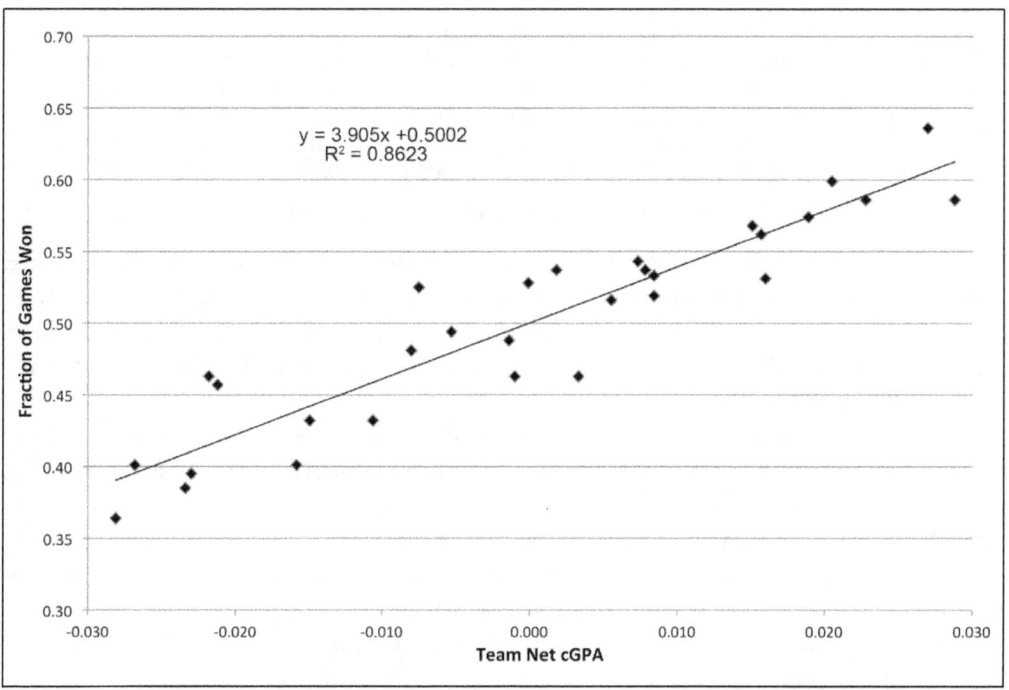

Figure 12. Team net cGPA vs fraction of games won for teams from the 2009 season.

How do actual team net cGPAs correlate with the number of wins they have during a single season?

Team	Batters GPA	Batters GPAbrc	Pitchers GPA	Pitchers GPAbrc	Net cGPA	WinFr	Wins	Pred Wins
Los Angeles	0.2693	0.0013	0.2395	0.0023	0.0288	0.586	95	97
New York (AL)	0.2901	0.0030	0.2631	0.0030	0.0270	0.636	103	95
Boston	0.2842	0.0034	0.2601	0.0046	0.0228	0.586	95	93
Anaheim	0.2863	0.0024	0.2636	0.0047	0.0205	0.599	97	92
Philadelphia	0.2748	0.0032	0.2581	0.0010	0.0189	0.574	93	91
Atlanta	0.2623	0.0009	0.2460	0.0011	0.0160	0.531	86	89
St. Louis	0.2624	0.0018	0.2475	0.0010	0.0157	0.562	91	89
Colorado	0.2742	0.0021	0.2588	0.0023	0.0151	0.568	92	88
Minnesota	0.2738	0.0029	0.2660	0.0023	0.0084	0.533	86	84
Tampa Bay	0.2727	0.0040	0.2660	0.0023	0.0084	0.519	84	84
Texas	0.2696	0.0037	0.2624	0.0031	0.0078	0.537	87	84
San Francisco	0.2478	0.0035	0.2416	0.0023	0.0073	0.543	88	84
Chicago (NL)	0.2586	0.0009	0.2518	0.0022	0.0055	0.516	84	83
Toronto	0.2698	0.0033	0.2683	0.0015	0.0033	0.463	75	81
Florida	0.2678	0.0027	0.2659	0.0028	0.0018	0.537	87	81
Detroit	0.2636	0.0018	0.2642	0.0012	−0.0001	0.528	85	79
Oakland	0.2631	0.0039	0.2659	0.0022	−0.0010	0.463	75	79
Chicago (AL)	0.2604	0.0022	0.2607	0.0033	−0.0014	0.488	79	79
Milwaukee	0.2701	0.0022	0.2751	0.0026	−0.0053	0.494	80	76
Seattle	0.2464	0.0023	0.2556	0.0006	−0.0075	0.525	85	75
Cincinnati	0.2503	0.0022	0.2609	−0.0004	−0.0080	0.481	78	75
Arizona	0.2590	0.0018	0.2675	0.0039	−0.0106	0.432	70	73
New York (NL)	0.2509	0.0034	0.2675	0.0017	−0.0149	0.432	70	71
Cleveland	0.2667	0.0029	0.2813	0.0041	−0.0158	0.401	65	70
Houston	0.2473	0.0022	0.2687	0.0020	−0.0212	0.457	62	67
San Diego	0.2450	0.0023	0.2661	0.0029	−0.0218	0.463	75	67
Baltimore	0.2638	0.0010	0.2855	0.0023	−0.0230	0.395	64	66
Pittsburgh	0.2460	0.0023	0.2694	0.0024	−0.0234	0.385	62	66
Kansas City	0.2535	0.0022	0.2785	0.0040	−0.0268	0.401	65	64
Washington	0.2587	0.0010	0.2843	0.0036	−0.0281	0.364	59	63
Average	0.2638	0.0024	0.2638	0.0024	0.0000	0.5000	81	

Table 16.9. Team net cGPAs from the 2009 season.

The observed team net cGPA and wins were well correlated ($R^2 = 0.862$). The simulated data was the result of 10,000,000 games while an actual season is only 162 games; a larger number of games would be expected to produce more accurate data. (See the "Chance in Baseball" chapter, which discusses how accurately the team net cGPA should predict the number of wins a team has for a season.)

Table 16.9 shows each team's net cGPA and fraction of games won from the 2009 season. The predicted number of wins for each team is calculated based on the formula, derived from simulated data, in Figure 11. For most teams, the number of wins in a season was within five of the total predicted based on the team net cGPA. Seattle won ten more games than predicted, which was the largest deviation seen for any of the 30 teams from the 2009 season. By chance alone, one of ten teams would be expected to be ten or more wins above or below the number of wins predicted. This topic is explored in the "Chance in Baseball" chapter.

In Summary, the team net cGPA is defined as the difference between the cGPA of the batters and the cGPA of pitchers on that team. The number of wins produced by a lineup is well correlated with the team's net cGPA. Over the range of team net cGPA seen in baseball from 1952 to 2012, there is a linear increase in the number of wins expected as net cGPA increases. A team expecting to win 0.600 of its games should have a net cGPA of 0.0256. A team expecting to win 0.550 of its games should have a net cGPA of 0.0128.

When examining data produced by the two-lineup game simulator it is important to remember the cGPA of the batters from the first lineup is the same as the cGPA of the pitchers from the second lineup. Conversely, the cGPA of the pitchers from the first lineup is the same as the cGPA of the batters from the second lineup.

Chance in Baseball

How important is it to be lucky in baseball?

Between 1997 and 2010, the New York Yankees made the playoffs 13 out of 14 seasons. How good would the Yankees have to be to make the playoffs that often? How much luck is involved in winning enough games in a season to make the playoffs?

Dustin Pedroia of the Red Sox won the 2007 American League Rookie of the Year Award with a total GPA (tGPA, which incorporates both ballpark and baserunning corrections) of 0.296. Pedroia won the 2008 AL MVP Award with a tGPA of 0.326. In 2009 his tGPA fell 0.030 points, settling again at 0.296. Was Pedroia lucky in 2008 or did his skills somehow decline in 2009?

Now consider a hypothetical, but familiar, scenario. A hitter has a strong start to the season, putting up a GPA of 0.400 in April, but by season's end has seen his GPA fall off to 0.268. Was the fast start merely luck? How much should an average hitter's results vary from week to week or month to month by chance alone?

A baseball season is 162 games long, and over the course of that season an individual hitter can amass 750 plate appearances, a team 6,000, and all 30 teams together about 180,000.

Using GPA to estimate the skill of a player, a team or the whole league is limited by the number of events sampled. The more events sampled, the more accurate the estimates. It is important to understand how much variation in GPA can be expected so that we know whether the differences seen are attributable to chance (luck) or differences in skill level.

Measures such as standard deviation can be used to gauge the accuracy of these estimates but tend to be complex and can lead to assumptions about the distribution of the data that might not be true. Simulation is easier to understand, and it provides a more accurate measure of the variation expected in a player's or team's production.

The skills of the players on a team should allow that team to win a certain fraction of its games. The true skill level of a team is impossible to know with certainty. Fans and baseball executives assume the number of wins a team has in a season reflects its talent level alone.

The regular baseball season is, at 162 games, much longer than the 82-game season of the NBA or the 16-game slate of the NFL. A major component of luck is still involved in determining the number of games a baseball team wins in a season.

Chance alone will result in a four- to 10-game variation from the expected number of wins. In Table 16.9, teams' cGPA is used to predict the number of wins in the 2009 season for each of the 30 MLB teams. For 21 of 30 teams, the actual number of wins was within four of the prediction, and for all 30 teams the actual number was within ten. Team cGPA performs as well as can be expected in predicting the number of wins a team had during a season.

Team Skill	\-\-\-\-\-\-\- Win Distribution by Percentile \-\-\-\-\-\-\-								
	1st	5th	10th	25th	50th	75th	90th	95th	99th
0.350	43	47	49	53	57	61	65	67	71
0.400	51	55	57	61	65	69	73	75	79
0.450	58	63	65	69	73	77	81	83	88
0.500	66	71	73	77	81	85	89	91	96
0.550	74	79	81	85	89	93	97	99	104
0.600	83	87	89	93	97	101	105	107	112
0.650	91	95	98	101	105	109	112	115	119

Table 17.1. Expected win distribution based on a 162-game season. Team Skill is the fraction of games that should be won based on the talent of the players on the team.

If the Yankees have a team skill level that should allow them to win 60 percent of their games, the actual number of wins will vary by chance alone from 87 to 107 during 90 percent of their seasons. One out of every 100 years they will win 83 or fewer games, almost certainly miss the playoffs, and the manager and general manager will probably both be fired. One out of every 100 years the same team, because of luck alone, will win 112 or more games and be compared to the best teams of all time.

Another way to view the same problem is to ask what is the chance a team with a certain level of skill will win enough games to make the playoffs.

Team Skill	\-\-\-\-\- Probability of Winning At Least This Many Games \-\-\-\-\-								
	82	85	88	91	94	97	100	103	106
0.350	0.0000	0.0000	0.0000	0.0000	0.0000	0.0000	0.0000	0.0000	0.0000
0.400	0.0040	0.0009	0.0002	0.0000	0.0000	0.0000	0.0000	0.0000	0.0000
0.450	0.0872	0.0338	0.0108	0.0028	0.0006	0.0001	0.0000	0.0000	0.0000
0.500	0.4684	0.2910	0.1535	0.0678	0.0246	0.0073	0.0017	0.0003	0.0000
0.550	0.8849	0.7667	0.6006	0.4138	0.2440	0.1209	0.0499	0.0167	0.0045
0.600	0.9939	0.9787	0.9394	0.8589	0.7249	0.5468	0.3578	0.1976	0.0908
0.650	0.9999	0.9996	0.9981	0.9920	0.9730	0.9256	0.8307	0.6805	0.4904

Table 17.2. Number of wins based on a 162-game season.

The number of wins needed to make the playoffs varies from year to year and from the AL to the NL. From 1997 to 2011, after the advent of interleague play, only one wildcard team made the playoffs from each league. Wild card teams that made the playoffs during that era won between 88 and 102 games, and the first teams excluded from the playoffs in each league won between 86 and 96 games. Every team with at least 97 wins made the playoffs and only one team with 94 or more wins was excluded. Teams with as few as 82 wins have made the playoffs by winning weak divisions.

A team with skill to win 50 percent of its games has between a 2 percent and 15 percent chance of making the playoffs each year (by winning 88 to 100 games); a team with skill to win 55 percent of its games has between a 24 percent and 60 percent chance; and a team with skills to win 60 percent of its games has between a 55 percent and 94 percent chance. Not until a team has the skill level to win 65 percent of its games is it all but assured of a playoff berth.

The average player from 1997 to 2009 had a GPA of 0.2684 and a BA of 0.2660. How much will a player's production vary, because of luck alone, from week to week, month to month and season to season?

Plate App	\-\-\-\-\-\-\-\-\-\- GPA Distribution by Percentile \-\-\-\-\-\-\-\-\-\-								
	1st	5th	10th	25th	50th	75th	90th	95th	99th
10	0.0000	0.0314	0.0761	0.1429	0.2565	0.3679	0.4794	0.5502	0.6941
50	0.1143	0.1565	0.1797	0.2201	0.2668	0.3159	0.3620	0.3906	0.4461
100	0.1536	0.1845	0.2013	0.2301	0.2632	0.2974	0.3292	0.3486	0.3859
250	0.1933	0.2134	0.2243	0.2429	0.2640	0.2855	0.3053	0.3172	0.3399
500	0.2136	0.2281	0.2359	0.2492	0.2642	0.2794	0.2933	0.3016	0.3176
750	0.2228	0.2348	0.2412	0.2521	0.2644	0.2768	0.2880	0.2948	0.3077

Plate App	\-\-\-\-\-\-\-\-\-\- BA Distribution by Percentile \-\-\-\-\-\-\-\-\-\-								
	1st	5th	10th	25th	50th	75th	90th	95th	99th
10	0.0000	0.0000	0.1000	0.1429	0.2500	0.3750	0.4444	0.5000	0.6667
50	0.1190	0.1591	0.1818	0.2222	0.2667	0.3111	0.3542	0.3778	0.4286
100	0.1585	0.1875	0.02043	0.2308	0.2614	0.2941	0.3226	0.3409	0.3750
250	0.1963	0.2150	0.2252	0.2430	0.2627	0.2826	0.3009	0.3122	0.3333
500	0.2151	0.2289	0.2362	0.2489	0.2628	0.2770	0.2899	0.2977	0.3125
750	0.2239	0.2352	0.2413	0.2515	0.2629	0.2745	0.2851	0.2914	0.3032

Table 17.3. Expected GPA and batting-average distribution based on the number of plate appearances by a hitter who is an average of all players from 1997 to 2009.

Consider a hypothetical situation: A manager decides to use our average hitter as a pinch hitter because he has a GPA of 0.479 in 10 PAs against a pitcher. By chance alone our hitter would have performed this well against 10 percent of pitchers. If our player had the best performance of 10 hitters the manager could have chosen to pinch hit, it was probably attributable to chance alone that he performed this well in the past against this pitcher.

The TV announcer claims our average player is in a slump with a GPA 0.156 on a 10-day road trip. If it's assumed that 10 days will yield 50 PAs, our average hitter's GPA can be expected to vary from 0.156 to 0.391. (Ten percent of the time, the variance will fall outside of that range.) If this was the only period during the season his GPA was so low, he was probably just unlucky and not in a slump.

Over the course of a season, a player who starts almost every game will make about 750 plate appearances. If his skill level is average, his GPA over a season should be between 0.235 and 0.295 at least 90 percent of the time. That degree of variation might be surprising. Many might consider a 0.295 season to be a strong performance for an average player and assume he must have worked hard to improve his baseball skills. Many might likewise consider a 0.235 season to be quite poor for an average player and assume he is losing his skills or not working hard enough. By chance alone on a team of 10 average players, one player's GPA for the season can be expected to be either below 0.235 or above 0.295.

The expected distribution of BA is similar to the expected distribution of GPA, as Table 17.3 demonstrates.

Team	Year	GPA	GPAbrc	tGPA	BA	OBP	SLG	PA
Boston	2007	0.290	0.008	0.298	0.317	0.380	0.442	581
Boston	2008	0.300	0.005	0.305	0.326	0.376	0.493	726
Boston	2009	0.285	0.002	0.287	0.296	0.371	0.447	714
Average		0.292	0.005	0.296	0.313	0.375	0.462	674

Table 17.4. Dustin Pedroia's statistics from 2007 to 2009.

Why did Pedroia's GPA fall from 0.300 to 0.285 and his BA from 0.326 to 0.296 from 2008 to 2009? It will be assumed that his 2,021 PAs from 2007 to 2009 accurately reflect his skill level. By chance alone, his GPA will vary from 0.280 to 0.303 during 50 percent of his seasons. His BA will vary from 0.290 to 0.336 during 90 percent of his seasons. The decrease in production from Pedroia's MVP season of 2008 to the 2009 season is easily explained by chance alone.

Plate App	GPA Distribution by Percentile								
	1st	5th	10th	25th	50th	75th	90th	95th	99th
10	0.0000	0.0602	0.1057	0.1857	0.2819	0.3873	0.4904	0.5565	0.6885
50	0.1424	0.1836	0.2061	0.2450	0.2897	0.3362	0.3795	0.4063	0.4580
100	0.1843	0.2147	0.2310	0.2589	0.2907	0.3234	0.3536	0.3722	0.4078
250	0.2228	0.2425	0.2531	0.2710	0.2913	0.3120	0.3309	0.3423	0.3640
500	0.2427	0.2568	0.2644	0.2772	0.2915	0.3061	0.3193	0.3273	0.3424
750	0.2514	0.2631	0.2693	0.2798	0.2916	0.3034	0.3142	0.3207	0.3331

Plate App	BA Distribution by Percentile								
	1st	5th	10th	25th	50th	75th	90th	95th	99th
10	0.0000	0.1000	0.1111	0.2000	0.3000	0.4000	0.5000	0.5714	0.7000
50	0.1591	0.2000	0.2245	0.2667	0.3111	0.3590	0.4043	0.4318	0.4783
100	0.2022	0.2333	0.2500	0.2791	0.3118	0.3448	0.3765	0.3953	0.4302
250	0.2420	0.2622	0.2731	0.2917	0.3125	0.3333	0.3529	0.3645	0.3865
500	0.2623	0.2770	0.2848	0.2980	0.3128	0.3275	0.3413	0.3493	0.3647
750	0.2716	0.2836	0.2900	0.3008	0.3129	0.3250	0.3359	0.3427	0.3552

Table 17.5. Expected GPA and BA distribution based on the number of PAs. Simulation based on the 2,021 PAs by Dustin Pedroia from 2007 to 2009.

Finally, we will look at how much league-wide statistics should vary from season to season, assuming the average skill levels of the players do not change. There were 2,425,389 PAs from 1997 to 2009, or an average of 186,568 per season.

Assuming the skill levels of the players do not change, the average GPA will in most seasons (90 percent of them) vary from 0.2673 to 0.2712, the average BA from 0.2649 to 0.2685 and the difference between GPA and BA from 0.0013 to 0.0038. Once the relationship between GPA and BA is set, the difference between GPA and BA should (again, in 90 percent of the seasons) remain within a window of 0.0025 points (0.0038 − 0.0013).

Plate App	Distribution by Percentile								
	GPA								
	1st	5th	10th	25th	50th	75th	90th	95th	99th
187K	0.2665	0.2673	0.2678	0.2685	0.2693	0.2700	0.2708	0.2712	0.2720
	BA								
	1st	5th	10th	25th	50th	75th	90th	95th	99th
187K	0.2642	0.2649	0.2653	0.2660	0.2667	0.2674	0.2681	0.2685	0.2692
	GPA−BA								
	1st	5th	10th	25th	50th	75th	90th	95th	99th
187K	0.0008	0.0013	0.0016	0.0020	0.0026	0.0031	0.0036	0.0038	0.0044

Table 17.6. Expected GPA and BA distribution by percentile, based on all 2,425,389 PAs from 1997 to 2009.

During the different eras from 1952 to 2012, the variation in GPA and GPA − BA from season to season has been much greater than would be expected by chance alone. The skills of the players were almost certainly changing over that period.

During the Pitching Era, defined in this book as 1971 to 1984, the difference between GPA and BA was −0.0039 to −0.0093 every year, a far greater variation than should be expected by chance alone. During the Steroid Era, from 1994 to 2004, the difference between GPA and BA was +0.0018 to +0.0073 every year — also a far greater variation than should be expected by chance alone. The differences between GPA and BA from 2005 to 2012 have remained within the 0.0025-point window of variation expected by chance alone.

Events	Type of Event	Measure	Range for 90 Pct.	Error
10	PAs for a Player in 2 Days	GPA	0.0602 to 0.5565	80.5%
162	Games for a Team in a Season	Wins	71 to 91	12.3%
750	PAs for a Player in a Season	GPA	0.2348 to 0.2948	11.3%
6,219	PAs for a Team in a Season	GPA	0.2588 to 0.2798	3.9%
186,568	PAs League Wide in a Season	GPA	0.2673 to 0.2712	0.7%

Table 17.7. Expected range of variation for selected events. Error is calculated as median ± error for 90 percent of range.

Using GPA to estimate the skill of a player, a team or the whole league will be limited by the number of events sampled. The accuracy of these estimates is proportional to the square root of the number of events sampled. For example, using GPA to estimate the skill of a player over 2 days will be about 137 times less accurate than using GPA to estimate the skill of the whole league over a season (square-root (186,568 / 10) = 137).

Understanding how much GPA can vary by chance alone helps place the significance of the observations made in this book in better perspective.

More than in most sports, statistics are used to measure a baseball player's skill level. It is important to understand how baseball statistics vary by chance alone so we do not become overconfident in our statistical measures. Even a "perfect" baseball statistic may not accurately measure a player's skill level over a limited period of time.

Should They Have Walked Bonds?

The next chapters of this book will use the statistics and techniques developed so far to examine three controversial topics involving baseball strategy: (1) the intentional walk; (2) the stolen base; and (3) optimal baserunning.

Team	Year	GPA	GPAbrc	cGPA	BA	BB	IBB	PA
Pittsburgh	1986	0.272	0.009	0.281	0.223	65	2	484
Pittsburgh	1987	0.271	0.003	0.274	0.261	54	3	611
Pittsburgh	1988	0.298	−0.000	0.298	0.283	72	14	614
Pittsburgh	1989	0.275	0.004	0.279	0.248	93	22	679
Pittsburgh	1990	0.349	0.009	0.357	0.301	93	15	621
Pittsburgh	1991	0.352	0.009	0.361	0.292	107	25	634
Pittsburgh	1992	0.365	0.008	0.373	0.311	127	32	612
San Francisco	1993	0.385	0.003	0.388	0.336	126	43	674
San Francisco	1994	0.349	0.005	0.354	0.312	74	18	474
San Francisco	1995	0.360	0.005	0.366	0.294	120	22	635
San Francisco	1996	0.401	0.008	0.409	0.308	151	30	675
San Francisco	1997	0.355	0.008	0.363	0.291	145	34	690
San Francisco	1998	0.365	0.002	0.367	0.303	130	29	697
San Francisco	1999	0.343	0.008	0.350	0.262	73	9	434
San Francisco	2000	0.380	0.003	0.383	0.306	117	22	607
San Francisco	2001	0.444	0.001	0.445	0.328	177	35	664
San Francisco	2002	0.457	0.004	0.461	0.370	198	68	612
San Francisco	2003	0.413	0.007	0.421	0.341	148	61	550
San Francisco	2004	0.471	0.005	0.476	0.362	232	120	617
San Francisco	2005	0.324	0.000	0.324	0.286	9	3	52
San Francisco	2006	0.372	0.004	0.376	0.270	115	38	493
San Francisco	2007	0.353	0.004	0.357	0.276	132	43	477
Average		0.365	0.005	0.370	0.298	2,558	688	12.6K

Table 18.1. Barry Bonds's statistics from 1986 to 2007.

This chapter will examine the intentional walk by looking at four simulated players of different skill levels:

1. 0.447 GPA. Barry Bonds's seasons from 2001 to 2004, the most dominant offensive performance in MLB history.
2. 0.360 GPA. Albert Pujols's seasons from 2001 to 2009, a high level of production but similar to league leaders most years.
3. 0.267 GPA. An average player from 1997 to 2009.
4. 0.117 GPA. When an average pitcher from 1997 to 2009 is due up next.

From this analysis, the optimal strategy for utilizing the intentional walk will be described for players of different skill levels in various game scenarios.

Barry Bonds's offensive production from 2001 to 2004 was the most dominant of any player in MLB history. During that period, Bonds walked 755 times in 2,443 plate appearances (30.9 percent). His 2004, 2002 and 2001 seasons rank as the top three single seasons in number of walks in history. These four seasons also contributed significantly to Bonds's career total of 2,558 walks, a figure that likewise ranks first in MLB history, ahead of second-place Rickey Henderson's career total of 2,190.

Many of these walks were intentional and others occurred after the pitcher very carefully pitched to Bonds with the intention of walking him unless he swung at a bad pitch. Intentional bases on balls have been an official MLB statistic only since 1955, but it will come as no surprise to most baseball fans that Bonds's 2004, 2002 and 2003 seasons rank as the top three single seasons in number of intentional walks from 1955 to 2012. Bonds's career total of 688 intentional walks dwarfs Hank Aaron's second-place career total of 293.

Did it make sense to intentionally walk Bonds so many times?

— — Before — —					Bonds's	BB		Int		Frac
Runners			Outs	BA	GPA	GPA	BB	BB	PA	BB
x	x	x	0	0.319	0.398	0.653	109	3	536	0.20
x	x	x	1	0.381	0.422	0.535	73	11	321	0.23
x	x	x	2	0.334	0.369	0.397	107	18	422	0.25
1B	x	x	0	0.425	0.615	0.871	24	0	98	0.24
1B	x	x	1	0.425	0.564	0.659	50	6	200	0.25
1B	x	x	2	0.237	0.349	0.489	59	13	197	0.30
x	2B	x	0	0.381	0.471	0.633	10	4	31	0.32
x	2B	x	1	0.394	0.514	0.507	53	41	86	0.62
x	2B	x	2	0.367	0.374	0.386	90	78	120	0.75
x	x	3B	0	0.250	0.428	0.686	2	0	6	0.33
x	x	3B	1	0.455	0.565	0.494	24	21	36	0.67
x	x	3B	2	0.313	0.408	0.411	19	15	35	0.54
1B	2B	x	0	0.314	0.565	1.090	9	0	45	0.20
1B	2B	x	1	0.371	0.620	0.920	17	1	80	0.21
1B	2B	x	2	0.250	0.473	0.598	33	14	70	0.47
1B	x	3B	0	0.286	0.320	0.795	3	0	11	0.27
1B	x	3B	1	0.714	0.736	0.661	10	4	28	0.36
1B	x	3B	2	0.375	0.614	0.542	14	9	30	0.47
x	2B	3B	0	0.250	0.551	0.572	7	7	12	0.58
x	2B	3B	1	0.000	0.441	0.449	25	25	26	0.96
x	2B	3B	2	0.000	0.404	0.456	14	14	15	0.93
1B	2B	3B	0	0.625	0.852	1.240	1	0	10	0.10
1B	2B	3B	1	0.500	1.012	1.250	2	0	14	0.14
1B	2B	3B	2	0.385	0.578	1.272	0	0	14	0.00
Total/Average				0.349	0.447		755	284	2,443	0.31

Table 18.2. Barry Bonds's statistics from 2001 to 2004 by base-out state. BB GPA is the GPA of a walk in that base-out state, and FracBB is the fraction of times Bonds walked in that base-out state.

Table 18.2 shows Bonds's statistics by base-out state from 2001 to 2004. The GPA of a walk in all 24 base-out states is listed alongside Bonds's actual GPA in each base-out state during this period. In only four base-out states does Bonds's actual GPA exceed the GPA of a walk: (1) with a man on second and one out; (2) with a man on and one out; (3) with men on first and third and one out; and (4) with men on first and third and two outs. Based on GPA, one can conclude that it rarely made sense to intentionally walk Bonds and that the intentional walks only added to his dominance during this period.

The number of PAs in each base-out state varied widely, ranging from six PAs with a man on third and no outs to 536 PAs with the bases empty and no outs. As discussed in the chapter "Chance in Baseball," the accuracy of a statistic is related to how many events are sampled.

Therefore, Bonds's GPA of 0.447 for all 2,443 PAs from 2001 to 2004 might be a more accurate measure of his production than the GPA for each base-out state.

The GPA of a walk was less than Bonds's overall GPA of 0.447 in only three base-out states: (1) with the bases empty and two outs; (2) with a man on second and two outs; and (3) with a man on third and two outs. Bonds walked 37.4 percent of the time in these three base-out states (19.2 percent of the time intentionally), more than his 30.9 percent average for this period.

Bonds was walked the highest percentage of times with men on second and third with one out and with men on second and third with two outs. Managers intentionally walked Bonds 95.1 percent of the time and only pitched to him twice (outs were recorded in both instances).

Of course Bonds's GPA and the GPA of a walk in both of those base-out states were similar since the PAs were almost all walks. The GPA of a walk in those base-out states was minimally higher than Bonds's overall GPA of 0.447 during this period, making the strategy of walking him for those base-out states a borderline call.

Gross Productivity Average is based on run expectancy (RE), which balances the chance of scoring one run with the chance of having a big inning. For most games in the early and middle innings the percentages discussed above apply.

At the end of a close game with the teams tied or trailing by a single run, the percentages will change because only one or two runs are needed. It is no longer necessary to consider the RE because a big inning is not needed. Rather, the chance of scoring a small number of runs is more important.

Might there have been times in a close game where walking Bonds was more beneficial? This question can be addressed by simulating the end of close games with the two-lineup simulator discussed in the chapter "Winning Games." One lineup will consist of players from the San Francisco Giants from 2001 to 2004, with Bonds batting forth. The second lineup will consist of average players from 2001 to 2004, with an average pitcher batting in the ninth position.

The Giants lineup changed on an almost daily basis from 2001 to 2004. The players chosen for the representative Giants lineup generally played the most games from 2001 to 2004 at each defensive position. The order in which they bat in the lineup was chosen to be as representative as possible. Bonds was placed fourth in the lineup because he batted in that position more than the third position during this era. The pitcher was placed ninth in the lineup and his statistics were the average of all MLB pitchers from 2001 to 2004.

The actual players chosen and order in which they bat only minimally affect the conclusion as to when Bonds should have been walked.

Lineup #1	Years	GPA	GPAbrc	cGPA	BA	OBP	RBI	HR
1st — Durham, Ray	2001–2004	0.287	0.003	0.290	0.280	0.359	58	15
2nd — Aurilira, Rich	2001–2004	0.265	0.001	0.266	0.280	0.331	65	18
3rd — Grissom, M.	2002–2004	0.282	0.004	0.286	0.287	0.322	57	15
4th — Bonds, Barry	2001–2004	0.447	0.004	0.452	0.349	0.559	110	52
5th — Snow, J.T.	2001–2004	0.301	0.003	0.305	0.273	0.381	49	8
6th — Santiago, Benito	2001–2004	0.243	0.000	0.243	0.273	0.312	49	10
7th — Alfonzo, Edgar	2001–2004	0.277	0.003	0.280	0.275	0.350	66	14
8th — Cruz, Jose	2001–2004	0.277	0.003	0.280	0.253	0.336	76	23
9th — Average Pitcher	2001–2004	0.117	0.001	0.118	0.144	0.176	18	2
Average		0.277	0.002	0.279	0.268	0.347	61	17
Lineup #2	Years	GPA	GPAbrc	cGPA	BA	OBP	RBI	HR
1st–8th — Average Batter	2001–2004	0.267	0.002	0.269	0.264	0.333	81	20
9th — Average Pitcher	2001–2004	0.117	0.001	0.118	0.144	0.176	18	2
Average		0.250	0.002	0.252	0.251	0.316	74	18

Table 18.3. Lineups used by the two-lineup simulator to evaluate the benefits of walking Bonds in various game scenarios.

The simulation is run with Bonds at bat in all 24 base-out states at various points in a close game with the Giants behind or ahead by up to two runs.

— — Before — —			— — — — — Top 9th — — — — —					— — — — Bottom 9th — — — —				
Runners		Outs	−2	−1	Tie	+1	+2	−2	−1	Tie	+1	+2
x	x	x	0	−5.64	−7.60	−4.66	−1.53	−0.58	−6.88	−8.58	−3.91	
x	x	x	1	−2.50	−1.74	−0.56	−0.29	−0.06	−3.09	−1.56	−0.01	
x	x	x	2	−1.74	−1.32	−0.33	−0.09	−0.01	−2.23	−1.32	0.44	
1B	x	x	0	−5.08	−5.60	−3.84	−1.20	−0.43	−5.73	−5.89	−3.39	
1B	x	x	1	−3.96	−3.93	−3.08	−0.90	−0.36	−4.20	−4.06	−2.81	
1B	x	x	2	−1.84	−3.64	−2.86	−0.87	−0.34	−2.10	−4.28	−2.94	
x	2B	x	0	−4.49	−1.33	0.16	−0.08	0.01	−5.05	−0.24	1.04	
x	2B	x	1	−2.23	−0.23	0.40	0.09	0.04	−2.35	0.67	0.95	
x	2B	x	2	−0.82	0.00	0.61	0.13	0.00	−1.01	0.25	0.91	
x	x	3B	0	−4.80	−2.95	−1.22	−0.46	−0.21	−5.15	−2.30	−0.35	
x	x	3B	1	−1.45	0.68	0.85	0.26	−0.12	−1.15	1.67	1.13	
x	x	3B	2	−0.16	0.23	0.02	0.02	0.02	0.01	0.49	0.05	
1B	2B	x	0	−11.33	−11.87	−6.52	−2.15	−0.90	−12.68	−12.41	−4.58	
1B	2B	x	1	0.47	−6.32	−6.89	−1.91	−0.80	1.20	−8.61	−8.05	
1B	2B	x	2	−3.46	−8.08	−5.83	−1.81	−0.80	−4.43	−10.17	−5.47	
1B	x	3B	0	−13.10	−8.13	−1.42	−0.80	−0.31	−14.96	−7.00	1.66	
1B	x	3B	1	3.29	6.60	5.34	1.61	0.71	4.34	8.19	5.29	
1B	x	3B	2	1.38	−1.92	−2.09	−0.54	−0.23	1.60	−3.06	−2.39	
x	2B	3B	0	−1.73	1.58	1.35	0.39	0.15	−0.99	3.09	1.63	
x	2B	3B	1	−0.29	0.36	0.45	0.10	0.06	−0.33	0.61	0.51	
x	2B	3B	2	−0.33	0.57	0.57	0.16	0.04	−0.22	0.89	0.72	
1B	2B	3B	0	−8.88	−9.02	−5.88	−1.84	−0.77	−9.26	−8.98	−4.76	
1B	2B	3B	1	−1.77	−8.46	−5.47	−1.76	−0.74	−3.70	−11.75	−5.09	
1B	2B	3B	2	−10.60	−28.77	−25.99	−7.57	−3.25	−13.03	−35.80	−27.34	

Table 18.4. Simulated results using the two lineups in Table 18.3. All 24 base-out states are shown for the Giants batting and Bonds at the plate in the top or bottom of the ninth inning.

The chance that the Giants are going to win the game is calculated for two scenarios: with the opposing team pitching to Bonds and with the opposing team walking him. The difference in win percentage is shown in the columns in the following tables. A negative percentage shows that walking Bonds reduces the opposing team's chance of winning the game by that percentage. A positive percentage (in bold) shows that walking Bonds increases the opposing team's chance of winning the game by that percentage.

Before Runners			Outs	Top 9th					Bottom 9th				
				−2	−1	Tie	+1	+2	−2	−1	Tie	+1	+2
x	x	x	0	−7.62	−11.49	−8.30	−2.49	−1.21	−9.48	−13.53	−7.39		
x	x	x	1	−5.07	−8.42	−6.08	−1.89	−0.90	−6.43	−10.05	−5.60		
x	x	x	2	−2.35	−4.38	−3.22	−1.03	−0.53	−3.07	−5.31	−3.11		
1B	x	x	0	−12.37	−15.96	−11.27	−3.56	−1.69	−14.63	−17.94	−10.01		
1B	x	x	1	−8.19	−11.13	−8.11	−2.56	−1.11	−9.77	−12.53	−7.31		
1B	x	x	2	−4.07	−6.41	−5.20	−1.65	−0.75	−4.94	−7.61	−4.85		
x	2B	x	0	−10.68	−8.00	−2.88	−1.24	−0.58	−12.52	−7.19	−0.54		
x	2B	x	1	−7.22	−5.64	−2.36	−0.92	−0.39	−8.65	−5.49	−0.73		
x	2B	x	2	−3.69	−2.94	−1.20	−0.50	−0.21	−4.51	−2.89	−0.35		
x	x	3B	0	−11.62	−8.83	−3.34	−1.45	−0.64	−13.66	−8.18	−0.90		
x	x	3B	1	−7.57	−5.01	−1.17	−0.66	−0.34	−8.93	−4.47	**0.65**		
x	x	3B	2	−4.20	−3.99	−1.98	−0.69	−0.30	−5.19	−4.15	−1.10		
1B	2B	x	0	−15.79	−19.65	−13.64	−4.36	−2.03	−17.70	−21.68	−11.75		
1B	2B	x	1	−11.52	−17.34	−13.34	−4.05	−1.89	−13.32	−20.03	−12.38		
1B	2B	x	2	−7.09	−9.22	−5.92	−1.93	−0.84	−8.34	−10.42	−4.85		
1B	x	3B	0	−14.08	−10.16	−3.47	−1.57	−0.72	−15.80	−9.20	−0.26		
1B	x	3B	1	−10.63	−8.57	−3.39	−1.44	−0.67	−12.04	−8.09	−1.17		
1B	x	3B	2	−6.50	−6.76	−3.45	−1.25	−0.57	−7.69	−7.07	−2.26		
x	2B	3B	0	−6.87	−2.95	−1.54	−0.59	−0.26	−6.31	−1.11	−0.34		
x	2B	3B	1	−5.04	−1.55	−0.21	−0.22	−0.11	−4.60	**0.12**	**0.75**		
x	2B	3B	2	−3.44	−3.61	−3.03	−0.82	−0.41	−3.49	−3.65	−3.02		
1B	2B	3B	0	−20.64	−19.06	−9.93	−3.59	−1.68	−23.10	−19.00	−6.33		
1B	2B	3B	1	−17.50	−25.10	−18.17	−5.63	−2.67	−20.79	−28.84	−16.16		
1B	2B	3B	2	−9.06	−29.58	−30.05	−8.55	−4.02	−10.29	−38.29	−33.41		

Table 18.5. Simulated results using two lineups of average players from 2001 to 2004.

The effect that walking Bonds had on the opposing team's chance of winning the game is shown in Table 18.4 with Bonds at bat in the ninth inning. There were many situations in the ninth inning of a close game in which it made strategic sense to walk Bonds. For comparison, the same simulation with two lineups of average players from 2001 to 2004 is shown in Table 18.5. In both tables, bold indicates that the walk worked to the advantage of the Giants' opponents.

The GPA of a walk is 0.411 or less in only three base-out states: (1) the bases empty and two outs; (2) a man on second and two outs; and (3) a man on third and two outs. Even in these base-out states, however, walking Bonds was not always the best strategy. The score and inning of the game were important in determining whether a walk was good strategy.

For average players, there were few scenarios in the bottom of the ninth inning of a close game in which it made strategic sense to walk the batter. There was a marginal benefit to the opposing team when they walked the batter in a tie game in the bottom of the ninth inning for two base-out states: a man on third with two outs and men on second and third with one out.

There were no scenarios in which walking a batter from a team of average players benefited opposing teams in the top of the ninth or in earlier innings. This is not surprising since the GPA of a walk is at least 0.386 for all base-out states, far higher than the GPA of an average batter.

Were there other times in a game that it made sense to walk Bonds? In the eighth inning there were still many scenarios in which walking Bonds benefited the opposing team, but that benefit shrank as earlier innings were evaluated. By the fifth inning, there were only two base-out states in which the opposing team stood to gain by walking Bonds: men on first and third with one and men on second and third with two outs. In the latter scenario, Bonds's GPA was 0.736 and the GPA of a walk was 0.661. It is reasonable to expect that an intentional walk in that base-out state could have benefited the opposing team.

When studying this data, whether the percentage is positive (helps opponents) or negative (hurts opponents) is most important. The size of the number is less important because it depends on chance that the opponent had of winning the game.

— — Before — —			— — — — — Top 8th — — — — — —					— — — — — Bottom 8th — — — — —				
Runners		Outs	−2	−1	Tie	+1	+2	−2	−1	Tie	+1	+2
x	x	x	0	−5.46	−6.28	−4.30	−2.05	−1.05	−6.20	−6.69	−3.77	−1.22	−0.52
x	x	x	1	−2.13	−1.59	−0.76	−0.34	−0.15	−2.52	−1.47	−0.51	−0.14	−0.09
x	x	x	2	−1.09	−0.60	−0.19	−0.15	0.02	−1.42	−0.49	−0.17	0.00	−0.04
1B	x	x	0	−4.72	−4.70	−3.53	−1.59	−0.90	−5.07	−4.98	−2.98	−0.98	−0.35
1B	x	x	1	−3.77	−3.52	−2.78	−1.30	−0.61	−3.84	−3.55	−2.35	−0.80	−0.31
1B	x	x	2	−1.81	−2.49	−2.27	−1.02	−0.61	−1.87	−2.72	−2.11	−0.65	−0.26
x	2B	x	0	−3.49	−1.63	−0.38	−0.23	−0.13	−3.78	−1.13	0.01	−0.04	−0.06
x	2B	x	1	−1.75	−0.62	0.02	0.03	−0.05	−1.77	−0.12	0.34	0.05	0.03
x	2B	x	2	−0.43	0.13	0.25	0.06	−0.05	−0.51	0.34	0.52	0.06	0.04
x	x	3B	0	−4.07	−3.00	−1.53	−0.74	−0.40	−4.36	−2.48	−1.01	−0.38	−0.18
x	x	3B	1	−1.23	0.28	0.36	0.11	0.18	−0.82	0.61	0.62	0.21	0.07
x	x	3B	2	−0.12	0.41	0.16	0.08	0.01	0.01	0.42	0.05	0.00	0.10
1B	2B	x	0	−9.82	−9.82	−6.23	−3.05	−1.50	−10.76	−10.02	−5.15	−1.72	−0.72
1B	2B	x	1	−1.22	−4.90	−5.30	−2.36	−1.24	−1.07	−6.08	−5.38	−1.56	−0.68
1B	2B	x	2	−3.46	−5.78	−4.71	−2.17	−1.14	−4.11	−6.72	−4.43	−1.41	−0.59
1B	x	3B	0	−10.46	−7.14	−2.72	−1.46	−0.72	−11.40	−5.98	−1.33	−0.66	−0.21
1B	x	3B	1	2.95	5.05	4.35	1.97	0.92	3.63	5.87	4.04	1.25	0.54
1B	x	3B	2	0.61	−1.13	−1.27	−0.53	−0.27	0.69	−1.74	−1.42	−0.33	−0.22
x	2B	3B	0	−1.58	0.59	0.74	0.32	0.22	−1.03	1.34	0.95	0.26	0.08
x	2B	3B	1	−0.17	0.23	0.12	0.17	0.11	−0.12	0.35	0.42	0.13	0.02
x	2B	3B	2	−0.18	0.41	0.43	0.07	0.15	0.00	0.64	0.56	0.11	0.10
1B	2B	3B	0	−8.40	−8.03	−5.46	−2.65	−1.35	−8.61	−7.91	−4.55	−1.52	−0.63
1B	2B	3B	1	−2.09	−5.86	−4.40	−2.08	−1.10	−3.36	−7.31	−4.28	−1.40	−0.57
1B	2B	3B	2	−11.83	−21.82	−20.17	−9.27	−4.80	−13.76	−25.80	−19.99	−5.93	−2.55

Table 18.6. Simulated results using the two lineups in Table 18.3. All 24 base-out states are shown for the Giants batting and Bonds at the plate in the top or bottom of the eighth inning.

For example, with the Giants trailing by 1 run in the bottom of the ninth inning and Bonds at bat with the bases loaded and two outs, the opponents had a 60.76 percent chance of winning the game. If the opponents walked Bonds, their chance of winning the game fell to 24.96 percent. With the Giants ahead by two runs and Bonds at bat with the bases loaded and two outs in the top of the ninth inning, opponents had a 5.26 percent chance of winning the game. If the opponents walked Bonds, their chance of winning the game fell to 2.01 percent. Walking Bonds in either scenario would have been a strategic blunder that lowered the chance of winning the game by about 60 percent. The magnitude of the percentage decline was much greater for the first scenario because the opponents had a much greater chance of winning the game.

-- Before --			------ Top 1st ------					------ Bottom 5th ------				
Runners		Outs	−2	−1	Tie	+1	+2	−2	−1	Tie	+1	+2
x	x	x	0	−2.65	−2.48	−2.22	−1.85	−1.32	−3.45	−3.51	−3.03	−2.26	−1.56
x	x	x	1	−0.87	−0.79	−0.77	−0.56	−0.34	−1.17	−1.15	−0.92	−0.64	−0.48
x	x	x	2	−0.56	−0.47	−0.35	−0.34	−0.16	−0.77	−0.77	−0.61	−0.48	−0.23
1B	x	x	0	−2.37	−2.13	−1.80	−1.44	−1.10	−3.09	−2.90	−2.48	−1.84	−1.27
1B	x	x	1	−1.92	−1.81	−1.50	−1.23	−0.94	−2.59	−2.53	−2.19	−1.65	−1.11
1B	x	x	2	−1.16	−1.23	−0.91	−0.88	−0.71	−1.59	−1.87	−1.56	−1.19	−0.74
x	2B	x	0	−1.23	−2.01	−0.75	−0.62	−0.38	−1.85	−1.29	−0.92	−0.58	−0.34
x	2B	x	1	−0.45	−0.33	−0.40	−0.26	−0.12	−0.80	−0.62	−0.33	−0.29	−0.09
x	2B	x	2	−0.17	0.03	0.01	0.08	−0.04	−0.28	−0.16	−0.06	0.01	0.00
x	x	3B	0	−1.69	−1.48	−1.23	−0.91	−0.66	−2.27	−2.03	−1.50	−1.04	−0.68
x	x	3B	1	−0.52	−0.41	−0.09	−0.19	0.00	−0.62	−0.32	−0.20	−0.14	−0.02
x	x	3B	2	−0.12	−0.26	−0.12	−0.07	0.01	−0.24	−0.09	−0.07	−0.10	−0.06
1B	2B	x	0	−4.89	−4.38	−3.68	−3.09	−2.19	−6.76	−6.23	−4.91	−3.66	−2.48
1B	2B	x	1	−2.09	−2.10	−1.88	−1.63	−1.22	−2.50	−2.79	−2.87	−2.17	−1.67
1B	2B	x	2	−2.18	−2.37	−2.10	−1.70	−1.27	−3.14	−3.25	−3.04	−2.27	−1.51
1B	x	3B	0	−4.28	−3.56	−2.81	−2.12	−1.54	−5.87	−4.95	−3.52	−2.49	−1.60
1B	x	3B	1	**1.61**	**1.72**	**1.66**	**1.25**	**1.00**	**2.08**	**2.37**	**2.34**	**1.82**	**1.26**
1B	x	3B	2	−0.44	−0.36	−0.37	−0.32	−0.33	−0.41	−0.78	−0.81	−0.65	−0.45
x	2B	3B	0	−0.60	−0.31	−0.14	−0.05	−0.03	−0.92	−0.54	−0.19	0.00	0.02
x	2B	3B	1	−0.04	−0.01	−0.16	0.02	0.05	−0.06	−0.03	**0.20**	0.08	−0.02
x	2B	3B	2	**0.14**	**0.15**	**0.19**	−0.01	0.08	0.07	**0.11**	**0.24**	**0.17**	0.08
1B	2B	3B	0	−4.65	−4.11	−3.49	−2.68	−1.94	−6.12	−5.48	−4.42	−3.13	−2.18
1B	2B	3B	1	−1.80	−1.83	−1.69	−1.38	−1.14	−2.13	−2.73	−2.53	−2.04	−1.44
1B	2B	3B	2	−8.86	−8.80	−7.87	−6.56	−5.18	−11.02	−12.43	−11.64	−9.00	−6.35

Table 18.7. Simulated results using the two lineups in Table 18.3. All 24 base-out states are shown for the Giants batting and Bonds at the plate in the bottom of the first or top of the fifth inning.

A drawback to using a very realistic simulation is that sometimes patterns occur that may be attributable to chance alone. Bonds's GPA with men on first and third and one out was based on only 28 PAs, of which 10 were walks. If one concludes that Bonds's GPA of 0.736 was a true reflection of his skills, then intentionally walking him was the correct strategy. A more likely conclusion is that Bonds was a bit lucky in that base-out state, and giving him a walk (which has a GPA of 0.661) was not the correct strategy.

The base-out states, men on second and third with one out and with two outs, are even more problematic for the simulation. All but one PA for each of these base-out states were walks. By comparing walking Bonds 100 percent of the time to walking him 95 percent of the time, no valid conclusion can be drawn.

Some of the choices managers made are particularly difficult to justify. Bonds was walked 47.1 percent of the time with men on first and second and two outs. In that base-out state, Bonds's GPA was 0.473 and the GPA of a walk was 0.598. Managers were so afraid of Bonds's potential production that they created a self-fulfilling prophecy. Giving Bonds a walk with a GPA of 0.598 contributed dramatically to his dominance. Because he was so dominant, they were afraid to pitch to him even when it was clearly the better strategic choice. Bonds's GPA of 0.614 with runners on third and less than two outs was attributable in part to managers walking him in 55.6 percent of those base-out states.

Is there a better way to determine whether walking Bonds in base-out states where he had few PAs was justified?

	GPA	BA	OBP	SLG	PA	Hits	RBI	HR
0 Outs	0.447	0.337	0.493	0.798	749	192	126	73
1 Out	0.517	0.405	0.601	0.950	791	211	195	79
2 Outs	0.387	0.308	0.577	0.687	903	170	117	57
Bases Empty	0.394	0.340	0.501	0.824	1,279	328	135	135
1st Only	0.488	0.353	0.537	0.743	495	125	84	34
2nd or 3rd	0.518	0.373	0.685	0.835	669	120	219	40
3rd,<2 Outs	0.614	0.492	0.727	1.102	143	29	79	10
Total	0.447	0.349	0.559	0.809	2,443	573	438	209

Table 18.8. Statistics for base-out states from Barry Bonds's 2001 to 2004 seasons.

Lineups	Years	GPA	GPAbrc	cGPA	BA	OBP	RBI	HR
1st–8th — Average Batter	2001–2004	0.268	0.002	0.270	0.266	0.335	74	18
9th — Average Pitcher	2001–2004	0.119	0.001	0.120	0.143	0.178	18	2
Average		0.251	0.002	0.253	0.252	0.318	68	16

Table 18.9. Lineups used by the two-lineup simulator to evaluate the benefits of walking the eighth batter in various base-out states.

Runners			Outs	Top 9th −2	−1	Tie	+1	+2	Bottom 9th −2	−1	Tie	+1	+2
x	x	x	0	−5.13	−9.43	−7.21	−2.22	−1.02	−6.37	−11.47	−6.98		
x	x	x	1	−2.63	−5.58	−4.22	−1.27	−0.61	−3.33	−6.80	−4.30		
x	x	x	2	−1.13	−1.45	−2.16	−0.57	−0.25	−1.37	−1.17	−2.32		
1B	x	x	0	−10.67	−15.88	−11.57	−3.57	−1.78	−12.84	−18.55	−10.80		
1B	x	x	1	−6.04	−8.72	−6.21	−1.91	−0.88	−7.32	−10.21	−5.63		
1B	x	x	2	−1.41	−1.76	−2.75	−0.74	−0.39	−1.57	−1.93	−3.13		
x	2B	x	0	−9.04	−8.44	−4.11	−1.59	−0.71	−10.70	−8.92	−2.44		
x	2B	x	1	−5.56	−4.19	−0.93	−0.55	−0.27	−6.78	−4.07	0.41		
x	2B	x	2	−1.27	1.73	1.50	0.42	0.22	−1.47	2.83	2.01		
x	x	3B	0	−10.28	−6.34	−0.58	−0.59	−0.32	−12.22	−5.34	2.07		
x	x	3B	1	−6.49	−0.36	3.90	0.72	0.33	−7.81	1.28	6.27		
x	x	3B	2	−1.54	1.43	1.38	0.38	0.12	−1.71	2.42	1.85		
1B	2B	x	0	−14.56	−19.65	−14.08	−4.41	−2.03	−16.36	−21.94	−12.60		
1B	2B	x	1	−8.33	−12.11	−8.90	−2.76	−1.37	−9.68	−14.03	−8.21		
1B	2B	x	2	−1.33	−0.26	−0.75	−0.18	−0.04	−1.52	−0.09	−0.60		
1B	x	3B	0	−12.88	−8.27	−2.10	−1.09	−0.58	−14.21	−7.01	2.07		
1B	x	3B	1	−7.72	−1.80	2.33	0.30	0.18	−8.78	−0.40	6.27		
1B	x	3B	2	−0.98	2.22	1.93	0.49	0.21	−0.99	3.47	1.85		
x	2B	3B	0	−6.57	−2.67	−1.05	−0.49	−0.23	−6.28	−0.96	0.80		
x	2B	3B	1	−3.30	2.64	3.81	0.92	0.48	−3.14	4.94	4.90		
x	2B	3B	2	2.12	4.71	1.77	0.69	0.34	3.28	6.22	2.14		
1B	2B	3B	0	−20.30	−21.41	−12.34	−4.18	−1.92	−23.10	−22.41	−9.16		
1B	2B	3B	1	−12.70	−22.56	−18.42	−5.51	−2.62	−14.81	−26.75	−18.58		
1B	2B	3B	2	−0.16	−23.91	−29.22	−7.74	−3.70	0.33	−32.43	−35.15		

Table 18.10. Simulated results using two lineups of average players from 1997 to 2009 batting in the first to eighth positions and an average pitcher from 1997 to 2009 batting in the ninth position. All 24 base-out states are shown for the ninth inning.

Probably the best approach is to look at the data for average players and extrapolate from there. With men on first and third and one out, it is a very bad strategic choice to walk an average player. Given the GPA of 0.661 of a walk in that base-out state, it is likely walking Bonds was also a poor choice.

The intentional walk was overused with Bonds and is rarely justified for a player with average skills. How about when the pitcher is due up next?

This question can be addressed by simulating games with the two-lineup simulator discussed in the chapter "Winning Games." Both lineups consist of average players from 1997 to 2009 batting in the first to eighth positions and an average pitcher from 1997 to 2009 batting in the ninth position.

The simulation was run for all 24 base-out states at various points in a close game with the team at bat behind or ahead by up to two runs.

— — Before — —			— — — — Top 8th — — — — —					— — — — Bottom 8th — — — —				
Runners		Outs	−2	−1	Tie	+1	+2	−2	−1	Tie	+1	+2
x x x		0	−4.71	−7.08	−5.83	−2.79	−1.46	−5.22	−7.96	−5.56	−1.74	−0.85
x x x		1	−2.57	−4.11	−3.43	−1.57	−0.86	−2.95	−4.65	−3.28	−0.97	−0.46
x x x		2	−1.90	−2.98	−2.40	−1.09	−0.60	−2.24	−3.37	−2.38	−0.64	−0.34
1B x x		0	−9.59	−12.38	−9.58	−4.06	−2.44	−10.79	−13.47	−9.09	−2.88	−1.39
1B x x		1	−5.45	−6.96	−5.45	−2.57	−1.36	−6.28	−7.68	−4.93	−1.63	−0.72
1B x x		2	−2.23	−3.35	−2.93	−1.42	−0.75	−2.54	−3.81	−2.87	−0.91	−0.48
x 2B x		0	−7.09	−6.72	−4.09	−2.01	−0.99	−7.81	−6.77	−3.24	−1.14	−0.59
x 2B x		1	−4.09	−3.41	−1.32	−0.80	−0.44	−4.59	−3.24	−0.72	−0.47	−0.19
x 2B x		2	−1.40	−0.61	0.21	0.02	−0.01	−1.45	−0.47	0.47	0.08	0.06
x x 3B		0	−7.40	−5.25	−1.78	−0.95	−0.42	−8.31	−4.71	−0.44	−0.52	−0.21
x x 3B		1	−3.86	−0.84	1.95	0.85	0.44	−4.30	0.14	3.01	0.52	0.31
x x 3B		2	−1.51	−0.78	0.21	−0.04	−0.01	−1.60	−0.59	0.32	0.03	0.00
1B 2B x		0	−13.35	−15.44	−11.91	−5.66	−2.90	−14.41	−16.40	−10.93	−3.52	−1.66
1B 2B x		1	−7.77	−9.84	−7.65	−3.60	−1.86	−8.68	−10.68	−7.15	−2.30	−1.10
1B 2B x		2	−1.98	−2.33	−1.38	−0.70	−0.38	−2.15	−2.46	−1.33	−0.49	−0.20
1B x 3B		0	−10.07	−7.19	−3.17	−1.66	−0.79	−10.47	−6.46	−1.75	−0.93	−0.45
1B x 3B		1	−5.21	−2.47	0.60	0.14	0.07	−5.62	−1.49	1.62	0.19	0.06
1B x 3B		2	−1.24	−0.49	0.48	0.10	0.07	−1.35	−0.09	0.75	0.07	0.08
x 2B 3B		0	−5.59	−2.99	−1.34	−0.67	−0.35	−5.16	−2.15	−0.62	−0.35	−0.13
x 2B 3B		1	−1.98	1.26	2.36	1.17	0.54	−1.60	2.49	3.08	0.70	0.41
x 2B 3B		2	0.91	1.63	0.85	0.46	0.18	1.35	2.00	0.73	0.26	0.15
1B 2B 3B		0	−17.44	−17.19	−11.58	−5.54	−2.86	−18.70	−17.43	−9.76	−3.38	−1.55
1B 2B 3B		1	−12.92	−17.77	−15.30	−7.10	−3.72	−19.62	−14.64	−4.47	−2.11	−2.11
1B 2B 3B		2	−6.35	−19.26	−22.20	−10.05	−5.23	−7.33	−23.85	−23.78	−6.62	−3.10

Table 18.11. Simulated results using two lineups of average players from 1997 to 2009 batting in the first to eighth positions and an average pitcher from 1997 to 2009 batting in the ninth position. All 24 base-out states are shown for the eighth inning.

The chance that the opposing team was going to win the game was calculated for scenarios in which the eighth batter was either pitched to or walked. The difference in win percentage is shown in the columns in the following tables. As in the previous tables in this chapter, a negative percentage shows that walking the eighth batter in the lineup reduced the opposing (pitching) team's chance of winning the game by that percentage; a positive percentage shows that walking the eighth batter increased the chance of winning the game by that percentage.

					-- Before --		------ Top 1st ------					------ Bottom 5th ------			
Runners			Outs	-2	-1	Tie	+1	+2	-2	-1	Tie	+1	+2
x	x	x	0	-2.91	-2.95	-2.90	-2.55	-1.99	-3.68	-4.17	-3.94	-3.08	-2.24
x	x	x	1	-1.67	-1.59	-1.48	-1.27	-1.12	-1.88	-2.43	-2.01	-1.78	-1.39
x	x	x	2	-1.06	-1.17	-1.06	-0.98	-0.72	-1.35	-1.49	-1.32	-1.05	-0.72
1B	x	x	0	-5.60	-5.68	-5.10	-4.28	-3.47	-6.96	-7.44	-6.84	-5.22	-3.67
1B	x	x	1	-3.06	-3.19	-2.78	-2.52	-1.93	-3.74	-4.19	-3.64	-2.88	-1.93
1B	x	x	2	-1.39	-1.30	-1.35	-1.08	-0.91	-1.64	-1.73	-1.63	-1.26	-1.04
x	2B	x	0	-3.54	-3.29	-2.97	-2.47	-1.82	-4.59	-4.33	-3.60	-2.75	-1.80
x	2B	x	1	-1.73	-1.59	-1.41	-1.05	-0.71	-2.31	-1.99	-1.61	-1.04	-0.77
x	2B	x	2	-0.23	-0.31	-0.17	0.02	0.02	-0.34	-0.23	0.06	-0.02	0.08
x	x	3B	0	-2.96	-2.62	-2.21	-1.84	-1.30	-4.26	-3.50	-2.67	-1.82	-1.25
x	x	3B	1	-0.80	-0.44	-0.09	-0.12	-0.01	-1.42	-0.63	-0.05	**0.13**	**0.24**
x	x	3B	2	-0.44	-0.37	-0.20	-0.41	-0.19	-0.55	-0.32	-0.13	-0.21	-0.09
1B	2B	x	0	-7.92	-7.70	-6.79	-5.72	-4.49	-10.13	-10.23	-9.00	-6.74	-4.80
1B	2B	x	1	-4.67	-4.63	-4.26	-3.61	-2.86	-4.26	-6.12	-5.44	-4.22	-2.99
1B	2B	x	2	-0.92	-0.95	-0.88	-0.74	-0.59	-1.42	-1.30	-1.10	-0.73	-0.60
1B	x	3B	0	-4.79	-4.27	-3.51	-2.76	-1.98	-6.42	-5.51	-4.13	-2.88	-1.95
1B	x	3B	1	-1.87	-1.55	-1.12	-0.77	-0.54	-2.70	-1.90	-0.97	-0.57	-0.38
1B	x	3B	2	-0.28	-0.05	-0.10	-0.10	-0.05	-0.29	-0.13	0.08	0.08	0.05
x	2B	3B	0	-2.86	-2.48	-1.98	-1.59	-1.05	-3.87	-3.12	-2.15	-1.52	-0.93
x	2B	3B	1	-0.32	-0.01	**0.25**	**0.35**	**0.27**	-0.62	**0.19**	**0.63**	**0.66**	**0.53**
x	2B	3B	2	**0.56**	**0.56**	**0.54**	**0.54**	**0.39**	**0.61**	**0.88**	**0.74**	**0.59**	**0.46**
1B	2B	3B	0	-9.88	-9.12	-8.05	-6.51	-4.92	-12.52	-11.95	-9.82	-7.39	-5.07
1B	2B	3B	1	-8.31	-8.42	-7.72	-6.62	-5.17	-10.18	-11.25	-9.98	-7.76	-5.60
1B	2B	3B	2	-7.50	-8.16	-8.19	-7.40	-6.14	-8.22	-11.02	-11.51	-9.24	-6.92

Table 18.12. Simulated results using two lineups of average players from 1997 to 2009 batting in the first to eighth positions and an average pitcher from 1997 to 2009 batting in the ninth position. All 24 base-out states are shown for the bottom of the first and top of the fifth innings.

At the beginning of a game, the simulation showed that in only two base-out states was intentionally walking the eighth hitter to face the pitcher potentially a good strategy: (1) with men on second and third and one out and with men on second and third with two outs. Walks in these base-out states had GPAs of 0.449 and 0.456. In three other base-out states in which a walk would have a GPA of 0.386 to 0.411, an intentional walk did not make strategic sense.

There are a number of reasons why walking the eighth hitter to face the pitcher is generally not a good strategy at the beginning of the game. The GPA of a walk is much higher than the GPA of an average hitter. Walking the eighth hitter to face the pitcher potentially sets up a big inning at the beginning of the game. The eighth hitter is often a weaker hitter than those at the top of the lineup. Pitching to the eighth hitter preserves the pitcher's at-bat for the current inning or to lead off the next inning, delaying the at-bats of the stronger hitters at the beginning of the lineup. The simulation is able to balance all of these complex interactions.

In the middle innings, only a few additional base-out states arise in which walking the eighth hitter to face the pitcher makes strategic sense.

In the late innings of a close game, the pitcher is often removed for a pinch hitter. More game scenarios arise in the last innings where intentionally walking the eighth hitter to face the pitcher might be beneficial, but the availability of pinch hitters and additional relief pitchers limit this strategy's usefulness. If a pinch hitter bats, the data on intentionally walking average hitters applies and the intentional walk is rarely a good strategy.

If the pitcher is forced to bat at the end of the game, there are more game scenarios in which intentionally walking the eighth hitter is good strategy, and the benefits of the strategy are significantly higher than in earlier innings. These scenarios arise more frequently when the team at bat is tied or ahead.

In two of the three simulations in this chapter, players with GPAs significantly higher than the batters who followed them were walked. Bonds (batting fourth) had a GPA that was 0.146 points higher than J.T. Snow (batting fifth). An average player (batting eighth) had a GPA that was 0.149 points higher than an average pitcher (batting ninth). In both of these cases, there were many scenarios in which intentionally walking a batter made strategic sense.

One simulation looked at a lineup of average hitters, all of whom had the same GPAs. There were few instances in that scenario in which intentionally walking a batter made strategic sense.

How about a hitter who falls somewhere in between these extremes?

From 2001 to 2009, Albert Pujols, batting third, had a GPA 0.057 points higher than the GPA of all hitters who batted in the fourth position of the lineup. Pujols is one of the today's dominant hitters and is often walked intentionally.

Team	Year	GPA	GPAbrc	cGPA	BA	BB	I-BB	PA
St. Louis	2001	0.350	0.000	0.350	0.329	69	6	676
St. Louis	2002	0.342	0.001	0.343	0.314	72	13	675
St. Louis	2003	0.375	0.003	0.378	0.359	79	12	685
St. Louis	2004	0.362	0.001	0.363	0.331	84	12	692
St. Louis	2005	0.346	0.005	0.351	0.330	97	27	700
St. Louis	2006	0.382	0.005	0.387	0.331	92	28	634
St. Louis	2007	0.338	−0.001	0.337	0.327	99	22	679
St. Louis	2008	0.375	0.005	0.380	0.357	104	34	641
St. Louis	2009	0.373	0.003	0.375	0.327	115	44	700
Average		0.360	0.003	0.363	0.334	811	198	6,082

Table 18.13. Albert Pujols's statistics from 2001 to 2009.

Albert Pujols's offensive production from 2001 to 2009 was second only to that of Barry Bonds, whose production during this period was unmatched in baseball history. From 2001 to 2009, no hitter except Bonds was able to maintain Pujols's high level of production over so many seasons. During the period, Pujols was walked 811 times in 6,082 PAs (13.3 percen). He never led the league in total walks but did lead the league in intentional walks in 2005, 2008 and 2009.

Table 18.14 shows Pujols's statistics by base-out state from 2001 to 2009. The GPA of a walk in all 24 base-out states is listed alongside Pujols's actual GPA in each base-out state during this period. In only two base-out states does Pujols's actual GPA exceed the GPA of a walk: man on first with two outs and men on second and third with two outs. Based on GPA, one can conclude that it rarely makes sense to intentionally walk Pujols and that the intentional walks only added to his dominance during this period.

The number of PAs in each base-out state varied widely from 22 PAs with bases loaded and no outs to 1,198 PAs with bases empty and two outs. Because the accuracy of a statistic is related to how many events are sampled, it can be assumed that Pujols's GPA of 0.360 for all 6,082 PAs from 2001 to 2009 is a more accurate measure of his production than the GPA for each base-out state.

| -- Before -- | | | | Pujols | BB | | Int | | Frac |
Runners		Outs	BA	GPA	GPA	BB	BB	PA	BB
x	x	x	0	0.344	0.341	0.653	90	0	1,085	0.08
x	x	x	1	0.313	0.337	0.535	93	1	810	0.11
x	x	x	2	0.332	0.316	0.397	137	2	1,198	0.11
1B	x	x	0	0.341	0.381	0.871	18	0	284	0.06
1B	x	x	1	0.316	0.336	0.659	62	0	652	0.10
1B	x	x	2	0.335	0.346	0.489	53	0	390	0.14
x	2B	x	0	0.357	0.356	0.633	6	3	90	0.07
x	2B	x	1	0.324	0.379	0.507	68	40	240	0.28
x	2B	x	2	0.353	0.422	0.386	87	59	210	0.41
x	x	3B	0	0.375	0.579	0.686	5	2	15	0.33
x	x	3B	1	0.438	0.414	0.494	32	20	90	0.36
x	x	3B	2	0.274	0.318	0.411	26	16	90	0.29
1B	2B	x	0	0.331	0.412	1.090	9	0	146	0.06
1B	2B	x	1	0.288	0.389	0.920	14	0	141	0.10
1B	2B	x	2	0.356	0.532	0.598	17	0	154	0.11
1B	x	3B	0	0.521	0.468	0.795	4	1	58	0.07
1B	x	3B	1	0.426	0.405	0.661	11	2	79	0.14
1B	x	3B	2	0.222	0.381	0.542	14	2	78	0.18
x	2B	3B	0	0.261	0.245	0.572	10	9	39	0.26
x	2B	3B	1	0.333	0.360	0.449	21	19	45	0.47
x	2B	3B	2	0.320	0.512	0.456	27	22	53	0.51
1B	2B	3B	0	0.471	0.508	1.240	1	0	22	0.05
1B	2B	3B	1	0.500	0.711	1.250	1	0	52	0.02
1B	2B	3B	2	0.339	0.555	1.272	5	0	61	0.08
Total/Average				0.334	0.360		811	198	6,082	0.13

Table 18.14. Albert Pujols's statistics from 2001 to 2009 by base-out state.

The GPA of a walk was more than Pujols's overall GPA of 0.360 in every base-out state, which suggests that it might in fact never make sense to intentionally walk Pujols.

But aren't there some times in a close game when walking Pujols was beneficial? This question can be addressed as it was for Bonds, by simulating close games with the two-lineup simulator discussed in the chapter "GPA and Winning Games." The St. Louis Cardinals lineup changed too much over the years to select a representative lineup; it's better instead to use the average of each position in the batting order from 1997 to 2009 throughout MLB, with Pujols batting third and an average pitcher batting ninth. The second lineup will consist of the average of each position in the batting order from 1997 to 2009 and with an average pitcher batting ninth. The players chosen and order in which they bat only minimally affect the data.

Lineup #1	Years	GPA	GPAbrc	cGPA	BA	OBP	RBI	HR
1st — Lineup Pos 1	1997–2009	0.267	0.004	0.270	0.275	0.343	64	14
2nd — Lineup Pos 2	1997–2009	0.271	0.003	0.274	0.276	0.339	74	16
3rd — Lineup Pos 3	1997–2009	0.306	0.003	0.309	0.288	0.370	105	28
4th — Lineup Pos 4	1997–2009	0.303	0.002	0.305	0.283	0.365	112	31
5th — Lineup Pos 5	1997–2009	0.283	0.002	0.284	0.272	0.344	98	25
6th — Lineup Pos 6	1997–2009	0.270	0.001	0.271	0.266	0.334	85	21
7th — Lineup Pos 7	1997–2009	0.257	0.001	0.258	0.258	0.322	77	17
8th — Lineup Pos 8	1997–2009	0.246	0.001	0.248	0.252	0.318	67	13
9th — Average Pitcher	1997–2009	0.119	0.001	0.120	0.143	0.178	10	1
	Average	0.263	0.002	0.265	0.261	0.331	61	17

Should They Have Walked Bonds?

Lineup #2	Years	GPA	GPAbrc	cGPA	BA	OBP	RBI	HR
1st — Lineup Pos 1	1997–2009	0.267	0.004	0.270	0.275	0.343	64	14
2nd — Lineup Pos 2	1997–2009	0.271	0.003	0.274	0.276	0.339	74	16
3rd — Pujols, Albert	2001–2009	0.360	0.003	0.363	0.334	0.427	124	41
4th — Lineup Pos 4	1997–2009	0.303	0.002	0.305	0.283	0.365	112	31
5th — Lineup Pos 5	1997–2009	0.283	0.002	0.284	0.272	0.344	98	25
6th — Lineup Pos 6	1997–2009	0.270	0.001	0.271	0.266	0.334	85	21
7th — Lineup Pos 7	1997–2009	0.257	0.001	0.258	0.258	0.322	77	17
8th — Lineup Pos 8	1997–2009	0.246	0.001	0.248	0.252	0.318	67	13
9th — Average Pitcher	1997–2009	0.119	0.001	0.120	0.143	0.178	10	1
Average		0.269	0.002	0.271	0.266	0.337	63	18

Table 18.15. Lineups used by the two-lineup simulator to evaluate the effect of walking Pujols in various game scenarios.

At the beginning a game, the simulation shows that in only two base-out states is intentionally walking Pujols potentially a good strategy: with a man on second with two outs and with men on second and third with two outs. Walks in these base-out states have GPAs of 0.386 and 0.456, lower than Pujols's actual GPAs of 0.422 and 0.512 in these base-out states.

As the game progresses, more and more scenarios arise in which walking Pujols makes strategic sense. The pattern is similar to the one seen for walking Bonds and walking the eighth hitter to face the pitcher, except that there are fewer scenarios in which walking Pujols is statistically justified. This is not surprising since Pujols's GPA was only 0.057 greater than the hitter that followed him in the simulated lineup.

— — Before — —			— — — — — Top 9th — — — — — —					— — — — Bottom 9th — — — —				
Runners		Outs	−2	−1	Tie	+1	+2	−2	−1	Tie	+1	+2
x	x	x	0	−6.74	−9.00	−5.98	−2.15	−0.91	−8.45	−10.70	−5.05
x	x	x	1	−4.80	−6.51	−3.99	−1.53	−0.69	−6.17	−7.79	−3.17
x	x	x	2	−2.37	−3.48	−1.67	−0.59	−0.36	−3.19	−4.27	−1.04
1B	x	x	0	−10.41	−12.76	−9.25	−3.09	−1.52	−12.28	−13.79	−8.37
1B	x	x	1	−7.27	−9.35	−6.77	−2.37	−1.13	−8.77	−10.53	−6.16
1B	x	x	2	−3.58	−5.15	−3.68	−1.30	−0.62	−4.27	−5.88	−3.51
x	2B	x	0	−9.33	−6.04	−1.98	−0.93	−0.40	−10.93	−5.13	0.33
x	2B	x	1	−5.17	−2.70	−0.33	−0.27	−0.10	−6.04	−1.93	1.08
x	2B	x	2	−1.33	0.94	1.58	0.44	0.23	−1.39	2.00	2.24
x	x	3B	0	−4.27	−0.83	0.28	−0.01	0.08	−4.42	0.29	1.38
x	x	3B	1	−4.48	−0.68	1.35	0.25	0.17	−5.20	0.44	2.84
x	x	3B	2	−3.95	−3.30	−1.25	−0.53	−0.29	−4.86	−3.42	0.03
1B	2B	x	0	−11.75	−16.52	−12.07	−4.20	−1.94	−12.86	−18.89	−11.11
1B	2B	x	1	−9.42	−15.07	−11.81	−3.97	−1.92	−10.50	−17.60	−11.33
1B	2B	x	2	−3.06	−3.21	−1.14	−0.54	−0.21	−3.12	−3.33	−0.11
1B	x	3B	0	−10.08	−5.90	−0.55	−0.52	−0.17	−11.37	−4.67	2.58
1B	x	3B	1	−8.49	−7.29	−3.10	−1.21	−0.56	−9.34	−7.15	−0.99
1B	x	3B	2	−5.23	−5.69	−3.02	−1.10	−0.58	−5.88	−6.12	−1.95
x	2B	3B	0	−6.99	−4.24	−2.37	−0.95	−0.39	−6.89	−2.72	−1.29
x	2B	3B	1	−2.98	−0.17	0.44	0.11	0.12	−2.73	1.09	1.11
x	2B	3B	2	1.23	2.33	1.66	0.58	0.27	2.05	3.06	1.71
1B	2B	3B	0	−15.00	−14.62	−8.00	−3.05	−1.34	−17.17	−15.25	−5.15
1B	2B	3B	1	−10.31	−15.64	−10.73	−3.80	−1.77	−12.43	−18.59	−9.57
1B	2B	3B	2	−4.61	−22.66	−24.59	−7.69	−3.73	−4.75	−29.22	−29.38

Table 18.16. Simulated results using the two lineups in Table 18.15. All 24 base-out states are shown with Pujols at the plate in the ninth inning with the score tied or his team leading or trailing by as many as two runs.

--Before--			------Top 8th------					------Bottom 8th------				
Runners		Outs	−2	−1	Tie	+1	+2	−2	−1	Tie	+1	+2
x	x	x	0	−6.22	−7.47	−5.51	−2.75	−1.47	−7.18	−7.99	−4.87	−1.77	−0.75
x	x	x	1	−4.28	−5.01	−3.63	−1.84	−0.95	−4.96	−5.33	−3.24	−1.14	−0.56
x	x	x	2	−1.56	−1.63	−1.10	−0.62	−0.28	−1.85	−1.75	−0.94	−0.34	−0.14
1B	x	x	0	−9.52	−10.46	−8.24	−4.11	−2.17	−10.42	−11.23	−7.27	−2.63	−1.16
1B	x	x	1	−6.41	−7.05	−5.50	−2.73	−1.36	−7.11	−7.60	−5.20	−1.77	−0.82
1B	x	x	2	−2.65	−2.92	−2.75	−1.31	−0.75	−3.01	−3.18	−2.64	−0.85	−0.38
x	2B	x	0	−7.69	−5.47	−2.53	−1.32	−0.73	−8.27	−4.68	−1.60	−0.79	−0.32
x	2B	x	1	−3.93	−2.28	−0.74	−0.40	−0.27	−4.05	−1.67	−0.14	−0.21	−0.03
x	2B	x	2	−0.36	**1.22**	**1.32**	**0.61**	**0.31**	−0.25	**1.91**	**1.55**	**0.48**	**0.22**
x	x	3B	0	−3.41	−1.22	−0.14	−0.21	−0.07	−3.14	−0.71	0.18	−0.02	0.05
x	x	3B	1	−2.92	−0.96	**0.58**	**0.26**	0.08	−3.23	−0.13	**1.15**	**0.26**	**0.19**
x	x	3B	2	−2.66	−1.97	−0.89	−0.54	−0.22	−2.95	−1.71	−0.71	−0.19	−0.15
1B	2B	x	0	−11.12	−13.38	−10.50	−5.21	2.69	−12.07	−14.44	−9.52	−3.39	−1.55
1B	2B	x	1	−9.00	−11.68	−9.82	−4.77	2.52	−9.85	−12.71	−9.16	−3.12	−1.44
1B	2B	x	2	−2.26	−1.61	−0.83	−0.51	−0.29	−2.22	−1.22	−0.59	−0.32	−0.03
1B	x	3B	0	−7.92	−5.00	−1.74	−1.01	−0.49	−8.52	−4.24	−0.54	−0.48	−0.15
1B	x	3B	1	−6.83	−5.71	−3.05	−1.66	−0.88	−7.44	−5.42	−2.27	−0.94	−0.43
1B	x	3B	2	−3.85	−3.52	−2.28	−1.18	−0.63	−4.27	−3.36	−2.07	−0.81	−0.33
x	2B	3B	0	−6.20	−4.08	−2.62	−1.31	−0.69	−5.99	−3.59	−1.89	−0.79	−0.31
x	2B	3B	1	−2.37	−0.65	0.08	−0.03	0.03	−2.18	0.09	**0.47**	**0.11**	0.09
x	2B	3B	2	**1.35**	**2.09**	**1.57**	**0.67**	**0.45**	**1.77**	**2.43**	**1.47**	**0.59**	**0.17**
1B	2B	3B	0	−12.84	−12.19	−7.87	−3.98	−2.13	−14.01	−12.18	−6.35	−2.48	−1.09
1B	2B	3B	1	−9.39	−12.01	−9.15	−4.53	−2.43	−10.61	−13.05	−8.43	−2.99	−1.36
1B	2B	3B	2	−7.55	−16.54	−18.43	−8.77	−4.71	−8.33	−19.99	−19.10	−6.22	−3.00

Table 18.17. Simulated results using the two lineups in Table 18.15. All 24 base-out states are shown with Pujols at the plate in the eighth inning with the score tied or his team leading or trailing by as many as two runs.

--Before--			------Top 1st------					------Bottom 5th------				
Runners		Outs	−2	−1	Tie	+1	+2	−2	−1	Tie	+1	+2
x	x	x	0	−3.20	−3.26	−3.00	−2.38	−1.95	−4.07	−4.34	−3.97	−2.96	−2.23
x	x	x	1	−2.19	−2.15	−1.99	−1.78	−1.37	−2.97	−3.07	−2.76	−2.12	−1.63
x	x	x	2	−0.89	−0.87	−0.88	−0.64	−0.50	−1.41	−1.41	−1.04	−0.89	−0.62
1B	x	x	0	−5.19	−5.00	−4.45	−3.77	−2.91	−6.63	−6.78	−5.99	−4.53	−3.30
1B	x	x	1	−3.44	−3.41	−3.18	−2.63	−2.08	−4.69	−4.89	−4.33	−3.29	−2.33
1B	x	x	2	−1.81	−1.66	−1.58	−1.19	−0.96	−2.39	−2.26	−2.05	−1.57	−1.21
x	2B	x	0	−3.17	−2.89	−2.40	−1.89	−1.51	−4.43	−3.96	−3.04	−2.10	−1.44
x	2B	x	1	−1.52	−1.32	−1.02	−0.92	−0.62	−2.28	−1.91	−1.35	−1.01	−0.56
x	2B	x	2	**0.11**	0.06	**0.33**	**0.23**	**0.15**	−0.14	**0.21**	**0.39**	**0.31**	**0.50**
x	x	3B	0	−1.39	−1.05	−0.82	−0.61	−0.48	−1.83	−1.57	−0.96	−0.59	−0.34
x	x	3B	1	−0.98	−0.92	−0.40	−0.34	−0.29	−1.59	−1.00	−0.39	−0.34	−0.12
x	x	3B	2	−1.37	−0.98	−0.93	−0.94	−0.56	−1.77	−1.55	−1.21	−0.94	−0.65
1B	2B	x	0	−6.77	−6.59	−5.82	−4.82	−3.87	−8.57	−8.73	−7.75	−5.84	−4.26
1B	2B	x	1	−5.86	−5.50	−5.03	−4.27	−3.46	−7.25	−7.65	−6.82	−5.32	−3.84
1B	2B	x	2	−1.30	−1.20	−0.88	−0.73	−0.64	−1.88	−1.68	−1.14	−0.89	−0.63
1B	x	3B	0	−3.49	−3.05	−2.43	−2.02	−1.33	−4.82	−3.99	−2.80	−2.01	−1.28
1B	x	3B	1	−3.39	−3.12	−2.70	−2.14	−1.65	−4.70	−4.30	−3.58	−2.51	−1.64
1B	x	3B	2	−2.15	−2.01	−1.70	−1.45	−1.18	−2.96	−2.79	−2.30	−1.72	−1.11
x	2B	3B	0	−3−39	−3.03	−2.52	−1.92	−1.33	−4.40	−3.73	−2.97	−2.09	−1.42
x	2B	3B	1	−1.10	−0.87	−0.67	−0.41	−0.32	−1.63	−0.96	−0.67	−0.50	−0.27
x	2B	3B	2	**0.47**	**0.55**	**0.55**	**0.36**	**0.52**	**0.45**	**0.84**	**0.86**	**0.69**	**0.51**
1B	2B	3B	0	−6.83	−6.26	−5.41	−4.40	−3.44	−8.95	−8.30	−6.87	−5.14	−3.61

		——Before——		——————Top 1st——————					—————Bottom 5th—————				
Runners	Outs	−2	−1	Tie	+1	+2	−2	−1	Tie	+1	+2
1B 2B 3B	1	−5.83	−5.63	−5.40	−4.22	−3.30	−7.26	−7.54	−6.78	−5.13	−3.59
1B 2B 3B	2	−7.33	−7.53	−7.32	−6.36	−5.27	−8.63	−10.23	−10.26	−8.39	−6.27

Table 18.18. Simulated results using the two lineups in Table 18.15. All 24 base-out states are shown with Pujols at the plate in the bottom of the first inning or top of the fifth inning with the score tied or his team leading or trailing by as many as two runs.

Some of the choices managers made are particularly difficult to justify. Pujols was walked 25.6 percent of the time with men on second and third and no one out. In that base-out state, Pulols' GPA was 0.245 and the GPA of a walk was 0.572. Pujols was also walked 28.3 percent of the time with a man on second and one out, a base-out state in which Pulols' GPA was 0.379 and the GPA of a walk was 0.507.

As they had been with Bonds, managers were so afraid of Pujols's potential production that they created a self-fulfilling prophecy. Giving Pujols a walk with a GPA of 0.507 to 0.572 contributes to his dominance; pitching to him was, according to the simulation, clearly the better option. Pujols's GPA of 0.447 with runners on third and fewer than two outs was partially attributable to managers walking him in 21.2 percent in that scenario.

	GPA	BA	OBP	SLG	PA	Hits	RBI	HR
Outs	0.360	0.349	0.406	0.656	1,739	545	315	120
1 Out	0.360	0.324	0.423	0.620	2,109	564	440	127
2 Outs	0.359	0.330	0.447	0.610	2,234	608	357	119
Bases Empty	0.330	0.331	0.407	0.627	3,093	908	196	196
1st Only	0.349	0.327	0.403	0.582	1,326	385	194	73
2nd or 3rd	0.425	0.345	0.483	0.673	1,663	424	722	97
3rd,<2 Outs	0.447	0.435	0.505	0.830	400	110	275	22
Total	0.360	0.334	0.427	0.628	6,082	1,717	1,112	366

Table 18.19. Statistics by base-out state for Pujols's 2001 to 2009 seasons.

It is clear why the intentional walk is such a controversial strategy. The score, inning and skills of the hitters due up next determine the few game scenarios in which the move makes sense. Without a sophisticated simulation, it would be nearly impossible to make the right call.

The Sacrifice Bunt

A batter is credited with a sacrifice bunt when, with fewer than two outs, advances one or more baserunners with a bunt and is either put out at first base or reaches on a fielding error. A sacrifice bunt does not count as an at-bat.

If the official scorer judges that the batter was bunting "exclusively" for a base hit, the batter is charged with a time at bat rather than a sacrifice bunt. If the batter gets a hit while attempting to sacrifice bunt, he is credited with a hit rather than a sacrifice bunt.

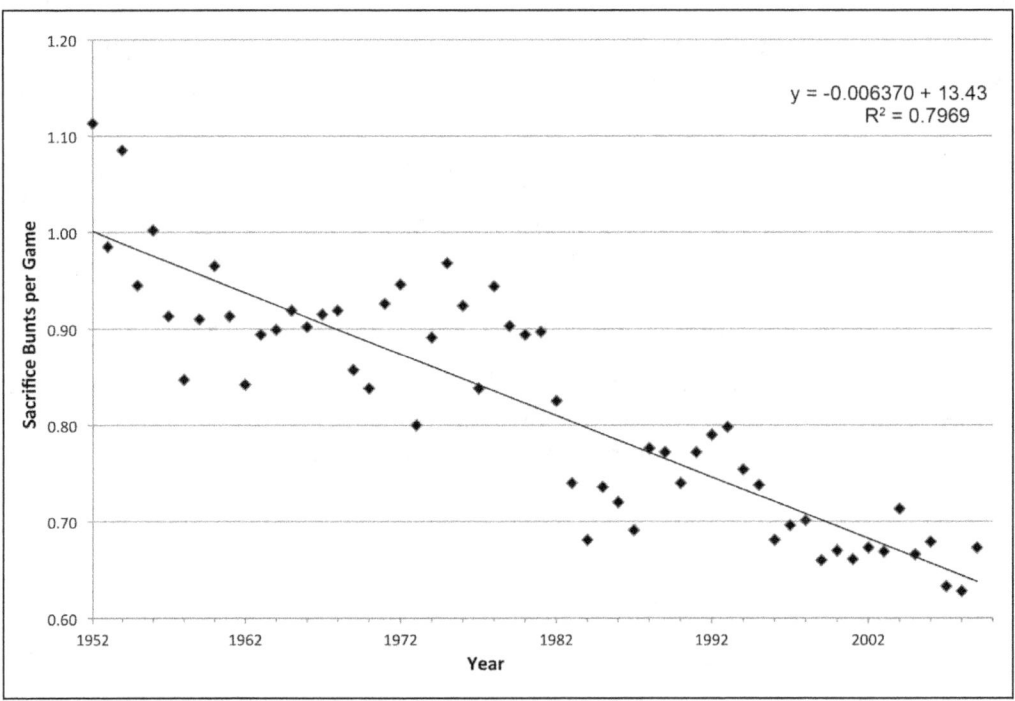

Figure 13. Sacrifice bunts per game from 1952 to 2009.

The sacrifice bunt is one of the most controversial strategies in baseball, especially when executed by a non-pitcher. As Figure 13 shows, it has become less popular over the years.

In only three base-out states does GPA suggest that a sacrifice bunt is a good strategy: (1) with a man on third and one out; (2) with men on first and third and one out; and (3) with the bases loaded and no one out. Successful sacrifice bunts in all three of these base-out states have GPAs between 0.324 and 0.410 and lead to a positive change in run expectancy.

—Before— Runners			Outs	—After— Runners			Outs	Runs	GPA of Sac Bunt	RE Before	RE After	Δ RE
1B	—	—	0	—	2B	—	1	0	0.053	0.921	0.706	−0.215
1B	—	—	1	—	2B	—	2	0	0.060	0.553	0.340	−0.213
—	2B	—	0	—	—	3B	1	0	0.089	1.166	0.981	−0.185
—	2B	—	1	—	—	3B	2	0	−0.060	0.706	0.372	−0.334
—	—	3B	0	—	—	—	1	1	0.139	1.440	1.288	−0.152
—	—	3B	1	—	—	—	2	1	0.401	0.981	1.111	+0.130
1B	2B	—	0	—	2B	3B	1	0	0.174	1.525	1.429	−0.096
1B	2B	—	1	—	2B	3B	2	0	−0.163	0.939	0.596	−0.343
1B	—	3B	0	—	2B	—	1	1	0.155	1.835	1.706	−0.129
1B	—	3B	1	—	2B	—	2	1	0.410	1.204	1.340	+0.136
—	2B	3B	0	—	—	3B	1	1	0.207	2.035	1.981	−0.054
—	2B	3B	1	—	—	3B	2	1	0.230	1.429	1.372	−0.057
1B	2B	3B	0	—	2B	3B	1	1	0.324	2.345	2.429	+0.084
1B	2B	3B	1	—	2B	3B	2	1	0.254	1.592	1.596	−0.004

Table 19.1. Successful sacrifice bunts along with their GPAs. Data from 1997 to 2009.

In three other scenarios, the strategic value of a sacrifice bunt is not clear-cut. With men on second and third with no one out, men on second and third with one out, and bases loaded with one out, successful sacrifice bunts have GPAs between 0.207 and 0.254 but bring a slightly negative change in run expectancy. For a below-average hitter, a sacrifice bunt in these base-out states may be good strategy, but otherwise it's a poor move.

Finally, for all but the weakest of hitters, the sacrifice bunt is clearly poor strategy with a man on third and no one out, men on first and second with no one out, and men on first and third with no one out. Successful sacrifice bunts in these three base-out states have GPAs between 0.139 and 0.174 and bring a negative change in run expectancy.

The statistics in Table 19.1 were calculated assuming that 100 percent of the sacrifice bunts were successful. In reality, some will of course fail, reducing the potential benefits of a sacrifice bunt even further.

It would be nice to use the Retrosheet database to carefully examine the outcomes of sacrifice bunts, but in the database, a failed bunt appears as an out, a superb bunt appears as a hit, a foul ball on a bunt attempt with two strikes appears as a strikeout, and accumulated strikes from attempting to bunt go unattributed if the batter abandons the attempt and swings away at subsequent pitches. Each of these limitations is worth considering at slightly greater length.

A bunt that would have failed without a fielding or throwing error appears as an out. The increased production from the error is not properly attributed to the bunt attempt.

Baseball announcers traditionally say the count is even when there is one ball and one strike or two balls and two strikes. Although in each instance the number of balls and strikes is the same, the balance between the hitter and pitcher is not even. With a count of one ball, one strike, hitters have a GPA of 0.293, which is 0.027 points higher than the average GPA of 0.266 for all PAs. The count slightly favors the hitter. With a count of two balls, two strikes, hitters have a GPA of 0.168, which is 0.098 points lower than the average GPA of 0.266. That count, then, strongly favors the pitcher.

Count	0 Balls	1 Ball	2 Balls	3 Balls	Average
0 Strikes	0.298	0.310	0.338	0.538	0.328
1 Strike	0.280	0.293	0.310	0.466	0.323
2 Strikes	0.131	0.148	0.168	0.325	0.198
Average	0.249	0.232	0.227	0.387	0.266

Table 19.2. GPA by count. Data from 1997 to 2012.

Count	0 Balls	1 Ball	2 Balls	3 Balls	Average
0 Strikes	0.332	0.339	0.354	0.376	0.337
1 Strike	0.319	0.326	0.338	0.354	0.329
2 Strikes	0.159	0.173	0.192	0.228	0.187
Average	0.282	0.259	0.250	0.257	0.264

Table 19.3. Batting average by count. Data from 1997 to 2012.

Three counts, in fact, strongly favor the pitcher, ranging from 0.098 to 0.135 GPA points below the 0.266 average: no balls, two strikes; one ball, two strikes; and two balls, two strikes. Two counts likewise strongly favor the batter by 0.200 to 0.272 GPA points: three balls, no strikes and three balls, one strike. The other seven counts slightly favor the hitter, boosting the GPA from 0.014 to 0.072 points above average. Batting average does not accurately reflect the dramatic differences in production seen with different ball and strike counts.

Batters are less productive as they accumulate strikes during a plate appearance. Table 19.2 shows that with counts of zero, one or two balls, batters are about half as productive with two-strike counts as they are with zero- or one-strike counts. A batter who accumulates strikes while attempting to bunt often abandons the bunt attempt and swings away at subsequent pitches so he does not strike out on a foul bunt attempt. In that scenario (the bunt attempt abandoned after one or more strikes), his PA would not appear as sacrifice bunt in the Retrosheet database and the lost production from the accumulated strikes would not properly be attributed to the bunt attempt.

Table 19.4 lists all successful sacrifice bunts with a man on first and no outs by outcome for the years 1997 to 2009. The goal in that base-out state is to advance the runner to second while "spending" one out. The double play is thereby avoided and the lead runner moved into scoring position. This outcome has a GPA of only 0.053, far lower than the GPA of an average pitcher. The actual GPA of all successful sacrifice bunts with a man on first and no outs was 0.104 because of the added benefit from defensive errors (ignoring the issues described above).

Based on GPA, one can conclude that a sacrifice bunt with a man on first and no outs is not good game strategy except possibly for very weak hitters such as pitchers.

Because GPA is based on run expectancy, it balances the chance of scoring one run with the chance of having a big inning. For most games in the early and middle innings the percentages discussed above apply. At the end of a close game with the teams tied or trailing by a single run, the percentages will change because only one or two runs are needed. It is no longer necessary to consider the RE because a big inning is not needed. Rather, the chance of scoring a small number of runs is more important.

Could there be more situations in close games when the sacrifice bunt is good game strategy?

The Sacrifice Bunt

— Before —		— After —				GPA of	RE	
Runners	Outs	Runners			Outs	Runs	Number	Play	After	Δ RE
1B — —	0	1B 2B —	0	0	306	0.871	1.525	+0.604
1B — —	0	1B — 3B	0	0	75	1.181	1.835	+0.914
1B — —	0	— 2B 3B	0	0	80	1.382	2.035	+1.114
1B — —	0	— 2B —	0	1	11	1.513	2.166	+1.245
1B — —	0	— — 3B	0	1	9	1.787	2.440	+1.519
1B — —	0	1B — —	1	0	2	−0.042	0.553	−0.368
1B — —	0	— 2B —	1	0	8,678	0.053	0.706	−0.215
1B — —	0	— — 3B	1	0	18	0.328	0.981	+0.060
1B — —	0	— — —	1	1	2	0.634	1.288	+0.367
1B — —	0	— — —	2	0	14	−0.542	0.111	−0.810
		Total/Average			9,195	0.104	0.758	−0.163

Table 19.4. Successful sacrifice bunts with a man on first and no outs, along with each outcome's GPA. The run expectency before the play was 0.921 runs. Data from 1997 to 2009.

This question can be addressed by simulating close games with the two-lineup simulator discussed in the chapter "Winning Games." Both lineups will consist of average players from 1997 to 2009.

The chance that the team at bat is going to win the game is calculated (1) with the team at bat not bunting; (2) with the team at bat executing a successful sacrifice bunt, after which the batter is out and the all runners advance one base; and (3) with the team at bat failing to execute a sacrifice bunt and the lead runner being thrown out.

The difference in win percentage between a successful sacrifice bunt and not bunting is shown in the columns of tables 19.5–19.8. A negative number shows bunting reduces the chance that the team at bat will win the game by that percentage. A positive number (in bold) shows that bunting increases the chance the team at bat will win the game by that percentage.

For those game scenarios for which the percentage is positive, a second percentage (not in bold) appears below the first; it indicates how often the sacrifice bunt needs to be successful to justify the risk.

— — Before — —		— — — — — Top 8th — — — — —					— — — — — Bottom 8th — — — — —				
Runners	Outs	−2	−1	Tie	+1	+2	−2	−1	Tie	+1	+2
1B x 3B	1	−2.30	5.26	8.36	4.11	2.27	−2.09	8.36	10.31	2.73	1.24
1B x 3B	1		76%	65%	66%	66%		71%	61%	63%	65%

Table 19.5. Sample table for data on successful sacrifice bunts The top row shows the change in a team's chances of winning and the bottom (with percentage symbol) shows the success rate required to justify the risk.

Table 19.5 shows how the sacrifice bunt data is displayed with men on first and third and one out in the top and bottom of the 8th inning of close games. For example:

1. With the game tied in the top of the eighth inning, the team at bat will increase its chance of winning the game by 8.36 percent if the sacrifice bunt is successful (resulting in a man on second with two outs and one run scoring). If the bunt fails (resulting in men on first and second with two outs) the team at bat would win 48.09 percent (data not shown) of the time. The team at bat would have to bunt successfully at least 65 percent (calculation below) of the time in this scenario to justify the risk.

2. Trailing by two runs in the bottom of the eighth inning, the team at bat will decrease its chance of winning the game by 2.09 percent (from 29.41 percent to 27.32 percent, data

not shown) if the sacrifice bunt is successful. A sacrifice bunt in this game scenario is a poor game strategy.

The formula to calculate the success rate needed to justify the risk of the sacrifice bunt is shown below. WinSH is the chance of winning the game with a successful sacrifice bunt (a species of sacrifice hit and so indicated by the same abbreviation, "SH"), WinNoSH the chance of winning with no bunt attempt, and WinFailedSH the chance of winning the game when the sacrifice bunt fails and the lead runner is thrown out.

Success Rate × (WinSH − WinNoSH) =
(100% − Percent-Success) × (WinNoSH − WinFailedSH)

Success Rate = (WinNoSH − WinFailedSH) / (WinSH − WinFailedSH) × 100%

For example, if a successful sacrifice bunt will win the game 60 percent of the time, a non-bunt will win the game 50 percent of the time and having the lead runner thrown out on a failed sacrifice bunt attempt will win the game 20 percent of the time, the success rate needed to justify the bunt attempt is:

Success Rate = (50% − 20%) / (60% − 20%) × 100% = 75%

In the first of the two examples above (men on first and third, one out and the game tied in the top of the eighth inning), the sacrifice bunt can be justified only if it is successful 65 percent of the time:

Success Rate = (63.80% − 48.09%) / (72.16% − 48.09%) × 100% = 65%

—— Before ——			—————— Top 9th ——————					———— Bottom 9th ————				
Runners		Outs	−2	−1	Tie	+1	+2	−2	−1	Tie	+1	+2
1B	x	x	0	−5.68	−5.44	−2.44	−0.86	−0.42	−6.97	−5.54	−1.37	
1B	x	x	1	−4.98	−6.32	−3.91	−1.23	−0.67	−6.29	−7.12	−2.91	
x	2B	x	0	−6.83	−4.04	−0.01	−0.34	−0.14	−8.13	−3.33	1.78	
x	2B	x	0								91%	
x	2B	x	1	−6.00	−10.30	−8.01	−2.47	−1.18	−7.46	−12.29	−7.43	
x	x	3B	0	−8.59	−1.46	4.52	0.80	0.35	−10.40	1.09	7.52	
x	x	3B	0			86%	91%	91%		97%	79%		
x	x	3B	1	−6.66	6.41	12.86	3.05	1.47	−8.27	11.23	16.73	
x	x	3B	1		79%	66%	69%	69%		74%	61%		
1B	2B	x	0	−4.16	0.27	1.55	0.27	0.08	−4.30	1.96	2.55	
1B	2B	x	0		98%	88%	93%			90%	80%		
1B	2B	x	1	−5.82	−8.76	−7.98	−2.32	−1.00	−6.46	−10.38	−7.83	
1B	x	3B	0	−6.26	1.69	4.63	0.96	0.50	−6.53	4.99	6.60	
1B	x	3B	0		94%	83%	86%	86%		87%	77%		
1B	x	3B	1	−6.42	8.46	13.64	3.41	1.55	−7.17	14.26	17.38	
1B	x	3B	1		73%	60%	64%	64%		67%	55%		
x	2B	3B	0	−4.17	5.43	5.52	1.42	0.76	−3.00	9.74	6.69	
x	2B	3B	0		86%	81%	84%	83%		80%	77%		
x	2B	3B	1	−10.66	3.06	11.01	2.36	1.16	−12.52	8.36	15.42	
x	2B	3B	1		91%	69%	75%	75%		82%	60%		
1B	2B	3B	0	1.14	6.81	5.92	1.70	0.81	3.34	9.83	6.33	
1B	2B	3B	0	93%	72%	67%	69%	69%	84%	67%	61%	
1B	2B	3B	1	−8.51	4.00	11.76	2.60	1.27	−9.82	8.66	16.23	
1B	2B	3B	1		85%	60%	68%	67%		75%	52%		

Table 19.6. Simulated results for two lineups of average players from 1997 to 2009. Game scenarios are from the ninth inning.

It is assumed that the benefits of defensive errors and bunts that turn into hits exactly offset the harm from accumulating strikes while attempting to bunt and making an out without advancing the runners. These assumptions probably result in a small bias in favor of the strategy of the sacrifice bunt.

From the beginning to middle innings of a close game, the simulation shows that in only three base-out states is a successful sacrifice bunt potentially a good strategy for an average hitter: (1) with a man on third and one out; (2) with men on first and third and one out; and (3) with bases loaded and no one out. Successful sacrifice bunts in all three of these base-out states have GPAs between 0.324 and 0.410.

The success rate needed to justify the risk of a sacrifice bunt in these base-out states was in simulation always above 73 percent and sometimes close to 100 percent. Few batters are skilled enough to bunt successfully even 85 percent of the time. In the early and middle innings, then, there are few game scenarios in which the success rate needed is low enough to justify the risk of the sacrifice bunt for an average hitter.

As the game moves into the later innings, more and more scenarios arise in which a sacrifice bunt might be good strategy, as the success rate needed to justify the risk drops into the 52–80 percent range. Many hitters are able to lay down successful sacrifice bunts this often. There are, however, a few scenarios that in earlier innings might have lent themselves to bunting but that now, with the game in its final frames, no longer do.

It is clear why the sacrifice bunt is such a controversial strategy for an average hitter. The scenarios in which it makes sense, or might, change with the score and from inning to inning. The simulations suggest, in other words, that the only answer to the question Does it make sense to sacrifice? is Well, it depends.

— — Before — —			— — — — — Top 8th — — — — — —					— — — — — Bottom 8th — — — — —				
Runners		Outs	−2	−1	Tie	+1	+2	−2	−1	Tie	+1	+2
1B	x	x	0	−4.48	−4.20	−2.51	−1.33	−0.63	−5.15	−4.31	−1.92	−0.71	−0.34
1B	x	x	1	−4.01	−4.66	−3.41	−1.80	−0.95	−4.81	−5.25	−3.02	−1.06	−0.52
x	2B	x	0	−4.73	−3.40	−1.17	−0.69	−0.39	−5.41	−2.90	−0.15	−0.32	−0.16
x	2B	x	1	−5.51	−7.60	−6.29	−3.19	−1.73	−6.46	−8.84	−6.12	−1.89	−0.94
x	x	3B	0	−5.25	−1.54	1.71	0.61	0.39	−5.83	−0.25	3.28	0.62	0.31
x	x	3B	0			92%	94%	93%			86%	91%	90%
x	x	3B	1	−2.44	4.31	7.52	3.55	2.06	−2.64	6.92	9.67	2.42	1.13
x	x	3B	1		80%	70%	72%	71%		76%	66%	69%	70%
1B	2B	x	0	−2.91	−0.56	0.56	0.21	0.05	−2.77	0.40	1.26	0.22	0.08
1B	2B	x	0			94%	96%			97%	88%	93%	
1B	2B	x	1	−5.45	−6.99	−6.27	−3.00	−1.73	−6.22	−7.70	−5.87	−1.87	−0.90
1B	x	3B	0	−4.03	0.25	2.21	1.01	0.59	−3.86	1.95	3.48	0.78	0.42
1B	x	3B	0		99%	88%	89%	89%		92%	83%	87%	85%
1B	x	3B	1	−2.30	5.26	8.36	4.11	2.27	−2.09	8.36	10.31	2.73	1.24
1B	x	3B	1		76%	65%	66%	66%		71%	61%	63%	65%
x	2B	3B	0	−2.55	2.46	3.29	1.61	0.96	−1.63	4.79	4.10	1.13	0.55
x	2B	3B	0		91%	85%	86%	85%		85%	82%	84%	83%
x	2B	3B	1	−5.68	1.40	5.64	2.64	1.50	−6.18	4.04	8.23	1.88	0.91
x	2B	3B	1		94%	77%	79%	78%		87%	69%	75%	75%
1B	2B	3B	0	0.99	4.12	4.08	2.16	1.19	2.46	6.01	4.53	1.37	0.67
1B	2B	3B	0	93%	78%	72%	72%	72%	85%	71%	67%	69%	68%
1B	2B	3B	1	−4.39	2.24	6.54	2.99	1.69	−4.48	4.84	8.74	2.15	1.01
1B	2B	3B	1		88%	69%	71%	72%		80%	61%	67%	66%

Table 19.7. Simulated results using two lineups of average players from 1997 to 2009. Game scenarios are shown for the eighth inning.

				Before	Bottom 1st					Top 5th				
Runners			Outs	−2	−1	Tie	+1	+2	−2	−1	Tie	+1	+2
1B	x	x	0	−2.17	−1.96	−1.90	−1.53	−1.16	−2.72	−2.66	−2.26	−1.62	−1.19
1B	x	x	1	−2.08	−1.99	−1.89	−1.58	−1.31	−2.75	−2.89	−2.40	−2.02	−1.46
x	2B	x	0	−1.76	−1.66	−1.40	−1.00	−0.82	−2.57	−2.20	−1.64	−1.31	−0.81
x	2B	x	1	−3.08	−3.10	−3.05	−2.64	−2.26	−3.99	−4.44	−4.09	−3.40	−2.51
x	x	3B	0	−1.32	−1.01	−0.71	−0.50	−0.20	−2.15	−1.38	−0.59	−0.16	0.00
x	x	3B	1	**1.02**	**1.43**	**1.66**	**1.63**	**1.51**	**0.76**	**1.94**	**2.67**	**2.57**	**2.11**
x	x	3B	1	87%	84%	81%	80%	78%	92%	84%	79%	76%	75%
1B	2B	x	0	−1.11	−0.78	−0.70	−0.34	−0.27	−1.54	−1.00	−0.56	−0.29	−0.19
1B	2B	x	1	−3.41	−3.22	−2.95	−2.66	−2.00	−4.13	−4.40	−4.02	−3.14	−2.37
1B	x	3B	0	−1.07	−0.81	−0.55	−0.33	−0.02	−1.75	−0.78	−0.09	**0.18**	**0.33**
1B	x	3B	0									98%	95%
1B	x	3B	1	**1.14**	**1.42**	**1.85**	**1.90**	**1.76**	**0.66**	**2.12**	**3.04**	**2.78**	**2.26**
1B	x	3B	1	86%	84%	79%	76%	74%	93%	83%	76%	74%	73%
x	2B	3B	0	−0.50	−0.13	0.07	**0.38**	**0.32**	−1.13	−0.01	**0.64**	**0.94**	**0.92**
x	2B	3B	0				96%	96%			95%	92%	89%
x	2B	3B	1	−0.64	−0.08	**0.35**	**0.62**	**0.62**	−1.43	−0.18	**1.03**	**1.35**	**1.17**
x	2B	3B	1			96%	93%	91%			92%	88%	86%
1B	2B	3B	0	**0.44**	**0.78**	**1.07**	**1.00**	**0.94**	**0.34**	**1.51**	**1.75**	**1.69**	**1.29**
1B	2B	3B	0	94%	90%	85%	84%	81%	97%	86%	82%	82%	78%
1B	2B	3B	1	−0.21	**0.24**	**0.75**	**0.91**	**0.94**	−1.01	**0.33**	**1.67**	**1.69**	**1.47**
1B	2B	3B	1		97%	91%	87%	84%		97%	85%	82%	80%

Table 19.8. Simulated results using two lineups of average players from 1997 to 2009. Game scenarios are shown for the bottom of the first and top of the fifth innings.

The power of the GPA statistic becomes apparent when examining the strategy of the sacrifice bunt. Instead of using a sophisticated computer simulation to determine when to sacrifice bunt, one can just look at the GPA of the anticipated play. In general, a successful sacrifice bunt is a good strategy when the GPA of the successful play is over 0.323. When the GPA of the play is 0.207 to 0.254, a sacrifice bunt is often good strategy with the team tied or ahead in the middle or late innings of a game. When the GPA of the play is 0.139 to 0.174, a sacrifice bunt is sometimes good strategy with the team tied or ahead in the late innings of a game. Rarely can sacrifice bunts be justified when the GPA of the play is less than 0.090.

How much better is the strategy of a sacrifice bunt when executed by a weak hitter such as a pitcher?

This question can be addressed by simulating games with the two-lineup simulator. Both lineups will consist of average players from 1997 to 2009 batting in the first to eighth positions and an average pitcher from 1997 to 2009 batting in the ninth position.

With the pitcher at bat, the chance the team at bat is going to win the game is calculated (1) with the pitcher not bunting; (2) with the pitcher executing a successful sacrifice bunt, with the batter out and all runners advancing one base; and (3) with the pitcher failing to execute a sacrifice bunt and the lead runner being thrown out.

The difference in win percentage between a successful sacrifice bunt and not bunting is shown in the middle of the following tables. A negative percentage shows bunting reduces the chance the team at bat will win the game by that percentage. A positive percentage (in bold) shows bunting increases the chance the team at bat will win the game by that percentage. For those game scenarios in which the percentage is positive, a second percentage

The Sacrifice Bunt 171

(not in bold) appears below the first percentage to indicate how often the sacrifice bunt needs to be successful to justify the risk.

There are only two base-out states in which a successful sacrifice bunt is always a bad strategy. The first is with a man on second and one out, for which the GPA is –0.060; the second is with men on first and second and one out, for which the GPA is –0.163. Even with the pitcher at bat, there is no scenario in which a sacrifice bunt is justified in these base-out states.

— Before —				— — — — — Top 9th — — — — —					— — — — Bottom 9th — — — —				
Runners			Outs	–2	–1	Tie	+1	+2	–2	–1	Tie	+1	+2
1B	x	x	0	–0.88	0.51	1.13	0.30	0.10	–0.99	0.96	1.58		
1B	x	x	0		91%	80%	81%			87%	76%		
1B	x	x	1	–0.95	–0.08	0.45	0.14	0.06	–1.13	0.16	0.75		
1B	x	x	1			89%	87%			97%	84%		
x	2B	x	0	–2.04	1.60	3.11	0.69	0.39	–2.39	2.86	4.28		
x	2B	x	0		89%	81%	85%	82%		86%	78%		
x	2B	x	1	–3.06	–4.94	–3.62	–1.13	–0.52	–3.83	–5.92	–3.41		
x	x	3B	0	–4.44	5.44	9.20	2.21	1.09	–5.26	8.73	12.09		
x	x	3B	0		80%	70%	73%	72%		76%	66%		
x	x	3B	1	–3.47	15.17	20.00	5.22	2.47	–4.16	21.92	24.49		
x	x	3B	1		52%	46%	47%	48%		50%	43%		
1B	2B	x	0	1.36	5.80	5.00	1.36	0.67	2.01	7.59	5.38		
1B	2B	x	0	80%	64%	62%	64%	63%	76%	62%	59%		
1B	2B	x	1	–0.86	–1.55	–1.91	–0.60	–0.25	–0.71	–1.78	–2.16		
1B	x	3B	0	–1.06	9.81	11.22	2.96	1.44	–0.76	14.27	13.35		
1B	x	3B	0		64%	57%	60%	58%		60%	53%		
1B	x	3B	1	–1.85	18.45	22.00	5.89	2.73	–1.87	26.03	26.31		
1B	x	3B	1		43%	35%	37%	39%		40%	31%		
x	2B	3B	0	2.24	13.16	10.25	3.00	1.42	4.48	18.04	10.62		
x	2B	3B	0	86%	66%	64%	66%	66%	79%	63%	63%		
x	2B	3B	1	–4.46	14.34	19.27	4.97	2.41	–5.13	21.23	23.81		
x	2B	3B	1		58%	44%	48%	47%		53%	38%		
1B	2B	3B	0	7.43	14.47	10.78	3.28	1.58	10.50	17.94	10.59		
1B	2B	3B	0	54%	42%	39%	41%	40%	49%	39%	35%		
1B	2B	3B	1	–0.44	16.47	20.36	5.44	2.56	–0.27	22.74	24.54		
1B	2B	3B	1		39%	31%	33%	33%		36%	27%		

Table 19.9. Simulated results of sacrifice bunts in the ninth inning and using two lineups of average players hitting first to eighth. An average pitcher is at bat and batting ninth. Data from 1997 to 2009.

For all other base-out states, there are scenarios in which a sacrifice bunt can be justified. From the beginning to middle innings of a close game with the pitcher at bat, the simulation shows that a sacrifice bunt is a bad strategy with a man on first and one out. In addition, the success rates needed with a man on first and no one out and a man on second with no one out are high enough it becomes a questionable move, in either situation, to sacrifice. Successful sacrifice bunts in all three of these base-out states have GPAs between 0.053 and 0.089, below the GPA of an average pitcher.

As the game progresses, more and more scenarios arise in which, with the pitcher at bat, a sacrifice bunt is a good strategy, with the success rate needed to justify the risk ranging from 27 percent to 85 percent. Many pitchers are able to lay down successful sacrifice bunts this often. The success rate needed to justify the risk of a sacrifice bunt is significantly lower for an average pitcher than for an average hitter in the same game scenarios.

--Before--			--------Top 8th--------				--------Bottom 8th--------				
Runners		Outs	-2	-1	Tie	+1	+2	-2	-1	Tie	+1	+2
1B	x	x	0	-0.45	0.30	0.68	0.19	0.22	-0.51	0.49	0.75	0.14	0.11
1B	x	x	0		93%	84%	90%	79%		90%	83%	88%	81%
1B	x	x	1	-0.55	-0.18	0.17	0.01	0.12	-0.64	0.08	0.24	0.13	0.03
1B	x	x	1			94%		84%			92%	86%	
x	2B	x	0	-0.91	0.88	1.97	0.91	0.55	-1.00	1.61	2.44	0.57	0.30
x	2B	x	0		92%	84%	84%	82%		88%	81%	85%	83%
x	2B	x	1	-2.79	-3.96	-3.04	-1.55	-0.81	-3.31	-4.23	-2.93	-1.01	-0.45
x	x	3B	0	-1.49	3.47	6.09	2.85	1.47	-1.53	5.37	7.18	1.87	0.88
x	x	3B	0		82%	72%	73%	73%		78%	70%	72%	73%
x	x	3B	1	1.23	10.71	13.89	6.49	3.40	1.74	14.24	15.51	4.25	2.06
x	x	3B	1	82%	53%	47%	48%	48%	79%	50%	46%	47%	46%
1B	2B	x	0	1.63	3.93	3.74	1.81	0.97	2.34	4.87	3.84	1.08	0.54
1B	2B	x	0	76%	66%	63%	64%	63%	72%	64%	62%	65%	62%
1B	2B	x	1	-1.01	-1.42	-1.45	-0.76	-0.45	-1.13	-1.51	-1.67	-0.51	-0.22
1B	x	3B	0	1.03	6.62	7.83	3.82	2.06	1.64	8.82	8.79	2.36	1.19
1B	x	3B	0	88%	66%	60%	59%	59%	85%	63%	57%	60%	58%
1B	x	3B	1	2.66	13.11	15.48	7.27	3.93	3.41	16.85	17.09	4.73	2.28
1B	x	3B	1	70%	44%	37%	38%	38%	68%	41%	35%	37%	36%
x	2B	3B	0	3.01	8.79	7.93	3.94	2.04	4.51	11.22	8.08	2.45	1.15
x	2B	3B	0	81%	68%	66%	65%	66%	77%	65%	64%	66%	66%
x	2B	3B	1	0.26	9.78	13.23	6.25	3.36	0.72	13.34	15.00	3.98	1.97
x	2B	3B	1	97%	60%	48%	48%	48%	94%	56%	44%	48%	47%
1B	2B	3B	0	6.57	10.53	8.87	4.27	2.27	8.47	12.21	8.60	2.73	1.26
1B	2B	3B	0	54%	45%	40%	42%	42%	50%	42%	38%	40%	40%
1B	2B	3B	1	3.15	11.65	14.25	6.81	3.64	3.94	15.11	15.84	4.38	2.09
1B	2B	3B	1	65%	41%	34%	34%	34%	62%	38%	31%	33%	33%

Table 19.10. Simulated results of sacrifice bunts in the eighth inning and using two lineups of average players batting first to eighth. An average pitcher is at bat and hitting ninth. Data from 1997 to 2009.

--Before--				-----Bottom 1st-----					----- Top 5th -----				
Runners			Outs	-2	-1	Tie	+1	+2	-2	-1	Tie	+1	+2
1B	x	x	0	-0.07	-0.01	0.17	0.09	0.11	-0.10	0.01	0.26	0.13	0.22
1B	x	x	0			90%		92%			89%	94%	85%
1B	x	x	1	-0.20	-0.04	-0.08	-0.06	0.10	-0.27	-0.26	-0.09	-0.14	-0.07
x	2B	x	0	0.12	0.37	0.35	0.44	0.31	0.00	0.43	0.63	0.68	0.52
x	2B	x	0	97%	92%	92%	89%	91%		93%	90%	87%	87%
x	2B	x	1	-1.77	-1.62	-1.62	-1.36	-1.02	-2.20	-2.24	-2.18	-1.62	-1.16
x	x	3B	0	0.89	1.17	1.60	1.42	1.19	0.64	1.68	2.43	2.16	1.61
x	x	3B	0	88%	86%	80%	81%	80%	92%	85%	79%	78%	77%
x	x	3B	1	3.92	4.40	4.39	4.13	3.50	3.76	5.95	6.68	5.63	4.30
x	x	3B	1	55%	54%	54%	52%	52%	60%	54%	52%	51%	49%
1B	2B	x	0	1.38	1.57	1.44	1.32	1.09	1.61	2.19	2.11	1.74	1.28
1B	2B	x	0	71%	68%	69%	67%	67%	72%	67%	67%	66%	65%
1B	2B	x	1	-0.87	-0.86	-0.64	-0.79	-0.53	-0.98	-0.98	-0.99	-0.64	-0.61
1B	x	3B	0	1.98	2.51	2.50	2.37	1.94	2.05	3.37	3.95	3.27	2.40
1B	x	3B	0	74%	70%	69%	67%	66%	76%	70%	65%	64%	64%
1B	x	3B	1	4.47	5.11	5.32	4.76	4.05	4.78	7.12	7.69	6.55	4.84
1B	x	3B	1	49%	47%	44%	44%	43%	52%	46%	43%	41%	41%
x	2B	3B	0	2.35	2.81	2.87	2.73	2.27	2.62	4.25	4.33	3.59	2.70
x	2B	3B	0	78%	75%	73%	71%	70%	79%	72%	71%	69%	69%
x	2B	3B	1	3.21	3.81	3.96	3.83	3.29	3.18	5.32	6.28	5.31	3.97

— Before —		——— Bottom 1st ———					——— Top 5th ———				
Runners	Outs	−2	−1	Tie	+1	+2	−2	−1	Tie	+1	+2
x 2B 3B	1	65%	62%	60%	56%	55%	70%	62%	56%	54%	53%
1B 2B 3B	0	3.75	4.05	3.91	3.43	2.80	4.74	5.77	5.57	4.31	3.22
1B 2B 3B	0	55%	51%	50%	47%	46%	54%	50%	47%	46%	42%
1B 2B 3B	1	4.40	4.92	5.07	4.47	3.85	4.72	6.70	7.31	5.88	4.50
1B 2B 3B	1	47%	44%	42%	41%	39%	51%	44%	40%	40%	38%

Table 19.11. Simulated results of sacrifice bunts in the bottom of the first and top of the fifth innings. Two lineups of average players bat in the first eight slots in the lineup; an average pitcher is at bat, hitting ninth. Data from 1997 to 2009.

In the ninth inning, the pitcher is often removed for a pinch hitter. If the pitcher does come to bat, a sacrifice bunt becomes an even better strategy as long as his team is behind by no more than one run. If the team at bat is behind by two runs, a sacrifice bunt is only clearly a good strategy with the bases loaded and no outs, and it is a marginal strategy with either men on first and second and no outs or men on second and third with no outs.

The sacrifice bunt is a widely used strategy with the pitcher at bat. But the advisability of that call changes with the score and from inning to inning, just as it does with position players at the plate. The game simulator helps select the game scenarios where a sacrifice bunt would be good strategy.

In summary, the game simulator is able to examine the complex interactions of the score, inning and skill of the hitter and calculate the success rate required to justify a sacrifice bunt attempt. The lower the success rate required, the better the strategy a sacrifice bunt becomes.

Baserunning Revisited

The first half of the chapter "Baserunning Strategies" provides general guidance for baserunning independent of the score and inning. The calculations found there are based on run expectancy, which balances the chance of scoring one run with the chance of having a big inning. For most games in the early and middle innings those guidelines will apply.

At the end of a close game, the guidelines change because only one or two runs may be needed. It is no longer necessary to consider the RE because a big inning is not needed. Scoring a small number of runs is more important.

Likewise, when a team is far behind the guidelines change because multiple runs are needed to have a chance of winning the game. It is no longer necessary to consider the RE because an inning when only one run scores is not very helpful. Rather, the chance of scoring a large number of runs is more important. Runners will need to be more conservative on the base paths in these situations.

The data presented in the second half of "Baserunning Strategies" is ideal for use in the bottom of the ninth inning when the home team knows exactly how many runs they need. It is possible to calculate similar data for each half inning, but the number of data points available is so small that calculations become unreliable.

Another approach is to simulate games with the two-lineup simulator described in the chapter "Winning Games." Both lineups will consist of average players from 1997 to 2009. The simulation is run for all 24 base-out states at various points in a close game with the team at bat behind or ahead by up to two runs.

The chance the team at bat is going to win the game is calculated for three scenarios: (1) with the runners not attempting to advance a base; (2) with all the runners successfully advancing one base; and (3) with the lead runner being thrown out and all other runners advancing one base.

The formula for calculating the success rate needed to justify the risk of advancing a base is shown below. WinAdv is the chance of winning the game with a successful base advancement, WinNoAdv is the chance of winning with no attempt to advance a base, and WinFailedAdv is the chance of winning the game when the lead runner is thrown out.

Success Rate × (WinAdv − WinNoAdv) =
$$(100\% - \text{Success Rate}) \times (\text{WinNoAdv} - \text{WinFailedAdv})$$

Success Rate = (WinNoAdv − WinFailedAdv) / (WinAdv − WinFailedAdv) × 100%

When multiple runners are on base there are more potential outcomes. Over 90 percent of the time, all the runners advance when the advance is successful. Only the lead runner advancing is the next most common successful outcome. About half the time the other runners are able to advance when an out is recorded on an attempt to advance a base.

In each set of tables in this chapter, the percentage success needed to justify the risk of advancing a base for various game scenarios appears in 10 columns of data. The middle column of each table is labeled **RE** and this bolded column of figures shows the success rate required to justify the attempt to advance a base. This is based on run expectancy, and the calculations were presented in the first half of "Baserunning Strategies." The right-most column in the tables with ninth-inning data is labeled **R-1** and is also bolded; it shows the success rate required to justify the attempt to advance a base if only one run is needed. These calculations were presented in the second half of "Baserunning Strategies."

The data in the first set of tables was calculated assuming that all the other runners advance whether the lead runner successfully advances or is thrown out.

At the beginning of the game, the score has only a small effect on the success rate needed to justify the advance attempt. The rate calculated by the baseball simulator and the rate calculated based on RE are almost the same. This fact confirms that using RE is an appropriate way to calculate the success rate needed to justify the risk of advancing a base. It also shows how accurate a tool the baseball simulator is for analyzing complex game scenarios.

——Before——			————Bottom 1st————					————Top 5th————				
Runners			Outs	−2	−1	Tie	+1	+2	**RE**	−2	−1	Tie	+1	+2
1B	x	x	0	73.8	71.3	72.7	69.4	70.4	**72.1**	74.8	72.6	70.0	67.9	68.6
1B	x	x	1	73.8	73.5	72.1	71.7	70.1	**74.3**	76.2	72.5	70.2	71.2	70.8
1B	x	x	2	73.5	68.3	67.0	69.8	66.8	**70.0**	72.6	73.0	69.5	68.1	68.3
x	2B	x	0	78.5	78.3	77.0	76.3	75.6	**76.2**	79.5	77.2	76.0	75.2	74.4
x	2B	x	1	69.0	67.9	67.3	66.8	66.7	**68.4**	71.5	68.8	66.4	66.3	65.7
x	2B	x	2	92.9	88.3	89.1	88.8	86.3	**91.4**	87.5	88.8	88.0	86.7	86.1
x	x	3B	0	91.7	90.0	90.2	88.5	88.8	**92.3**	91.3	90.0	88.8	88.3	88.1
x	x	3B	1	74.3	74.1	73.5	72.4	71.4	**73.9**	76.2	73.2	71.8	70.9	71.1
x	x	3B	2	34.7	34.9	33.6	32.7	33.2	**33.5**	36.6	33.3	33.0	31.5	30.7
1B	2B	x	0	61.7	61.6	61.1	60.0	59.2	**61.6**	63.4	60.4	59.5	58.5	58.2
1B	2B	x	1	57.9	56.9	55.7	54.5	55.2	**55.0**	58.8	56.5	54.2	52.7	52.6
1B	2B	x	2	74.5	74.3	74.4	77.0	74.6	**76.5**	73.1	75.9	73.7	75.3	74.9
1B	x	3B	0	76.7	75.9	75.5	74.9	75.7	**77.3**	76.3	75.2	75.3	75.4	74.6
1B	x	3B	1	64.0	62.8	62.3	61.7	61.1	**63.2**	64.4	62.7	61.5	60.1	59.8
1B	x	3B	2	40.0	38.9	37.9	37.3	36.8	**38.1**	41.3	38.3	37.3	36.7	35.9
x	2B	3B	0	73.1	71.9	71.8	71.0	70.1	**72.2**	74.0	71.3	69.9	69.5	68.4
x	2B	3B	1	64.8	64.6	63.0	63.1	62.0	**65.7**	66.3	63.5	62.7	61.9	61.1
x	2B	3B	2	45.1	43.3	41.9	41.3	39.8	**43.4**	47.7	43.8	40.8	39.4	39.2
1B	2B	3B	0	58.9	58.1	57.6	57.1	56.1	**57.0**	58.3	57.6	56.9	56.1	55.9
1B	2B	3B	1	54.9	55.3	53.9	54.1	54.6	**54.3**	56.0	54.1	54.5	54.1	53.7
1B	2B	3B	2	49.1	48.0	47.3	46.5	45.9	**49.1**	52.1	48.7	46.0	45.2	43.5

Table 20.1. Simulated results using two lineups of average players from 1997 to 2009. Game scenarios are shown from the bottom of the first inning and top of the fifth inning.

By the middle of the game, the score has a small to moderate effect on the success rate needed to justify the advance attempt. For most game scenarios, the difference in success rate needed ranges by 3 percent to 8 percent, depending on whether a team is ahead or behind by two runs. The calculations based on RE are now close to those made by the baseball simulator when the team at bat is behind by one run. When the team is tied or ahead, a success rate as high as that calculated based on RE is no longer needed to justify the attempt.

— — Before — —			— — — — Top 8th — — — — —						— — — — Bottom 8th — — — —				
Runners		Outs	–2	–1	Tie	+1	+2	RE	–2	–1	Tie	+1	+2
1B	x	x	0	80.4	70.8	65.1	66.4	64.0	**72.1**	79.6	69.2	62.6	64.7	63.0
1B	x	x	1	81.1	72.8	67.8	69.8	71.4	**74.3**	80.8	70.8	66.1	69.6	67.2
1B	x	x	2	79.5	70.4	66.6	65.2	66.3	**70.0**	79.6	68.6	63.1	66.4	65.2
x	2B	x	0	86.0	76.9	72.6	72.8	72.7	**76.2**	84.6	75.0	70.3	72.8	72.3
x	2B	x	1	79.5	67.6	63.3	63.3	62.7	**68.4**	79.6	66.2	61.0	61.8	63.1
x	2B	x	2	91.0	89.2	87.6	86.6	88.5	**91.4**	93.7	88.2	86.6	84.2	84.1
x	x	3B	0	97.1	88.7	85.8	85.3	85.8	**92.3**	96.5	87.5	83.9	85.3	84.6
x	x	3B	1	85.6	72.7	65.3	68.9	68.2	**73.9**	85.4	70.7	66.2	67.5	67.3
x	x	3B	2	47.6	33.7	29.7	30.1	29.4	**33.5**	46.4	32.4	28.6	30.3	28.9
1B	2B	x	0	65.1	58.0	55.0	55.4	56.0	**61.6**	63.7	55.6	53.1	54.9	53.7
1B	2B	x	1	62.6	54.4	50.2	50.5	51.9	**55.0**	61.4	51.6	48.0	49.5	47.4
1B	2B	x	2	71.4	72.8	77.5	78.4	78.4	**76.5**	69.4	73.3	80.1	78.8	78.5
1B	x	3B	0	75.3	72.8	74.5	73.5	75.0	**77.3**	73.2	71.4	75.1	73.8	73.5
1B	x	3B	1	67.7	60.5	58.1	58.6	58.1	**63.2**	66.7	58.7	57.1	58.0	58.6
1B	x	3B	2	50.9	37.4	33.4	34.4	33.6	**38.1**	50.0	35.8	31.3	32.5	33.6
x	2B	3B	0	75.1	68.1	65.9	67.1	66.4	**72.2**	72.7	65.4	64.0	65.7	66.0
x	2B	3B	1	67.5	60.6	60.1	60.0	59.2	**65.7**	65.4	59.2	59.2	59.3	59.2
x	2B	3B	2	61.4	42.9	35.1	36.3	35.5	**43.4**	60.7	40.0	31.8	34.2	33.8
1B	2B	3B	0	55.6	54.3	56.0	55.7	55.0	**57.0**	53.3	53.0	56.3	54.1	53.5
1B	2B	3B	1	53.3	52.2	54.0	53.8	53.4	**54.3**	51.7	51.9	53.9	53.0	53.3
1B	2B	3B	2	60.1	47.5	40.9	41.7	41.6	**49.1**	59.6	45.4	37.7	40.4	40.5

Table 20.2. Simulated results using two lineups of average players from 1997 to 2009. Game scenarios are shown from the eighth inning.

— — Before — —			— — — — Top 9th — — — — —						— — — — Bottom 9th — — — —				
Runners		Outs	–2	–1	Tie	+1	+2	RE	–2	–1	Tie	+1	R-1
1B	x	x	0	88.3	70.8	62.5	64.9	64.0	**72.1**	88.6	67.8	59.0		56.0
1B	x	x	1	88.3	72.1	65.0	67.5	70.7	**74.3**	88.2	70.5	62.1		60.6
1B	x	x	2	92.6	70.0	62.7	65.2	65.7	**70.0**	92.8	68.4	60.1		57.4
x	2B	x	0	94.0	76.1	70.0	71.9	72.5	**76.2**	94.0	74.0	67.6		67.6
x	2B	x	1	93.5	67.4	60.4	62.5	64.1	**68.4**	93.8	65.1	57.4		56.6
x	2B	x	2	99.4	88.9	86.0	87.0	87.0	**91.4**	98.9	87.9	84.4		88.2
x	x	3B	0	100.0	88.3	83.9	85.2	84.9	**92.3**	100.0	86.6	81.8		81.7
x	x	3B	1	100.0	71.7	66.1	68.0	67.6	**73.9**	100.0	70.0	63.9		64.4
x	x	3B	2	100.0	33.3	28.3	29.3	29.4	**33.5**	100.0	31.8	26.7		25.5
1B	2B	x	0	66.7	56.0	53.1	54.9	54.3	**61.6**	64.8	53.4	49.5		49.6
1B	2B	x	1	66.5	52.3	47.5	49.2	49.6	**55.0**	65.3	49.4	43.6		41.9
1B	2B	x	2	66.8	72.5	80.4	77.7	78.0	**76.5**	65.6	73.1	85.2		88.6
1B	x	3B	0	73.6	70.6	75.6	74.2	73.7	**77.3**	70.5	69.7	77.3		77.0
1B	x	3B	1	73.0	59.1	56.8	57.8	58.3	**63.2**	70.6	57.2	55.3		54.7
1B	x	3B	2	70.3	36.8	31.2	32.9	32.9	**38.1**	68.2	34.5	35.6		27.5
x	2B	3B	0	75.7	65.4	64.1	65.5	65.2	**72.2**	72.7	62.2	60.0		59.6
x	2B	3B	1	68.8	59.2	59.2	59.7	58.8	**65.7**	66.2	57.3	57.9		58.3
x	2B	3B	2	86.5	42.0	31.7	34.6	34.7	**43.4**	85.9	38.7	27.4		26.3
1B	2B	3B	0	53.1	52.6	56.3	55.8	55.7	**57.0**	49.9	51.7	59.3		59.1
1B	2B	3B	1	51.4	51.3	53.9	52.9	53.6	**54.3**	48.9	50.6	55.6		55.6
1B	2B	3B	2	73.1	47.4	37.4	40.4	40.3	**49.1**	73.0	44.4	33.2		32.2

Table 20.3. Simulated results using two lineups of average players from 1997 to 2009. Game scenarios are shown from the ninth inning.

At the end of the game, the score can have a large effect on the success rate needed to justify the advance attempt. For some scenarios, there is a 30 percent to 74 percent difference, depending on whether a team is tied or behind by two runs. The calculations based on RE are now close to those made by the baseball simulator when the team at bat is behind by either one or two runs. When the team is tied or ahead, a success rate as high as that calculated based on RE is no longer needed to justify the attempt.

When a game is tied in the bottom of the ninth inning, the success rate is similar to that calculated based on the chance of scoring one or more runs in a half inning, which was presented in the second half of "Baserunning Strategies" (column labeled **R-1**).

The previous tables show data from representative half innings throughout the game. Figure 14 shows the success rate needed to justify the advance attempt in a tie game with a man on first and no one out, which is the most commonly encountered base-out state, and the one in which runners most often try to advance. The calculation is made for every half inning of the game.

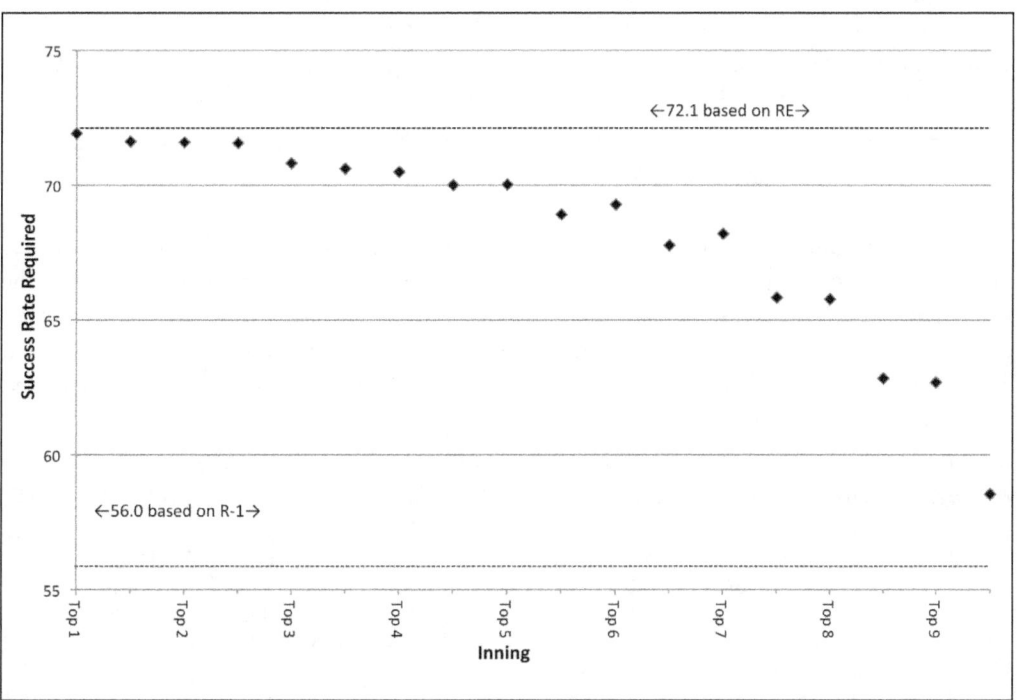

Figure 14. The success rate needed to justify an advance attempt, shown for each half inning, always with a man on first and no one out. Simulated with two lineups of average players from 1997 to 2009.

At the beginning of the game, the success rate required to justify the risk of advancing a base is very close to that predicted based on RE. As the game progresses the success needed falls, especially in the later innings. By the bottom of the ninth inning, the success rate needed approaches that predicted based on the probability of scoring at least one run in a half inning.

When multiple runners are on base, there are more potential outcomes. The data in the first set tables in this chapter were calculated based on all the runners attempting to advance a base; the data in the next set of tables were calculated with only the lead runner successfully advancing or being thrown out. The pattern is similar to that seen with all the runners advancing, but the success rate needed to justify the attempt is higher.

— Before —			— — Bottom 1st — —					— — Top 5th — —			
Runners		Outs	−2	−1	Tie	+1	+2	RE	−2	−1	Tie	+1	+2
1B 2B	x	0	78.5	75.7	74.9	75.3	73.5	75.8	80.0	76.9	74.9	74.1	72.7
1B 2B	x	1	75.2	72.1	71.2	70.1	71.0	72.6	77.6	72.9	72.1	69.4	69.6
1B 2B	x	2	87.2	86.1	84.2	86.5	84.0	89.4	87.7	86.0	85.0	85.7	86.2
1B x 3B		0	92.7	92.6	92.3	91.9	90.5	93.7	95.0	92.5	90.6	89.0	88.5
1B x 3B		1	75.2	73.1	72.6	71.5	70.1	73.5	76.8	73.4	70.9	69.8	69.2
1B x 3B		2	43.3	41.4	40.3	39.8	39.6	41.2	45.5	42.1	39.0	38.9	38.1
x 2B 3B		0	92.1	91.4	89.5	89.3	87.7	91.0	93.6	90.4	89.1	88.2	86.5
x 2B 3B		1	80.4	77.9	76.5	75.7	74.5	79.7	82.4	78.4	75.5	73.8	73.4
x 2B 3B		2	44.6	44.0	44.2	43.1	42.0	44.5	49.6	45.0	41.5	40.5	39.2
1B 2B 3B		0	90.6	89.7	89.0	88.2	87.9	88.6	91.2	90.0	88.0	87.0	86.6
1B 2B 3B		1	78.6	76.0	75.0	74.0	73.2	76.6	79.7	76.4	73.5	72.5	71.3
1B 2B 3B		2	55.9	53.2	51.6	50.3	49.9	53.8	58.3	53.2	49.7	48.6	47.6

Table 20.4. Simulated results using two lineups of average players from 1997 to 2009. Game scenarios are shown from the bottom of the first and top of the fifth innings.

At the beginning of the game, the score has only a small effect on risk-reward considerations. The success rate calculated by the baseball simulator and based on RE are almost the same.

By the middle of the game, the score has a small-to-moderate effect on the success rates needed. For most game scenarios, there is a 5 percent to 9 percent difference in the rates, depending on whether a team is ahead or behind by two runs. The calculations based on RE are now close to those made by the baseball simulator when the team at bat is behind by one or two runs. When the team is tied or ahead, a success rate as high as that calculated based on RE is no longer needed to justify the attempt.

— Before —			— — Top 8th — —					— — Bottom 8th — —			
Runners		Outs	−2	−1	Tie	+1	+2	RE	−2	−1	Tie	+1	+2
1B 2B	x	0	85.3	74.9	69.5	70.1	69.5	75.8	84.7	72.8	66.2	67.8	69.1
1B 2B	x	1	89.0	71.3	65.2	66.1	63.7	72.6	83.4	68.8	61.3	63.9	63.1
1B 2B	x	2	97.3	86.4	84.9	81.6	84.2	89.4	89.6	84.6	82.6	88.9	82.9
1B x 3B		0	99.2	90.6	86.6	87.6	87.3	93.7	98.5	88.9	84.8	85.8	85.9
1B x 3B		1	85.9	71.7	66.1	66.9	66.3	73.5	84.5	69.3	63.4	65.5	64.3
1B x 3B		2	60.6	41.0	34.7	35.2	34.7	41.2	60.1	38.2	32.3	33.9	33.4
x 2B 3B		0	96.5	88.5	85.0	84.9	84.9	91.0	95.8	86.7	82.0	84.2	83.1
x 2B 3B		1	90.7	76.9	69.6	70.5	69.2	79.7	89.5	73.6	65.6	68.0	68.1
x 2B 3B		2	64.5	44.2	35.9	36.9	36.6	44.5	63.8	41.2	32.0	35.0	35.3
1B 2B 3B		0	94.4	87.8	84.3	84.2	84.8	88.6	93.6	86.4	81.8	83.0	82.8
1B 2B 3B		1	88.1	74.5	67.1	68.2	68.1	76.6	87.0	71.0	63.5	66.8	65.4
1B 2B 3B		2	73.0	51.5	42.6	43.7	42.4	53.8	72.2	47.7	38.5	42.7	41.5

Table 20.5. Simulated results using two lineups of average players from 1997 to 2009. Game scenarios are shown from the eighth inning.

At the end of the game, the score can have a large effect on the risk associated with an advance attempt. For some late-inning scenarios, there is a 30 percent to 71 percent difference in the success rate needed, depending on whether a team is tied or behind by two runs. The calculations based on RE are now close to those made by the baseball simulator when the team at bat is behind by either one or two runs. When the team is tied or ahead, a success rate as high as that calculated based on RE is no longer needed to justify the attempt.

When a game is tied in the bottom of the ninth inning, the success rate is similar to that calculated based on the chance of scoring one or more runs in a half inning (see the second half of the "Baserunning Strategies").

— — Before — —			— — — — Top 9th — — — —					— — — — Bottom 9th — — — —			
Runners		Outs	−2	−1	Tie	+1	+2	RE	−2	−1	Tie	+1	R-1
1B 2B x	0	91.8	73.9	65.9	68.2	67.8	75.8	91.1	70.6	61.1		49.6
1B 2B x	1	93.8	70.5	61.6	64.3	64.0	72.6	93.2	67.2	57.1		41.9
1B 2B x	2	93.3	85.2	82.6	85.2	85.7	89.4	94.2	84.7	81.3		88.6
1B x 3B	0	100.0	89.9	84.5	86.6	85.8	93.7	100.0	87.4	81.4		77.0
1B x 3B	1	100.0	70.7	63.4	65.8	64.1	73.5	100.0	68.0	60.0		54.7
1B x 3B	2	100.0	40.2	32.1	33.8	33.1	41.2	100.0	35.6	28.7		27.5
x 2B 3B	0	100.0	87.7	81.7	83.8	83.6	91.0	99.1	85.0	77.1		59.6
x 2B 3B	1	100.0	75.2	65.6	68.7	68.5	79.7	100.0	71.8	60.2		58.3
x 2B 3B	2	98.6	43.5	32.0	34.7	35.2	44.5	97.5	40.0	27.3		26.3
1B 2B 3B	0	96.5	86.7	81.3	83.5	83.2	88.6	96.1	84.4	77.9		59.1
1B 2B 3B	1	98.5	73.0	63.1	65.5	66.4	76.6	97.9	69.3	57.8		55.6
1B 2B 3B	2	100.0	50.1	38.2	41.6	42.5	53.8	100.0	45.9	33.1		32.2

Table 20.6. Simulated results using two lineups of average players from 1997 to 2009. Game scenarios are shown from the ninth inning.

In summary, the data in this chapter provides guidelines for when a team should consider an attempt to advance a base. A lead runner should attempt to advance if the chance he will be successful exceeds the percentage listed in the tables in this chapter for that game scenario. Although the runner's decision will need to be made in a split second, knowing approximately how often he needs to reach the next base safely can help him decide whether the attempt is appropriate.

The simulations in this chapter used average hitters in all nine lineup positions. If the next hitter due to bat is a below-average hitter or a pitcher, the percentages listed in this chapter will still apply. If the next hitter has a GPA over 0.300—even well over it, as in the cases of Pujols and Bonds—the success rate needed to justify the attempt will generally be 5 percent to 10 percent higher than those listed in this chapter.

Part IV. Using GPA

GPA AND WINS ABOVE REPLACEMENT

Wins Above Replacement (WAR) is the number of wins a team would lose if a player were replaced with a top minor leaguer or someone from the bench with marginal major league skills. The concept of WAR was probably first described by Bill James in his 1987 *Baseball Abstract*, but the actual implementation has been hampered by a number of problems, most notably the lack of a standardized formula for its calculation.

The measure is similar to GPA in that it attempts to value each player's contribution to his team with a single, all-encompassing statistic for both hitters and pitchers. Additional wins is an attractive way to gauge a player's contributions to his team since it is easy for the average fan understand. This chapter will show how GPA can be used to calculate WAR.

The "Winning Games" chapter showed how the number of games a team wins is tightly correlated with the team's cGPA (GPA + GPA-base-running correction). Teams with cGPAs between 0.223 and 0.292 have a linear increase in wins as their team's cGPA increases. From the "Run Production" chapter we know that the way in which a team increases its team GPA does not matter. Adding one player with a high GPA is the same as adding two players with a moderately high GPA as long as the total GPA of the team increases by the same amount. The GPA statistic, then, provides an ideal method of calculating WAR.

Using GPA to calculate WAR (1) incorporates all the advantages of GPA, including baserunning and ballpark corrections; (2) requires the number of PAs to be taken into account; (3) can reflect the defensive contributions of each player to his team by adjusting for the defensive positions he played; and (4) will *not* reflect the smaller differences in fielding skill among players at the same defensive position.

From the "Winning Games" chapter we know that an average team has a cGPA of 0.2704 and wins half of its 162 games. The fraction of games won (FracGW) is calculated using the following formula:

$$\text{FracGW} = 3.7779 \times \text{team cGPA} - 0.5213$$

Using that formula, the additional increase in team GPA required for each additional win can be determined. In the example below, the increase in cGPA to go from 81 to 82 wins for a 162 game season is calculated:

$$81/162 = 3.7779 \times \text{team cGPA} - 0.5213 \quad \text{team cGPA} = 0.2703357$$
$$82/162 = 3.7779 \times \text{team cGPA} - 0.5213 \quad \text{team cGPA} = 0.2719693$$

Each 0.001634 increase in team cGPA produces one additional win.

These formulas can ignore ballpark corrections because only a change is being calculated. An actual player's contribution to his team's total production will be determined by tGPA, which includes both a baserunning and ballpark correction.

tGPA	Wins Above Average	— WAR at Replacement Level —		
		0.2263	0.2337	0.2410
0.4175	10.0	13.0	12.5	12.0
0.4028	9.0	12.0	11.5	11.0
0.3880	8.0	11.0	10.5	10.0
0.3733	7.0	10.0	9.5	9.0
0.3586	6.0	9.0	8.5	8.0
0.3439	5.0	8.0	7.5	7.0
0.3292	4.0	7.0	6.5	6.0
0.3145	3.0	6.0	5.5	5.0
0.2998	2.0	5.0	4.5	4.0
0.2851	1.0	4.0	3.5	3.0
0.2704	0.0	3.0	2.5	2.0
0.2557	−1.0	2.0	1.5	1.0
0.2410	−2.0	1.0	0.5	0.0
0.2263	−3.0	0.0	−0.5	−1.0
0.2116	−4.0	−1.0	−1.5	−2.0
0.1969	−5.0	−2.0	−2.5	−3.0
0.1822	−6.0	−3.0	−3.5	−4.0

Table 21.1. Total GPA converted to Wins Above Average and WAR for a position player with 692 PAs (one-ninth of his team's total).

tGPA	Wins Above Average	— WAR at Replacement Level —		
		0.3117	0.3060	0.3003
0.1792	8.0	11.9	11.4	10.9
0.1906	7.0	10.9	10.4	9.0
0.2020	6.0	9.9	9.4	8.0
0.2134	5.0	8.9	8.4	7.0
0.2248	4.0	7.9	7.4	6.0
0.2362	3.0	6.9	6.4	5.0
0.2476	2.0	5.9	5.4	4.0
0.2590	1.0	4.9	4.4	3.0
0.2704	0.0	3.9	3.4	2.0
0.2818	−1.0	2.9	2.4	1.0
0.2932	−2.0	1.9	1.4	0.0
0.3046	−3.0	0.9	0.4	−1.0
0.3160	−4.0	−0.1	−0.6	−2.0
0.3274	−5.0	−1.1	−1.6	−3.0
0.3388	−6.0	−2.1	−2.6	−4.0
0.3502	−7.0	−3.1	−3.6	−5.0
0.3616	−8.0	−4.1	−4.6	−6.0
0.3730	−9.0	−5.1	−5.6	−7.0
0.3844	−10.0	−6.1	−6.6	−8.0
0.3958	−11.0	−7.1	−7.6	−9.0
0.4072	−12.0	−8.1	−8.6	−10.0

Table 21.2. Total GPA converted to Wins Above Average and WAR for a starting pitcher with 893 batters faced, or one-seventh of his team's total.

From 1997 to 2010, each team had an average of 6,230 PAs per year. Each player's contribution to his team's tGPA is determined by the fraction of those 6,230 PAs that were attributed to the player. The tGPA and PAs can be converted to wins above the average position player as follows:

(tGPA − 0.2704) × (PAs / 6230) / 0.001634 = Wins Above Average

The tGPA and PAs can be converted to Wins Above Average for a pitcher as follows:

(0.2704 − tGPA) × (PAs / 6230) / 0.001634 = Wins Above Average

Notice that first term in the formula for pitchers (0.2704 − tGPA) is the negative of the same term in the formula for position players. This compensates for the fact that productive pitchers have low GPAs while productive position players have high GPAs.

tGPA	Wins Above Average	— WAR at Replacement Level —		
		0.3117	0.3060	0.3003
0.1694	3.0	4.3	4.2	4.0
0.2021	2.0	3.3	3.2	3.0
0.2349	1.0	2.3	2.2	2.0
0.2676	0.0	1.3	1.2	1.0
0.3003	−1.0	0.3	0.2	0.0
0.3331	−2.0	−0.7	−0.8	−1.0
0.3658	−3.0	−1.7	−1.8	−2.0
0.3985	−4.0	−2.7	−2.8	−3.0
0.4313	−5.0	−3.7	−3.8	−4.0

Table 21.3. Total GPA converted to Wins Above Average and WAR for a relief pitcher with 311 batters faced (one twenty-first of his team's total).

There are a number of problems with the WAR statistic. Each will be discussed in the next few pages, along with potential solutions. Other attempts to calculate WAR incorporate numerous "fudge factors" to deal with these issues, making the WAR calculation even more difficult for the average fan understand.

1. The replacement level (the R in WAR) is arbitrary.

WAR was created to show how much each player is worth to his team compared to an easily obtained replacement player from the bench or minor leagues. Choosing a replacement level is difficult because (1) some players in the minor leagues are better than players in the majors and (2) some less-skilled MLB players have unlucky seasons in which their production falls below that of top minor league players (see the chapter "Chance in Baseball").

Any replacement level will be arbitrary, and there will be some MLB players whose WAR will be less than 0 unless the replacement level is set at an unrealistically low level.

An average team wins half of its games, or 81 games in a season. The number of wins each team should expect can be calculated by adding the Wins Above Average for each player on the team to 81. If Wins Above Average were used rather than WAR, it would not be necessary to define an arbitrary replacement level.

In the previous three tables, arbitrary replacement levels were chosen which correspond to teams expected to win 54, 58.5 and 63 games during a 162-game season. The following table shows how often teams and individual players fell below those arbitrary replacement levels from 1997 to 2010, and that data will be used to help select the replacement level used in this book.

	———— WAR at Replacement Level ————		
tGPA for Position Players	0.2263	0.2337	0.2410
tGPA for Pitchers	0.3117	0.3060	0.3003
Team Wins for a 162-Game Season	54.0	58.5	63.0
Wins Above Average (692 PAs)	−3.0	−2.5	−2.0
	——— Worse Than the Above Levels ———		
Team Wins	3 (0.8%)	9 (2.3%)	25 (6.4%)
Team Hitting	0	1 (0.3%)	7 (1.8%)
Team Pitching	0	0	0
Individual Batters (PA>250)	270 (6.3%)	493 (11.5%)	723 (16.8%)
Individual Pitchers (PA>250)	320 (8.0%)	433 (10.8%)	560 (14.0%)

Table 21.4. At top, total wins expected for a team with various tGPAs for position players or pitchers. At bottom, teams whose win total, batting and pitching fell below these levels for a season, along with individual batters and pitchers who fell below these levels. Data from 1997 to 2010.

A team made up of position players with a Wins Above Average of −3.0 in 692 PAs (corresponding to a tGPA of 0.2263) and average pitchers would be expected to win 54 games in a 162-game season. A team made up of pitchers with a Wins Above Average of −3.0 in 692 PAs (corresponding to a tGPA of 0.3117) and average hitters would also be expected to win 54 games in a 162-game season.

The three teams that actually won 54 or fewer games in a season from 1997 to 2010 had a combination of bad hitting and bad pitching rather than either one alone. No team from 1997 to 2010 had a tGPA below 0.2263 for its hitters or a tGPA above 0.3117 for its pitchers, the levels required for an individual player with 692 PA to have a Wins Above Average of −3.0.

Team	Year	— Batters —		— Pitchers —		Net tGPA	WinFr	Wins	Pred Wins
		GPA	GPAbrc	GPA	GPAbrc				
Seattle	2010	0.2223	0.0034	0.2550	0.0032	−0.0325	0.376	61	60
Florida	1998	0.2481	0.0023	0.2907	0.0022	−0.0425	0.333	54	54
Arizona	2004	0.2406	0.0018	0.2882	0.0029	−0.0487	0.315	51	51
Detroit	2003	0.2360	0.0008	0.2927	0.0020	−0.0579	0.265	43	45

Table 21.5. Teams with 54 or fewer wins or a tGPA of less than 0.2337 for batters from 1997 to 2010. Pred Wins is the predicted number of wins based on net tGPA using the formula in Figure 11.

Individual batters often have tGPAs below 0.2263 and individual pitchers often have tGPAs above 0.3117, the levels required for a player with 692 PA to have a Wins Above Average of −3.0. From 1997 to 2010, 7.1 percent of players with at least 250 PAs have had production low enough to reach these levels. That works out to an average of one to two players on each 25-man roster, probably the level of skill of a top minor league player.

It is quite common for individual batters to have tGPAs below 0.2410 and individual pitchers to have tGPAs above 0.3003, the levels required for a player with 692 PA to have a Wins Above Average of −2.0. From 1997 to 2010, 15.5 percent of players with at least 250 PAs have had production low enough to reach these levels. That works out to an average of three to four players on each 25-man roster, probably the level of skill of an average major league bench player.

Although it is an arbitrary choice, a Wins Above Average of −3.0 for a player with 692 PAs was chosen as the replacement level used to calculate WAR in this book. This corresponds to perhaps the skill level of top minor league players.

2. Different positions have different value to the team.

A player's defensive position is an important consideration when building a team. Few catchers could successfully replace a shortstop, and few right fielders could successfully replace a second baseman.

Teams accept tradeoffs between players' defensive skills and their offensive production. The information in the Retrosheet database does provide enough information to judge the relative value teams place on different defensive positions.

Position	GPA	GPAbrc	cGPA	cGPA − 0.2748	WAA	WAR
Catcher	0.2537	0.0012	0.2550	−0.0199	−1.35	1.65
First Base	0.2966	0.0018	0.2984	0.0236	1.60	4.60
Second Base	0.2643	0.0027	0.2670	−0.0078	−0.53	2.47
Third Base	0.2725	0.0017	0.2742	−0.0006	−0.04	2.96
Shortstop	0.2557	0.0027	0.2584	−0.0164	−1.12	1.88
Left Field	0.2842	0.0025	0.2867	0.0119	0.81	3.81
Center Field	0.2704	0.0029	0.2733	−0.0015	−0.10	2.90
Right Field	0.2869	0.0020	0.2889	0.0141	0.96	3.96
Designated Hitter	0.2829	0.0017	0.2846	0.0098	0.67	3.67
Pinch Hitter	0.2363	0.0024	0.2387	−0.0361	−2.45	0.55
Average	0.2726	0.0022	0.2748	0.0000	0.00	3.00

Table 21.6. Average production by defensive position, excluding pitchers. Data from 1997 to 2010.

Table 21.6 lists the average GPA of players by defensive position excluding pitchers. Between 1997 and 2010, the average catcher had a cGPA of 0.2550 which is 0.0199 points below the average MLB position player and 0.0434 points (0.2550 − 0.2984) below the average first baseman. Teams gave up 1.35 offense-generated wins (assuming that player made 692 PA) to obtain the defensive skills of the average catcher, more than any other position. Teams also highly valued the defensive skills of shortstops (1.12 wins) and second basemen (0.53 wins).

The average first basemen had a cGPA of 0.2984 which is higher than any other position player. That cGPA was 0.0236 points above the average MLB position player, which corresponds to 1.60 more wins for the team (assuming that player made 692 PA). Teams expect the average first baseman to be more productive offensively because they value a first baseman's defensive skills less than for other positions. Teams also highly valued the offensive production of right fielders (1.41 wins), left fielders (1.19 wins) and designated hitters (0.98 wins).

Center field is the most difficult defensive position to play in the outfield because there is more ground to cover. The average center fielder had a cGPA of 0.2733, which is 0.0156 points (0.2733 − 0.2889) lower than the average right fielder. Teams gave up 1.56 offense-generated wins (−0.15 − 0.141) to obtain the defensive skills of the average center fielder compared to the average right fielder (assuming that player made 692 PA).

It is possible that right fielders' 0.022-point cGPA advantage over left fielders is attributable to teams having chosen better athletes to play that position, which has the outfield's longest throw (to third) and requires right handers to reach across their bodies on balls in the right-center gap. Using average cGPA to value each defensive position is probably as accurate and objective a measure as can be obtained from the Retrosheet database. If there are errors, they are likely small compared with the large difference in relative value teams place on the defensive skills of a catcher compared with a first baseman. Other methods of calculating WAR have chosen values for each defensive position based more on opinion than objective data.

Whether teams realize they are placing these relative values on different defensive positions does not matter. The differences seen are probably due to the physical tradeoffs required for an athlete to play a more demanding defensive position such as catcher or shortstop. These relative values are reflected in the market for replacement players — exactly what WAR values.

Position	GPA	GPAbrc	cGPA	cGPA − 0.2748	WAA	WAR
All Positions	0.2511	0.0024	0.2535	−0.0213	−1.45	1.55
As Pinch Hitter	0.2363	0.0024	0.2387	−0.0361	−2.45	0.55

Table 21.7. All PAs of players as both pinch hitters and position players compared with the PAs of those same players when they were pinch hitters. Data from 1997 to 2010.

Pitch hitters had a cGPA of 0.2387, far below the cGPA of 0.2748 for all position players. Is it difficult to pinch hit or are pinch hitters less skilled than average players?

Players who pinch hit had an average cGPA of 0.2535 as both pinch hitters and position players (adjusted for the number of PAs each player made as a pinch hitter). The numbers suggest that pinch hitters are less skilled than average players since they had a cGPA that was 0.0213 points (0.2535 − 0.2748) lower than the average position player. But pinch hitting is clearly also difficult since players had a cGPA 0.0148 points (0.2387 − 0.2535) lower when they pinch hit compared to their overall productivity.

The calculations for WAR in this book adjust each player's tGPA to reflect the different defensive positions he actually played. For example, a player who made half of his PAs while playing third base and half while playing first base will have a tGPA adjustment of −0.0115 points (−(−0.0006 + 0.0236) / 2) used to calculate his WAR.

The information in the Retrosheet database does not provide enough information to compare an individual player's defensive skills with others who played his position. Calculated using tGPA, WAR will largely reflect the defensive contributions of each player by adjusting for the defensive positions he played, but smaller differences between players who play the same position will be lost.

3. The average GPA changes from year to year.

From 1997 to 2010, the average cGPA was 0.2704 and it has ranged from a low of 0.2658 during the 2005 season to a high of 0.2798 during the 2000 season. (See the "Baseball Eras, 1952–2012" chapter for a list of average cGPAs for each season.)

To accurately calculate WAR, it is necessary to take into account the average cGPA for the period being evaluated. If WAR for the 2000 season had been calculated based on a 0.2704 average, a team of average players (with tGPAs of 0.2798, 0.0094 above average) would be expected to win 86.8 games rather than 81 games.

The calculations for WAR in this book compare each player's tGPA to the average cGPA during the period being evaluated. If a period of multiple years is being evaluated, the average cGPA during that period (adjusted for the number of PAs by the player each year) will be used. With this correction, a player's production as measured by WAR can be accurately compared from year to year.

4. *Relief pitchers are undervalued compared with starting pitchers.*

From 1997 to 2010, the top relief pitchers each season faced about 300 batters while the top starting pitchers faced about 900 batters. The calculation for WAR is proportional to the number of batters faced. All thing being equal, a starting pitcher facing 900 batters will have a WAR that is three times higher than a relief pitcher facing 300 batters.

Relief pitchers are allowed to face hitters whom they have the best chance of getting out and can throw at maximum velocity on nearly every pitch since their appearances are often short. For these reasons, top relief pitchers tend to have tGPAs slightly lower than those of top starting pitchers. This small difference in tGPA is not enough to make up for the many fewer batters faced by relief pitchers when calculating WAR.

Does this large difference in valuation based on WAR between relief and starting pitchers make sense? In 2010 the highest-paid starting pitchers were Barry Zito, John Lackey, Johan Santana and C.C. Sabathia, who made between $18 million and $23 million per season. The highest-paid relief pitchers were Francisco Rodriquez, Brad Lidge and Mariano Rivera, who made between $12 million and $15 million per season. The average starting pitcher made $4.6 million and the average reliever made $2.1 million.

Teams clearly value starting pitchers more than relief pitchers since they are paid between 1.5 to 2.2 times as much per season. This is below the 3.0 level that would be expected if salary were based on batters faced (again, top starting pitchers face three times as many batters as top relief pitchers).

Teams win about half of the games started by an average starting pitcher, but the team (obviously) does not know in advance if that particular game will be won or lost. By the time a relief pitcher enters the game, the team has some sense of whether the game will be won, lost or could go either way. Teams are able to use their best relief pitchers in game scenarios that are critical to the outcome of the game while they can use less skilled pitchers when the game is not close and the outcome largely decided.

To properly calculate WAR for starting and relief pitchers, it is necessary to take into account how important each batter faced by a pitcher is to the team. At the start of the game, a batter faced has a moderate value because either team could win. If either team is far ahead, however, the batter's PA has less relative value because the outcome of the game is unlikely to change no matter what happens. At the end of a close game, the PA has a much higher value because the outcome of the game is much more likely to depend on what happens.

Top Inning	Outs	— Visiting Team Behind —				0	— Visiting Team Ahead —			
		−4	−3	−2	−1		+1	+2	+3	+4
1	0 1 2	x	x	x	x	0.457	0.564	0.656	0.735	0.837
2	0 1 2	0.098	0.192	0.278	0.357	0.459	0.576	0.676	0.755	0.841
3	0 1 2	0.111	0.180	0.264	0.346	0.460	0.581	0.701	0.769	0.848
4	0 1 2	0.109	0.165	0.241	0.350	0.468	0.588	0.712	0.787	0.864
5	0 1 2	0.094	0.138	0.218	0.326	0.472	0.615	0.733	0.818	0.891
6	0 1 2	0.069	0.115	0.194	0.306	0.472	0.639	0.765	0.854	0.916
7	0 1 2	0.047	0.092	0.158	0.280	0.464	0.686	0.806	0.893	0.947
8	0 1 2	0.028	0.049	0.112	0.228	0.470	0.750	0.866	0.932	0.964
9	0 1 2	0.007	0.018	0.055	0.130	0.468	0.847	0.930	0.972	0.989
10+	0 1 2	x	x	x	x	0.478	0.861	0.930	0.977	0.984

Bottom Inning	Outs	—— Home Team Behind ——				0	—— Home Team Ahead ——			
		−4	−3	−2	−1		+1	+2	+3	+4
1	0 1 2	0.185	0.303	0.385	0.487	0.594	0.692	0.764	0.827	0.889
2	0 1 2	0.194	0.278	0.358	0.462	0.585	0.694	0.766	0.855	0.910
3	0 1 2	0.172	0.269	0.347	0.480	0.588	0.705	0.797	0.852	0.915
4	0 1 2	0.159	0.240	0.327	0.463	0.594	0.719	0.814	0.880	0.927
5	0 1 2	0.124	0.219	0.311	0.439	0.600	0.745	0.834	0.904	0.946
6	0 1 2	0.104	0.169	0.282	0.421	0.611	0.769	0.871	0.928	0.962
7	0 1 2	0.070	0.126	0.225	0.375	0.627	0.816	0.914	0.959	0.978
8	0 1 2	0.042	0.081	0.160	0.301	0.649	0.893	0.955	0.989	0.993
9	0 1 2	0.015	0.036	0.086	0.180	0.662	1.000	1.000	1.000	1.000
10+	0 1 2	0.022	0.031	0.069	0.168	0.661	1.000	1.000	1.000	1.000

Table 21.8. The probability that the team at bat they will win the game. Data shown by inning and score based on 2,616,602 PAs from 1997 to 2010.

One way to value a PA is to determine how likely the outcome of the game will change based on the results. Table 21.8 shows the probability that a team will win the game depending on the inning and score from close games. Every PA that occurred in that inning (with no outs, one out or two) and with that score differential is counted as a separate event. This data allows us to begin to see which PAs are the most important to a team's chance of winning a game.

From 1997 to 2010, the visiting team made 49,499 PAs in the top of the first inning with the score tied and, after 24,123 (or 45.7 percent) of them, won the game. By scoring one run in the top of the first inning, the visiting team increases its chance of winning the game from 45.7 percent to 56.4 percent, a 10.7 percent increase. By scoring one run in the top of the ninth inning of a tied game, the visiting team increases its chance of winning the game from 46.8 percent to 84.7 percent, a 37.9 percent increase. By this measure, scoring one run in the top of ninth inning of a tied game is 3.5 times (37.9 / 10.7) as valuable as scoring a run in the top of the first inning.

With the home team trailing by four runs in the bottom of the ninth inning, scoring one run increases the home team's chance of winning the game from 1.5 percent to 3.6 percent, a 2.1 percent increase. With the game tied in the bottom of the ninth inning, scoring one run cinches the game for the home team, which had had a 66.1 percent chance of winning. This 33.9 percent difference (from 66.1 to 100) means that scoring one run with the game tied in the bottom of the 9th inning is 16 times (33.9 / 2.1) as valuable as when trailing by four runs.

Table 21.10 shows how scoring one run changes the team at bat's chance of winning the game. The calculation is shown for every combination of inning and score from close games. The probabilities vary widely depending on the inning and score. This is one way of determining the value a PA for the team.

———————— *Run Distribution in an Inning* ——————————

Runs	0	1	2	3	4	5	6	7	8
Probability	0.7101	0.1554	0.0723	0.0343	0.0159	0.0071	0.0030	0.0011	0.0005

Table 21.9. The probability of scoring no runs to eight runs during an inning. Data from 1997 to 2009.

The calculations in Table 21.10 ignore the possibility that more than one run could score during an inning. From 1997 to 2009, teams scored more than one run in 13.45 percent of the innings played. The same calculation can be made eight times — once each for one to eight runs scoring. Table 21.11 shows an average of all eight calculations (weighted by the probability that many runs would score) and provides a relative measure of how likely the outcome of the game is to change with the remaining PAs in the game.

Top Inning	Outs	— Visiting Team Behind —				0	— Visiting Team Ahead —			
		−4	−3	−2	−1		+1	+2	+3	+4
1	0 1 2	x	x	x	x	0.107	0.092	0.079	0.102	−0.007
2	0 1 2	0.094	0.086	0.079	0.102	0.118	0.099	0.079	0.087	0.015
3	0 1 2	0.069	0.084	0.082	0.114	0.121	0.119	0.068	0.079	0.041
4	0 1 2	0.056	0.076	0.109	0.118	0.120	0.125	0.075	0.076	0.048
5	0 1 2	0.045	0.079	0.108	0.146	0.143	0.118	0.085	0.073	0.043
6	0 1 2	0.046	0.079	0.112	0.166	0.167	0.126	0.089	0.062	0.028
7	0 1 2	0.045	0.067	0.122	0.184	0.222	0.119	0.088	0.053	0.018
8	0 1 2	0.021	0.063	0.117	0.241	0.281	0.116	0.066	0.031	0.018
9	0 1 2	0.011	0.037	0.075	0.339	0.532	0.153	0.070	0.028	0.011
10+	0 1 2	x	x	x	x	0.522	0.139	0.070	0.023	0.016

Bottom Inning	Outs	—— Home Team Behind ——				0	—— Home Team Ahead ——			
		−4	−3	−2	−1		+1	+2	+3	+4
1	0 1 2	0.119	0.081	0.102	0.107	0.099	0.071	0.063	0.062	0.020
2	0 1 2	0.085	0.079	0.104	0.123	0.109	0.072	0.089	0.054	0.009
3	0 1 2	0.097	0.078	0.134	0.107	0.118	0.092	0.054	0.063	0.027
4	0 1 2	0.081	0.088	0.135	0.131	0.125	0.095	0.065	0.047	0.034
5	0 1 2	0.094	0.092	0.128	0.160	0.146	0.088	0.070	0.041	0.026
6	0 1 2	0.065	0.113	0.140	0.189	0.159	0.102	0.057	0.035	0.010
7	0 1 2	0.056	0.099	0.150	0.252	0.189	0.098	0.045	0.019	0.014
8	0 1 2	0.039	0.079	0.141	0.348	0.245	0.061	0.035	0.004	0.004
9	0 1 2	0.021	0.050	0.094	0.482	0.338	x	x	x	x
10+	0 1 2	0.009	0.038	0.099	0.493	0.339	x	x	x	x

Table 21.10. The change in probability of the team at bat of winning the game if one run scores. Data shown by inning and score based on 2,616,602 PAs from 1997 to 2010.

The data in Table 21.10 can be calculated for scoring two runs, three runs, and so on. The average of those calculations is shown in Table 21.11 weighted for the probability of scoring that many runs (from Table 21.9).

Table 21.11 shows the relative importance of each PA to the team depending on the inning and score, but the valuations are low when one team is far ahead. In the bottom of the seventh inning, the value of a PA with the game tied is 14 times greater than when the home team is ahead by four runs (0.215 / 0.015). Teams rarely overcome large deficits in games because the team ahead continues to use skilled pitchers to maintain the lead. To properly value a PA for the team, it is necessary to balance the chance that a team might overcome the deficit with the need to get the remaining hitters out.

Top Inning	Outs	— Visiting Team Behind —				0	— Visiting Team Ahead —			
		-4	-3	-2	-1		+1	+2	+3	+4
1	0 1 2	x	x	x	x	0.134	0.116	0.103	0.106	0.017
2	0 1 2	0.120	0.112	0.111	0.136	0.146	0.123	0.101	0.094	0.032
3	0 1 2	0.095	0.111	0.117	0.150	0.154	0.140	0.090	0.091	0.051
4	0 1 2	0.081	0.110	0.145	0.154	0.154	0.147	0.095	0.089	0.054
5	0 1 2	0.071	0.115	0.152	0.187	0.176	0.142	0.104	0.085	0.049
6	0 1 2	0.073	0.117	0.162	0.213	0.202	0.151	0.105	0.070	0.035
7	0 1 2	0.071	0.108	0.179	0.244	0.256	0.143	0.101	0.058	0.023
8	0 1 2	0.046	0.107	0.190	0.314	0.312	0.133	0.074	0.036	0.020
9	0 1 2	0.029	0.078	0.176	0.432	0.401	0.094	0.046	0.018	0.002
10+	0 1 2	x	x	x	x	0.402	0.081	0.049	0.011	0.016

Bottom Inning	Outs	— — Home Team Behind — —				0	— — Home Team Ahead — —			
		-4	-3	-2	-1		+1	+2	+3	+4
1	0 1 2	0.145	0.112	0.134	0.135	0.120	0.090	0.079	0.067	0.021
2	0 1 2	0.111	0.112	0.139	0.154	0.132	0.096	0.103	0.059	0.019
3	0 1 2	0.124	0.116	0.166	0.141	0.143	0.108	0.071	0.071	0.035
4	0 1 2	0.111	0.128	0.174	0.167	0.151	0.113	0.079	0.056	0.038
5	0 1 2	0.125	0.133	0.175	0.200	0.171	0.107	0.082	0.048	0.029
6	0 1 2	0.102	0.158	0.194	0.233	0.186	0.117	0.066	0.038	0.016
7	0 1 2	0.091	0.150	0.221	0.302	0.215	0.109	0.050	0.023	0.015
8	0 1 2	0.070	0.134	0.236	0.408	0.261	0.070	0.036	0.005	0.004
9	0 1 2	0.045	0.103	0.225	0.561	0.338	x	x	x	x
10+	0 1 2	0.031	0.092	0.232	0.572	0.339	x	x	x	x

Table 21.11. The change in probability of the team at bat of winning the game if one to eight runs score. Data shown by inning and score based on 2,616,602 PA from 1997 to 2010.

The average relative value of a PA in Table 21.11 is 0.143, similar to the relative value of a PA at the start of a tied game. To balance the chance a team might overcome the deficit with the need to get the remaining hitters out, 0.143 is added to the valuations in Table 21.11, with the results shown in Table 21.12. Plate appearances from extra innings are included in the ninth inning since their valuations are almost identical, as one might expect.

The calculations for WAR in this book for pitchers are adjusted to reflect the importance of the batters faced. The relative values in Table 22.12 are used (those where one team is ahead by five or more runs are not shown). The total WAR for each team does not change, but the WAR for individual pitchers may go up or down. Adjusting for the relative value of a PA results in the average starting pitcher's WAR changing by less than 10 percent, a top relief pitcher's WAR increasing by about 50 percent, and a typical middle reliever's WARs declining by 10 percent to 20 percent.

A similar relative valuation could be made for each out in an inning (rather than combining the data for one, two, or no outs), but the values do not change enough to justify the added complexity. No additional adjustments are needed to account for the runners on base and outcome of the PA since GPA already takes these into account.

GPA and Wins Above Replacement

Top Inning	Outs	— Visiting Team Behind —					— Visiting Team Ahead —			
		−4	−3	−2	−1	0	+1	+2	+3	+4
1	0 1 2	x	x	x	x	0.277	0.259	0.246	0.249	0.160
2	0 1 2	0.263	0.255	0.254	0.279	0.289	0.266	0.244	0.237	0.175
3	0 1 2	0.238	0.254	0.260	0.293	0.297	0.283	0.233	0.234	0.194
4	0 1 2	0.224	0.253	0.288	0.297	0.297	0.290	0.238	0.232	0.197
5	0 1 2	0.214	0.258	0.295	0.330	0.319	0.285	0.247	0.228	0.192
6	0 1 2	0.216	0.260	0.305	0.356	0.345	0.294	0.248	0.213	0.178
7	0 1 2	0.214	0.251	0.322	0.387	0.399	0.286	0.244	0.201	0.166
8	0 1 2	0.189	0.250	0.333	0.457	0.455	0.276	0.217	0.179	0.163
9+	0 1 2	0.172	0.222	0.323	0.590	0.526	0.235	0.189	0.160	0.145

Bottom Inning	Outs	—— Home Team Behind ——					—— Home Team Ahead ——			
		−4	−3	−2	−1	0	+1	+2	+3	+4
1	0 1 2	0.288	0.255	0.277	0.278	0.263	0.233	0.222	0.210	0.164
2	0 1 2	0.254	0.255	0.282	0.297	0.275	0.239	0.246	0.202	0.162
3	0 1 2	0.267	0.259	0.309	0.284	0.286	0.251	0.214	0.214	0.178
4	0 1 2	0.254	0.271	0.317	0.310	0.294	0.256	0.222	0.199	0.181
5	0 1 2	0.268	0.276	0.318	0.343	0.314	0.250	0.225	0.191	0.172
6	0 1 2	0.245	0.301	0.337	0.376	0.329	0.260	0.209	0.181	0.159
7	0 1 2	0.234	0.293	0.364	0.445	0.358	0.252	0.193	0.166	0.158
8	0 1 2	0.213	0.277	0.379	0.551	0.404	0.213	0.179	0.148	0.147
9+	0 1 2	0.188	0.247	0.373	0.710	0.468	x	x	x	x

Table 21.12. Relative value of PAs used to calculate WAR. The values balance the chance that the outcome of the game will change from the PA with the need to get the remaining hitters out. Data shown by inning and score based on 2,616,602 PA from 1997 to 2010.

A similar adjustment for relative value could be applied to hitters' PAs, which would yield a "clutch hitting" adjusted GPA and WAR, but there is no need to make this adjustment. A position player already faces PAs that vary widely in importance to his team's chance of winning the game (unlike some relief pitchers). The adjustments would have little effect on position player's GPA and WAR calculations.

Top Inning	Outs	— Visiting Team Behind —					— Visiting Team Ahead —			
		−4	−3	−2	−1	0	+1	+2	+3	+4
7	0 1 2	0	0	0	0	0	0	0	0	0
8	0 1 2	6	13	33	36	6	5	0	1	0
9+	0 1 2	134	300	346	348	393	130	41	19	15

Bottom Inning	Outs	—— Home Team Behind ——					—— Home Team Ahead ——			
		−4	−3	−2	−1	0	+1	+2	+3	+4
7	0 1 2	0	0	0	0	3	0	3	0	0
8	0 1 2	20	36	44	59	21	4	1	8	7
9+	0 1 2	168	283	373	428	156	x	x	x	x

Table 21.13. Mariano Rivera's batters faced by inning and score from 1997 to 2010. An additional 416 of his 3,856 batters were faced with a score differential of more than four runs.

Mariano Rivera almost always appears at the end of games and usually when the game is tied or the Yankees are ahead by a small margin. Table 21.13 shows Rivera's batters faced by inning and score from 1997 to 2010. The Yankees used Rivera exactly as one would expect if the relative values for PAs shown in Table 21.12 are correct.

5. Calculating WAR for AL versus NL teams.

When pitchers' PAs (as batters) are excluded, the average NL batter had, from 1997 to 2010, a GPA of 0.2734; the average AL batter had a nearly identical GPA of 0.2726. Unlike other methods of calculating WAR, using GPA to calculate WAR requires no corrections for the league in which the player played.

Position	GPA	GPAbrc	cGPA	cGPA − 0.2759	WAA	WAR
Pitchers	0.1187	0.0007	0.1194	−0.1565	−10.64	−7.64
Position Players	0.2737	0.0022	0.2759	0.0000	0.00	3.00

Table 21.14. Average production of pitchers (as batters) compared with position players. Data from 1997 to 2010.

From 1997 to 2010, pitchers had an average of 358 PAs (as batters) per season for each NL team (5.7 percent of PAs) and 22 per season for each AL team. For an NL team, these PAs for pitchers account for 1.55 WAR while for an AL team these PAs account for a 0.10 WAR.

Wins Above Replacement can be calculated for each pitcher-batter, as the position correction for a pitcher is +0.1544 (0.2748 − 0.1194). For NL teams, even pitchers who are strong batters rarely make more than 90 PAs in a season, which would translate to a 0.39 WAR for the average pitcher. Ignoring the PAs by NL pitchers introduces only a small error when calculating the WAR.

It is not clear that a skilled major league pitcher is a better batter than a replacement player from the minor leagues. The whole concept WAR for pitchers as batters, then, may not be very useful. The WAR calculations in this book therefore ignore PAs by pitchers.

Wins Above Replacement is calculated for batters as follows: GPA is corrected for the ballparks played in (GPAbpc) and baserunning production (GPAbrc), yielding the tGPA. The tGPA is then adjusted for the player's defensive positions (GPApc), yielding the total position-adjusted GPA (t_{pa}GPA). The t_{pa}GPA is compared with the average tGPA for all players that season, and the difference is used to calculate Wins Above Average. Wins Above Average is then converted to WAR. The following formulas are used:

$$\text{GPA} + \text{GPAbpc} + \text{GPAbrc} + \text{GPApc} = t_{pa}\text{GPA}$$
$$(t_{pa}\text{GPA} - \text{average tGPA}) \times (\text{PA} / 6230) / 0.001634 = \text{Wins Above Average}$$
$$\text{Wins Above Average} + (\text{PA} / 692) \times 3 = \text{WAR}$$

Wins Above Replacement is calculated for pitchers as follows: GPA is corrected for the ballparks pitched in (GPAbpc) and the baserunning production allowed (GPAbrc), yielding tGPA. The tGPA is compared with the average tGPA for all players that season and corrected for the value (importance) of the PAs the pitcher faced (GPArv), thereby calculating Wins Above Average. Wins Above Average is then converted to WAR. The following formulas are used (C=Correction:

$$\text{GPA} + \text{GPAbpc} + \text{GPAbrc} = \text{tGPA}$$
$$(\text{Average tGPA} - \text{tGPA}) \times (\text{PA} / 6230) / 0.001634 \times \text{GPArv} = \text{Wins Above Average}$$
$$\text{Wins Above Average} + (\text{PA} / 692) \times 3 = \text{WAR}$$

The best seasons as measured by WAR for batters, starting pitchers and relief pitchers from 1952 to 2012 are presented in the following tables. There are a few games missing from the Retrosheet database from 1952 to 1973 and the statistics listed here may differ slightly from the official statistics for those years.

GPA is an absolute measure of productivity that does not depend on how other players performed during the season. Wins Above Replacement, on the other hand, measures productivity relative to the average player during that season. The best seasons as measured by WAR will tend to be more evenly distributed across eras than those measured by GPA.

For batters, the Steroid Era from 1994 to 2004 accounted for 55 of 108 (50.9 percent) of the top seasons as measured by GPA, but only 36 of 108 (33.3 percent) of the top seasons as measured by WAR. Although this is 55 percent more of the top seasons as measured by WAR than would be expected by chance alone, it is similar to the era from 1952 to 1971. The Pitching Era from 1972 to 1993 still accounts for fewer of the top seasons as measured by WAR than would be expected by chance alone.

Seasons	Top 108 Batters GPA	Top 108 Batters WAR	Pct. Top 108 Batters GPA	Pct. Top 108 Batters WAR	Expected Pct. Batters	Team Seasons
1952 to 1961	16	19	14.8%	17.6%	10.8%	162
1962 to 1971	9	22	8.3%	20.4%	14.1%	212
1972 to 1981	7	14	6.5%	13.0%	16.7%	250
1982 to 1993	7	7	6.5%	6.5%	20.9%	314
1994 to 2004	55	36	50.9%	33.3%	21.5%	322
2005 to 2012	14	10	13.0%	9.3%	16.0%	240

Table 21.15. The top 108 seasons as measured by GPA and WAR for batters with at least 500 PAs from 1952 to 2012.

For starting pitchers, the era from 1962 to 1971 accounted for 46 of 108 (42.6 percent) of the top seasons as measured by GPA, but only 29 of 108 (26.8 percent) of the top seasons as measured by WAR. This is 90 percent more of the top seasons as measured by WAR than would be expected by chance alone. The Steroid Era from 1994 to 2004 accounts for about as many of the top seasons as measured by WAR as would be expected by chance alone.

Seasons	Top 108 Pitchers GPA	Top 108 Pitchers WAR	Pct. Top 108 Pitchers GPA	Pct. Top 108 Pitchers WAR	Expected Pct. Pitchers	Team Seasons
1952 to 1961	6	11	5.6%	10.2%	10.8%	162
1962 to 1971	46	29	42.6%	26.8%	14.1%	212
1972 to 1981	22	24	20.4%	22.2%	16.7%	250
1982 to 1993	17	16	15.7%	14.8%	20.9%	314
1994 to 2004	11	25	10.2%	23.1%	21.5%	322
2005 to 2012	6	3	5.6%	2.8%	16.0%	240

Table 21.16. The top 108 seasons as measured by GPA and WAR for pitchers with at least 500 batters faced from 1952 to 2012.

For relief pitchers, the top 71 seasons as measured by WAR are distributed in a pattern that reflects the evolving role of the relief pitcher. Before 1960, it was uncommon for the same pitcher to regularly finish close games. Not a single relief pitcher from 1952 to 1961 made the list of top 71 seasons by relief pitchers as measured by GPA. The era from 1962 to 1981 accounts for 35 of 71 (49.3 percent) top seasons as measured by WAR. Top relief pitchers from this era typically faced 450 to 600 batters compared with only about 300 batters for top relievers since 2000. Since WAR is proportional to the number of batters faced, a modern reliever must have a historic season to make the list of top seasons. The top 24 seasons measured by WAR all came from the era from 1960 to 1984, with Brad Linge's 2004 season and Eric Gagne's 2003 season the only exceptions.

Seasons	Top 71 Pitchers GPA	Top 71 Pitchers WAR	Pct. Top 71 Pitchers GPA	Pct. Top 71 Pitchers WAR	Expected Pct. Pitchers	Team Seasons
1952 to 1961	0	6	0.0%	8.4%	10.8%	162
1962 to 1971	5	17	7.0%	23.9%	14.1%	212
1972 to 1981	9	18	12.7%	25.4%	16.7%	250
1982 to 1993	13	10	18.3%	14.1%	20.9%	314
1994 to 2004	20	14	28.2%	19.7%	21.5%	322
2005 to 2012	24	6	33.8%	8.5%	16.0%	240

Table 21.17. The top 71 seasons as measured by GPA and WAR for relief pitchers with at least 200 batters faced from 1952 to 2012.

The relative value of the batters faced (in the column under "GPA RV" in the tables at the end of this chapter) tends to be higher for relievers of recent years because they face only a few batters in the most critical game situations for their teams.

John Hiller's 1973 season for the Tigers was the best since 1952 for a reliever measured by his WAR of 9.02 (tGPA 0.149). Hiller faced 498 batters with an average relative value of 1.33. B.J. Ryan's 2006 season for the Blue Jays had a tGPA of 0.145, the lowest ever by a pitcher with at least 200 batters faced. Ryan's WAR was only 5.90 because he faced 270 batters with a relative value of 1.41. Trevor Hoffman's 1996 season for the Padres had a relative value of 1.66, the eighth highest ever. Hoffman's WAR was only 5.75 because his tGPA was 0.202 and he faced 348 PAs.

In summary, GPA can be used to calculate WAR and will incorporate all the advantages of GPA, including baserunning and ballpark corrections. Unlike GPA, WAR will be proportional to the number of PAs. For position players, WAR is corrected for the defensive positions played; for pitchers, it is corrected for the importance of the batters faced.

Gross Productivity Average comes closer to being the "perfect" single statistic than WAR because it adjusts for the number of opportunities each player has and is easier for the average fan to understand. Still, WAR can be a useful way to value a player's contribution to the team. The methods used to calculate GPA can be used to provide a standardized and accurate method of calculating WAR.

Table 21.18. Batters with 500+ Plate Appearances

Player	Team	Year	BA	GPA	GPA brc	GPA bpc	tGPA	GPA pc	WAR	PA
Bonds, Barry	SFG	2004	0.362	0.471	0.005	0.002	0.478	−0.011	14.57	617
Bonds, Barry	SFG	2002	0.370	0.457	0.004	0.001	0.463	−0.012	13.79	612
Bonds, Barry	SFG	2001	0.328	0.444	0.001	0.000	0.446	−0.011	13.57	664
Mantle, Mickey	NYY	1956	0.353	0.412	0.006	0.003	0.422	0.002	13.15	652
Morgan, Joe	CIN	1976	0.320	0.390	0.016	0.003	0.409	0.008	12.51	599
Mantle, Mickey	NYY	1957	0.365	0.404	0.007	0.003	0.414	0.002	12.48	623
Mantle, Mickey	NYY	1961	0.317	0.406	0.004	0.002	0.412	0.002	12.26	646
Morgan, Joe	CIN	1972	0.293	0.354	0.010	0.008	0.372	0.008	12.14	674
Morgan, Joe	CIN	1975	0.327	0.373	0.017	0.003	0.393	0.008	11.96	639
Rodriguez, Alex	NYY	2007	0.314	0.385	0.006	0.001	0.393	0.000	11.60	708
Bonds, Barry	SFG	1996	0.308	0.401	0.008	0.005	0.414	−0.011	11.34	675

GPA and Wins Above Replacement

Player	Team	Year	BA	GPA	GPA brc	GPA bpc	tGPA	GPA pc	WAR	PA
Torre, Joe	STL	1971	0.363	0.361	0.004	−0.001	0.364	0.001	11.30	707
Aaron, Hank	MLB	1963	0.319	0.363	0.007	0.008	0.379	−0.014	11.10	700
Rodriguez, Alex	SEA	1996	0.358	0.376	0.006	−0.002	0.380	0.016	10.94	677
Killebrew, H.	MIN	1969	0.276	0.371	0.004	−0.003	0.372	−0.009	10.84	709
Mays, Willie	SFG	1958	0.345	0.358	0.014	0.002	0.373	0.002	10.81	680
Piazza, Mike	LAD	1997	0.362	0.372	0.003	0.004	0.379	0.019	10.69	633
Sosa, Sammy	CHC	2001	0.328	0.395	0.001	−0.003	0.393	−0.014	10.68	711
Giambi, Jason	OAK	2000	0.333	0.413	0.004	0.003	0.420	−0.021	10.66	664
Rodriguez, Alex	SEA	2000	0.316	0.370	0.003	0.007	0.380	0.016	10.64	672
Rosen, Al	CLE	1953	0.336	0.382	0.000	−0.003	0.379	0.001	10.63	688
Yastrzemski, Carl	BOS	1967	0.326	0.376	0.001	−0.009	0.369	−0.012	10.61	680
Bonds, Barry	SFG	1993	0.336	0.385	0.003	0.005	0.393	−0.012	10.57	674
Giambi, Jason	OAK	2001	0.342	0.399	0.005	0.003	0.407	−0.022	10.49	671
Yount, Robin	MIL	1982	0.331	0.341	0.006	0.001	0.347	0.016	10.45	704
McGwire, Mark	STL	1998	0.299	0.404	0.002	0.000	0.405	−0.023	10.40	681
Rodriguez, Alex	NYY	2005	0.321	0.362	0.004	0.003	0.369	0.001	10.38	715
Rodriguez, Alex	TEX	2001	0.318	0.351	0.007	−0.005	0.354	0.016	10.30	732
Martinez, Edgar	SEA	1995	0.356	0.400	0.003	−0.002	0.401	−0.010	10.25	639
Rodriguez, Alex	TEX	2002	0.300	0.351	0.004	−0.006	0.349	0.016	10.25	725
Jeter, Derek	NYY	1999	0.349	0.350	0.006	0.002	0.359	0.016	10.21	739
Cash, Norm	DET	1961	0.361	0.398	0.005	−0.006	0.398	−0.023	10.19	673
Snider, Duke	BRO	1953	0.336	0.374	0.006	−0.008	0.373	0.002	10.16	680
Bonds, Barry	SFG	2003	0.341	0.413	0.007	0.004	0.424	−0.012	10.14	550
Mantle, Mickey	NYY	1962	0.321	0.413	0.009	0.003	0.424	−0.001	10.13	502
Brett, George	KCR	1980	0.390	0.408	0.005	−0.001	0.412	0.001	10.10	515
Williams, Billy	CHC	1972	0.333	0.368	0.004	−0.006	0.366	−0.012	10.04	650
McCovey, Willie	SFG	1969	0.320	0.388	0.004	0.002	0.395	−0.024	10.03	623
Aaron, Hank	MLB	1957	0.322	0.363	0.003	0.005	0.370	−0.007	10.02	675
Murcer, Bobby	NYY	1971	0.331	0.354	0.003	0.005	0.363	0.002	9.95	624
Mays, Willie	SFG	1964	0.296	0.348	0.007	0.002	0.357	0.002	9.95	665
Snider, Duke	BRO	1955	0.309	0.381	−0.001	−0.008	0.372	0.002	9.93	653
Williams, Ted	BOS	1957	0.389	0.427	0.003	−0.009	0.420	−0.011	9.91	513
Berkman, Lance	HOU	2002	0.292	0.370	0.001	−0.002	0.369	−0.002	9.88	692
Delgado, Carlos	TOR	2000	0.344	0.400	0.000	−0.001	0.400	−0.024	9.82	711
Porter, Darrell	KCR	1979	0.291	0.346	0.003	−0.001	0.348	0.017	9.82	679
Dietz, Dick	SFG	1970	0.300	0.352	0.003	0.002	0.357	0.020	9.80	612
Cedeno, Cesar	HOU	1972	0.322	0.338	0.011	0.008	0.356	0.002	9.79	616
Ripken, Cal	BAL	1991	0.323	0.326	0.006	0.004	0.336	0.016	9.79	717
Morgan, Joe	CIN	1973	0.290	0.330	0.013	0.004	0.346	0.008	9.75	693
Mantle, Mickey	NYY	1958	0.304	0.353	0.007	0.003	0.363	0.001	9.72	654
Mays, Willie	SFG	1962	0.304	0.349	0.005	0.002	0.356	0.002	9.72	706
Alomar, Roberto	CLE	2001	0.336	0.356	0.007	0.001	0.364	0.008	9.71	677
Campanella, Roy	BRO	1953	0.312	0.377	0.001	−0.008	0.370	0.020	9.71	590
Mantle, Mickey	NYY	1955	0.306	0.367	0.001	0.004	0.372	0.002	9.71	638
Snider, Duke	BRO	1954	0.341	0.365	0.002	−0.008	0.359	0.002	9.71	679
Jackson, Reggie	OAK	1969	0.275	0.358	0.002	0.005	0.365	−0.013	9.68	678
Ramirez, Manny	CLE	1999	0.333	0.401	0.000	0.002	0.402	−0.014	9.64	640
Rose, Pete	CIN	1965	0.312	0.324	0.006	−0.004	0.326	0.008	9.64	757
Ortiz, David	BOS	2005	0.300	0.372	0.002	−0.004	0.370	−0.010	9.62	713
Kemp, Matt	LAD	2011	0.324	0.342	0.006	0.005	0.353	0.001	9.62	689
Berkman, Lance	HOU	2001	0.331	0.381	−0.002	−0.003	0.377	−0.008	9.60	688
Mathews, Eddie	MLB	1959	0.314	0.358	0.002	0.005	0.365	0.001	9.59	653
Alomar, Roberto	CLE	1999	0.323	0.356	0.010	0.002	0.367	0.008	9.58	694

Player	Team	Year	BA	GPA	GPA brc	GPA bpc	tGPA	GPA pc	WAR	PA
Jeter, Derek	NYY	2006	0.343	0.339	0.008	0.002	0.349	0.016	9.58	715
Mathews, Eddie	MLB	1960	0.276	0.353	0.002	0.005	0.361	0.001	9.56	657
Kent, Jeff	SFG	2000	0.334	0.368	0.001	0.001	0.370	0.006	9.55	695
Mantle, Mickey	NYY	1964	0.303	0.373	0.000	0.004	0.377	−0.001	9.46	567
Brett, George	KCR	1985	0.335	0.356	0.003	−0.001	0.358	0.001	9.44	665
Mays, Willie	SFG	1965	0.317	0.346	0.006	0.001	0.353	0.002	9.44	638
Sheffield, Gary	ATL	2003	0.330	0.374	0.004	0.002	0.380	−0.014	9.42	678
Schmidt, Mike	PHI	1974	0.282	0.344	0.001	0.002	0.347	0.001	9.40	686
Bonds, Barry	PIT	1992	0.311	0.365	0.008	0.003	0.376	−0.012	9.38	612
Cabrera, Miguel	FLA	2006	0.339	0.364	−0.001	0.006	0.369	0.001	9.37	676
Griffey, Ken	SEA	1997	0.304	0.356	0.002	0.002	0.360	0.001	9.37	704
Robinson, Frank	CIN	1962	0.342	0.369	0.002	−0.004	0.368	−0.014	9.36	701
Biggio, Craig	HOU	1997	0.309	0.336	0.007	0.004	0.346	0.008	9.36	744
Herr, Tom	STL	1985	0.302	0.328	0.009	0.005	0.343	0.008	9.35	696
Robinson, Frank	BAL	1966	0.316	0.358	−0.001	0.001	0.358	−0.014	9.34	680
Gwynn, Tony	SDP	1997	0.372	0.376	0.000	0.008	0.385	−0.014	9.30	651
Pujols, Albert	STL	2003	0.359	0.375	0.003	0.000	0.378	−0.015	9.29	685
Rodriguez, Alex	SEA	1998	0.310	0.326	0.008	0.003	0.337	0.016	9.29	748
Banks, Ernie	CHC	1959	0.307	0.352	0.001	−0.009	0.344	0.016	9.27	653
Williams, Billy	CHC	1970	0.322	0.358	0.006	−0.007	0.358	−0.012	9.26	714
Carew, Rod	MIN	1977	0.388	0.374	0.006	−0.004	0.376	−0.023	9.25	694
Bonds, Barry	SFG	1998	0.303	0.365	0.002	0.006	0.373	−0.012	9.25	697
Rose, Pete	CIN	1969	0.348	0.346	0.001	−0.003	0.344	−0.008	9.23	731
Maris, Roger	NYY	1961	0.269	0.362	0.003	0.002	0.367	−0.013	9.22	698
Mays, Willie	SFG	1961	0.308	0.361	0.002	−0.002	0.361	0.002	9.22	659
Knoblauch, Chuck	MIN	1996	0.341	0.357	0.007	−0.005	0.359	0.008	9.22	701
Simmons, Ted	STL	1975	0.332	0.329	0.003	0.005	0.336	0.019	9.21	649
Stargell, Willie	PIT	1971	0.295	0.367	0.002	−0.001	0.368	−0.012	9.20	606
Jeter, Derek	NYY	1998	0.324	0.335	0.008	0.002	0.344	0.016	9.16	694
Parker, Dave	PIT	1978	0.334	0.358	0.007	0.002	0.368	−0.014	9.16	642
Bench, Johnny	CIN	1974	0.280	0.317	0.003	0.003	0.324	0.016	9.16	708
Ellsbury, Jacoby	BOS	2011	0.321	0.337	0.006	−0.005	0.338	0.002	9.15	732
Allen, Dick	CHW	1972	0.308	0.364	0.006	0.001	0.371	−0.023	9.14	609
Ordonez, Magglio	DET	2007	0.363	0.373	0.002	0.002	0.377	−0.014	9.14	679
Belle, Albert	CLE	1996	0.311	0.370	0.005	−0.001	0.374	−0.012	9.13	715
Mauer, Joe	MIN	2009	0.365	0.362	0.001	−0.001	0.362	0.014	9.12	606
Gonzalez, Luis	ARI	2001	0.325	0.372	0.001	−0.008	0.366	−0.012	9.12	728
Allen, Dick	PHI	1966	0.317	0.362	0.001	−0.001	0.362	−0.003	9.10	599
Helton, Todd	COL	2000	0.372	0.418	0.004	−0.030	0.392	−0.023	9.10	697
Clemente, Roberto	PIT	1967	0.355	0.361	0.006	0.002	0.370	−0.014	9.09	586
Pujols, Albert	STL	2009	0.327	0.373	0.003	0.002	0.378	−0.023	9.09	700
Bautista, Jose	TOR	2011	0.302	0.364	0.002	−0.001	0.365	−0.012	9.06	655
Mays, Willie	SFG	1966	0.288	0.345	0.004	0.001	0.350	0.001	9.05	629
Clark, Will	SFG	1989	0.333	0.356	0.005	0.008	0.368	−0.023	9.03	675

Table 21.19. Pitchers with 500+ Batters Faced

Player	Team	Year	ERA	BA	GPA	GPA brc	GPA bpc	tGPA	GPA rv	WAR	PA
Perry, Gaylord	CLE	1972	1.92	0.205	0.191	0.002	0.000	0.192	1.15	13.16	1345
Gooden, D.	NYM	1985	1.53	0.201	0.180	−0.003	0.008	0.185	1.11	13.09	1065
Gibson, Bob	STL	1968	1.12	0.184	0.172	0.000	−0.001	0.171	1.14	13.03	1161
Carlton, Steve	PHI	1972	1.97	0.207	0.195	0.001	0.001	0.197	1.12	12.33	1351

Player	Team	Year	ERA	BA	GPA	GPA brc	GPA bpc	tGPA	GPA rv	WAR	PA
Ellsworth, Dick	CHC	1963	2.11	0.210	0.202	−0.003	−0.009	0.191	1.13	12.33	1160
Clemens, Roger	TOR	1997	2.05	0.213	0.200	−0.003	−0.003	0.194	0.99	12.29	1044
Johnson, Randy	ARI	1999	2.48	0.208	0.214	0.001	−0.006	0.208	1.02	12.23	1079
Gibson, Bob	STL	1969	2.18	0.219	0.204	0.002	−0.002	0.204	1.13	12.23	1270
Koufax, Sandy	LAD	1963	1.88	0.189	0.186	0.002	0.007	0.195	1.12	12.19	1210
Martinez, Pedro	BOS	2000	1.74	0.167	0.182	0.000	−0.003	0.179	1.05	12.04	817
Koufax, Sandy	LAD	1966	1.73	0.205	0.190	0.001	0.009	0.201	1.06	11.86	1274
Chance, Dean	LAA	1964	1.65	0.195	0.182	0.001	0.008	0.192	1.13	11.84	1093
Palmer, Jim	BAL	1975	2.09	0.216	0.203	0.001	0.003	0.207	1.04	11.74	1268
Maddux, Greg	ATL	1995	1.63	0.197	0.173	0.003	−0.002	0.173	1.09	11.68	785
Johnson, Randy	ARI	2001	2.49	0.203	0.209	0.000	−0.010	0.199	1.05	11.62	994
Blue, Vida	OAK	1971	1.82	0.189	0.192	0.000	0.006	0.197	1.08	11.52	1207
Brown, Kevin	FLA	1996	1.89	0.220	0.198	0.000	−0.001	0.197	1.06	11.41	906
McLain, Denny	DET	1969	2.80	0.237	0.211	0.002	−0.003	0.210	1.07	11.38	1304
Koufax, Sandy	LAD	1965	2.04	0.179	0.197	0.003	0.009	0.209	1.11	11.24	1297
Carlton, Steve	PHI	1980	2.34	0.218	0.211	−0.002	0.003	0.212	1.09	11.22	1228
Johnson, Randy	ARI	2002	2.32	0.208	0.210	−0.001	−0.007	0.203	1.03	11.17	1035
Seaver, Tom	NYM	1971	1.76	0.206	0.190	−0.001	0.002	0.191	1.05	11.14	1103
Perry, Gaylord	CLE	1974	2.51	0.204	0.210	0.001	0.000	0.211	1.08	11.04	1263
Palmer, Jim	BAL	1977	2.91	0.229	0.226	−0.007	0.003	0.222	1.12	11.00	1269
Johnson, Randy	ARI	2000	2.64	0.224	0.223	0.000	−0.007	0.216	1.06	10.99	1001
Martinez, Pedro	MON	1997	1.90	0.184	0.202	0.001	−0.002	0.201	1.08	10.99	947
Maddux, Greg	ATL	1994	1.56	0.207	0.188	−0.002	−0.005	0.181	1.08	10.96	774
Seaver, Tom	NYM	1973	2.08	0.206	0.197	0.002	0.006	0.205	1.07	10.93	1147
Guidry, Ron	NYY	1978	1.74	0.193	0.194	−0.003	0.002	0.193	1.02	10.90	1057
Maddux, Greg	ATL	1993	2.36	0.232	0.212	0.002	−0.003	0.210	1.08	10.84	1064
Lolich, Mickey	DET	1971	2.92	0.237	0.225	0.000	−0.004	0.221	1.10	10.84	1538
Wood, Wilbur	CHW	1971	1.91	0.222	0.205	0.004	0.001	0.210	1.07	10.80	1316
Hunter, Jim	NYY	1975	2.58	0.208	0.215	−0.001	0.002	0.217	1.07	10.78	1294
Marichal, Juan	SFG	1966	2.23	0.202	0.201	0.003	0.000	0.204	1.10	10.76	1180
Maddux, Greg	ATL	1997	2.20	0.236	0.194	0.000	0.003	0.197	1.07	10.75	893
McLain, Denny	DET	1968	1.96	0.200	0.195	0.001	−0.004	0.193	1.03	10.73	1288
Clemens, Roger	BOS	1987	2.97	0.235	0.225	0.002	−0.008	0.219	1.00	10.71	1157
Blyleven, Bert	MIN	1973	2.52	0.242	0.217	0.002	−0.002	0.217	1.01	10.69	1321
Tiant, Luis	BOS	1974	2.92	0.241	0.220	0.000	−0.007	0.213	1.06	10.64	1266
Tudor, John	STL	1985	1.93	0.209	0.196	0.000	0.007	0.203	1.03	10.59	1062
Marichal, Juan	SFG	1965	2.13	0.205	0.200	0.001	0.001	0.202	1.06	10.56	1153
Schilling, Curt	ARI	2001	2.98	0.245	0.224	−0.003	−0.009	0.213	1.06	10.53	1021
Maddux, Greg	CHC	1992	2.18	0.210	0.201	−0.002	−0.001	0.199	1.06	10.55	1061
Roberts, Robin	PHI	1954	3.00	0.232	0.223	−0.001	−0.004	0.219	1.06	10.53	1224
Martinez, Pedro	BOS	1999	2.07	0.205	0.200	0.001	−0.004	0.196	1.02	10.51	835
Messersmith, A.	LAD	1975	2.29	0.213	0.206	0.001	0.011	0.218	1.06	10.46	1276
McDowell, Sam	CLE	1970	2.92	0.213	0.222	0.000	0.000	0.221	1.09	10.46	1258
Pierce, Billy	CHW	1953	2.72	0.218	0.226	−0.004	−0.001	0.221	1.12	10.42	1113
Palmer, Jim	BAL	1973	2.40	0.211	0.207	0.000	0.003	0.210	1.01	10.41	1190
Clemens, Roger	BOS	1990	1.93	0.228	0.200	−0.002	−0.007	0.191	1.08	10.40	920
Bunning, Jim	PHI	1966	2.41	0.223	0.210	0.000	0.000	0.209	1.02	10.37	1254
Maddux, Greg	ATL	1998	2.22	0.220	0.213	−0.002	0.000	0.210	1.04	10.36	987
Drysdale, Don	LAD	1964	2.18	0.207	0.204	0.000	0.009	0.213	1.05	10.34	1264
Wood, Wilbur	CHW	1972	2.51	0.235	0.218	−0.004	0.001	0.216	1.07	10.33	1490
McDowell, Sam	CLE	1965	2.18	0.185	0.203	0.003	−0.002	0.204	1.12	10.32	1116
Palmer, Jim	BAL	1970	2.71	0.231	0.215	0.004	0.003	0.221	1.05	10.31	1258
Seaver, Tom	NYM	1969	2.21	0.207	0.203	0.000	0.000	0.204	1.09	10.25	1089

Player	Team	Year	ERA	BA	GPA	GPA brc	GPA bpc	tGPA	GPA rv	WAR	PA
Drysdale, Don	LAD	1960	2.84	0.215	0.218	−0.001	−0.006	0.210	1.09	10.14	1083
Clemens, Roger	BOS	1986	2.48	0.195	0.211	−0.002	−0.007	0.203	1.04	10.13	997
Niekro, Phil	ATL	1974	2.38	0.225	0.211	0.005	−0.002	0.214	1.04	10.10	1219
Rijo, Jose	CIN	1993	2.48	0.230	0.212	−0.001	0.000	0.211	1.03	10.10	1029
Marichal, Juan	SFG	1969	2.10	0.222	0.213	−0.003	0.003	0.212	1.11	10.10	1176
Garcia, Mike	CLE	1954	2.64	0.230	0.216	0.001	−0.004	0.213	1.14	10.05	1051
Lemon, Bob	CLE	1952	2.51	0.209	0.217	0.001	−0.003	0.215	1.04	10.04	1217
Antonelli, John	NYG	1954	2.30	0.219	0.215	0.000	−0.003	0.212	1.07	10.02	1071
Scott, Mike	HOU	1986	2.22	0.186	0.198	0.002	0.012	0.212	1.07	9.98	1065
Wynn, Early	CLE	1956	2.69	0.228	0.221	0.001	−0.001	0.221	1.08	9.98	1142
Brown, Kevin	SDP	1998	2.38	0.235	0.213	0.000	0.007	0.220	1.08	9.95	1032
Hands, Bill	CHC	1969	2.49	0.237	0.224	−0.002	−0.006	0.215	1.08	9.93	1220
Greinke, Zack	KCR	2009	2.16	0.230	0.207	−0.003	−0.003	0.201	1.02	9.92	915
Lolich, Mickey	DET	1972	2.50	0.234	0.214	0.000	−0.003	0.210	1.06	9.88	1321
Garcia, Mike	CLE	1952	2.30	0.249	0.223	−0.003	−0.002	0.218	1.10	9.87	1201
Maddux, Greg	ATL	1996	2.72	0.241	0.222	0.002	−0.004	0.220	1.04	9.83	978
Smoltz, John	ATL	1996	2.94	0.216	0.229	−0.001	−0.007	0.221	1.02	9.82	995
Clemens, Roger	HOU	2005	1.87	0.198	0.198	−0.001	−0.002	0.196	1.07	9.80	838
Ryan, Nolan	CAL	1973	2.82	0.203	0.220	0.004	0.002	0.226	1.03	9.78	1356
Dierker, Larry	HOU	1969	2.33	0.214	0.211	−0.001	0.006	0.216	1.06	9.70	1207
Hunter, Jim	OAK	1974	2.49	0.229	0.214	−0.004	0.008	0.218	1.04	9.70	1240
Stieb, Dave	TOR	1984	2.83	0.221	0.220	−0.003	−0.003	0.214	1.10	9.68	1085
Appier, Kevin	KCR	1993	2.56	0.212	0.213	−0.001	−0.001	0.211	1.08	9.67	953
Tiant, Luis	CLE	1968	1.60	0.168	0.186	−0.003	0.000	0.183	1.12	9.65	987
Maddux, Greg	ATL	2000	3.00	0.238	0.226	0.003	0.000	0.229	1.04	9.63	1012
Jenkins, F.	CHC	1971	2.77	0.246	0.226	−0.001	−0.007	0.218	1.09	9.62	1299
Lee, Bill	BOS	1973	2.75	0.257	0.223	0.001	−0.007	0.217	1.05	9.61	1173
Cuellar, Mike	BAL	1969	2.38	0.204	0.213	−0.001	0.002	0.213	1.10	9.60	1137
Halladay, Roy	PHI	2010	2.44	0.245	0.209	0.000	−0.002	0.207	1.02	9.58	993
Marichal, Juan	SFG	1963	2.41	0.216	0.218	−0.002	0.001	0.218	1.11	9.57	1271
Rogers, Steve	MON	1982	2.40	0.237	0.216	−0.002	0.005	0.220	1.14	9.55	1122
Brown, Kevin	LAD	2000	2.58	0.213	0.218	0.002	0.002	0.221	1.04	9.54	921
Seaver, Tom	NYM	1975	2.38	0.214	0.208	0.000	0.007	0.215	1.08	9.53	1115
Caldwell, Mike	MIL	1978	2.36	0.234	0.215	−0.001	0.001	0.216	1.03	9.52	1176
Jenkins, F.	TEX	1974	2.82	0.232	0.222	0.001	0.002	0.225	1.09	9.52	1305
Santana, Johan	MIN	2004	2.61	0.192	0.206	0.000	−0.001	0.206	1.01	9.50	881
Saberhagen, B.	KCR	1989	2.16	0.217	0.208	−0.003	0.001	0.205	1.06	9.46	1021
Kile, Darryl	HOU	1997	2.57	0.225	0.218	0.003	0.004	0.225	1.05	9.44	1056
Wynn, Early	CLE	1954	2.73	0.225	0.224	−0.004	−0.001	0.219	1.06	9.44	1102
Johnson, Randy	ARI	2004	2.60	0.197	0.224	0.001	−0.007	0.218	1.05	9.43	964
Glavine, Tom	ATL	1998	2.47	0.238	0.213	−0.002	0.002	0.212	1.01	9.42	934
Stieb, Dave	TOR	1985	2.48	0.213	0.221	−0.001	−0.003	0.216	1.05	9.42	1087
Reuschel, Rick	CHC	1977	2.79	0.247	0.221	−0.004	−0.001	0.217	1.09	9.42	1030
Hentgen, Pat	TOR	1996	3.22	0.241	0.239	−0.002	−0.003	0.234	1.01	9.42	1100
Key, Jimmy	TOR	1987	2.76	0.221	0.229	−0.002	−0.005	0.222	1.03	9.40	1033
Clemens, Roger	BOS	1991	2.62	0.221	0.223	−0.002	−0.007	0.215	1.04	9.39	1077
Gromek, Steve	DET	1954	2.74	0.246	0.222	−0.001	−0.007	0.214	1.03	9.37	1049
Garcia, Mike	CLE	1953	3.25	0.250	0.232	0.002	−0.003	0.231	1.11	9.37	1133
Bunning, Jim	PHI	1965	2.60	0.232	0.216	0.000	−0.001	0.215	1.07	9.35	1191
Brown, Kevin	FLA	1997	2.69	0.240	0.216	0.003	−0.002	0.217	1.00	9.33	976
Hunter, Jim	OAK	1972	2.04	0.189	0.196	0.003	0.007	0.206	1.12	9.33	1149

Table 21.20. Relief Pitchers with 200+ Batters Faced

Player	Team	Year	ERA	BA	GPA	GPA brc	GPA bpc	tGPA	GPA rv	WAR	PA
Hiller, John	DET	1973	1.44	0.198	0.152	−0.002	−0.001	0.149	1.33	9.02	498
Gossage, Rich	PIT	1977	1.62	0.170	0.177	0.002	0.002	0.182	1.44	8.21	523
Corbett, Doug	MIN	1980	1.98	0.213	0.177	0.002	−0.004	0.176	1.33	7.89	531
Marshall, Mike	MON	1973	2.63	0.252	0.211	0.001	−0.004	0.207	1.29	7.73	742
Gossage, Rich	CHW	1975	1.84	0.201	0.195	0.000	−0.001	0.194	1.39	7.36	583
Radatz, Dick	BOS	1964	2.29	0.186	0.208	−0.002	−0.008	0.197	1.36	7.22	634
Campbell, Bill	BOS	1977	2.96	0.224	0.210	−0.004	−0.008	0.199	1.31	7.22	583
Hernandez, G.	DET	1984	1.92	0.194	0.187	0.002	−0.001	0.188	1.27	7.01	548
Kern, Jim	TEX	1979	1.57	0.198	0.191	0.004	0.001	0.196	1.19	6.98	578
Sutter, Bruce	CHC	1977	1.34	0.183	0.178	0.003	−0.001	0.180	1.47	6.60	411
Sutter, Bruce	STL	1984	1.54	0.245	0.180	0.003	0.005	0.188	1.42	6.60	477
Lidge, Brad	HOU	2004	1.90	0.174	0.177	0.000	−0.002	0.175	1.44	6.59	369
McDaniel, Lindy	STL	1960	2.09	0.208	0.186	0.003	−0.010	0.179	1.32	6.49	448
Miller, Stu	BAL	1965	1.89	0.207	0.180	−0.002	0.002	0.180	1.41	6.39	462
Miller, Stu	SFG	1961	2.66	0.215	0.195	−0.003	−0.001	0.191	1.22	6.39	487
Radatz, Dick	BOS	1963	2.04	0.201	0.199	0.004	−0.010	0.193	1.38	6.35	541
Wilhelm, Hoyt	CHW	1965	1.80	0.175	0.175	0.012	0.001	0.188	1.21	6.33	549
Sanders, Ken	MIL	1971	1.91	0.227	0.193	−0.006	0.002	0.189	1.31	6.29	538
Radatz, Dick	BOS	1962	2.24	0.211	0.201	0.004	−0.009	0.195	1.25	6.29	504
Gossage, Rich	NYY	1978	2.01	0.187	0.194	0.003	0.001	0.198	1.34	6.26	543
Selma, Dick	PHI	1970	2.75	0.226	0.208	0.000	−0.001	0.207	1.38	6.23	553
Black, Joe	BRO	1952	2.15	0.201	0.204	−0.004	−0.005	0.195	1.18	6.21	560
Quisenberry, D.	KCR	1983	1.81	0.229	0.200	0.001	−0.001	0.200	1.29	6.19	536
Gagne, Eric	LAD	2003	1.20	0.133	0.158	0.001	0.006	0.165	1.56	6.18	306
Rivera, Mariano	NYY	1996	2.09	0.189	0.190	−0.000	0.002	0.191	1.21	6.16	425
Stanley, Bob	BOS	1982	3.10	0.255	0.225	−0.001	−0.007	0.216	1.13	6.15	694
Murphy, Tom	MIL	1974	1.90	0.224	0.190	0.004	0.001	0.195	1.42	6.12	497
Henry, Bill	CHC	1959	2.67	0.225	0.202	0.003	−0.011	0.194	1.15	6.04	512
McGraw, Tug	NYM	1971	1.70	0.189	0.168	0.006	0.001	0.174	1.31	5.99	441
Fisher, Eddie	CHW	1965	2.40	0.205	0.202	0.006	0.000	0.208	1.25	5.99	646
Bedrosian, Steve	ATL	1982	2.42	0.206	0.206	0.001	−0.001	0.206	1.24	5.97	567
Ryan, B.J.	TOR	2006	1.37	0.169	0.141	0.006	−0.001	0.145	1.41	5.95	270
Papelbon, J.	BOS	2006	0.92	0.167	0.150	0.005	−0.004	0.151	1.57	5.92	257
Wilhelm, Hoyt	CHW	1964	1.99	0.202	0.182	0.015	−0.001	0.196	1.35	5.91	510
Foulke, Keith	CHW	1999	2.22	0.188	0.195	−0.002	−0.003	0.190	1.15	5.88	411
Tekulve, Kent	PIT	1979	2.75	0.222	0.208	0.004	0.002	0.214	1.33	5.87	550
Thigpen, Bobby	CHW	1990	1.83	0.195	0.173	0.004	−0.001	0.176	1.57	5.82	347
Taylor, Ron	STL	1963	2.84	0.243	0.200	−0.001	−0.008	0.192	1.17	5.77	540
Hoffman, T.	SDP	1996	2.25	0.161	0.196	0.000	0.006	0.202	1.66	5.75	348
Leskanic, Curtis	COL	1995	3.40	0.226	0.217	0.004	−0.035	0.185	1.14	5.72	406
Stanley, Bob	BOS	1983	2.79	0.266	0.220	0.004	−0.007	0.218	1.31	5.69	602
McDaniel, Lindy	NYY	1970	2.01	0.217	0.196	−0.001	0.003	0.198	1.47	5.68	436
Quisenberry, D.	KCR	1980	3.02	0.265	0.214	−0.002	−0.001	0.211	1.42	5.68	528
Aker, Jack	KCA	1966	1.99	0.200	0.188	−0.002	−0.004	0.183	1.30	5.66	444
Minton, Greg	SFG	1982	1.83	0.244	0.200	0.001	0.007	0.209	1.49	5.65	496
McGraw, Tug	PHI	1980	1.46	0.194	0.168	0.001	0.002	0.171	1.36	5.60	355
Graves, Danny	CIN	1999	3.08	0.227	0.207	0.003	−0.002	0.207	1.13	5.57	454
Rodney, F.	TBR	2012	0.60	0.167	0.142	0.006	0.003	0.151	1.46	5.57	282
Lopez, Aurelio	DET	1979	2.41	0.210	0.209	0.001	−0.001	0.208	1.21	5.56	519
Clippard, Tyler	WAS	2011	1.83	0.162	0.171	−0.007	0.001	0.165	1.37	5.51	329
Lee, Bob	LAA	1964	1.51	0.182	0.193	0.004	0.006	0.203	1.21	5.42	547

Player	Team	Year	ERA	BA	GPA	GPA brc	GPA bpc	tGPA	GPA rv	WAR	PA
Monge, Sid	CLE	1979	2.27	0.209	0.213	0.006	0.000	0.218	1.32	5.42	542
Betancourt, R.	CLE	2007	1.47	0.183	0.163	−0.004	0.002	0.160	1.33	5.42	289
Wagner, Billy	HOU	2003	1.78	0.169	0.175	0.007	−0.002	0.181	1.36	5.41	335
Wagner, Billy	HOU	1999	1.57	0.135	0.167	0.008	0.004	0.179	1.49	5.40	286
Grissom, Marv	NYG	1954	2.05	0.225	0.202	0.001	−0.005	0.198	1.21	5.38	461
Worrell, Todd	STL	1986	2.08	0.229	0.206	−0.003	0.005	0.208	1.57	5.34	430
Gordon, Tom	NYY	2004	2.21	0.180	0.182	0.002	0.002	0.186	1.35	5.34	342
Wetteland, John	MON	1993	1.37	0.188	0.178	0.009	0.005	0.192	1.54	5.33	344
Marshall, Mike	MON	1972	1.78	0.202	0.190	−0.002	0.001	0.190	1.43	5.33	465
Perranoski, Ron	LAD	1963	1.67	0.231	0.197	0.003	0.007	0.207	1.38	5.32	541
Gagne, Eric	LAD	2002	1.97	0.189	0.175	0.003	0.006	0.184	1.54	5.28	314
Tatum, Ken	CAL	1969	1.36	0.172	0.147	0.011	0.006	0.165	1.31	5.28	342
Wilhelm, Hoyt	CLE	1958	2.34	0.204	0.204	0.010	−0.005	0.208	1.17	5.27	526
McGraw, Tug	NYM	1972	1.70	0.197	0.188	−0.004	−0.001	0.183	1.46	5.27	419
Perranoski, Ron	MIN	1969	2.11	0.205	0.208	0.001	−0.002	0.207	1.51	5.26	485
Bell, Heath	SDP	2007	2.02	0.185	0.179	0.003	0.009	0.191	1.29	5.23	363
Hoffman, T.	SDP	1998	1.48	0.165	0.158	0.006	0.009	0.174	1.55	5.20	274
Hernandez, Rob	CHW	1996	1.91	0.208	0.200	0.004	0.004	0.208	1.54	5.20	355
Benitez, A.	NYM	1999	1.85	0.148	0.177	0.007	0.002	0.186	1.35	5.17	312
Sutter, Bruce	CHC	1979	2.22	0.186	0.194	0.011	0.000	0.205	1.51	5.17	403

Who Should Have Won the Cy Young Award?

The Cy Young Award (CYA) is an honor given to the best pitcher. From 1956 to 1966 only one pitcher in the major leagues was honored. Since 1967, one pitcher in each league has been honored.

The award is chosen by the Baseball Writers Association of America (BBWAA), who select two baseball writers who cover each team to vote. From 1956 to 1969, each writer had a single vote for the award. From 1970 to 2009, each writer ranked the three best pitchers in his league from one to three with the first ranked pitcher receiving five points, the second three points and the third one point. Since 2010, each writer has ranked the five best pitchers from one to five, with the top ranked player receiving seven points, the second five points, the third three points, the forth two points and the fifth one point. The player in each league with the most points wins the Cy Young.

Criteria for selecting a Cy Young winner are minimal, with the ballot instructing the sportswriters to "list in order the five (5) pitchers he/she feels had the best seasons in their league" (personal communication, Jack O'Connell, secretary-treasurer, BBWAA).

Total GPA (again, calculated by adding the GPA baserunning correction and the GPA ballpark correction to GPA) should identify the best pitcher. Criteria such as how many games a pitcher won, how well his team played, how well he was liked by the writers, what team he played for and how many statistical categories he led are ignored by tGPA. These less objective criteria have often had considerable influence writers' choices for the Cy Young Award.

The table at the end of this chapter lists the Cy Young winners along with the pitchers whom tGPA identifies as the most deserving. Here as elsewhere in the book it should be pointed out that there are a few games missing from the Retrosheet database from 1952 to 1973, and the statistics listed here may differ slightly from the official statistics for those years.

The goal of this chapter is to show who should have won the Cy Young Award. The choice of a starting or relief pitcher for the award is somewhat arbitrary. When a starting pitcher has been given the Cy Young, the merits of other starting pitcher are considered; when a reliever has been the recipient, all other pitchers are considered.

In the early years of the award, the number of games won by the pitcher appears to have been the most important criterion for selection. Every winner from 1956 to 1972, except Dean Chance in 1964, was within one win of the leader in games won that year. Cy

Young Award winners during this era were limited to starting pitchers from top teams since other pitchers could not generate enough wins to be seriously considered by the writers.

Seasons	*Cy Young Winner Trailed League Leader in tGPA By*			
	None	1 to 9	10 to 19	20+
1956 to 1960	0	1	2	2
1961 to 1970	3	7	3	2
1971 to 1980	11	2	3	5
1981 to 1990	10	2	5	3
1991 to 2000	15	2	1	2
2001 to 2012	10	7	2	5

Table 22.1. Number of tGPA points the Cy Young winner trailed the pitcher with the best (lowest) tGPA from 1956 to 2012.

The 1964 season was also the first time that the pitcher with the best tGPA, Chance, was chosen by the writers. The pitcher with the best tGPA won only three of 20 CYAs (15.0 percent) before 1971, but from 1971 to 2012 won 46 of 84 times (54.8 percent). Pitchers whose tGPAs trailed the league leader by 20 or more points have been chosen by the writers less frequently from 1971 to 2012 (25.0 percent vs. 17.9 percent).

In the past four decades, the writers still made occasional choices that seem hard to justify, such as their selection of Bob Welch over Roger Clemens in 1990. Clemens had a tGPA of 0.191 that season, the seventh best for a starting pitcher from 1952 to 2012. Welch's tGPA was 0.240, or 0.049 GPA points worse than Clemens' tGPA—the largest margin in the Cy Young Award's history. Many writers could not see past Welch's 27 wins (compared with 21 wins for Clemens), despite Clemens' far superior ERA (1.93 vs. 2.95) and number of strikeouts (209 vs. 127).

Mgn	Year	Won CYA	Team	tGPA	Lost CYA	Team	tGPA
0.049	1990AL	Welch, Bob	OAK	0.240	Clemens, Roger	BOS	0.191
0.038	2003AL	Halladay, Roy	TOR	0.239	Martinez, Pedro	BOS	0.201
0.038	2012NL	Dickey, R.A.	NYM	0.223	Medlen, Kris	ATL	0.185
0.035	1959	Wynn, Early	CHW	0.241	Wilhelm, Hoyt	BAL	0.206
0.032	1993AL	McDowell, Jack	CHW	0.243	Appier, Kevin	KCR	0.211
0.031	1984NL	Sutcliffe, Rick	CLE*	0.254	Rhoden, Rick	PIT	0.223
0.028	1962	Drysdale, Don	LAD	0.241	Aguirre, Hank	DET	0.213
0.027	1971NL	Jenkins, Ferguson	CHC	0.218	Seaver, Tom	NYM	0.191
0.026	1977AL	Lyle, Sparky(r)	NYY	0.225	Campbell, Bill(r)	BOS	0.199
0.026	1980AL	Stone, Steve	BAL	0.246	Norris, Mike	OAK	0.220
0.025	1967AL	Lonborg, Jim	BOS	0.220	Horlen, Joe	CHW	0.195
0.025	1978NL	Perry, Gaylord	SDP	0.240	Swan, Craig	NYM	0.215
0.025	1978NL	Perry, Gaylord	SDP	0.240	Rogers, Steve	MON	0.215
0.024	2005AL	Colon, Bartolo	ANA	0.243	Santana, Johan	MIN	0.219
0.024	1996NL	Smoltz, John	ATL	0.221	Brown, Kevin	FLA	0.197
0.023	1957	Spahn, Warren	MLB	0.227	Sullivan, Frank	BOS	0.204
0.021	1974NL	Marshall, Mike(r)	LAD	0.233	Capra, Buzz	ATL	0.212
0.021	1982AL	Vuckovich, Pete	MIL	0.248	Palmer, Jim	BAL	0.227
0.021	2005NL	Carpenter, Chris	STL	0.217	Clemens, Roger	HOU	0.196

Table 22.2. Largest margins (Mgn) and year the Cy Young winner trailed the pitcher with the best tGPA in the league. (Relievers are designated by "(r).")

With more sources for baseball statistics available today, writers are willing to look more objectively at a pitcher's production when making selections. Felix Hernandez won the 2010 AL Cy Young with only 13 wins, the lowest total by a starting pitcher in the award's history. It is unlikely writers from the 1950s or 1960s would have been willing to vote for a starting pitcher with only 13 wins.

Mike Marshall's 1974 Cy Young was the first won by a relief pitcher. He appeared in 106 games, had 15 wins and 21 saves. His 857 batters faced were more than some starting pitchers who have won the award. Even though Marshall's 1974 season was therefore out of the ordinary and he played for a Dodgers team that won an MLB-high 102 games, Buzz Capra and especially Phil Niekro of the Braves had significantly more productive 1974 seasons. Niekro's total of 1,219 batters faced and a tGPA of 0.214 were both second in the NL that year.

In 1977 Sparky Lyle of the Yankees became the second relief pitcher to win the award. Lyle's candidacy was helped when the Yankees won their division and Lyle posted an ERA of 2.17. Yet Bill Campbell of the Red Sox had a more productive season, at least as measured by his 0.199 tGPA, which was 0.026 better than Lyle's tGPA of 0.225. Campbell also led Lyle in saves (31 to 26) and batters faced (583 to 554). In the NL that year, Rich Gossage had a tGPA of 0.182, an ERA of 1.62, 26 saves and 523 batters faced, yet did not receive a single vote for the Cy Young.

Seven other relief pitchers have won the award since 1979. Each had a superior season, leading all starting and relief pitchers in their leagues in tGPA. The exception is Mark Davis in 1989, whose fine tGPA of 0.191 trailed only Rob Dibble's 0.181. Dibble was used as a set-up man in 1989 and had only two saves to Davis's 44 saves.

Relief pitchers have won nine of 104 Cy Youngs (8.6 percent) from 1956 to 2012. Today the best relief pitchers tend to have lower (better) GPAs than the best starting pitchers but face far fewer batters.

The following table lists pitchers who won or should have won multiple Cy Young Awards from 1952 to 2012 based on tGPA. Pitchers whose tGPA led the Cy Young winner by 20 or more points were almost certainly more deserving of the award than the pitcher chosen by writers. Pitchers who led by 10 to 19 points were probably more deserving of the award, and an argument can at least be made for the pitchers who led by one to nine points.

Consider the case of Roger Clemens. By adding the number of Cy Youngs won to the number of years that he both led the league in tGPA and led the Cy Young winner by 20 or more GPA points, then subtracting the number of years he won the award but trailed another pitcher in the league by 20 or more GPA points (**20+** column), it can be determined that Clemens could easily have won two more awards, for a total of nine over the course of his career.

If having the best tGPA is the criteria used to determine who should have won the award (**0+** column), Clemens's Cy Young count falls back to eight while Greg Maddux's (four to six) and Dave Stieb's (none to two) increase by two. Randy Johnson would gain one, moving from five to six, which would tie him with Maddux for the, second most behind Clemens.

Table 22.3 lists pitchers who won or should have won multiple Cy Young Awards from 1952 to 2012 based on tGPA. The **Won** column is the number of awards won from 1956 to 2012. The **20+** column includes awards won but is adjusted to reflect (1) the number of years that pitcher led the league in tGPA and led the Cy Young winner by 20 or more GPA points; and (2) the number of years he won the Cy Young and trailed another pitcher in the league by 20 or more GPA points. The **10+** column is the same as the **20+** column, but with the cutoff lowered to 10 GPA points.; and the **0+** column lowers the cutoff still further, to to 0 GPA points. The data is based on at least 3.1 batters faced per game in the season for starting pitchers.

Player	*Won*	*20+*	*10+*	*0+*	*Player*	*Won*	*20+*	*10+*	*0+*
Clemens, Roger	7	9	8	8	Glavin, Tom	2	2	2	1
Johnson, Randy	5	5	5	6	McLain, Denny	2	2	1	1
Carlton, Steve	4	4	2	2	Perry, Gaylord	2	1	1	1
Greg Maddux	4	4	4	6	Saberhagen, Bret	2	2	2	1
Koufax, Sandy	3	3	3	0	Santana, Johan	2	3	3	3
Martinez, Pedro	3	4	4	3	Lincecum, Tim	2	2	1	1
Palmer, Jim	3	4	5	3	Halladay, Roy	2	1	1	1
Seaver, Tom	3	4	4	4	Ford, Whitey	1	1	2	1
Gibson, Bob	2	2	2	1	Stieb, Dave	0	0	1	2

Table 22.3. Leading pitchers, their Cy Young Awards totals, and the number that each should have won according the number of tGPA points they led or trailed the writers' selection.

The following table presents Cy Young voting by year and league with the players listed by tGPA. An **s** after the year indicates a strike-shortened season. A number after the pitcher's name is his rank in the league based on tGPA. A pound sign (#) before his name indicates that more than 5 percent of the PAs for that season are missing from the Retrosheet database and WAR and GPA are adjusted for the missing games. An **r** after the win total indicates the pitcher was primarily a reliever. An asterisk (*) after team abbreviation indicates the pitcher played for two teams that year. An underlined ERA indicates that the relief pitcher lead all relief pitchers in the league in ERA. The data is based on at least 3.1 batters faced per game for starting pitchers.

22.4. Cy Young Winners and Pitchers with the Best tGPA by Year and League

Player 1956	*Team*	*SO*	*Wins*	*ERA*	*WAR*	*GPA*	*GPA brc*	*GPA bpc*	*Total GPA*	*Cy Young Points*	*Rank*
Maglie, Sal	CLE	110	13	2.89	6.96	0.225	−0.000	−0.008	0.217	4	2
Score, Herb	CLE	*263*	20	2.53	9.02	0.218	0.004	−0.002	0.220		
Ford, Whitey(4)	NYY	141	19	*2.47*	7.95	0.223	−0.006	0.004	0.221	1	3
Newcombe, D.(6)	BRO	139	*27*	3.06	8.92	0.229	0.000	−0.008	0.221	10	1
# Spahn, W.(7)	MLB	128	20	2.78	*9.44*	0.222	−0.001	0.004	0.225	1	3

Player 1957	*Team*	*SO*	*Wins*	*ERA*	*WAR*	*GPA*	*GPA brc*	*GPA bpc*	*Total GPA*	*Cy Young Points*	*Rank*
# Sullivan, Frank	BOS	127	14	2.73	*9.89*	0.217	−0.001	−0.012	0.204		
Podres, Johnny	BRO	109	12	*2.66*	7.56	0.214	0.000	−0.009	0.206		
Drysdale, Don	BRO	148	17	2.69	7.62	0.221	0.003	−0.008	0.217		
Donovan, Dick(6)	CHW	88	16	2.77	7.21	0.220	0.000	−0.000	0.220	1	2
Spahn, W.(8)	MLB	111	*21*	2.69	8.24	0.225	−0.002	0.004	0.227	15	1

Player 1958	*Team*	*SO*	*Wins*	*ERA*	*WAR*	*GPA*	*GPA brc*	*GPA bpc*	*Total GPA*	*Cy Young Points*	*Rank*
Ford, Whitey	NYY	145	14	*2.01*	7.78	0.211	−0.005	0.006	0.212		
Pierce, Billy	CHW	144	17	2.68	8.03	0.226	−0.003	−0.000	0.222		
Lary, Frank	DET	131	16	2.90	*8.65*	0.226	0.000	−0.004	0.223		
Turley, Bob	NYY	168	21	2.97	7.53	0.226	−0.002	0.003	0.227	5	1
# Spahn, W.(11)	MLB	150	*22*	3.07	8.05	0.233	−0.002	0.004	0.235	4	2

Player 1959	Team	SO	Wins	ERA	WAR	GPA	GPA brc	GPA bpc	Total GPA	Cy Young Points	Rank
Wilhelm, Hoyt	BAL	139	15	*2.19*	*9.21*	0.200	0.005	0.001	0.206		
Shaw, Bob	CHW	89	18	2.69	8.65	0.219	-0.001	-0.001	0.216		
Jones, Sam(12)	SFG	209	*21*	2.83	8.29	0.230	0.000	0.001	0.232	2	2
Wynn, Early(19)	CHW	179	*22*	3.17	6.79	0.241	0.001	-0.001	0.241	13	1

Player 1960	Team	SO	Wins	ERA	WAR	GPA	GPA brc	GPA bpc	Total GPA	Cy Young Points	Rank
Broglio, Ernie	STL	188	*21*	2.74	8.63	0.219	-0.003	-0.009	0.206	1	t3
Drysdale, Don	LAD	*246*	15	2.84	*10.14*	0.218	-0.001	-0.006	0.210		
Baumann, Frank	CHW	71	13	*2.67*	6.28	0.219	0.001	-0.001	0.219		
Law, Vern(6)	PIT	120	20	3.08	8.29	0.225	0.000	-0.000	0.225	8	1
Spahn, W.(21)	MLB	74	*21*	3.50	6.58	0.238	-0.003	0.007	0.242	4	2

Player 1961	Team	SO	Wins	ERA	WAR	GPA	GPA brc	GPA bpc	Total GPA	Cy Young Points	Rank
Stafford, Bill	NYY	101	14	2.68	6.59	0.222	-0.003	0.004	0.223		
Ford, Whitey	NYY	209	*25*	3.21	*8.90*	0.228	0.001	0.002	0.232	9	1
Kralick, Jack	MIN	137	13	3.61	7.86	0.234	0.004	-0.006	0.232		
O'Toole, Jim	CIN	178	19	3.10	8.00	0.237	0.001	-0.006	0.233		
Spahn, W.(9)	MLB	115	21	*3.02*	7.97	0.226	-0.001	0.010	0.236	6	2

Player 1962	Team	SO	Wins	ERA	WAR	GPA	GPA brc	GPA bpc	Total GPA	Cy Young Points	Rank
Aguirre, Hank	DET	156	16	*2.21*	8.58	0.215	0.001	-0.003	0.213		
Gibson, Bob	STL	208	15	2.85	8.53	0.222	0.004	-0.006	0.220		
Purkey, Bob(5)	CIN	141	23	2.81	*9.32*	0.228	0.004	-0.005	0.227	1	3
Drysdale, Don(16)	LAD	*232*	*25*	2.83	8.22	0.233	-0.002	0.010	0.241	14	1
Sanford, Jack(17)	SFG	147	24	3.43	6.86	0.241	-0.001	0.002	0.242	4	2

Player 1963	Team	SO	Wins	ERA	WAR	GPA	GPA brc	GPA bpc	Total GPA	Cy Young Points	Rank
Ellsworth, Dick	CHC	185	22	2.11	*12.33*	0.202	-0.003	-0.009	0.191		
Koufax, Sandy	LAD	*306*	25	*1.88*	12.19	0.186	0.002	0.007	0.195	20u	1
Peters, Gary	CHW	189	19	*2.33*	8.56	0.203	0.002	0.000	0.205		
Pascual, Camilo	MIN	202	21	2.46	8.09	0.214	0.001	-0.003	0.211		
Nuxhall, Joe	CIN	169	15	2.61	6.80	0.225	-0.004	-0.006	0.215		

Player 1964	Team	SO	Wins	ERA	WAR	GPA	GPA brc	GPA bpc	Total GPA	Cy Young Points	Rank
Chance, Dean	LAA	207	20	*1.65*	*11.84*	0.182	0.001	0.008	0.192	17	1
Koufax, Sandy	LAD	223	19	1.74	8.45	0.191	-0.000	0.010	0.201	1	3
Horlen, Joe	CHW	138	13	1.88	7.73	0.204	-0.001	-0.000	0.202		
Short, Chris	PHI	181	17	2.20	7.58	0.203	0.005	-0.000	0.208		
Jackson, Larry(18)	CHC	148	*24*	3.14	8.00	0.230	0.002	-0.004	0.227	2	2

Player 1965	Team	SO	Wins	ERA	WAR	GPA	GPA brc	GPA bpc	Total GPA	Cy Young Points	Rank
Marichal, Juan	SFG	240	22	2.13	10.56	0.200	0.001	0.001	0.202		
McDowell, Sam	CLE	325	17	*2.18*	10.32	0.203	0.003	-0.002	0.204		
Koufax, Sandy	LAD	*382*	*26*	*2.04*	*11.24*	0.197	0.003	0.009	0.209	20	1
Maloney, Jim	CIN	244	20	2.54	8.24	0.214	0.003	-0.002	0.215		
# Law, Vern	PIT	101	17	2.15	6.80	0.215	-0.002	0.002	0.215		

Player 1966	Team	SO	Wins	ERA	WAR	GPA	GPA brc	GPA bpc	Total GPA	Cy Young Points	Rank
Peters, Gary	CHW	129	12	**1.98**	7.55	0.198	0.003	−0.001	0.200		
Koufax, Sandy	LAD	***317***	***27***	***1.73***	***11.86***	0.190	0.001	0.009	0.201	20u	1
Marichal, Juan	SFG	222	25	2.23	10.76	0.201	0.003	0.000	0.204		
Bunning, Jim	PHI	252	19	2.41	10.37	0.210	0.000	−0.000	0.209		
Gibson, Bob	STL	225	21	2.44	8.62	0.215	0.002	−0.001	0.216		

Player 1967	Team	SO	Wins	ERA	WAR	GPA	GPA brc	GPA bpc	Total GPA	Cy Young Points	Rank
Horlen, Joe	CHW	124	19	**2.06**	9.21	0.197	−0.002	−0.000	0.195	2	2
Peters, Gary	CHW	215	16	2.28	7.80	0.214	0.001	−0.001	0.214		
Lolich, Mickey	DET	174	14	3.04	5.82	0.217	0.001	−0.002	0.215		
Lonborg, Jim(6)	BOS	246	***22***	3.16	7.47	0.225	0.003	−0.008	0.220	**18**	1
Niekro, Phil	ATL	129	11r	***1.87***	6.64	0.202	0.010	−0.004	0.208		
Short, Chris	PHI	142	9	2.39	6.54	0.212	−0.002	−0.001	0.209		
Hughes, Dick	STL	161	16	2.67	6.66	0.214	−0.001	−0.002	0.212		
Jenkins, F.(7)	CHC	236	20	2.80	***8.60***	0.227	−0.006	−0.009	0.213	1	2
McCormick, M. (10)	SFG	150	***22***	2.85	6.79	0.222	−0.000	0.001	0.223	**18**	1

Player 1968	Team	SO	Wins	ERA	WAR	GPA	GPA brc	GPA bpc	Total GPA	Cy Young Points	Rank
Tiant, Luis	CLE	264	21	***1.60***	9.65	0.186	−0.003	−0.000	0.183		
McLain, Denny	DET	280	***31***	1.96	10.73	0.195	0.001	−0.004	0.193	20u	1
McNally, Dave	BAL	202	22	1.95	8.14	0.191	0.004	0.003	0.197		
Nash, Jim	OAK	169	13	2.28	6.19	0.203	0.004	0.003	0.209		
Gibson, Bob	STL	***268***	22	***1.12***	***13.03***	0.172	−0.000	−0.001	0.171	20u	1
Seaver, Tom	NYM	205	16	2.20	8.26	0.206	−0.002	0.000	0.203		
Koosman, Jerry	NYM	178	19	2.08	7.76	0.205	−0.001	−0.000	0.204		
# Jarvis, Pat	ATL	157	16	2.60	7.71	0.206	0.002	−0.004	0.204		

Player 1969	Team	SO	Wins	ERA	WAR	GPA	GPA brc	GPA bpc	Total GPA	Cy Young Points	Rank
McLain, Denny	DET	181	24	2.80	11.38	0.211	0.002	−0.003	0.210	10	1
Bosman, Dick	WAS	99	14	**2.19**	6.32	0.210	0.000	0.002	0.212		
Cuellar, Mike	BAL	182	23	2.38	9.60	0.213	−0.001	0.002	0.213	10	1
Perry, Jim	MIN	153	20	2.82	8.16	0.222	0.000	−0.004	0.218	3	3
Koosman, Jerry	NYM	180	17	2.28	9.32	0.198	0.003	0.002	0.202		
Gibson, Bob	STL	269	20	2.18	***12.23***	0.204	0.002	−0.002	0.204		
Seaver, Tom	NYM	208	***25***	2.21	10.25	0.203	0.000	0.000	0.204	23	1
Carlton, Steve	STL	210	17	2.17	8.67	0.211	−0.005	0.000	0.207		

Player 1970	Team	SO	Wins	ERA	WAR	GPA	GPA brc	GPA bpc	Total GPA	Cy Young Points	Rank
Palmer, Jim	BAL	199	20	2.71	10.31	0.215	0.004	0.003	0.221	11	5
McDowell, Sam	CLE	***304***	20	2.92	***10.46***	0.222	−0.000	−0.000	0.221	45	3
Culp, Ray	BOS	193	17	3.04	7.77	0.236	0.002	−0.010	0.228		
McNally, Dave	BAL	185	***24***	3.22	8.40	0.230	−0.000	0.003	0.233	47	2
Perry, Jim(6)	MIN	168	***24***	3.04	7.59	0.240	−0.002	−0.002	0.236	**55**	1
Seaver, Tom	NYM	283	18	**2.82**	8.85	0.222	0.004	0.001	0.227		
Gibson, Bob	STL	274	***23***	3.12	***8.88***	0.229	0.003	−0.002	0.230	118	1
Nolan, Gary	CIN	181	18	3.27	7.39	0.238	−0.001	−0.005	0.232	5	6
Jenkins, F.	CHC	274	22	3.39	8.63	0.237	0.001	−0.005	0.233	16	3

Player 1971	Team	SO	Wins	ERA	WAR	GPA	GPA brc	GPA bpc	Total GPA	Cy Young Points	Rank
Blue, Vida	OAK	301	24	**1.82**	*11.52*	0.192	0.000	0.006	0.197	98	1
Wood, Wilbur	CHW	210	22	1.91	10.80	0.205	0.004	0.001	0.210	23	3
Hedlund, Mike	KCR	76	15	2.71	6.37	0.219	-0.005	0.001	0.215		
Lolich, Mickey(5)	DET	**308**	**25**	2.92	10.84	0.225	0.000	-0.004	0.221	85	2
Seaver, Tom	NYM	**289**	20	**1.76**	11.14	0.190	-0.001	0.002	0.191	61	2
Jenkins, F.	CHC	263	24	2.77	9.62	0.226	-0.001	-0.007	0.218	97	1
Roberts, Dave	SDP	135	14	2.10	7.92	0.209	0.002	0.009	0.220	2	6
Wilson, Don	HOU	180	16	2.45	7.48	0.210	0.001	0.008	0.220		

Player 1972s	Team	SO	Wins	ERA	WAR	GPA	GPA brc	GPA bpc	Total GPA	Cy Young Points	Rank
Perry, Gaylord	CLE	234	24	1.92	*13.16*	0.191	0.002	-0.000	0.192	64	1
Palmer, Jim	BAL	184	21	2.07	9.05	0.198	0.003	0.001	0.203	20	5
Hunter, Jim	OAK	191	21	2.04	9.33	0.196	0.003	0.007	0.206	26	4
Lolich, Mickey	DET	250	22	2.50	9.88	0.214	-0.000	-0.003	0.210	27	3
Carlton, Steve	PHI	**310**	**27**	**1.97**	12.33	0.195	0.001	0.001	0.197	120u	1
Gibson, Bob	STL	208	19	2.46	8.45	0.208	0.003	-0.001	0.210	3	9
Matlack, Jon	NYM	169	15	2.32	6.86	0.217	-0.000	0.001	0.217	6	5
Blass, Steve(5)	PIT	117	19	2.49	6.71	0.220	-0.002	0.000	0.218	35	2

Player 1973	Team	SO	Wins	ERA	WAR	GPA	GPA brc	GPA bpc	Total GPA	Cy Young Points	Rank
Palmer, Jim	BAL	158	22	**2.40**	10.41	0.207	0.000	0.003	0.210	88	1
Blyleven, Bert	MIN	258	20	2.52	*10.69*	0.217	0.002	-0.002	0.217	1	7
Lee, Bill	BOS	120	17	2.75	9.61	0.223	0.001	-0.007	0.217		
Ryan, Nolan(5)	CAL	**383**	21	2.82	9.78	0.220	0.004	0.002	0.226	62	2
Seaver, Tom	NYM	**251**	19	**2.08**	*10.93*	0.197	0.002	0.006	0.205	71	1
Sutton, Don	LAD	200	18	2.42	8.15	0.206	0.004	0.011	0.221	7	2
Twitchell, Wayne	PHI	169	13	2.50	7.09	0.220	-0.001	0.003	0.222		
Koosman, Jerry	NYM	156	14	2.84	7.35	0.226	-0.003	0.007	0.230		

Player 1974	Team	SO	Wins	ERA	WAR	GPA	GPA brc	GPA bpc	Total GPA	Cy Young Points	Rank
Perry, Gaylord	CLE	216	21	2.51	*11.04*	0.210	0.001	0.000	0.211	90	1
Tiant, Luis	BOS	176	22	2.92	10.64	0.220	0.000	-0.007	0.213	8	4
Hunter, Jim	OAK	143	**25**	**2.49**	9.70	0.214	-0.004	0.008	0.218		
Jenkins, F.(5)	TEX	225	**25**	2.82	9.52	0.222	0.001	0.002	0.225	75	2
Capra, Buzz	ATL	137	16	**2.28**	7.47	0.214	0.000	-0.002	0.212	1	9
Niekro, Phil	ATL	195	20	2.38	*10.10*	0.211	0.005	-0.002	0.214	15	3
Matlack, Jon	NYM	195	13	2.41	8.46	0.212	0.001	0.006	0.219		
Marshall, Mike(9)	LAD	143	15r	2.38	5.66	0.224	-0.001	0.010	0.233	96	1

Player 1975	Team	SO	Wins	ERA	WAR	GPA	GPA brc	GPA bpc	Total GPA	Cy Young Points	Rank
Palmer, Jim	BAL	193	**23**	**2.09**	*11.74*	0.203	0.001	0.003	0.207	98	1
Tanana, Frank	CAL	**269**	16	2.62	8.83	0.217	-0.005	0.004	0.216	7	4
Hunter, Jim	NYY	177	**23**	2.58	10.78	0.215	-0.001	0.002	0.217	74	2
Eckersley, Dennis	CLE	152	13	2.60	5.67	0.220	0.006	0.001	0.227		
Seaver, Tom	NYM	243	22	2.38	9.53	0.208	0.000	0.007	0.215	98	1
Messersmith, A.	LAD	213	19	2.29	*10.46*	0.206	0.001	0.011	0.218	1	5
Reuss, Jerry	PIT	131	18	2.54	7.89	0.216	0.002	0.001	0.219		
Jones, Randy	SDP	102	20	**2.24**	7.88	0.217	0.002	0.011	0.230	80	2

Player 1976	Team	SO	Wins	ERA	WAR	GPA	GPA brc	GPA bpc	Total GPA	Cy Young Points	Rank
Fidrych, Mark	DET	97	19	**2.34**	8.23	0.218	−0.004	−0.002	0.213	51	2
Tanana, Frank	CAL	269	16	2.43	9.10	0.214	−0.002	0.003	0.215	18	3
Blue, Vida	OAK	166	18	2.35	**9.29**	0.209	−0.001	0.009	0.217	8	6
Palmer, Jim	BAL	159	**22**	2.51	8.93	0.220	−0.002	0.004	0.222	**108**	1
Seaver, Tom	NYM	**235**	14	2.59	7.39	0.214	0.003	0.008	0.225	1	8
Denny, John	STL	74	11	**2.52**	5.69	0.222	−0.001	0.005	0.226		
Zachry, Pat	CIN	143	14	2.74	5.38	0.228	−0.004	0.004	0.228		
Koosman, Jerry	NYM	200	21	2.69	6.36	0.224	−0.001	0.006	0.229	69	2
Jones, Randy	SDP	93	**22**	2.74	7.59	0.219	0.002	0.011	0.232	**96**	1

Player 1977	Team	SO	Wins	ERA	WAR	GPA	GPA brc	GPA bpc	Total GPA	Cy Young Points	Rank
Campbell, Bill	BOS	114	13r	2.96	7.22	0.210	−0.004	−0.008	0.199	25	5
Tanana, Frank	CAL	205	15	**2.54**	8.95	0.213	−0.001	0.002	0.214	3	9
Blyleven, Bert	TEX	182	14	2.72	8.03	0.219	0.000	0.001	0.221		
Palmer, Jim	BAL	193	20	2.91	**11.00**	0.226	−0.007	0.003	0.222	48	2
Guidry, Ron	NYY	176	16	2.82	6.89	0.223	−0.002	0.003	0.224	5	7
Lyle, Sparky	NYY	68	13r	**2.17**	4.89	0.223	−0.001	0.003	0.225	**56**	1
Gossage, Rich	PIT	151	11r	**1.62**	8.21	0.177	0.002	0.002	0.182		
Candelaria, John	PIT	133	20	**2.34**	9.03	0.211	−0.004	0.001	0.209	17	5
Seaver, Tom	CIN*	196	21	2.58	9.27	0.206	0.003	0.007	0.216	18	3
Reuschel, Rick	CHC	166	20	2.79	**9.42**	0.221	−0.004	−0.001	0.217	18	3
Carlton, Steve	PHI	198	**23**	2.64	8.88	0.226	−0.001	0.003	0.227	**104**	1
John, Tommy(10)	LAD	123	20	2.78	6.15	0.229	−0.001	0.010	0.239	54	2

Player 1978	Team	SO	Wins	ERA	WAR	GPA	GPA brc	GPA bpc	Total GPA	Cy Young Points	Rank
Guidry, Ron	NYY	248	**25**	**1.74**	**10.90**	0.194	−0.003	0.002	0.193	**140u**	1
Caldwell, Mike	MIL	131	22	2.36	9.52	0.215	−0.001	0.001	0.216	76	2
Goltz, Dave	MIN	116	15	2.49	7.30	0.225	−0.002	−0.005	0.218		
Tiant, Luis	BOS	114	13	3.31	6.84	0.228	−0.002	−0.007	0.219		
Swan, Craig	NYM	125	9	**2.43**	6.95	0.209	−0.001	0.008	0.215		
Rogers, Steve	MON	126	13	2.47	7.30	0.215	−0.004	0.005	0.215		
Hooton, Burt(5)	LAD	104	19	2.71	6.38	0.218	−0.001	0.013	0.229	38	2
Niekro, Phil(10)	ATL	248	19	2.88	**8.95**	0.224	0.009	−0.000	0.232	10	6
Perry, Gaylord(15)	SDP	154	21	2.73	6.05	0.232	−0.003	0.011	0.240	**116**	1

Player 1979	Team	SO	Wins	ERA	WAR	GPA	GPA brc	GPA bpc	Total GPA	Cy Young Points	Rank
Kern, Jim	TEX	136	13r	**1.57**	6.98	0.191	0.004	0.001	0.196	25	4
Lopez, Aurelio	DET	106	10r	2.41	5.56	0.209	0.001	−0.001	0.208	1	7
Eckersley, D.(4)	BOS	150	17	2.99	**8.79**	0.225	0.004	−0.008	0.220		
Guidry, Ron(5)	NYY	201	18	**2.78**	7.87	0.225	−0.003	0.002	0.224	26	3
Flanagan, M.(13)	BAL	190	**23**	3.08	7.14	0.238	−0.002	0.004	0.240	**136**	1
Sutter, Bruce	CHC	110	6r	**2.22**	5.17	0.194	0.011	0.000	0.205	72	1
Tekulve, Kent	PIT	75	10r	2.75	5.87	0.208	0.004	0.002	0.214		
Richard, J.R.(8)	HOU	**313**	18	**2.71**	8.68	0.216	0.004	0.013	0.234	41	3
Seaver, Tom(13)	CIN	131	16	3.14	5.77	0.235	−0.001	0.006	0.239	20	4
Niekro, Joe(19)	HOU	119	21	3.00	6.62	0.226	0.007	0.012	0.246	66	2

Player 1980	Team	SO	Wins	ERA	WAR	GPA	GPA brc	GPA bpc	Total GPA	Cy Young Points	Rank
Norris, Mike	OAK	180	22	2.53	*9.31*	0.214	−0.000	0.006	0.220	91	2
Burns, Britt	CHW	133	15	2.84	7.48	0.223	0.002	−0.000	0.224		
Haas, Moose	MIL	146	16	3.10	6.92	0.234	−0.003	0.002	0.233		
Stone, Steve(10)	BAL	149	*25*	3.23	5.67	0.245	−0.004	0.004	0.246	100	1
Carlton, Steve	PHI	*286*	24	2.34	*11.22*	0.211	−0.002	0.003	0.212	118	1
Sutton, Don	LAD	128	13	*2.20*	7.56	0.200	0.001	0.011	0.212		
Reuss, Jerry	LAD	111	18	2.51	6.43	0.218	0.001	0.011	0.230	55	2
Soto, Mario	CIN	182	10r	3.07	5.46	0.216	0.011	0.004	0.230	1	5

Player 1981s	Team	SO	Wins	ERA	WAR	GPA	GPA brc	GPA bpc	Total GPA	Cy Young Points	Rank
Fingers, Rollie	MIL	61	6r	*1.04*	4.94	0.164	0.000	−0.001	0.163	126	1
McCatty, Steve	OAK	91	*14*	2.33	*6.25*	0.206	−0.004	0.008	0.210	84	2
Lamp, Dennis	CHW	71	7	2.41	3.89	0.214	0.003	−0.001	0.216		
Morris, Jack(5)	DET	97	*14*	3.05	5.77	0.223	0.001	−0.002	0.222	21	3
Sambito, Joe	HOU	41	5r	1.84	3.23	0.179	−0.008	0.012	0.183		
Ryan, Nolan	HOU	68	11	*1.69*	5.34	0.185	0.009	0.010	0.204	28	4
Reuss, Jerry	LAD	51	10	2.30	4.89	0.210	−0.005	0.009	0.214		
Valenzuela, F.	LAD	*180*	13	2.48	*6.22*	0.203	−0.001	0.013	0.214	70	1
Carlton, Steve	PHI	179	13	2.42	5.93	0.213	0.001	0.002	0.215	50	3

Player 1982	Team	SO	Wins	ERA	WAR	GPA	GPA brc	GPA bpc	Total GPA	Cy Young Points	Rank
Palmer, Jim	BAL	103	15	3.13	6.73	0.228	−0.003	0.003	0.227	59	2
Sutcliffe, Rick	CLE	142	14	*2.96*	6.23	0.234	−0.005	0.000	0.230	14	5
Stieb, Dave	TOR	141	17	3.25	7.87	0.241	−0.004	−0.003	0.234	36	4
Vuckovich, P.(10)	MIL	105	18	3.34	5.10	0.247	−0.000	0.001	0.248	87	1
Niekro, Joe	HOU	130	17	2.47	8.89	0.200	0.007	0.012	0.219		
Rogers, Steve	MON	179	19	*2.40*	9.55	0.216	−0.002	0.005	0.220	29	2
Andujar, Joaquin	STL	137	15	2.47	8.50	0.215	0.001	0.005	0.221	1	7
Carlton, Steve(6)	PHI	*286*	23	3.10	7.73	0.235	−0.003	0.004	0.236	112	1

Player 1983	Team	SO	Wins	ERA	WAR	GPA	GPA brc	GPA bpc	Total GPA	Cy Young Points	Rank
Stieb, Dave	TOR	187	17	3.04	*8.61*	0.227	0.003	−0.004	0.226		
Dotson, Rich	CHW	137	22	3.23	7.01	0.228	0.005	−0.001	0.232	9	4
Honeycutt, Rick	TEX	74	16	3.03	5.77	0.238	−0.007	0.002	0.233		
Hoyt, Lamarr(9)	CHW	148	*24*	3.66	6.24	0.244	−0.001	−0.001	0.242	116	1
Denny, John	PHI	139	19	2.37	8.16	0.220	−0.004	0.003	0.219	103	1
Soto, Mario	CIN	242	17	2.70	*8.55*	0.223	0.001	0.003	0.227	61	2
Candelaria, John	PIT	157	15	3.23	6.02	0.228	−0.003	0.002	0.227		
McMurtry, Craig	ATL	105	15	3.08	6.20	0.239	−0.003	−0.001	0.235	3	7

Player 1984	Team	SO	Wins	ERA	WAR	GPA	GPA brc	GPA bpc	Total GPA	Cy Young Points	Rank
Hernandez, G.	DET	112	9r	*1.92*	7.01	0.187	0.002	−0.001	0.188	88	1
Quisenberry, Dan	KCR	41	6r	2.64	5.15	0.214	−0.002	−0.001	0.211		
Stieb, Dave	TOR	198	16	2.83	*9.68*	0.220	−0.003	−0.003	0.214	1	7
Blyleven, Bert	CLE	170	19	2.87	7.60	0.221	0.003	−0.001	0.223	45	3

(Player 1984)	Team	SO	Wins	ERA	WAR	GPA	GPA brc	GPA bpc	Total GPA	Cy Young Points	Rank
Rhoden, Rick	PIT	136	14	2.72	**7.53**	0.223	−0.003	0.002	0.223		
Gooden, Dwight	NYM	**276**	17	2.60	6.64	0.205	0.012	0.008	0.225	45	2
Pena, Alejandro	LAD	135	12	**2.48**	6.06	0.218	−0.000	0.010	0.227		
Sutcliffe, Rick(28)	CLE*	213	**20**	3.64	4.70	0.258	−0.003	−0.001	0.254	120u	1

Player 1985	Team	SO	Wins	ERA	WAR	GPA	GPA brc	GPA bpc	Total GPA	Cy Young Points	Rank
Stieb, Dave	TOR	167	14	**2.48**	**9.42**	0.221	−0.001	−0.003	0.216	2	7
Saberhagen, Bret	KCR	158	20	2.87	7.92	0.221	−0.002	−0.000	0.219	127	1
Key, Jimmy	TOR	85	14	3.00	6.55	0.226	0.003	−0.003	0.226		
Guidry, Ron(9)	NYY	143	22	3.27	6.63	0.236	−0.002	0.003	0.237	88	2
Gooden, D.	NYM	**268**	**24**	**1.53**	**13.09**	0.180	−0.003	0.008	0.185	120u	1
Tudor, John	STL	169	21	1.93	10.59	0.196	−0.000	0.007	0.203	65	2
Reuschel, Rick	PIT	138	14	2.27	6.94	0.216	−0.003	0.001	0.214		
Hershiser, Orel	LAD	157	19	2.03	7.22	0.212	0.001	0.013	0.226	17	3

Player 1986	Team	SO	Wins	ERA	WAR	GPA	GPA brc	GPA bpc	Total GPA	Cy Young Points	Rank
Clemens, Roger	BOS	238	**24**	2.48	**10.13**	0.211	−0.002	−0.007	0.203	140u	1
Higuera, Ted	MIL	207	20	2.79	8.07	0.226	−0.001	0.001	0.226	42	2
Witt, Mike	CAL	208	18	2.84	8.15	0.226	−0.001	0.002	0.228	35	3
Morris, Jack	DET	223	21	3.27	7.74	0.232	0.003	−0.001	0.234	13	5
Scott, Mike	HOU	**306**	18	**2.22**	9.98	0.198	0.002	0.012	0.212	98	1
Rhoden, Rick	PIT	159	15	2.84	8.48	0.221	−0.002	0.002	0.220	2	5
Ojeda, Bob	NYM	148	18	2.57	6.80	0.217	0.001	0.009	0.226	9	4
Valenzuela, F.(11)	LAD	200	21	3.14	6.46	0.233	0.001	0.012	0.245	88	2

Player 1987	Team	SO	Wins	ERA	WAR	GPA	GPA brc	GPA bpc	Total GPA	Cy Young Points	Rank
Clemens, Roger	BOS	256	**20**	2.97	**10.71**	0.225	0.002	−0.008	0.219	124	1
Key, Jimmy	TOR	161	17	**2.76**	9.40	0.229	−0.002	−0.005	0.222	64	2
Viola, Frank	MIN	197	17	2.90	9.27	0.230	−0.001	−0.004	0.225	5	6
Saberhagen, Bret	KCR	163	18	3.36	8.43	0.233	−0.001	−0.001	0.231		
Burke, Tim	MON	58	7r	**1.19**	4.24	0.202	0.001	0.006	0.208		
Tekulve, Kent	PHI	60	6r	3.09	4.15	0.213	0.000	0.002	0.216		
Alexander, D.(4)	ATL	108	14	3.01	7.32	0.227	−0.002	−0.002	0.223		
Bedrosian, S.(7)	PHI	74	5r	2.83	3.79	0.219	0.005	0.003	0.227	57	1
Ryan, Nolan(10)	HOU	**270**	8	**2.76**	6.66	0.217	0.008	0.013	0.237	12	5
Welch, Bob(15)	LAD	196	15	3.22	7.52	0.231	−0.003	0.011	0.239	3	8
Sutcliffe, Rick(24)	CHC	174	18	3.68	6.58	0.246	0.003	−0.002	0.247	55	2

Player 1988	Team	SO	Wins	ERA	WAR	GPA	GPA brc	GPA bpc	Total GPA	Cy Young Points	Rank
Higuera, Ted	MIL	192	16	**2.45**	7.88	0.211	−0.001	0.001	0.211		
Viola, Frank	MIN	193	**24**	2.64	**8.58**	0.218	−0.000	−0.004	0.214	138	1
Anderson, Allan	MIN	83	16	**2.45**	6.65	0.221	−0.001	−0.004	0.216		
Clemens, Roger	BOS	**291**	18	2.93	8.57	0.220	0.002	−0.006	0.217	8	6
Gubicza, Mark(6)	KCR	183	20	2.70	7.93	0.223	0.003	−0.001	0.226	26	3
Hershiser, Orel	LAD	178	**23**	2.26	**9.03**	0.206	−0.002	0.011	0.215	120u	1
Tudor, John	STL	87	10	2.32	6.23	0.220	−0.007	0.007	0.220		
Cone, David	NYM	213	20	2.22	7.12	0.205	0.008	0.008	0.221	42	3
Jackson, Danny	CIN	161	**23**	2.73	7.59	0.217	0.004	0.003	0.223	54	2

Who Should Have Won the Cy Young Award?

Player 1989	Team	SO	Wins	ERA	WAR	GPA	GPA brc	GPA bpc	Total GPA	Cy Young Points	Rank
Montgomery, J.	KCR	94	7r	*1.37*	4.36	0.181	0.005	−0.000	0.186		
Saberhagen, B.	KCR	193	**23**	*2.16*	**9.46**	0.208	−0.003	0.001	0.205	138	1
Blyleven, Bert	CAL	131	17	2.73	7.72	0.213	0.002	0.003	0.218	9	4
Stewart, Dave(17)	OAK	155	21	3.32	5.28	0.239	0.001	0.008	0.247	80	2
Dibble, Rob	CIN	141	10r	2.09	5.16	0.166	0.012	0.004	0.181		
Davis, Mark	SDP	92	4r	1.85	4.78	0.180	−0.000	0.011	0.191	107	1
Garrelts, Scott	SFG	119	14	*2.28*	5.90	0.209	0.003	0.007	0.219	4	6
Hershiser, Orel	LAD	178	15	2.31	**8.03**	0.208	0.001	0.012	0.221	7	4
Scott, Mike(33)	HOU	172	**20**	3.10	4.80	0.221	0.010	0.014	0.244	65	2

Player 1990	Team	SO	Wins	ERA	WAR	GPA	GPA brc	GPA bpc	Total GPA	Cy Young Points	Rank
Clemens, Roger	BOS	209	21	*1.93*	**10.40**	0.200	−0.002	−0.007	0.191	77	2
Finley, Chuck	CAL	177	18	2.40	7.87	0.221	−0.003	0.003	0.221	1	7
Wells, David	TOR	115	11	3.14	5.92	0.229	−0.004	−0.002	0.223		
Welch, Bob(12)	OAK	127	**27**	2.95	5.87	0.231	0.002	0.007	0.240	107	1
Drabek, Doug	PIT	131	**22**	2.76	7.02	0.220	0.000	0.003	0.223	118	1
Viola, Frank	NYM	182	20	2.67	**7.81**	0.216	−0.000	0.007	0.223	19	3
Rijo, Jose	CIN	152	14	2.70	6.11	0.219	0.000	0.005	0.224		
Martinez, R.(10)	LAD	223	20	2.92	5.44	0.234	−0.003	0.012	0.243	70	2

Player 1991	Team	SO	Wins	ERA	WAR	GPA	GPA brc	GPA bpc	Total GPA	Cy Young Points	Rank
Clemens, Roger	BOS	**241**	18	2.62	**9.39**	0.223	−0.002	−0.007	0.215	119	1
Candiotti, Tom	CLE	167	13	2.65	8.09	0.217	0.005	−0.002	0.220		
Tapani, Kevin	MIN	135	16	2.99	7.77	0.222	0.003	−0.005	0.220	6	7
Erickson, Scott(7)	MIN	108	**20**	3.18	5.91	0.236	−0.002	−0.004	0.231	56	2
Glavine, Tom	ATL	192	**20**	2.55	7.72	0.219	0.002	0.001	0.222	110	1
Martinez, Dennis	MON	123	14	2.39	7.19	0.216	0.001	0.006	0.222	4	5
Rijo, Jose	CIN	172	15	2.51	6.13	0.218	0.004	0.003	0.225	13	4
Harnisch, Pete	HOU	172	12	2.70	6.42	0.215	0.004	0.012	0.231		

Player 1992	Team	SO	Wins	ERA	WAR	GPA	GPA brc	GPA bpc	Total GPA	Cy Young Points	Rank
Eckersley, Dennis	OAK	93	7r	*1.91*	4.66	0.162	0.003	0.008	0.173	107	1
Guthrie, Mark	MIN	76	2r	2.88	3.28	0.190	0.001	−0.004	0.186		
Appier, Kevin(6)	KCR	150	15	2.46	7.60	0.209	0.001	−0.001	0.208		
Mussina, Mike(8)	BAL	130	18	2.54	8.39	0.211	−0.001	−0.001	0.209	26	4
Clemens, R.(11)	BOS	208	18	*2.41*	8.49	0.219	−0.001	−0.008	0.210	48	3
McDowell, J.(23)	CHW	178	20	3.18	6.65	0.232	−0.002	0.004	0.234	51	2
Maddux, Greg	CHC	199	20	2.18	**10.55**	0.201	−0.002	−0.001	0.199	112	1
Tewksbury, Bob	STL	91	16	2.16	7.97	0.205	−0.001	0.005	0.210	22	3
Schilling, Curt	PHI	147	14	2.35	7.39	0.210	−0.000	0.002	0.212		
Glavine, Tom(7)	ATL	129	20	2.76	6.72	0.226	−0.001	−0.003	0.223	78	2

Player 1993	Team	SO	Wins	ERA	WAR	GPA	GPA brc	GPA bpc	Total GPA	Cy Young Points	Rank
Appier, Kevin	KCR	186	18	*2.56*	**9.67**	0.213	−0.001	−0.001	0.211	30	3
Key, Jimmy	NYY	173	18	3.00	7.89	0.224	−0.000	0.002	0.226	14	4
Johnson, Randy	SEA	**308**	19	3.24	8.29	0.228	0.004	−0.002	0.230	75	2
McDowell, J.(11)	CHW	158	**22**	3.37	7.08	0.243	−0.004	0.004	0.243	124	1

(Player 1993)	Team	SO	Wins	ERA	WAR	GPA	GPA brc	GPA bpc	Total GPA	Cy Young Points	Rank
Maddux, Greg	ATL	197	20	**2.36**	**10.84**	0.212	0.002	−0.003	0.210	119	1
Rijo, Jose	CIN	227	14	2.48	10.10	0.212	−0.001	0.000	0.211	8	5
Avery, Steve	ATL	125	18	2.94	7.71	0.230	−0.002	−0.004	0.224		
Swift, Bill	SFG	157	21	2.82	7.75	0.222	−0.000	0.004	0.226	61	2

Player 1994s	Team	SO	Wins	ERA	WAR	GPA	GPA brc	GPA bpc	Total GPA	Cy Young Points	Rank
Clemens, Roger	BOS	168	9	2.85	7.09	0.226	−0.002	−0.006	0.218		
Cone, David	KCR	132	16	2.94	6.75	0.220	−0.000	−0.001	0.218	108	1
Johnson, Randy	SEA	**204**	13	3.19	6.30	0.233	−0.006	−0.001	0.225	24	3
Key, Jimmy(7)	NYY	97	**17**	3.27	5.34	0.237	0.002	0.002	0.241	96	2
Maddux, Greg	ATL	156	**16**	**1.56**	**10.96**	0.188	−0.002	−0.005	0.181	140u	1
Saberhagen, Bret	NYM	143	14	2.74	6.68	0.224	−0.004	0.006	0.225	42	3
Trachsel, Steve	CHC	108	9	3.21	5.52	0.241	−0.006	−0.007	0.228		
Hill, Ken(7)	MON	85	**16**	3.32	5.11	0.231	0.005	0.003	0.238	56	2

Player 1995s	Team	SO	Wins	ERA	WAR	GPA	GPA brc	GPA bpc	Total GPA	Cy Young Points	Rank
Johnson, Randy	SEA	**294**	18	2.48	9.26	0.209	0.002	−0.002	0.209	136	1
Mussina, Mike	BAL	158	**19**	3.29	7.78	0.230	−0.001	−0.001	0.228	14	5
Wakefield, Tim	BOS	119	16	2.95	6.91	0.236	0.001	−0.007	0.229	29	3
Martinez, Dennis	CLE	92	11	3.08	6.37	0.231	0.001	−0.001	0.232		
Maddux, Greg	ATL	181	**19**	**1.63**	**11.68**	0.173	0.003	−0.002	0.173	140u	1
Glavine, Tom	ATL	140	13	3.08	7.63	0.230	0.003	−0.008	0.225	30	3
Navarro, Jaime	CHC	128	14	3.28	7.55	0.232	0.001	−0.007	0.225		
Schourek, Pete(5)	CIN	69	7r	3.22	6.45	0.234	−0.002	−0.003	0.229	55	2

Player 1996	Team	SO	Wins	ERA	WAR	GPA	GPA brc	GPA bpc	Total GPA	Cy Young Points	Rank
Guzman, Juan	TOR	165	11	**2.93**	7.22	0.223	0.005	−0.003	0.224		
Hentgen, Pat	TOR	177	20	3.22	**9.42**	0.239	−0.002	−0.003	0.234	110	1
Appier, Kevin	KCR	207	14	3.62	7.46	0.234	0.002	−0.001	0.235		
Pettitte, Andy(8)	NYY	162	21	3.87	6.22	0.252	−0.002	0.003	0.253	104	2
Brown, Kevin	FLA	159	17	**1.89**	**11.41**	0.198	−0.000	−0.001	0.197	88	2
Leiter, Al	FLA	200	16	2.93	8.94	0.221	−0.002	−0.001	0.218	1	9
Maddux, Greg	ATL	172	15	2.72	9.83	0.222	0.002	−0.004	0.220	4	5
Smoltz, John	ATL	**276**	**24**	2.94	9.82	0.229	−0.001	−0.007	0.221	136	1

Player 1997	Team	SO	Wins	ERA	WAR	GPA	GPA brc	GPA bpc	Total GPA	Cy Young Points	Rank
Clemens, Roger	TOR	292	21	2.05	**12.29**	0.200	−0.003	−0.003	0.194	134	1
Johnson, Randy	SEA	291	20	2.28	9.12	0.209	−0.002	0.001	0.209	77	2
Cone, David	NYY	222	12	2.82	7.29	0.218	0.007	0.000	0.225		
Thompson, Justin	DET	151	15	3.02	7.97	0.226	0.000	−0.001	0.225		
Maddux, Greg	ATL	177	19	2.20	10.75	0.194	0.000	0.003	0.197	75	2
Martinez, Pedro	MON	305	17	**1.90**	10.99	0.202	0.001	−0.002	0.201	134	1
Brown, Kevin	FLA	205	16	2.69	9.33	0.216	0.003	−0.002	0.217		
Glavine, Tom	ATL	152	14	2.96	9.20	0.221	−0.001	−0.001	0.219		

Who Should Have Won the Cy Young Award?

Player 1998	Team	SO	Wins	ERA	WAR	GPA	GPA brc	GPA bpc	Total GPA	Cy Young Points	Rank
Clemens, Roger	TOR	271	**20**	2.65	**9.03**	0.218	0.003	−0.001	0.220	140u	1
Martinez, Pedro	BOS	251	19	2.89	8.54	0.225	0.003	−0.004	0.224	65	2
Rogers, Kenny	OAK	138	16	3.17	7.65	0.237	−0.002	0.001	0.236		
Wells, David	NYY	163	18	3.49	6.47	0.234	0.000	0.002	0.237	31	3
Maddux, Greg	ATL	204	18	**2.22**	**10.36**	0.213	−0.002	0.000	0.210	10	4
Leiter, Al	NYM	174	17	2.47	8.23	0.205	0.001	0.006	0.212	3	6
Glavine, Tom	ATL	157	**20**	2.47	9.42	0.213	−0.002	0.002	0.212	99	1
Brown, Kevin	SDP	257	18	2.38	9.95	0.213	0.000	0.007	0.220	76	3

Player 1999	Team	SO	Wins	ERA	WAR	GPA	GPA brc	GPA bpc	Total GPA	Cy Young Points	Rank
Martinez, Pedro	BOS	313	**23**	**2.07**	**10.51**	0.200	0.001	−0.004	0.196	140u	1
Moyer, Jamie	SEA	137	14	3.87	7.24	0.249	−0.001	−0.002	0.245	3	6
Mussina, Mike	BAL	172	18	3.50	6.39	0.244	−0.001	0.003	0.246	54	2
Radke, Brad	MIN	121	12	3.75	6.54	0.250	0.000	0.000	0.250		
Johnson, Randy	ARI	**364**	17	2.48	**12.23**	0.214	0.001	−0.006	0.208	134	1
Millwood, Kevin	ATL	205	18	2.68	8.66	0.224	0.001	0.002	0.227	36	3
Hampton, Mike	HOU	177	**22**	2.90	9.07	0.225	0.001	0.004	0.229	110	2
Daal, Omar	ARI	148	16	3.65	7.84	0.246	−0.002	−0.009	0.235		

Player 2000	Team	SO	Wins	ERA	WAR	GPA	GPA brc	GPA bpc	Total GPA	Cy Young Points	Rank
Martinez, Pedro	BOS	284	18	**1.74**	**12.04**	0.182	−0.000	−0.003	0.179	140	1
Castillo, Frank	TOR	104	10	3.59	4.94	0.239	−0.002	−0.001	0.236		
Mussina, Mike	BAL	210	11	3.79	7.44	0.244	0.002	0.002	0.248	1	6
Colon, Bartolo	CLE	212	15	3.88	5.85	0.249	0.000	0.001	0.250		
Hudson, Tim(9)	OAK	169	**20**	4.14	4.84	0.254	0.006	0.005	0.265	54	2
Johnson, Randy	ARI	**347**	19	2.64	**10.99**	0.223	0.000	−0.007	0.216	133	1
Brown, Kevin	LAD	216	13	**2.58**	9.54	0.218	0.002	0.002	0.221	4	6
Maddux, Greg	ATL	190	19	3.00	9.63	0.226	0.003	0.000	0.229	59	3
Glavine, Tom	ATL	152	**21**	3.40	8.26	0.240	−0.002	0.001	0.240	64	2

Player 2001	Team	SO	Wins	ERA	WAR	GPA	GPA brc	GPA bpc	Total GPA	Cy Young Points	Rank
Buehrle, Mark	CHW	126	16	3.29	7.47	0.233	−0.002	−0.003	0.229		
Mays, Joe	MIN	123	17	3.16	**7.95**	0.228	0.002	0.000	0.230		
Mussina, Mike	NYY	214	17	3.15	7.49	0.231	−0.002	0.002	0.232	2	5
Mulder, Mark	OAK	153	**21**	3.45	7.24	0.234	−0.001	0.003	0.236	66	2
Clemens, Roger(8)	NYY	213	20	3.51	6.16	0.237	0.006	0.003	0.246	122	1
Johnson, Randy	ARI	**372**	21	2.49	**11.62**	0.209	−0.000	−0.010	0.199	156	1
Schilling, Curt	ARI	293	**22**	2.98	10.53	0.224	−0.003	−0.009	0.213	98	2
Kile, Darryl	STL	179	16	3.09	8.51	0.231	−0.004	−0.002	0.225		
Maddux, Greg	ATL	173	17	3.05	7.75	0.231	−0.003	0.002	0.230		

Player 2002	Team	SO	Wins	ERA	WAR	GPA	GPA brc	GPA bpc	Total GPA	Cy Young Points	Rank
Lowe, Derek	BOS	127	21	2.58	**8.82**	0.205	0.002	−0.003	0.204	41	3
Martinez, Pedro	BOS	239	20	**2.26**	7.75	0.212	0.000	−0.002	0.209	96	2
Zito, Barry	OAK	182	**23**	2.75	7.83	0.223	−0.001	0.003	0.225	114	1
Colon, Bartolo	CLE	149	20	2.93	8.03	0.231	−0.003	−0.001	0.227		

(Player 2002)	Team	SO	Wins	ERA	WAR	GPA	GPA brc	GPA bpc	Total GPA	Cy Young Points	Rank
Johnson, Randy	ARI	*334*	*24*	*2.32*	*11.17*	0.210	−0.001	−0.007	0.203	160u	1
Schilling, Curt	ARI	316	23	3.23	9.28	0.226	0.001	−0.009	0.218	90	2
Perez, Odalis	LAD	155	15	3.00	7.43	0.223	−0.002	0.004	0.224		
Maddux, Greg	ATL	118	16	2.62	6.96	0.221	0.003	0.001	0.225		

Player 2003	Team	SO	Wins	ERA	WAR	GPA	GPA brc	GPA bpc	Total GPA	Cy Young Points	Rank
Martinez, Pedro	BOS	206	14	*2.22*	8.47	0.203	0.001	−0.002	0.201	20	3
Loaiza, Esteban	CHW	207	21	2.90	*8.78*	0.223	−0.002	−0.004	0.218	63	2
Hudson, Tim(4)	OAK	162	16	2.70	7.97	0.226	0.000	0.005	0.230	15	4
Halladay, Roy(5)	TOR	204	*22*	3.25	7.93	0.237	0.003	−0.001	0.239	136	1
Gagne, Eric	LAD	137	2r	*1.20*	6.18	0.158	0.001	0.006	0.165	146	1
Cormier, Rheal	PHI	67	8r	1.70	4.76	0.172	−0.001	0.004	0.175		
Schmidt, Jason(4)	SFG	208	17	*2.34*	8.70	0.199	0.005	0.002	0.206	73	2
Webb, Brando(11)	ARI	172	10	2.84	7.19	0.221	0.002	−0.007	0.216		
Prior, Mark(12)	CHC	245	18	2.43	8.33	0.220	−0.001	−0.002	0.217	60	3

Player 2004	Team	SO	Wins	ERA	WAR	GPA	GPA brc	GPA bpc	Total GPA	Cy Young Points	Rank
Santana, Johan	MIN	265	20	2.61	*9.50*	0.206	−0.000	−0.001	0.206	140u	1
Schilling, Curt	BOS	203	*21*	3.26	8.23	0.226	0.001	−0.005	0.222	82	2
Radke, Brad	MIN	143	11	3.48	7.17	0.238	−0.003	0.000	0.235		
Lopez, Rodrigo	BAL	121	14	3.59	5.84	0.229	0.002	0.002	0.234		
Martinez, Pedro	BOS	227	16	3.90	6.26	0.248	0.001	−0.003	0.245	1	4
Johnson, Randy	ARI	*290*	16	2.60	9.43	0.224	0.001	−0.007	0.218	97	2
Clemens, Roger	HOU	218	18	2.98	8.14	0.224	0.002	−0.003	0.223	140	1
Sheets, Ben	MIL	264	12	2.70	8.39	0.225	0.001	−0.002	0.224	1	8
Zambrano, Carlos	CHC	188	16	2.75	7.63	0.225	0.004	−0.003	0.225	8	5

Player 2005	Team	SO	Wins	ERA	WAR	GPA	GPA brc	GPA bpc	Total GPA	Cy Young Points	Rank
Santana, Johan	MIN	*238*	16	2.87	8.42	0.217	0.002	−0.001	0.219	51	2
Millwood, Kevin	CLE	146	9	*2.86*	6.01	0.227	0.005	0.002	0.234		
Garland, Jon	CHW	115	18	3.50	6.54	0.241	−0.000	−0.003	0.237	1	6
Buehrle, Mark	CHW	149	16	3.12	7.09	0.239	0.001	−0.003	0.237	5	5
Colon, Bartolo(9)	ANA	157	*21*	3.48	5.93	0.241	−0.001	0.003	0.243	118	1
Clemens, Roger	HOU	185	13	*1.87*	9.80	0.198	−0.001	−0.002	0.196	40	3
Pettitte, Andy	HOU	171	17	2.39	8.86	0.210	−0.001	−0.002	0.207	1	6
Carpenter, Chris	STL	213	21	2.83	8.83	0.220	−0.002	0.000	0.217	132	1
Martinez, Pedro	NYM	205	15	2.82	7.59	0.212	0.002	0.006	0.220		
Willis, Dontrelle	FLA	170	*22*	2.63	8.17	0.219	−0.001	0.007	0.225	112	2

Player 2006	Team	SO	Wins	ERA	WAR	GPA	GPA brc	GPA bpc	Total GPA	Cy Young Points	Rank
Santana, Johan	MIN	*245*	19	2.77	9.10	0.221	−0.002	−0.001	0.218	140u	1
Halladay, Roy	TOR	132	16	3.19	7.28	0.231	0.002	0.000	0.232	48	3
Verlander, Justin	DET	124	17	3.63	5.95	0.242	−0.005	0.001	0.239		
Wang, C.-M.(6)	NYY	76	*19*	3.63	6.08	0.247	−0.001	0.003	0.249	51	2
Oswalt, Roy	HOU	166	15	*2.98*	8.37	0.227	−0.001	−0.002	0.223	31	4
Carpenter, Chris	STL	184	15	3.09	7.87	0.230	−0.002	0.001	0.229	63	3
Webb, Brandon	ARI	178	*16*	3.10	8.16	0.233	0.003	−0.007	0.229	103	1
Arroyo, Bronson	CIN	184	14	3.29	7.92	0.238	−0.002	−0.002	0.235		

Who Should Have Won the Cy Young Award?

Player 2007	Team	SO	Wins	ERA	WAR	GPA	GPA brc	GPA bpc	Total GPA	Cy Young Points	Rank
Bedard, Erik	BAL	221	13	3.16	6.37	0.220	0.005	0.004	0.229	1	5
Beckett, Josh	BOS	194	*20*	3.27	6.81	0.232	0.001	−0.003	0.230	86	2
Santana, Johan	MIN	235	15	3.33	6.71	0.237	−0.001	0.001	0.236	1	5
Sabathia, C.C.	CLE	209	19	3.21	7.71	0.235	−0.001	0.002	0.237	119	1
Buehrle, Mark	CHW	115	10	3.63	6.43	0.241	−0.001	−0.002	0.237		
Greinke, Zack	KCR	106	7	3.47	3.87	0.242	−0.000	−0.004	0.237		
Peavy, Jake	SDP	*240*	19	*2.54*	7.95	0.209	0.003	0.014	0.226	160u	1
Webb, Brandon	ARI	194	18	3.01	*8.43*	0.232	0.002	−0.005	0.229	94	2
Smoltz, John	ATL	197	14	3.11	7.09	0.228	0.002	0.001	0.231	2	6
Oswalt, Roy	HOU	154	14	3.18	7.41	0.235	0.001	−0.003	0.233		

Player 2008	Team	SO	Wins	ERA	WAR	GPA	GPA brc	GPA bpc	Total GPA	Cy Young Points	Rank
Lee, Cliff	CLE	170	*22*	2.54	8.64	0.210	0.002	0.002	0.214	132	1
Duchscherer, J.	OAK	95	10	2.54	4.97	0.219	−0.001	0.003	0.221		
Matsuzaka, D.	BOS	154	18	2.90	6.27	0.224	0.002	−0.004	0.222	10	4
Halladay, Roy	TOR	206	20	2.78	8.49	0.224	0.002	−0.001	0.225	71	2
Lester, Jon	BOS	152	16	3.21	7.03	0.232	−0.000	−0.004	0.228		
Lincecum, Tim	SFG	*265*	18	2.62	9.00	0.205	0.008	0.001	0.214	137	1
Sabathia, C.C.	MIL*	251	17	2.70	*9.31*	0.218	0.001	0.001	0.220	9	5
Santana, Johan	NYM	206	16	*2.53*	8.69	0.216	0.000	0.004	0.220	55	3
Haren, Dan	ARI	206	16	3.33	7.35	0.229	0.002	−0.006	0.225		
Webb, Brando(10)	ARI	183	*22*	3.30	6.96	0.239	0.003	−0.004	0.237	73	2

Player 2009	Team	SO	Wins	ERA	WAR	GPA	GPA brc	GPA bpc	Total GPA	Cy Young Points	Rank
Greinke, Zack	KCR	242	16	*2.16*	9.92	0.207	−0.003	−0.003	0.201	134	1
Halladay, Roy	TOR	208	17	2.79	8.43	0.220	0.002	−0.001	0.221	11	5
Hernandez, Felix	SEA	217	*19*	2.49	7.84	0.221	0.002	0.008	0.231	80	2
Lester, Jon	BOS	225	15	3.41	6.56	0.235	0.001	−0.004	0.232		
Carpenter, Chris	STL	144	17	*2.24*	8.42	0.200	−0.003	0.002	0.199	94	2
Lincecum, Tim	SFG	*261*	15	2.48	8.66	0.208	0.003	0.004	0.215	*100*	1
Wainwright, Adam	STL	212	*19*	2.63	*9.09*	0.215	0.001	0.002	0.218	90	3
Jurrjens, Jair	ATL	152	14	2.60	8.10	0.217	0.001	0.000	0.218		

Player 2010	Team	SO	Wins	ERA	WAR	GPA	GPA brc	GPA bpc	Total GPA	Cy Young Points	Rank
Buchholz, Clay	BOS	120	17	2.33	6.45	0.216	−0.000	−0.003	0.213	20	6
Duensing, Brian	MIN	78	10	2.62	4.56	0.216	−0.000	0.001	0.216		
Hernandez, Felix	SEA	232	13	*2.27*	8.38	0.213	0.002	0.006	0.220	167	1
Price, David	TBR	188	19	2.72	6.55	0.221	0.003	0.004	0.228	111	2
Sabathia, C.C.	NYY	197	*21*	3.18	7.24	0.229	0.003	−0.004	0.228	102	3
Weaver, Jered	ANA	*233*	13	3.01	6.75	0.222	0.005	0.003	0.229	24	5
Jimenez, Ubaldo	COL	214	19	2.88	9.05	0.219	−0.001	−0.014	0.204	90	3
Halladay, Roy	PHI	219	*21*	2.44	*9.58*	0.209	0.000	−0.002	0.207	224	1
Wainwright, Adam	STL	213	20	2.42	8.03	0.211	−0.001	0.003	0.213	122	2
Hudson, Tim	ATL	139	17	2.83	8.35	0.217	−0.004	0.002	0.214	39	4
Johnson, Josh	FLA	186	11	*2.30*	6.73	0.208	−0.001	0.007	0.214	34	5
Oswalt, Roy	PHI	193	13	2.76	7.43	0.217	−0.000	−0.001	0.216	14	6

Player 2011	Team	SO	Wins	ERA	WAR	GPA	GPA brc	GPA bpc	Total GPA	Cy Young Points	Rank
Weaver, Jered	ANA	198	18	2.41	8.81	0.206	−0.003	0.003	0.207	97	2
Verlander, Justin	DET	*250*	*24*	*2.40*	*8.84*	0.208	0.001	0.000	0.209	196	1
Beckett, Josh	BOS	175	13	2.89	6.64	0.212	0.007	−0.004	0.215	3	9
Shields, James	TBR	225	16	2.82	7.93	0.221	−0.005	0.003	0.219	66	3
Sabathia, C.C.	NYY	230	19	3.00	7.46	0.230	−0.001	−0.006	0.224	63	4
Romero, Ricky	TOR	178	15	2.92	6.93	0.223	0.003	−0.002	0.225	2	10
Halladay, Roy	PHI	220	19	2.35	*9.21*	0.203	0.002	−0.001	0.204	133	2
Lee, Cliff	PHI	238	17	2.40	8.60	0.207	0.001	−0.001	0.207	90	3
Kennedy, Ian	ARI	198	*21*	2.88	8.22	0.214	0.004	−0.007	0.210	76	4
Kershaw, Clayton	LAD	*248*	*21*	*2.28*	8.23	0.207	−0.001	0.005	0.212	207	1
Hamels, Cole	PHI	194	14	2.79	7.38	0.211	0.004	0.000	0.214	17	5
Cueto, Johnny	CIN	104	9	2.31	5.38	0.220	−0.001	−0.001	0.218		

Player 2012	Team	SO	Wins	ERA	WAR	GPA	GPA brc	GPA bpc	Total GPA	Cy Young Points	Rank
Price, David	TBR	205	20	2.56	7.58	0.211	0.000	0.001	0.212	153	1
Sale, Chris	CHW	192	17	3.05	6.73	0.219	−0.001	−0.002	0.216	17	6
Verlander, Justin	DET	*239*	17	2.64	*7.81*	0.218	0.002	0.001	0.221	149	2
Weaver, Jered	ANA	142	20	2.81	5.97	0.221	−0.003	0.003	0.221	70	3
Morrow, Brandon	TOR	108	10	2.96	3.88	0.227	0.001	−0.001	0.226		
Harrison, Matt	TEX	133	18	3.29	6.54	0.232	−0.001	−0.004	0.226		
Medlen, Kris	ATL	120	10	*1.57*	5.89	0.185	−0.001	0.001	0.185		
Kershaw, Clayton	LAD	229	14	2.53	*8.07*	0.212	−0.004	0.006	0.214	96	2
Cueto, Johnny	CIN	170	19	2.78	7.52	0.225	−0.004	−0.003	0.217	75	4
Gonzalez, Gio	WAS	207	*21*	2.89	6.40	0.219	0.004	−0.000	0.223	93	3
Dickey, R.A.	NYM	*230*	20	2.73	7.29	0.218	0.001	0.004	0.223	209	1
Zimmermann, Jor	WAS	153	12	2.94	6.15	0.224	0.002	−0.000	0.226		
Lohse, Kyle	STL	143	16	2.86	6.66	0.225	−0.001	0.001	0.226	6	7

Who Should Have Won the MVP Award?

Like the Cy Young Award, the Most Valuable Player (MVP) Award is chosen by the Baseball Writers Association of America (BBWAA). In 1938, the BBWAA instituted the "ranked choice" method of voting for each league. Two baseball writers (three from 1928–1960) who cover each team vote. They rank the 10 most valuable players in their league from 1 to 10. The first-ranked player receives 14 points, the second-ranked player receives nine, the third-ranked player receives eight, and so on until the 10th-ranked player receives one point. The player in each league with the most points wins the MVP Award.

Writers are instructed to select the best pitcher for the Cy Young. The criteria for selecting a most valuable player are more subjective. Clearly offense, defense and leadership need to be taken into account.

Should the best player get the award or should it be the best player on a contending team? The writers tend to select players from contending teams, but players with truly exceptional seasons on losing teams have won the MVP Award.

Total GPA should identify the most productive offensive player. Criteria such as how well his team played, how well he was liked by the writers, what city he played for and how many statistical categories he led will be ignored by tGPA. These less-objective criteria have often had, even by the admission of some writers, a major influence on voting.

The table at the end of this chapter lists the MVP Award winners along with the players whose tGPAs suggest they were among the most deserving. Defense and leadership are not measured by tGPA. These criteria are somewhat subjective (although great strides are now being made in the analysis of defense) and generally do not overwhelm an exceptionally productive offensive season by a player. There are a few games missing from the Retrosheet database from 1952 to 1973 and the statistics listed here may differ slightly from the official statistics for those years.

The goal of this chapter is to show who should have won the MVP Award, as it was in the previous chapter, on the Cy Young Award. The choice of a position player or a pitcher is somewhat arbitrary. For the years that a pitcher won the MVP, we will consider whether other pitchers who might have been more deserving; in the instances that a position player won the award, the alternative candidates will be confined to other position players.

	— MVP Award Winner Trailed League Leader in tGPA By —			
Seasons	None	1 to 19	20 to 39	40+
1952 to 1960	3	5	3	5
1961 to 1970	6	3	1	7
1971 to 1980	10	4	1	5
1981 to 1990	6	5	5	1
1991 to 2000	6	3	4	6
2001 to 2012	13	3	3	4

Table 23.1. The number of tGPA points the MVP Award winner trailed the position player with the best tGPA from 1952 to 2012.

The writers' ability to choose the most deserving pitcher (with the lowest tGPA) for the Cy Young improved significantly after 1970. With the MVP Award, the writers' ability has modestly improved over the years. The position player with the highest tGPA won nine of 33 MVP Awards (27.3 percent) before 1971, but since has won 35 of 79 times (44.3 percent). Fewer MVPs whose tGPAs trailed the league leader by 40 or more points have been selected since 1971 (36.4 percent vs. 20.2 percent).

Mgn	Year	Won MVP	Team	tGPA	Led in tGPA	Team	tGPA
0.099	1999AL	Rodriguez, Ivan	TEX	0.303	Ramirez, Manny	CLE	0.402
0.079	2001AL	Suzuki, Ichiro	SEA	0.328	Giambi, Jason	OAK	0.407
0.075	1987NL	Dawson, Andre	CHC	0.308	Clark, Jack	STL	0.383
0.073	1995AL	Vaughn, Mo	BOS	0.328	Martinez, Edgar	SEA	0.401
0.073	1954AL	Berra, Yogi	NYY	0.326	Williams, Ted	BOS	0.407
0.071	1960NL	Groat, Dick	PIT	0.290	Mathews, Eddie	MLB	0.361
0.068	1962NL	Wills, Maury	LAD	0.300	Robinson, Frank	CIN	0.368
0.062	2002AL	Tejada, Miguel	OAK	0.333	Ramirez, Manny	BOS	0.395
0.062	1955AL	Berra, Yogi	NYY	0.310	Mantle, Mickey	NYY	0.372
0.056	1965AL	Versalles, Zoilo	MIN	0.282	Killebrew, Harmon	MIN	0.338
0.056	1979NL	Stargell, Willie	PIT	0.302	Hernandez, Keith	STL	0.358
0.053	1991NL	Pendleton, Terry	ATL	0.311	Bonds, Barry	PIT	0.364
0.053	1964AL	Robinson, Brooks	BAL	0.324	Mantle, Mickey	NYY	0.377
0.052	1972NL	Bench, Johnny	CIN	0.320	Morgan, Joe	CIN	0.372
0.050	1952NL	Sauer, Hank	CHC	0.296	Kluszewski, Ted	CIN	0.346
0.045	1970NL	Bench, Johnny	CIN	0.330	McCovey, Willie	SFG	0.375
0.045	1961AL	Maris, Roger	NYY	0.367	Mantle, Mickey	NYY	0.412
0.045	1973NL	Rose, Pete	CIN	0.322	Stargell, Willie	PIT	0.367
0.044	1998NL	Sosa, Sammy	CHC	0.361	McGwire, Mark	STL	0.405
0.044	1964NL	Boyer, Ken	STL	0.313	Mays, Willie	SFG	0.357
0.043	2008AL	Pedroia, Dustin	BOS	0.301	Quentin, Carlos	CHW	0.344
0.042	2006AL	Morneau, Justin	MIN	0.338	Hafner, Travis	CLE	0.380
0.041	1976NL	Munson, Thurmon	NYY	0.280	Carew, Rod	MIN	0.321
0.041	1996NL	Caminiti, Ken	SDP	0.373	Bonds, Barry	SFG	0.414
0.041	1979AL	Baylor, Don	CAL	0.322	Lynn, Fred	BOS	0.363
0.040	1958NL	Banks, Ernie	CHC	0.333	Mays, Willie	SFG	0.373
0.040	1963AL	Howard, Elston	NYY	0.299	Kaline, Al	DET	0.339
0.040	1996AL	Gonzalez, Juan	TEX	0.360	McGwire, Mark	OAK	0.400

Table 23.2. The largest differences in tGPA points between the MVP Award winner and the position player with the best tGPA. Data by year and league from 1952 to 2012.

The writers continue to make choices that seem hard to justify, however. Their selection of Ivan Rodriquez over Manny Ramirez for the AL MVP Award in 1999 is a case in point. Ramirez had a tGPA of 0.402 during his 1999 season, the 19th highest from 1952 to 2012.

Rodriquez's tGPA was 0.303, or 0.099 GPA points lower than Ramirez's tGPA — the largest margin of any of the 122 MVP Award ballots from 1952 to 2012. Both the Rangers and Indians won their divisions that year and both players had similar BAs. Ramirez had superior HR (44 vs. 35), RBI (165 vs. 113) and walk (99 vs. 24) totals, but had more strikeouts (131 vs. 64).

Rodriguez's defense behind the plate was outstanding in 1999, and he had a productive season offensively at a position that more often produces weak or league-average hitters. From the information in Table 21.6 we know an average catcher is worth 0.032 GPA points more to his team than an average left fielder. From the "Winning Games" chapter we know that adding 0.099 additional GPA points to a lineup should yield 0.41 more runs per game and 6.7 more wins per season. It is doubtful Rodriquez's defense and leadership skills were enough to justify his selection for the MVP Award over Ramirez.

Pitchers have won 11 of 123 MVP awards (8.9 percent) from 1952 to 2012. Every pitcher who won the MVP since 1956 also won the Cy Young. Except for Don Newcombe in 1956, all pitchers who won the MVP had truly outstanding seasons as measured by tGPA. Only award winners Newcombe in 1956, Sandy Koufax in 1963 and Denny McLain in 1968 did not lead all starting pitchers in tGPA.

The absence of any superior seasons by position players in the NL in 1956 helped Newcombe win. With the exception of Hank Aaron's tGPA of 0.379 in 1963 (Koufax won), Bobby Murcer's tGPA of 0.363 in 1971 (Vida Blue won) and Miguel Cabrera's tGPA of 0.368 in 2011 (Justin Verlander won), most pitchers won their MVP Award in years when no position players in their leagues had superior seasons.

Certain players' skills have repeatedly been underappreciated by the writers. Ted Williams won two MVPs but, according to tGPA, deserved to win in 1954 (Yogi Berra won), probably deserved to win in 1957 (Mickey Mantle won) and may have deserved to win in 1958 (Jackie Jensen won). Mickey Mantle won three MVP awards but also deserved the hardware on three other occasions, in 1955 (Yogi Berra won), 1961 (Roger Maris won) and 1964 (Brooks Robinson won). He may not have deserved to win in 1957, however.

Willie Mays won two MVP awards and deserved to win two more in 1958 (Ernie Banks won) and 1964 (Ken Boyer won), according to tGPA. Mays may have deserved the 1961 award (Frank Robinson won), but his 1954 award may have more deservingly gone to Ted Kluszewski.

Hank Aaron won a single MVP but may have deserved to win in 1959 (Ernie Banks won) and 1971 (Joe Torre won). Both Mays and Aaron had many seasons in which their tGPA was among the league best, but rarely did the writers give them the MVP votes their strong seasons deserved. It is unclear whether their skills were simply underappreciated by the writers or race was a significant factor in the voting.

Ted Kluszewski never won the MVP Award but deserved to win in 1952 (Hank Sauer won) and may have deserved to win in 1954 (Willie Mays won). Eddie Mathews never won the MVP Award, either, but he deserved to win in 1960 (Dick Groat won) and may have deserved to win in 1953 (Roy Campanella won).

In more recent decades, certain players' skills continue to be underappreciated by the writers. Almost without exception, Mark McGwire and Manny Ramirez did not receive the MVP votes that their strong seasons deserved, and neither ever won the MVP Award. According to tGPA, McGwire deserved to win in 1996 (Juan Gonzalez won) and 1998 (Sammy Sosa won) and probably deserved to win in 1999 (Chipper Jones won). Ramirez deserved to win in 1999 (Derek Jeter won) and 2002 (Miguel Tejada won) and probably deserved to win in 2004 (Vladimir Guerrero won). McGwire's superior seasons may have been harder for the writers to recognize since his BA was so much lower than his tGPA. Ramirez put up superior numbers across the board but had a reputation with the writers for being uncooperative. Barry Bonds won seven MVP awards and deserved two more, one in 1991 (Terry Pendleton won) and one 1996 (Ken Caminiti won). Frank Thomas won two MVP awards but probably deserved to win in 1997 (Ken Griffey won) and may have in 1991 (Cal Ripken won). No other player since 1952 deserved multiple MVP awards that he did not receive, at least according to tGPA.

From 1952 to 2012 there were five players who won at least two MVP awards that they might not have deserved. Roy Campanella probably did not deserve to win in 1955 and may not have been deserving in 1953. Ernie Banks did not deserve to win in 1958 and may not have in 1959. Johnny Bench did not deserve to win in 1970 or 1972. Juan Gonzalez did not deserve to win in 1996 and may not have deserved to win in 1998. Alex Rodriguez probably did not deserve to win in 2003 and may not have deserved to win in 2005 although he did deserve the award he won in 2007.

Player	Won	40+	20+	0+	Player	Won	40+	20+	0+
Bonds, Barry	7	9	9	9	Gonzalez, Juan	2	1	1	0
Berra, Yogi	3	1	1	1	Aaron, Hank	1	1	1	3
Mantle, Mickey	3	6	6	5	Clemente, Robert	1	1	2	1
Schmidt, Mike	3	3	4	3	Yastrzemski, Carl	1	1	1	2
Rodriguez, Alex	3	3	2	1	Killebrew, Harmon	1	2	2	2
Pujols, Albert	3	3	3	4	McCovey, Willie	1	2	2	2
Mays, Willie	2	4	4	4	Allen, Dick	1	1	1	2
Campanella, Roy	2	1	1	0	Jackson, Reggie	1	1	1	2
Banks, Ernie	2	1	1	0	Lynn, Fred	1	2	2	2
Maris, Roger	2	1	1	0	Carew, Rod	1	2	2	2
Robinson, Frank	2	3	3	2	Giambi, Jason	1	2	2	2
Bench, Johnny	2	0	0	0	Williams, Ted	0	1	2	3
Morgan, Joe	2	3	3	3	Kluszewski, Ted	0	1	1	2
Yount, Robin	2	2	2	1	Mathews, Eddie	0	1	1	2
Murphy, Dale	2	2	1	1	McGwire, Mark	0	2	3	3
Ripken, Cal	2	2	1	0	Ramirez, Manny	0	2	3	3
Thomas, Frank	2	2	3	4					

Table 23.3. Leading position players, their MVP Award totals, and the number that each should have won according to the number of tGPA points they led or trailed the writers' selection. Data based on at least 3.1 plate appearances per game in the season.

Table 23.3 lists position players who either won or should have won multiple MVP awards from 1952 to 2012. Players whose tGPA led the MVP Award winner by 40 or more points were almost certainly more deserving than the player chosen by writers, while those who led by 20 to 39 points were probably more deserving, and those who led by 1 to 19 points may have been more deserving.

The thresholds for saying a player was more deserving of the MVP than the player who won were increased by 100 percent over the thresholds used when evaluating who was most deserving of the Cy Young. These higher thresholds help compensate for the higher GPA of an exceptional hitter. Defense and leadership are not measured by GPA, and these higher thresholds allow more leeway in evaluating the writers' selections.

The following table presents the top candidates for MVP by year and league with the players ranked by tGPA. An "**s**" after the year indicates a strike shortened season. A number after the player's name is his rank in the league by tGPA. A pound sign (#) before a player's name indicates that more than 5 percent of the PAs for that season are missing from the Retrosheet database and WAR and GPA are adjusted for the missing games. An asterisk (*) after team abbreviation indicates the pitcher played for 2 teams that year. Data based on at least 3.1 plate appearances per game.

Table 23.4. MVP Winners and Players with the Best tGPA by Year and League

Player 1952	Team	HR	RBI	BA	WAR	GPA	GPA brc	GPA bpc	Total GPA	—MVP— Points	Rank
# Shantz, Bobby	PHA	Pitcher Won			10.33	0.213	−0.001	−0.006	0.206	280	1
# Mantle, Mickey	NYY	23	87	0.311	7.41	0.330	−0.002	0.003	0.331	143	3
Doby, Larry	CLE	32	104	0.276	7.29	0.332	0.001	−0.003	0.330	46	12
Robinson, Eddie	CHW	22	104	0.296	5.71	0.319	0.001	−0.002	0.318	47	11
# Kluszewski, T.	CIN	16	86	0.320	6.18	0.353	−0.002	−0.004	0.346	16	17
# Musial, Stan	STL	21	91	**0.336**	7.26	0.335	−0.002	−0.007	0.325	127	5
Robinson, Jackie	BRO	19	75	0.308	*7.74*	0.331	0.002	−0.007	0.325	31	7
Hodges, Gil	BRO	32	102	0.254	5.50	0.334	−0.003	−0.008	0.324		
# Sauer, Hank(10)	CHC	*37*	*121*	0.270	4.83	0.308	−0.003	−0.009	0.296	226	1

Player 1953	Team	HR	RBI	BA	WAR	GPA	GPA brc	GPA bpc	Total GPA	—MVP— Points	Rank
Rosen, Al	CLE	43	145	0.336	*10.63*	0.382	0.000	−0.003	0.379	336u	1
Boone, Ray	DET*	26	114	0.296	7.86	0.356	0.003	−0.004	0.355	59	8
# Mantle, Mickey	NYY	21	92	0.295	7.31	0.344	0.001	0.003	0.349	4	22
Vernon, Mickey	WAS	15	115	**0.337**	6.46	0.345	−0.001	−0.000	0.343	162	3
# Berra, Yogi	NYY	27	108	0.296	7.35	0.323	0.001	0.002	0.326	167	2
# Mathews, Eddie	MLB	*47*	135	0.302	9.38	0.373	0.000	0.004	0.377	216	2
# Musial, Stan	STL	30	113	0.307	8.60	0.386	0.000	−0.011	0.376	62	8
Snider, Duke	BRO	42	126	0.312	*10.16*	0.374	0.006	−0.008	0.373	157	3
Campanella, Roy	BRO	41	142	0.336	9.71	0.377	0.001	−0.008	0.370	297	1
Robinson, Jackie	BRO	12	95	0.329	6.50	0.343	0.009	−0.007	0.344	19	12
# Irvin, Monte	NYG	21	97	0.329	5.41	0.344	0.002	−0.003	0.344	11	15

Player 1954	Team	HR	RBI	BA	WAR	GPA	GPA brc	GPA bpc	Total GPA	—MVP— Points	Rank
Williams, Ted	BOS	29	89	**0.345**	8.90	0.416	0.001	−0.010	0.407	65	7
Minoso, Minnie	CHW	19	116	0.320	8.69	0.359	−0.000	−0.002	0.357	186	4
Mantle, Mickey	NYY	27	102	0.300	8.45	0.351	0.000	0.003	0.354	16	15
Berra, Yogi	NYY	22	125	0.307	8.36	0.328	0.003	0.002	0.334	230	1
Doby, Larry	CLE	32	126	0.272	7.81	0.334	0.001	−0.003	0.332	210	2
Kluszewski, Ted	CIN	*49*	*141*	0.326	8.18	0.372	0.000	−0.007	0.366	217	2
Snider, Duke	BRO	40	130	0.341	*9.71*	0.365	0.002	−0.008	0.359	135	4
# Musial, Stan	STL	35	126	0.330	8.50	0.372	−0.004	−0.009	0.358	97	6
# Mays, Willie	NYG	41	110	**0.345**	8.97	0.360	−0.001	−0.003	0.357	283	1

Player 1955	Team	HR	RBI	BA	WAR	GPA	GPA brc	GPA bpc	Total GPA	—MVP— Points	Rank
Mantle, Mickey	NYY	37	99	0.306	*9.71*	0.367	0.001	0.004	0.372	113	5
Kaline, Al	DET	27	102	**0.340**	7.53	0.353	−0.003	−0.004	0.346	201	2
Boone, Ray	DET	20	*116*	0.284	5.70	0.322	0.004	−0.005	0.321	16	16
Smith, Al	CLE	22	77	0.306	6.11	0.313	0.002	−0.002	0.314	200	3
Berra, Yogi	NYY	27	108	0.272	6.73	0.306	0.000	0.004	0.310	218	1

(Player 1955)	Team	HR	RBI	BA	WAR	GPA	GPA brc	GPA bpc	Total GPA	—MVP— Points	Rank
Snider, Duke	BRO	42	*136*	0.309	*9.93*	0.381	−0.001	−0.008	0.372	221	2
# Mays, Willie	NYG	*51*	127	0.319	9.62	0.356	0.006	−0.004	0.359	165	4
# Mathews, Eddie	MLB	41	101	0.301	6.95	0.338	0.000	0.005	0.343	6	18
# Musial, Stan	STL	33	108	0.311	6.55	0.349	−0.001	−0.009	0.339	46	8
Campanella, Roy	BRO	32	107	0.318	7.09	0.344	0.002	−0.008	0.337	*226*	1

Player 1956	Team	HR	RBI	BA	WAR	GPA	GPA brc	GPA bpc	Total GPA	—MVP— Points	Rank
Mantle, Mickey	NYY	*52*	*130*	*0.353*	*13.15*	0.412	0.006	0.003	0.422	336u	1
Williams, Ted	BOS	24	82	0.345	7.64	0.392	0.001	−0.010	0.382	70	6
Skowron, Bill	NYY	23	90	0.308	5.52	0.344	0.000	0.003	0.347		
Berra, Yogi(6)	NYY	30	105	0.298	8.20	0.335	0.000	0.003	0.338	186	2
Newcombe, Don	BRO	Pitcher	Won		8.92	0.229	0.000	−0.008	0.221	*223*	1
# Adcock, Joe	MLB	38	103	0.294	4.92	0.337	0.001	0.004	0.342	54	11
Mathews, Eddie	MLB	37	95	0.272	6.03	0.321	0.003	0.005	0.329		
Snider, Duke	BRO	43	101	0.292	6.84	0.331	−0.000	−0.008	0.323	55	10

Player 1957	Team	HR	RBI	BA	WAR	GPA	GPA brc	GPA bpc	Total GPA	—MVP— Points	Rank
# Williams, Ted	BOS	38	87	*0.388*	10.50	0.427	0.003	−0.009	0.420	209	2
Mantle, Mickey	NYY	34	94	0.365	*12.48*	0.404	0.007	0.003	0.414	*233*	1
Sievers, Roy	WAS	42	114	0.302	7.55	0.339	0.001	0.000	0.341	205	3
Fox, Nellie(8)	CHW	6	61	0.317	7.34	0.307	0.002	−0.001	0.308	193	4
Aaron, Hank	MLB	*44*	*132*	0.322	10.02	0.363	0.003	0.005	0.370	*239*	1
# Mays, Willie	NYG	35	97	0.333	8.94	0.346	0.006	−0.003	0.348	174	4
Musial, Stan	STL	29	102	*0.351*	6.21	0.352	0.002	−0.009	0.345	230	2
Mathews, Eddie	MLB	32	94	0.292	7.75	0.323	0.003	0.004	0.330	45	8
Schoendienst (10)	NYG	15	65	0.309	6.20	0.294	−0.002	0.003	0.295	221	3

Player 1958	Team	HR	RBI	BA	WAR	GPA	GPA brc	GPA bpc	Total GPA	—MVP— Points	Rank
Williams, Ted	BOS	26	85	*0.328*	7.72	0.378	0.003	−0.011	0.369	89	7
Mantle, Mickey	NYY	42	97	0.304	*9.72*	0.353	0.007	0.003	0.363	127	5
Colavito, Rocky	CLE	41	113	0.303	7.12	0.354	0.000	−0.002	0.352	181	3
Cerv, Bob	KCA	38	104	0.305	6.32	0.347	−0.001	−0.004	0.342	164	4
Jensen, Jackie	BOS	35	*122*	0.286	7.10	0.346	0.000	−0.009	0.336	*233*	1
Mays, Willie	SFG	29	96	0.347	*10.81*	0.358	0.014	0.002	0.373	185	2
Banks, Ernie	CHC	*47*	*129*	0.313	9.42	0.343	−0.001	−0.009	0.333	*283*	1
Musial, Stan	STL	17	62	0.337	4.90	0.333	0.002	−0.009	0.326	39	12
Aaron, Hank	MLB	30	95	0.326	6.69	0.311	0.005	0.005	0.321	166	3

Player 1959	Team	HR	RBI	BA	WAR	GPA	GPA brc	GPA bpc	Total GPA	—MVP— Points	Rank
Woodling, Gene	BAL	14	77	0.300	5.43	0.333	−0.000	0.001	0.333	18	16
Lemon, Jim	WAS	33	100	0.279	5.90	0.325	0.005	0.001	0.331	4	25
Mantle, Mickey	NYY	31	75	0.285	7.14	0.318	0.006	0.003	0.328	13	17
Kuenn, Harvey	DET	9	71	*0.353*	6.03	0.324	0.008	−0.005	0.327	64	8
Fox, Nellie(13)	CHW	2	70	0.306	6.76	0.304	0.002	−0.001	0.304	*295*	1
Aaron, Hank	MLB	39	123	*0.355*	9.08	0.352	0.004	0.006	0.362	174	3
Mathews, Eddie	MLB	*46*	114	0.306	*9.57*	0.354	0.002	0.005	0.361	189	2
Mays, Willie	SFG	34	104	0.313	8.67	0.343	0.006	0.002	0.350	85	6
Banks, Ernie	CHC	45	*143*	0.304	9.20	0.352	0.001	−0.009	0.344	*232*	1

Player 1960	Team	HR	RBI	BA	WAR	GPA	GPA brc	GPA bpc	Total GPA	—MVP— Points	Rank
Gentile, Jim	BAL	21	98	0.292	6.10	0.364	0.001	0.000	0.366	21	15
Maris, Roger	NYY	39	**112**	0.283	7.30	0.352	−0.000	0.003	0.355	**225**	1
Mantle, Mickey	NYY	40	94	0.275	**8.69**	0.341	0.005	0.003	0.349	222	2
Sievers, Roy	CHW	28	93	0.295	5.48	0.341	0.002	−0.002	0.341	58	7
Mathews, Eddie	MLB	39	124	0.277	**9.56**	0.353	0.002	0.005	0.361	52	10
Aaron, Hank	MLB	40	**126**	0.292	6.99	0.329	0.002	0.005	0.336	49	11
Mays, Willie	SFG	29	103	0.319	7.73	0.330	0.001	−0.002	0.329	155	3
Robinson, Frank	CIN	31	83	0.297	5.16	0.332	−0.003	−0.005	0.324	2	20
Groat, Dick(15)	PIT	2	50	**0.325**	5.71	0.289	0.001	−0.000	0.290	276	1

Player 1961	Team	HR	RBI	BA	WAR	GPA	GPA brc	GPA bpc	Total GPA	—MVP— Points	Rank
Mantle, Mickey	NYY	54	128	0.317	**12.26**	0.406	0.004	0.002	0.412	198	2
Cash, Norm	DET	41	132	**0.361**	10.19	0.398	0.005	−0.006	0.398	151	4
Gentile, Jim	BAL	46	**141**	0.302	8.70	0.391	−0.000	−0.001	0.390	157	3
Maris, Roger	NYY	**61**	**141**	0.269	9.22	0.362	0.003	0.002	0.367	202	1
Mays, Willie	SFG	40	123	0.308	**9.22**	0.361	0.002	−0.002	0.361	70	6
Cepeda, Orlando	SFG	46	**142**	0.311	7.27	0.355	0.001	−0.002	0.354	117	2
Robinson, Frank	CIN	37	124	0.323	7.03	0.343	0.008	−0.006	0.345	219	1
Aaron, Hank	MLB	34	120	0.327	7.47	0.330	0.004	0.005	0.339	39	8

Player 1962	Team	HR	RBI	BA	WAR	GPA	GPA brc	GPA bpc	Total GPA	—MVP— Points	Rank
Mantle, Mickey	NYY	30	89	0.321	**10.13**	0.413	0.009	0.003	0.424	234	1
Siebern, Norm	KCA	25	117	0.308	8.05	0.357	0.003	−0.003	0.356	53	7
Killebrew, H.	MIN	**48**	**126**	0.243	6.60	0.336	−0.002	−0.004	0.331	99	3
Kaline, Al	DET	29	94	0.304	4.31	0.329	0.004	−0.004	0.329	58	6
Robinson, Frank	CIN	39	136	0.342	9.36	0.369	0.002	−0.004	0.368	164	4
# Aaron, Hank	MLB	45	128	0.323	8.91	0.352	0.000	0.008	0.361	72	6
Mays, Willie	SFG	**49**	141	0.304	**9.72**	0.349	0.005	0.002	0.356	202	2
Davis, Tommy	LAD	27	**153**	**0.346**	8.96	0.345	0.001	0.009	0.355	175	3
Wills, Maury(21)	LAD	6	48	0.299	7.39	0.267	0.025	0.009	0.300	209	1

Player 1963	Team	HR	RBI	BA	WAR	GPA	GPA brc	GPA bpc	Total GPA	—MVP— Points	Rank
Kaline, Al	DET	27	101	0.312	7.41	0.339	0.005	−0.005	0.339	148	2
Allison, Bob	MIN	35	91	0.271	6.40	0.323	0.002	−0.004	0.321	15	15
Yastrzemski, Carl	BOS	14	68	**0.321**	6.68	0.326	−0.000	−0.009	0.317	81	6
Tresh, Tom	NYY	25	71	0.269	6.31	0.303	0.003	0.005	0.311	38	11
Howard, Elsto(10)	NYY	28	85	0.287	6.02	0.293	0.002	0.004	0.299	248	1
Koufax, Sandy	MLB		Pitcher Won		**12.19**	0.186	0.002	0.007	0.195	237	1
Aaron, Hank	MLB	44	**130**	0.319	11.10	0.363	0.007	0.008	0.379	135	3
Mays, Willie	SFG	38	103	0.314	8.74	0.333	0.001	0.001	0.334	102	5
Groat, Dick(17)	STL	6	73	0.319	7.33	0.297	0.003	−0.007	0.293	190	2

Player 1964	Team	HR	RBI	BA	WAR	GPA	GPA brc	GPA bpc	Total GPA	—MVP— Points	Rank
Mantle, Mickey	NYY	35	111	0.303	**9.46**	0.373	0.000	0.004	0.377	171	2
Powell, Boog	BAL	39	99	0.290	7.09	0.356	0.001	0.003	0.360	28	3
Robinson, Brooks	BAL	28	**118**	0.317	7.99	0.318	0.004	0.002	0.324	269	1
Allison, Bob	MIN	32	86	0.287	5.82	0.321	0.006	−0.004	0.322	5	23

(Player 1964)	Team	HR	RBI	BA	WAR	GPA	GPA brc	GPA bpc	Total GPA	—MVP— Points	Rank
Mays, Willie	SFG	*47*	111	0.296	**9.95**	0.348	0.007	0.002	0.357	66	6
Carty, Rico	MLB	22	88	0.330	6.54	0.337	0.004	0.007	0.348		
Torre, Joe	MLB	20	109	0.321	8.54	0.330	−0.001	0.009	0.339	85	5
Boyer, Ken(10)	STL	24	*119*	0.295	7.46	0.316	0.004	−0.007	0.313	243	1

Player 1965	*Team*	*HR*	*RBI*	*BA*	*WAR*	*GPA*	*GPA brc*	*GPA bpc*	*Total GPA*	—*MVP*— *Points*	*Rank*
Killebrew, H.	MIN	25	75	0.269	5.58	0.337	0.004	−0.004	0.338	15	15
Oliva, Tony	MIN	16	98	*0.321*	*7.02*	0.329	0.002	−0.004	0.328	174	2
Blefary, Curt	BAL	22	70	0.260	5.66	0.314	0.004	0.002	0.319		
Versalles, Zoil(17)	MIN	19	77	0.273	6.73	0.280	0.006	−0.004	0.282	275	1
Mays, Willie	SFG	*52*	112	0.317	9.44	0.346	0.006	0.001	0.353	224	1
Williams, Billy	CHC	34	108	0.315	7.80	0.327	0.006	−0.006	0.327	21	12
Rose, Pete	CIN	11	81	0.312	*9.64*	0.324	0.006	−0.004	0.326	67	6
McCovey, Willie	SFG	39	92	0.276	6.16	0.322	0.002	0.001	0.325	25	10

Player 1966	*Team*	*HR*	*RBI*	*BA*	*WAR*	*GPA*	*GPA brc*	*GPA bpc*	*Total GPA*	—*MVP*— *Points*	*Rank*
Robinson, Frank	BAL	*49*	122	0.316	*9.34*	0.358	−0.001	0.001	0.358	280u	1
Powell, Boog	BAL	34	109	0.287	5.97	0.332	0.002	0.001	0.335	122	3
Kaline, Al	DET	29	88	0.288	6.89	0.337	−0.002	−0.004	0.331	66	7
Killebrew, H.	MIN	39	110	0.281	7.65	0.332	−0.001	−0.004	0.326	96	4
Robinson, Brooks	BAL	23	100	0.269	6.42	0.294	0.004	0.001	0.299	153	2
Allen, Dick	PHI	40	101	0.317	9.10	0.362	0.001	−0.001	0.362	107	4
Mays, Willie	SFG	37	103	0.288	9.05	0.345	0.004	0.001	0.350	111	3
McCovey, Willie	SFG	36	96	0.295	7.00	0.344	0.003	0.001	0.348	12	17
# Clemente, R.(5)	PIT	29	119	0.317	8.24	0.336	0.004	0.003	0.343	218	1

Player 1967	*Team*	*HR*	*RBI*	*BA*	*WAR*	*GPA*	*GPA brc*	*GPA bpc*	*Total GPA*	—*MVP*— *Points*	*Rank*
Yastrzemski, Carl	BOS	*44*	*121*	0.326	*10.61*	0.376	0.001	−0.009	0.369	275	1
Robinson, Frank	BAL	30	94	0.311	7.56	0.346	0.001	0.002	0.349	31	11
Killebrew, H.	MIN	*44*	113	0.269	7.54	0.333	0.003	−0.004	0.333	161	2
Kaline, Al	DET	25	78	0.308	6.45	0.325	0.011	−0.004	0.332	88	5
# Clemente, R.	PIT	23	110	*0.357*	9.95	0.361	0.006	0.002	0.370	129	3
Aaron, Hank	ATL	*39*	109	0.307	8.83	0.348	0.002	−0.003	0.347	79	5
Cepeda, Orlando	STL	25	*111*	0.325	7.70	0.337	0.007	−0.001	0.343	280u	1
McCarver, T.(17)	STL	14	69	0.295	6.03	0.294	−0.001	−0.001	0.292	136	2

Player 1968	*Team*	*HR*	*RBI*	*BA*	*WAR*	*GPA*	*GPA brc*	*GPA bpc*	*Total GPA*	—*MVP*— *Points*	*Rank*
McLain, Denny	DET	Pitcher Won			10.73	0.195	0.001	−0.004	0.193	280u	1
Yastrzemski, Carl	BOS	23	74	*0.301*	*8.05*	0.323	0.010	−0.009	0.324	50	9
Howard, Frank	WAS	*44*	106	0.274	6.96	0.303	0.005	0.003	0.311	63	8
Freehan, Bill(5)	DET	25	84	0.263	8.25	0.306	0.003	−0.003	0.306	161	2
Gibson, Bob	STL	Pitcher Won			13.03	0.172	−0.000	−0.001	0.171	20u	1
McCovey, Willie	SFG	*36*	*105*	0.293	7.08	0.326	0.003	0.001	0.330	135	3
Mays, Willie	SFG	23	79	0.289	6.96	0.305	0.004	0.001	0.310	14	13
Allen, Dick	PHI	33	90	0.263	6.32	0.311	−0.005	−0.001	0.305		
Williams, Billy	CHC	30	98	0.288	*7.10*	0.306	0.005	−0.007	0.304	48	8

Who Should Have Won the MVP Award?

Player 1969	Team	HR	RBI	BA	WAR	GPA	GPA brc	GPA bpc	Total GPA	—MVP— Points	Rank
Killebrew, H.	MIN	*49*	*140*	0.276	*10.84*	0.371	0.004	−0.003	0.372	294	1
Jackson, Reggie	OAK	47	118	0.275	9.68	0.358	0.002	0.005	0.365	110	5
Robinson, Frank	BAL	32	100	0.308	8.41	0.347	0.006	0.002	0.355	162	3
Powell, Boog	BAL	37	121	0.304	7.30	0.347	0.002	0.002	0.351	227	2
McCovey, Willie	SFG	45	*126*	0.320	*10.03*	0.388	0.004	0.002	0.395	265	1
Wynn, Jim	HOU	33	87	0.269	9.02	0.334	0.007	0.005	0.346	8	15
Rose, Pete	CIN	16	82	*0.348*	9.23	0.346	0.001	−0.003	0.344	127	4
Clemente, Robert	PIT	19	91	0.345	6.81	0.331	0.008	0.003	0.342	51	8
Aaron, Hank	ATL	44	97	0.300	7.16	0.339	−0.002	−0.002	0.335	188	3

Player 1970	Team	HR	RBI	BA	WAR	GPA	GPA brc	GPA bpc	Total GPA	—MVP— Points	Rank
Yastrzemski, Carl	BOS	40	102	0.329	8.44	0.359	0.005	−0.008	0.355	136	4
Powell, Boog	BAL	35	114	0.297	7.42	0.351	0.001	0.002	0.354	234	1
Howard, Frank	WAS	44	*126*	0.283	*8.65*	0.349	0.002	0.003	0.354	91	5
White, Roy	NYY	22	94	0.296	7.55	0.322	0.007	0.005	0.334	25	15
Oliva, Tony	MIN	23	107	0.325	6.57	0.331	−0.001	−0.003	0.327	157	2
McCovey, Willie	SFG	39	126	0.289	8.61	0.370	0.003	0.002	0.375	47	9
Carty, Rico	ATL	25	101	*0.366*	7.46	0.363	0.001	−0.002	0.361	43	10
Williams, Billy	CHC	42	129	0.322	9.26	0.358	0.006	−0.007	0.358	218	2
Dietz, Dick	SFG	22	107	0.300	*9.80*	0.352	0.003	0.002	0.357		
Bench, Johnny(12)	CIN	*45*	*148*	0.293	8.62	0.332	0.003	−0.005	0.330	326	1

Player 1971	Team	HR	RBI	BA	WAR	GPA	GPA brc	GPA bpc	Total GPA	—MVP— Points	Rank
Blue, Vida	OAK	Pitcher	Won		11.52	0.192	0.000	0.006	0.197	268	1
Murcer, Bobby	NYY	25	94	0.331	*9.95*	0.354	0.003	0.005	0.363	72	7
Rettenmund, M.	BAL	11	75	0.318	7.42	0.335	0.002	0.002	0.339	8	19
Bando, Sal(12)	OAK	24	94	0.271	6.08	0.294	−0.002	0.005	0.298	182	2
Aaron, Hank	ATL	47	118	0.327	8.62	0.370	0.002	−0.001	0.371	180	3
Stargell, Willie	PIT	*48*	125	0.295	9.20	0.367	0.002	−0.001	0.368	222	2
Torre, Joe	STL	24	*137*	*0.363*	*11.30*	0.361	0.004	−0.001	0.364	318	1
Mays, Willie	SFG	18	61	0.271	6.62	0.322	0.009	0.003	0.334	11	19

Player 1972	Team	HR	RBI	BA	WAR	GPA	GPA brc	GPA bpc	Total GPA	—MVP— Points	Rank
Allen, Dick	CHW	37	113	0.308	*9.14*	0.364	0.006	0.001	0.371	321	1
Mayberry, John	KCR	25	100	0.298	6.63	0.330	0.002	0.002	0.334	27	12
Murcer, Bobby	NYY	33	96	0.292	8.30	0.317	0.002	0.005	0.324	89	5
Rudi, Joe(10)	OAK	19	75	0.305	5.28	0.285	−0.000	0.005	0.290	164	2
Morgan, Joe	CIN	16	73	0.292	*12.14*	0.354	0.010	0.008	0.372	197	4
Williams, Billy	CHC	37	122	*0.333*	10.04	0.368	0.004	−0.006	0.366	211	2
Cedeno, Cesar	HOU	22	82	0.320	9.74	0.336	0.011	0.008	0.354	112	6
Bench, Johnny(8)	CIN	*40*	*125*	0.270	8.86	0.314	−0.002	0.008	0.320	263	1

Player 1973	Team	HR	RBI	BA	WAR	GPA	GPA brc	GPA bpc	Total GPA	—MVP— Points	Rank
Jackson, Reggie	OAK	32	117	0.293	7.98	0.345	0.002	0.007	0.353	336u	1
Mayberry, John	KCR	26	100	0.278	6.45	0.333	0.004	−0.001	0.336	76	7
Scott, George	MIL	24	107	0.306	5.52	0.316	0.001	0.001	0.317	25	14
Bando, Sal	OAK	29	98	0.287	7.24	0.308	0.002	0.007	0.317	83	4

(Player 1973)	Team	HR	RBI	BA	WAR	GPA	GPA brc	GPA bpc	Total GPA	−MVP− Points	Rank
Stargell, Willie	PIT	**44**	**119**	0.299	8.70	0.361	0.005	0.001	0.367	250	2
Aaron, Hank	ATL	40	96	0.301	6.22	0.354	0.001	−0.001	0.353	35	12
Morgan, Joe	CIN	26	82	0.290	**9.75**	0.330	0.013	0.004	0.346	102	4
Bonds, Bobby	SFG	39	96	0.283	8.63	0.329	0.008	0.007	0.343	174	3
Rose, Pete(11)	CIN	5	64	**0.338**	7.28	0.316	0.003	0.003	0.322	274	1

Player 1974	Team	HR	RBI	BA	WAR	GPA	GPA brc	GPA bpc	Total GPA	−MVP− Points	Rank
Jackson, Reggie	OAK	29	93	0.289	6.87	0.325	0.005	0.007	0.337	119	4
Burroughs, Jeff	TEX	25	**118**	0.301	7.20	0.331	0.001	0.001	0.333	248	1
Carew, Rod	MIN	3	55	**0.364**	8.22	0.316	0.008	−0.003	0.322	70	7
Rudi, Joe(11)	OAK	22	99	0.293	4.81	0.289	0.002	0.007	0.298	161	2
Schmidt, Mike	PHI	**36**	116	0.282	**9.40**	0.344	0.001	0.002	0.347	136	6
Zisk, Richie	PIT	17	100	0.313	7.28	0.339	0.003	0.002	0.344	54	9
Stargell, Willie	PIT	25	96	0.301	7.35	0.340	0.001	0.002	0.344	43	10
Garvey, Steve(7)	LAD	21	111	0.312	6.20	0.310	0.003	0.010	0.324	270	1
Brock, Lou(17)	STL	3	48	0.306	5.31	0.279	0.013	0.004	0.297	233	2

Player 1975	Team	HR	RBI	BA	WAR	GPA	GPA brc	GPA bpc	Total GPA	−MVP− Points	Rank
Lynn, Fred	BOS	21	105	0.331	**8.47**	0.354	0.005	−0.007	0.352	326	1
Carew, Rod	MIN	14	80	**0.359**	7.98	0.333	0.007	−0.003	0.338	54	9
Mayberry, John	KCR	34	106	0.291	6.70	0.331	0.001	−0.000	0.332	157	2
Harrah, Toby	TEX	20	93	0.293	7.85	0.328	−0.005	0.001	0.324	16	15
Morgan, Joe	CIN	17	94	0.327	**11.96**	0.373	0.017	0.003	0.393	321	1
Stargell, Willie	PIT	22	90	0.295	8.47	0.346	0.004	0.001	0.351	69	7
Watson, Bob	HOU	18	85	0.324	5.49	0.325	0.002	0.010	0.338	8	20
Luzinski, Greg(12)	PHI	34	**120**	0.300	6.51	0.314	0.001	0.002	0.317	154	2

Player 1976	Team	HR	RBI	BA	WAR	GPA	GPA brc	GPA bpc	Total GPA	−MVP− Points	Rank
Carew, Rod	MIN	9	90	0.331	6.33	0.321	0.003	−0.003	0.321	71	5
Jackson, Reggie	BAL	27	91	0.277	5.66	0.307	0.009	0.004	0.320	17	16
Brett, George(9)	KCR	7	67	**0.333**	6.63	0.299	0.000	−0.000	0.299	217	2
Munson, T.(25)	NYY	17	105	0.302	5.82	0.276	0.001	0.002	0.280	304	1
Morgan, Joe	CIN	27	111	0.320	**12.51**	0.390	0.016	0.003	0.409	311	1
Griffey Sr., Ken	CIN	6	74	0.336	7.77	0.334	0.007	0.003	0.343	49	8
Madlock, Bill	CHC	15	84	**0.339**	7.23	0.332	−0.001	−0.003	0.329	51	6
Schmidt, Mike	PHI	**38**	107	0.262	8.16	0.319	0.001	0.002	0.322	179	3
Foster, George(9)	CIN	29	**121**	0.306	6.41	0.310	0.004	0.003	0.317	221	2

Player 1977	Team	HR	RBI	BA	WAR	GPA	GPA brc	GPA bpc	Total GPA	−MVP− Points	Rank
Carew, Rod	MIN	14	100	**0.388**	9.25	0.374	0.006	−0.004	0.376	273	1
Singleton, Ken	BAL	24	99	0.328	7.31	0.341	0.001	0.003	0.346	200	3
Page, Mitchell	OAK	21	75	0.307	6.12	0.314	0.012	0.008	0.334		
Cowens, Al(7)	KCR	23	112	0.312	6.26	0.327	−0.001	−0.001	0.325	217	2
Luzinski, Greg	PHI	39	130	0.309	8.28	0.354	0.003	0.003	0.360	255	2
Schmidt, Mike	PHI	38	101	0.274	**8.48**	0.337	0.006	0.003	0.346	48	10
Smith, Reggie	LAD	32	87	0.307	6.75	0.330	0.003	0.011	0.345	112	4
Foster, George(5)	CIN	**52**	**149**	0.320	7.80	0.339	0.000	0.004	0.342	**291**	1

Player 1978	Team	HR	RBI	BA	WAR	GPA	GPA brc	GPA bpc	Total GPA	—MVP— Points	Rank
Rice, Jim	BOS	*46*	*139*	0.315	8.51	0.338	0.005	−0.007	0.336	352	1
Otis, Amos	KCR	22	96	0.298	7.08	0.329	0.006	−0.001	0.334	90	4
Hisle, Larry	MIL	34	115	0.290	6.87	0.333	0.001	0.000	0.334	201	3
Piniella, Lou	NYY	6	69	0.314	5.02	0.314	0.003	0.002	0.319	11	21
Parker, Dave	PIT	30	117	*0.334*	*9.16*	0.358	0.007	0.002	0.368	320	1
Smith, Reggie	LAD	29	93	0.295	6.29	0.328	0.004	0.011	0.343	164	4
Burroughs, Jeff	ATL	23	77	0.301	6.70	0.330	0.002	−0.001	0.331	7	19
Garvey, Steve(5)	LAD	21	113	0.316	6.45	0.315	0.001	0.011	0.327	194	2

Player 1979	Team	HR	RBI	BA	WAR	GPA	GPA brc	GPA bpc	Total GPA	—MVP— Points	Rank
Lynn, Fred	BOS	39	122	*0.333*	8.95	0.367	0.004	−0.008	0.363	160	4
Lezcano, Sixto	MIL	28	101	0.321	6.90	0.353	0.002	0.001	0.356	18	15
Porter, Darrell(3)	KCR	20	112	0.291	*9.82*	0.346	0.003	−0.001	0.348	52	9
Brett, George(4)	KCR	23	107	0.329	8.84	0.342	0.005	−0.001	0.347	226	3
Singleton, Ken(7)	BAL	35	111	0.295	7.09	0.329	0.003	0.003	0.336	241	2
Baylor, Don(10)	CAL	36	*139*	0.296	6.60	0.318	0.002	0.002	0.322	347	1
Hernandez, Keith	STL	11	105	*0.344*	7.98	0.350	0.002	0.006	0.358	216	1
Winfield, Dave	SDP	34	*118*	0.308	*8.18*	0.342	0.000	0.011	0.353	115	3
Foster, George	CIN	30	98	0.302	5.51	0.337	−0.000	0.004	0.340	34	12
Stargell, Willie(23)	PIT	32	82	0.281	2.93	0.301	−0.002	0.002	0.302	216	1

Player 1980	Team	HR	RBI	BA	WAR	GPA	GPA brc	GPA bpc	Total GPA	—MVP— Points	Rank
Brett, George	KCR	24	118	*0.390*	*10.10*	0.408	0.005	−0.001	0.412	335	1
Jackson, Reggie	NYY	41	111	0.300	7.82	0.353	0.002	0.002	0.357	234	2
Cooper, Cecil	MIL	25	122	0.352	7.42	0.341	0.005	0.001	0.347	160	5
Singleton, Ken	BAL	24	104	0.304	7.06	0.327	0.002	0.003	0.332	4	21
Simmons, Ted	STL	21	98	0.303	8.08	0.331	0.003	0.005	0.339		
Schmidt, Mike	PHI	*48*	121	0.286	8.02	0.333	0.002	0.002	0.337	336	1
Hernandez, Keith	STL	16	99	0.321	6.64	0.329	−0.000	0.005	0.334	29	11
Carter, Gary(20)	MON	29	101	0.264	6.05	0.286	0.001	0.005	0.292	193	2

Player 1981s	Team	HR	RBI	BA	WAR	GPA	GPA brc	GPA bpc	Total GPA	—MVP— Points	Rank
Fingers, Rollie	MIL	Pitcher	Won		4.94	0.164	0.000	−0.001	0.163	319	1
Evans, Dwight	BOS	22	71	0.296	5.48	0.333	0.003	−0.007	0.329	140	3
Murray, Eddie	BAL	22	78	0.294	3.96	0.318	0.001	0.005	0.324	137	5
Henderson, R.(13)	OAK	6	35	0.319	3.86	0.292	−0.002	0.007	0.296	308	2
Schmidt, Mike	PHI	*31*	*91*	0.316	*7.36*	0.372	0.002	0.003	0.377	321	1
Foster, George	CIN	22	90	0.295	6.06	0.335	0.007	0.005	0.347	146	3
Raines, Tim	MON	5	37	0.304	4.61	0.312	0.029	0.004	0.346	15	19
Matthews, Gary	PHI	9	67	0.301	4.57	0.314	0.009	0.002	0.325	31	13
Dawson, Andre	MON	24	64	0.302	5.00	0.303	0.010	0.005	0.318	215	2

Player 1982	Team	HR	RBI	BA	WAR	GPA	GPA brc	GPA bpc	Total GPA	—MVP— Points	Rank
Yount, Robin	MIL	29	114	0.331	*10.45*	0.341	0.006	0.001	0.347	385	1
McRae, Hal	KCR	27	*133*	0.308	8.26	0.349	−0.001	−0.001	0.347	175	4
Murray, Eddie	BAL	32	110	0.316	6.16	0.330	0.003	0.003	0.336	228	2
Lynn, Fred	CAL	21	86	0.299	6.39	0.327	0.000	0.003	0.330		

(Player 1982)	Team	HR	RBI	BA	WAR	GPA	GPA brc	GPA bpc	Total GPA	—MVP— Points	Rank
Guerrero, Pedro	LAD	32	100	0.304	7.49	0.322	0.005	0.011	0.338	175	3
Oliver, Al	MON	22	109	0.331	6.17	0.321	0.001	0.005	0.328	175	3
Madlock, Bill	PIT	19	95	0.319	6.81	0.316	0.003	0.002	0.321	37	11
Murphy, Dale(9)	ATL	36	109	0.281	6.86	0.314	0.003	−0.001	0.316	283	1
Smith, Lonnie(10)	STL	8	69	0.307	6.23	0.300	0.010	0.005	0.315	218	2

Player 1983	Team	HR	RBI	BA	WAR	GPA	GPA brc	GPA bpc	Total GPA	—MVP— Points	Rank
Boggs, Wade	BOS	5	74	0.361	8.98	0.351	0.002	−0.007	0.346	25	12
Murray, Eddie	BAL	33	111	0.306	7.25	0.340	0.002	0.003	0.345	290	2
Henderson, R.	OAK	9	48	0.292	6.09	0.296	0.021	0.007	0.324	1	24
Ripken, Cal(9)	BAL	27	102	0.318	8.07	0.306	0.001	0.003	0.310	322	1
Murphy, Dale	ATL	36	121	0.302	8.50	0.332	0.009	−0.001	0.340	318	1
Raines, Tim	MON	11	71	0.298	7.66	0.309	0.019	0.005	0.333	83	5
Guerrero, Pedro	LAD	32	103	0.298	7.84	0.317	0.004	0.011	0.333	182	4
Dawson, A.(16)	MON	32	113	0.299	5.55	0.285	0.003	0.005	0.293	213	2

Player 1984	Team	HR	RBI	BA	WAR	GPA	GPA brc	GPA bpc	Total GPA	—MVP— Points	Rank
Hernandez, G.	DET	Pitcher Won			7.01	0.187	0.002	−0.001	0.188	306	1
Murray, Eddie	BAL	29	110	0.306	7.72	0.340	0.004	0.004	0.347	197	4
Davis, Alvin	SEA	27	116	0.284	6.74	0.337	0.001	−0.001	0.336	26	12
Evans, Dwight	BOS	32	104	0.295	7.64	0.336	0.003	−0.007	0.332	39	11
Hrbek, Kent	MIN	27	107	0.311	5.93	0.333	0.002	−0.004	0.331	247	2
Ripken, Cal(8)	BAL	27	86	0.304	8.80	0.314	0.003	0.004	0.321	1	27
Gwynn, Tony	SDP	5	71	0.351	7.83	0.333	0.001	0.010	0.344	184	3
Hernandez, Keith	NYM	15	94	0.311	6.61	0.325	0.006	0.008	0.338	195	2
Cruz, Jose	HOU	12	95	0.312	7.31	0.318	0.002	0.012	0.333	53	8
Sandberg, Ryne(7)	CHC	19	84	0.314	7.83	0.316	0.004	−0.001	0.318	326	1

Player 1985	Team	HR	RBI	BA	WAR	GPA	GPA brc	GPA bpc	Total GPA	—MVP— Points	Rank
Brett, George	KCR	30	112	0.335	9.44	0.356	0.003	−0.001	0.358	274	2
Henderson, R.	NYY	24	72	0.314	8.80	0.327	0.021	0.002	0.350	174	3
Murray, Eddie	BAL	31	124	0.297	7.28	0.341	0.002	0.004	0.347	130	5
Mattingly, Don	NYY	35	145	0.324	7.49	0.339	0.002	0.002	0.343	367	1
Guerrero, Pedro	LAD	33	87	0.320	7.51	0.338	0.003	0.013	0.353	208	3
Herr, Tom	STL	8	110	0.302	9.35	0.328	0.009	0.005	0.343	119	5
McGee, Willie(4)	STL	10	82	0.353	8.05	0.322	0.011	0.005	0.338	280	1
Parker, Dave(7)	CIN	34	125	0.312	6.13	0.320	−0.006	0.004	0.318	220	2

Player 1986	Team	HR	RBI	BA	WAR	GPA	GPA brc	GPA bpc	Total GPA	—MVP— Points	Rank
Clemens, Roger	BOS	Pitcher Won			10.13	0.211	−0.002	−0.007	0.203	339	1
Boggs, Wade	BOS	8	71	0.357	8.80	0.351	0.000	−0.007	0.345	87	7
Mattingly, Don	NYY	31	113	0.352	6.72	0.326	0.004	0.002	0.332	258	2
Gibson, Kirk	DET	28	86	0.268	5.10	0.322	0.008	−0.000	0.330		
O'Brien, Pete	TEX	23	90	0.290	5.54	0.321	0.006	0.001	0.327	5	17
Schmidt, Mike	PHI	37	119	0.290	7.77	0.337	0.001	0.003	0.341	287	1
Raines, Tim	MON	9	62	0.334	6.68	0.307	0.018	0.005	0.330	99	6
Hernandez, Keith	NYM	13	83	0.310	5.60	0.319	0.001	0.007	0.327	179	4
Davis, Glenn(11)	HOU	31	101	0.265	4.31	0.292	0.002	0.013	0.307	231	2

Who Should Have Won the MVP Award?

Player 1987	Team	HR	RBI	BA	WAR	GPA	GPA brc	GPA bpc	Total GPA	—MVP— Points	Rank
Molitor, Paul	MIL	16	75	0.353	7.23	0.353	0.011	0.000	0.364	125	5
Evans, Dwight	BOS	34	123	0.305	6.83	0.353	0.003	−0.007	0.349	127	4
Trammell, Alan	DET	28	105	0.343	**8.68**	0.334	0.007	−0.001	0.340	311	2
Bell, George(7)	TOR	47	**134**	0.308	6.07	0.327	0.005	−0.003	0.329	**332**	1
Clark, Jack	STL	35	106	0.286	7.42	0.375	0.002	0.006	0.383	186	3
Strawberry, D.	NYM	39	104	0.284	**8.97**	0.366	0.008	0.008	0.381	95	6
Davis, Eric	CIN	37	100	0.293	8.11	0.353	0.014	0.004	0.370	73	9
Dawson, A. (20)	CHC	**49**	**137**	0.287	4.50	0.307	0.002	−0.001	0.308	269	1

Player 1988	Team	HR	RBI	BA	WAR	GPA	GPA brc	GPA bpc	Total GPA	—MVP— Points	Rank
Winfield, Dave	NYY	25	107	0.322	7.60	0.338	0.005	0.002	0.345	164	4
Canseco, Jose	OAK	**42**	**124**	0.307	**8.10**	0.331	0.001	0.007	0.339	392	1
Greenwell, Mike	BOS	22	119	0.325	8.04	0.344	0.002	−0.007	0.339	242	2
Brett, George	KCR	24	103	0.306	7.27	0.330	0.009	−0.001	0.338	29	12
Davis, Eric	CIN	26	93	0.273	6.71	0.315	0.014	0.004	0.333	14	13
Daniels, Kal	CIN	18	64	0.291	6.45	0.315	0.012	0.004	0.332		
McReynolds, Kev	NYM	27	99	0.288	6.17	0.306	0.011	0.008	0.325	162	3
Strawberry, D.(5)	NYM	**39**	101	0.269	6.35	0.315	0.001	0.007	0.323	236	2
Gibson, Kirk(7)	LAD	25	76	0.290	5.86	0.295	0.009	0.011	0.315	272	1
Larkin, Barry(14)	CIN	12	56	0.296	**6.85**	0.284	0.012	0.004	0.299		

Player 1989	Team	HR	RBI	BA	WAR	GPA	GPA brc	GPA bpc	Total GPA	—MVP— Points	Rank
Davis, Alvin	SEA	21	95	0.305	7.13	0.344	0.006	−0.000	0.349	2	23
Henderson, R.	NYY	12	57	0.274	7.57	0.315	0.014	0.006	0.335	67	9
Yount, Robin	MIL	21	103	0.318	**8.41**	0.325	0.005	0.002	0.333	256	1
Sierra, Ruben(5)	TEX	29	**119**	0.306	6.65	0.318	0.001	0.002	0.321	228	2
Clark, Will	SFG	23	111	0.333	**9.03**	0.356	0.005	0.008	0.368	225	2
Smith, Lonnie	ATL	21	79	0.315	7.38	0.351	0.001	−0.001	0.351	34	11
Mitchell, Kevin	SFG	**47**	**125**	0.291	8.05	0.341	−0.000	0.008	0.348	314	1
Davis, Eric	CIN	34	101	0.281	7.09	0.329	0.007	0.005	0.341	44	9

Player 1990	Team	HR	RBI	BA	WAR	GPA	GPA brc	GPA bpc	Total GPA	—MVP— Points	Rank
Henderson, R.	OAK	28	61	0.325	7.48	0.333	0.012	0.006	0.352	317	1
Fielder, Cecil	DET	**51**	**132**	0.277	6.53	0.333	0.001	−0.001	0.333	286	2
Brett, George	KCR	14	87	0.329	5.60	0.324	0.003	−0.001	0.326	60	7
Canseco, Jose	OAK	37	101	0.274	5.57	0.317	0.002	0.007	0.326	26	12
Bonds, Barry	PIT	33	114	0.301	8.29	0.349	0.009	0.002	0.360	331	1
Daniels, Kal	LAD	27	94	0.296	6.64	0.340	0.001	0.011	0.352	1	27
Sandberg, Ryne	CHC	40	100	0.306	**8.55**	0.329	0.005	−0.001	0.334	151	4
Bonilla, Bobby(29)	PIT	32	120	0.280	4.44	0.285	0.004	0.002	0.292	212	2

Player 1991	Team	HR	RBI	BA	WAR	GPA	GPA brc	GPA bpc	Total GPA	—MVP— Points	Rank
Thomas, Frank	CHW	32	109	0.318	8.63	0.347	0.002	0.004	0.353	181	3
Tartabull, Danny	KCR	31	100	0.316	6.89	0.348	0.005	−0.000	0.353	32	12
Canseco, Jose	OAK	44	122	0.266	7.39	0.326	0.005	0.007	0.339	145	4
Ripken, Cal(5)	BAL	34	114	0.323	**9.79**	0.326	0.006	0.004	0.336	318	1
Fielder, Cecil(11)	DET	**44**	**133**	0.261	6.38	0.323	0.001	−0.001	0.324	286	2

(Player 1991)	Team	HR	RBI	BA	WAR	GPA	GPA brc	GPA bpc	Total GPA	−MVP− Points	Rank
Bonds, Barry	PIT	25	116	0.292	8.68	0.352	0.009	0.002	0.364	259	2
Clark, Will	SFG	29	116	0.301	7.23	0.343	0.003	0.009	0.355	118	4
Sandberg, Ryne	CHC	26	100	0.291	**9.00**	0.334	0.006	−0.001	0.339	2	17
Pendleton, T.(10)	ATL	22	86	**0.319**	6.27	0.309	0.003	−0.000	0.311	274	1

Player 1992	*Team*	*HR*	*RBI*	*BA*	*WAR*	*GPA*	*GPA brc*	*GPA bpc*	*Total GPA*	*−MVP− Points*	*Rank*
Eckersley, Dennis	OAK	Pitcher	Won		4.66	0.162	0.003	0.008	0.173	306	1
Thomas, Frank	CHW	24	115	0.323	**8.37**	0.345	0.002	0.004	0.351	108	8
Tartabull, Danny	NYY	25	85	0.266	6.31	0.339	0.001	0.002	0.342		
McGwire, Mark	OAK	42	104	0.268	6.16	0.331	0.003	0.007	0.341	155	4
Puckett, Kirby(10)	MIN	19	110	0.329	7.36	0.315	0.003	−0.004	0.315	209	2
Bonds, Barry	PIT	34	103	0.311	**9.38**	0.365	0.008	0.003	0.376	**304**	1
Sheffield, Gary	SDP	33	100	**0.330**	8.40	0.336	−0.002	0.011	0.346	204	3
Daulton, Darren	PHI	27	**109**	0.270	8.96	0.338	0.003	0.003	0.344	100	6
Pendleton, T.(9)	ATL	21	105	0.311	7.24	0.311	0.004	−0.001	0.314	232	2

Player 1993	*Team*	*HR*	*RBI*	*BA*	*WAR*	*GPA*	*GPA brc*	*GPA bpc*	*Total GPA*	*−MVP− Points*	*Rank*
Thomas, Frank	CHW	41	128	0.317	**8.65**	0.368	0.003	0.004	0.375	392u	1
Olerud, John	TOR	24	107	**0.363**	8.37	0.370	0.000	−0.002	0.369	198	3
Hoiles, Chris	BAL	29	82	0.310	7.92	0.362	0.001	−0.001	0.362	10	16
Molitor, Paul(6)	TOR	22	111	0.332	7.80	0.336	0.009	−0.002	0.343	209	2
Bonds, Barry	SFG	*46*	123	0.336	**10.57**	0.385	0.003	0.005	0.393	272	1
Piazza, Mike	LAD	35	112	0.318	8.76	0.339	0.001	0.009	0.350	49	9
Daulton, Darren	PHI	24	105	0.257	8.88	0.337	0.006	−0.000	0.343	79	7
Dykstra, L.(13)	PHI	19	66	0.305	7.65	0.315	0.005	0.000	0.321	267	2

Player 1994s	*Team*	*HR*	*RBI*	*BA*	*WAR*	*GPA*	*GPA brc*	*GPA bpc*	*Total GPA*	*−MVP− Points*	*Rank*
Thomas, Frank	CHW	38	101	0.353	**7.99**	0.402	0.003	0.004	0.409	372	1
Belle, Albert	CLE	36	101	0.357	7.03	0.387	0.004	−0.001	0.391	225	3
O'Neill, Paul	NYY	21	83	**0.359**	5.84	0.371	0.003	0.002	0.377	150	5
Griffey, Ken	SEA	40	90	0.323	6.68	0.363	0.006	−0.002	0.367	233	2
Bagwell, Jeff	HOU	39	*116*	0.368	7.73	0.401	0.006	0.010	0.417	392u	1
Walker, Larry	MON	19	86	0.322	5.32	0.354	0.009	0.004	0.367	23	11
Mitchell, Kevin	CIN	30	77	0.326	4.45	0.356	0.003	0.001	0.360	86	9
Bonds, Barry	SFG	37	81	0.312	5.52	0.349	0.005	0.006	0.360	144	4
Williams, Matt(15)	SFG	*43*	96	0.267	4.20	0.316	−0.004	0.006	0.318	281	2

Player 1995s	*Team*	*HR*	*RBI*	*BA*	*WAR*	*GPA*	*GPA brc*	*GPA bpc*	*Total GPA*	*−MVP− Points*	*Rank*
Martinez, Edgar	SEA	29	113	**0.356**	**10.25**	0.400	0.003	−0.002	0.401	244	3
Salmon, Tim	CAL	34	105	0.330	8.73	0.377	0.002	0.001	0.381	110	7
Thomas, Frank	CHW	40	111	0.308	7.21	0.354	0.002	0.004	0.360	86	8
Belle, Albert	CLE	*50*	126	0.317	6.85	0.349	0.002	−0.001	0.350	300	2
Vaughn, Mo(14)	BOS	39	126	0.300	4.80	0.335	0.001	−0.007	0.328	**308**	1
Piazza, Mike	LAD	32	93	0.346	7.82	0.367	0.004	0.005	0.375	214	4
Bonds, Barry	SFG	33	104	0.294	**8.07**	0.360	0.005	0.004	0.369	21	12
Sanders, Reggie	CIN	28	99	0.306	6.72	0.359	0.004	−0.002	0.361	120	6
Gwynn, Tony	SDP	9	90	***0.368***	5.92	0.333	0.004	0.009	0.346	72	9
Larkin, Barry	CIN	15	66	0.319	7.43	0.326	0.019	0.000	0.345	**281**	1
Bichette, D.(22)	COL	40	*128*	0.340	3.87	0.340	−0.000	−0.036	0.304	251	2

Player 1996	Team	HR	RBI	BA	WAR	GPA	GPA brc	GPA bpc	Total GPA	−MVP− Points	Rank
McGwire, Mark	OAK	*52*	113	0.312	7.90	0.393	0.003	0.004	0.400	100	7
Martinez, Edgar	SEA	26	107	0.327	8.71	0.381	0.003	−0.002	0.382		
Thomas, Frank	CHW	40	134	0.349	8.03	0.374	0.004	0.003	0.382	88	8
Rodriguez, Alex	SEA	36	123	0.358	*10.94*	0.376	0.006	−0.002	0.380	287	2
Gonzalez, Juan	TEX	47	*144*	0.314	6.64	0.361	0.003	−0.004	0.360	290	1
Bonds, Barry	SFG	42	129	0.308	*11.34*	0.401	0.008	0.005	0.414	132	5
Sheffield, Gary	FLA	42	120	0.314	8.90	0.380	0.002	−0.002	0.380	112	6
Caminiti, Ken	SDP	40	130	0.326	8.87	0.365	0.002	0.005	0.373	392u	1
Bagwell, Jeff	HOU	31	120	0.315	7.92	0.354	0.005	0.009	0.368	59	9
Piazza, Mike	LAD	36	105	0.336	8.96	0.350	−0.000	0.007	0.357	237	2

Player 1997	Team	HR	RBI	BA	WAR	GPA	GPA brc	GPA bpc	Total GPA	−MVP− Points	Rank
Thomas, Frank	CHW	35	125	*0.347*	8.89	0.385	0.003	−0.004	0.384	172	3
Griffey, Ken	SEA	*56*	*147*	0.304	*9.37*	0.356	0.002	0.002	0.360	392u	1
Justice, David	CLE	33	101	0.329	6.91	0.359	−0.003	0.001	0.357	90	5
Martinez, T.(10)	NYY	44	141	0.296	5.46	0.327	0.002	0.001	0.330	248	2
Gwynn, Tony	SDP	17	119	*0.372*	9.30	0.376	0.000	0.009	0.385	113	6
Piazza, Mike	LAD	40	124	0.362	*10.69*	0.372	0.003	0.004	0.379	263	2
Walker, Larry	COL	*49*	130	0.366	8.95	0.397	0.010	−0.030	0.377	359	1
Bonds, Barry	SFG	40	101	0.291	8.94	0.355	0.008	0.006	0.370	123	5

Player 1998	Team	HR	RBI	BA	WAR	GPA	GPA brc	GPA bpc	Total GPA	−MVP− Points	Rank
Belle, Albert	CHW	49	152	0.328	8.37	0.360	0.002	−0.003	0.359	98	8
Williams, Bernie	NYY	26	97	*0.339*	7.09	0.345	0.004	0.001	0.350	103	7
Jeter, Derek(5)	NYY	19	84	0.324	*9.16*	0.335	0.008	0.002	0.344	180	3
Gonzalez, Juan(7)	TEX	45	*157*	0.318	6.73	0.346	0.004	−0.008	0.342	357	1
Garciaparra, N(16)	BOS	35	122	0.323	7.14	0.322	0.003	−0.004	0.321	232	2
McGwire, Mark	STL	*70*	147	0.299	*10.40*	0.404	0.002	−0.000	0.405	272	2
Bonds, Barry	SFG	37	122	0.303	9.25	0.365	0.002	0.006	0.373	66	8
Sosa, Sammy	CHC	66	*158*	0.308	8.56	0.362	0.001	−0.002	0.361	438	1
Bagwell, Jeff	HOU	34	111	0.304	6.74	0.345	0.006	0.003	0.354		

Player 1999	Team	HR	RBI	BA	WAR	GPA	GPA brc	GPA bpc	Total GPA	−MVP− Points	Rank
Ramirez, Manny	CLE	44	*165*	0.333	9.64	0.401	−0.000	0.002	0.402	226	3
Palmeiro, Rafael	TEX	47	148	0.324	8.58	0.382	0.001	−0.007	0.376	193	5
Alomar, Roberto	CLE	24	120	0.323	9.58	0.356	0.010	0.001	0.367	226	3
Jeter, Derek(7)	NYY	24	102	0.349	*10.21*	0.350	0.006	0.002	0.359	177	6
Rodriguez, I.(32)	TEX	35	113	0.332	5.49	0.306	0.004	−0.007	0.303	252	1
McGwire, Mark	STL	*65*	147	0.278	8.30	0.383	0.002	0.001	0.386	115	5
Bagwell, Jeff	HOU	42	126	0.304	8.60	0.372	0.002	0.004	0.378	276	2
Walker, Larry	COL	37	115	*0.379*	6.55	0.405	0.003	−0.030	0.377	35	10
Giles, Brian	PIT	39	115	0.315	8.53	0.371	0.004	−0.000	0.375	11	19
Jones, Chipper(7)	ATL	45	110	0.319	*8.78*	0.355	0.007	−0.000	0.361	432	1

Player 2000	Team	HR	RBI	BA	WAR	GPA	GPA brc	GPA bpc	Total GPA	−MVP− Points	Rank
Giambi, Jason	OAK	43	137	0.333	*10.66*	0.413	0.004	0.003	0.420	317	1
Ramirez, Manny	CLE	38	122	0.351	8.51	0.406	0.003	0.002	0.412	97	6
Delgado, Carlos	TOR	41	137	0.344	9.82	0.400	0.000	−0.001	0.400	206	4
Thomas, Frank(5)	CHW	43	143	0.328	8.83	0.378	−0.000	−0.003	0.375	285	2

(Player 2000)	Team	HR	RBI	BA	WAR	GPA	GPA brc	GPA bpc	Total GPA	—MVP— Points	Rank
Helton, Todd	COL	42	*147*	*0.372*	9.10	0.418	0.004	−0.030	0.392	198	5
Bonds, Barry	SFG	49	106	0.306	8.16	0.380	0.003	0.001	0.384	279	2
Sheffield, Gary	LAD	43	109	0.325	7.53	0.370	−0.000	0.003	0.373	71	9
Kent, Jeff	SFG	33	125	0.334	*9.55*	0.368	0.001	0.001	0.370	*392*	1
Piazza, Mike	NYM	38	113	0.324	8.18	0.362	0.003	0.004	0.369	271	3

Player 2001	Team	HR	RBI	BA	WAR	GPA	GPA brc	GPA bpc	Total GPA	—MVP— Points	Rank
Giambi, Jason	OAK	38	120	0.342	10.49	0.399	0.005	0.003	0.407	281	2
Alomar, Roberto	CLE	20	100	0.336	9.71	0.356	0.007	0.001	0.364	165	4
Thome, Jim	CLE	49	124	0.291	7.07	0.356	0.003	0.001	0.360	107	7
Suzuki, Ichiro(16)	SEA	8	69	*0.350*	6.41	0.313	0.009	0.007	0.328	*289*	1
Bonds, Barry	SFG	*73*	137	0.328	*13.57*	0.444	0.001	0.000	0.446	438	1
Sosa, Sammy	CHC	64	*160*	0.328	10.68	0.395	0.001	−0.003	0.393	278	2
Berkman, Lance	HOU	34	126	0.331	9.60	0.381	−0.002	−0.003	0.377	125	5
Gonzalez, Luis	ARI	57	142	0.325	9.12	0.372	0.001	−0.008	0.366	261	3

Player 2002	Team	HR	RBI	BA	WAR	GPA	GPA brc	GPA bpc	Total GPA	—MVP— Points	Rank
Ramirez, Manny	BOS	33	107	*0.349*	8.25	0.395	0.003	−0.003	0.395	39	9
Thome, Jim	CLE	52	118	0.304	8.45	0.382	0.001	0.001	0.384	69	7
Giambi, Jason	NYY	41	122	0.314	8.99	0.366	0.005	0.002	0.373	162	5
Rodriguez, Alex	TEX	*57*	*142*	0.300	10.25	0.351	0.004	−0.006	0.349	254	2
Tejada, Miguel(11)	OAK	34	131	0.308	8.94	0.325	0.003	0.003	0.333	*356*	1
Bonds, Barry	SFG	46	110	*0.370*	*13.79*	0.457	0.004	0.001	0.463	448u	1
Giles, Brian	PIT	38	103	0.298	8.74	0.369	0.002	0.001	0.372	27	13
Berkman, Lance	HOU	42	*128*	0.292	9.88	0.370	0.001	−0.002	0.369	181	3
Pujols, Albert(8)	STL	34	127	0.314	7.36	0.342	0.001	0.000	0.343	276	2

Player 2003 AL	Team	HR	RBI	BA	WAR	GPA	GPA brc	GPA bpc	Total GPA	—MVP— Points	Rank
Delgado, Carlos	TOR	42	*145*	0.302	8.56	0.369	0.003	−0.001	0.371	213	2
Posada, Jorge	NYY	30	101	0.281	7.91	0.339	0.001	0.002	0.342	194	3
Giambi, Jason	NYY	41	107	0.250	6.38	0.331	0.003	0.002	0.336	36	13
Rodriguez, Alex(8)	TEX	*47*	118	0.298	*8.73*	0.336	0.003	−0.006	0.333	242	1
Bonds, Barry	SFG	45	90	0.341	*10.14*	0.413	0.007	0.004	0.424	426	1
Sheffield, Gary	ATL	39	132	0.330	9.42	0.374	0.004	0.002	0.380	247	3
Pujols, Albert	STL	43	124	*0.359*	9.29	0.375	0.003	−0.000	0.378	303	2
Helton, Todd	COL	33	117	0.358	8.44	0.382	0.004	−0.015	0.371	75	7

Player 2004	Team	HR	RBI	BA	WAR	GPA	GPA brc	GPA bpc	Total GPA	—MVP— Points	Rank
Ramirez, Manny	BOS	43	130	0.308	7.44	0.358	−0.002	−0.004	0.353	238	3
Hafner, Travis	CLE	28	109	0.311	6.53	0.349	0.001	0.002	0.352	2	24
Mora, Melvin	BAL	27	104	0.340	7.85	0.344	0.005	0.003	0.352	5	18
Sheffield, Gary(8)	NYY	36	121	0.290	6.31	0.332	0.000	0.002	0.334	254	2
Tejada, Migue(12)	BAL	34	*150*	0.311	*8.56*	0.325	0.004	0.002	0.331	123	5
Guerrero, Vla(13)	ANA	39	126	0.337	5.91	0.322	0.004	0.003	0.329	*354*	1
Bonds, Barry	SFG	45	101	*0.362*	*14.57*	0.471	0.005	0.002	0.478	407	1
Edmonds, Jim	STL	42	111	0.301	8.39	0.363	0.002	−0.000	0.365	160	5
Pujols, Albert	STL	46	123	0.331	7.67	0.362	0.001	−0.001	0.363	247	3
Rolen, Scott	STL	34	124	0.314	7.94	0.362	0.001	−0.000	0.362	226	4
Beltre, Adrian(9)	LAD	*48*	121	0.334	7.63	0.336	0.005	0.004	0.344	311	2

Player 2005	Team	HR	RBI	BA	WAR	GPA	GPA brc	GPA bpc	Total GPA	−MVP− Points	Rank
Ortiz, David	BOS	47	*148*	0.300	9.42	0.372	0.002	−0.004	0.370	307	2
Rodriguez, Alex	NYY	48	130	0.321	*10.38*	0.362	0.004	0.003	0.369	*331*	1
Hafner, Travis	CLE	33	108	0.305	7.60	0.362	0.002	0.002	0.365	151	5
Giambi, Jason	NYY	32	87	0.271	6.63	0.358	0.002	0.003	0.363	5	18
Pujols, Albert	STL	41	117	0.330	7.32	0.346	0.005	−0.000	0.351	378	1
Giles, Brian	SDP	15	83	0.301	*7.73*	0.337	0.004	0.010	0.351	48	9
Lee, Derrek	CHC	46	107	*0.335*	7.08	0.347	0.004	−0.001	0.350	263	3
Jones, A.(22)	ATL	*51*	128	0.263	5.68	0.304	0.001	0.001	0.306	351	2

Player 2006	Team	HR	RBI	BA	WAR	GPA	GPA brc	GPA bpc	Total GPA	−MVP− Points	Rank
Hafner, Travis	CLE	42	117	0.308	7.82	0.377	0.001	0.002	0.380	64	8
Ortiz, David	BOS	54	137	0.287	8.07	0.359	0.003	−0.003	0.359	193	3
Jeter, Derek(7)	NYY	14	97	0.343	*9.58*	0.339	0.008	0.002	0.349	306	2
Morneau, J.(10)	MIN	34	130	0.321	5.62	0.339	0.000	−0.001	0.338	*320*	1
Pujols, Albert	STL	49	137	0.331	8.60	0.382	0.005	0.003	0.390	347	2
Howard, Ryan	PHI	*58*	*149*	0.313	8.84	0.377	0.002	0.001	0.380	*388*	1
Berkman, Lance	HOU	45	136	0.315	8.18	0.379	0.001	−0.003	0.378	230	3
Beltran, Carlos	NYM	41	116	0.275	8.96	0.366	0.005	0.004	0.375	211	4
Cabrera, Miguel	FLA	26	114	0.339	*9.37*	0.364	−0.001	0.006	0.369	170	5

Player 2007	Team	HR	RBI	BA	WAR	GPA	GPA brc	GPA bpc	Total GPA	−MVP− Points	Rank
Rodriguez, Alex	NYY	*54*	*156*	0.314	*11.60*	0.385	0.006	0.001	0.393	382	1
Ordonez, Magglio	DET	28	139	*0.363*	9.14	0.373	0.002	0.002	0.377	258	2
Ortiz, David	BOS	35	117	0.332	8.64	0.367	0.005	−0.003	0.369	177	4
Pena, Carlos	TBR	46	121	0.282	6.87	0.358	0.003	0.003	0.364	64	9
Jones, Chipper	ATL	29	102	0.337	7.66	0.352	0.003	0.002	0.356	107	6
Cabrera, Miguel	FLA	34	119	0.320	7.96	0.336	0.003	0.006	0.345	18	15
Utley, Chase	PHI	22	103	0.332	7.62	0.339	0.005	0.001	0.345	89	8
Fielder, Prince	MIL	*50*	119	0.288	6.12	0.341	0.000	−0.000	0.341	284	3
Holliday, Matt(6)	COL	36	137	*0.340*	6.67	0.347	0.002	−0.016	0.334	336	2
Rollins, J.(20)	PHI	30	94	0.296	*8.29*	0.308	0.010	0.001	0.319	*353*	1

Player 2008	Team	HR	RBI	BA	WAR	GPA	GPA brc	GPA bpc	Total GPA	−MVP− Points	Rank
Quentin, Carlos	CHW	36	100	0.288	6.12	0.341	0.005	−0.003	0.344	160	5
Youkilis, Kevin	BOS	29	115	0.312	5.97	0.341	0.001	−0.002	0.340	201	3
Bradley, Milton	TEX	22	77	0.321	5.27	0.344	−0.000	−0.006	0.338	9	17
Mauer, Joe(5)	MIN	9	85	0.328	*7.98*	0.329	0.003	−0.000	0.332	188	4
Morneau, Justin(6)	MIN	23	129	0.300	5.93	0.328	0.003	−0.000	0.330	257	2
Pedroia, D.(25)	BOS	17	83	0.326	6.16	0.300	0.005	−0.003	0.301	*317*	1
Pujols, Albert	STL	37	116	0.357	*8.57*	0.375	0.005	0.002	0.382	*369*	1
Ramirez, Manny	LAD*	37	121	0.332	8.43	0.360	0.006	0.000	0.365	138	4
Jones, Chipper	ATL	22	75	*0.364*	7.13	0.355	0.003	0.000	0.358	44	12
Howard, Ryan(12)	PHI	*48*	*146*	0.251	5.12	0.320	0.001	−0.001	0.320	308	2

Player 2009	Team	HR	RBI	BA	WAR	GPA	GPA brc	GPA bpc	Total GPA	−MVP− Points	Rank
Mauer, Joe	MIN	28	96	*0.365*	*9.12*	0.362	0.001	−0.001	0.362	*387*	1
Zobrist, Ben	TBR	27	91	0.297	7.28	0.339	0.002	0.003	0.344	34	8
Bay, Jason	BOS	36	119	0.267	6.81	0.341	0.006	−0.005	0.343	78	7
Youkilis, Kevin	BOS	27	94	0.305	6.15	0.343	0.004	−0.005	0.342	150	6
Teixeira, Mark(6)	NYY	39	*122*	0.292	5.86	0.332	0.002	−0.005	0.330	225	2

(Player 2009)	Team	HR	RBI	BA	WAR	GPA	GPA brc	GPA bpc	Total GPA	−MVP− Points	Rank
Pujols, Albert	STL	*47*	135	0.327	9.09	0.373	0.003	0.002	0.378	448u	1
Fielder, Prince	MIL	45	*141*	0.279	8.09	0.361	−0.000	−0.000	0.360	203	4
Votto, Joey	CIN	25	84	0.322	5.78	0.354	0.004	−0.004	0.354	4	22
Lee, Derrek	CHC	35	111	0.306	6.51	0.354	0.001	−0.001	0.353	66	9
Ramirez, Hanley	FLA	24	106	**0.342**	8.80	0.336	0.002	0.005	0.343	233	2

Player 2010	Team	HR	RBI	BA	WAR	GPA	GPA brc	GPA bpc	Total GPA	−MVP− Points	Rank
Hamilton, Josh	TEX	32	100	**0.359**	7.51	0.362	0.003	−0.007	0.358	358	1
Cabrera, Miguel	DET	38	*126*	0.328	7.53	0.357	0.000	0.001	0.358	262	2
Bautista, Jose	TOR	*54*	124	0.260	7.68	0.341	0.002	−0.002	0.340	165	4
Konerko, Paul	CHW	39	111	0.312	6.11	0.336	0.003	−0.003	0.336	130	5
Crawford, Carl	TBR	19	90	0.307	6.36	0.316	0.006	0.003	0.325	98	7
Choo, Shin-Soo	CLE	22	90	0.300	5.80	0.316	0.004	0.002	0.321	9	14
Cano, Robinson	NYY	29	109	0.319	*7.64*	0.323	0.003	−0.006	0.320	229	3
Votto, Joey	CIN	37	113	0.324	*8.02*	0.368	0.000	−0.003	0.365	443	1
Gonzalez, Adrian	SDP	31	101	0.298	7.23	0.332	0.003	0.011	0.346	197	4
Pujols, Albert	STL	42	*118*	0.312	6.90	0.332	0.006	0.002	0.340	279	2
Heyward, Jason	ATL	18	72	0.277	6.32	0.328	0.004	0.001	0.333	11	20
Utley, Chase	PHI	16	65	0.275	5.95	0.324	0.004	−0.001	0.327		
Gonzalez, Carlos	COL	34	117	0.336	6.18	0.335	0.003	−0.016	0.322	240	3

Player 2011	Team	HR	RBI	BA	WAR	GPA	GPA brc	GPA bpc	Total GPA	−MVP− Points	Rank
Verlander, Justin	DET	Pitcher	Won			0.211	−0.002	−0.007	0.203	280	1
Cabrera, Miguel	DET	30	105	*0.344*	8.88	0.361	0.005	0.001	0.367	193	5
Bautista, Jose	TOR	*43*	103	0.302	9.03	0.364	0.002	−0.002	0.364	231	3
Martinez, Victor	DET	12	103	0.330	7.10	0.336	0.003	0.001	0.339	7	16
Ellsbury, Jacoby	BOS	32	105	0.321	*9.15*	0.337	0.006	−0.005	0.338	242	2
Gonzalez, Adrian	BOS	27	117	0.338	6.69	0.333	0.003	−0.005	0.331	105	7
Braun, Ryan	MIL	33	111	0.332	8.26	0.351	0.008	−0.001	0.358	388	1
Kemp, Matt	LAD	39	*126*	0.324	*9.62*	0.342	0.006	0.005	0.353	332	2
Berkman, Lance	STL	31	94	0.301	6.98	0.348	−0.002	0.002	0.348	118	7
Fielder, Prince	MIL	38	120	0.299	7.42	0.345	0.002	−0.001	0.345	229	3
Votto, Joey	CIN	29	103	0.309	7.50	0.345	0.000	−0.003	0.342	135	6

Player 2012	Team	HR	RBI	BA	WAR	GPA	GPA brc	GPA bpc	Total GPA	−MVP− Points	Rank
Encarnacion, Edw	TOR	42	110	0.280	7.58	0.350	0.002	−0.002	0.350	33	11
Trout, Mike	ANA	30	83	0.326	*8.09*	0.328	0.015	0.003	0.345	281	2
Fielder, Prince	DET	30	108	0.313	6.70	0.333	0.003	0.001	0.336	56	9
Mauer, Joe	MIN	10	85	0.319	7.80	0.334	0.001	0.000	0.335	6	19
Cabrera, Miguel	DET	44	*139*	0.330	8.03	0.329	0.002	0.001	0.331	362	1
Hamilton, Josh	TEX	43	128	0.285	6.95	0.334	0.002	−0.006	0.330	127	5
Posey, Buster	SFG	24	103	0.336	8.17	0.333	0.004	0.002	0.339	422	1
Headley, Chase	SDP	31	*115*	0.286	*8.52*	0.322	0.006	0.010	0.338	127	5
Braun, Ryan	MIL	41	112	0.319	7.22	0.333	0.003	−0.001	0.335	285	2
Stanton, G.	MIA	37	86	0.290	5.07	0.329	0.005	−0.003	0.331	7	24
McCutchen, A.	PIT	31	96	0.327	7.74	0.333	−0.004	0.001	0.330	245	3

GPA and Free Agency

Gross Productivity Average can be a useful tool at a number of points along the free-agency pathway.

When a top prospect is drafted by a team, he must sign a contract with that team in a designated period of time. The drafted player has some leverage because the team will lose the right to sign him after this time is up. Many high baseball draft picks never become good major league players, so the player's future worth is uncertain. These factors keep salaries low during the first few years of a player's career relative to the salaries of more experienced big leaguers. If he quickly becomes a star player, he has little leverage to renegotiate his contract during the first three years.

Once a player has three years of major league service he becomes eligible for arbitration. The 17 percent of players with at least two years but less than three years of major league service who have the most time in the major leagues may also be eligible for arbitration.

Once an arbitration-eligible player's contract expires, his team can either offer him binding arbitration, in which the team and player each submit a salary table and an arbiter chooses one, or decline to offer arbitration and instead grant the player unrestricted free-agent status. Approximately 90 percent of players and teams agree on a salary before the arbitration process is complete.

Once a player has been in the major leagues for six or more years, he becomes an unrestricted free agent when his contract expires. His team can offer him binding arbitration, but the player can decline and his team will receive compensation in the form of draft picks if he is a top free agent and signs with another team. If the player declines arbitration, he can negotiate with the club only until January 7, after which no further negotiation can take place until May 1, well after the next season starts.

The actual draft picks given in compensation depend on where the club signing the free agent will pick in the amateur draft and the rank of the free agent.

The 2007–2011 basic agreement describes a document entitled "A Statistical System for the Ranking of Players," which is used to evaluate a player's performance over the previous two years, but the formula in this document has not been disclosed. (See page 73 of the agreement for the reference.) Some of the details have been leaked over the years including the information in Table 24.1, which was first reported by Keith Law of the MLB Trade Rumors site in 2007.

Group	Criteria Used to Rank Players
1B, OF, DH	PA, BA, OBP, HR, RBI
2B, 3B, SS	PA, BA, OBP, HR, RBI, Fielding Percentage, Total Fielding Chances
C	PA, BA, OBP, HR, RBI, Fielding Percentage, Assists
Starting P	Games (starts + 0.5 × relief appearances), Innings Pitched, Wins, Win/Loss ratio, ERA, SO
Relief P	Games (2 × starts + relief appearances), Innings Pitched, Wins + Saves, IP/H ratio, K/BB ratio, ERA

Table 24.1. Position-based criteria used to rank free agent players.

The Elias Sports Bureau uses this secret formula to rank all players, including those who are not free agents, on a scale of 0 to 100 at their position and within their league. The top 20 percent of players at each position are classified as "Type A" free agents, and their former teams get two draft picks as compensation when they sign with another team. The top 21–40 percent are "Type B" free agents, and their former teams get one draft pick as compensation. No compensation is given to the former teams of players ranking in the 41st to 100th percentiles.

How accurate are the Elias rankings? All NL outfielders and first basemen with at least 400 PAs over two years are shown with their Elias rank plotted against their tGPA (including baserunning and ballpark corrections) in Figure 15. The Elias rankings do not accurately reflect a player's production as measured by tGPA. The R^2 (again, a statistical measure of how well the regression line approximates the real data points, with 0.0 denoting that it does not explain any variation and 1.0 denoting that it perfectly explains the observed variation) of 0.65 indicates that the regression line fits the data moderately well. The Elias rankings for 2008 to 2009 for other position players show a similar pattern.

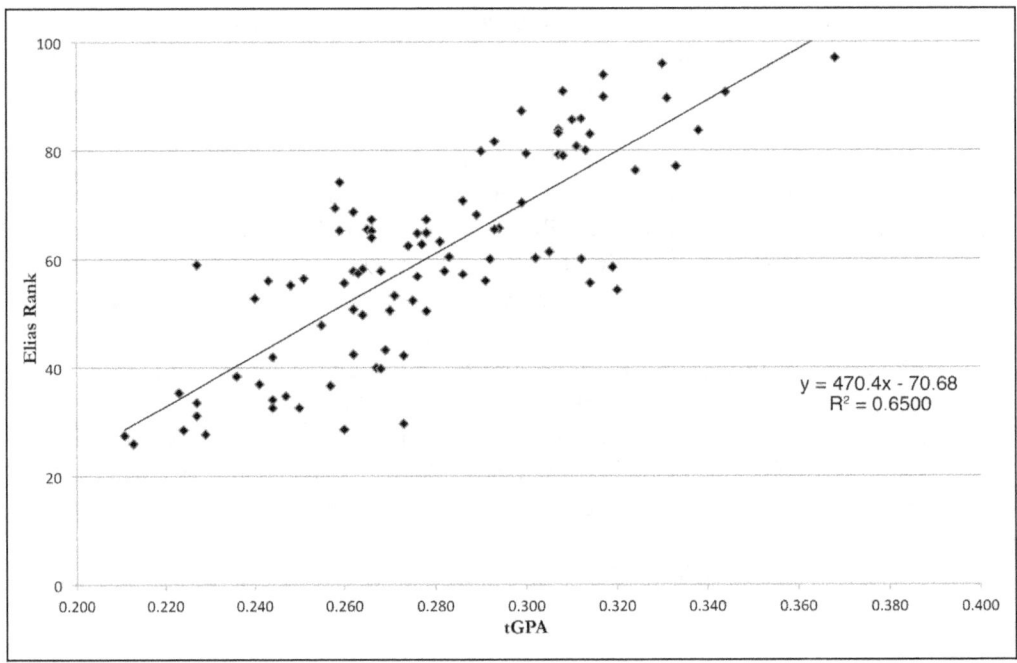

Figure 15. Elias Rank vs. tGPA for the NL outfielder and first baseman position group. Only players with 400 or more PAs from 2008 to 2009 are shown. Elias rank from usatoday.com.

GPA and Free Agency

Considering only players who have at least 400 PAs over two years sets a low standard for eliminating fringe players. Using this standard, the Elias rankings classify 26 of 128 (20.3 percent) players as Type A free agents and 24 of 128 (18 percent) players as Type B free agents.

A tGPA of 0.300 to 0.368 would include the top 26 players among NL outfielders and first baseman. A total GPA of 0.273 to 0.299 would include the next 24 players in this position group.

Table 24.2 shows the top players and the 26 players misclassified (based on tGPA) using the Elias rankings. The most glaring misclassifications include Hunter Pense, who was identified as a Type A free agent but should have been an uncompensated free agent, and Jim Thome and Andrew McCutchen, who were uncompensated free agents and should have been Type A free agents.

Player	Elias Rank		tGPA	Player	Elias Rank		tGPA
Pujols, Albert	97.037	A	0.368	Loney, James	65.185	B ?x	0.266
Holliday, Matt	95.960	A	0.330	Rowand, Aaron	63.939	B ?x	0.266
Braun, Ryan	93.939	A	0.317	Smith, Seth	61.313	B ?A	0.305
Lee, Carlos	90.909	A	0.308	Coghlan, Chris	60.202	B ?A	0.302
Ramirez, Manny	90.707	A	0.344	Delgado, Carlos	60.000	B ?A	0.312
Ethier, Andre	87.273	A ?B	0.299	Francoeur, Jeff	58.990	B ?x	0.227
Kemp, Matt	81.616	A ?B	0.293	Johnson, Nick	58.519	B ?A	0.319
Victorino, Shane	79.798	A ?B	0.290	Headley, Chase	58.182	B ?x	0.264
Votto, Joey	77.037	A	0.333	Spilborghs, Ryan	57.778	B	0.282
Pence, Hunter	74.141	A ?x	0.259	Infante, Omar	57.172	B	0.286
Willingham, Josh	70.707	A ?B	0.286	Pagan, Angel	55.960	x ?B	0.291
Helton, Todd	70.370	A ?B	0.299	Thome, Jim	55.556	x ?A	0.314
Schumaker, Skip	69.394	B ?x	0.258	McCutchen, A.	54.242	x ?A	0.320
Soriano, Alfonso	68.687	B ?x	0.262	Harris, Willie	52.323	x ?B	0.275
Giles, Brian	67.273	B ?x	0.266	Garko, Ryan	50.370	x ?B	0.278
Anderson, Garret	65.455	B ?x	0.265	Murphy, Dan	42.222	x ?B	0.273
Hart, Corey	65.253	B ?x	0.259	Ishikawa, Travis	29.630	x ?B	0.273

Table 24.2. Select players from the 2008 to 2009 Elias NL outfielder and first baseman position group. ("A" indicates a Type A free agent, "B" a Type B free agent and "x" an uncompensated free agent.)

All starting AL pitchers with at least 400 batters faced over two years are shown with their Elias rank plotted against their tGPA (including baserunning and ballpark corrections) in Figure 16. The Elias rankings do not accurately reflect a pitcher's production as measured by tGPA. An R^2 of 0.5716 indicates that the regression line fits the data moderately well.

As with the NL outfielders and first basemen, the inclusion criteria — all pitchers must have faced at least 400 batters over two years — sets a very low standard for eliminating fringe players. Using this standard, the Elias rankings classify 19 of 95 (20.0 percent) players as Type A free agents and 19 of 95 (20.0 percent) as Type B free agents.

A tGPA of 0.212 to 0.249 would include the top 17 AL starting pitchers, and a tGPA of 0.250 to 0.260 would include the next 17 best. Table 24.3 shows the top AL pitchers and the 25 who were misclassified (based on tGPA) by the Elias rankings. The most glaring misclassification was Brad Bergesen, who was an uncompensated free agent and should have been Type A free agent.

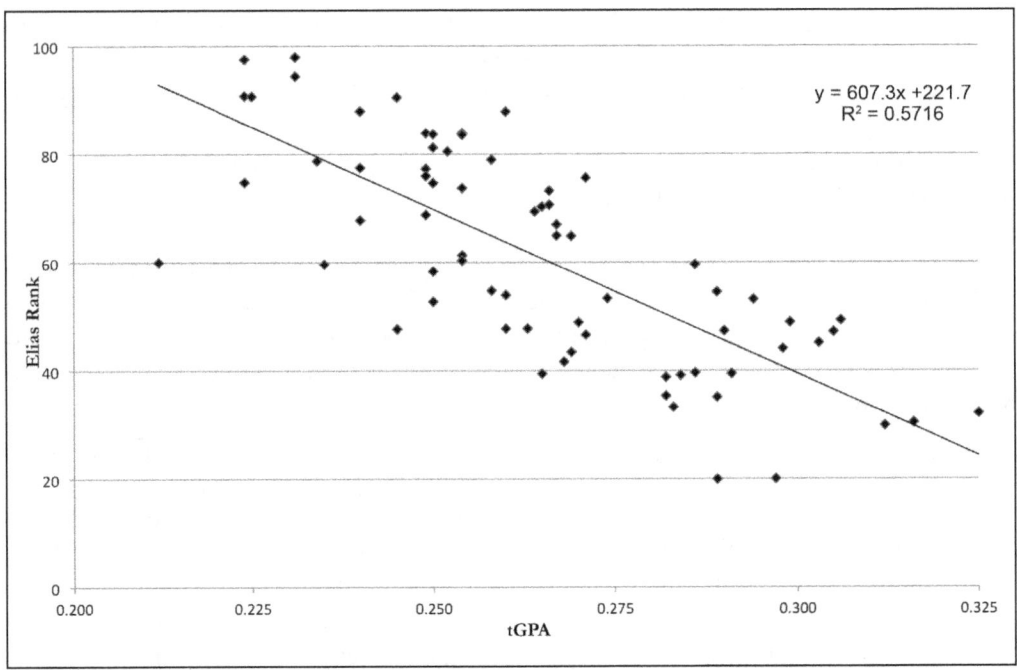

Figure 16. Elias Rank vs. tGPA for AL starting pitchers. Only players with 400 or more batters faced from 2008 to 2009 are shown. Elias rank from usatoday.com.

Major League Baseball and the MLB Players Association agreed to these rankings, but the results are embarrassingly poor. From the "Run Production" chapter we know that GPA correlates tightly with run production ($R^2 = 0.9913$). Slugging average ($R^2 = 0.8389$), OBP ($R^2 = 0.7238$) and BA ($R^2 = 0.5671$) have a moderate correlation with production. The accuracy of the Elias rankings falls somewhere between that of OBP and BA. Using OBP instead of the Elias formula would more accurately reflect a player's offensive production.

Player	Elias Rank			tGPA	Player	Elias Rank			tGPA
Sabathia, C.C.	97.961	A		0.231	Chamberlain, J.	70.656	B	?x	0.266
Holliday, Roy	97.518	A		0.224	Slowey, Kevin	70.301	B	?x	0.265
Hernandez, Felix	94.415	A		0.231	Blackburn, Nick	69.415	B	?x	0.264
Greinke, Zack	90.780	A		0.224	Wakefield, Tim	68.794	B	?A	0.249
Lester, Jon	90.691	A		0.225	Bedard, Erik	67.819	B	?A	0.240
Baker, Scott	90.514	A		0.245	Guthrie, Jeremy	67.021	B	?x	0.267
Saunders, Joe	83.865	A	?B	0.254	Feldman, Scott	64.982	B	?x	0.267
Verlander, Justin	83.688	A	?B	0.250	Meche, Gil	64.894	B	?x	0.269
Santana, Ervin	83.599	A	?B	0.254	Duchscherer, J.	60.018	B	?A	0.212
Buehrle, Mark	81.206	A	?B	0.250	Marcum, Shaun	59.663	B	?A	0.235
Shields, James	80.496	A	?B	0.252	Pavano, Carl	59.663	B	?x	0.286
Floyd, Gavin	78.989	A	?B	0.258	Washburn, Jarrod	54.787	x	?B	0.258
Matsuzaka, D.	78.723	A		0.234	Romero, Ricky	53.989	x	?B	0.260
Pettitte, Andy	75.621	B	?x	0.271	Porcello, Rick	52.748	x	?B	0.250
Peavy, Jake	74.823	B	?A	0.224	Anderson, Brett	47.784	x	?B	0.260
Millwood, Kevin	73.227	B	?x	0.266	Bergesen, Brad	47.695	x	?A	0.245

Table 24.3. Select pitchers from the 2008 to 2009 Elias AL starting pitcher position group.

Switching to GPA would provide a much more accurate measurement of offensive production, take baserunning into account and correct for the effects of playing in different ballparks. The GPA formula would not be a secret and the results would be easy to understand.

Although GPA does not take into account the number of PAs or a player's defensive skills, it could be adjusted slightly to take both of these factors into account if MLB or the Players Association felt it was needed (see the "GPA and Wins Above Replacement" chapter). Adding inaccurate measures of defensive skill to a GPA-based formula could make the GPA formula a less accurate measure of overall player skill, however.

Position players with the most expensive free-agent contracts of all time, by average annual value, are listed in Table 24.4, along with their performances in the three years prior to the new contracts. (The contract details in this table and Table 24.5 are from a January 2012 Baseball Prospectus article by Jeff Euston.) Seven players had tGPAs of 0.302 or less and appear to have been overpaid. In Table 24.5, data on the performance of these players and their teams is presented.

None of the seven players significantly improved his performance after signing the new contract, and two of them, Andruw Jones and Alfonso Soriano, performed significantly worse.

Player	Years	BA	GPA	GPA brc	GPA bpc	Total GPA	Average Salary
Rodriguez, Alex	2005–2007	0.309	0.357	0.004	0.004	0.365	$27.5
Rodriguez, Alex	1998–2000	0.305	0.341	0.006	0.002	0.349	$25.2
Howard, Ryan	2007–2009	0.266	0.326	0.001	−0.001	0.326	$25.0
Pujols, Albert	2009–2011	0.313	0.335	0.004	0.001	0.340	$24.0
Mauer, Joe	2007–2009	0.332	0.336	0.003	0.001	0.340	$23.0
Ramirez, Manny	2006–2008	0.317	0.340	0.003	−0.002	0.341	$22.5
Teixeira, Mark	2006–2008	0.298	0.332	0.004	−0.003	0.334	$22.5
Gonzalez, Ad.	2009–2011	0.306	0.330	0.002	0.005	0.337	$22.0
Braun, Ryan	2009–2011	0.318	0.330	0.006	−0.001	0.336	$21.0
Crawford, Carl	2008–2010	0.297	0.294	0.008	0.003	0.305	$20.3
Ramirez, Manny	1998–2000	0.324	0.378	0.002	−0.002	0.378	$20.0
Kemp, Matt	2009–2011	0.290	0.302	0.003	0.004	0.308	$20.0
Cabrera, Miguel	2005–2007	0.327	0.339	0.001	0.000	0.341	$19.0
Jeter, Derek	1998–2000	0.337	0.338	0.007	0.004	0.349	$18.9
Jones, Andruw	2005–2007	0.249	0.290	0.002	0.009	0.302	$18.1
Bonds, Barry	1998–2000	0.293	0.365	0.004	−0.002	0.367	$18.0
Howard, Ryan	2006–2008	0.277	0.343	0.002	−0.001	0.343	$18.0
Hunter, Torii	2005–2007	0.279	0.279	0.005	0.001	0.285	$18.0
Sosa, Sammy	1998–2001	0.305	0.355	−0.001	−0.008	0.346	$18.0
Suzuki, Ichiro	2005–2007	0.327	0.285	0.011	−0.001	0.294	$18.0
Wells, Vernon	2005–2007	0.273	0.282	0.003	−0.001	0.283	$18.0
Werth, Jason	2004–2006	0.247	0.277	0.006	0.003	0.286	$18.0
Reyes, Jose	2009–2011	0.306	0.274	0.009	0.003	0.285	$17.7
Giambi, Jason	1999–2001	0.330	0.388	0.004	−0.006	0.385	$17.1
Bagwell, Jeff	1999–2001	0.301	0.364	0.003	−0.002	0.365	$17.1
Beltran, Carlos	2002–2004	0.281	0.318	0.008	−0.001	0.324	$17.0
Delgato, Carlos	1998–2000	0.303	0.350	0.001	−0.001	0.351	$17.0
Soriano, Alfons	2004–2006	0.275	0.294	0.005	−0.001	0.299	$17.0

Table 24.4. Highest-paid position players in MLB history by average annual value. Average Salary is for the new contract that began after the years listed.

Vernon Wells appears to be the most overpaid of the players listed. Wells's production is slightly above average, yet the Blue Jays are paying him $18.0 million annually. During the period from 2005 to 2007, there were 102 players with tGPAs of at least 0.283 and at least 1,000 PAs. Many of these players could have been signed for far less than $18.0 million per year. Wells's salary represented 21.0 percent of the Blue Jays' payroll from 2008 to 2010, a clear misallocation of team resources. The Yankees had a league leading $208.0 annual payroll, and the Red Sox a $141.1 million annual payroll from 2008 to 2010. To compete against division rivals with far more resources, the Blue Jays needed to allocate their limited resources more wisely.

From 2008 to 2010, the Blue Jays' offense had a tGPA of 0.267 and their pitchers had a tGPA of 0.257. From the "Winning Games" chapter we know a net tGPA of +0.010 should result in an average of 85.4 wins per season. The Blue Jays actually won 86, 75 and 85 games during this period and finished in fourth place within their division each year.

Player	Years	BA	GPA	GPA brc	GPA bpc	Total GPA	Average Salary
Jones, Andruw	2005–2007	0.249	0.290	0.002	0.009	0.302	$13.5
	2008–2009	0.260	0.264	0.002	−0.003	0.264	$18.1
LA Dodgers	2008	0.264	0.255	0.004	0.004	0.263	$118.6
Hunter, Torii	2005–2007	0.279	0.279	0.005	0.001	0.285	$10.2
	2008–2010	0.285	0.294	0.001	0.002	0.297	$18.0
LA Angels	2008–2010	0.277	0.277	0.003	−0.001	0.278	$118.0
Suzuki, Ichiro	2005–2007	0.327	0.285	0.011	−0.001	0.294	$12.5
	2008–2010	0.325	0.276	0.007	0.007	0.290	$18.0
Seattle	2008–2010	0.262	0.248	0.002	−0.001	0.250	$102.6
Wells, Vernon	2005–2007	0.273	0.282	0.003	−0.001	0.283	$5.4
	2008–2010	0.275	0.270	0.002	−0.001	0.270	$18.0
Toronto	2008–2010	0.265	0.264	0.003	−0.001	0.267	$85.7
Soriano, A.	2004–2006	0.275	0.294	0.005	−0.001	0.299	$7.6
	2007–2010	0.271	0.278	0.001	−0.001	0.278	$17.0
Chicago Cubs	2007–2010	0.268	0.269	0.002	−0.008	0.262	$124.3
Lee, Carlos	2004–2006	0.290	0.300	0.004	−0.002	0.302	$7.7
	2007–2010	0.289	0.289	0.001	−0.003	0.287	$16.7
Houston	2007–2010	0.261	0.256	0.002	−0.002	0.255	$93.1
Young, Michael	2006–2008	0.304	0.292	0.005	−0.001	0.295	$4.3
	2009–2010	0.322	0.293	0.002	−0.006	0.290	$16.0
Texas	2009–2010	0.260	0.270	0.004	−0.006	0.268	$66.5

Table 24.5. The most overpaid players according to tGPA. Average Salary is for the period listed. Data through 2010.

Torii Hunter appears to be the second-most overpaid of the players listed. Hunter's production is above average, but not at a level that would justify the $18.0 million annually the Angels agreed to pay him. During the period from 2005 to 2007, there were 98 players with comparable tGPAs (all at least 0.285 and at least 1000 Pas), and many of these players could have been signed for far less than $18.0 million per year. Hunter's salary represented 15.2 percent of the Angels' payroll. The Angels had the eighth highest payroll in MLB, which allowed them to overcome this misallocation of team resources. It also helped that the other teams in the AL West had lower payrolls than the Angels during this period.

From 2008 to 2010, the Angels' offense had a tGPA of 0.278 and their pitchers' had a tGPA of 0.261. From the "Winning Games" chapter we know a net tGPA of +0.017 should result in an average of 89.6 wins per season. The Angels actually won 100, 97 and 80 games during this period and finished in first place within their division twice.

One of the most overrated players in the game, according to tGPA, has been Ichiro Suzuki in his time with the Mariners. Suzuki had a tGPA of 0.328 during his MVP season of 2001, which trailed league leader Jason Giambi's total GPA of 0.407 by 0.079 GPA points, the second-largest margin from 1952 to 2012. Suzuki's baserunning skills and the value of his hits are consistently overrated by both his team and the writers who vote for the MVP Award. Although he strikes out less often and hits into fewer double plays than the average player, his production from walks and extra base hits is substantially below average.

	Ichiro Suzuki 2001–2011			*MLB Average 2001–2011*		
	aGPA	× FracPA	= GPA	aGPA	× FracPA	= GPA
Any Out	0.005	0.6190	0.003	−0.016	0.6621	−0.011
Strike Out	−0.001	0.0928	−0.000	−0.017	0.1722	−0.003
Double/Tr Play	−0.538	0.0117	−0.006	−0.560	0.0242	−0.014
Walk	0.538	0.0618	0.033	0.572	0.0851	0.049
HBP/Interference	0.603	0.0058	0.004	0.608	0.0094	0.006
Error	0.727	0.0119	0.009	0.776	0.0093	0.007
Any Hit	0.778	0.3015	0.235	0.913	0.2342	0.214
Single	0.695	0.2458	0.171	0.731	0.1551	0.113
Double	0.962	0.0347	0.033	1.038	0.0472	0.049
Triple	1.274	0.0092	0.012	1.325	0.0049	0.006
Home Run	1.587	0.0118	0.019	1.666	0.0270	0.045
Extra Base Hit	1.146	0.0557	0.064	1.270	0.0791	0.100
Total	0.283	1.0000	0.283	0.265	1.0000	0.265

Table 24.6. Ichiro Suzuki's production by event compared with the major league average from 2001 to 2011.

The Seattle Mariners' five-year, $90.0 million contract with Suzuki represented a poor allocation of team resources. During the period from 2005 to 2007, there were 72 players with comparable tGPAs (at least 0.294 and at least 1000 PAs), many of whom could have been signed for less than $18.0 million per year. Suzuki's salary represented 17.6 percent of the Seattle payroll from 2008 to 2010. The Mariners had the ninth-highest payroll in MLB but were not able to overcome this and other misallocations of their resources.

From 2008 to 2010, the Mariners' offense had a tGPA of 0.250 and their pitchers' had a tGPA of 0.266. From the "Winning Games" chapter we know a net tGPA of −0.016 should result in an average of 70.0 wins per season. The Mariners actually won 61, 85 and 61 games during this period and finished in third or fourth place within their division each year.

Pitchers with the most expensive free agent contracts by average annual value are listed in Table 24.7 along with their performance in the three years leading up to their new contract. Five had tGPAs of 0.250 or higher and appear to have been overpaid. Each of these pitchers is listed in Table 24.8 along with their performance and their team's performance through 2010.

Player	Years	ERA	BA	GPA	GPA brc	GPA bpc	Total GPA	Average Salary
Clemens, Roger	2004–2006	2.40	0.210	0.210	0.001	−0.002	0.209	$28.0
Sabathia, C.C.	2009–2011	3.18	0.242	0.233	0.001	−0.006	0.228	$24.4
Lee, Cliff	2008–2010	2.98	0.255	0.226	0.001	0.001	0.228	$24.0
Sabathia, C.C.	2006–2008	3.03	0.247	0.230	0.000	−0.002	0.228	$23.0
Santana, Johan	2005–2007	2.99	0.217	0.225	−0.000	0.001	0.226	$22.9
Clemens, Roger	2003–2005	2.92	0.221	0.223	0.001	−0.000	0.224	$22.0
Halladay, Roy	2008–2010	2.78	0.247	0.222	0.002	−0.000	0.224	$20.0
Zambrano, C.	2005–2007	3.54	0.218	0.245	−0.001	−0.009	0.235	$18.3
Zito, Barry	2004–2006	4.05	0.247	0.257	0.000	−0.007	0.250	$18.0
Peavy, Jake	2007–2009	2.83	0.217	0.218	0.002	−0.002	0.218	$17.3
Weaver, Jered	2009–2011	3.03	0.226	0.224	0.000	0.002	0.227	$17.0
Burnett, A.J.	2006–2008	3.94	0.242	0.249	0.005	−0.000	0.254	$16.5
Lackey, John	2007–2009	3.48	0.259	0.241	0.003	−0.002	0.243	$16.5
Verlander, Justin	2007–2009	3.95	0.243	0.252	−0.000	−0.004	0.247	$16.0
Schmidt, Jason	2004–2006	3.67	0.227	0.243	0.003	−0.002	0.244	$15.7
Hernandez, F.	2007–2009	3.23	0.255	0.236	0.003	−0.001	0.238	$15.6
Wilson, C.J.	2009–2011	3.09	0.226	0.233	0.003	−0.006	0.231	$15.5
Hampton, M	1998–2000	3.12	0.253	0.239	0.000	0.003	0.242	$15.1
Lowe, Derek	2006–2008	3.58	0.254	0.248	0.001	−0.007	0.241	$15.0
Rivera, Mariano	2005–2007	2.08	0.215	0.198	0.002	0.004	0.203	$15.0
Oswalt, Roy	2004–2006	3.14	0.262	0.234	−0.001	−0.001	0.232	$14.6
Buehrle, Mark	2005–2007	3.87	0.278	0.257	−0.001	−0.001	0.254	$14.0
Halladay, Roy	2005–2007	3.20	0.251	0.227	0.002	−0.002	0.228	$13.3
Dempster, Ryan	2006–2008	3.69	0.237	0.247	0.004	−0.010	0.241	$13.0
Carpenter, Chris	2005–2007	3.01	0.234	0.226	−0.002	−0.011	0.213	$12.7
Arroyo, B.	2006–2008	4.05	0.267	0.260	−0.001	−0.007	0.253	$12.5
Millwood, K.	2003–2005	3.83	0.257	0.249	0.004	−0.001	0.253	$12.0

Table 24.7. Highest-paid pitchers in MLB history by average annual value. Average Salary is for the contract that began after the years listed.

Player	Years	ERA	BA	GPA	GPA brc	GPA bpc	Total GPA	Average Salary
Zito, Barry	2004–2006	4.05	0.247	0.257	0.000	−0.007	0.250	$5.5
	2007–2010	4.56	0.254	0.270	−0.000	−0.002	0.268	$18.0
San Francisco	2007–2010	4.04	0.252	0.255	0.003	−0.002	0.256	$86.4
Burnett, A.J.	2006–2008	3.94	0.242	0.249	0.005	−0.000	0.254	$9.5
	2009–2010	4.04	0.247	0.255	0.005	0.003	0.263	$16.5
NY Yankees	2009–2010	4.26	0.251	0.263	0.003	0.002	0.269	$207.4
Buehrle, Mark	2005–2007	3.87	0.278	0.257	−0.001	−0.001	0.254	$7.8
	2008–2010	3.81	0.278	0.252	−0.002	0.000	0.250	$14.0
Chi. White Sox	2008–2010	4.10	0.261	0.259	0.003	−0.001	0.262	$106.8
Arroyo, B.	2006–2008	4.05	0.267	0.260	−0.001	−0.007	0.253	$3.9
	2009–2010	3.84	0.256	0.253	−0.001	−0.003	0.249	$12.5
Cincinnati	2009–2010	4.18	0.258	0.261	−0.000	−0.003	0.257	$74.9
Millwood, K.	2003–2005	3.83	0.257	0.249	0.004	−0.001	0.253	$9.3
	2006–2009	4.57	0.284	0.269	0.003	−0.006	0.267	$12.0
Texas	2006–2009	4.77	0.275	0.278	0.002	−0.001	0.279	$68.1

Table 24.8. The most overpaid pitchers according to tGPA. Average Salary is for the period and listed in millions.

During the three years before their new contracts were signed, all five pitchers had similar (slightly above average) production, and none improved significantly during his new contract. Barry Zito and Kevin Millwood each performed significantly worse.

From 2003 to 2009 there were on average 54 pitchers each year who had tGPAs of 0.254 or lower and at least 1000 batters faced during the preceding three years. Many of these pitchers could have been signed for far less than $12.0 to $18.0 million per year.

Millwood's salary represented 17.6 percent of the Rangers' payroll. Texas had one of the lowest payrolls in MLB and could not afford to misallocate their limited resources. From 2007 to 2009 the Rangers won 75, 79 and 87 games and finished second to fourth in their division. It was not until Millwood was traded before the 2010 season that they freed up enough resources to win 90 games and win their division.

A.J. Burnett's salary represented 8.0 percent of the Yankees payroll from 2009 to 2010. Although his production was perhaps average, the Yankees have the resources to overpay for players and still make the playoffs almost every year. Most teams could not justify $16.5 million per year for Burnett's production, but for the Yankees the cost may have been acceptable.

GPA could be a useful tool for setting a player's salary. Most of a player's production is represented by his tGPA. Defense and other intangibles represent a much smaller portion of most players' production. His tGPA can be used to calculate WAR and take into account both the number of PAs and the defensive positions played when calculating a player's value to the team (see the "GPA and Wins Above Replacement" chapter).

Salary disputes might be settled before going to arbitration, and cases in arbitration more fairly and objectively decided, if tGPA were the main measure of productivity. Players could be compared to other players at their positions and to players who have a similar level of experience. Either tGPA or WAR calculated from tGPA would provide an objective guide for teams signing free-agent players.

Ideally, players would be paid according to production, with, a substantial portion of each player's salary determined by his productivity during the past season. But in the real world, both owners and players would have objections to this system.

Star players would be reluctant to give up their large guaranteed contracts. Even if a fixed pool of money were allocated to the players, the Players Association might object because it could slow the rising salaries of the players.

Owners of poorer teams, moreover, would be concerned by unexpectedly high salary awards. This objection could be overcome if the productivity awards were paid out of a pool of money derived from revenue sharing. Poorer teams might then be better able to compete, but richer teams might object to the loss of some of their economic advantage.

Finally, the value of a player may not be the same to every team. The Padres' 2010 Opening Day payroll of $37.8 million was the lowest in MLB that year, and their batters' tGPA of 0.245 was likewise a major league low from 2008 to 2009. If the Padres had signed Albert Pujols, who had a career tGPA of 0.353, the team tGPA might have risen to 0.257 (($0.245 \times 8 + 0.353) / 9$). Alternatively, the Padres could have achieved the same offensive boost by signing two players with tGPAs of 0.299 or three players with tGPAs of 0.281. Either option would likely have been far cheaper than signing Pujols to a contract of $25.0 million or more per year. From the "GPA and Winning Games" chapter, we know an increase of 0.012 in team net tGPA will result in an average increase of 7.1 wins per season.

The Yankees' 2010 Opening Day payroll of $213.4 million, on the other hand, was the highest in baseball that year, and their tGPA of 0.288 led MLB from 2008 to 2009. If the

Yankees had signed Albert Pujols, their tGPA might have risen to 0.295 ((0.288 × 8 + 0.353) / 9). As in the previous scenario with the Padres, though, New York could also have signed two players with a total GPA of 0.320 or three players with a total GPA of 0.310 to achieve the same increase in team tGPA. But for the Yankees, neither alternative signing is likely to have been cheaper than signing Pujols. An increase of 0.007 in team net tGPA would result in an average increase of 4.1 wins per season.

For a poor team, signing an elite player is neither affordable nor cost effective. When a rich team signs an elite player, on the other hand, it can still be a cost-effective way to increase the number of games it wins. It is no surprise, then, that rich teams accumulate star players and less well-off teams struggle to sign even their homegrown, elite free agents.

Jim Rice's 1984 Season

Returning to a motivation behind this book and the invention of GPA, it is time to consider Jim Rice's 1984 season. Rice was elected to the Hall of Fame in 2009 for a stellar offensive career that lasted from 1974 to 1989 and included 382 home runs and a 0.298 lifetime batting average. During the 1984 season, he had a 0.280 BA with 122 RBI and 28 home runs. Ralph Houk, the Red Sox manager that year, clearly was happy with the production, as he batted Rice third in the lineup for most of his 708 PAs and rarely rested the slugger. Even though the Red Sox led the league with a 0.283 team BA, they won only 86 games and came in fourth place in the American League East, some 18 games behind the Detroit Tigers.

	—— Jim Rice 1984 ——			— MLB Average 1984 —		
	aGPA ×	FracPA =	GPA	aGPA ×	FracPA =	GPA
Any Out	−0.043	0.6667	−0.029	−0.013	0.6667	−0.009
Strike Out	−0.038	0.1441	−0.005	−0.015	0.1393	−0.002
Double/Tr Play	−0.550	0.0537	−0.030	−0.563	0.0244	−0.014
Walk	0.554	0.0621	0.034	0.567	0.0830	0.047
HBP/Interference	0.653	0.0014	0.001	0.606	0.0043	0.003
Error	0.617	0.0099	0.006	0.760	0.0132	0.010
Any Hit	1.014	0.2599	0.263	0.876	0.2328	0.204
Single	0.780	0.1751	0.137	0.730	0.1677	0.122
Double	1.053	0.0353	0.037	1.020	0.0387	0.039
Triple	1.756	0.0099	0.017	1.331	0.0061	0.008
Home Run	1.825	0.0395	0.072	1.676	0.0203	0.034
Extra Base Hit	1.495	0.0847	0.127	1.254	0.0651	0.082
Total	0.276	1.0000	0.276	0.255	1.0000	0.255

Table 25.1. Production by event from Jim Rice's 1984 season compared with the MLB average from 1984.

We can use GPA and the other techniques discussed in this book to evaluate the benefits of having Rice hit in the heart of a potent lineup and determine whether they were outweighed by the rallies he killed and runners he left on base throughout the year. Should the Red Sox have won more than 86 games in 1984? Would the team have won more games with someone else hitting third in the lineup?

A closer look at Rice's 1984 season shows his GPA of 0.276 was below his BA of 0.280 because he walked only 44 times while striking out 102 times and hitting into a then-record 36 double plays. Rice's production was above average, but not spectacular for someone hitting in the middle of the lineup. Although his 122 RBIs and 28 HRs overstate his production and value to the team, it does not appear Rice was primarily responsible for the 1984 Red Sox demise.

	GPA	BA	OBP	SLG	PA	Hits	RBI	HR
0 Outs	0.233	0.268	0.300	0.439	210	53	30	5
1 Out	0.317	0.302	0.347	0.539	268	74	61	15
2 Outs	0.267	0.266	0.317	0.411	230	57	31	8
Bases Empty	0.252	0.248	0.291	0.386	316	74	9	9
1st Only	0.300	0.300	0.328	0.535	177	51	23	10
2nd or 3rd	0.291	0.312	0.367	0.534	215	59	90	9
3rd,<2 Outs	0.407	0.429	0.464	0.690	56	18	41	2
Total	0.276	0.280	0.323	0.467	708	184	122	28

Table 25.2. Statistics by base-out state for Jim Rice's 1984 season.

Why did the Red Sox finish fourth in their division? The AL East division was loaded with good teams in 1984, with five of seven teams finishing well over 0.500. One might have assumed that the 1984 Red Sox had a potent lineup since they led baseball with a 0.283 BA, but the Red Sox hitters had a tGPA of 0.269 which was only fifth best that year and trailed the Tigers by 0.009 GPA points. Their BA over-represented their production by an MLB-high 0.014 GPA points that year. The Red Sox pitchers had a tGPA of 0.262, which was 17th best in the big leagues, and trailed the Tigers by 0.016 GPA points.

The Tigers won 104 games in 1984 and it would have been difficult for any team in the division to finish ahead of them. From the "Winning Games" chapter we know the Tigers' net tGPA of +0.032 should result in an average of 98.4 wins per season. The Tigers won six more games than expected based on their net team tGPA. The Red Sox's net tGPA of +0.007 should result in an average of 83.6 wins per season. Boston won two more games than expected based on their net team tGPA.

1984 Team Hitting	GPA W	GPA L	Total BA	GPA	brc	bpc	GPA	RBI	HR
Detroit Tigers	104	58	0.271	0.279	0.000	−0.001	0.278	788	187
Boston Red Sox	86	76	0.283	0.275	0.001	−0.007	0.269	767	181
New York Yankees	87	75	0.276	0.266	0.001	0.002	0.269	725	130
Toronto Blue Jays	89	73	0.263	0.263	0.003	−0.003	0.263	702	143
Baltimore Orioles	85	77	0.252	0.255	0.001	0.004	0.259	647	160

1984 Team Pitching	GPA W	GPA L	Total BA	GPA	brc	bpc	GPA	ERA	SO
Detroit Tigers	104	58	0.246	0.246	0.001	−0.001	0.246	3.49	914
Toronto Blue Jays	89	73	0.257	0.255	0.001	−0.004	0.253	3.71	875
New York Yankees	87	75	0.264	0.254	−0.000	0.002	0.256	3.78	992
Baltimore Orioles	85	77	0.256	0.252	0.001	0.004	0.257	3.85	714
Boston Red Sox	86	76	0.270	0.269	−0.000	−0.007	0.262	4.18	927

1984 Team Summary	W	L	Predicted Wins	Team tGPA Hitting	Team tGPA Pitching	Team tGPA Net
Detroit Tigers	104	58	98.4	0.278	0.246	+0.032
Toronto Blue Jays	89	73	85.4	0.263	0.253	+0.010
New York Yankees	87	75	87.2	0.269	0.256	+0.013
Boston Red Sox	86	76	83.6	0.269	0.262	+0.007
Baltimore Orioles	85	77	80.7	0.259	0.257	+0.002

Table 25.3. Select teams from the AL East Division. Predicted Wins was calculated using net team tGPA using the formula in Figure 11.

Red Sox players hit into more double plays and walked fewer times than average, but they also struck out less often than the league average. Their hitters' GPA was 0.275, 0.020 points above the MLB average in 1984, a difference largely attributable to their production from extra base hits. To understand why the Red Sox GPA was so much lower than their BA it is necessary to look at each player's statistics.

	—— Red Sox 1984 ——			— MLB Average 1984 —		
	aGPA × FracPA = GPA			aGPA × FracPA = GPA		
Any Out	−0.020	0.6509	−0.013	−0.013	0.6667	−0.009
Strike Out	−0.017	0.1344	−0.002	−0.015	0.1393	−0.002
Double/Tr Play	−0.569	0.0280	−0.016	−0.563	0.0244	−0.014
Walk	0.579	0.0800	0.046	0.567	0.0830	0.047
HBP/Interference	0.697	0.0034	0.002	0.606	0.0043	0.003
Error	0.700	0.0102	0.007	0.760	0.0132	0.010
Any Hit	0.911	0.2555	0.233	0.876	0.2328	0.204
Single	0.730	0.1781	0.130	0.730	0.1677	0.122
Double	1.060	0.0413	0.044	1.020	0.0387	0.039
Triple	1.375	0.0072	0.010	1.331	0.0061	0.008
Home Run	1.699	0.0290	0.049	1.676	0.0203	0.034
Extra Base Hit	1.328	0.0774	0.103	1.254	0.0651	0.082
Total	0.275	1.0000	0.275	0.255	1.0000	0.255

Table 25.4. Production by event for the 1984 Red Sox compared with the MLB average that season.

1984 Red Sox Lineup	Pos	GPA	GPA brc	GPA bpc	Total GPA	BA	OBP	RBI	HR
1st — Boggs, Wade	3B	0.286	0.004	−0.007	0.283	0.295	0.388	64	14
2nd — Evans, Dwight	RF	0.336	0.003	−0.007	0.332	0.276	0.339	74	16
3rd — Rice, Jim	LF	0.276	0.002	−0.007	0.271	0.280	0.323	105	28
4th — Armas, Tony	CF	0.287	0.001	−0.007	0.280	0.268	0.300	112	31
5th — Easler, Mike	DH	0.301	−0.000	−0.007	0.293	0.293	0.376	98	25
6th — Buckner, Bill	1B	0.258	−0.000	−0.006	0.252	0.272	0.313	85	21
7th — Gedman, Rich	C	0.283	0.000	−0.007	0.276	0.269	0.312	77	17
8th — Barrett, Marty	2B	0.261	−0.000	−0.007	0.254	0.303	0.358	67	13
9th — Gutierrez, Jackie	SS	0.187	0.003	−0.007	0.183	0.263	0.284	10	1
Team Average/Total		0.275	0.001	−0.007	0.269	0.283	0.341	767	181

Table 25.5. The most common starting lineup for the 1984 Red Sox.

Table 25.5 shows the most common lineup for the Red Sox in 1984. All players shown in the sample lineup appeared in 133–162 games except for Bill Buckner, who appeared in 114 games. Collectively, their 5,480 PAs represented 87.7 percent of the 6,250 PAs for the team in 1984. No bench player had more than 141 PAs.

Red Sox shortstop Jackie Gutierrez had an extraordinarily unproductive 1984 season despite his BA of 0.263. He hit into many double plays and walked infrequently. He also had little production from extra-base hits and had few clutch hits with runners in scoring position. Gutierrez had only 10 RBI despite having 480 PAs. His tGPA of 0.183 was 0.080 points below his BA and was the major reason the Red Sox hitters had a team tGPA that was 0.016 points below their batting average.

Finally, we can determine whether it would have mattered if Rice had been moved from third to sixth in the lineup.

	—Jackie Gutierrez 1984—			——MLB Average 1984——		
	aGPA	× FracPA	= GPA	aGPA	× FracPA	= GPA
Any Out	−0.044	0.7042	−0.031	−0.013	0.6667	−0.009
Strike Out	0.020	0.1021	0.002	−0.015	0.1393	−0.002
Double/Tr Play	−0.601	0.0438	−0.026	−0.563	0.0244	−0.014
Walk	0.658	0.0313	0.021	0.567	0.0830	0.047
HBP/Interference	0.000	0.0000	0.000	0.606	0.0043	0.003
Error	0.695	0.0188	0.013	0.760	0.0132	0.010
Any Hit	0.751	0.2458	0.185	0.876	0.2328	0.204
Single	0.711	0.2104	0.150	0.730	0.1677	0.122
Double	1.002	0.0250	0.025	1.020	0.0387	0.039
Triple	0.745	0.0063	0.005	1.331	0.0061	0.008
Home Run	1.269	0.0042	0.005	1.676	0.0203	0.034
Extra Base Hit	0.988	0.0354	0.035	1.254	0.0651	0.082
Total	0.187	1.0000	0.187	0.255	1.0000	0.255

Table 25.6. Production by event for Jackie Gutierrez in 1984 compared with the MLB average that season.

	GPA	BA	OBP	SLG	PA	Hits	RBI	HR
0 Outs	0.185	0.241	0.274	0.297	180	38	7	1
1 Out	0.207	0.292	0.316	0.340	152	42	10	1
2 Outs	0.170	0.259	0.264	0.313	148	38	12	0
Bases Empty	0.248	0.279	0.299	0.357	251	68	2	2
1st Only	0.162	0.226	0.265	0.269	109	21	3	0
2nd or 3rd	0.084	0.259	0.269	0.268	120	29	24	0
3rd,<2 Outs	0.059	0.300	0.280	0.300	25	6	11	0
Total	0.187	0.263	0.284	0.316	480	118	29	2

Table 25.7. Statistics by base-out state for Jackie Gutierrez in 1984.

Table 25.8 shows a simulation of the 1984 season using the most common lineup the Red Sox fielded. Table 25.9 shows a second simulation with the same players, but the batting order has been changed so that the hitters batting in the second to ninth positions are placed in order from highest to lowest GPA.

1984	——Simulated Lineup 1——				——Simulated For Team——			
Red Sox Lineup	PA	GPA	GPAbrc	RBI+	PA	GPA	GPAbrc	RBI+
1st — Boggs, Wade	771	0.285	0.003	55	702	0.2802	0.0013	93.1
2nd — Evans, Dwight	755	0.345	0.003	117				
3rd — Rice, Jim	739	0.281	−0.003	138				
4th — Armas, Tony	720	0.283	0.000	136				
5th — Easler, Mike	700	0.301	0.000	93				
6th — Buckner, Bill	686	0.256	0.001	82				
7th — Gedman, Rich	669	0.286	0.001	103				
8th — Barrett, Marty	650	0.262	0.003	63				
9th — Gutierrez, J.	631	0.209	0.003	51				

Table 25.8. The most common lineup the Red Sox fielded during the 1984 season was used for Simulated Lineup 1. The production of each batter over a 162-game season (left) and the average production of each batter on the team (right) was calculated by the single-lineup simulator.

Moving Rice from third (Simulated Lineup 1) to sixth (Simulated Lineup 2) in the batting order resulted in an increase in tGPA of 0.0017 for the Red Sox as a team. With this increase, the 1984 Red Sox would have been expected to win one additional game that season — not enough to catch the Tigers in the AL East.

Most players' actual GPAs (Table 25.5) and their GPAs in both simulated lineups are very similar. However, Mike Easler's GPA was 0.334 in Simulated Lineup 2 while his actual GPA was 0.301. This deviation demonstrates the limitations of running a realistic simulation with the limited data available from a single season. If the base-out states the player faces in the simulated lineup differ significantly from the actual base-out states he faced, his simulated and actual GPAs can diverge. The simulations run in the preceding chapters of this book combined data from many seasons to minimize this error.

1984 Red Sox Lineup	— — Simulated Lineup 2 — —				— — Simulated For Team — —			
	PA	GPA	GPAbrc	RBI+	PA	GPA	GPAbrc	RBI+
1st — Boggs, Wade	774	0.281	−0.003	60	704	0.2825	0.0007	94.5
2nd — Evans, Dwight	756	0.346	0.000	118				
3rd — Easler, Mike	740	0.334	0.000	126				
4th — Armas, Tony	724	0.284	0.001	158				
5th — Gedman, Rich	705	0.273	0.001	112				
6th — Rice, Jim	688	0.275	0.002	96				
7th — Barrett, Marty	670	0.263	0.001	56				
8th — Buckner, Bill	651	0.246	0.002	67				
9th — Gutierrez, J.	631	0.222	0.003	57				

Table 25.9. Simulated Lineup 2 includes the same players as in Simulated Lineup 1, but the hitters in the second to ninth slots are placed in order from highest to lowest GPA.

In Summary, the 1984 Red Sox finished in fourth place because of their average pitching and, at least most noticeably, Gutierrez's poor production at the plate. The Tigers were somewhat lucky to have won 102 games, but this was still far more than the Red Sox should have won based on their team's tGPA. Moving Rice from third to sixth in the lineup would have made little difference in the outcome.

Conclusion

In summary, this book describes a new baseball statistic called Gross Productivity Average (GPA), which measures a hitter's or pitcher's production. Reported on a scale similar to the one used for batting average (BA), GPA is easy for the average fan to understand. Adjusting the average GPA to equal the average BA from 2005 to 2008 sets a modern standard untainted by steroids. It works out well that the average GPA and BA of all major league players from 1952 to 2012 are virtually identical at 0.259.

Gross Productivity Average appropriately values extra base hits and RBIs, moving runners over, and reaching base by means other than a hit. It also appropriately penalizes batters for leaving runners on base and hitting into double plays. It measures production by pitchers and hitters equally well and on the same scale.

A ballpark correction can be applied to GPA that accurately compensates for the mix of ballparks and the era in which a hitter or pitcher played. Most ballparks from 1952 to 2012 have had ballpark corrections of between –0.010 and +0.010 GPA points. Of the 30 ballparks in use in the major leagues today, Colorado's Coors Field (since the introduction of a baseball humidor), with a ballpark correction of –0.034 GPA points, is the park most favorable to hitters; San Diego's PETCO Park, with a ballpark correction of +0.024 GPA points, is the park most favorable to pitchers.

The ballpark can have a dramatic effect on a hitter's or pitcher's production. Many of the greatest seasons by hitters were aided by playing in ballparks favorable to offense. Many of the greatest seasons by pitchers were likewise aided by playing in ballparks that suppressed offense.

A baserunning correction can be applied to GPA that accurately measures a player's contribution to his team from stealing bases or advancing on the base paths in other ways. The average player from 1997 to 2012 has had a baserunning correction of +0.002 GPA points. Rickey Henderson's 1988 season with 93 stolen bases had a baserunning correction of +0.031 GPA points, the highest of any player from 1952 to 2012. His production on the base paths accounted for a substantial portion of his total production as measured by GPA.

Baserunning can significantly affect a hitter's or pitcher's production for his team, but the number of stolen bases does not necessarily correlate with the baserunning correction. Rickey Henderson set a modern record with 130 stolen bases in 1982, yet his baserunning correction was only +0.007 GPA points. His desire to set a major league record may have encouraged him to steal when the opportunities were not as good. The average production from baserunning has slowly risen from around 0.000 in the early 1950s to over +0.002

GPA points during the past few years. Today's players are more productive on the base paths than at any time since 1952 even though they attempt fewer stolen bases than in previous eras.

As this book describes the creation of the GPA statistic, it explains why GPA is more than merely an effective statistic. A complex and accurate baseball simulator is then used to demonstrate that GPA behaves in much the way the "perfect" baseball statistic should behave.

The simulator shows that the GPA of the whole lineup accurately predicts offensive productivity as measured by runs scored. Adding a single player with a high GPA to the lineup will produce the same increase in production as adding multiple players with lower GPAs, as long as the average GPA of the whole lineup is the same. The GPA of a team's pitching staff accurately predicts the opponent's offensive productivity as measured by runs allowed.

From these simulated lineups, it appears the best lineup is constructed by placing the best hitters at the top of the order, although the advantage over the traditional batting order, with the best hitters in the middle, is admittedly small. Players can contribute to their team's production by creating opportunities for others or driving in runs.

None of the traditional offensive statistics used in baseball comes close to the very tight correlation seen between the GPA of the team's batters and run production. Team ERA is a good measure of the opponent's productivity, but is not as tightly a correlated with runs allowed as is the GPA of the team's pitchers.

The simulator shows the number of wins produced by a lineup is well correlated with the team's net GPA, defined as the difference between the GPA of the batters and the GPA of pitchers on that team. There is a linear increase in the number of wins expected as a team's net GPA increases.

The simulator is able to examine the complex interactions of the score, inning and skill of the hitters due to bat. With tools as powerful as GPA and the simulator, it becomes possible to settle long-standing controversies in baseball. This book provides the first definitive guidelines for when to intentionally walk a batter, when a runner should attempt to advance a base and when a hitter should attempt a sacrifice bunt.

The intentional walk is such a controversial strategy because the score, inning and skills of the hitters due up next determine the few game scenarios in which it qualifies as good strategy. Without a sophisticated simulation, it would be almost impossible to use the intentional walk in a way that is consistently effective.

When the hitter at bat has a much higher GPA than the hitter on deck, there are many scenarios in which intentionally walking the hitter at bat makes strategic sense. One example of this situation is when a pitcher is on deck. Another, historical example is when Barry Bonds was at bat during the era from 2001 to 2004 when his production was higher than any player in modern baseball history. Managers were so afraid of Bonds's potential production, in fact, that they intentionally walked him far more frequently than could be justified.

When the hitter at bat has a GPA moderately higher than the hitter on deck, there are fewer scenarios in which intentionally walking the hitter at bat makes strategic sense. A current example of this situation is when Albert Pujols bats. But, as with Bonds, managers walk Pujols more frequently than can be justified.

When the hitter at bat has a similar GPA to the one on deck, there are few times that it pays to issue an intentional walk.

The sacrifice bunt is also a controversial strategy for an average hitter, and for the same reasons — because the score and inning determine the few game scenarios in which the sacrifice bunt doesn't come with too high a cost. For an average hitter, the simulator shows that there are few situations in the early and middle innings that it makes sense to sacrifice bunt. As the game progresses, more scenarios arise in which a sacrifice bunt is good strategy, and the success rate needed to justify the risk falls as low as 52 percent.

The sacrifice bunt is a widely used strategy with the pitcher at bat, and the simulator shows that there are many scenarios in the early and middle innings of a game that the move makes sense. As the game progresses, still more good opportunities arise, and the success rate needed to justify the risk of the sacrifice bunt by a pitcher falls as low as 27 percent.

Guidelines for determining when to attempt an advance, based on the success rate needed to justify the risk, can be determined using run expectancy (RE), the foundation on which GPA is based. These guidelines are easy to remember, but it should be noted that they do not apply at the end of close games or when one team is far behind. The baseball simulator can also calculate the specific success rates needed in a given scenario, taking into account the inning, score and base-out state. These percentages are far more accurate but also more difficult to remember since they change as the game progresses.

The difference between GPA and BA provides a unique measure of added production attributable to extra base hits, clutch hitting and walks. It removes most of the "noise" that makes other statistics hard to interpret from season to season. The mix of ballparks, changes in game strategy, and changes in rules tend to cancel out, allowing the long term trends to emerge. The increased muscle mass and power attributed to steroid use should increase production in a way accurately measured by the GPA — BA difference.

Multiple factors probably came together to create what this book refers to as the Pitching Era (1971-1984). Despite three major rule changes from 1969 to 1973 to boost offensive production, the difference between GPA and BA continued to be negative throughout those 14 years. New ballparks accounted for about a third of the falloff in offensive production, but the emergence of relief pitchers and the five-man rotation likely contributed more heavily to the dominance of pitching during this era. There is fair evidence the baseball was less lively during these years, and its composition changed with the end of the era.

Why the Pitching Era ended is less clear. One interpretation of the data is that from 1985 to 1993, the balance between hitting and pitching returned to the level seen in the 1950s and since 2005 when the difference between GPA and BA was close to zero. Another interpretation is that the Pitching Era faded and the Steroid Era favoring hitting slowly took over.

This book defines the Steroid Era as the unprecedented string of 11 years from 1994 to 2004 in which the difference between GPA and BA for a whole season was positive. From the analysis presented, perhaps only 38.5 percent of the added production seen during the Steroid Era was attributable to steroid use. Improved athletic performance explained at least in part by better training techniques probably accounted for 41.8 percent of the improvement and improved baserunning another 7.7 percent.

GPA can be used to reexamine every Most Valuable Player and Cy Young Award from 1952 to 2012 to determine who truly deserved their awards and who might have been a more deserving choice. Many of the greatest players in baseball history did not receive the votes they deserved, especially early in their careers. The analysis shows that from 1952 to 2012 the writers have slowly become better at choosing the most deserving players for these awards. Still, even in the past few years, some of the award winners chosen by the writers are difficult to justify.

Wins Above Replacement (WAR) can be calculated using GPA in an accurate and reproducible manner. WAR allows the number of plate appearances and the defensive positions played to be taken into account while incorporating all the advantages of GPA including baserunning and ballpark corrections. Smaller differences in fielding skill among players who play the same defensive position will be lost when WAR is calculated using GPA.

GPA can have a major impact on the business of baseball. Free agents can be appropriately ranked using GPA rather than the inaccurate and secret formula used by MLB today. Players who participate in salary arbitration can have their worth accurately valued using GPA. Most importantly, GPA provides teams with the tools to evaluate which players are most likely to be productive for them within the budget available.

More than in most sports, statistics are used to measure a baseball player's skill level. Many points of view are supported by selectively choosing among various imperfect statistics. This book revisits a small selection of these controversies and uses GPA to try and finally settle the issues.

A major goal in writing this book is to establish GPA as the new standard for evaluating a major league player's productivity. My hope is that baseball professionals and average fans will use GPA as the primary tool to examine other controversies in baseball.

Before GPA appears in every newspaper's sports section and on every baseball broadcast, the detailed play-by-play information used to calculate GPA will have to be made more available. This book used the information in the Retrosheet database, but it is only released well after the baseball season ends. MLB and the Elias Sport Bureau have access to this information, but in the past have been unwilling to make it widely available to the public.

GPA comes as close to being the "perfect" baseball statistic as has ever been created to judge a major league baseball player's productivity. It is important to understand how baseball statistics vary due to chance alone so we do not become overconfident in our statistical measures. Even a "perfect" baseball statistic may not accurately predict a player's production over a limited period of time such as one baseball season.

I know from my years of rooting for the Red Sox — the best team may not always win!

Glossary

ΔRE *see* Change in Run Expectancy

aGPA *see* Average GPA

Average GPA (aGPA) The average GPA for all major leaguers over a specified period.

Average Change in Run Expectancy (aΔRE) The mean change in run expectancy from a number of events.

Average tGPA The average tGPA for all players over a specified period.

Base-Out State The number of outs and the bases occupied with a player at bat. There are seven possible ways the bases can be occupied: man on first, man on second, man on third, men on first and second, men on first and third, men on second and third, and bases loaded. The bases, however, can also be empty, which yields an eighth bases-occupied scenario. There are likewise three possibilities for the number of outs: none, one or two. There are, therefore, a total of 24 base-out states.

Baserunning Event Any advancement or putout on the base paths that is not the result of a batted ball. Baserunning events include the stolen base, caught stealing, pickoff, defensive indifference, error, wild pitch, passed ball or balk.

Batting Average Distribution The fraction of times various batting averages occur across the range of batting averages seen for those events.

Ballpark Correction (BPC) Correction that accounts for the differences between ballparks, and specifically for the effect each has on hitting and pitching. A ballpark-corrected statistic is one that has been adjusted to compensate for park advantages or disadvantages, with the goal of neutralizing their effects on statistics. In this book, ballpark correction is discussed primarily in terms of the GPA ballpark correction (GPAbpc).

Baseball Game Simulator A computer program that can simulate large numbers of baseball games.

Batters Faced (BF) The number of batters who made a plate appearances against a pitcher.

Base on Balls GPA (BB GPA) The GPA of a walk in a specified base-out state.

BB GPA The GPA value for a base on balls in a specified base-out state.

BF *see* Batters Faced

BPC *see* Ballpark Correction

Calculated Run Expectancy Calculated by taking the average run expectancy of the base-out state after the play occurred, subtracting the average run expectancy of the base-out state before the play occurred, then adding the number of runs that scored.

Calculated Success Rate Calculated percent of attempts that need to be successful to justify the risk.

cGPA *see* Corrected GPA.

Change in Run Expectancy (ΔRE) The run expectancy after an event minus the run expectancy before that event.

Corrected GPA (cGPA) The GPA after it is corrected for either the ballparks in which the plate appearances occurred or the base running events that occurred (depending on the context).

CS Caught Stealing.

Cy Young Points Total points from the writers who voted for the Cy Young Award.

Cy Young Rank A player's rank in the voting for the Cy Young Award, with 1 being the winner.

Early DH Era Includes the seasons from 1973 (when the DH rule was implemented) to 1996 (the year before interleague play began).

Elias Rank A ranking, published after each season, that places free agents (along with non-free agents) into one of three categories (A, B, or C) based on their performance over the previous two seasons. The category determines the level of compensation a team receives if its free-agent player signs elsewhere.

Event A plate appearance or a base running play from the Retrosheet database.

Expected Pct. Batters Percentage of batters expected in a specified context (e.g., the percentage of all-time great offensive seasons from a given era) based on chance alone. Calculated by dividing the number of team seasons in the subset of years listed by the total number of team seasons.

Expected Pct. Pitchers Percentage of pitchers expected in a specified context (e.g., the percentage of all-time great pitching seasons from a given era) based on chance alone. Calculated by dividing the number of team seasons in the subset of years listed by the total number of team seasons.

Expected Pct. Runners Percentage of runners expected in a specified context (e.g., the percentage of all-time great base-stealing seasons from a given era) based on chance alone. Calculated by dividing the number of team seasons in the subset of years listed by the total number of team seasons.

FracPA The fraction calculated by dividing a subset of plate appearances by the total number of plate appearances. For example, 52 of 100 plate appearances is a FracPA of 0.52 which is the same as 52 percent.

FracBB The fraction of times a batter walked relative to the total number of plate appearances. For example, a batter who walked 14 of 100 plate appearances has a FracBB of 0.14 which is the same as 14 percent.

FracGW The fraction of games won with 1.0 representing 100 percent of games won and 0.0 representing no games won.

Game Scenario The combination of base-out state, game score and half inning being played.

GPA *see* Gross Productivity Average

GPA – BA The difference between GPA and batting average, which represents production not reflected by the batting average.

GPA – BA Distribution The fraction of times various differences between GPA and batting average occur across the range of differences seen for those events.

GPAbpc *see* GPA Ballpark Correction

GPAbrc *see* GPA Baserunning Correction

GPA Ballpark Correction (GPAbrc) Correction for the mix of ballparks in which the plate appearances occurred. Each plate appearance has a GPA correction value added based on the ballpark and year the PA took place. The total correction is divided by the number of PAs, yielding a ballpark correction in GPA points. Players who have a GPA Ballpark Correction greater than zero played in a mix of ballparks that favored pitchers over batters while those who have a GPA Ballpark Correction less than zero played in a mix of ballparks that favored batters over pitchers.

GPA Ballpark Correction Value Correction for each ballpark applied to GPA to compensate how that ballpark's balance between pitching and hitting compared to other ballparks over a number of seasons. A negative correction is seen in ballparks that favor batters over pitchers while a positive correction is seen in ballparks that favor pitchers over batters. GPA Ballpark Correction Values are listed in the Table at the end of "Ballpark Corrections" chapter.

GPA Baserunning Correction (GPAbrc) Correction applied to GPA to reflect the production from base running events for runners or the base running production allowed for pitchers.

GPA Correction A correction applied to GPA to compensate for a factor that affects a player's production or its measurement by statistics. In this book GPA corrections are described for (1) the ballparks in which the plate appearances occurred, (2) the production from base running events, (3) the defensive positions played by a non-pitcher, and (4) the relative-value of the at-bats faced for a pitcher.

GPA Distribution The fraction of times various GPAs occur across the range of GPAs seen for those events.

GPApc *see* GPA Position Correction

GPA Position Correction (GPApc) Correction for the defensive positions played (non-pitchers only).

GPArv A GPA correction for the relative value (importance) of at-bats faced by a pitcher to the outcome of the game for his team. The relative value of each PA to the team depends on the inning and score. The relative value is low when one team is far ahead and far higher in the late innings of a close game. See Relative Value of a Plate Appearance.

GPA Value The valuation for a plate appearance used to calculate GPA. For each of the 311 base-out state and play-result combinations, the change in run expectancy is calculated by comparing the outcome for that combination to the average outcome for all plate appearances from 1997 to 2009 for that base-out state. The change in run expectancy is adjusted up by 0.26833, the correction factor required to make the batting average and GPA of all major league players from 2005 to 2008 nearly equal at 0.26642, yielding a GPA value for each base-out state and play-result combination. (The table at the end of the "Creating GPA" chapter provides the GPA values for all 311 base-out state and play result combinations.)

Gross Productivity Average (GPA) A measure of the change in run expectancy. For all 311 base-out states and play-result combinations, the change in run expectancy is calculated by comparing the outcome of each combination to the average outcome for all plate appearances from 1997 to 2009 for that base-out state. The change in run expectancy is adjusted up by 0.26833, the correction factor required to make the batting average and GPA of all major league players from 2005 to 2008 nearly equal at 0.26642, yielding a GPA value for each base-out state and play result combination. (The table at the end of the "Creating GPA" chapter provides the GPA values for all 311 base-out state and play-result combinations.) The GPA is the average GPA value for all plate appearances. The relative value of each plate appearance to the team is reflected in the range of GPA values for that base-out state.

HmRdDifferential *see* Home-Road Differential.

Home-Road Differential (HmRdDifferential) The difference between an average player's GPA at his home ballpark and his GPA on the road.

HR/PA Home runs per plate appearance.

IAP *see* Improved Athletic Performance.

Improved Athletic Performance (IAP) the improved athletic performance of players over time that may be attributable to medical and technological advances, including better training methods, but not to the effects of steroids and other purportedly performance-enhancing drugs.

Interleague Era Includes the seasons from 1997, when a rule allowing interleague play during the regular season went into effect, to the current season.

MVP Points Total points from the writers who voted for the Most Valuable Player Award. In 1938, the BBWAA instituted the "ranked choice" method of voting for each league. Two baseball writers (three from 1928–1960) who cover each team vote. They rank the 10 most valuable players in their league from 1 to 10. The top-ranked player receives 14 points, the second-ranked player receives nine points, the third-ranked player receives eight points, and so on, with the 10th-ranked player receiving one point. The player in each league with the most points wins the MVP Award.

MVP Rank A player's rank in the voting for the Most Valuable Player Award, with 1 being the winner.

Net cGPA *see* Net Corrected GPA.

Net Corrected GPA (Net cGPA) The difference between the cGPA of the batters and the cGPA of pitchers on a team.

Observed Data Historical data from major league games, as opposed to simulated data.

Observed Run Expectancy Run expectancy calculated from actually observed (i.e., historical) plate appearances, as opposed to a calculated run expectancy derived from the run expectancy of the base-out states before and after the play occurred.

OPS On-base percentage plus slugging average. A widely used sabermetric statistic, OPS measures a player's ability to both get on base and hit for power.

Other Advance Advancing on the base paths in ways other than a stolen base or a batted ball. The possibilities include defensive indifference, error, wild pitch, passed ball or balk.

Other Out Making an out on the base paths in ways other than being caught stealing or as the result of a batted ball. Most other outs are the result of pickoff plays.

PA *see* Plate Appearance.

Pitching Era Defined in this book as the years 1971 to 1984, over which there was an unprecedented string of 14 years in a row where the difference between GPA and BA for all PAs for a season was negative (average −0.0057 points).

Plate Appearance A statistic that accounts for every appearance at the plate that a batter makes that results in that player making an out or reaching base. Unlike at-bats, plate appearances include walks, hit-by-pitches, sacrifices, and interference calls.

Play Result The outcome after a batter's plate appearance or the outcome after a runner's attempt to advance on the base paths.

Pre-DH Era For this book, the period includes the years from 1952 (the earliest year for full statistical coverage in the Retrosheet database) to 1972 (the year before the DH rule was implemented).

Predicted RBI+ Number of RBI+ predicted for a lineup based on a formula, found in Table 16.1 derived from simulated lineups.

R-1 The success rate required to justify an advance attempt when only one run is needed to win the game.

R^2 A statistical measure of how well a regression line approximates the real data points, with 0.0 denoting that it does not explain any variation and 1.0 denoting that it perfectly explains the observed variation.

RBI+ Runs batted in plus other runs that score on errors and double plays (runs scored).

RE *see* Run Expectency.

Relative Value of a Plate Appearance Measures the relative value of a plate appearance by its effect on a team's chances of winning the game. The chance a team might overcome a deficit is balanced with the need to get the remaining hitters out. The average plate appearance has a relative value of 1.0, more important plate appearances relative values greater than 1.0 and less important plate appearances relative values less than 1.0.

Retrosheet An organization that provides a free comprehensive play-by-play database covering almost all major league baseball games played from 1947 to the current season. After each season is complete, the database is updated, primarily with the help of volunteers. Additional coverage extended back through time is added as it becomes available. The first draft of this book was written during the 2010 Major League Baseball (MLB) season. By the end of 2012, the Retrosheet database had been updated to include most of the games from the 1947 and 1951 seasons and all games from the 2010 through 2012 seasons. Chapters have been updated to include the 2010 through 2012 data if its inclusion was helpful or significant. There are a few games missing from the Retrosheet database from 1947 to 1973, especially from the earlier seasons in that date range.

Run Distribution The fraction of times that half innings produce 0 up to the maximum number of runs scored (in a half inning).

Run Expectancy The average number of runs that are expected to score for the rest of that half-inning for that base-out state. Run expectancy includes the runs that result from the current plate appearance and all subsequent runs that score during the half-inning.

Run Production The number of runs that score from a lineup of batters.

SBa Stolen bases allowed by a pitcher.

Sacrifice Hit (SH) For the purposes of this book, a sacrifice hit is always a sacrifice bunt, defined as a bunt **with fewer than two outs** that advances one or more base runners and results with the bunter-runner's either having been put out at first base or reaching on an error. A sacrifice bunt does not count as a charged at-bat.

SH *see* sacrifice hit

Simulated Data For the purposes of this book, "simulated data" always refers to data created from a computer program that simulates major league games.

Simulated Player Used by a computer program to simulate a batter's production based on all plate appearances and attempts to advance on the base paths from an era (from a single player or group of players). The actual play results for all 311 combinations of base-out states and the actual play results for all base running situations are used to accurately simulate that batter's production.

Single-Lineup Game Simulator A computer program that simulates large numbers of baseball games using a single nine-batter lineup of hitters.

SLG *see* Slugging Average

Slugging Average Also called slugging percentage, slugging average measures a player's propensity for extra-base hits. The formula: (singles + doubles × 2 + triples × 3 + homers × 4)/at-bats.

Steroid Era Defined in this book as the years 1994 to 2004, which saw an unprecedented string of 11 years in a row in which the difference between GPA and BA for all PAs for a season was positive (average +0.0034 points).

Glossary

Success Rate The percentage of attempts that need to be successful to justify the risk of making an out.

Team Net GPA The difference between the GPA of the batters and the GPA of pitchers on a team.

Team Seasons The average number of teams playing during an era multiplied by the number of seasons in that era.

Team Skill The fraction of games that should be won based on the talent of the players on the team.

tGPA *see* Total GPA.

Total Change in Run Expectancy (Total ΔRE) The aggregate change in run expectancy from a number of events.

Total ΔRE *see* Total Change in Run Expectancy.

Total GPA (tGPA) GPA after it is corrected for both the ballparks in which the plate appearances occurred and the base running events that occurred.

Total Position-Adjusted GPA (t_{pa}GPA) GPA corrected for the ballparks in which a position player played, his base running production and the defensive positions he played.

t_{pa}GPA *see* Total Position-Adjusted GPA

Two-Lineup Game Simulator A computer program that simulates large numbers of baseball games using two nine-batter lineups of hitters.

WAA *see* Wins Above Average

WAR *see* Wins Above Replacement

WinAdv The chance of winning the game when the attempt to advance a base is successful.

WinFailedAdv The chance of winning the game when the attempt to advance a base fails and the runner is put out.

WinFailedSH The chance of winning the game when the sacrifice bunt fails.

WinFr Fraction of games won.

Winning Margin Distribution The fraction of times that the winning margin of games is 1 up to the maximum winning margin seen (in runs).

WinNoAdv The chance of winning the game when no attempt is made to advance a base.

WinNoSH The chance of winning the game with no bunt attempt.

Win Percentage The percentage of times a team should win the game in a specific game scenario.

Wins Above Average (WAA) The number of wins a team would lose if a player was replaced with an average Major League player.

Wins Above Replacement (WAR) The number of wins a team would lose if a player were replaced with a top minor leaguer or a bench player with marginal major league skills.

WinSH The chance of winning the game with a successful sacrifice bunt.

INDEX

Aaron, Hank 150, 219
arbitration 235
athletic performance 108, 114

ballpark correction 56
ballpark correction values 57, 58, 60, 63
ballpark factor 56
ballparks, new 106, 113
Banks, Ernie 220
base on balls, GPA 150
base-out state 9, 14, 117
baseball eras 9, 100
baseball game simulator 117
baseball statistics 5
baseballs 110
baserunning corrections 73, 83; by season 103
baserunning events 73; by season 100
baserunning strategies 66, 174
batters best seasons 48, 193; by GPA 49; by WAR 194
batting average (BA) 6, 93, 132; by ball/strike count 165, 166; by season 103, 146
Bay, Jason 124
Beckert, Glenn 96
Bench, Johnny 220
best lineup 121
Bonds, Barry 48, 93, 149, 220
Bourn, Michael 75
Braun, Ryan 23, 25
Buckner, Bill 1
bunt 164
Burnett, A.J. 243

Cabrera, Miguel 24, 82, 219
calculated run expectancy 16
calculating GPA 14
Campanella, Roy 220
Campbell, Bill 203
Capra, Buzz 203
Cash, Dave 97

Chadwick, Henry 5
Chance, Dean 201
chance in baseball 144
change in run expectancy (ΔRE) 12
Clark, Jack 62
Clemens, Roger 202
Collins, Dave 85
conclusion 251
constructing the best lineup 121
Contreras, Jose 78, 80
Coors Field 48, 56, 58
Crawford, Carl 75
creating GPA 9
Cy Young Award 26, 201; by season 203, 204

Davis, Mark 203
defensive position correction to WAR 192
defensive position, value to the team 185
DeJesus, David 77, 79
designated hitter (DH) 9, 10
Dibble, Rob 203
Dickey, R.A. 26
difference between GPA and BA 93, 98, 147; by season 102, 103, 147
dilution of MLB talent 107

earned run average (ERA) 7, 135; by season 103
Elias Sports Bureau 2, 236, 254
Ellsbury, Jacoby 26, 75, 79
Encarnacion, Edwin 24
expansion 107

Fenway Park 58
Figgins, Chone 77
Fireman of the Year Award 108
Ford, Whitey 109
fraction inning distribution 136, 137

fraction run distribution by inning 119
fraction winning margin 137
Free Agency 235
free agent player rankings 236

Garvin, Jerry 86
Giambi, Jason 241
Gonzalez, Gio 26
Gonzalez, Juan 220
Gossage, Rich 203
GPA by ball/strike count 165
GPA by defensive position played 185
GPA by season 103, 146, 186
GPA relative value 192
GPA values 14, 18
Granderson, Curtis 26
Gutierrez, Jackie 247
Gwynn, Tony 59

Halladay, Roy 27
Henderson, Ken 85
Henderson, Ricky 2, 83, 150, 251
Hernandez, Felix 27
home run (HR) 6
home runs per plate appearance (HR/PA) 101, 103
Houk, Ralph 1, 245
Hunt, Ron 97
Hunter, Torii 240

improved athletic performance 108, 114
interleague play 10
intentional walk 149; GPA of 151

James, Bill 2, 181
Jepsen, Kevin 80
Jones, Andruw 239

Kauffman Stadium 57
Kershaw, Clayton 26, 27

Kluszewski, Ted 219
knuckleball 79, 87
Koufax, Sandy 26

Lanier, Hal 96
league correction for WAR 192
Lee, Carlos 125
Lee, Cliff 27
LeFlore, Ron 84
Lyle, Sparky 203

Mantle, Mickey 48, 219
Marshall, Mike 203
Mathews, Eddie 219
Mays, Willie 219
McCutchen, Andrew 23
McGuire, Mark 48, 219
Medlen, Kris 26
Millwood, Kevin 243
Moreno, Omar 85
Morgan, Joe 1, 97
Morgan, Nyjer 77
most expensive free agent contracts 239
Murcer, Bobby 219
MVP Award 23, 217; for pitchers 219; by season 221

Nash, Jim 62
Newcombe, Don 219
NFL Passer Rating 8
Niekro, Joe 87
Niekro, Phil 203

observed run expectancy 15
on-base percentage (OBP) 7, 132; by season 103
on-base percentage + slugging average (OPS) 7
one-lineup baseball game simulator 117
other advances 67
overpaid players 240, 241, 242

Pedroia, Dustin 144, 146
Pena, Carlos 125
"perfect" baseball statistic 5, 17, 148, 252
PETCO Park 59
Piazza, Mike 59
pinch hitter 186
pitcher bunting 170

pitching era 102, 105, 148
play result 11, 117
Posey, Buster 23
position group (Elias) 236
Price, David 27
Progressive Field 57
Project Scoresheet 2
Pujols, Albert 122, 123, 149, 159, 243

QuesTec Umpire Information System 109

R-1 179
Radatz, Dick 62
Ramirez, Manny 48, 114, 218
random chance in baseball 144
relationship between GPA and BA 93, 98, 147; by season 102, 103, 147
relative value of a PA 192
relief pitching 109, 187, 193, 203; best seasons by GPA 53; best seasons by WAR 199
replacement level (R in WAR) 183
Retrosheet 2
Rice, Jim 1, 245
Rodriguez, Alex 220
Rodriquez, Ivan 218
run expectancy 11, 15, 66
run production 129
runs batted in (RBI) 6
runs batted in + (RBI+) 119

sabermetrics 2
sacrifice bunt 164
salaries 243
save 109
Scott, Mike 86
Sexson, Richie 125
simulated lineup 119, 136
single-lineup baseball game simulator 117
slugging average (SLG) 7, 133; by season 103
Smith, Dave 2
Soriano, Alfonso 239
starting pitching 187, 193; best season by WAR 196; best seasons by GPA 49, 51; Elias rank 239

stealing bases 67, 73, 83; by season 100, 101
steroid era 103, 112, 148
steroids 114
strike zone 109
success rate needed for bunts 168, 169
Suzuki, Ichiro 241

team cGPA 131, 134, 138
team net cGPA 140
team skill 144
Tenace, Gene 93
Thomas, Frank 124, 220
Trout, Mike 24, 82
two-lineup baseball game simulator 136, 151, 157, 171, 174

Uggla, Dan 75
University of Rhone Island Forensic Science Partnership 110
unrestricted free agent 235

Verlander, Justin 25, 27, 28, 79

Wakefield, Tim 79, 87
Walker, Larry 59
WAR 181; calculated from GPA 192
Weaver, Jered 26–28
Welch, Bob 202
Wells, Vernon 240
Wilhelm, Hoyt 87
Williams, Ted 48, 96, 219
Wilson, Mookie 1
Wilson, Willie 85
win distribution 145
win percentage 152, 153
winning games 136
winning margin 137
wins above average (WAA) 182
wins above replacement (WAR) 181; calculated from GPA 192
Witt, Bobby 87
Wrigley Field 56, 57

Yankee Stadium, New 59

Zavagno, David 110
Zito, Barry 243

www.ingramcontent.com/pod-product-compliance
Lightning Source LLC
Chambersburg PA
CBHW081547300426
44116CB00015B/2784